A History of British Mollusca, and Their Shells, Volume 1

A

HISTORY

OF

BRITISH MOLLUSCA,

AND THEIR SHELLS.

A

HISTORY

OF

BRITISH MOLLUSCA,

AND THEIR SHELLS.

BY

PROFESSOR EDWARD FORBES, F.R.S.,

OF KING'S COLLEGE, LONDON;

AND

SYLVANUS HANLEY, B.A., F.L.S.,

OF WADHAM COLLEGE, OXFORD.

VOLUME I.

INCLUDING THE TUNICATA, AND THE FAMILIES OF LAMELLI-
BRANCHIATA AS FAR AS CYPRINIDÆ.

LONDON:

JOHN VAN VOORST, PATERNOSTER ROW.

———

M.DCCC.LIII.

271126

.

.

LONDON:
Printed by SAMUEL BENTLEY and Co.
Bangor House, Shoe Lane.

PREFACE.

ALTHOUGH our work is long, our Preface need not be so;
nor, indeed, need it be more than a grateful record of the
obligations we are under to the many friends who have
assisted in our task. That a History of the British Mollusca in accordance with the present state of Natural History Science, and of the present knowledge of our native
species was required, will, we are confident, be denied
by no person qualified to offer an opinion upon the matter.
Materials for such a work have long been in course of
collection, and amply amassed by ourselves and others.
We entered upon the task diffidently, and not before the
field was fairly open, those best qualified for the labour
urging us to attempt what had almost become a duty.
The invaluable and classical collection of British shells in
the possession of Mr. Gwyn Jeffreys, and the extensive
experience of its liberal proprietor, placed within the reach
of that energetic investigator, materials for a work like
this, such as no other naturalist could command, but the
imperious demands of professional avocations withheld the
leisure where there was both will and ample knowledge.
Mr. Alder, too, profoundly versed in British Malacology,
and gifted with the power of delineating, at once accu-
rately and artistically, the animals whose external clothing
and internal structure had alike engaged his attention,
was already occupied with a section of the subject that

had become the work of years. Mr. Clark had aban-
doned the field in which he had years ago laboured so
diligently and skilfully, though now, fortunately for
science, he has returned to it with renewed vigour and
enthusiasm. To all these gentlemen we offer our warmest
thanks for their most generous contributions of original
materials. The choicest specimens in Mr. Jeffreys' cabinet have been placed at our disposal for figuring, without
reserve, and the pencil of Mr. Alder has, in many instances, embellished our illustrations with figures exceedingly precious, since from no other source could they be
procured.

Our valued and lamented friend, the late William
Thompson, of Belfast, who had devoted years of study to
the British Mollusks, aided us, as long as he lived, with
every possible assistance that lay in his power. In all
that concerns the distribution of Irish species, his hand
may be traced, and advice, notes and specimens were constantly coming from him for our use. For many of the
details that we are enabled to give respecting the distribution and range of the species described, we owe the
fullest thanks to Mr. M'Andrew, of Liverpool, who, with
a zeal too rarely imitated, has for years spared neither
expense nor labour in searching out marine animals in
their deepest recesses, a work, often-times, of no small risk
and danger.

The veteran conchologist of Scarborough, Mr. William
Bean, has liberally aided us in numerous instances. The
precious cabinets of Mr. Cuming have been opened to us
most freely for consultation. Specimens of peculiar value
and interest, have been confided to us by Sir Walter Trevelyan, Dr. Robert Ball, Dr. Farran, Mr. Albany Hancock, Mr. Warren of Dublin, and Mr. Couch. We owe

many obligations to the liberality of labourers in the same
field, and heartily thank (as we do all who have assisted
in this work), the veteran investigators of British Mollusca,
Dr. Fleming, Capt. Thomas Brown, and the Rev. Leonard
Jenyns. To Lieut. Thomas, R.N., Mr. Spence Bate,
Mr. Barlee, Mr. W. Thomson of London, and Dr.
Knapp, we are indebted for extensive information on
subjects of much consequence to the completion of our
inquiries. To three ladies, *viz.*, the Marchioness of Hastings, Mrs. Griffiths, and Mrs. Gulson, we return many
thanks for their interesting communications. A long list
of friends who have contributed valuable notes or specimens
remains unenumerated. Professor Allman, Professor Bell,
Dr. Battersby, Mr. Byerly, Mr. W. H. Baily, Mr. Cocks
of Falmouth, Mr. Darbyshire, Mr. W. C. Eyton, Mr.
Gibbs, Mr. Howse, Mr. Hyndman, the Rev. T. Hincks,
Mr. Hopkins of Dublin, Dr. Johnston of Berwick, Prof.
King of Galway, Mr. Lowe of Nottingham, Mr. F. D.
Lukis of Guernsey, the Rev. David Landsborough, Mr.
Metcalfe, Mr. Mackie of Folkstone, Mr. Pickering, Mr.
R. Patterson of Belfast, Mr. Peach, Mr. Reeve of Wor-
cester, Mr. Smith of Jordan-hill, Mr. J. de C. Sowerby,
Professor Strickland, and Mr. S. P. Woodward.

We may have omitted to mention some to whom thanks
are equally due, and whose names are mentioned in the
body of the work.

INTRODUCTION.

———

Of the great or primary assemblages into which all animals may be grouped, the MOLLUSCA constitute one. They rank inferior to the VERTEBRATA, partially inferior to the ARTICULATA, and mainly superior to the RADIATA and AMORPHOZOA. From the vertebrate animals they are conspicuously distinguished by their limb-less bodies, and the absence of a jointed internal skeleton; from the articulate animals, by their inarticulated exoskeleton, and bodies not divided into segments; from the radiate animals, zoophytes and sponges, by their more complex organization and subsymmetrical non-radiated forms. Between them and certain animals of all the other groups, there are, however, striking resemblances of analogy. The mollusks are all provided with a well-defined nervous system, the distinctive feature of which is that of being heterogangliate. They possess distinct organs of digestion, respiration, and circulation. The rapid anamorphosis of the entire group, shown by the progression from a low type of organization, such as is seen in the *Bryozoa*, to one comparatively very high, as exhibited by the *Cephalopoda*, necessarily implies varied manifestations of internal structure and external form. Hence the subdivisions of the Mollusca display remarkable contrasts in their diagnostic characters, and the aspect of a member of one of the lower divisions is singularly different from that of its relative among the higher orders of its class. The more important sections are distinguished by the absence, presence, or degree of development of a distinct head, a character correspondent to the degree of the development of the nervous system, and consequent degree of perfection of the organs of sense, and by modifications of the respiratory organs. Most Mollusca are furnished with a shell, which is usually composed of a single piece in the higher groups, and is bivalve in the lower. This shell, whether internal or external, may be regarded as a pneumoskeleton, its principal office being that of serving as a shield, or case, for the protection of the respiratory organs, although it often serves as a defensive covering for the whole of the soft parts. The names *Testacea*, and "shell-fish," have been bestowed upon the Mollusca on account of their shells, whose elegance of form, richness of sculpture, beauty of colouring and durability of substance have for ages attracted the notice of the curious, and led to their collection and study by lovers of Nature. But whilst the shelly portion of the body of the Mollusk was carefully inspected, treasured, and delineated, the more perishable parts were sadly neglected, and although some of our earlier English naturalists, especially the illustrious Lister, attended to the organization of the entire creature, the shell alone occupied the attention of the majority of observers, even from the time of Linnæus until within comparatively few years ago. The indefatigable and acute Montagu was indeed inclined to be an honourable exception, and the anatomical studies of Leach led this energetic naturalist to a truer appreciation of the subjects of his researches. The works of Turton, Donovan, and others, frequently cited in the following pages, are monuments of the attention, on the other hand, devoted almost exclusively to the shells. The naked Mollusks of all tribes were but seldom sought for. Montagu and Leach, it is true, called attention in England to the beauty and peculiarities of these animals ; Jameson and Fleming did the same service for these and still less attractive tribes in Scotland, but until within the last twenty years neither the Mollusks without shells, nor the soft parts of the testaceous families could be said to be estimated at their due importance, or to be regarded with systematic attention. How much has been done since, and how much is being done now, we have endeavoured to record, as far as our limits would admit, in the following history.

In like manner, but little was known of the habits, range, and distribution, geographical and bathymetrical, of the Mollusks indigenous to our seas. They were looked upon too frequently as objects of mere elegant curiosity, to be made the subjects of laborious research and observations conducted amid their native haunts. The importance of a knowledge of the facts of their mode of life, and the physical conditions affecting their diffusion, was not understood, nor indeed, until geology called loudly for information so necessary to the progress of that world-dissecting science, was the inquiry deemed of sufficient interest to attract the attention of more than some half a dozen observers. British naturalists can now boast of having investigated the phenomena of the molluscous fauna of their native islands more thoroughly than has been done by their colleagues in any foreign country. The number of facts now recorded respecting the distribution of the species inhabiting our seas is very considerable, and sufficient to warrant extensive generalizations. We offer the following brief review of the principal results of our present acquaintance with this peculiarly interesting branch of inquiry, as an appropriate introduction to the descriptive details that follow.

The Mollusca of the British seas are numerous and abundant. The varied conformation of the coasts of Great Britain and Ireland, and of the sea-bed surrounding these islands, is peculiarly favourable for the nourishment of a multiplicity of kinds of these animals. The climatal conditions of our area are such as to encourage the presence and perpetuation of both northern and southern temperate types, and the influence of very different ancient conditions is manifested by the presence among them of not a few shell-fish of boreal or arctic origin. Our Mollusca are, when taken collectively, not remarkable for brilliancy of painting, magnitude of dimensions, or singularity of contour; although in all these respects we can boast of striking exceptions, and among our minute species can show many of exquisite elegance and curious sculpture. By far the larger part of our marine Mollusks are tiny species. Our nudibranchs are, however, distinguished for the beauty of their colouring, and even among the despised ascidians there are some whose coats are tinged with the brightest or else the most delicate hues. The cuttle-fishes that live around us are too excursive and oceanic in their habits to be claimed as exclusively, or even chiefly, our own. Those that frequent our sea-bed are mostly animals of considerable size for Mollusca, and certainly among the most astonishing and beautiful of the inhabitants of the sea. They are, however, seldom seen by the casual observer, whose knowledge of our Molluscan treasures is mainly derived from sorry specimens of shells, cast upon the sea-beach by the waves.

The land-shells of the British islands are still less striking than the testacea of the surrounding seas. Their hues

are dull when compared with those of more southern
countries, and their shapes but seldom attractive for eccen-
tricity of outline or ornament.   They exhibit but few
peculiarities, and reckon among their number but few
rarities.   This is not the case with our marine species,
among which are numerous sorts that have either not been
noticed elsewhere, or are rarely to be met with, and which,
even when of pigmy dimensions, are among the most
prized gems of a good conchological cabinet.   In the grand
system of Nature size is of small account, and elephants
and mites, however different in bigness, reckon of equal
value as links in the chain of organization.   God's works
are never left unfinished.   None is too minute for the
display of infinite perfection.   The microscope has exhibited to our wondering eyes beauties of structure that have
been concealed from mortal sight for long ages.   It would
almost seem as if only glimpses of those excellencies of
creation are permitted to man to behold, whilst the full
contemplation of such wondrous charms is reserved for
immortal and invisible admirers.

Although, in consequence of the great number of Mollusks that are common to all parts of the British seas, provided we compare localities where conditions of sea-bottom
and depth are similar, it might seem that there is little
evidence of a peculiar distribution within the limits of our
area, if we regard its shell-fish either in mass or analyze
the relations of the several species to foreign and surrounding regions, we shall find very distinct manifestations
of peculiarities within the boundaries of our own.   Were
a conchologist desirous of accumulating personally and
rapidly a complete collection of British shells, he would
fail in his object if he confined his researches to any one
locality, even though it embraced a considerable reach of

coast and variety of sea-bottom. Four districts, at least, would have to be visited. To the Channel Islands he would have to go for several forms that are almost extra-British. On the south-west coasts of England he would find not a few shells that he would seek for in vain in more northern or eastern seas. Only on the west coasts of Scotland, many species of great interest and peculiarity could be readily obtained. In the extreme province of the Zetland Isles he would gather some of our most remarkable rarities; and possibly, after all, he would have to visit as much of the northern half of the German Ocean as may be claimed for our natural history province, and the west coasts of Ireland, before his cabinets could be fairly filled.

In reality, our Molluscan fauna is a composite assemblage, in which immigrants from the north and from the south intermingle with the aboriginal inhabitants, and descendants of a pre-Adamite fauna survive amongst them. Those forms that have travelled northwards and those that have journeyed southwards have not all made their way with equal speed. Consequently as we proceed either way we find a number of species gradually disappear, and differences instituted, both positive, by the presence of peculiar types, and negative by the absence of others, that serve to mark a sub-division of provinces within our area. Even among many of the species that are widely and almost universally spread throughout our seas, we find the frequency of their occurrence diminishing one way or other according to their origin. As a general rule the northern influence prevails over the southern in the British fauna, and gives greater peculiarities to the zoology of the Scottish than to that of the English seas. The central portion of our area—the Irish sea—is a sort of neutral ground, from which several forms are absent that are to be found both to the south and to the north of it. But such types, mostly of southern origin, can be traced in the course of their migration along the Atlantic coasts of Ireland, where their progress northwards has been favoured by the genial influence of warm currents. The most unproductive district is the southern half of the eastern coast,

Our marine Molluscan fauna, when considered with respect to its home arrangements, may be said to be composed of examples of no fewer than nine types ;—

I. The LUSITANIAN type, exemplified in species which are to be met with only in the extreme south, members of the Lusitanian and Mediterranean faunas, whose northern limits just impinge upon our area. *Haliotis tuberculata, Murex corallinus, Lachesis minima, Rissoa lactea* and *striatula, Pandora rostrata, Donax politus, Ervilia castanea, Lucina divaricata, Mactra helvacea, Avicula Tarentina, Galeomma Turtoni, Trochus striatus, Truncatella Montagui,* and *Onchidium Celticum,* may be cited as the principal representatives of this assemblage.

II. The SOUTH-BRITISH type ; to this belong species of southern origin with a somewhat wider diffusion than the last, occupying a limited but well-marked range along the southern and south-western coasts of England, and southern and western shores of Ireland, many of them entering St. George's Channel, but few passing the confines of South Wales. Such are *Adeorbis subcarinata, Bulla hydatis, Cardium aculeatum* and *rusticum, Chiton discrepans, Cytherea Chione, Dentalium Tarentinum, Diodonta fragilis, Diplodonta rotundata, Emarginula rosea, Gastrochæna Modiolina, Lepton squamosum, Modiola barbata, Nassa pygmæa, Ovula patula, Petricola lithophaga, Pholadidea papyracea, Rissoa costulata, Trochus exiguus* and *lineatus, Venerupis Irus,* and *Venus verrucosa.*

III. The Euɪᴏᴘᴇᴀɴ type, represented by species that
are equally diffused and abundant in most parts of the
British Seas, and which at the same time have a wide
range along the shores of Europe, although none of them
cross the Atlantic. To this section belong, among others,
the *Aporrhais pes-pelecani, Artemis exoleta* and *lincta, Cardium echinatum, edule, fasciatum* and *Norvegicum, Chiton
fascicularis, Corbula nucleus, Cylichna cylindracea, Cypræa
Europæa, Donax anatinus,Emarginula reticulata,Kellia suborbicularis, Lucinopsis undata, Lutraria elliptica, Mactra
solida, stultorum* and *subtruncata, Mangelia linearis, Nassa
reticulata, Natica nitida, Nucula nucleus, Patella vulgata, Pecten opercularis* and *pusio, Pectunculus glycimeris,
Pileopsis Hungaricus, Psammobia Ferroensis, Solen siliqua,
Syndosmya alba, Tapes virginea, Tellina Donacina, tenuis*
and *solidula, Tornatella fasciata, Trochus cinerarius, tumidus* and *zizyphinus, Turritella communis, Venus fasciata,
ovata* and *striatula.* Several of our Nudibranchiate Mollusks, and some Ascidians, probably belong to this group.
Many of the above-cited species are remarkably prolific,
and the individuals of them often constitute a large proportion of the contents of the dredge, or are to be gathered
numerously on the shore.

IV. Along with the last, and most of them as plentiful,
are the members of the Cᴇʟᴛɪᴄ type, a group especially
characteristic of our area. This assemblage consists of
species that are essentially Atlantic. They are most prolific and at home within the Celtic province, of which the
British Islands constitute an important portion. They
have a tendency to diffuse themselves rather northwards
than southwards, multiplying rather in the boreal than in the
Lusitanian province. Many of them are of ancient origin,
and well known in the fossil state. As examples we may

cite *Acmæa virginea, Astarte sulcata, Buccinum undatum, Chiton cinereus* and *ruber, Orenella decussata* and *discors, Fusus antiquus* and *Islandicus*; the various species of *Lacuna, Littorina littoralis, littorea* and *rudis, Lucina borealis, Mactra elliptica* and *solida, Mangelia turricula, Modiola modiolus, Mya arenaria* and *truncata, Mytilus edulis, Natica monilifera, Nassa incrassata, Ostrea edulis, Patella pellucida, Pecten maximus, Pholas crispata* and *candida, Purpura lapillus, Rissoa cingillus* and *striata, Saxicava arctica* and *rugosa, Scaphander lignarius, Skenea planorbis, Solen ensis, Syndosmya prismatica, Tapes pullastra, Thracia distorta, Trophon clathratus* and *muricatus, Velutina lævigata* and *Venus casina.* Many of our naked Mollusks take their place here.

V. Peculiarly BRITISH may be styled the assemblage of species little known elsewhere, or even unknown out of our own seas. The list is considerable but very fallacious, since it is swelled by minute or critical forms, that in all probability enjoy a wider range, but have as yet escaped observation on stranger shores. In this category we may place many of the *Odostomiæ* and *Montacutæ,* hitherto unrecognised on other coasts than our own. Every year discovers that the parentage of some cherished species is not so exclusively British as patriotic naturalists fondly imagined. Excluding, however, all critical types or forms liable from resemblance to others to be overlooked, the following remarkable Testacea have not as yet been noticed beyond our limits:—*Assiminea Grayana, Astarte crebricostata* (probably arctic), *Buccinum fusiforme, Fusus Berniciensis, Fusus Turtoni* (the three last will probably prove to be members of a more northern Fauna); the species of *Jeffreysia, Lepton Clarkiæ, Megathyris cistellula, Natica Kingii* (probably arctic); *Otina otis, Pecten niveus, Pro-*

pilidium Ancyloide (probably arctic) ; a few species of *Rissoa*, and of so-called *Skeneæ, Stylifer Turtoni, Syndosmya tenuis* and *Thracia villosiuscula*, the two last probably much more diffused. Species well known in a few localities elsewhere, but most abundant in the British seas, such as *Trochus Montagui* and *millegranus, Scalaria Trevelyana, Natica Montagui, Astarte triangularis,* and *Pecten tigrinus* and *striatus*, might possibly be cited with even more propriety as representatives of a British type.

VI. A considerable number of our marine Mollusca are sufficiently common on the western coasts of Britain, though scarce in the Irish Sea, and for the most part absent from the German Ocean, or, at least, from the more central portions of our eastern coast. Most of these have a considerable range to the southward of the British Islands. Some of them, however, such as *Trochus umbilicatus*, are confined to the oceanic coasts of Europe. The whole assemblage seems to have a spread, in part indicative of an ancient trend of land westwards, and in part of the course and influence of the extension of the Gulf stream. This assemblage may be styled the ATLANTIC type. Many instances may be adduced, such as *Akera bullata, Arca tetragona, Cerithiopsis tuberculare, Cerithium adversum* and *reticulatum, Circe minima, Fissurella reticulata, Isocardia cor, Lima hians* and *subauriculata, Lucina spinifera, Mangelia attenuata, gracilis* and *purpurea, Modiola tulipa, Natica sordida*, the species of *Neæra ?, Nucula decussata, Nucula radiata ?, Pinna pectinata, Psammobia costulata* and *tellinella, Rissoa labiosa, rufilabrum* and *vitrea, Scalaria clathratula, Solen marginatus, Solecurtus candidus* and *coarctatus, Tapes aurea* and *decussata, Tellina balaustina* and *incarnata, Terebratula caput serpentis.*

VII. The few Pelagic Mollusca that are driven towards

or habitually frequent our seas are also to be found mainly upon our western boundaries. They constitute an OCEANIC type. Our native and occasional Pteropods, as *Hyalæa trispinosa*, and the three species of *Spirialis*; our few pelagic Gasteropods, as *Ianthina communis*, *exigua* and *pallida*, and, just possibly, *Scissurella crispata*; the Nudibranchous Mollusk, *Scyllæa pelagica*; the tunicated swimmer, *Salpa runcinata*; borers in floating wood, such as the various species of *Teredo* and the *Xylophaga dorsalis*; and, lastly, our twelve species of Cephalopods may be ranked in this interesting group.

VIII. We have before remarked that in the northern division of the British Seas there are many species either not found more to the south, or else becoming rarer as we proceed southwards. Some of them, too, are only to be met with in peculiar and limited localities, grouped together like isolated colonists. The majority of these northern forms belong to an assemblage that constitutes the BOREAL type of our Molluscan fauna. They are all species that thrive best in seas to the north of Britain, and many of them range across the Boreal Atlantic, or, at least, are found on both sides, but only within cold waters. They are not, however, to be considered as strictly Arctic. To this group we may assign such examples as *Acmæa testudinalis*, *Astarte compressa* and *elliptica*, *Cardium Suecicum*, *Cerithium metula*, *Chemnitzia fulvocincta?* *Chiton Hanleyi* and *marmoreus*, *Crania anomala*, *Crenella nigra*, *Cyprina Islandica*, *Emarginula crassa*, *Fusus Norvegicus* and *propinquus*, *Hypothyris psittacea*, *Leda caudata* and *pygmæa*, *Mangelia nana*, *Natica Helicoides*, *Nucula tenuis*, *Panopæa Norvegica*, *Pecten Danicus?* *Philine quadrata* and *scabra*, *Pilidium fulvum*, *Puncturella Noachina*, *Syndosmya intermedia*, *Thracia convexa*, *Trichotropis borealis*,

Trochus alabastrum, helicinus and *undulatus*, and *Volutina flexilis*. A considerable portion of our Ascidians belong to this type.

IX. A few of our most northern shells may be regarded as belonging to a still more northern, an Arctic type. *Astarte arctica, Natica pusilla, Scalaria Grænlandica* and *Terebratula cranium*, may be accepted as representatives of this group.

Our land and freshwater Mollusks may likewise be grouped under several types, which, however, we shall sufficiently indicate hereafter when noticing their foreign relations.

The main text of this work is occupied with the descriptions and history of the species which are true and indigenous members of these several types. Only such can fairly be considered as British Mollusca. In this division of the animal kingdom, unlike what may happen in the higher and more mobile sections of our fauna, there is little danger of the intrusion of stragglers, although a few of oceanic habits, or else transported through the unconscious agency of man, acting as their carrier through the medium of his sea-traversing ships, do find their way legitimately into our seas. A few land-snails also transported in timber, or about the roots of plants, have established themselves, though only for a limited period, on our soil. Such legitimised foreigners we have, in almost every instance, described in a supplementary shape at the end of the genera to which they belong. A residue of unlawful and confusing intruders remains to be accounted for.

The number of exotic shells erroneously introduced into our fauna is very large, our earlier writers having frequently considered them as indigenous upon very slender grounds of evidence. When once the species was inserted in our lists,

it was admitted as a native into the cabinets of local collectors with even a less degree of circumspection than
previously, and subsequent authors, misled by the assertions
of their self-deceived friends (too often willingly deceived,
for a specimen worthless as exotic, was quickly metamor-
phosed into a rarity, when supposed to represent a locally
scarce species), added the weight of their authority to
promulgate the original error. Montagu, in one of his
letters, written subsequently to the publication of his great
quarto work on "British Conchology," laments the too
easy credence he had given to the accounts of his friends,
and earnestly deprecates any further attempts at augment-
ing our fauna, without strict investigation and mature
deliberation.

Peculiar pains have been bestowed, throughout this work,
to arrive at sound conclusions in regard to the retention or
rejection as indigenous of the many species hitherto doubtfully allowed to remain in our catalogues. The original
specimens of the hypothetically spurious species have been
sought for and examined, that their worn or perfect condition might serve as an auxiliary means of eliminating the
truth, in balancing the probabilities of their having been
tempest-driven upon our coast (the spoils of some wrecked
merchantman), or calmly wafted upon our sands from their
native depths. The importance of this actual examination
may be inferred from the fact that Dr. Leach took fragments
of foreign coral* from several of Montagu's own specimens!
The different value at which we must rate the testimony†

---

* "It is well known that some Conchologists shamefully imposed upon Montagu, and that Dr. Leach took fragments of foreign coral from several of the
shells that had been in his possession." (Bean's Letter.) "General Bingham
was notorious for being imposed on as to indigenousness." (Jeffreys' Letter.)

† As a general rule, the unsupported testimony of Laskey or Bryer is not to
be depended upon.

of each individual informant of an author, has been estimated upon the opinion entertained by surviving contemporaries, of his veracity and caution; the several shades
of difference between an author's positive declaration, that
he himself has dredged the species in a living state, and
the mere picking up, by some unlearned friend of his,
of single valves upon the beach, are duly taken into our
estimate; the competency for the determination of species,
at the date of publication, of parties who have re-admitted
such into their local catalogues, has been, as far as possible,
scrutinized; the improbability of a Boreal species being
discovered on our Southern shores, or of a tropical one upon
our Northern coast, the unlikelihood of a known littoral
shell being dredged in deep water at many miles from the
land, has been poised in the balance of conflicting testi-
monies: in fine, an almost unanimous verdict from the
chief living writers upon British Conchology, and the most
zealous and trustworthy collectors, has preluded and sanc-
tioned our expulsion of any species which has ever been
improperly regarded as a veritable inhabitant of the soil
or waters of our Islands.

Were we to preface such species with a circumstantial
detail of the evidences upon which our conclusions have
been grounded, a larger portion of our work would be
occupied by the spurious than by the genuine British Testacea. With a similar view of economising space, without
the omission of any matter important to Conchology, those
of the former, which are universally known, are simply
defined by a synonomy based upon the re-examination of
the types (or where that was impracticable, careful study
of the published descriptions), and not merely founded upon
the surmise that the British writer had correctly divined
the previous names bestowed upon them by Linnæus and

the earlier writers. To other rejected species, where deemed
advisable, a more or less brief description has been appended,
that continental authors may at length definitively ascertain
what was actually intended by Montagu, Turton, their
predecessors and contemporaries.

The distribution, in depth, of Mollusca in the British
seas, has been made the subject of numerous and minute
researches. Under each marine species described in this
work, full particulars of its bathymetrical range are usually
given, and instances illustrative of its habitat at different
and distant points. Those of our readers who would study
this interesting subject in all its bearings, should consult
the essay " On the Connection between the Distribution of
the existing Fauna and Flora of the British Isles, with the
Geological Changes that have affected their Area," contained in the first volume of the " Memoirs of the Geological Survey of Great Britain," and the "Report on the
Investigation of British Marine Zoology by means of the
Dredge," in the volume of " British Association Reports
for 1850." There is also a very interesting paper on this
subject detailing the results of extensive experience, by Mr.
M'Andrew, published in the "Transactions of the Literary
and Philosophical Society of Liverpool."

A few remarks will serve to explain the notes on bathymetrical range, appended to our descriptions of species.
Marine Mollusca are mentioned as inhabiting a depth of
water of so many fathoms, or as having been dredged from
such a depth. We need scarcely remind our readers that
the term *fathom*, in depth, is applied to a vertical measure
of six feet. It is employed in preference to other terms,
because it is in general use among sailors, and is the measure
commonly inscribed upon hydrographical charts. Marine
Mollusca are also mentioned as inhabiting different *Zones*

or *Regions of Depth*. By this phrase is understood the several belts or spaces margining the land, or occupying the floor of the sea, distinguished from each other by the presence of peculiar features dependent on arrangements of their animal and vegetable inhabitants.

The highest of these belts is the space between tide-marks, an interval of very great importance in the marine Fauna of our Islands, and inhabited by numerous peculiar species of plants as well as animals. It is termed the LITTORAL ZONE. Its features vary with the geological or rather mineralogical character of the coast, and its population, both as to kinds and numbers, varies correspondently. Where it is rocky, it is inhabited by numerous gasteropodous mollusks; where muddy, or sandy, by burrowing bivalves, or, in such localities, is not unfrequently devoid of testacea. The common limpet, *Patella vulgata*, the various species of periwinkle (*Littorina*), the dog-whelk, *Purpura lapillus*, certain forms of *Trochus* and *Rissoa*, the little *Skenea planorbis*, the common mussel and the minute *Kellia rubra* inhabit this zone on hard rocky ground universally in the British seas. Local forms and occasional stragglers from lower regions are here and there mingled with them. On sandy and muddy shores numerous bivalves are often thrown up by the waves, not a few of which are to be found alive in the lower division of this zone. In places where the water is brackish, it swarms with *Rissoa ulvæ*. It is capable of being divided into several sub-regions, each marked by prevailing forms of animals and plants. The uppermost is distinguished by the presence of the smaller varieties of *Littorina rudis* and *L. Neritoides*; a second belt by the abundance of *Mytilus edulis*, and the larger forms of *Littorina rudis*; a third by the prevalence of *Littorina littorea* and *Purpura lapillus*; a fourth, and lowermost, by the dominance of *Littorina littoralis*, various *Rissoæ*, especially *Rissoa parva*, and *Trochus cinerarius*, accompanied in the west by *Trochus umbilicatus*, and in the south-west by *Trochus lineatus*.

A second region is the CIRCUM-LITTORAL or LAMINARIAN ZONE; so called from the abundance of tangles or sea-weeds of the genus *Laminaria*, that flourish in it around the shores of Europe. On sandy ground these are replaced by the Grass-Wrack or *Zostera*. Vegetable-feeding shell-fish and naked Mollusca are exceedingly numerous in this space. It is indeed highly productive of various types of animal and also of vegetable life. Its usual vertical extent may be stated as between low-water mark and fifteen fathoms. In its lower portion the coral-weed, or *Nullipora*, becomes very abundant, and furnishes a ground often chosen by fishes for their spawning haunts. The genera *Lacuna* (except one species), *Calyptrea*, *Aplysia*, *Scrobicularia* and *Donax* do not range, in our seas, below this belt; and *Rissoa*, *Chiton*, *Bulla*, *Trochus*, *Mactra*, *Venus* and *Cardium* have the majority of their British representatives within its precincts. The sub-genus of *Patella*, called *Patina*, is entirely confined to it.

A third region is the MEDIAN or CORALLINE ZONE, occupying the space between fifteen and fifty fathoms. Sea-weeds, properly so called, are scarce within it, and absent from its greater portion, but much of it is clothed with an animal-vegetation, so to speak, in the shape of corallines, or hydroid-zoophytes. It abounds in shell-fish, and many of our rarest and most valued kinds are procured from it. In its upper portion *Trochus ziziphinus* and *tumidus*, *Chiton asellus*, *Acmæa virginea*, *Turritella communis*, *Venus ovata* and *V. fasciata*, *Pecten opercularis*, *Modiola modiolus*, the common form of *Crenella*, *Pectunculus glycimeris* and *Nucula nucleus*, are characteristic testacea, and in its lower half *Solen pellucidus*, *Pecten varius*, *Modiola modiolus*, *Dentalium* and *Mactra elliptica*. It is marked more by the peculiarities of its species than by the exclusive presence of genera.

The fourth region is the INFRA-MEDIAN, also called the region of deep-sea corals, since in our seas (though not in those of the tropics) the principal stony corals, whether of zoophytic or bryozoan production, are procured from it. Its most characteristic portions, within the British area, are in the extreme north. There appear, however, to be very few species of Mollusks peculiar to it within our seas. Those that are found are, for the most part, of rather small dimensions, and remarkable for being of dull or pale colouring.

Beneath this zone is the ABYSSAL REGION, which can scarcely be said to be developed within the British area.

The greater part of the floor of the British seas is occupied by the Coralline or Median zone. The Infra-median belt is of less, though considerable, extent. The Abyssal or deep-sea region occupies but an insignificant portion of their area. Hence the very small number of our Mollusks that can be fairly regarded as characteristic abyssal species. The coast-line of the British Islands is exceedingly varied, in consequence of the numerous formations of various mineral constitution and geological age of which the land is composed. A corresponding variety in the species, and abundance of distinct specific types, are the result, and our Molluscan fauna, in consequence, becomes an exceedingly rich one. The very shallowness of a considerable extent of our seas is in favour of their richness, when combined, as it is, with considerable variety of sea-bed. An inspection of hydrographical charts will readily illustrate this

feature, since the letters inscribed upon them, indicative of
a bottom consisting of sand, sandy mud, rock, stones,
gravel, muddy gravel, shelly ground, and " coral," *i. e.*,
nullipore or vegetable coral, mark as many spaces in which
certain forms of Mollusks multiply or prevail in preference
to other types.   As a general rule univalve testacea and
naked Mollusca flourish most upon hard, bivalve testacea
upon soft ground, and this appears to hold true, at least
with respect to the species described in this work, through
all gradations of depth.

Besides these several sub-divisions of the floor of the
Ocean, there are the high levels of the sea-water itself,
inhabited by a small assemblage of Mollusks.   The genera
Ianthina and *Spirialis*, among our testacea, and our solitary
species of *Salpa*, as well as the curious and anomalous
Appendicularia among Tunicata, are inhabitants of this
marine atmosphere.   All these forms are, however, very
local around our coasts.   In more southern seas, the waves
often swarm with pelagic Mollusca.

To the two uppermost zones are confined all the representatives of several genera, whilst the species which live
in the lower belts belong to genera which have also members in the Littoral and Laminarian zones.   In the two
uppermost zones the great majority of testaceous species
is found ; in the second, or Laminarian belt the majority of
naked and tunicated Mollusks.   In the higher zones many
of the species, both of univalve and bivalve testacea, are exceedingly prolific, and their individuals gregarious, so that
large numbers of one kind of shell are found assembled together within a limited area, sometimes almost to the exclu-
sion of other sorts.   The proportion of gregarious species to
those of solitary or scattered diffusion is much greater in the
littoral than in any of the other belts.   All the zones of

depth are in a manner linked together by species common to
two or more of them. Bivalve Mollusks would appear to
be more extensively distributed in depth, and to constitute
more constant links between zone and zone than univalves.

The foreign relations of our marine Molluscan fauna may
be stated approximately as follows :—

Our catalogue of *Tunicata*, a group to which comparatively little attention has been given, and of which our
account is intended to serve only as a Prodromus, includes
seventy-four species. There are, doubtless, many more
inhabiting the British seas. Out of those which we have
enumerated, more than one-third are unnoticed as members
of any extra-British fauna, and of those that have been
observed elsewhere, the majority is Celtic or else boreal.
In the main we may regard our Ascidians as immigrants
from more northern seas.

The number of our indigenous *Acephala*, or bivalved
shell-fish, may be stated at a hundred and sixty species,
after expunging doubtful, introduced, and spurious forms.
Out of this number very few indeed, not more than about
seven species, are known only as inhabitants of the British
seas, and as these are critical or very rare types, they may
fairly be considered as having escaped notice on foreign
coasts, rather than as peculiar to our own. About eighty
of our bivalves extend their range in the European seas
both northwards and southwards of our area; forty range
southwards into the Lusitanian province, but are not known
to the north of the Celtic area; thirteen inhabit the Scandinavian seas, but do not range to the south of Britain,
nor, so far as known, across the Atlantic; twenty-seven
are common to the seas of Boreal and Arctic America, and
those of Boreal and Celtic Europe. The few remaining
species are such as have been only observed so far with-

out an area on the continental coasts of the Celtic
province.

The distribution of the four *Pteropoda* that find a place
in this work is oceanic. Two of them are, however, as
yet unrecorded as extra-British, though it is probable that
they will be found widely diffused in the Atlantic, if indeed
they be not identical with the oceanic forms referred to in
our descriptions.

The number of our species of testaceous marine *Gasteropoda* may be stated at two hundred and thirty-two. Out
of these a considerable proportion, not fewer than fifty-five,
has no place in any account of foreign Mollusca. It is
exceedingly unlikely that all of this number can be peculiarly British, though in all probability many of them are
peculiarly Celtic. The members of some of our genera of
minute univalves, especially *Odostomia*, have not yet received sufficient attention from foreign naturalists to enable
us to say, with any approach to certainty, whether they
are found on continental coasts or not; and out of the
fifty-five species above mentioned no fewer than nineteen
are *Odostomiæ*. There are fifty-four species common to
the seas both north and south of Britain, mostly ranging
southwards to the Mediterranean, the few exceptions
ceasing on the coast of Spain, certain kinds of *Littorina*
and *Patella* especially. No fewer than fifty-two species
range to the southwards of the British Islands, but do not
occur northwards of them; whilst thirty-four range northwards into the Boreal and European province, but do not
extend south of our area. Some twenty-eight or thirty
are inhabitants of arctic and boreal seas, and are common
to both sides of the Atlantic, within those provinces. The
few remaining are species observed in extra-British portions
of the Celtic province, but not elsewhere.

We have enumerated and characterized ninety British Nudibranchiate and Pellibranchiate Gasteropoda. Of these more than two-thirds have as yet been noticed only in the British seas. It is quite impossible to institute any comparison of this portion of our fauna with the accounts of the corresponding portion of any extra-British fauna, since the minute and elaborate researches of Messrs. Alder and Hancock have given us an overwhelming advantage.

Our single marine naked pulmonated Mollusk is not known at present, we believe, out of the Celtic province; but, as it has been seldom sought for, may have escaped notice. Our two testaceous marine Pulmonifera range southward of Britain, and one of them is found on the opposite shores of the Atlantic.

Our fourteen species of *Cephalopoda* are, with one exception, found beyond our limits. At least four of them may be regarded as common to all the seas around us, whilst six are apparently immigrants from more southern, and three from more northern provinces. There are still hopes of our acquiring, in the course of natural history research, a few additions to our list in this interesting portion of the fauna, one that has been in a great measure neglected. The interesting and curious genus *Onychoteuthis* especially may be expected to furnish a British representative. We would urgently press upon our younger naturalists to let no cuttle-fish pass unexamined.

Our land and fresh-water Mollusks present but few peculiarities, and are almost all continental. The *Helix fusca* was supposed to be exclusively British, and is stated to be so in our text, but it appears now that the shell referred to under the name of *Helix revelata* (a very distinct species) by Bouchard Chantereaux is really *fusca*. It is indeed very doubtful whether any of our land shells can be

claimed as truly confined to the British Islands. One remarkable slug, the *Geomalacus maculosus*, has never been
met with out of the south-west of Ireland, and is there
exceedingly scarce. We think it not unlikely that this
curious animal will eventually be found to be a member of
the Lusitanian fauna. A very curious fresh-water shell,
Lymneus involutus, is also, at present, confined to the same
portion of Ireland, and another species of the same genus,
L. Burnetti, is reputed peculiar to Britain. In these
instances we are possibly dealing with monstrosities, or
extreme varieties of the widely distributed *L. pereger*. One
fresh-water bivalve, a species of *Pisidium*, has not been
noticed beyond our limits ; but in this genus the characters
are too critical to warrant our inferring that it has not been
passed over abroad. Within our own areas, several of our
land and fresh-water shells do not range north to Scotland.

At least fifty species of our land and fresh-water Mollusks
may be regarded as generally distributed throughout Europe,
and as ranging both to the north and south of the British
Isles. None can be said to come from the north exclusively. About eighteen are members of the fauna of Northern and Central Europe ; some fourteen are Central European species, not ranging far northwards or southwards ;
about sixteen belong to Central and Southern Europe ; not
more than four are decidedly of southern origin exclusively ;
some seven or eight species are reported to extend their
range into the New World ; but, except in the instances of
one or two aquatic types, they have probably been introduced through the agency of man. Indeed, some of our
smaller snails have found their way through the same unconscious assistance even into Australia. Several of our aquatic
species have a wide range into the further parts of the
Asiatic continent. The provinces of Asia and Africa that

e

border on the Mediterranean, participate in the presence of such of our species as form part of the fauna of that region.

In alpine regions, of higher elevation than those that diversify the surface of the British Islands, a distinct and positive distribution in altitude of land and fresh-water Mollusca may be clearly made out, peculiar species appearing for the first time in definite zones of elevation. On our mountains, deficiencies only can be observed; they can boast of no peculiar types. The few Mollusks that are found on their higher portions are such as may be collected in the northernmost regions of Europe; but, at the same time, are equally members of the fauna of our low districts, and the neighbourhood of our shores.

Whilst the early history of our naked and unpreservable Mollusks has perished without a record, the genealogy of not a few of our testacea may be traced unerringly in fossiliferous formations. The area of the British Islands exhibits a long series of ancient seabeds that tell unmistakably of the changes that have taken place within its bounds. By far the greater part of these show, in their contents, no instances of specific identity with our existing Mollusca, and the farther we recede in time, the more different was our submarine population. The first approach to an existing British species is seen in the *Terebratula striatula*, of the upper cretaceous strata, a form scarcely distinguishable in essential features from the *Terebratula caput-serpentis*. It is not, however, until we seek among our tertiary strata, that we find true homologues of our living Mollusca. Some three or four Eocene shells, especially forms of *Eulima* and *Cylichna*, come exceedingly close to recent species, and are possibly identical. There is a doubt, however; the forms themselves being what are termed critical types, and their

Eocene associates of less questionable character, being assuredly wholly distinct from any now living. Our Eocene land and fresh-water shells (as well as the fresh-water forms of previous epochs), although several, especially certain *Paludinæ* and *Planorbides*, very closely, almost too closely, approach existing types, are all regarded as distinct from those that live upon our land now. It is a very remarkable fact, that among them, as shown by Mr. Searles Wood and Mr. Frederic Edwards, there are species which cannot be separated from existing American forms. The true source of our Molluscan fauna was first manifested by the assemblage of testacea preserved in the deposit called Coralline Crag, a formation at first regarded as Miocene, but now held to be of older Pliocene age. In that ancient sea-bed are to found many of the ancestors of our living shell-fish, mostly of them forms which we regard as southern types. Some of these seemed to have lived on continuously to our own time, but the majority, after struggling with the advent of less favourable conditions during the deposition of the succeeding Red Crag, were banished from our seas, when the frigid conditions of the glacial epoch set in, and did not return until the restoration of new ages of summer. With glacial conditions came Arctic species, many of which linger still within our area. It seems very probable that some of these are gradually being extinguished, and that a few of our testacea, such as *Pecten Danicus*, of which the number of dead specimens taken is quite disproportioned to the rarity of living examples, are close upon the time of their final extirpation, whilst others, such as *Pecten Islandicus*, and *Leda oblonga*, may have been blotted from the lists of the living, even since the occupation of the British Isles by man.

Our land and fresh-water testacea, although we cannot

track them as far back in time as we can our marine species,
have, nevertheless, survived in many instances prodigious
changes, and been the companions of larger animals that
have long ceased to inhabit our earth. Some of our commonest snails, such as *Helix nemoralis*, *H. hispida*, *Zonites
collaria*, and *Zua lubrica*, occur abundantly in deposits
buried beneath the gravel, in which the remains of extinct
elephants, and other quadrupeds, strikingly different from
the wild beasts now living in Central Europe, are abundantly found. Still older, possibly, are those that are associated with the *Cyrena* of the Nile, and the *Unio littoralis*
in the fresh-water deposits of the valley of the Thames.
Geology has, as yet, scarcely approached towards an estimate of the vast duration of these comparatively modern
epochs. They have but lately received anything like a due
share of attention, and the nearer we approach our own
times in our gropings amid geological antiquity, the more
complex seem to become our calculations of the length of
those periods during which the progenitors of still-existing
forms of life flourished, along with creatures that have disappeared for ever. When we learn how long has been the
existence upon the world's surface of some of our little
shell-fish, our wonder is not that they should be so widely
spread over it now, but rather that there should be any
spot capable of supporting their life from which they should
be absent.

GENERAL INDEX.

THE SYNONYMS ARE IN ITALICS.

h

i

ERRATA.

Index, page lxvii, line 17, *for* Greenlandica *read* Grœnlandica.
　　"　　　　"　　　　"　18, 　"　*Grœnlandica*　"　*Greenlandica*.
　　"　　lxviii, 　"　27, 　"　S. Hebridicus　"　Hebridicus.
In Plates of Animals, page 483, vol. i., line 18, *for* 7, *read* 7 ; .
　　　　"　　　　"　484, 　"　　"　6, *for* 3. *M. (Bela septangularis)*
　　　　　　　　read 3. *M. (Bela) septangularis.*
　　　　"　　　　"　485, 　"　　"　37, 　"　*Ancylus* read *Conovulus bidentatus.*

CONTENTS OF THE FIRST VOLUME,

EXHIBITING THE FINAL CORRECTIONS AND ADDITIONS.

Species of questionable indigenousness are printed in italics ; spurious and unrecognised species in nonpareil. The addition of (A. i.) to a species refers the reader to the first Appendix, or Supplementary Notes on the Acephala, in the Second Volume, (A. ii.) to the Appendix at the end of the work.

BRITISH MOLLUSCA.

ACEPHALA TUNICATA.

In every class of organised beings there are creatures so constituted as to link the group to which they belong with some other, or even to render their true position a matter of question. Especially at the extremities, at the lowest and highest portions of considerable sections, do we find such beings. In so great a subdivision of the animal kingdom as the Mollusca, we must expect to meet with anomalous or connecting creatures; and were we to begin this history of our native species, in which we propose to treat of them in the order of their ascent in the animal series, with such as seem to us to mark the commencement of their type, we should have to extract a very considerable chapter from our esteemed friend Dr. Johnston's "History of the British Zoophytes." For the curious beings called Bryozoa, or Ascidian Polypes, present so many characters in common with certain undoubted Mollusca, especially with the Tunicata, and so few comparatively with true zoophytes, that in a natural classification they could not with propriety be separated from the former class. Even that which was supposed essentially to distinguish them from true Mollusca, the absence of ganglia in their nervous system, has been shewn to be incorrect, since Van Beneden and Professor Allman have demonstrated the presence of a distinct nervous system with a ganglion in certain species of Bryozoa.

Still the Bryozoa may be regarded as a lowest order of Mollusca, linking that great class with the Zoophyta, and distinguished from the true tunicated mollusks by the

crown of long ciliated tentacula surrounding their mouths,
and forming so conspicuous a part of the animals, which,
aggregated, constitute the plant-like bodies familiar to all
frequenters of the sea-shore, and known as *Flustræ*. Some
of these bodies, such as the *Alcyonidium*, are extremely
difficult to distinguish at a glance from masses or systems
of organisms belonging to the true Tunicata. And were
activity to be the test of a creature's position in the animal
series, the little Bryozoa, which form the corallines called
Flustra, would stand higher than the Compound Tunicata,
for they are infinitely more lively creatures, and apparently
even more intelligent. Though their existence be fixed it
is active; whereas the majority of tunicated mollusks,
even of the higher and more independent forms, lead a
passive and apathetic life, at least when they have attained
their perfect development, for, like many other invertebrated
animals, they are much more free and lively in their earlier
stages, passing through a tadpole state, but eventually un-
dergoing what, in some respects, may be regarded as a
retrograde metamorphosis.

Some very distinguished authorities would separate the
whole of the Tunicata from the Mollusca, and place them
as an intermediate class, or sub-class, between that great
group and the Zoophyta. Professor Milne-Edwards,
whose researches on Ascidians are second in point of merit
only to those of Savigny, and, indeed, equal in value, has
come to such a conclusion. In his admirable memoir on
the "Ascidiens Composées," printed in the eighteenth volume of the "Memoirs of the Institute of France," (1842,) he
sums up as follows :—" The facts which I have made known
in this memoir shew that the Ascidians have less intimate
analogies with the Mollusca, properly so called, than is
usually believed. They resemble, it is true, these animals
in the arrangement of their digestive apparatus, and in
some peculiarities of the respiratory system ; but they de-
part from the Molluscan type in mode of circulation, in the
metamorphosis which the fry undergo, and, above all, in the
singular power which most of them possess, of multiplying

by gemmation. In these latter characters, so very important in a physiological point of view, they approach closely polypes ; and if we compare the general conformation of their bodies with that of the Escharæ, Vesiculariæ, Halodactyles, Pedicellariæ, and other zoophytes, for which I have proposed the designation of 'Polypes Tuniciers,' one cannot but perceive other analogies not less striking— the mode of aggregation through which most of them are united in societies, and their phytoid aspect. To harmonise the zoological classification with our anatomical knowledge, it seems to me convenient no longer to confound, with Cuvier, the Tunicata with the Mollusca, but to follow Lamarck, and constitute for them a special division intermediate between the bivalve Mollusca and the polypes." The force of this proposal, however, depends mainly upon the view to be taken of the classification of the zoophytes themselves. And, in the present state of our knowledge, a blank would occur in such a series of works on the Natural History of Britain as that of which this forms a part, unless some account of the Ascidians were therein given.

We shall commence, then, our history with a short notice of the Mollusca of the order Tunicata. Our main object in this work is to give a full account of the Testaceous Mollusks of the British Islands, but it is necessary, in order to connect them in zoological order, to notice the shell-less tribes. To treat the latter fully, or on nearly the same scale with the shelled species, would be to extend these volumes to an encyclopædic length; nor is it necessary, for the beautiful monograph of the "Nudibranchiate Mollusca," by our friends Mr. Alder and Mr. Hancock, exhausts one portion of the subject, whilst for the other, equal in extent, that of the Tunicated Mollusks of the British seas, which we are now about to outline, though great masses of materials have been collected by the combined labours of many naturalists, and are now safely in charge of Professor Goodsir, by whom, we trust, they will before long be worthily examined and made known, to work them will be a labour of several years, and many more ob-

servations must be made upon them in the living state
before they can be published.   Nevertheless, an outline of the present extent of our knowledge of British
species may be serviceable, as directing attention to a very
interesting and but partially explored department of our
native zoology, and as furnishing some guide for future
researches.

The Tunicata are Mollusca which have no true shell, but
are enveloped in a coriaceous tunic or mantle ; whence their
name.   This is constructed in the form of a sac with two
openings, or else is shaped like a tube, of greater or less
dimensions, open at both ends.   Within the tunic we find
the viscera, consisting of well-defined organs of respiration,
circulation, and digestion, and a muscular and a nervous
system.   The branchial organ is usually in the form of a
sac, placed at the commencement of the alimentary canal,
of which it forms, as it were, the antechamber, and is
never arranged in distinct leaflets, as it is in the lamellibranchiate Conchifera.   The circulation of their blood is
remarkable, on account of its fluctuations and periodical
changes of direction.   They have no distinct head, and no
organs serving as arms or feet.   Sometimes they are free,
more usually fixed ; but in all cases free during some portion of their existence.   Some are simple, some present
various degrees of combination ; some are simple in one
generation, combined in another.   They are all dwellers in
the sea.   Their various states and structures enable naturalists to group them under several well-marked tribes, of
most of which we have examples in the British seas.   The
best classification of them is that proposed by Professor
Milne-Edwards.   He divides them into three sub-orders,
of which the Salpa, the Ascidia, and the Pyrosoma are the
types, and subdivides the Ascidians proper into simple,
social, and compound.   Of all, except the Pyrosoma, we
have British examples.

These animals attracted the notice of the all-observing
Aristotle.   Like most philosophic naturalists, the question
of the distinction between the animal and vegetable king-

doms had for him great attractions. The Ascidia (Τηθυα) was one of the many creatures which he examined, in the hopes of gaining definite information respecting such distinction. Its inert and sponge-like form, rooted to the ground, seemed to indicate a vegetable nature; but Aristotle was not content with a mere external survey—he explored its internal structure, and soon perceived its highly animal condition. His description of the Τηθυα is wonderfully correct: it occurs in the fourth book of his "History of Animals." There he distinctly recognises the Ascidians to be Mollusca, of which, he says, "they are the only kind whose whole body is enclosed in the shell, and that shell of a substance between true shell and leather : it may be cut like dry leather." What comparison could be more graphic or more true ! "They are attached to rocks by their shell. They have two separate openings, which are very small and difficult to notice, the one to take in, the other to eject the water.* * * * If we open them, we find a nervous membrane lining this leathery case, and fixed to it at two points corresponding to the openings, one of which may be looked upon as the mouth and the other as the vent." And then he makes further remarks on their anatomy. His appreciation of the nature of the Ascidians is an interesting proof of the wonderful sagacity and minute observation of the great Father of Natural History.

It is worthy of remark, that very lately the Ascidians have again played a part in that much-vexed question of the distinction between animals and vegetables. After Aristotle's demonstration of their affinity with ordinary Mollusca, they had escaped being dragged into this very unsatisfactory discussion. As the sciences have progressed they have approximated, and chemistry has been called to the aid of natural history for the solving of this knotty point. The Ascidians have been obliged to submit to a new cross-examination, and with very unexpected results ; for they have shewn in the composition of their tissues an unlooked-for relation with vegetable structures. In 1845, Dr. Schmidt, in a work entitled " Zur vergleichenden

Physiologie der wirbellosen Thiere," put forward the novel statement, that he had discovered in the tunic of an Ascidian mollusk (the *Phallusia mammillaris*) a ternary substance identical with cellulose. He inferred thence that no chemical distinction could be drawn between animals and vegetables; and, as he had previously shewn that on no other structural or physiological ground any line between the two kingdoms could be drawn, he put forward the somewhat bold dogma, that " Psychology only is competent to trace a limit between plants and animals; and that the only difference admissible is, that the animal possesses, besides the vegetable form—*i. e.* cellule—a ψυχη."

Whatever naturalists might think of Dr. Schmidt's hypothetical definition, it became them to look to his statement respecting the presence of cellulose in the Ascidian tunic. Fortunately the inquiry was undertaken by two most competent observers, Professors Löwig and Albert Kolliker: the result was to confirm the statement and extend it. They found cellulose undoubtedly present in the envelopes of many Tunicata, both simple and compound, including the genera Phallusia, Cynthia, Clavelina, Diazona, Botryllus, Pyrosoma, and Salpa. But they sought in vain for cellulose in animals of inferior organisation, although in some of the above-named creatures it formed a very considerable part of the animal tissues.*

The explanation offered by Löwig and Kolliker of these very anomalous facts is extremely ingenious, and probably very near the truth. It is to the following effect:—Tunicata

---

* The memoir of MM. Löwig and Kolliker was examined by a committee of the French Institute, consisting of Dumas, Milne-Edwards, Boussingault, and Payen: the last-named eminent philosopher drew up the report. In it he gives the following formula of the composition of the envelopes of the Tunicata:—

Cellulose	60·34
Azotised substance . .	27·00
Inorganic matter . .	12·66
	100·00

He remarks that the establishment of the existence of cellulose in the Tunicata is a "fait capital" in science, very important in its bearing on future researches into the comparative physiology of the two kingdoms.

live entirely upon vegetable organisms. The contents of
the stomachs of the Phallusiæ, Clavelinæ, and Diazonæ
examined consisted of particles of florideous algæ, which
had probably found their way there by chance, and a great
quantity of microscopic plants of low position in the series,
species of Navicula, Frustulia, Baccilaria, Closterium, &c.
These minute vegetable organisms have been shewn by
Nageli and Schmidt to contain cellulose. This is probably
dissolved by the gastric juice, that is to say, changed into
sugar or gum; in which state it circulates with the blood,
and is afterwards introduced into the tunics, either directly
by the sanguiferous canals (as in Phallusia), or by their prolongations ramified in the walls of the common body (as in
Diazona and Botryllus), which thus, as Milne-Edwards has
shewn, contain also blood in their cavity, probably penetrating
by imbibition when the envelopes have no blood-vessels. The
presence of cellulose in the tunics of the Ascidian Mollusca,
then, cannot be taken as an evidence of an approach to a
vegetable nature in those bodies. It affords us, however,
a wholesome warning against the placing of confidence in
asserted chemical distinctions between the great kingdoms
of nature.

If we consider our British Ascidians in ascending order,
they will rank as follows: — 1st, those lower and compound forms which constitute the " Ascidiens Composées "
of Milne-Edwards; 2nd, a few species belonging to his
social group; 3rd, a considerable number of simple Ascidians, properly so called; 4th, a genus (*Pelonaia*) of
Tunicata, including as yet only two forms, which, on
account of important peculiarities of organisation to be
hereafter noticed, cannot take its place in any of Milne-Edwards's sections, but must rank as the type of a special
section; and, 5th, a solitary example of the great and very
numerous tribe of *Salpidæ*.

8

I. BOTRYLLIDÆ;

OR, TRUE COMPOUND ASCIDIANS.

If, when walking on the sea-shore about low-water mark, we turn over large stones, or look under projecting eaves of rock, we are almost sure to see translucent jelly-like masses of various hues of orange, purple, yellow, blue, grey, and green, sometimes nearly uniform in tint, sometimes beautifully variegated, and very frequently pencilled as if with stars of gorgeous device; now encrusting the surface of the rock, now depending from it in icicle-like projections. These are Compound Ascidians. A tangle, or broad-leaved fucus, torn from its rocky bed, or gathered on the sands where the waves have cast it after storms, will shew us similar bodies, mostly those star-figured, investing its stalks, winding among the intricacies of its roots, or clothing with a glary coat the expanse of its foliated extremities. If we keep some of these bodies alive in a vessel of sea-water, we find them lie there as apathetic as sponges, giving few signs of vitality beyond the slightly pouting out of tube-like membranes, around apertures which become visible on their surfaces, though a closer and microscopic examination will shew us currents in active motion in the water around those apertures, streams ejected and whirlpools rushing in, indicating, that, however torpid the creature may externally appear, all the machinery of life, the respiratory wheels and circulatory pumps, are hard at work in its inmost recesses. In the course of our examination, especially if we cut up the mass, we find that it is not a single animal which lies before us, but a commonwealth of beings, bound together by common and vital ties. Each star is a family, each group of stars a community. Individuals are linked together in systems, systems combined into masses. Each member of the commonwealth has its own peculiar duties, but shares also in operations which relate to the interest and well-being of the mass. Anatomical investigation shews us the details of these curious structures and arrangements, beautiful as wise. Indeed, few bodies among the lower forms of animal life exhibit such exquisite and kaliedoscopic figures as those which we see displayed in the combinations of the compound Ascidians.

The merit of first understanding and interpreting the true nature of these curious bodies is due to Jules César Savigny, an illustrious French naturalist, whose zeal in the cause of minute investigation eventually deprived him of sight, and the world of many profound and philosophical researches. Savigny carried on his enquiries chiefly in Egypt, when a member of the band of philosophers, whom Napoleon, anxious to palliate the crime of conquest by extending, through their aid, the realms of knowledge, gathered around him in the land of the Pharaohs. The account of Savigny's researches among the Tunicata is contained in his celebrated " Mémoires sur les Animaux sans Vertèbres," to which the author might well, indeed, prefix his motto of " Patientia." Two parts only of that laborious work appeared, though more were promised to be issued at *irregular* intervals ; " for," wrote the noble-spirited naturalist, " obligations too imperious paralyse the faculties, and seem to alter the will itself. If good observations are the fruit of patience, they are also that of full and entire liberty. *Venena servitus, libertas poma.*" Alas ! the sad catastrophe already mentioned prevented the realisation of the many labours he had planned.

Before Savigny's time the Botryllidæ had been confounded with polypes, and regarded as forms of the genus *Alcyonium,* to which, indeed, the masses bore a striking resemblance. The earliest distinct figures of these forms appeared in the "Philosophical Transactions" for 1757, where they were published by Schlosser ; and in 1758, that curious observer, Borlase, gave descriptions sufficiently graphic; and rude but unmistakeable figures of several species, in his interesting folio on "The Natural History of Cornwall." The first naturalist who indicated their compound nature, and held forth a clue to their true affinities, was the famous botanist Gaertner, whose zoological observations on marine animals, communicated to, and published by Pallas, (in 1774,) are of the highest degree of merit. Gaertner, however, did not follow up his enquiries in these bodies, though to him we owe the generic groups *Botryllus* and *Distomus*. The Italian naturalist, Renieri, (in 1793,) had a similar obscure perception of their affinities.

The memoir of Savigny, published in 1816, however, threw entirely new and unanticipated light on their nature. He shewed that they were essentially Ascidians, differing from the simple forms only in being united into more or less complicated systems. The researches of Milne-Edwards "On the Compound Ascidiæ of the Channel," read before the Institute of France, 1839, have fully confirmed those of Savigny, and have also greatly extended our knowledge of these creatures. The figures given by both these naturalists are among the most beautiful and minutely accurate that have ever illustrated and adorned natural history essays.

APLIDIUM, Savigny.

This genus belongs to the constellated section of the tribe of "Polycliniens" in the arrangement of Milne-Edwards. The individual animals of that tribe have a body composed of three distinct parts : 1st, a thorax, with branchial apparatus ; 2nd, a superior abdomen, with digestive organs ; and, 3rd, a post-abdomen, with heart and reproductive organs.

"The common mass of the Aplidia is sessile, gelatinous or cartilaginous, polymorphous, and composed of very numerous, slightly prominent, annular, sub-elliptic systems, which have no central cavity, but have a distinct circumscription. The animals (three to twenty-five) are placed in a single row, at equal distances from the centre and their common axis. Each has a six-rayed branchial, and a simple indistinct anal orifice."—SAVIGNY.

The British species of this genus require careful re-examination. We have thought it best to reprint the original descriptions of them. In pl. A, fig. 1, we have figured an Aplidium from the Isle of Man, apparently identical with *A. fallax*, and in pl. B, fig. 1, one of the separated Ascidians of this genus, as drawn by Savigny.

1. A. FICUS, Linnæus, (Sp.)

Alcyonium ficus, Linnæus S. N. 12th ed. t. i. p. 1295.—Alcyonium pulmonis instar lobatum, Ellis, Corallines, p. 82, pl. 17, fig. *b*, B. C. D.—Alcyonium pulmonarie, Solander and Ellis, p. 175, No. 2.—Aplidium ficus, Savigny, Mém. pt. 2, p. 183.—Alpidium ficus, Fleming, Brit. An. p. 470.

" This sea production is of a dark olive-colour, of a fleshy substance, and smells very disagreeably when it is opened; the inside is full of little oblong yellow particles, from whence it borrows its name of sea-fig among the fishermen, from whom it was procured, with many other things of the same kind, at Whitstable. When I applied my glass to it, I found the whole surface covered with small stars of six rays, like small polypes of six claws. Upon opening it, I found the inside consisted of little bags of a yellowish colour, full of a clear viscid liquor; in the midst of this was a small duct, leading to the centre of the star at the top of each. On examining one of these bags attentively, I discovered several regular figures like shells in this inner tube or duct, placed upon one another; but whether they are the food of the animal in the gut or stomach, or whether it is the ovary, I am not certain."— ELLIS.

2. A. FALLAX, Johnston.

Mag. Nat. Hist. 1st series, vol. vii. p. 15, fig. 4.

" Common body sub-globose or papillary, gelatinous, of a clear honey-yellow colour, marked on the upper surface with white and brown specks, from the contained animals; orifices circular, protuberant, plain, and entire. Animals distinct, scattered irregularly, each in its proper cell, perpendicular, about two lines long. Branchial aperture divided into six equal short segments; the sac large, white, netted on the sides with minute square meshes, which, however, are very obscure; œsophagus narrow, entering laterally at the upper side of the stomach, which is large, yellowish-brown, and mottled ; intestine dark-coloured, wide, flexuose, recurved, and winding up at the base of the branchial sac ; anal aperture elongate, linear, entire, lateral, and near the mouth ; ovary white, cellulose, at the base of the intestine, with a long white tubular canal running up and along the middle of the intestine, and terminating in the branchial cavity. Differs from the *Aplidium ficus* in having the apertures in the common envelope entire, whereas in the *A. ficus* they are distinctly cut into six equal rays. (See Ellis, Corall. tab. 17, fig. B. C. D.) Hab., affixed to old shells, &c. from deep water in Berwick Bay."—JOHNSTON.

3. A. NUTANS, Johnston.

Mag. Nat. Hist. 1st series, vol. vii. p. 16, fig. 5.

" Common body adherent by a broad base, knob-like or pear-shaped, nearly an inch high, and half that in diameter, smooth, gelatinous, pellucid, of a straw-yellow colour, tinted with brown, and marked with whitish streaks from the immersed animal. There are no fibres nor spicula to strengthen this common mass ; neither are there any visible orifices on the surface ; but by ripping up the skin with a needle, the contained animals may be removed entire without difficulty. These are of a long thread-like shape, with a bulging and nutant head, scattered irregularly in the substance of the jelly, in which they lie horizontally, or nearly so. The length of a single individual is about four-tenths of an inch. The mouth is cut into six equal segments, and placed on the upper side of the large branchial sac, which is an oval bag filled in the specimens examined with innumerable minute granules. When the animalcule was compressed between plates of glass, these granules escaped abundantly from the mouth, and from a prominent aperture a little below it on the side. The walls of the branchial sac are marked with several lines or plaits in a longitudinal direction, but I saw no traces of any vascular network. On the inner side of the branchial sac there is an obscure appearance of an intestine or vessel winding up it, to end at the anal aperture ; and near the base of the sac there is a considerable orange-coloured spot marked with longitudinal lines, and presumed to be the stomach. Immediately below this, the body is suddenly contracted into a very long and linear tail, as it may be called, in which, when compressed, we perceive a dark intestine-like mark, mottled with darker and lighter shades on each side, and a clear space between them; but I cannot trace any distinct termination of these organs (which are the ovaries) in the branchial sac, although the shadings at the base of this part indicate the existence and situation of some distinct organs. This species has a great resemblance to *Aplidium effusum* of Savigny, but I cannot consider them identical.—Hab., Berwick Bay, in deep water."— JOHNSTON.

In the twenty-sixth volume of the "Edinburgh New Philosophical Journal," (p. 152,) Sir John Dalyell gives an account of a compound Ascidian, from the Frith of Forth, under the name of "*Aplidium verrucosum*." He describes it as "a gelatinous-looking, but solid, compact substance, which, being suspended by silk threads in a jar of sea-water, proved of an olive-green colour, and approached the form of an irregular parallelopiped above three inches long, and equalling perhaps three cubical inches of solid contents. The whole mass covered with very low prominences, almost even with the surface. In a short time the prominences developed as a profusion of short, projecting, cylindrical orifices, each fashioned as a lip, with a smooth, even edge, wherein were attracted by a powerful current, and absorbed, the neighbouring buoyant particles."

SIDNYUM, SAVIGNY.

This genus was made known by Savigny in a note supplementary to his memoir. He founded it for a British Ascidian received from Dr. Leach, but did not figure the species. It belongs to the unistellated section of the tribe "Polycliniens" in the arrangement of Milne-Edwards.

The mass presents the appearance of a number of heads of madrepore or cladocora, each formed of a simple cone truncated and starred at the summit, rising from a common encrusting base,

the whole being grouped closely together. Each cone is composed
of a fascicle of individuals, varying in number from five or six to
ten or twelve, and forming a margin round a depressed centre.
The whole mass is translucent, gelatinous, and of a rich amber or
orange colour; the individuals are somewhat paler, but marked
by dark visceral specks; they partake of the characters of those
of *Synoicum* and *Aplidium*, resembling the former in the structure of their stomach, and the latter in their branchial sac. Each
has an 8-toothed branchial orifice, and a simple tubulose vent
folded against the thorax. The ovary is peduncled, and very
conspicuous at the extremity of the animal.

S. TURBINATUM, Savigny.

Mem. pt. ii. p. 238. Flem. Br. An. p. 469.
Plate A, fig. 2, and plate B, fig. 2.

The above description is taken from this species, which occurs
abundantly on the under surface of shelving rocks, exposed at
low-water during spring-tides, on the north coast of the Isle of
Man, isle of Islay, Dr. Fleming; Strangford Lough, W. Thompson; Belfast Bay, Dr. Drummond. Dr. Leach probably procured
it on the south coast of England.

POLYCLINUM, Savigny.

" Mass sessile, gelatinous, or cartilaginous, polymorphous, composed of more or less multiplied systems, convex, radiated, each
having a central cavity, and being more or less distinctly circumscribed. Individuals (ten to one hundred and fifty) placed at
very unequal distances from a common centre: branchial orifice
6-angled and 6-rayed; anal prolonged horizontally, irregularly
cut, and aiding in forming the prominent and fringed border of
the cavity of the system."—SAVIGNY.

P. AURANTIUM, Milne-Edwards.

Mem. Asc. Comp. p. 292, pl. 1, fig. 6.
Plate A, fig. 3, and plate B, fig. 3.

" Little orange masses, more or less spherical, fixed to rocks by
a short and thick peduncle; the animals composing them undis-

tinguishable by the naked eye, but when the surface is examined with a lens, a number of little holes, ranged in linear series, are seen ; the mouths of the animals united in a common mass grouped round one or many systems, each opening into a common cloaca ; tegument coriaceous."—MILNE-EDWARDS.

Mr. Alder finds a species, which seems to be a pale, fuscous, yellow variety of this, at Cullercoats.

AMOUROUCIUM, MILNE-EDWARDS.

Mass lobed or encrusting, sessile or pedunculated, fleshy or cartilaginous, composed of many systems, more or less circumscribed, each having a central cavity; the individuals, more or less numerous, placed at unequal distances from the common centre ; their anal orifices open into a common cloaca ; branchial orifice six-rayed ; post-abdomen not pedunculate, but following superior abdomen, as in *Aplidium.* [See pl. B, fig. 4.]

1. A. PROLIFERUM, Milne-Edwards.

Mem. Asc. Comp. p. 267, pl. 1, fig. 3, and pl. 3, fig. 2.

Yellowish or red fleshy masses, sometimes encrusting, sometimes lobed, with orange elongated spots on their upper surface. Individuals with a red thorax.

"Belfast Bay," W. Thompson, in Ann. N. Hist. vol. xiii. (1844) p. 485. " Not uncommon in Cornwall," Mr. Alder.

2. A. NORDMANNI, Milne-Edwards.

Mem. Asc. Comp. p. 289, pl. 1, fig. 5.

" Thick encrusting masses, broader than high, of a light rosecolour, tinged with yellow towards the base. Systems few, and usually arranged in a single row, so as to represent a more or less elongated ellipsoid, usually several in a mass, and distinctly circumscribed. The oral opening of these Ascidians is but slightly prominent, and the lobes of the membranous border are obtuse and white, so as to constitute a circle of six white rounded spots around the mouth, contrasting with the general rose-colour ; the tegumentary tissue is yellowish, and the prevailing rose-colour depends on the tint of the thoracic portion of the bodies of the Ascidians."—M.-E.

At Falmouth, Mr. Alder.

3. A. Argus, Milne-Edwards.

Mem. Asc. Comp. p. 291, pl. 1, fig. 4ª.

Plate A, fig. 4.

General colour olive-yellow towards the base of the mass, passing into orange near its free extremity, which is nearly white, speckled with little red points. The individuals are grouped nearly circularly round a common cloaca, usually a single system of them to a mass. Each individual is prominent on the common surface, and the border of the buccal opening is deeply divided into six nearly triangular lobes ; around these are ranged the red eye-like spots, four to each animal.

At Falmouth, Mr. Alder. This species appears to have a wide range : it occurs in the Ægean, E. F.

LEPTOCLINUM, Milne-Edwards.

Mass thin, sessile, encrusting, polymorphous, coriaceous or gelatinous, composed of many systems. Anal orifices of the individuals opening into a common cloaca, more or less ramified. Branchial orifices 6-lobed. [Pl. B, fig. 5.]

This genus belongs to the tribe of "Didemniens" in the arrangement of Milne-Edwards, composed of those compound Ascidians which have the body distinctly divided into two portions, a thorax and an abdomen : "They approach very nearly the Clavellinæ, and are distinguished from the Polycliniens by the absence of a post-abdomen, and by the position of the generative apparatus and heart, which are placed beside the intestine."—M.-E.

1. L. maculosum, Milne-Edwards.

Mem. Asc. Comp. p. 297, pl. 8, fig. 2.

A thin, hard, leathery crust, investing the roots of Laminariæ, variegated with white and blue. The substance of the crust is strengthened with calcareous raphides.

Common on most parts of our coast, but first recorded as British by Mr. W. Thompson, who noted it as occurring plentifully on the roots of Laminariæ in Belfast Bay and the north of Ireland generally, in the 13th volume of the "Annals of Natural History," (1844.)

2. L. ASPERUM, Milne-Edwards.

Mem. Asc. Comp. p. 298, pl. 8, fig. 3, 3ᵃ.

Closely resembling the last, with which it occurs, but usually
white or pale, and rough with conical tubercles placed near each
of the buccal orifices.

Common ; first recorded as British by Mr. W. Thompson, who
found it in the same localities with the last species.

3. L. AUREUM, Milne-Edwards.

Mém. Asc. Comp. p. 298, pl. 8, fig. 4, 4ᵃ.

Similar to the two last species, but distinguished by its uniform
chamois-yellow colour. The buccal orifices are closer than in *L.
asperum*, and more deeply lobed.

Dredged in Strangford Lough by Mr. Hyndman and Mr. W.
Thompson.

4. L. GELATINOSUM, Milne-Edwards.

Mém. Asc. Comp. p. 299, pl. 8, fig. 1, 1ᵃ.

Plate A, fig. 5.

Distinguished from all the other species by its gelatinous consistence, and the semi-transparency of the common integument.
The individuals have yellow abdominal viscera, and are arranged
irregularly around a common cloaca.

" On the roots of Laminariæ in Belfast Bay," W. Thompson,
Ann. Nat. Hist., 1844. " A gelatinous compound Ascidian,
probably *L. gelatinosum*, is common on the south coast of England," Mr. Alder.

5. L. LISTERIANUM, Milne-Edwards.

" Polyclinum," Lister, Philosophical Transactions for 1834, pt. 2, p. 382, pl.
12, fig. 1.

A grey slimy crust, speckled with white and black ; a circle of
dark spots around the buccal orifice of each individual.

Investing algæ at Brighton, Mr. Lister. An interesting account
of the structure and economy of this species is given by the most
accurate microscopical observer who first discovered it.

6. L. PUNCTATUM, Forbes.

A thin, shining, translucent crust, investing stones at low water. The animals, minute, are placed in pairs, each individual marked with a conspicuous black spot.

Isle of Man, E. F.   Cullercoats, Mr. Alder.

DISTOMA, GAERTNER.

This genus, which is one of the two genera of Compound Ascidians distinguished by Gaertner, belongs to the uni-stellated section of the group styled by Milne-Edwards " Didemnians."

The common body, or mass, of Distoma is sessile, semi-cartilaginous, polymorphous, and composed of many systems, usually circular.   The individual animals are placed in one or two ranks, at unequal distances from a common centre.   They present the striking and distinctive character of having both branchial and anal orifices regularly and equally six-rayed.   The species inhabit the European seas.

1. D. RUBRUM, Savigny.

Mém. 2nd part, p. 177, pl. 3, fig. 1, and pl. 13.

Plate A, fig. 6, and plate B, fig. 6.

" Mass compressed; various shades of red, with slightly-prominent, oval, yellowish points (individuals) scattered on the two sides, and grouped in systems of from three to twelve.   Orifices obtusely rayed, tinted with purple.

" Mass four to five inches across, and half an inch thick.   Individuals, two lines."—SAVIGNY.

This species was communicated to Savigny by Dr. Leach.   To it the French naturalist referred the " Alcyonium rubrum, pulposum, conicum plerumque " of Plancus. (Conch. Min. Not. t. 10, f. B. d.) Mr. W. Thompson has recorded it as occurring on Laminaria digitata in Belfast Bay, where it was found by Mr. Getty. He remarks that the specimens are not so lively in colour as those figured by Savigny. (Ann. Nat. Hist. vol. v. p. 95.)

2. D. variolosum, Gaertner.

Alcyonium ascidioïdes, Pallas, Sp. Zool. f. 10, p. 40, f. 4, f. 7, a, A. — A. distomum, Brugière, Enc. Méth. — Distoma variolosum, Savigny, Mém. 2nd part, p. 178.—Polyzona variolosa, Fleming, Br. An. p. 469.

Mass coriaceous, not thick, flat beneath, warty above; pale reddish, or yellowish-white. Individuals orange-red. Systems not distinctly circumscribed.

"Common on Fucus palmatus, and on that plant only, enveloping sometimes the entire stem," according to Gaertner. "A Distoma, apparently, from description, of this species, has occurred to me investing Fucus serratus in Belfast Bay: the colour was always whitish-yellow," W. Thompson, Ann. N. H. vol. v. p. 95.

BOTRYLLUS, Gaertner.

This genus, one of the first established among the Compound Ascidians, is the type of the tribe of "Botryllians" in the arrangement of Milne-Edwards. The individual animals present no distinction between abdomen and thorax. Their viscera are accumulated in the thoracic cavity, and form with it an ovoid mass. Their branchial orifices are simple: they are ranged round a common cloaca. In the genus Botryllus they are grouped in simple stars, and lie horizontally, with the vent far from the branchial orifice.

1. B. Schlosseri, Pallas, (Sp.)*

Schlosser, Phil. Trans. vol. xlix. pt. 2, 1757, p. 447, t. 14, fig. A—c ; Borlase, Nat. Hist. Cornwall, p. 254, t. 25, f. 1, 2, 3, 4.—Alcyonium Schlosseri, Pallas, Elench. Zooph. No. 208.—Botryllus stellatus, Gaertner in Pallas, Spic. Zool. fasc. 10, p. 37, t. 4, f. 1 — 5.— B. stellatus, Brugière, Enc. Méth. 1 ; Lamarck.—B. Schlosseri, Savigny, Mém. pt. 2, p. 200, pl. 20, f. 5 ; Fleming, Brit. An. p. 470.—Alcyonium Schlosseri, Linnæus, Syst. Nat. 12th ed. — A. Schlosseri, Ellis and Solander, Nat. Hist. Zooph. p. 177.

Plate A, fig. 7, and plate B, fig. 7.

Mass a thick, gelatinous, semi-transparent, glaucous crust, with yellow marginal tubes. Systems numerous, composed of from ten

* In the forty-ninth volume of the "Philosophical Transactions" (for 1756) occurs the first notice of the Compound Ascidians, being the description of this Botryllus, with a very characteristic figure. The paper is entitled, "An account of a curious

to twenty or more individuals, yellowish and reddish. Branchial
aperture white, surrounded by a circle of broad ferruginous spots;
a red spot on the centre of each individual. Mass often measuring several inches across; individuals one-twentieth of an inch
in diameter.

---

fleshy, coral-like substance; in a letter to Mr. Peter Collinson, F.R.S., from Dr.
Albert Schlosser, M.D., F.R.S., with some observations on it communicated to
Mr. Collinson by Mr. John Ellis, F.R.S." Being short, we quote it :—

"' Dear Sir,—I hired some fishermen to dredge for me in this harbour, in order to
examine the small English coral, or *Corallium nostras* of Ray's "Synopsis," recent
in the microscope. The first time they hauled in the dredge, I discovered a most
extraordinary sea production surrounding the stem of an old Fucus teres: it was
of a hardish but fleshy substance, and more than an inch thick, of a light brown
or ash-colour, the whole surface covered over with bright yellow, shining, and
star-like bodies, which induced me to believe it to be an undescribed species of
Alcyonium. I put it immediately into a bucket of sea-water, expecting every
moment that the polypes, which I thought to lodge in those little stars, would
extend and shew themselves like those of the Alcyonium No. 2 of Ray's "Synopsis," commonly called " dead man's hand;" but after more than half-an-hour's
attention, the vessel lying very quiet all the time, I did not perceive the least appearance of any polypes; upon which I brought them to shore in the sea-water,
and then, by means of my microscope, I discovered every one of those stars to be
a true animal, and much more beautiful than any polype, but quite of a different
structure, which I shall now describe to you.

"' Every one of those stars is composed of many thin hollow radii, of a pear-shape
form, from five to twelve or more in number, all united intimately at their smaller
end; every radius appears broad at the extreme part from the centre, and a little
convex in the middle of this raised broad part. When the animal is alive there
appears a circular little hole, which contracts and opens itself frequently. All the
radii are of this structure; but their common centre, which is formed by a combination of the small converging extremities, exhibits an opening of a circular,
oval, or oblong figure, forming a kind of rising rim like a cup, which, when the
animal is alive and at rest, contracts and expands itself to many different degrees,
with great alertness and velocity, though sometimes it remains a great while expanded or contracted. In all these holes, the central large one, as well as the
smaller ones, (which last I take to be the mouths of the animals,) I could not perceive any tentacula, or claws, on the outside; but, by looking into them very nar-
rowly, I saw something like very tender little fibres moving at the bottom of their
insides.

"' By comparing and examining all the various pieces I had collected of this fleshy
substance, with its shining stars, I observed that the size and colour, as well as
the very figure of these stars, varied greatly, but the structure of the leaf-like
radii, and that of their mouths, and their motions, were perfectly the same in
every one individual.

Very common on stones and sea-weeds near low water-mark, all round the British Islands.*

2. B. POLYCYCLUS, Savigny.

"Botryllus stellatus, Renieri, Le Sueur, and Desmarest."—Polycyclus, Lamarck, Mém. du Mus. t. i. p. 340. — Botryllus polycyclus, Savigny, Mém. pt. 2, p. 202, pl. 4, fig. 5, and pl. 21.

A gelatinous, translucent, grey crust, with reddish and purple marginal tubes. Systems numerous, of from eight to twenty or more individuals. Oval; bluish or purple. Orifices bordered by purple; the branchial aperture surrounded by eight large white or bluish spots, divided by deep purple spaces: radial line similarly coloured. Mass grows to several inches. Individuals one-twelfth of an inch or less.

"Much more common in the north of Ireland than B. Schlosseri : chiefly on the leaves of Laminaria digitata," W. Thomp-

---

" ' Many of these bodies I have found so thick and large as to resemble the great branched madrepore coral, especially as they are generally to be met with covering and enclosing the stem and branches of this stiff, ramose fucus.' Thus far Dr. Schlosser.

" ' I have had an opportunity lately of examining this curious, fleshy, coral-like figure in the microscope, and find that all the interstices between the stars are filled with eggs of different sizes, each adhering by one end to a very fine capillary filament. The smallest eggs are globular, and as they advance in size, change to an oval figure ; from thence they assume the shape of one of the radii of the stars.

" In several of these stars I have observed a smaller radius, as it were, endeavouring to get into the circle ; and notwithstanding their seeming connexion in the centre as one animal, I believe I shall soon be able to shew you, in a drawing from the microscope, that each radius is a distinct animal by itself.

" I am, dear Sir,
" Your most affectionate friend,
" JOHN ELLIS."

* BOTRYLLUS CONGLOMERATUS, Gaertner.

Gaertner in Pallas, Spic. Zool. fasc. 10, p. 39, t. 4, f. 6, a. A.— Alcyonium conglomeratum, Gmelin.—Botryllus conglomeratus, Lamarck ; Savigny, Mém. pt. 2, p. 204 ; Fleming, Brit. An. 470.

" B. dactylis conglomeratis osculis edentulis terminalibus ; corpus gelatinosum, molle, convexum ; plantis marinis adnatum." The true nature of this Ascidian, if it be one, is very doubtful. It was taken by Gaertner on the Cornish coast. The " Alcyonium Borlasii" and "A. constellatum" are supposed species of Botryllus, instituted by Dr. Turton from the rude figures of Borlase.

son. Very generally distributed around our shores : it ranges to
the Mediterranean.

3. B. GEMMEUS, Savigny.

Mém. pt. ii. p. 203.

" Body forming a thin, gelatinous, sub-orbicular greyish crust,
with yellowish marginal tubes. Systems isolated, or few and
scattered, commonly composed of from five to twelve or more individuals, with oval summits of a yellow or golden-grey colour.
Orifices terminated with white ; radial line bordered with white."
—SAVIGNY.

Diameter of mass, according to Savigny, not exceeding an
inch ; but it occurs much larger. Individuals one-thirtieth of an
inch.

"Adhering to fuci dredged in Belfast Bay by Mr. Getty," W.
Thompson, Annals, 1844. Ballaugh, Isle of Man, adhering to
stones at low-water, E. F.

4. B. VIOLACEUS, Milne-Edwards.

Mém. Asc. Comp. p. 306, pl. 6, fig. 4, 4*.

Common integument pale greenish-grey. Tunics of individuals
deep blue, except around the cloacal opening, where they are yellowish-white ; and between that opening and the mouth there is
a radiating space of the same colour, divided by a violet line, so
that each system forms a blue rosette, with a yellow central star.
Animals small.

" Common on the Cornish coast," Mr. Alder.

5. B. SMARAGDUS, Milne-Edwards.

Mém. Asc. Comp. p. 307, pl. 6, fig. 6, 6*.

General integument yellowish-green. Individuals much larger
than in the last species; their tunics apple-green or yellowish,
bright yellow round the mouth, and between the mouth and the
cloacal orifice presenting an oval yellow space, divided by green
lines, radiating from a central vermilion or orange spot.

On fuci. " A green species, which I think is the *smaragdus*,
is common on the Cornish coast," Mr. Alder. "North of Ireland,"
Mr. Thompson.

6. B. BIVITTATUS, Milne-Edwards.

Mém. Asc. Comp. p. 308, pl. 6, fig. 7, 7ᵃ.

General integument ash-grey. Systems appearing as small stars, with linear yellow rays and dark centres. Individuals coloured like the common integument, but marked between and around their mouths and the common cloaca with two narrow yellow bands.

Belfast Bay, Mr. W. Thompson. At Torquay and Falmouth, Mr. Alder.

BOTRYLLOÏDES, MILNE-EDWARDS.

This genus belongs to the same tribe as the last, but the stars formed by the systems of animals are irregular and ramifying. The individuals also differ in position and structure, having their bodies placed vertically and their two orifices approximated. [Pl. B, fig. 8.]

1. B. LEACHII, Savigny, (Sp.)

Botryllus Leachii, Sav. Mém. 2nd part, p. 199, pl. 4, fig. 6, and pl. 20, fig. 4.

" Mass forming a gelatinous crust, hyaline, with a purple tint, ornamented with a great number of yellowish vascular tubes. Systems very numerous and closely packed, composed commonly of from ten to twelve individuals, and sometimes of from twenty-five to thirty ; their summits claviform and variegated with white and yellow. Branchial orifice white, with a yellow collar encircled by white ; the radial line bordered with white."—SAVIGNY.

Mass two to three inches across ; size of individuals one-fourth of a line.

Communicated to Savigny by Leach, probably from the English coast. " North-east coast of Ireland, occasionally investing the roots of Laminaria digitata, &c. When dried it has somewhat the appearance of a sponge," W. Thompson in Ann. Nat. Hist. vol. v. p. 95. ! Common on the Northumberland coast, Mr. Alder.

2. B. ALBICANS, Milne-Edwards.

Mém. p. 304, pl. 6, fig. 2.

Plate A, fig. 8.

White stars on a transparent ground.

"On June 16th, 1846, I found this species attached to the
under side of a stone in a pool, between tide-marks, at Springvale,
county of Down. It was likewise attached to fuci (Fucus vesicu-
losus, &c.) growing in the rock-pools, and was in much smaller
masses than the following species ; generally but one system of
individuals existed in each mass. On the small branches of fuci
to which it was attached, there was not room for more ; nor was
there, indeed, on the broadest portion of the main stem, whence
the leading branches of the plant issued : the latter is its favourite position," W. Thompson, Ann. Nat. Hist. 1846, vol. xviii.
p. 385.

3. B. ROTIFERA, Milne-Edwards.

Mém. Asc. Comp. p. 301, pl. 6, fig. 1 and 1ᵃ.

Mass gelatinous, yellowish ; individuals having semi-transparent tunics, speckled with red ; the red specks form a ring round
the mouth.

"On the under side of the same stone with the last, and covering several square inches of its surface. I mark it with doubt,
on account of some little difference in colour. The 'consistence
gelatineuse' was hyaline rather than 'jaunâtre.' The individual forms were more of a uniform red than in Edwards's figure,
and were each as brightly coloured as in *B. rubrum*, Edw., and of
the tint that it is represented to be. The individuals being arranged in a scattered manner, and not thrown into masses as in
B. rubrum, was a striking character," W. Thompson, *loc. cit.*
"There is a species with wheel-like rays on this (Northumberland)
and the Cornish coast, but it is yellow without red markings, as
in *B. rotifera*," Mr. Alder in letter.

4. B. RUBRUM, Milne-Edwards.

Mém. Asc. Comp. p. 304, pl. 6, fig. 3, 3ᵃ.

Common tunic opaque, and throughout of an intense orpiment
red. Systems more distinct than in the last species.

Common at Falmouth, Mr. Alder.

II. CLAVELINIDÆ;

OR, SOCIAL ASCIDIANS.

The Compound Ascidians are not so far removed from the Simple as to be unconnected by intermediate forms. It was supposed until very lately that the curious animals of this class, of which one species had been described by Pallas under the name of *Ascidia clavata*, and another by Otho Frederic Müller under that of *Ascidia lepadiformis*, belonged to the latter section ; but Milne-Edwards has shewn that the individuals of the genus *Clavelina*, to which Savigny referred the species first named, are not always, nor, indeed, usually separated from each other, but spring, as it were, from a common creeping root, and multiply by gemmation in the manner of the truly compound Ascidians. Some years previously, Mr. Lister, in his valuable paper on "The structure and functions of tubular and cellular Polypi and of Ascidiæ,"* described and figured a remarkable Ascidian which he had found at Brighton on Conferva elongata, and which seemed to combine the characters of simple and compound *Tunicata*. He described it as occurring in groups consisting of several individuals, each having its own heart, respiration, and system of nutrition, but fixed on a peduncle that branches from a common creeping stem, and all being connected by a circulation that extends throughout. Their parts are of such transparency, that their interior is easily seen. Their external shape resembles a pouch, compressed at the sides and fixed at the hind part of the base upon the peduncle.

The affinity of this curious animal, or rather group of animals, with *Clavelina* was demonstrated by Milne-Edwards in the memoir already cited, wherein he elevated

* Philosophical Transactions, 1834.

these two genera into a separate and most natural group,
under the name of "Ascidies sociales."

CLAVELINA, Savigny.

Individuals and groups connected by creeping, radiciform
prolongations; the Ascidians arising from them having
elongated, erect, more or less pedunculated bodies. Branchial and anal orifices without rays. Outer tunic smooth
and transparent. Thorax usually marked with coloured
lines.

C. LEPADIFORMIS, O. F. Müller, (Sp.)

Ascidia lepadiformis, O. F. Müller, Zool. Dan. t. 79, f. 5.—Clavelina lepadiformis, Savigny, Mém. pt. 2, p. 174 ; Fleming, Brit. An. p. 468 ; Milne-
Edwards, (Mém. Asc. Comp.,) Mém. Inst. vol. xviii. p. 266, pl. 1, fig. 1, and pl. 2,
fig. 1, 1ᵇ.

Plate E, fig. 1.

Thorax forming a third part of the length of the adult individual, and marked with yellow lines ; stomach of a bright orange,
placed near the middle of the abdominal portion of the animal ;
part of the intestine of the same colour.

Usual length from one-half to three-fourths of an inch. Abundant on rocks and stones at low-water in many places, especially
on the west coast of Scotland. Strangford Lough, Mr. W.
Thompson. Connemara. "Very generally diffused ; I have met
with it on the Devonshire, Cornish, and Northumberland coasts,
and in Lamlash, Rothesay, and Oban bays in Scotland," Mr. Alder.

The mode of germination of this species has been well described
by Milne-Edwards. "If we examine with care the foot of a *Clavelina lepadiformis*, we see that the animal adheres to the soil
by more or less numerous radiciform prolongations of the tegumentary tunic ; and usually we find also cylindrical filaments,
which, mingled with these roots, and formed externally by the
same tissue, creep also on the surface of the soil, but are hollow,
and internally furnished with a membranous tube. This tube is
continuous with the internal tunic of the Ascidian ; and the circulation which is seen in the interior of the abdomen of the latter is
equally continued into the appendicular canal. This stalk-like

body, which is closed at the extremity, is at first simple, but ramifies as it elongates. When its growth is more advanced, we see developing at the extremities of its branches, or even at different points of its length, tubercles containing in their interior a little organised mass in connexion with the internal tube. These tubercles elongate, elevate themselves vertically, and become claviform; the blood which circulates in the stem penetrates the soft and pyriform central mass; but this mass, at first pedunculated and adhering to the inner tunic of the principal canal, soon separates itself, and no longer participates in the circulation of the individual to which it owed its origin. Nevertheless, its development continues, and we soon distinguish in it all the principal characteristic traits of Ascidian structure; the branchial sac becomes perfectly outlined without being as yet in communication with the interior; a curved digestive tube is seen beneath the thorax. At length a buccal opening is formed, and the general shape of the young animal approaches more and more nearly that of the adult. Thus there is produced, by process of budding, a new individual, linked with its parent by a radiciform prolongation of the tegumentary tunic, and which, during the first years of its life, has a circulation in common with the mother-ascidian, but in the end enjoys an independent existence. Still, however, it may remain in connexion with the individual which produced it, through the medium of its roots, or it may become completely free by their rupture, without any change of consequence in its mode of life." (Mémoires de l'Institut, vol. xviii. p. 262.)

In the memoir cited, Milne-Edwards has distinguished several species of *Clavelina*, most of which are likely to occur on our coast. One is the *Clavelina Savigniana*, the abdominal portion of whose body is four or five times as long as the thorax, and the thoracic lines probably white. A second, *Clavelina producta*, has the thorax very short and as broad as long, and the abdomen very long. *Clavelina pumilio*, on the other hand, is nearly sessile and square. We have gathered a species, probably identical with the last, though much larger than the specimens described by Milne-Edwards, at low water in the island of Herm. *Clavelina Rissoana* is a Mediterranean species, resembling

C. lepadiformis, but having white thoracic lines: as the latter, on our own coast, has these lines very frequently so pale as to be nearly white, this may be only a variety. The figure usually quoted from Müller, of the original *lepadiformis*, does not so closely represent the common appearance of British specimens as that given under the name of *Ascidia gelatinosa*, in the fourth part of the "Zoologia Danica," edited by Rathke.

PEROPHORA, Wiegmann.

Individuals pedunculated, suborbicular, compressed, attached by their pedicles to creeping tubular processes of the common tunic, through which the blood circulates. Thorax not lineated by granular bands.

P. Listeri, Wiegmann.

J. Lister, on the Structure and Functions of tubular and cellular Polypi and of Ascidiæ, Philosophical Transactions, 1834. [The author gave no name to his Ascidian. When his paper was translated into the German journals, Professor Wiegmann proposed the appellations here adopted.]

Plate E, fig. 2.

We have already noticed the characters of this curious little animal or group of animals, so well described by Mr. Lister. His account of the structure and economy of Perophora may be studied with advantage for its minute accuracy. It threw light on the true nature of *Clavelina*, which had previously been referred to the Simple Ascidians. The *Perophora Listeri* is a minute creature. It occurs not rarely on the south coast of England, and we have taken it in the Irish Sea. Mr. M'Andrew and Professor E. Forbes dredged it adhering to weed on the coast of Anglesey in 1843. It is beautifully transparent, appearing in the weed like little specks of jelly dotted with orange and brown, and linked by a winding silvery thread. When dried, as it may often be met with on sea-weed cast on shore, these bodies appear like the minute ova of some mollusk.

III. ASCIDIADÆ.

Rarely is the dredge drawn up from any sea-bed at all prolific in sub-marine creatures, without containing few or many irregularly shaped leathery bodies, fixed to sea-weed, rock, or shell by one extremity or by one side, free at the other, and presenting two more or less prominent orifices, from which on the slightest pressure the sea-water is ejected with great force. On the sea-shore, when the tide is out, we find similar bodies attached to the under surface of rough stones. They are variously, often splendidly coloured, but otherwise are unattractive or even repulsive in aspect. These creatures are *Ascidiæ*, properly so called. Numbers of them are often found clustering among tangles, like bunches of some strange semi-transparent fruit. They are very apathetic and inactive, living upon microscopic creatures drawn in with currents of water by means of their ciliated respiratory organs.

The leathery case is often encrusted with stones and shells, decorated with parasitical though ornamental plumes of corallines, and not seldom perforated by bivalves, which lodge themselves snugly in the tough but smooth skin; it is the analogue of the true shell of conchiferous Mollusca. It is a sac, closed except at two orifices, one of which is branchial, the other anal. This elastic gelatinous or coriaceous envelope is called the test, and encloses a second tunic or mantle, which is muscular and adheres to the first only near the orifices. The branchial sac lines the interior of the mantle in part. It is both respiratory and pharyngeal. The remainder of the cavity is occupied with the principal organs of digestion, circulation, and generation. The chief nervous centre is situated between the two openings of the muscular tunic. The sexes of *Ascidiæ* are distinct.

In 1828 Milne-Edwards and Audouin[*] made the important discovery that the Compound Ascidians did not begin their life as fixed animals, but originated from independent tadpole-like embryos. In 1835 a similar account of their early history was given by the Norwegian naturalist, Sars;[†] and in 1839 Sir John Graham Dalyell,[‡] of Edinburgh, published his observations on the development of *Ascidiæ*, both simple and compound, with the same results. Since then many observers have noticed the metamorphoses of the *Tunicata*—metamorphoses which account for the wide diffusion of these apparently sedentary animals. The tadpole as it appears in the egg is at first an oval disk; a tail is soon after observed; arm-like projections spring from the head of the creature, which then presents a striking analogy with the form of a hydroid zoophyte; it becomes free and swims about by means of its rapidly vibrating tail; it fixes itself to rocks or sea-weeds by its arms; the tail disappears; that which was the head, or nucleus, sends out root-like projections; orifices appear in it, and its final form as an Ascidian begins to be manifested. Such are the successive stages of the metamorphosis.[§]

ASCIDIA, BASTER.

(*arsæ*, a leather bag.)

Body sessile, covered with a coriaceous or gelatinous tunic. Branchial orifice 8-lobed and 6-lobed. [Branchial sac not plicated, surmounted by a circle of simple tentacular filaments; meshes of the respiratory sac papillated.] This is the genus PHALLUSIA of Savigny.

[*] Annales des Sciences Naturales, t. xv. p. 10.
[†] Sars, Beskrivelser ag jagttagelser, &c. Bergen, 1835.
[‡] Edinburgh New Philosophical Journal, 1835.
[§] For a clear and full abstract of the observations on this subject, see Owen's Lectures on the Invertebrata, p. 273.

1. A. INTESTINALIS, Linnæus.

Ascidia intestinalis, Lin. Syst. Nat. 12th ed. (previously described by Bohadsch,
An. Mar. p. 132, t. x. f. 4–5) ; Cuvier, Mém. du Mus. t. ii. pl. 2, f. 4–7.—
A. corrugata, Müller, Zool. Dan. t. 79, f. 3–4.—A. virescens, Brugière, Enc.
Méth. pl. 64, f. 4–6.—Phallusia intestinalis, Savigny, Mém. pt. 2, p. 169,
pl. 11, f. 1.—Ciona intestinalis, Fleming, Brit. An. p. 468.—Ascidia intesti-
nalis, Macgillivray, Mol. Aberdeen, p. 313.

Body elongated, cylindrical; outer tunic thin, soft, gelatinous,
smooth, transparent, usually pale green or yellow. Orifices terminal, placed close together on rather short tubes, usually bordered with bright yellow: the branchial with eight lobes and
eight red ocelli; the anal with six. Elongated fibrous bands
shine through the outer tunic.

It grows to the length of five or six inches, but commonly to
not more than three. It adheres to rocks, shells, fuci at various
depths. It is found on most parts of our coast, but is especially
abundant in the north.

2. A. CANINA, O. F. Müller.

Zool. Dan. t. 55, fig. 1–6 (copied in Enc. Méth. pl. 64, f. 1–3).—Phallusia
canina, Savigny, Mém. pt. 2, p. 171.

Body elongated, cylindrical, flaccid; outer tunic stronger than
that of the last species, more or less tinged with red, especially
about the approximated, terminal, and much corrugated orifices.
Three to four inches in length. Adhering to fuci in from three to
seven fathoms water.

Strangford Lough, W. Thompson. Clew Bay, County Mayo,
W. T., R. Ball, E. F. Kirkwall Bay, Orkney, J. Goodsir and E.F.
(1839). In the Solent, (1847,) Capt. James, R. E., and E. F.

3. A. VENOSA, O. F. Müller.
Zool. Dan. t. 25.

Body elongated, sub-cylindrical; outer tunic sub-cartilaginous,
smooth, pellucid, so lineated with red vascular ramifications as to
appear of a red hue all over. Branchial orifice terminal, anal
lateral; both sessile, tinged with red, and more or less corrugated.
Inner tunic crimson. Length about two inches. Usually gregarious.

"Obtained by dredging in the loughs of Strangford and Belfast. First distinguished as an Irish species by Dr. J. L. Drummond," W. Thompson, Ann. Nat. Hist. vol. v. 1840. Bay of Killery, Connemara, W. T., R. Ball, E. F. (1840). Hebrides, R. M'Andrew and E. F. (1845.)

4. A. MENTULA, O. F. Müller.

Zool. Dan. t. 8, f. 1–4 (copied in Enc. Méth. pl. 62, f. 2–4).—Ascidia mona- chus, Cuvier, Mém. du Mus. t. ii. p. 32.—Phallusia monachus, Savigny, Mém. pt. 2, p. 167, pl. 10, f. 2.—Pandocia conchilega and Phallusia mentula, Fleming, Brit. An. p. 468.?—Ascidia prunum, Macgillivray, Mol. Ab. p. 312.?

Plate C, fig. 1.

Body oblong. Outer tunic very thick, cartilaginous, translu- cent, varying in colour from pale greenish-white to dark brown ; [often containing imbedded Modiola marmorata, and frequently covered by investing corallines.] Orifices distinct, sessile ; the branchial terminal, 8-lobed ; the indentations of the lobes pre- senting the ocelli, which are yellow, with a red central spot ; the tentacular filaments are very conspicuous between the ocelli, as they are also in the 6-lobed and 6-ocellated anal orifice, which is placed laterally at a considerable distance from the branchial, and usually on a bulging of the side. Grows to the length of six inches, and even longer. This is the commonest of our deep- water Ascidians, occurring plentifully in from fifteen to twenty fathoms water in many parts of the coast. Müller's description of his A. mentula applies so well to it, that, although the figure be rather puzzling, and not good at best, one can hardly doubt their identity ; " Ascidiarum singularissima. Massu informis cinereo- flavescens, quadratum irregulare sistens ; substantia crassa gela- tinosa, duriuscula, subpellucida, rejectamentis corallinarum et fucorum passim obsita."

" Belfast Bay ; Roundstone Bay, County Galway, adhering to a stone between tide-marks (? if the same) ; Ascidia communis, Forbes' MSS., Clew Bay," W. Thompson, in Ann. Nat. Hist., 1844. Isle of Man, Zetland, Orkney, east and west coasts of Scotland, E. F.

5. A. ARACHNOÏDEA, E. Forbes.

Oblong, resembling the last in form. Outer tunic very thick, cartilaginous, hard, smooth, undulated as if obsoletely tuberculated, opaline, with a porcelain-like lustre, either milk-white, or marked with reticulating lines, as if it were covered by a spider's web. Branchial orifice terminal ; anal lateral and distinct; both with very strongly-marked lobes : ocelli inconspicuous. " Inner tunic soft and dark blue."—(Mr. Alder.)

Three inches in length. A very beautiful species. On the south coast of England, Mr. Bowerbank. " Not uncommon on the Cornish and Devonshire coasts. I have also found it at Lamlash, Arran," Mr. Alder. [Taken in the Ægean, E. F., 1842.]

6. A. scabra, O. F. Müller.

Zool. Dan. t. 65, f. 3.

Plate C, fig. 3.

Body ovate, compressed, adhering by the side. Test tough, white, transparent, scabrous, shewing the reddish branchial sac shining through. Orifices sessile, approximate, near one extremity. An inch to an inch and a half in length.

Strangford and Belfast Loughs, W. Thompson. On fronds of Laminaria in Killery Bay, west coast of Ireland, W. Thompson, R. Ball, E. F. (1840). Irish Sea, not rare ; west coast of Scotland, E. F.

7. A. virginea, O. F. Müller.

Zool. Dan. t. 49, f. 4.—A. opalina, Macgillivray, Mol. Ab. p. 312.

Plate C, fig. 2.

Body irregularly tetragonal, compressed, adhering by base, and sometimes partly by the side. Tunic smooth, glossy, crystalline, firm, yellowish-hyaline. Through it the branchial sac, beautifully marbled with crimson, and banded with white, is seen. Orifices terminal, sessile, rather distant; ocelli red. Length and breadth often two inches.

" Hæc frustam glaciei visu, tactu et ipso frigore refert, vix ulli pulchritudine secunda."—Müller.

Dredged, adhering to dead shells, in twenty fathoms, four miles from land, Ballaugh, Isle of Man, (1839,) E. F. Hebrides and Zetland, R. M'Andrew and E. F. Moray Firth, Captain Otter, R.N. " Abundant in deep water off Aberdeen," Macgillivray.

8. A. PARALLELOGRAMMA, O. F. Müller.

Zool. Dan. t. 49, f. 1, 2, 3.

Body more or less tetragonal, sub-compressed, adhering by base. Tunic smooth, glossy, pellucid, exhibiting the branchial sac ornamented conspicuously with rectangular reticulating white lines, and occasionally bright yellow or crimson spots. Orifices terminal, rather distinct, not conspicuously ocellated. About an inch and a half in length.

"Ascidiarum pelluciditate, consistentiâ, colorumque splendore spectatissimus."—MÜLLER.

Attached to algæ in Strangford Loch, W. Thompson, Ann. Nat. Hist. vol. v. (1840) p. 94. Roundstone Bay, Connemara, W. T., R. Ball, E. F. (1840). Zetlands, (1845,) R. M'Andrew and E. F.

9. A. PRUNUM, Müller!

O. F. Müller, Zool. Dan. t. 34, f. 1, 2, 3.—Pirena prunum, Fleming, Brit. An. p. 468?

Body ovate, depressed, adhering to the side. Tunic very smooth, hyaline, the branchial sac shining white through the tunic. Orifices sessile, or nearly so, approximate, bordered with yellow, the branchial with eight red ocelli and eight tubercles in the tunic around it; the anal with six red ocelli and six surrounding tubercles. Usually about an inch in length.

Common on most parts of our coast, adhering to the under surface of stones at low-water; often gregarious. Isle of Man, Bristol Channel, west and east coast of Scotland, Zetlands, E. F. Dredged in the Lochs of Strangford and Belfast, W. Thompson. Northumberland, Mr. Alder, who objects to this species being referred to the *prunum* of Müller.

10. A. ORBICULARIS, Müller.

Zool. Dan. t. 79, f. 1, 2.

Body orbicular, depressed, adhering. Tunic hyaline, pellucid, with an opaque disk, "scabrous." Orifices approximate, sessile. One inch across.

"On Zostera marina in Strangford Lough," W. Thompson, Ann. Nat. Hist. vol. v. (1840) p. 94.

11. A. ASPERSA, Müller.

Zool. Dan. t. 65, f. 2.

Body ovate, sub-compressed, adhering obliquely at base. Tunic slightly scabrous, white, transparent, shewing the red spotted branchial sac. Orifices papillose, nearly sessile, terminal. Gregarious. An inch in length.

Loughs of Strangford and Belfast, W. Thompson, Ann. Nat. Hist. vol. v. (1840) p. 94.

12. A. VITREA, Van Beneden.

Mem. Acad. Roy. Belg. t. xx. (1847) p. 59, pl. 4, f. 1–5.

Body globose or sub-compressed, attached by a very small base. Outer tunic thin, transparent, membranous, hyaline; tubes terminal, placed rather apart, the branchial projecting most, but both short. Orifices with red ocelli. Half an inch in length.

On Alcyonidium in Killery Bay, (1840,) R. Ball, W. Thompson, and E. F. Probably not uncommon on many parts of our coast.

13. A. CONCHILEGA, O. F. Müller.

Zool. Dan. t. 30, A, f. 4, 5, 6.

"Compressed, infested with fragments of shells; inner tunic white, passing to blue." This species requires elucidation.

"Coast of Down and Antrim," W. Thompson, in Ann. Nat. Hist., 1844.

14. A. ECHINATA, Linnæus.

Zool. Dan. t. 130, f. 1.
Plate C, fig. 4.

Body globose, adhering by base. Tunic tough, yellowish, opaque-white, studded with conical eminences or papillæ, which bear upon their summits a circle of from four to seven radiating bristles. Orifices sessile, tinged and rayed with deep crimson; the oral with eight, the anal with six rays or notches; the interspaces tubercular: the branchial orifice is much the most conspicuous. About an inch in height.

Zetland, (1837,) J. Goodsir and E. F. "Parasitic on one of the larger *Ascidiæ*; dredged in Strangford Lough," W. Thompson, Ann. Nat. Hist. vol. v. (1840) p. 91.

MOLGULA, E. Forbes.

(Diminutive of Μολγος, a bag of skin.)

Body more or less globular, attached or free, with a membranous tunic, usually invested with extraneous matter; orifices on very contractile and naked tubes; the branchial 6-lobed, the anal 4-lobed.

1. M. oculata, E. Forbes.

Plate D, fig. 6.

Body globose, adhering by base; test closely encrusted with sand, shells, and gravel, except a smooth, oblong, reniform, regularly bounded, depressed space, within which the very short but rather wide orifices project. This space is very tender, translucent, bluish or purplish, mottled with orange; the orifices are short tubes, similarly coloured, the one 6-lobed, the other 4-lobed; lobes acute. Two inches and a half across.

This curious species, the orifices of which seem like dark eyes within a spectacle-formed frame, was dredged off Plymouth, adhering to a scallop, in twenty-five fathoms, (1846,) R. M'Andrew and E. F.

2. M. tubulosa, Rathke, (Sp.)

Ascidia tubulosa, Zool. Dan. t. 130, f. 3.

Plate C, fig. 5.

Body perfectly globular, not adhering, but buried in sand or mud. Test hyaline, encrusted with fine sand, smooth, except the short conical approximated orifices, which are naked, bluish, and beautifully reticulated; their edges are bordered with yellowish tubercles, (6+4.) The branchial opening is the largest.

This curious species occurs abundantly in muddy lochs and bays on the west coast of Scotland. When it comes up in the dredge, it resembles a little ball of sand; when the sand is rubbed away, it seems like a little transparent bullet, in the interior of which the viscera are seen winding. The description in the Zoologia Danica does not agree with our species so well as the figure.

CYNTHIA, Savigny.

Body sessile, covered with a coriaceous tunic; branchial and
anal orifices opening in four rays or lobes. [Branchial sac
longitudinally plicated, surmounted by a circle of tentacular
filaments; meshes of the respiratory tissue not furnished with
papillæ.]

1. C. microcosmus, Savigny.

Cynthia microcosmus, Sav. Mém. pt. 2, p. 144, pl. 2, f. 1, and pl. 6, f. 2.—
Ascidia microcosmus, Cuv. Mém. Mus. t. ii. pl. 1, f. 1–6 ?

Body tuberous; test deeply and unequally wrinkled across,
glabrous, yellowish-grey, hard, opaque; orifices 4-cleft, small,
on prominent, tuberculated, conical, hirsute projections, rayed in-
teriorly with blue and purple. British specimens are rarely larger
than two or three inches in height.

South coast of England? Ireland, W. Thompson.

2. C. claudicans, Savigny.

Sav. Mém. pt. ii. p. 150, pl. 2, f. 1.

Body tuberous; test wrinkled and furrowed in every direction, finely bristly, of a greyish or ashy-red or brownish colour,
thick, opaque, often encrusted with sand and fragments of
shells; orifices small, deeply 4-lobed, reddish, placed on slightly prominent conical projections. Usually about an inch in
height.

On oysters, especially in the south. " Not uncommon on oysters and other shell-fish taken on the north coast of Ireland," W.
Thompson. West coast of Scotland, R. M'Andrew and E. F.

3. C. tuberosa, Macgillivray.

Macg. Mollusca of Aberdeen, p. 311.

" Greyish-white or grey, sessile, sub-ovate and hemispheric, very
densely cartilaginous, covered with irregular prominences or tubercles of various sizes. Length one inch."—Macgillivray.

Deep water off Aberdeen. A reddish-brown Cynthia with red

apertures, having a very thick outer tunic, in which Modiola marmorata is generally embedded, is not uncommon at Cullercoats, according to Mr. Alder, and is probably the adult of Professor Macgillivray's species.

4. C. QUADRANGULARIS, E. Forbes.

Pl. D, fig. 1.

Body conical; test thick, coriaceous, dark reddish-brown, warty; orifices rather large, on produced conical quadrangular eminences, the angles formed by strong ribs composed of united warts; rims of orifices white, with a fine crimson bordering line. Length nearly two inches.

Dredged in Loch Fine, from a depth of thirty fathoms, (1845,) R. M'Andrew and E. F.

5. C. INFORMIS, E. Forbes.

Body rudely conical, subtuberous; test thick, coriaceous, crimson, covered with rather undefined, oblong, large warts; orifices on conical, obtuse projections, 4-lobed, deep crimson. Length two inches.

Dredged in from seven to nine fathoms water in Zetland and in Stromness Bay, Orkneys, J. Goodsir and E. F. (1839.)

6. C. TESSELLATA, E. Forbes.

Pl. D, fig. 3.

Body transversely ovate, and shaped not unlike the *Psolus squamatus*; test coriaceous, tessellated by regular, smooth, hexagonal, oblong, depressed spaces or warts, each of which is darkly tinted in the centre, so that the creature appears to be tawny, speckled with regular purple spots; orifices quadrangular, with deep crimson margins, on rather short and distinct conical eminences, which are more deeply tinted with purple than the body. Length half an inch.

Dredged, adhering to a stone, in twenty-five fathoms water, Mount's Bay, Cornwall, (1846,) R. M'Andrew and E. F.

7. C. LIMACINA, E. Forbes.

Plate D, fig. 4.

Body depressed, expanded, doridiform ; test coriaceous, orange, with dark-brown reticulating markings, enclosing numerous small depressed warts of various sizes ; orifices quadrangular, papillose, almost sessile, brown. Three-quarters of an inch in length.

On a dead shell in twenty-five fathoms, Mount's Bay, Cornwall, (1846,) R. M'Andrew and E. Forbes.

8. C. MORUS, E. Forbes.

Plate D, fig. 2.

Body oblong, attached throughout the length of its base, rugose, with more or less rounded tubercular spaces, rose-red ; orifices nearly sessile, distinct, placed at about the same level, banded with alternate stripes of orange and red ; tunic very tough.

Length three-quarters of an inch, height half an inch.

Mounts Bay, Cornwall, on stones in twenty-five fathoms water, R. M'Andrew and E. Forbes. "Taken on an oyster at Fowey by Mr. Peach. Very like a raspberry when contracted," Mr. Alder.

9. C. RUSTICA, Linnæus, (Sp.)

Ascidia rustica, Müller, Zool. Dan. pl. 15, f. 1.—Phallusia rustica, Fleming, Brit. An. p. 469.

Body more or less globular or botryoidal, rugose, usually of a rusty red ; apertures sessile, placed apart, deeply tinged with rose-red. From half an inch to two inches in length.

A coriaceous, white, smooth, but nodulose, botryoidal ascidian occurs in deep water on the coast of Cornwall, apparently a variety of this species. There is considerable confusion, however, about *Cynthia rustica*. It is very doubtful whether the figures of Müller really represent only one species. Lamarck has wrongly referred *Ascidia scabra*, *A. aspersa*, and *A. patula* to varieties of *rustica*.

Common on most parts of our coast, on fuci.

10. C. GROSSULARIA, Van Beneden, (Sp.)

Ascidia grossularia, Van Beneden, Mém. Acad. Roy. Belg. t. xx. (1847) p. 61,
pl. 4, f. 7–11.

Body oval, depressed, often lenticular, sessile, and attached by
the entire lower surface ; outer tunic corneous, smooth, rose-red ;
apertures sessile. Forming disks about a quarter of an inch
across. Very common on oysters everywhere, and on stones at
low water. Usually regarded in this country as the fry of *C.
rustica*, but probably distinct. Professor Van Beneden states
that the branchial sac is without folds.

11. C. AMPULLA, Brugière, (Sp.)

Baster, Opusc. p. 84, t. 10, f. 5, a, b, c, d. (cop. in Encyc. Méth. pl. 63, f. 1–3.)
Ascidia ampulla, Lamarck, An. sans Vert. vol. iii. (in 2nd ed. p. 528.)

Body more or less ovate or globular, unattached ; outer tunic
hairy ; orifices tubular, produced, placed close together, yellowish,
speckled with red. About an inch in length.
"Common at Cullercoats, Northumberland ; brought in on
fishermen's lines. Unattached, and sometimes covered with sand
to the depth of half an inch," Mr. Alder.

12. C. MAMMILLARIS, Pallas, (Sp.)

Ascidia mammillaris, Pallas, Sp. Zool. fasc. 10, p. 24, t. 1, f. 15, (copied in
Encyc. Méth. f. 62, f. 1.)

Body oblong, depressed, sessile, attached throughout its length,
rugose, gibbous ; the outer tunic coriaceous, clothed with soft
hairs ; colour dirty white or pale yellow ; orifices nearly sessile,
approximate, scarlet within. About an inch in length. Very
irritable.
"On submarine rocks in Cornwall," Gaertner. This species
requires to be sought for and re-observed.

13. C. AGGREGATA, Rathke. (Sp.)

Ascidiâ aggregata.   Rathke, Zool. Dan. t. 130, f. 2.

Plate D. f. 5.

Body bottle-shaped, cylindrical, with terminal approximate orifices ; base of attachment small, sending out many fibres ; outer tunic membranous, smooth, of an uniform brilliant orange ; the orifices quadrangular, bordered with still brighter orange and edged with red ; the anal placed more obliquely than the branchial : no ocelli.   About an inch in height.

Gregarious in vast numbers under large stones in twelve fathoms water at Dartmouth, R. M'Andrew and E. F. (1846.) Sometimes forming large free bunches, in consequence of the interlacing of the rootfibres.   The description in the "Zoologia Danica" well expresses this habit :—" Siquidem nunquam solitariam, semper vero plures, sæpius viginti ad triginti, mediantibus radiculis tendineis invicem junctas deprehenderit, eam aggregatam appellari voluit."

On many of the branching root-fibres are small, tough, globular, imperforate, orange bodies, of various sizes, full of granules.   Are not these intermediate states of this Ascidian 1   The Ascidians we examined were full of tadpoles in various stages of development.

This form seems intermediate between the simple and social Ascidians, and should probably rank as the type of a distinct genus.

IV. PELONAIADÆ.

We have now to notice the British species of a very curious group of *Tunicata*, one which seems to have escaped the observation of most naturalists, and hitherto to have been omitted from systematic arrangements of the Mollusca, partly through the rarity of the creatures themselves, partly from the only published account of them having been overlooked. These are two animals, both inhabitants of the Scottish seas, one of which was first observed by Professor E. Forbes, and the other by Professor Goodsir, who jointly constituted for their reception the genus *Pelonaia*.* Whilst in many of their characters they approach the true Ascidians, especially the unattached species of the genus *Cynthia*, in others they indicate a relationship with the cirrhograde *Echinodermata*. They present the remarkable positive anatomical character of a union of mantle with test; so that there can be little question of their right to be regarded as members of a distinct family of *Tunicata*.† As no account of them is to be found out of the original paper, we reprint it entire :—

"Among the Ascidian Mollusca which we have collected together, with a view to a complete investigation of the British *Tunicata*, are two remarkable animals, which appear to represent a very natural genus, as yet unrecorded.

"They differ from their allies in the tribe chiefly by their not being fixed, and by their form, which reminds one more of that of a *Siphunculus* than of an *Ascidia;* indeed, they may be re-

* See Jameson's Ed. New Phil. Journal, vol. xxxi. (for 1841), p. 29.
† It is worthy of notice, that Mr. Macleay, in his valuable remarks on the arrangement of the *Tunicata*, (Linnæan Trans. vol. xiv. ,) had hypothetically indicated such a group as this now constituted.

garded as analogous to certain *Siphunculidæ*, and in that point
of view the details of their form and structure are of much interest to the naturalist.

" They are both of a cylindrical shape, having their orifices on
the same plane, elevated on papillose eminences at one extremity
of the body. No rays or tentacula surround either of the [4-
cleft] orifices. Their posterior extremities terminate in a blunt
point. They live buried in mud, quite unattached to any other
body, and are extremely apathetic animals, presenting scarcely
any appearance of motion.

" We have styled the genus *Pelonaia*, and define it as follows :—
" Test cylindrical, unattached.

" Orifices without rays, on two equal approximated papillose
eminences at the anterior extremity.

" Species I. P. CORRUGATA [Pl. E, fig.4.].—Test deep brown,
much elongated, rudely wrinkled transversely.

" In the mud-filled cavities of old shells from deep water, An-
struther. It has also been taken by Dr. Johnston at Berwick.
[Northumberland, Mr. Alder.]

" Sp. II. P. GLABRA [Pl. E, fig. 3.].—Test greenish-yellow,
smooth, pilose, not nearly so much elongated as the last.

" Dredged in seven fathoms water, in mud, Rothesay Bay.

Anatomy of P. glabra.

" 1. *Muscular System.*—The mantle is similar to that of other
Ascidiæ, possessing longitudinal and circular fibres. A strong
band of transverse fibres passes round it, immediately below the
anal orifice, encroaching on the cavity principally on that side.
The chief peculiarity of the mantle is its firm adhesion to the
test.

" 2. *Digestive and Respiratory Systems.* — The respiratory
opening is of small size, and exhibits no folds or tentacular
fringes. The respiratory sac is elongated, cylindrical, contracting
rather suddenly towards one side to become continuous with the
œsophagus. On the external surface of the sac there are about
thirty parallel transverse ridges, which give it the appearance of
a plaited frill. These plaits are less apparent along the course of
the branchial artery and branchial vein, but midway between

them on each side they are very prominent, and are tied each by a minute cord to the inner surface of the mantle. The internal surface of the sac exhibits along one side the serpentine double cord which contains the branchial vein; along the other side the branchial artery; and from these primary and secondary perpendicular branches proceed, as in the other *Ascidiæ*. The transverse plaits on the external surface of the sac correspond to the primary or tranverse branches of the vessels on the internal surface. The animal was not examined while alive, but cilia, without doubt, exist in great abundance on the edges of the lozenge-shaped spaces of the sac.

"The œsophagus commences by a white plicated opening at the lower end, and on one side of the sac. It is curved in a sigmoidal form, and exhibits longitudinal rugæ through its coats. Near the lower end of the mantle-cavity it terminates by suddenly dilating into the stomach, which is pear-shaped, and directed obliquely upwards towards the side opposite to the œsophagus. The internal surface of the stomach presents longitudinal plicæ, and is succeeded by the intestine, which at first curves upward, then down to the bottom of the mantle cavity, up along the œsophageal side of that cavity, and between its walls and the branchial artery, terminating about the anterior third of the animal in a funnel-shaped anus, which is cut into ten or eleven processes, like the petals of a flower. The first part of the intestine is white and longitudinally plicated; the rectum is dilated with attenuated coats.

"3. *Vascular System.*—The vascular system resembles that of the true *Ascidiæ*, except that there is no heart. It consists of two sets of vessels, with four sets of capillaries, a circle in fact twice interrupted, once in the respiratory sac, and again throughout the body. The branchial veins run along the transverse plaits of the sac, receiving secondary and ternary twigs at right angles. The primary branchial venous branches empty themselves on each side into the branchial trunk, which runs in the substance of the double cord which coasts the superior aspect of the sac. This double cord terminates in an abrupt manner anteriorly near the oral orifice, and in a similar manner, but after becoming smaller near the orifice leading to the œsophagus. At this point the vein becomes an artery, and probably sends back vessels to nourish the sac. It now runs along the œsophagus, supplying the stomach and intestine, and giving off in its course branches to the cloak. The veins arising from the arterial capillaries of the body meet near the commencement of the œsophagus in one trunk, which, passing along the inferior wall of the respiratory sac, opposite to the branchial vein, performs the functions of a branchial artery. It is interesting to observe here the differences between the modes in which the branches enter the branchial vein, and strike off from the branchial artery. In the former, just before the branches enter the trunk, they give off a number of vessels, which enter the trunk alongside of the parent trunk, the combination forming a sort of delta: in the latter they leave the trunk singly, and send off their branches in a radiating direction. At a little distance from the trunks of both artery and vein, the secondary branches become parallel to one another, and perpendicular to their primary branches, the more minute divisions following the same mode of ramification.

" Not having examined the animal when alive, we have no information as to the nature of its blood.

" 4. *Nervous System.*—This system consists, as in other *Ascidiæ*, of a ganglion situated in the substance of the mantle, between the oral and anal orifices. It is globular, and sends off nervous twigs, 1. to the respiratory orifice of the mantle ; 2. to the respiratory sac, where it begins to exhibit the transverse plaits ; and, 3, to the anal orifice of the mantle.

" 5. *Generative System.*—The generative organs consist of two elongated tubes, closed at one end, open at the other, and having a great number of close-set parallel cæca arranged at right angles, and opening into them along each side. These tubes are attached to the internal surface of the mantle ; their mouths are free for a short distance, and prominent, the rest of their extent and the attached cæca adherent. The orifices of these organs are situate at the junction of the first with the second quarter of the animal, and one third of the other end of each turns in toward its neighbour, and then proceeds forward parallel to itself. The branchial vein runs midway between the generative tubes above, and the branchial artery in a corresponding course below, so that the threads of attachment of the plaits on the external surface of the sac are fixed into the tubes in a series on each side.

Anatomy of P. corrugata.

"The structure of this species differs very little from that of *P. glabra*. The animal being elongated, the organs are placed more longitudinally. The respiratory sac is longer; the stomach is longer, and is not placed so much across the body. The œsophagus runs down to the bottom of the sac before it terminates. The rectum is very long, and of considerable width, but just before it terminates in the anus it becomes very much contracted. The mantle exhibits no ridge or shelf below the anal orifice, but its longitudinal fibres are very strong, and form a thick bundle at their origin round the respiratory opening. The test, instead of being thin and diaphanous like parchment, as in *P. glabra*, is thick and cartilaginous, coloured brown, and transversely wrinkled externally.

"From the details of structure which we have now given, it is evident that the *Pelonaiæ* are *Ascidiæ*. Their anatomy is important, as it explains the nature of the parts and organs in the *Tunicata*. They differ from the other *Ascidiæ* more particularly in being bi-lateral. The generative organs are symmetrical, and open one on each side of the anus, which is directed toward the ventral surface of the animal, in a line with the mouth and nervous ganglion. The latter is thus proved to be an abdominal or sub-œsophageal ganglion, corresponding to, or forming one of the chains of ganglia on the abdominal surface of the *Articulata*. In the same manner, the branchial artery or heart is proved to be the pulsating dorsal vessel, and the branchial vein the abdominal vessel (when that vessel exists), in the *Annulosa*. It is interesting also to perceive, that, co-existing with this decided approach to the annular type of form, we have the transverse plaits of the respiratory sac corresponding to the rings of an articulated animal. The disappearance of a separate test is also a departure from the plan of formation in the *Ascidiæ*, and an approach to other types of form, and more particularly to the cirrhograde *Echinodermata*, with certain of which *Pelonaia* has at least an analogical relation, in the water-filled body and in the external form.

"*Pelonaia*, in fine, is one of those connecting genera so valuable as filling up gaps in the system, and supplying links in the chain of structures which runs through the series of organised bodies."

V. SALPIDÆ.

Very different from the simple, the social, or true compound Ascidians, are the animals of the genus *Salpa*. They are free, and habitually swim in the waters of the ocean. In form they resemble short but rather wide tubes, often of considerable size. The tube is composed of the test or tunic, semi-cartilaginous or gelatinous in structure, seeming as if carved in crystal, lined with the mantle, which in this tribe is adherent throughout. Each end of the tube is open, often terminating in a conical more or less produced process. Within we find two narrow, oblique, unequal, leaf-like branchiæ, attached to the anterior and posterior walls of the respiratory cavity. The branchial orifice is protected by a valve. Near one extremity is the principal visceral mass or nucleus, conspicuous owing to the brilliant orange, brown, or reddish hues of the liver. Not unfrequently we find *Salpæ* making their way through the waters deprived of their nuclei by birds or fishes, retaining their vitality for a considerable time, and exercising their muscular powers when the organs of digestion, circulation, and reproduction have been torn away. Peculiar crustaceans make use of the cavity of the *Salpa* as a dwelling-place and carriage; and the number of minute phosphorescent animals which lodge themselves within it is often so great, as to mislead the observer into the belief that it is the mollusk itself which gives out phosphorescent flashes.

A great interest is attached to the natural history of the *Salpæ*, on account of their singular mode of reproduction, discovered by the German naturalist Chamisso, and the extraordinary generalisation to which that discovery in a great measure gave rise. Previous observers had noticed that these animals were sometimes found solitary, at others

united together in long chains, composed of numerous individuals of similar form, each an independent being, though
constantly associated, and linearly aggregated, with its
companions. These long chains swim through the tranquil
water with regular serpentine movements, for the creatures
of which they are composed contract and expand simultaneously, keeping time, as it were, like a regiment of sol-
diers upon parade. Each chain seems consequently to be
a single being, acting through the influence of an unique
will, and hence sailors often look upon it as a reptile, and
in many seas the salpa-chains are called sea-serpents. But
when taken out of the water, the links of the chain fall
asunder, the several distinct animals of which it is composed suddenly losing their power of adhesion. In consequence of accidents, broken-up chains and separated
members of such communities are not unfrequently met in
seas where *Salpæ* are numerous. But other *Salpæ* are also
met with very dissimilar in form, and never united together
in chains. Now, the discovery of Chamisso was, that such
constantly solitary *Salpæ* did not belong to species distinct
from those united in chains, however dissimilar, (and they
are so dissimilar usually as to appear even generically distinct,) but were either the parents or the progeny, as the
case might be, of the aggregate forms; that chained *Salpæ*
did not produce chained *Salpæ*, but solitary *Salpæ*, which,
in their turn, did not produce solitary beings, but chained.
Consequently, as Chamisso graphically observed, " A *Salpa*
mother is not like its daughter or its own mother, but resembles its sister, its granddaughter, and its grandmother."
So surprising, so paradoxical an assertion, a statement so
contrary to what naturalists fancied to be the laws of nature,
could scarcely expect to be received with credulity. Nor
was it. There was a general outcry against it; it was
treated as a wild assertion resulting from the incorrect
observations of a man with more imagination than judgment. In vain Chamisso offered the most careful researches
and minute details of his observations. The heavy-headed
in science stigmatised him as a poet and romancer, who

carried his day-dreams into the world of reality, and thus
conjured up his wonderful vision of *Salpæ*. More than
twenty years had to pass away before his statements were
fairly treated. Men ungifted with the poetic insight which
characterised Chamisso, collected and watched *Salpæ* in
vain. Working in a spirit of unbelief, they saw what they
wished, and what was accordant with their ideas of what
ought to be; whereas the poet-naturalist had worked in the
spirit of faith, and therefore was unsurprised when he met
with facts and phenomena inconsistent with received human
knowledge. Working before his time, he was misunderstood; but the time came when not only were his observations proved to be true, but when a great impulse was given
to natural history through them. It was the history over
again of all great impulses in our science. Linnæus pro-
claimed the metamorphosis of plants unlistened to; Goethe,
more happy in his time, unravelled the same great mystery,
and was understood, though not by all. The poetic spirit,
working alike in Linnæus and in Goethe, did these things;
so also in Chamisso. It required a similar spirit to renew the
impulse in the zoological instance, as in the botanical. That
spirit has appeared in Steenstrup, the germ of whose theory
of the alternation of generations is to be found in Chamisso's discovery of the alternation of generations in the
Salpæ.*

The recent researches of Krohn on the *Salpæ* of the coast
of Sicily† fully confirm the statements of Chamisso. Krohn
found that every *Salpa* which came under his observation
was viviparous, and that each species propagated itself by
an alternate succession of dissimilar generations. One of
these generations is represented by isolated, the other by
aggregate individuals (forming chains). Each isolated in-

* Chamisso's observations were published in 1819 : " De animalibus quibus-
dam a classe vermium Linnæana, fasc. i. de Salpa." We owe to the Ray
Society and Mr. Busk an English version of Steenstrup's most interesting treatise.

† Krohn, Observations sur la Génération et le Développement des Biphores
Ann. Sc. Nat., August, 1846.

dividual produces an aggregate assemblage, and each of the members of such a group produces isolated individuals. The members of the one generation are very dissimilar from those of the other; consequently specific names have been doubly multiplied.

The recently published observations on *Salpæ* by the Norwegian naturalist, Sars, one of the most original and philosophical of living zoologists, have thrown great light on the habits and development of these curious creatures. They are to be found in the first part of his beautiful " Fauna littoralis Norwegiæ," and should be carefully studied by the British naturalist who may be fortunate enough to meet with our native species.

Salpæ were first observed in the British seas by the eminent geologist, Dr. Macculloch. His account of them is given in his work on the Western Islands, in that part which relates to the natural history of Jura.* It is accompanied by a very rude figure, insufficient for the determination of the species, but putting the genus beyond question. The description which the doctor there gives is so interesting and original, that we think it right to extract it entire in his own words :—

" Some marine animals occur in these seas which remain still unrecorded in the catalogue of British zoology. Among these, indeed, it is probable that a few will be found still undescribed by naturalists, since fresh additions are even yet occasionally made to our catalogue of these obscurer parts of the creation. Many of these animals have occasionally fallen under my notice, but amid pursuits which rendered it impossible to attend either to their examination or preservation. I have, however, preserved a memorial of one, as it appears to form a new species in a tribe of which no individual has yet been observed within the limits of the British seas. It belongs apparently to the genus *Salpa*, and the accompanying drawing would be sufficient to distinguish it, even without a specific definition.†

* Western Isles, vol. ii. p. 187.   † Plate 29.

"The mode in which the *republic* is linked together is observed to be constant in each species; and it is sufficiently remarkable in this one to distinguish it from the rest of the genus as far as it is yet described. Each individual adheres to the preceding by a regular sequence of superposition lengthwise, so that the whole forms a long simple chain; the adhesion continuing, as in the ovarium, for some time after hatching. They were found from the middle to the latter end of August, and always linked together. It is probable that their separation takes place at a later season of the year, but I did not observe them in that state. The individual is amongst the most simple in shape of those yet described, presenting an oval-lanceolate and slightly rhomboidal flattened figure, without appendages. The anal opening is of a bright brown and circular, being placed at some distance from the extremity; and when the chain is linked together, all these apertures are directed the same way. The animal is perfectly hyaline and tender, and the adhesion of the chain so slight, that the individuals are easily separated. The act of swimming is known to result from the introduction and emission of water by each animal; and as the republic swims together by an undulating motion resembling that of a serpent, the chain often extending to many feet in length, it is evident that this motion must arise from the unequal manner in which the different individuals act throughout the whole line.

"The species now described is most analogous to the *S. polycratica* and to the *S. confederata* of Forskahl. It differs, however, from the former in the want of the caudal denticle, in its hyaline appearance, and in the absence of the rigid portion which attends that one. From the latter it is readily distinguished by its longitudinal concatenation, since, in that species, the individuals adhere by their sides, so as to form a row in a lateral direction, while there are at the same time important differences in the structure of the two.

"I had occasion to remark of this animal, that, like the *Medusæ* and analogous tribes, it cannot bear to be confined in a limited portion of water, as it died, even in the ship's bucket, in less than half an hour; a very remarkable circumstance in the economy of these imperfect animals.

"Hitherto, this genus is only known as the inhabitant of hot

climates and of the Mediterranean Sea. I found it in great
abundance in the harbours of Canna and Campbeltown, rising to
the surface in calm weather, and crowding the water, as the *Medusæ* often do at the same time of the year. It may be called
Salpa moniliformis, and defined as follows :—

"S. ovato-lanceolata, ano fusco, absque appendice terminali.

"I was desirous of observing whether this animal, like many
other of the marine worms, emitted light, but had no opportunity
of ascertaining the fact, as they seemed always to retire to the
bottom at sunset, and those which were taken on board died, as I
have already observed, in a very short time."

During a voyage round the coast of Scotland, in 1821,
Dr. Fleming, who gave a very interesting account of his
journey in the "Edinburgh Philosophical Journal," observed *Salpæ* in great numbers on the coast of Caithness.
He describes them as occurring abundantly in spring, when
they form chains of a foot and more in length. The
separated individuals are about an inch in length, and
shaped like a cylinder, with a long conical process at
each extremity, the anteal one being rather more produced
than the other. The nucleus is of a dark brownish-orange
colour, and, as well as the branchial band, is distinctly
seen through the transparent gelatinous body. The *Salpæ*
are gregarious, in company with "*Eulimena quadrangularis*" (*Beroe cucumis*). They seem, however, to be very
capricious in their appearance. During three voyages which
we have made in the Scottish seas, although continually and
anxiously on the look-out for these creatures, we have never
encountered them. Lately they have been met with, but
only occasionally, by Mr. M'Andrew; and Lieutenant
Thomas, R.N., has taken them in the Orkneys, and succeeded in preserving them in both their solitary and aggregate forms. An examination of specimens, kindly communicated by that active officer and observant naturalist, has
enabled us to identify them certainly with the *Salpa runcinata,* which Sars has found so abundantly, and figured so
well, from the coast of Norway. The figures we have given

we have taken from Lieutenant Thomas's preserved specimens, guided and corrected by the drawing from the living
animal by Sars, whose description we think it best to
follow.

SALPA RUNCINATA, Chamisso.

Chamisso, de Salpa, p. 16, f. 5.—Quoy and Gaimard, Voy. Astrol. Zool. 3, pl. 87,
f. 1–5.—Sars, Fauna littoralis Norwegiæ, pl. 8, f. 44, 45, and pl. 9, f. 1–24.

Solitary State. (Pl. E, fig. 5.)—Body oblong, anterior extremity rounded, posterior truncated, beneath gelatinous and flat,
above depressed in front, elevated and cartilaginous behind, where
it is furnished with seven keels, gradually disappearing anteally,
produced into short spines posteally.   Both apertures of the
branchial sac terminal.   Muscles of respiration nine, placed in
the ventral side, three anterior and three posterior, approximated
in the middle.

Aggregate State. (Pl. E, fig. 6: the individuals represented
are not so elongated as when full grown.)—Body gelatinous,
ovate, slightly depressed; beneath plane, above convex, produced
at each extremity into a conical acuminated appendage.   Orifices of the branchial sac beneath, at the bases of the appendages.
Muscles of respiration (besides those of the apertures) six, placed
in the ventral side, four anterior and two posterior, approximated
in the middle.

Sars has found another species, which he refers to the
Salpa spinosa of Otto, in the Norwegian seas.   It will very
probably be found also among the Hebrides.   The posterior
extremity of the solitary individual is furnished with two
long straight spines; the aggregate individuals have an ovate
body, rounded anteriorly, produced into a short pyramidal
cartilaginous spine posteriorly.   These characters will enable our naturalists to recognise it.

The preceding enumeration of the British species of
TUNICATA, though far exceeding in detail any account of
them hitherto published, is offered as a mere outline of a

very extensive and interesting tribe of Mollusca, one so
little examined, that the identification of well-known
species with the figures and descriptions of O. F. Müller,
and other authors quoted, is disputed by some of our ablest
naturalists.   The whole subject has to be re-investigated:
the brief notices and slight figures given by the older naturalists are insufficient for accurate determination.   Several
years must elapse before the task can be undertaken with
success.   In the mean time this outline may be serviceable.

ACEPHALA LAMELLIBRANCHIATA.

WERE the test of an Ascidia to be converted into hard shell, symmetrically divided into two plates connected together dorsally by cartilage, and capable of separation so as to expose the mantle along a ventral mesial line, whilst the orifices protruded at one extremity, it would present the closest similarity with many bivalve shell-fish. We pass by a very natural transition from the Ascidians to the Lamellibranchiate *Acephala*.

This great section of the headless mollusks is so styled, because of the peculiar arrangement of the respiratory organs in the creatures composing it. The branchial leaflets are four in number, usually forming expanded laminæ, arranged in pairs on each side of the main mass of viscera. If the number, as in a few species, appear fewer than four, it is so by habitual suppression ; if more, by reduplication.

This peculiar respiratory apparatus is included within the mantle, but quite free from it. The mantle secretes and is protected by a bivalve shell, the two valves of which are applied to the two sides of the animal. These valves are almost always moveably articulated together at their dorsal edges by a more or less complicated hinge, connected by a more or less developed ligament, and are held close by powerful adductor muscles passing from the inner surface of one valve to that of the opposite, either one or two in number. The edges of the lobes of the mantle are more or less united, and in certain genera and families are free. Its extreme margin, in a great many, is prolonged in the shape of two

tubes, forming the so-called siphons, capable of being retracted by special muscles. Through one of the tubes water
is inhaled, through the other ejected. In such of the *La-
mellibranchiata* as have only one adductor muscle, there
are no tubes, and in several of those with two adductors.
The mass of the body is placed in the deeper and central
part of the cavity of the shell, and consists of variously
modified digestive, reproductive, and secretory organs,
vessels, and nerves. The liver and generative glands constitute the greater part. In a majority of species, a single
linguiform muscular organ is developed for locomotion on
the ventral side of the viscera. This is the foot. It has
been observed that the development of the nervous and respiratory systems corresponds in degree with that of the
locomotive organ. The degree of the development of the
nervous system varies much among these bivalves. The
principal ganglion (the branchial) is present in all, so are
usually two labial ganglia. The presence of a pedal ganglion depends on the presence of a foot. The organs of
sense are very variously developed. There are almost always around the mouth, which is to be sought for at the
opposite extremity of the body from that where the siphons
project, more or less developed lips, usually four in number.
Ocelli, imperfect organs of sight, are present in the majority
of bivalves, and very conspicuous in some genera, arranged
along the margin of the mantle, or dotting the edges of the
siphonal orifices, exactly as in the *Ascidiæ*. Minute sacs,
with vibrating otolites (rudimentary organs of hearing),
have been observed in several species, and are possibly present in all. The sexes are either separate or combined.
All the lamellibranchiate bivalves undergo an imperfect
metamorphosis. They live upon infusoriæ and microscopic
plants.

I. PHOLADIDÆ.

THE PHOLAS TRIBE.

The first tribe of lamellibranchiate bivalves is that of which the *Pholas* is the type. Such an arrangement does not exactly imply that the *Pholas* and its allies are lower in organisation than all other *Conchifera*, but rather that they are among an assemblage of tribes which seem to take their place as it were at the bottom of the table, and to link the *Tunicata* with the higher mollusks. In many respects a *Mya* resembles more nearly an Ascidian, than a *Pholas* does; but the customary arrangement is most convenient, and not so far from the truth as to call for alteration.

The *Pholadidæ* are shelled acephalous mollusks, having more or less elongated bodies, produced posteriorly into a long siphonal tube, divided at its extremity, the orifices being cirrhated. Anteriorly the mantle is closed, except where a small orifice is left for the passage of a clavate and truncate, sometimes nearly obsolete, foot. Other characters are such as belong to the class, or are peculiar to particular genera. The shells are equivalve and inequilateral, always more or less gaping. They have no true hinge, and the ligament is almost or altogether suppressed. Beneath the summit of each valve there is a curved calcareous process.

All the members of this tribe are borers into stone, clay, wood, or other substances. Their habits and history are described under the several genera.

Shell globular or annular, regular, composed of two equal much-curved polygonal valves, their outer surfaces striated in various directions, the inner surface presenting only one distinct muscular impression. No true hinge; ligament obsolete; a curved process beneath the beaks of each valve. No accessory valves at the back of the shell.

Animal vermiform; mantle tubular, slightly open anteriorly; siphons very long, bifurcating at their extremities, orifices fringed; a muscular ring, into which are inserted two variously shaped calcareous ossicles (pallets), at the part where the siphons divide; branchiæ continued into the siphonal tube; foot rudimentary, sucker-shaped.

Tube calcareous, cylindrical, lining the cell in which the animal is lodged.

The genus *Teredo* is the most abnormal of all the lamellibranchiate bivalves; nor is it to be wondered at that the ancients, and the older writers among the moderns, regarded it as a worm rather than as a mollusk. The resemblance of its tube to that constructed by the *Serpula*, and the worm-shaped body of the creature itself, naturally suggested the notion that it was an annellid, while even the valves of the shell seemed rather like the jaws of some curious and voracious worm, which, by means of them, eat its way into the planks of ships and piles of harbours, than like the shells familiar to casual observers. The powers of the creature to do mischief aided the prevalent fancy; and the terror which its ravages seem in all ages to have inspired, blinded the half-instructed naturalists, who curiously examined it, to its true affinities.

The researches of anatomists during the last and present

century, however, have made known to us its true organisation, and have proved that it is a true mollusk, and a
bivalve, closely allied to the *Pholas*. The supposed head is
now known to be the main part of the body, including all
the viscera except a portion of the respiratory organs; the
fancied tongue, or sucker, is the foot; the reputed "jaws"
are the valves of the shell; the "body" is the main part of
the siphonal tubes; the "tail" their bifurcated extremity;
whilst the tube, upon which so much stress was laid, turns
out to be the least important part of the whole creature,
and, in fact, a mere appendage. Most "chimæras dire,"
when thus closely pressed, and forced to dwindle into their
true proportions, lose all their ancient terrors; not so with
the *Teredo*. It still pursues its destructive course, unmind-
ful of the scalpel of the naturalist, sinking many a goodly
ship, and shaking many a stately pier. With the evil,
however, comes good, for it acts as a clearer of the seas,
breaking down into small fragments the useless masses of
floating timber and fragments of wreck, which might otherwise prove serious and dangerous impediments to navigation.

The abnormal character of the animal of *Teredo* does not
lie merely in its vermiform shape, of which we had a parallel instance in the Ascidian genus *Pelonaia*, but also in
peculiarities of its internal organisation. Thus, whilst in
other lamellibranchiate bivalves the gills inclose the intes-
tines and other viscera, in this they are in a great measure
placed apart, so that the intestinal sac comes directly into
contact with the mantle, whilst the respiratory organs are
continued posteriorily, or into the tubes. In this relative
position of the branchiæ and the mass of the viscera, we
see an affinity with the *Tunicata* indicated, borne out
by the minute structure of the external covering or mantle,
which, according to the observations of Frey and Leuck-

hart, remarkably resembles that of the tunic in the genus
Ascidia. The gills themselves are very peculiar, presenting the appearance of long, brown, fleshy cords; so different,
indeed, from the usual appearance of those organs, that Sir
Everard Home mistook portions of them for male reproductive bodies, and Sellius and Delle Chiaji for the ovaria,
misled in part by finding the eggs lodged there after protrusion. The true ovarium is a bright white, fatty, cylindrical body, placed in the main mass of the viscera. The
heart, as Professor Van Beneden has shewn, is placed quite
distinct from the intestine, and is not pierced by the latter.
The circulating system is extremely simple. The blood was
stated by Home to be red, but this is denied by recent observers. The mouth is furnished with labial processes, and
internally with a curious cartilaginous club-shaped body,
which is peculiar to the *Teredo*, but may possibly be analogous to the tongue of higher *Mollusca*. The œsophagus is a
long thin tube, furnished with a salivary gland; there are
two distinct stomachs, one of which is invested with the liver.
The foot is very rudimentary, and shaped like a sucker,
so that Deshayes, we think wrongly, describes the animal as
having no foot. The anterior adductor muscle is strongly
developed, and the posterior but slightly, so as to leave
scarcely any traces in the shells. The presence of two calcareous styles, called "pallettes" by Adanson, "calamules"
by Deshayes, in the muscular ring which surrounds the base
of the bifurcating extremities of the siphons, is a remarkable
feature, and, as will be seen in the following descriptions of
the species, one of no small importance as a source of specific distinction.

On the ground of the many peculiarities of the anatomy
of *Teredo*, M. Deshayes has constituted it the type of a
distinct family. Nevertheless, the relations of this genus

with *Xylophaga* and *Pholas* are so evident and close, that we prefer placing it along with them, regarding the differences, however important, rather as such as mark the rapid anamorphoses of organisation exhibited by most outlying families of every order, than as grounds for the establishment of this genus alone as the type of an isolated group.

The *Teredo* was known to the ancients, though it is difficult to separate the allusions made to it in Greek and Latin authors from those alluding to wood-perforating insects. Aristotle has frequently been quoted as mentioning the *Teredo* under the name of Τϵρϵηδων, in the ninth book of the " History of Animals ;" but the animal there spoken of is evidently some flying vespiform insect. The mention by Theophrastus, of " worms which corrupt wood in the sea," is more likely to refer to our animal. Of Pliny's large-headed *Teredo*, " which gnaws with teeth, and lives only in the sea," there can be no mistake; nor respecting the allusion to ship-worms by Ovid. The question, whether the *Teredo* was known to the ancients, was once much discussed, for it was a popular fancy, at the commencement of the last century, that this mollusk had been newly imported into Europe from the Eastern seas—evidently one of those rapid and absurd conclusions every now and then taken up by great bodies of people without ground or inquiry; for, as Deshayes has pointed out, Dutch writers, as long ago as 1580, complained that the shipworm was damaging Holland. The argument of Deshayes, that the presence of fossil *Teredines* in the tertiaries of Europe is proof sufficient of their constant presence from antiquity in our seas, is not so sound, although it has been very generally received with favour. For it is now known that numerous *Mollusca*, identical with existing species, retired from the seas of Europe in the interval between the miocene and pliocene epochs, on the one hand, and the present, on the other, not returning until after the close of the glacial period.

The modern history of the *Teredo* dates chiefly from the commencement of the eighteenth century. In 1715 we find it alluded to by the celebrated Valisnieri, and, in 1720, mistakes were made about it by Deslandes. It attained its majority, and came out with great *éclat*, however, in 1733, when no fewer than three elaborate treatises on the *Teredo* were published, by as many authors. In that year Holland was seriously threatened by the boring of our little shell-fish, and Dutchmen by that of its biographers. Strange to say, its history, "civil and natural," was worked out not by zoologists, but by political writers; and with much credit did they execute their task. The investigators were Pierre Massuet, Jean Rousset, and Godfrey Sellius. They worked independently of each other. All three were remarkable men, worthy of a passing notice. Massuet was a Belgian, and had been a Benedictine monk, but became a Protestant, and took refuge in Holland, where he studied medicine under Boerhaave. He was fortunate; for, dividing his time between his patients and his researches, he saved enough to buy a *seigneurie* and to die rich. He wrote on history and natural philosophy. Rousset began life as a soldier, and quitted the sword for the birch. Ruling school-boys, however, did not satisfy his ambition; he turned politician, and lectured kings and states. He was successful for a time, but, like most politicians, got at length into trouble, and was obliged to conceal himself, which he did effectually, for nobody knows where he died. He wrote many works, geographical, historical, and political, and edited a translation of " Paradise Lost." He would not have meddled with the *Teredo*, but that it took part itself in the political prospects of Europe, by undermining the piles and interests of Holland. Sellius was a native of Dantzic, very learned, but very unfortunate. He began life wealthy, but ruined himself by the expenses of his studies and travels. He was versed in all ancient and modern literature, and wrote many learned works on law and history, besides very numerous translations. He was at one time a professor in the university of Gottingen, and afterwards in Halle, but his difficulties would not let him remain long in one place: he retreated to Paris, and, sad to tell, died mad in the hospital at Charenton. His work on the *Teredo*, a small quarto of 360 pages, is a most remarkable production. In it all the learning of the ancients and of the moderns, up to his time, is brought to bear upon the history of the ship-worm, or to ornament, by apt quotation, the digressions suggested by his subject. Nearly two hundred authors are cited. More than once, among the many scraps of ancient poetry with which he lightens the tedium of his monograph, he quotes with admiration those lines of Ovid in which the poet makes unquestionable mention of the *Teredo*; they were singularly applicable to his own history:—

" Estur ut occulta vitiata teredine navis ;
    Æquorei scopulos ut cavat unda salis ;
    Roditur ut scabra positum rubigine ferrum ;
    Conditus ut tineæ carpitur ore liber :
    Sic mea perpetuos curarum pectora morsus,
        Fine quibus nullo conficiantur, habent."*

---

* Ovid. Epist. ex Pont. Lib. 1, Ep. 1.

An imitation, though rude, may not be unacceptable :—

    For as the ship by hidden shipworm spoil'd ;
        Or as the rock by briny wavelet mined
    Or as the rested sword by rust is soil'd ;
        Or book unread the tiny moths unbind :
    So gnawed and nibbled, without hope of rest,
    By cares unceasing, is my tortured breast.

The essay of Sellius is highly original : it is a very perfect monograph for its time.   He was the first to attempt
to develope the organisation, internal and external, of the
Teredo, and he illustrated his book with elaborate figures
from his own drawings, which, as well as his descriptions, are executed in good faith and with judgment.
It must be borne in mind that the nature of the *Teredo*
was entirely misunderstood, and its history lost in obscurity and fable, at the time when Sellius attempted to work
out the subject in all its details.   No after-writer had
equal difficulties to contend with, for he cleared the way.
Few monographs on single species are even now attempted
to be worked in such elaboration; and the example set by
this civil historian, turning his attention suddenly to a difficult zoological research, is too remarkable an event in malacology to be passed over without full praise.   He was the
first to hold and prove that the *Teredo* is a mollusk, thus anti-
cipating Adanson, and shewing more sagacity than Linnæus,
who long after persisted in placing the ship-worm alongside
of the *Dentalium* and the *Serpula*.   Adanson was not aware
of the determination of Sellius; and in his "Natural History
of Senegal," (1757,) claims to have arranged the *Teredo*
among bivalve *Testacea*.   With his usual ability he at once
recognised both the true nature of the several external parts
of the animal, and the true position of the genus alongside of
Pholas.   The truth of Adanson's view was more completely
demonstrated by Cuvier, and tardily admitted by Lamarck.
Except in England, where the followers of Linnæus forgot
the spirit and adhered to the letter of the works of the illustrious Swede—a proceeding most contrary to the example
he had set in his own course—the molluscan nature of *Teredo*, and its place alongside of *Pholas*, was everywhere understood, in the early part of the present century.   The

important researches of Sir Everard Home * redeemed us,
however, from the slur of neglect of the study of the animal, and were the greatest steps made towards a knowledge of its anatomy. Lately, M. Deshayes has given an
elaborately detailed account of its organisation,† with
gorgeous, but often redundant, figures; and an excellent
essay, in which full justice is done to the labours of Sellius
on the same subject, has been published by Drs. Frey and
Leuckhart.‡

The older writers give many details of the habits and
ravages of this destructive mollusk. They believed that it
ate up the wood into which it bored, a notion which has
long been disproved, and which was first opposed by Adanson. How the *Teredo* bores is a much disputed point even
now, and very conflicting opinions have been put forward
on this interesting subject, the examination of which it is
convenient to defer until we come to treat of kindred mollusks, the *Pholades*. It is a question of no small importance, in an economic as well as in a physiological point of
view. The operations of the *Teredo* in 1730 threatened to
submerge Holland, and, as we have seen, led to the first
careful researches into the structure of the animal. Our
friend Mr. W. Thompson has given a very full account of
its proceedings on the British coast, especially in the harbour of. Port Patrick ;§ and previously Sir Everard Home
and Mr. Osler had, in the "Philosophical Transactions," noticed many instances of its destructive power. It does not
appear that the kind of wood makes very much difference
with the *Teredo*. Its rule of boring seems to be to follow
the grain if possible, though when an impediment comes in

---

* Philosophical Transactions.　　　　　† Mollusques d'Algérie.
‡ Beitrage zur Kenntniss Wiebelloser Thiere, 1847.
§ Edinburgh New Phil. Journ., 1835.

the way, it can change its course, and work round the ob-
stacle. The tube is the lining of the tunnel in which it lives
and conducts its operations. The destructive character of
its work is well illustrated by an instance narrated by Mr.
Thompson. A piece of pine wood nine inches in diameter,
after having been employed as a pile for five years and a
half, was so reduced by the perforations of *Teredines*, as to
contain not more than about an inch of solid timber in any
part, and in several places was completely bored through.
This pole was placed fifteen feet below high water-mark,
and left dry only during low water at spring-tides. Montagu remarks that sound piles will be found completely
perforated by *Teredines* after four or five years submer-
gence. Well might Linnæus style it " calamitas navium !"
Remedies and preventives of many kinds have been proposed, most of them various ways of preparing timber. It
is doubtful whether any have proved successful, though it
has lately been asserted that creasoted timber is not touched by the ship-worm. Baster, who published a paper on
the subject in the "Philosophical Transactions" for 1739-40,
mentions, that most of the proposed specifics against the
Teredo in his day were mercurial; but states they had
proved of no use, and recommends varnishing the wood.
The only efficient protection for piles seems to be the studding of their surface closely with broad-headed nails.

1. Teredo norvagica, Spengler.

Valves :—Body or fang-shaped portion of moderate length, not
slender and produced ; auricle seated on the posterior shoulder,
not dilated nor defined externally; internally parted off by a distinct carina ; its base scarcely, if at all, lower than that of the
projecting front triangle. Subumbonal blade rather wide, presenting its broader surface to the inner disk.

Pallets testaceous, flask-shaped, not forked at the base.

Tube semi-concamerated at its narrower end; posterior aperture contracted in the middle.

Plate IV. figs. 1–5.

Teredo norvagicus, SPENGLER, Skrivter af Naturhistorie selskabet, (1792) vol.
ii. pt. 1, p. 102, pl. 2, f. 4, 5, 6, B.
„   *navalis* (not of Linnæus, Home, nor Spengler), MONTAGU, Testac. Brittan.
p. 527, and Supplement, p. 7.—TURT. Conch. Diction. p. 183.
—TURT. Dithyra Brit. p. 14, pl. 2, f. 1–3.—FLEMING, Brit.
Anim. p. 454.—Brit. Marine Conch. p. 28.—BROWN, Ill.
Conch. G. Brit. p. 116, pl. 50, f. 3, 6, 7.—CROUCH, Introd.
Lam. Conch. pl. 2, f. 10.—SOWERBY, Genera Shells.—Magaz.
Nat. Hist. vol. ii. p. 23, f. 7.—Conch. Systemat. pl. 21.—
MAWE, Conch. pl. 35.—LAMARCK, Anim. s. Vert. ed. 2, vol.
vi. p. 88 (not synonyms).—GOULD, Invert. Masach. p. 26.—
GRAY, Philosoph. Magaz. 1827, p. 410.—HUMPHREY's Conch.
pl. 10, f. 2, 3.—SOWERBY, Conch. Manual, f. 48.—HANLEY,
Recent Shells, p. 3.—DEKAY, New York Moll. p. 84, f. 325.
„   *Brugieri*, Delle Chiaje Memorie, vol. iv. pp. 28, 82, pl. 54, f. 9–12.—
PHILIPPI, Moll.   Sicil. vol. i. p. 2, and vol. ii. p. 3.

The united valves of the *Teredines* have fancifully, and not inaptly, been compared to a helmet, the bodies or middle fang-shaped portions constituting the headpiece, the two trigonal areas of the anterior side composing the crown, and the posterior auricle forming a kind of rude ornament, or support for the crest.

This similitude we have adopted, not alone from its conveying the best idea of the general contour of the valves, but also from its indicating the three external component parts, viz. the triangular area or anterior commencement, the body or central unguiform surface, and the auricle or posterior extremity.

The first of these is typically rather large, but varies greatly in relative size, increasing usually with age at the expense of the auricle, which is generally best developed in individuals which have not quite attained to maturity. Its base is not particularly oblique, and displays but little convexity, being nearly, but not quite, rectilinear. The body, although far less broad in some individuals than in others, and generally narrower than in the two following species, is never slender and produced, as in *bipennata*. In specimens which have advanced to maturity under circumstances apparently favourable to the developement of the natural proportions, the distance from the beaks to the ventral apex decidedly exceeds that from the angular tip of the triangle to the opposite edge of the auricle. The lower edge of the anterior side is straight, and inclines but very slightly hinderward, forming with the lower posterior one, which slopes (at first somewhat retusely, and then a little convexly) to meet it, a rather blunt but gradually attenuated apex. The auricle, which is never peculiarly large, rarely exceeding the size of the front triangle, is always situated high up on the posterior side, its base being nearly on the same level with that of the triangular area : the lower posterior margin is consequently longer in proportion than in the two succeeding species. It is ordinarily rather narrow, is more or less ear-shaped, and although usually a little below the level of the beaks, will occasionally be found rising slightly above them ; but even in that case no risk is incurred of confounding it with *megotara*, as the auricle in that species descends likewise far below the base of the triangular area. No abrupt lowering of surface indicates, as in *navalis*, its anterior commencement; a slight concavity precedes its terminal reflexion. Internally it is sharply defined by a more or less oblique carina, which, although projecting near the beaks a little over the inner disc, neither forms a continuous shelf-like ledge, nor an appressed overlapping margin. Both dorsal edges are concave; the front one is decidedly sloping, and not remarkably abbreviated.

The texture is tolerably firm, and in large specimens even solid; the surface is rather glossy, and covered, in fine and typical specimens, (more so in foreign than in strictly British examples,) with an olivaceous epidermis, beneath which it is equally devoid of colour with the rest of its genus. The front triangular area is concentrically traversed by elevated and rather closely-set striæ, which diverge from the anterior dorsal edge : to these succeed another series of the most crowded and exquisitely engraved lines imaginable, which under a powerful glass exhibit a distinct microscopic subgranular decussation ; these latter, uninterrupted by either linear callosity or impressed striæ, unite almost at right angles with the former, and occupy a more or less narrow triangular strip of surface, extending from the beaks to the ventral tubercle. Posteriorly these fine lines diverge, and form concentric and rather distant arches, with occasionally intermediate striulæ, which very quickly become obsolete, leaving the hinder side comparatively smooth and destitute of any decided sculpture ; there is, nevertheless, a not unfrequent tendency in the surface of the auricle and immediately adjacent parts to rise up in confluent verrucose granules.

Internally, there is a kind of prolongation of the beaks, in the shape of a protuberant callosity, which leans towards the interior, and does not project above the dorsal line ; this is terminated in the right valve by a narrow shelf-like rim, and in the left by a projecting and recurved tubercular lamina, which juts out rather obliquely from the posterior side of the callosity. The subumbonal blade is moderately but not peculiarly oblique, and presents its broader side to the inner disc. It is very thin, and rather wide, swelling out a little at its anterior edge, which is simple and not jagged, but usually bending back again near its termination, so that the apex is not broadly clavate, but a little attenuated. The tubercle which terminates the ventral edge is very solid, and not broad. The tube is long, slender, tapering, and flexuous, divided at the narrow end by thin, close-set, transverse, circular partitions, ten or twelve in number, which do not occupy the entire area, but leave a large oval orifice in the middle; the posterior aperture is contracted in the middle. The pallets, or caudal appendages, are somewhat spoon-shaped, being convex on one side, and concave on the other; a rib-like elevation running down the centre of the latter projects above it, and forms a slender, cylindrical, and oftentimes flexuous handle opposite to the straightish or slightly convex base.

The length of the valves in our British or Irish specimens rarely exceeds half, and the breadth four-sevenths of an inch; and tubes exceeding a foot in length are very seldom, if ever, to be met with in our cabinets.

The opinion appears to be prevalent among British naturalists, that the *Teredo norvagica* was originally of foreign importation, and that, although decidedly naturalised for a season in the harbours of Plymouth and Falmouth, it has at length, through the strenuous exertions of government, become entirely extirpated. Mr. Osler, in the "Philosophical Transactions" for 1826, remarks, that in the abovementioned harbours, where it was once so perniciously abundant, it is now no longer to be found; and at Devonport the few specimens long ago extracted from one of the piles, are now, from its utter extinction, treasured and exhibited as curiosities. Several of our earlier writers, indeed, (Pulteney, Da Costa, &c.,) only knew it as obtained from foreign timbers, and consequently regarded it as a doubtful native, and Pennant, who first introduced it into systematic Conchology as an inhabitant of Great Britain, defined it by neither figure nor description. Montagu, however, who described the characters from naturalised

Plymouth examples, and Turton, who furnishes an admirable diagnosis from specimens living in a tree of British oak, regained at Teignmouth after a long immersion, satisfy us by their descriptions that it is not only indigenous, or, at least, long naturalised, but that it is the true *T. norvagica* of Spengler, a fact not ascertainable from the language or the drawings of any of our previous writers upon British Conchology; the delineation in Donovan's " British Shells," vol. v. pl. 145, and that in Pulteney's "Dorset Catalogue, pl. 18, f. 21, being equally suitable to any species of this genus. In truth, the microscopic scrutiny, so peculiarly demanded for the valves of this genus, has rarely been bestowed upon them; writers of the Linnæan school, both British and foreign, (with the honourable exception of Spengler,) contenting themselves with classing all the ship-worms under the one appellation *navalis*, describing the tube, but neglecting the more important anterior valves and the characteristic pallets. But whether extinct or not in those spots from which our cabinets were formerly supplied, its devastations are continued to the present day in the little harbour of Port Patrick, on the coast of Wigtonshire, where several of the piles used in the formation of the pier have been materially injured, and some even utterly destroyed. The tubes in this locality had, in some cases, attained the extraordinary length of nearly two feet and a half; and the valves of three-quarters of an inch in diameter. Mr. Thompson, in the interesting paper* from which we have derived our knowledge of this habitat, thus describes them :—

" The greatest diameter of the testaceous tube or case, at the larger end, is seven-eighths of an inch; at the smaller, it varies from one and a half to two lines. All of the spe-

---

* W. Thompson, in the Edinburgh New Philos. Journal, January, 1835.

cimens have from one and a half to two inches and upwards
of the smaller end of the tube greatly contracted within
by laminæ, also the partition producing the double aperture
extending but a few lines from the very extremity.   The
greatest thickness of the shell is at the smaller end, where,
at the commencement of the laminæ, its consistence is from
one-twentieth to one-fortieth part of an inch: from this
it becomes gradually thinner towards the greater end, which
in the very largest specimens is found to be closed up; but
in several others there is no deposition whatever of testa
ceous matter for some distance from the termination of the
cell.   In one perforation, about twenty inches long, the
body of the animal has had no testaceous covering for the
last three and a half inches; in two other cells, of about
two feet, no deposition appears for four and a half and
four inches and three-quarter from their termination.   All
the timber at Portpatrick in which the *Teredo* had formed
its habitation is pine; and perhaps to this circumstance the
superior size of the animal may chiefly be attributed.
Though it is well known that the *Teredo* bores in the direction of the grain, it may be observed that it does so whether the position of the wood be perpendicular or otherwise.
Captain Fayrer remarked that it has a decided disposition
to work horizontally.   It is, however, often obliged to deviate from a straightforward course, to avoid such obstruc-
tions as nails, timber-knots, and the tubes of its fellows, and
make a winding or angular habitation, according as such
impediments occur; but these circumstances seem not eventually to impede the progress of the animal, as some of the
very largest specimens I have examined are the most tortuous.   During the nine or ten years that the *Teredo* has
been established at Portpatrick, it has not degenerated, as
specimens just received, which were alive in their native

element a few days ago, are of equal size to those sent from the same place five years since, shewing that it has not been affected by the cold of the winter season, as we might reasonably expect were the animal truly exotic. If this animal had been originally introduced, and has been preserved only by occasional importations, should we not rather look for it in those ports of the United Kingdom where vessels from every quarter of the globe are congregated, than in the obscure harbour of Portpatrick, which has never been visited by a foreign craft."

That the species is not extinct also in England, was clearly proved during a recent visit to Torquay,* when a large stalk of timber, to which the cables of vessels were wont to be attached, having been removed as unsound, a living specimen was extracted from it, and several individuals have since been discovered in the same log, and forwarded to Mr. Hanley by Mrs. Griffiths, with the important information that it was by that species the late destruction of the bridge at Teignmouth had been effected. Almost all our evidence tends to prove that the *T. norvagica*, so far from being an exotic species, imported from warmer climates, and lingering for a few generations in our less congenial waters, is actually more abundant as we proceed northwards, its distribution extending to England and other temperate countries of Europe, where it propagates now at least, even if not strictly indigenous from the most ancient periods. Nevertheless, it must be regarded as one of our rarer shells, the greater number of collections being only provided with individuals taken from ships' timbers and other foreign sources, and very few indeed with specimens derived from the piles of jetties, submerged trees, or other legitimately indigenous habitats. Hence great caution is required in

* S. H.

the mention of localities; individuals, however, have been
taken by Mr. Jeffreys, near Swansea, in floating wood, of
so immature a growth as to render their foreign origin at
least questionable; and others are recorded by Mr. Thompson as having been met with at Achill, in the west of Ireland. Dr. Turton states " that fragments of a wreck known
to have been buried in the ocean for nearly half a century
have lately (1822) been dragged up filled with magnificent
specimens in their most perfect state."

2. T. NAVALIS, Linnæus.

Valves :—Body short, and rounded at its lower extremity ;
auricle in typical examples projecting laterally, never dorsally,
externally defined by the abrupt sinking of the level of its surface, internally by a broad overlapping margin, which is more or
less appressed.

Pallets small, testaceous, forked, and very solid at the base;
stalk cylindrical.

Tube simple, strong, not chambered at its narrow end.

Plate. IV. figs. 7, 8, and Plate XVIII. figs. 3, 4.

Beschreibung Holländischen, See oder Pfahl-Wurms, (Nurnberg, 1733,) plate 3,
    f. 19, 20.—ROUSSET, Observations sur les Vers de Mer, pp. 15, 16, 17, f. 1,
    2, 3, 4, 10.—Ditto, English Translat., (1733,) pp. 13, 14, figs. 1, 2, 3, 4, 10.
    —BELKMEER, Natuur-kundige Verhandel. Zee Worm, pl. 2, f. 7, 8, 9.—
    SELLIUS, Hist. Nat. Teredin. pl. 2, f. 2, 3, 6.

Teredo navalis, LINN. Syst. Nat., ed. 12, p. 1267 (not of British authors).—
        HOMK, Phil. Trans. 1806, pl. 12, f. 7, 8, 9, 10.—CHIAJE Me-
        morie, vol. iv. pp. 23, 32, pl. 54, f. 2, 3.—PHILIPPI, Moll.
        Sicil. vol i. p. 2, and vol. ii. p. 3.

    „   *Batava*, SPENGLER, Skrivt. Naturhist. Selskab. (1792), vol. ii. pt. 1,
        p. 103, pl. 2, fig. C.

The widely overlapping margin of the auricle, as viewed
internally, readily distinguishes the true *navalis* of Linnæus, from that erroneously regarded as it by the earlier
British conchologists ; a mistake which we are enabled to
rectify, not only by a careful comparison of the *Teredines*
with the figures of Sellius, on whose iconography the spe-

cies, inadequately defined by the language of its author, and only specifically limited by his references to the engravings of that author and of Vallisnieri, the latter irrecognisable, depends, but also by personal examination of the examples still preserved in the cabinet of the illustrious Swede.

The casque-shaped valves (as well as the tube and pallets) are of an uniform white; the sculpture of the former exhibits no peculiar features, the front triangular area being finely and rather closely lyrated concentrically; the succeeding, oblique, and crowded striæ, which run parallel to the lower anterior edge, and subrectangularly to the lyræ, being minutely decussated, or even subgranulated, and the remainder of the surface comparatively smooth, although, in some of the younger examples, the striæ of growth are so developed, as almost to give a finely plicated appearance to that portion of the shell.

The front triangular area is in general rather large, abruptly severed, as it were, from the body by a more or less impressed line, and having its base more convex than in the succeeding or preceding species, not particularly oblique, and always much above the level of that of the auricle. The lower anterior edge slopes a little backwards, and forms a rounded point with the short and somewhat arcuated lower margin of the hinder side. The auricle, whose commencement is easily perceived by the *abrupt* sinking of the level, is of a moderate size, somewhat pear-shaped internally, laterally and never dorsally projecting, and in typical examples seated low down, so that the general inclination of the posterior hinge margin is more sloping than in most of the known *Teredines*. Its lower edge is more or less arched; its upper, whether it runs retusely, straightly, or more rarely convexly to the beaks, forms an uninterrupted line with the

dorsal margin, and is never seemingly truncated in front by
any abrupt ascension of the dorsal margin. Its anterior
limit is most distinctly indicated internally by a broad and
appressed rim, which overlaps the edge of the body or medial portion of the valves. This latter is never greatly elongated, the breadth and length of the valves being frequently
equal to each other.

The subumbonal blade, or tooth-like apophysis, is thin,
broad, arched, and nearly of equal breadth throughout,
neither being clavate nor much attenuated at its termination, nor jagged along its edge, which runs nearly parallel
to the lower front, and presents its sharp and not its broader
surface to the inner disc. The cardinal denticle and lunate
rim, and likewise the ventral tubercle, do not appear to
differ much from those of *Norvagica*. The pallets, or caudal
appendages, are each composed of a thick, suboval, shelly
plate, bifurcated at its extremity, and seated upon a slender
and more or less short, flexuous, cylindrical stalk. This
plate is flat upon one side, and convex upon the other, but
devoid of any central rib.

The tube or sheath is long, flexuous, tapering, and devoid
of internal concameration; it is usually rather solid.

We are not aware that this has hitherto been published
as British, although individuals may exist in some of the
less noted collections, mixed up with those of *Norvagica*.
The only locality we know, is in the piles of the pier at
Herne Bay, from whence Mr. Hanley took them, along
with their animals, about four years ago. The tubes
were about eight inches long, and about one-sixth of an
inch in diameter at their broader extremity. The valves
did not (even those which wore the appearance of age) very
much exceed a quarter of an inch, which latter measurement was the full length of the caudal appendages.

3. T. MEGOTARA,* Hanley.

Valves rather short, rapidly diminishing to a moderately attenuated extremity ; auricles very large, rising dorsally above the
level of the beaks, and extending ventrally far below the base of
the triangular area, concave near the body, strongly reflected at
their extremities, not marginated internally, nor abruptly defined
externally.

Pallets nearly resembling those of *T. Norvagica.*

Tube simple, not concamerated posteriorly.

Plate IV. fig. 6, and Plate XVIII. figs. 1, 2.

Teredo nana, TURT. Dithyr. Brit. p. 16, pl. 2, f. 6, 7.—FLEM. Brit. Anim. p. 455.
—Brit. Marine Conch. p. 29.—BROWN, Ill. Conch. G. B. p. 116,
pl. 50, f. 14, 15.—GRAY, Philosoph. Magas. (1827,) p. 410.—
HANL. Recent Shells, p. 4, suppl. pl. 11, f. 23, 24 (copied from
Turton).

   „   *navalis,* CUVIER, Règne Animal, ed. gr., pl. 114, f. 2.

It is with reluctance that we have changed the name of
this beautiful and comparatively large species, from the
prior, but very inappropriate name of *T. nana,* bestowed
upon its young by the late Dr. Turton, whose specimens
were so small and imperfect, that nothing but actual comparison of them with a series commencing with perfect individuals of a similar size, could have proved their identity
with the magnificent examples from whence our drawings
and descriptions have been derived. So broken were they,
that their most characteristic feature, the ample auricles,
were denied to them in the body of his work, (Conchylia
Dithyra, p. 16;) this statement is, however, corrected in
the Addenda.

The entire surface of the valves is of an ivory-white, and
often highly polished. The triangular area, or anterior extremity, which is not severed from the body by any impressed line, is marked, as in the other *Teredines,* with

* From μίγα, greatly; ἄτρςὰ, eared.

elevated concentric approximate lines, which are more
closely set as they recede from the apex of the valves; the
slightly raised, narrow, ray-like strip, which skirts the
lower half of the anterior side, passing upwards to the.
beaks, is likewise crowded with very delicate elevated
oblique lines, decussated (though scarcely so closely as in
Norvagica) with microscopic striulæ. Behind these, another narrow ray-like space appears, extending from the
beaks to the most projecting part of the ventral margin,
and usually lying about the middle of the valves. This
area is rather distantly traversed, in a concentric direction,
by arched and imbricated elevated striæ, and obsoletely
and radiatingly subdivided by the hinder portion being distinctly concave, and the front rendered slightly duller in
surface, from the intervals of the striæ being filled up in
the adult with microscopic striulæ. The remaining or
posterior surface, which is smooth and glossy, but sometimes traversed by remote and obsolete lines of growth, is
again convex, the gradual cessation of which convexity
marks the commencement of the auricle, which is not
otherwise externally defined, and is only so internally by
its immediate reflexion, and the previous thickening of
the body or middle part of the valves at that point; there
being neither carination present, nor the slightest appearance of an overlapping margin. The extraordinary development of the auricle is evidently the typical characteristic
of the species. Decidedly reflected at its outer extremity,
its surface, in consequence, is retuse or concave; its margin,
arching out laterally in one uninterrupted sweep from its
base to its summit, towers a little above the beaks, and
being met, not far from them, by the short, ascending, and
deeply incurved dorsal edge, seems retusely subtruncated
near its highest elevation. It thus projects both laterally

and dorsally, and (in the adult, at least) occupies more than one-half of the posterior side. The front triangular area is small, and acutely pointed; its base, which is peculiarly straight and oblique, lying much above the level of that of the auricle. The front dorsal line is very short, and scarcely, if at all, declining; the lower anterior edge is rectilinear, and rarely inclining inwards to meet the more or less convex and rapidly sloping margin of the posterior side, with which it forms a somewhat rounded point.

The subumbonal blade is so placed as to present its broader surface to the inner disc; it is narrow, not particularly elongated, tapering, and not at all jagged at the edge. The callosity of the hinge-margin is well developed, projects above the dorsal level, and slants with a strong posteriorward inclination: the ventral callosity is solid and prominent, but not widely expanded.

The pallets, which, like those of *Norvagica*, resemble the shape of a battledore, approach so nearly to those of that species, as with difficulty to be distinguished, except by direct comparison. We may then perceive that the handle or stalk is much less elongated in proportion, and tapers to a fine point at its apex, (in the other it is blunt at its termination, and solid throughout.) In the only five specimens of this portion which we have hitherto seen, and which, not being above a quarter of an inch long, we cannot pronounce adult, the position of the stalk upon the interior surface of the broader terminal plate is most distinctly manifested throughout, and externally there is a distinct groove on either side of it at its insertion in the plate. The latter, which is somewhat abbreviated in form, has its sides curling inwards, somewhat in the fashion of those of *malleolus*, (the stalk is, however, not bent as in that rare species;) and, although the base is almost straight, there is rather a large triangular depressed basal surface, and in the young, a small, but deep incurvation in the middle.

The tubes are strong, and without concameration.

The finest specimens we have ever met with were obtained by Mr. Hanley from timber, which, having formed a portion of the piles of the pier at Herne Bay, in Kent, had been removed in consequence of its destruction by these animals. One tube was nearly half a yard in length, and the valves rather more than half an inch in diameter in each direction, their length and breadth being nearly equal. The locality mentioned by Turton is simply " wood in Torbay :" to this may be added,—from wood drifted on shore at Exmouth, (Clark;) from drifted wood in Swansea Bay, (Jeffreys;) and from some stakes near the jetty at Broadstairs, (Metcalfe.)

Species not proved to be of British origin.

4. T. BIPENNATA, Turton.

Valves with the body or medial portion narrow and elongated. Auricle typically projecting higher than the beaks: its upper internal edge most strongly reflected outwards ; the lower internal edge scarcely sloping, and projecting shelf-fashion over the body. Triangular area extending as low down as the auricle, not large, its outer edge very oblique ; tooth-like apophysis greatly slanting posteriorwards. Pallets very large, quill-shaped, of a spongy texture.

Plate IV. figs. 9, 10, 11.

Teredo bipennata, TURTON, Conch. Dictionary, p. 184, f. 38, 39, 40.—TURT. Dithyra. Britann. p. 15.—FLEM. Brit. Anim. p. 454; Brit. Marine Conch. p. 28.— BROWN, Ill. Conch. G. Brit. p. 116. —GRAY, Philosoph. Magaz. (1827,) p. 411. —HANLEY, Ill. and Desc. Cat. Recent Sh. p. 4; suppl. pl. 9, f. 51.

„ *navalis*(?), SPENG. Skrivt.af Naturhis. Selsk. vol. ii. pt. 1, pl. 2, f. 1, 2, 3, A.

The indigenousness of this very interesting ship-worm is by no means satisfactorily established, although, from its being frequently found alive in floating wood, it is by no means improbable that it may have established itself equally with the two preceding in the timber of our jetties, &c.; unfortunately, too many who have the opportunities of taking these animals upon the renewal of the piles, satisfy their curiosity by preserving merely the perforated wood, or the testaceous tubes, leaving us still in doubt by what species the cavities have been effected. It is with some little hesitation, then, that we include this and the succeeding in our Fauna, which we are induced to do, rather from the example of preceding writers, and the fact that they are not noticed in any known continental work as natives of another country, than from any positive proof of strict naturalisation.

The shape of the valves is very different from that of *Norvagica* or *Batava*, the medial portion being decidedly more elongated, and the lower end of the auricle slightly more remote from the ventral tubercle than is that of the front triangle. This latter occupies less than two-fifths of an imaginary line drawn from the beaks to the base of the shell, and is concentrically traversed by raised striæ, or narrow lyræ, which are moderately close-set, and not much arcuated below, but more distant and more curved towards the commencement of the series. These are succeeded by another set of minutely decussated striæ, which occupy the narrow strip situated between the lateral triangle and the internal radiating groove, and are produced thence along the front margin of the shell. Then follows a still narrower strip, which, together with the preceding, is elevated towards the beaks above the remainder of the surface, covered with very oblique, distant, raised, concentric striulæ, often with finer intermediate ones, which, after passing the central, shallow, groove-like, radiating area, are more or less distinctly continued over the remainder of the surface as far as the auricle. This latter, which is smooth, small, and ear-shaped, projects at its upper part above the summit of the beak, and is internally cut off as it were from the body of the shell by its lower edge, which almost straight, and scarcely declining, projects like a ledge over the subumbonal region. Its basal line is thus almost at right angles to the hinder margin, whilst its much arcuated posterior outline runs nearly parallel to the base of the lateral triangle. This ear-shaped appendage is also most strongly reflected outwards, and is internally rather closely grooved with concentric costellæ; its hinder termination is attenuately rounded, and its front extremity is in the adult concavely, in the young subrectilinearly, more or less obliquely subtruncated.

The entire shell is white, and faintly glossy; there is an extremely oblique lamina surmounted by a tooth-like process upon the hinge margin, running at acute angles to the very oblique and flat subumbonal blade, which latter is clavate, and in the most perfect specimens we have met with either tuberculated or jagged at its edge near its termination. Both the posterior and anterior edges of the valves, which are inclined to solidity, are rectilinear, the front being nearly perpendicular, the hinder much more oblique; but in the young these sides are rather more parallel, and the central, or linguiform portion of the shell, much more narrow. The ventral apex is narrow, but not acute, and its internal tubercle rather broad and compressed. The pallets are very curious, and of a sponge-like look and colour. They are remarkably large, in some measure resemble a quill in shape, are usually more or less curved, and have their stalk or unbarbed portion most minutely tuberculated. The upper portion, which is usually about one half of the entire length, and even at its broadest part scarcely wider than the stalk, is closely articulated; the upper and concave edge of each joint terminating at either extremity in an ascending filament, is adorned on one side with a very fine fringe of similar, but more minute filaments. The joints towards the extremity appear in the few specimens we have seen, to lose their lateral filament, and the concavity of the upper edges so increases as to form a decided angle near their middle.

The tube, which we have not seen ourselves, is declared by Dr. Turton to be thicker and stronger than that of *Norvagica*, and simple at its outer orifice; and by Mr. Gray, in the Annals of Philosophy for 1827, to be not concamerated. The diameter of the valves from whence our description was drawn up, is about four-sevenths of an inch, whilst the pallets are actually three inches in length, and about two lines broad at the widest part. These dimensions, however, especially that of the pallet, are greatly exceeded in the Sumatran examples, from whence we may reasonably conclude that that country is in all probability its native habitat. Specimens are extremely rare; those of Dr. Turton, are recorded by him to have been taken from a piece of fir timber, which, covered with *Anatifa lævis*, had been drifted into the river Ex. Mr. Bean writes us word that he has met with it on the coast of Scarborough; and Mr. Thompson informs us that he has only acquired his from wood washed upon shore at Youghal, and at Miltown Malbay in Clare, at the former of which places it was found by Mr. R. Ball, and at the latter by Mr. Harvey. Valves marked "Waterford" are likewise to be seen in a collection formed by Mr. Humphreys, of Cork, and now in the possession of Mr. Jeffreys. The British Museum, and the extensive collection of Mr. Metcalfe, equally include it; the specimens of the former were taken by Mr. Bulwer

from drifted wood in the British Channel. Mr. Bean, of
Scarborough, has taken it alive from a plank of oak.

5. T. MALLEOLUS, Turton.

Valves similar to those of *bipennata*.

Pallets testaceous, consisting of a mallet-shaped plate, or a more
or less expanded, thin, incurved lamina surmounting, at an obtuse
angle, a short and filiform stalk.

Plate I. Figs. 12, 13, 14.

Teredo malleolus, TURTON, Dithy. Brit. p. 255, pl. 2, f. 19.—BROWN, Illus.
Conch. G. Brit. p. 116, pl. 50, f. 16.—FLEM. Brit. Anim. p.
454.—Brit. Mar. Conch. p. 28.—GRAY, Philosoph. Magaz.
1827, p. 410.—HANLEY, Des. and Ill. Cat. Recent Sh. p. 4,
suppl. pl. 11, f. 25 (copied from Turton).

The valves of this very rare *Teredo*, are so precisely
similar to those of *bipennata*, that it has been conjectured
that Turton fabricated this species from the young anterior
appendages of that shell, and some distorted tail plates of
Norvagica. An examination of the interesting collection of
Mrs.Griffith of Torquay, disproves this erroneous impression,
as that lady possesses several specimens with the valves
and pallets united by the shrivelled animals. The few individuals we have been enabled to inspect, and which possibly may not be adult, although several exhibited all the
indications of maturity, only appear to differ from *bipennata*
in respect to their valves, by being invariably much smaller,
with their auricle less developed, and running in a concave
line above, almost on a level with the apices of the beaks;
internally, too, it does not seem plicated or scarcely so, and
is much excavated and but little reflected outwards. The
external surface is smooth posteriorly, and the subumbonal
tooth-like apophysis, is typically most strongly clavate at its
termination. The pallet, which is white and of a testaceous
substance, frequently, but not necessarily, bears a consider-

able likeness to a mallet, from which resemblance the name
malleolus is derived.   It consists of a thin plate or lamina,
varying much in shape, but always laterally enlarging towards its base, and more or less angular above.   From the
upper portion of it springs a short, compressed, filiform
stalk, which rises centrally about an equal distance from
the angle, to that of the latter from the basal termination
of the lamina.   This stalk is not in the same plane with
the plate, but forms a more or less obtuse angle with it, an
important character for distinguishing it from all the stages
of growth in the caudal appendage of *Norvagica*.   The two
sides which form the angle of the lamina, are usually in the
younger and more symmetrical examples (for the pallets of
the *Teredines* vary with their growth), much incurved near
the stalk, and bowed out as they recede from it; the basal
line appears sinuous and not rectilinear, in some specimens
being incurved in the middle, and convex or arcuated at
one or both extremities; in others, swollen in the centre,
and concave at the extremities.   The sides of the lamina
bend towards the more concave area.   The tube is stated
by Dr. Turton to be composed of a slight testaceous deposit on the inside of the chamber it has excavated, the
terminal portion of which is slightly semi-concamerated.

We cannot regard this species as strictly indigenous,
since hitherto it has been almost exclusively extracted from
foreign wrecks or floating timber from uncertain localities.
The native habitat is Sumatra, (so prolific in *Teredines*,)
and it is by no means probable that a species from so warm
a climate should ever become naturalised in our less genial
waters.   The original describer of *malleolus*, obtained it
from a piece of spar supposed to have formed part of
the *Venerable* man-of-war which was drifted into Torquay
during the prevalence of some heavy gales, that vessel having

been wrecked in Torbay about fifteen years previously. The other authors we have cited have evidently solely derived their knowledge of it from the *Conchylia Dithyra* of Dr. Turton. We are acquainted only with four collections which contain it, that of Mrs. Griffith, who similarly procured it from Torquay; the original types now in the cabinet of Mr. Jeffreys, some very fine ones, without any indicated habitat, which, formerly in the possession of the Rev. F. Stainforth, now belong to Mr. Metcalfe, of Lincoln's-inn, and some decidedly exotic ones in our National Museum.

6. T. palmulata, Lamarck.

Valves similar to those of *Navalis*.

Pallets small, in shape resembling a short stalk of barley; their stem short and filiform, their broader end pinnately articulated and compressed.

Plate II. figs. 9, 10, 11.

Taret de Pondichorry, Adanson, Acad. Roy. des Sciences, 1759, p. 276, pl. 9, f. 11, 12.

Teredo palmulata, Lamarck, Anim. a. Vert. ed. 2, vol. vi. p. 38.—Gray, Philosoph. Magaz. 1827, p. 410.—Cuvier, Règne Anim. (ed. Henders.) pl. 40, f. 8.—Hanley, Recent Shells, p. 4, suppl. pl. 11, f. 13 (copied from Blainv.)—Philippi, Moll. Sicil. vol. i. p. 2, pl. 1, f. 8, and vol. ii. p. 3?

„ *bipalmulata*, Delle Chiaje Memorie, vol. iv. p. 28, pl. 54, f. 18, 22, 23, 24.—Thompson in Annals N. Hist. October, 1847, (corrected from T. malleolus in the September number).

Taret bipalmulé, Blainville, Man. Malacolog. pl. 80, bis, f. 8 (copied from Adanson).—Griffith's Anim. K. vol. 12. pl. 7. f. 5 (pallet).

So closely do the valves of this species resemble those of *navalis*, not merely in general aspect but in separate features, that it is almost impossible to distinguish it from the latter, excepting by the aid of its characteristic pallets. Their surface, however, appears of scarcely so pure and glossy a white, and the overlapping internal edge of the auricle is not so closely appressed, but a little elevated.

This ear-shaped appendage varies in its outlines similarly to *navalis*, rising, in the adult, above the dorsal line, and, in the immature shells, sinking far below the level of the beaks, owing to the then greatly declining curve of the dorsal edge.

There is one fact with regard to the shipworms which has rendered their investigation peculiarly laborious, namely, that no reliance can be placed upon the relative proportions of their several parts for specific definition. If we take at random about fifty valves of *norvagica* for instance, we shall find that in some the oblique decussated striæ occupy twice the space of the succeeding strip, in others this is reversed, in many these are both contracted, and a large posterior smooth area is exhibited ; in others again, almost the entire surface is occupied by the two former, to the great diminution of the hinder portion. Hence it is absolutely necessary to examine very numerous examples, in order to elicit the real and permanent specific characters, and the valves alone are rarely adequate for the determination of the species.

The pallets, which are extremely fragile, and never attain to any considerable dimensions, closely resemble diminutive specimens of those of *bipennata*. They vary much with age and circumstances in regard to the number of articulations, their closeness or laxity of approach to each other, and even in their individual shapes. In the smaller specimens, (and almost all hitherto taken in our seas belong to this class, not exceeding half an inch in length,) the stem resembles a piece of fine thread, and is about equally long with the broader pinnated portion which surmounts it. This latter is composed of numerous somewhat triangular pieces, of which the narrower end is jointed as it were to the broader opposite extremity of the preceding one, which is more or less deeply incurved in the middle, and has, in consequence, its lateral terminations more or less strongly forked. The basal articulation is often peculiarly graceful in shape, the lateral outline being formed by two convex lines of corresponding curve on either side. The number of these joints may average about a dozen, some apparently having only eight distinct ones, whilst others (chiefly the larger) have nearly twice that number. The articulated portion is usually about three times as broad as the stalk, and tapers towards its termination, where the joints likewise are smaller and more closely set. In the larger pallets, where the articulations are more remote from each other, their forked extremities, instead of embracing (as in the young) the succeeding joint, project on either side beyond the narrow bases, so as to cause the lateral edges to appear serrated; in certain specimens where the joints are peculiarly distant, and their subtrigonal forms have become in consequence less distinct, these forked terminations are produced in narrow filaments, and the central concavities are clothed with a more or less fringed membrane, which in some measure conceals the depth of incurvation. So various then are the aspects of both the pallets and the valves of this interesting *Teredo*, that nothing but the long suite of specimens in various stages of growth which we have had the good fortune to inspect and mutually compare, could have enabled us to detect their specific identity. None of the valves we have hitherto seen at all equal the dimensions of our three first species, and the longest pallet was under two inches in length. Those which have been delineated in our plates, are very young, and are some of a large number extracted by Mr. Thompson, in Ireland, from the timbers of a vessel returned from a foreign voyage. Some finer ones are in Mr. Jeffrey's collection, taken by Mr. Clark, at

Exmouth, and others in Mr. Hanley's cabinet, which he procured from ship-timber at Bristol. Strictly speaking then, this ought not to be included in our Fauna, as we have no evidence of its propagation in this country. The terminal portion of the tube was concamerated in the wood which accompanied Mr. Clark's examples; we confess, however, we perceived no indication of such structure in the very small perforations of the Irish specimens; in both the testaceous matter was sparingly deposited.

XYLOPHAGA, Turton.

Shell globular, closed posteriorly, much and angularly open anteriorly, composed of two equal, much-curved, anteriorly emarginate valves, their outer surfaces divided into various ornamented and smooth portions, the inner strengthened by a strong longitudinal rib or apophysis running from beak to ventral margin; muscular impressions two, posterior large, round, anterior small, submarginal. A single distinct and curved denticle beneath, but not under, the beak. Back of the shell anteriorly furnished with two (complicated) accessory valves. No tube.

The animal of our British species, according to a note kindly communicated by the Rev. David Landsborough, is, with the exception of the siphons, entirely included within the shell. The foot is large, and pillar-shaped; its extremity tinged with buff. It occupies the greater part of the anterior opening, and may be protruded to some length. The margin of the mantle around it appears to be plicated. The rest of the animal is white. The siphons are very extensible; sometimes assuming a length of three-quarters of an inch, more usually resting at about the third of those dimensions. Such an animal has evidently much closer

affinity with *Pholas* than with *Teredo*, though at first
glance the shell bears most resemblance to the latter. The
tertiary fossil genus, *Jouanettia*, is in some respects intermediate between *Teredo* and *Xylophaga*, of which no
extinct species are known.

XYLOPHAGA DORSALIS, Turton.

Plate II. figs. 3, 4.

Teredo dorsalis, TURT. Conch. Diction. p. 185, (erroneously as to tube) ; Dithyr.
            Brit. p. 16, pl. 2, f. 4, 5.
Xylophaga,   TURT. Dithyra Brit. p. 253.—FLEM. Brit. Anim. p. 455.—Brit.
            Marine Conch. p. 32.—Annals of Nat. Hist. Septem. 1847.—
            BROWN, Ill. Conch. G. B. p. 117, pl. 50, f. 8 to 13.—SOW-
            ERBY, Genera Shells.—REEVE, Conch. Syst. vol. i. pl. 22.—
            Sow. Conch. Manual. f. 50, 51.—HANL. Recent Shells, p.
            10, supp. pl. 11, f, 21, 22.
Pholas xylophaga, DESH. Lam. Anim. s. Vert. ed. 2, vol. vi. p. 47.
Xylophage dorsal. CHENU. Traité Elem. p. 40. f. 122, 123.

A hasty glance at this interesting and uncommon shell
would induce us to place it with *Teredo*, and the closing of
its posterior side, where there is not the slightest gape, will
probably be the first differential point to attract our attention to its generic as well as specific distinctness. The
general shape (allowing for the subrectangular incision at
the anterior side) is subrotund, the distance from the extreme points of the front and hinder margins being at least
equal to that from the umbo to the opposite edge. The
texture is remarkably fragile, devoid of colour, and but
little glossy, even when the specimens are fresh. The valves
are tumid, but not quite hemispherical, and strengthened
internally by a narrow, but strong, prominent, somewhat
jointed rib, which, running perpendicularly from the umbo
to the ventral margin, divides the shell into two very unequal portions, the hinder being thrice the bigness of the
anterior one. The surface is externally marked with two

nearly vertical, slightly-diverging, approximate costellæ, which radiate from the anterior side of the umbones to the greatly arcuated ventral margin, and vary greatly in size and elevation in different examples. The hinder is, however, invariably the most distinct, the anterior one being, in some specimens, almost entirely obsolete. The narrow space between them is usually depressed; which is also not unfrequently the case with that portion of the shell which immediately succeeds the posterior rib. The perfect smoothness of the general surface is relieved by the fine and crowded elevated lines which striate the front triangular area and the strip which lies between that and the anterior costella; those of the former (whose base is scarcely convex, and but little oblique) are concentric, and closely set; those of the latter, which are delicate, crowded, and not at all crenulated (as in the *Teredines*), run obliquely downwards, diverging slightly as they advance. The umbones are broad, and very prominent. The dorsal edge, which is scarcely at all sloping, is very short, and reflected in front, and nearly straight (but, in the young, tumid) behind. The posterior side is simply and exactly rounded in the young; but in fine specimens is slightly subangulated at the upper extremity. The rectilinear lower margin of the anterior side, (which, as in *Teredo*, is furnished with a subrect-angular incision, leaving a triangular area near the beaks,) contrary to its direction in that genus, is nearly vertical, almost forming a rectangle with the ascending ventral, which latter being more tumid posteriorly, renders the contour of the valves a little oblique. The hinge margin presents a single, distinct, and curved, tusklike denticle, just beneath the beaks, which, springing from beneath the margin in one valve, leans over to the opposite one.

The accessory plates, which, however, are rarely present

in cabinet specimens, being very easily detached, are rather
complicated in structure, and are situated dorsally in front
of the shell.   They are two in number, covered with a
yellow skin, and nearly smooth; their surface, except centrally, is a little depressed; in form they remind us of the
single valves, examined laterally, of that common exotic
shell, the *Cardium cardissa*. They are not simple plates, or
laminæ, as in most of the *Pholades*, but double; the edge
where they fold forming an acute carina, from the intensity
of the compression. Each, examined separately and externally, may be likened to a short wing; the two longer
sides, of which the more produced is arcuated, and the
other retuse or incurved, forming a more or less acute or
obtuse point at their junction.   The posterior extremity, or
beak, as it were, resembles the outer angles of a quarter of
a circle, beneath which, internally, is a very sharp, tooth-
like projection.   In front of this the inner margin, which at
this point is not greatly compressed, and adapts itself to the
shape of the reflected front dorsal edges of the shell, is most
strongly incurved, again swelling out, however, near its
front extremity, a little beyond the line of the corresponding external edge.

Like the *Teredines*, it penetrates wood which has been
immersed for any considerable period in salt water; wherein it forms for itself an oval receptacle, or cavity, having a
small and single external orifice, and nowhere lined with
any shelly deposition.

The original types were procured by Dr. Turton from the
fragments of a wreck known to have been submerged for
nearly fifty years off Berry Head, near the entrance of
Torbay; other specimens have been taken by Mr. Clark
off Exmouth in floating timber.   It is occasionally obtained
at Scarborough (Bean); Mr. M'Andrew has taken it in

Loch Fyne; but our cabinets have hitherto been chiefly
supplied from Ireland ("Ringsend in Dublin Bay, Waterford, and Bantry Bay," Thompson and Humphreys) : a
new and prolific habitat has just been communicated by
Mr. Thompson, in the September number of the "Annals
of Natural History for 1847."

"Early in the month of May last, Major Martin of Ardrossan, in Ayrshire—a gentleman well known as a lover of
natural history, and as a successful collector of objects of
zoological and botanical interest—sent me a piece of wood
perforated by the *Xylophaga dorsalis*, and labelled as from
the dock-gates, Ardrossan. Not having before heard of this
animal attacking the *fixed* timber of our harbours (it has been
found in drift-wood, or portions of vessels cast ashore), I
made immediate inquiry respecting it. The piece of wood
sent was a portion of the dock-gates. The *Xylophaga* has
been known to be consuming them since the docks were
opened in March, 1844. It has been known for a very
considerable time along this coast, where there is no fresh
water. It attacks timber of all kinds : for instance, the
wooden pier (the supporters of which are nearly destroyed)
and other timbers that are under water about the quays,
and have been placed there without any preservative coating. It appears to prefer black birch to any other timber,
but does not like African or American oak. The only successful preventive made use of for preserving the dock-gates
against the *Teredo*, *Xylophaga*, &c., is Muntz's patent
yellow metal sheathing, which is put on to the height of
thirteen feet; it lasts for ten or twelve years. The timber
that is perforated is always covered by water. The depth
of water in the docks is from sixteen to eighteen feet. It
may give some idea of the frequency of the *Xylophaga's*
perforations in the different pieces of wood, to mention,

that on an average at least one-half is occupied by its burrows. The *Xylophaga* has never, like the *Teredo*, been observed by my correspondent to form a testaceous tube, or lining to its cell. Many of the chambers of the *Xylophaga* before me are one inch and a half in length, thus exceeding by one-half the longest noticed by Turton. The shells of my largest specimens are 5½ lines in length : the two valves joined at the hinge occupy a space of 5½ lines in diameter. This species differs from *Teredo navalis* (Turton), by boring *against* the grain of the wood (all of which is pine), in a diagonal manner."

Löven enumerates *Xylophaga dorsalis* among the inhabitants of the seas of Norway.

Only one more species of this genus (*X. globosa*) is as yet known to us, which, judging from its very brief diagnosis in the Zoological Proceedings for 1835, appears principally to differ from our own by the greater slope of its posterior dorsal margin.

PHOLAS, Linnæus.

Valves oval or elongated, (rarely suborbicular,) equivalve, inequilateral, gaping, especially anteriorly ; external surfaces of the shell more or less ornamented by transverse laminated ridges and longitudinal furrows ; the inner surfaces presenting two distinct muscular impressions, very distant, the posterior one largest, connected by a pallial impression, which is deeply sinuated posteriorly, narrow, oblique, and tongue-shaped centrally. A curved free spoon-shaped apophysis springing from beneath the beaks in each valve, and directed forwards. Beaks covered by a callosity reflected from the interior. No hinge. Ligament obscure or rudimentary. Accessory valves or plates more or less developed at the back of the shell.

Animal thick and claviform; the lobes of the mantle united in front, except for a small space anteriorly, through which the foot is protruded; reflected dorsally to cover the beaks, and form callosities and accessory valves. Siphonal tube long, very extensile, divided externally only nearer the extremity; orifices bordered with cirrhi, but not surrounded by a cirrhigerous disk. Foot often considerably developed, thick, short, and truncated at its extremity. No tube.

The genus *Pholas*, and its immediate allies, *Xylophaga* and *Pholadidea*, form a natural and graduated link between such abnormal and worm-like mollusks as the *Teredo*, and the more ordinary and typical genera of Lamellibranchiate Mollusca. The shells of some *Pholades* very closely resemble those of certain *Petricolæ*. The animal, whilst it retains some of the peculiarities of the *Teredo*, especially in its branchial arrangements, in most respects assimilates closely to the normal lamellibranchiate types. Its mantle is more highly organised than that of *Teredo*, and the visceral mass more concentrated. The latter, including the liver, the digestive organs, the large reproductive glands, &c., is surmounted by a well-developed, but peculiar foot, having a sucker-shaped truncated disk which, however, is not provided with a foliaceous border like that of *Teredo*. The stomach of *Pholas* is simple. The anterior adductor muscle, in this genus, makes up for the deficiency of ligament. The labial tentacles are largely developed.

The species of *Pholas* are numerous and widely distributed. The genus may be said to be cosmopolitan. Its range in depth extends from low water, between tides, where the majority of the species are found, to twenty-five, or, perhaps, thirty fathoms. Geologically, it dates from the oolitic period. The species increase in numbers as they

approach existing times. Some of those now living commenced their existence within our area as far back as the
epoch of the coralline crag. Extinct, like recent species,
lived in cavities excavated by themselves, and fitting their
dimensions.

All the species of *Pholas* are endowed with the remarkable power of perforating various substances of considerable
hardness, such as stone, shale or wood; some indifferently,
some selecting one or other for their habitations. They
are never naturally found free. This habit of boring is
common to the whole tribe of which *Pholas* is the type,
and is presented also by certain members of other tribes.
The majority of Lamellibranchiate Mollusca may be said
to be borers, so far as the power of burying themselves in
sand, clay, mud, or gravel, can give them a claim to such
appellation, but the boring of the *Pholas, Teredo, Xylophaga, Pholadidea,* of the *Gastrochæna,* and its allies, and
of certain species of *Mytilidæ,* appears to be effected by
very different means. The question how the boring
mollusca excavate their dwelling-places has long been discussed, and is still at issue among naturalists; and the
name *Pholas,* (from φωλεω, to bore,) was applied by the
ancients to certain shell-fish whose power of perforating
the solid rock attracted their notice. A shell-fish is mentioned by Athenæus under the name of *Pholas,* probably
not one of the members of the genus now so called, but
the *Lithodomus lithophagus,* or date-shell, which is very
abundant in the seas of Greece, and used by the people for
food, whilst the true *Pholades* are very scarce in the
Ægean, and not likely to have attracted popular attention.

The earliest observations made upon the boring of
Pholas were those by the celebrated Reaumur, one of the
most excellent of practical naturalists. They are published

in the Memoirs of the French Academy for 1812. He
figures the *Pholas candidus* in its cavity, and attempts to
account for its presence there. He remarks that it is always found in cavities, either of soft stone or clay; that
these are made by the efforts of the animal itself, and by
means of its foot, for when it was placed by him upon soft
clay, it buried itself in that substance by the action of its
foot. He argues that they bore only in soft clay, and that
their presence in stone (soft stone, which he terms "la
Banche,") is owing to the former having petrified around
the *Pholades.* He shews that the dimensions of the cavity
in which the full-grown *Pholas* is found are, as compared
with shell and aperture, such that the former must have
remained in it since it first perforated, and could not have
changed its habitation. He states that the young are always found in clay, and the old in stone, and concludes
that the stone is only clay petrified by means of a viscous
matter derived from sea-water. It need not be said now
that Reaumur's observations and conclusions were fallacious, but as a first step in the inquiry they had great
merit.

Mr. John Edward Gray, in an interesting paper on the
habits of Mollusca, published by him in the "Philosophical
Transactions," for 1833, gives his opinion on this question.
He holds that *Pholades, Petricola, Venerupis,* and *Lithodomus,* bore into shells and calcareous rocks by dissolving
them. His reasons for holding this opinion are several;—
1st. because the animals of most of them are furnished
with a large foot more or less expanded at the end; 2nd.
because the holes fit the shell—in *Petricola* and *Gastrochæna*
—so as to prevent rotation, and the use of the asperities on its surface; 3rd. because all borers are covered with
a periostracum, (thin in *Teredo, Pholas,* and *Lasea*; thick

in *Lithodomus;*) which would be rubbed off during the
operation of boring; 4th. because, though some borers
have spiny shells, others have smooth ones: 5th. because
all bore into calcareous substances, wood excepted; and
into sandstone only when it has lain a long time under the
sea, and become as soft as clay. These objections of Mr.
Gray to the mechanical theory are some good, some bad;
several not consistent with a correct knowledge of the habits
and structure of the genera he quotes. The same naturalist, in a paper on the structure of *Pholades,* in the 1st
volume of the "Zoological Journal," 1825, held an opposite view to that quoted above; for he here maintains that
the *Pholades* bore by means of rasping. Dr. Fleming's
most recently-expressed opinion on this subject,* is in
favour of rasping and rotatory motion.

Among the best memoirs on the subject of the boring
mollusks, is that by Mr. Osler, published in the "Philosophical Transactions" for 1826.† It is entitled "On Burrowing and Boring Marine Animals," and contains the
fruit of much careful and original observation. According
to this gentleman, the instinct to bore is exhibited at a very
early stage of the animal's life. He found *Pholades* completely buried when so minute as to be almost invisible.
He regards the curved processes, or apophyses, within the
shell of *Pholas,* as characteristic of an animal which bores
mechanically by employing its shell as a rasp, holding that
the shell is the chief instrument by means of which *Pholas*
bores. He remarks with respect to *Pholas candidus,* a
species whose habits he observed with great care, that it is
by means of the anterior and lower part of the shell, which
is thicker and spiny, the boring is effected. He considers
the peculiar arrangement of the muscles, and the suppres-

* Molluscous Animals, p. 114.   † Vol. cxvii. p. 356.

sion of the ligament in this genus, as peculiarities in its organisation connected with its perforating habits. *Teredo*, he holds, bores in like manner with *Pholas*, and by the same means, effecting the stroke during the operation by the contraction of the posterior adductor muscle. The boring of *Saxicava*, however, Mr. Osler maintains to be effected by very different means, most probably by an acid solvent. Its hole is not round; and if there are siliceous particles in the stone they are left projecting into the cavity. Mr. Osler was unable, nevertheless, to detect any direct evidences of free acid, either by the test of litmus-paper, or by any experiments he could devise.

The account given by Mr. Osler of the operations of *Pholas* when boring is so circumstantial, that we quote it in his own words:—

"The *Pholas* has two methods of boring. In the first, it fixes itself by the foot, and raises itself almost perpendicu-larly, thus pressing the operative part of the shell upon the substance to which it adheres: it now proceeds to execute a succession of partial rotatory motions, effected by the alter-nate contraction of the lateral muscles, employing one valve only, by turning on its side, and immediately regain-ing the erect position. I have observed that this method is almost exclusively employed by the very young animals; and it certainly is peculiarly adapted for penetrating in a direction nearly perpendicular, so that they may be com-pletely buried in the shortest possible time. It may be observed that the posterior extremities of the valves are much less produced in the very minute *Pholades* than they afterwards become; and thus the time required to complete a habitation is still further diminished.

"But when the *Pholades* have exceeded two, or at the most three, lines in length, I have never observed them to

work in the manner I have described; the altered figure of
the shell, and the increased weight of that part of the
animal behind the hinge, would prevent it from raising
itself so perpendicularly as at first, independent of the
narrow space which it occupies. In the motions required
to enlarge its habitation, the adductors perform a very
essential part. The animal being attached by the foot,
brings the anterior part of the shell into contact. The
lateral muscles now contract, and, raising the posterior adductor, bring the dorsal margins of the valves into contact,
so that the strong rasp-like portions are suddenly separated,
and scrape rapidly and forcibly over the substance on
which they press. As soon as this is effected, the posterior
extremity sinks, and the stroke is immediately repeated by
the successive contraction of the anterior adductor, the
lateral, and the posterior adductor muscles.

"The particles rubbed off, and which, in a short time,
completely clog the shell, are removed in a very simple
manner. When the projected syphon is distended with
water, the *Pholas* closes the orifices of the tubes, and
retracts them suddenly. The water, which they contained,
is thus ejected forcibly from the opening in the mantle;
and the jet is prolonged by the gradual closure of the
valves, to expel the water contained within the shells.
The chamber occupied by the animal is thus completely
cleansed; but as many of the particles washed out of it
will be deposited before they reach the mouth of the hole,
the passage along which the *Pholas* projects its siphon
is constantly found to be lined with a soft mud."

In a valuable paper on the anatomy of the lamellibranchiate mollusca published by Mr. Garner in the second
vol. of the Zoological Transactions, that excellent observer
has some short remarks on the means by which *Pholas* and

other mollusks bore. He mentions that the boring is
effected by currents produced by vibratile cilia, aided in
some cases by rasping. He remarks that the valves of
Lithodomus are not adapted for mechanical boring; that
the crypts of *Saxicava* are not circular; that the valves of
Teredo probably do not correspond to the bore; that *Pholas conoides* is often found in hard timber, though its valves
are not adapted for any boring or filing. He further observes " there is a cartilage between the two small spinous
processes of the hinge in the *Pholas candidus*: in other species of *Pholas* which have no rudiment of it, and allied
genera which have a particular character of articulation,
I consider the motion of the valves as but a secondary
cause in the perforation of the substances in which the animals are found." *

Mr. G. B. Sowerby objected to the notion that the cavities of *Pholas* were produced by rotatory motions of the
shell, since they are fitted to the latter, and since some of
the shell bones are externally smooth. He also objected to
the notion of a solvent.

Mr. W. Thompson, in his paper on *Teredo* cited under
the account of that genus, expresses his belief that the
smoothly rounded termination of the cell made by that
animal, is due to " the action of a solvent supplied by the
proboscis, which thus acts as a pioneer in mining the passage that is afterwards increased to its final dimensions by
the boring action of the primary valves."

Dr. Drummond, in his "Letters to a Young Naturalist,"
suggested the possibility of the animal of the boring mollusks decomposing the sea salt, as its wants may require,
and applying the liberated muriatic acid to the solution
of the calcareous rock.

* Loc. cit. p. 89.

M. Deshayes, in his splendid work upon the mollusca of
Algeria, maintains that the *Teredo* bores by means of a
solvent. The foot (which, however, he regards not as
such, but as a special secreting organ) presents a circular
smooth surface surrounded by a thick fleshy ring, so as to
constitute a sucker, by means of which the animal attaches
itself to the wood, and denudes the anterior extremity of the
gallery it inhabits. He believes that the contact long prolonged of this part of the animal with the wood, macerates
and renders it friable, by the action of a special secretion, of
which the product impregnates the leaflets of the fleshy ring,
and does not diffuse itself, or become dissolved in water.

M. F. Caillaud* holds a similar opinion with respect to
the perforating power of animals of the genus *Clavagella*,
which he maintains perforate by a solvent acid. This acid
he supposes to be developed in very small quantities at a
time, for otherwise the shell itself would be attacked by it.
He believes the animal has the power of applying the acid
to the point where it wishes to work, and that it can dilute
the solvent with water in case it threatens to endanger the
shell.

In the "Annales des Sciences Naturelles" for 1839,
M. L. A. Necker published some very interesting and important observations on the mineralogical nature of the
shells of mollusca, in which he points out differences of
structure as indicated by polarization of light. In it he
has the following observations on the subject in question :
"It is very remarkable that two genera of perforating
shells, the *Pholas* and the *Venerupis*, radiate strongly calc-
spar. Thus the asperities which roughen their shells may
with the aid of the acids with which they are provided,
excavate the calcareous rocks inhabited by them. The

* Mag. de Zoologie, 1842.

notion that their shells are formed of calc-spar (*chaux car-
bonate spathique*) seems to render impossible the perforation
by the shells themselves, of calcareous rocks equally hard
with the bodies perforating. But now that we know these
shells are composed of arragonite, it is plain that they can
act mechanically even on the hardest lime-stones."

Sir Henry de la Beche has given a table of the specific
gravity of some shells, as observed by himself,* in which
he states that of *Pholas crispata* to be 2·82, and of a number
of other bivalves and univalves to be nearly the same;
indicating a constitution which, allowance being made for
amount of animal matter, approximates their shells much
more nearly to arragonite than to calc-spar, the former having a specific gravity of 2·93, and the latter of 2·71.†

Mr. Albany Hancock‡ has put forward one of the most
definite and important opinions ever expressed on this disputed question. He states that—" The excavating instrument of *Pholas* and *Teredo* is formed of the anterior portion of the animal, in the surface of which are imbedded
siliceous particles. The particles penetrating the skin, give
to it much the character of rasping paper. The whole
forms a rubbing surface, which being applied closely to the
bottom of the cavity by the adhesion of the foot, enables
the animal to rub down, and so penetrate, shale, chalk,
wood, or even the hardest lime-stones and marble.

" *Saxicava rugosa* is also furnished with a rasping surface covered with silicious particles. This surface, however, in this species, is formed entirely of the anterior portion of the mantle, the margins of which being united, are

* Theoretical Researches, p. 75.

† Mr. Trenham Reeks has lately examined the specific gravity of several species
of *Pholas*, and has kindly communicated the results: he finds that of *P. crispata*
to be 2·76; *P. dactylus*, 2·45; *P. candida*, 2·70; and *Pholadidea papyracea*
2·64. ‡ An. Nat. Hist. vol. xv. p. 114.

so much thickened, forming a sort of cushion capable of considerable protrusion at the will of the animal. The foot is small, and passing through a much constricted orifice, gives origin to a byssus, which anchors the shell close to the base of the excavation, and thus holds the rubbing apparatus in immediate contact with the part to be excavated."

Such are the opinions expressed on this subject, worthy of note for their own weight, or on account of the reputation of their authors, of whose chemical acquirements, at least, several of them are not favourable specimens. They may all be classed under five conclusions: 1st. That the boring mollusca perforate by means of the rotation of the valves of their shells, which serve as augers. 2nd. That the holes are made by rasping effected by siliceous particles studding the substance of certain parts of the animals. 3rd. That currents of water, set in action by the motions of vibratile cilia, are the agents. 4th. That the animal secretes a chemical solvent, an acid which dissolves the substance into which it bores. 5th. That the combined action of a secreted solvent, and rasping by the valves, effects the perforations.

Of all these theories, the chemical one, so far as a secreted solvent is concerned, bears least examination in the case of the *Pholadidæ*. The substances perforated are wood, limestones hard and soft, argillaceous shales, clays, sandstone, and, in the case of a *Pholas* in the magnificent collection of Mr. Cuming, wax. The notion of a secreted solvent, that would act indifferently on all these substances, is, at present at least, purely hypothetical; and, since all attempted tests have failed to detect an acid, gratuitously so; for we can hardly suppose that any of those who have taken this view of the cause would maintain that

the animals have the power of secreting different acids at
will, according to the substance they have to attack. Yet
this notion has been most favoured by naturalists, who,
sceptical as to the perforating power of such fragile instruments as are the shells of many of these creatures, endowed
the animals with supernatural chemical qualifications.
Even good experimental observers,—Mr. Osler for one,—
whilst they proved that the *Pholas* could bore mechanically
by the rotation of its valves, could not free their minds
from the prejudice in favour of a solvent. The important
statement put forward by Mr. Albany Hancock respecting
the instruments by which mollusca bore, and which, so
far as Gasteropoda are concerned, appear to furnish us
with a true explanation, namely, that it was effected
by means of siliceous particles, variously arranged in
certain portions of the animal's body, led us to hope
that a better cause than any yet alleged had been discovered. But we cannot bear it out with respect to the
Pholadidæ. We can find no such particles in the mantle of *Teredo*, nor have any been noticed by Home or
Deshayes, or by the most recent observers, Frey and
Leuckart, who paid especial attention to the structure of
the tissues in this genus. Nor could we, although aided
by the anatomical and microscopical skill of Mr. Busk,
detect any siliceous particles in either the mantle, foot, or
siphon tube of *Pholas candida*. If present in any species,
therefore, they are exceptional, so far as the genus *Pholas* and
its allies are concerned. The shells of several British species
of *Pholas*, and that of *Pholadidea*, have been chemically
examined by our friend, Mr. Trenham Reeks, with a negative result as regards the presence of particles of silex in
their substance, where, after the statement of Mr. Hancock
respecting the structure of the mantle, we thought they

might possibly be found. On the other hand, taking into
consideration its mineralogical nature, as stated by M.
Necker, there is no reason for supposing that the shell of
the *Pholadidæ* is so weak a perforating instrument as some
have fancied. With its peculiar form, and the saw-like
asperities of its surface, especially of its anteal extremity,
it is well adapted for an auger, when wielded fresh and
elastic by its well-muscled animal inhabitant, whose foot in
all the members of this tribe, even in *Teredo*, where it is
least developed, seems specially organized to serve as a fulcrum. We have no evidence that they perforate any substances essentially harder than their shells, or so hard. The
sandstones in which they occasionally occur are either friable
or marly when fresh, though cabinet specimens seem so solid.
The explanation of Necker accounts for their perforations
in the hardest limestones. Wood, wax, and other substances in which they occur, offer no difficulty. The statements put forward respecting their boring in lava and granite have long ago been shewn to be mistakes. That they
exhibit a rotatory motion during the action of boring, has
been proved by competent observers ; and the cavities they
excavate, if examined when fresh, invariably show transverse groovings, which could have been caused only by
such motions. Currents of water set in motion by cilia
doubtless aid materially the animal's operations, and possibly may be the means by which the larvæ effect their first
lodgement ; but, considering the arrangements of the parts
of the body in the adult animal, it seems to us that Mr.
Garner's view of their being the primary cause of the perforation, whilst the rasping of the valves is secondary,
should be reversed. Such currents must be most effective
in clearing away loosened and loosening particles. If there
be any chemical action aiding, it must be due to the carbo-

nic acid set free during the respiratory process.   Evidence
of a secreted solvent there is none.

Pholades are often described as occurring in sand, in instances where their true habitat is in clays or soft rock, as
lias or pleistocene marl, immediately beneath the sand.
This was first noticed, in the case of *Pholas candida* and
P. dactylus, by Audouin and Milne Edwards.[*] The wood
and peat in which they occur not unfrequently on the
British shores, are usually the remains of submerged
forests.

A remarkable property of the animals of this genus, and
one which has long attracted notice, is their phosphorescence
when placed in the dark.   This phenomenon is exhibited
by some other acephalous mollusks, and by the compound
tunicated genus *Pyrosoma*.   The light is of a bluish-white
hue, and is regarded by Mayen to proceed from a luminous
mucous, like that given off by the *Medusæ*.   This mucus
is thrown off into the surrounding water, so that the currents proceeding from the animal are luminous.   Dr. Cold-
stream states[†] that the light is given out most strongly by
the internal surfaces of the respiratory tubes, and that it is
strongest in summer.   Professor John Müller has observed
that when *Pholades* are placed in a vacuum the light disappears, but re-appears on the admission of air ; also, that
when dried, they recover their luminous property on being
rubbed or moistened.

All our *Pholades* might be used as articles of food,
though we are not aware of their being eaten in this
country.   A very large West Indian species, the *Pholas
costata*, is much prized as such, and is regularly sold in the
markets of Havannah.

[*] Hist. Nat. du Littoral de France, t. i. p, 233.
[†] Cyclopædia of Anatomy and Physiology.—Art. Luminous Animals.

PHOLAS DACTYLUS, Linnæus.

Valves beaked : umbonal region crested by a series of subquadrangular cells: dorsal plates 4 in number.*

Plate III.

Pholas dactylus, LINN. Syst. Nat. ed. 12, p. 1110.—PENN. Br. Zool. ed. 1, 177,
vol. iv. p. 76. pl. 39, f. 10.—DA COSTA, Br. Conch. p. 244.
pl. 16, f. 2.—DONOV. Br. Shells, vol. iv, pl. 118.—MONT.
Test. Brit. p. 20 and 526.— Linn. Trans. vol. viii. p. 30.
Dorset Catal. p. 27, pl. 3, f. 2.—TURT. Conch. Dict. p. 143.
Dithyr. Brit. p. 8. — FLEM. Brit. Anim. p. 457. — Brit.
Marine Conch. p. 31.—BROWN, Ill. Conch. G. B. p. 115, pl.
49, f. 1, 2, 3.—BORN, Mus. Cæs. p. 14. pl. 1, f. 7.—CHEMN.
Conch. Cab. viii. p. 353, pl. 101, f. 859. — SPENGL. Skrivt.
Naturhist. Selsk. vol. ii. part 1, p. 85.—POLI, Test. Sicil.
pl. 1, f. 1 to 5.—WOOD, General Conch. p. 77, pl. 13.—
DILLW. Recent Shells, vol. i. p. 35.—LAM. Anim. s. Vert.
ed. 2, p. 43.—MAWE, Conch. pl. 3, f. 3.— Index Testac. pl.
2, Phol. f. 1.—SOWERB. Gen. Sh. Pholas. f. 1.—REEVE,
Conch. System, pl. 24.—Sow. Conch. Manual, f. 55.—PHIL.
Moll. Sicil. vol. i. p. 3, and vol. ii. p. 4.—DESH. Exp. Sci.
Algér. Moll. p. 107, pl. ix. C. E. and G., f. 1, 2, 3 (animal).

Pholas hians, PULTEN, Dorset, p. 26.
„   *callosa*, CUV. R. Anim. ed. Croch. pl. 113, f. 1.
Pholade dactyle, CHENU, Traité Elem. p. 38, f. 111.
LISTER, Hist. Conch. pl. 433, f. 276.

This ancient and universally-known species of *Pholas* is
much elongated in shape, rather inflated, not very fragile,
dull white, and extremely inequilateral. The entire surface
is sculptured by concentric lamellar striæ, which, moderately
distant posteriorly, become approximated in front, where
they form short vaulted spines, arranged in close-set radiating rows. The convexity of the valves is simple, that is
to say, they are not divided into distinct areas by a
radiating furrow, or concavity. The anterior side, which
is the more tumid, is very short, and forms a distinct beak,
through the large ventral hiatus incurving that margin ; the
posterior side is much produced, and tapers to a rounded

* These diagnoses refer to the British species only.

extremity ; the gape is moderate, and both the margins are
slightly convex. The front dorsal edge is incurved, and
moderately sloping ; its edge recurved, and spread over the
umbonal region, the summit of which is crested by a series
of about a dozen deeply-excavated, square-mouthed cells,
formed by a dorsal arch supported by perpendicular laminæ.
The accessory valves are four in number ; the two principal, which are exactly similar, large, peculiarly fragile,
membranaceous, elongated, somewhat wedge-shaped, and
almost smooth, or merely marked with the lines of increase,
are in fine specimens divided into areas by an oblique posterior line, and a more or less shallow or profound anterior
excavation, which runs to the extremities of the inner
margin (where the valves touch each other), from a slight-
ly-projecting point, situated not far from the middle of the
opposite margin. Their exact contour varies according to
age, the lateral edges being more nearly parallel in the
adult ; the anteal extremity, however, is always attenuated
to an obtuse point, and the hinder so biangulated that the
outer angle is the more prominent ; the interior lateral edge
is nearly straight, with a slight retusion near the middle,
the exterior one convex and sloping in front, subretuse and
straight behind. A solid, transverse, hammer-shaped, testaceous plate, most closely attached to their hinder termination, and dove-tailed above into the inner posterior
angles, completes the concealment of the cells and umbonal
region. This is immediately followed by a narrow and very
thin shelly plate, which extends thence more than half-way
the distance to the end of the shell. Subumbonal blade is
rather large, and moderately wide and elongated, spatulate,
curved, flat, broader at its termination, where in expanding
it becomes thinner, and internally concave : the hinge-plate
is marked with several raised sulci.

A stunted variety is found, which is abbreviated posteriorly, and has its beak narrow, and peculiarly prominent. Its striæ, too, are so crowded as to present no interstices.

This is by far the largest of our British *Pholades*, the shell attaining to five or six inches in length, and one and a half in breadth. The number of the accessory plates, and the possession of dorsal cells, are its salient characteristics.

" Animal elongated, subcylindrical, pale-bluish white, having the mantle closed throughout, except a passage in the anterior ventral range for an oval foot, with a thick, fleshy, subcylindrical base. The mantle posteriorly is prolonged into a very long, thick, rounded tube, which terminates in two orifices, whereof the branchial one is the largest, having from ten to fourteen large rays, each of which have three, four, five, six, or seven cilia on one side ; besides the principal rays, there are between each one or two minor ones. The anal, or upper tube, is short, just separate at its extremity from the branchial one, curves a little upwards, and has its orifice plain. This tube is eminently contractile, capable of great extension ; sometimes to double the length of the shell, sometimes it is shortened and inflated with water to a diameter as great, or even greater, than the thickest part of the shell. When contracted it has a corrugated aspect ; when extended it is of a pearly-white colour, with the orifices and rays dusky. For an inch or two towards the extremity it is papillose, the papillæ so disposed as to have a squamous aspect."— CLARK's *MSS.*, *communicated by Mr. Jeffreys.*

On the south coasts of England it is not only the commonest species of the genus, but one of the most abundant of shells, being found in profusion near low-water mark, imbedded in chalk, red-sandstone, lias, decayed wood, and even in pure sand, &c. Among its numerous localities we may mention Margate, and most parts of the Kentish coast (S. H.); Hastings (S. H.), Weymouth (S. H.), Exmouth (Clark), Lyme Regis (E. F.). In Wales it is found in Cardigan and Swansea Bays (Jeffreys). In Ireland, at Belfast and Dublin Bays (Thompson), coast of Cork (R. Ball), and Ballycotton Bay (Jeff. Cab.). It is of rare occurrence on the coast of Scotland; Frith of Forth (Laskey), Clyde (Smith). It occurs fossil in (true) raised beaches on the coast of Ayrshire. It ranges throughout the European seas.

PHOLAS PARVA, Pennant.

Valves beaked; surface not divided by a radiating sulcus front dorsal edge recurved, but not cellular; dorsal plate single.

Plate IV. figs. 1, 2, and Plate II. fig. 2, and (Animal) Plate F. f. 3, and 3, A.

Pholas parva, PENN. Brit. Zool. ed. 1, vol. iv. p. 77, pl. 40, f. 13.—MONT. Test. Brit. p. 22, pl. 1, f. 7, 8.—LINN. Trans. viii. p. 35.—TURT. Conch. Dict. p. 143; Dithyr. Brit. p. 9.—FLEM. Br. Anim. p. 457.—Br. Marine Conch. p. 32, f. 71.—BROWN, Ill. Conch. G. B. p. 115, pl. 48, f. 11, 12.—WOOD, General Conch. p. 82.— DILLW. Recent Shells, vol. i. p. 38.—HANL. Recent Shells, p. 5.

  „ *crenulata*, SPENGL. Skrivt. Naturhis. Selsk. vol. ii. part 1. p. 92.

  „ *dactyloides*, LAM. Anim. s. Vert. ed. 2, vol. vi. p. 45, (description not note).

  „ *ligamentina*, DESH. Elem. Conch. pl. 3, f. 11, 12.

  „ *tuberculata*, TURT. Dithyr. Brit. p. 5, pl. 1, f. 7, 8.—FLEM. Br. Anim. p. 457.—BROWN, Ill. Conch. G. B. p. 115, pl. 49, f. 12, 13. —Brit. Marine Conch. p. 30.—Ind. Testac. sup. pl. 1, Phol. f. 2.—HANL. Recent Shells, p. 9, sup. pl. 1, Phol. f. 2.

In common with all our English *Pholades*, and, indeed, with the mass of known species in this genus, the shell we are describing is of a lustreless white, often stained, however, with brick-red, from the nature of its habitat. It is elongated oblong, thin, fragile, gibbous in front, and then at

about two-fifths the distance from that extremity, without
any intervening radiating channel, suddenly diminishes in
convexity.   The anterior space is more or less closely set
with radiating lines and concentric elevated striæ, of which
the former are generally the more strongly marked, and the
latter in typical examples are usually remarkably delicate.
Neither of these traverse the entire surface; but, after
muricating by their intersection the gibbous portion of the
shell, become obsolete shortly after passing it, and leave the
posterior third smooth, or merely wrinkled with the lines of
increase.   The sides, although unequal, are less so than is
usual with the *Pholades*; the posterior is attenuated, but
rounded at its extremity (and more rarely abbreviated,
scarcely tapering, and broadly rounded at its termination,)
its arcuated dorsal and convex ventral edges sloping with
almost equal inclination.   The anterior end forms a short
and obtuse beak, the ventral edge, which encloses an hiatus
which occupies one-half the length of the shell, being
greatly incurved, and the dorsal moderately but decidedly
sloping, and very slightly retuse.   The accessory valve is
solitary, umbonal, excessively fragile, and resembling that of
P. candida, but is proportionally narrower, and the central
excavation almost or entirely invisible.   The hinge-margin,
which is reflected slightly over the umbones and anteriorward, but not generally appressed, is internally provided
with a callous tubercle; but is destitute of teeth.   The
subumbonal blade is slender, curved, and not concave, and
expands but little at its apex.

   Animal elongated, white; body oblong; mantle white
anteally, tinged with fawn-colour posteally, open centrally
at the widest part, for the passage of a thick, nearly round,
or widely oval truncated white foot. Line of suture of sides
of mantle anteriorly strongly marked by a whitish band.

Siphonal tubes tawny; their orifices very unequal; the margin of the branchial bordered by scalloped lobes, which are not prolonged into rays, except a pair contiguous to each other on each side, on a line with the anal. The orifice of the branchial tube and the foot distinguish it from all its British congeners.

We regard this as not only a more local species than *dactylus, candida* or *crispata*, but as specifically less abundant. We have found it in company with the two former; but in a wide disproportion of number. The only spot where Montagu met with it—and more successfully than our subsequent collectors,—in considerable abundance, was near the town of Salcombe in South Devon, in decayed wood, a substance greatly affected by most of the species of this genus. Pennant, the original discoverer and describer of it, states that he found it in fossil-wood at Abergelly in Denbighshire. It is not uncommon on the shores at Torquay, embedded in red sandstone (S. H.); is taken also at Exmouth, and other places on the Devonshire coast (Clark); likewise, though rarely, at Margate (S. H.), and has been dredged alive in fifteen fathoms water in hard turf, at the west bay of Portland (M'Andrew). Pridmouth, near Fowey, in Cornwall (C. W. Peach), Oxwich, in Glamorganshire (Jeffreys), Belfast Bay (Thomps. in Ann. N. H., vol. 13, p. 434), may also be included among its habitats; a single example (perhaps from ballast) is likewise recorded by Captain Brown as taken at St. Cyrus, in Kincardineshire. Although scarcely mentioned in foreign works, the species is not confined to the British Isles; Mr. M'Andrew has taken it also on the coast of Spain. In general appearance it is intermediate between *crispata* and *dactylus*; but, besides differing in the dorsal plate, which, from its extreme brittleness, is too frequently broken in cabinets, is devoid of the cells of the former, and of the channel of the latter ; compared to which, it is narrower and smaller, the average size rarely exceeding an inch and a quarter in length, and about half an inch in breadth. The *Pholas tuberculata* of Turton is only a monstrosity of this species, as we have ascertained by the examination of his own unique specimen, which, together with the rest of his collection, is now in the possession of Mr. Gwyn Jeffreys, of Norton, near Swansea.

The description given by Lamarck of his *Ph. callosa* sufficiently accords with the characteristics of this species ; the synonymy of the recent edition of the " Animaux sans Vertebres" indicates, however, a mere variety of *dactylus*.

PHOLAS CRISPATA, Linnæus.

Valves abbreviated, beaked, divided by a radiating grove without dorsal cells : dorsal plate rudimentary.

Plate IV. figs. 3, 4, 5.

Pholas crispata, LINN. Syst. Nat. p. 1111.—PENN. Br. Zool. ed. 1, vol. iv. p 77, pl. 40, f. 12.—DONOV. Br. Shells, vol. ii. pl. 62—PULTENEY, Dorset, p. 27.—MONT. Test. Brit. p. 23.—Linn. Trans. vol. viii. p. 32.—TURT. Conch. Dict. p. 146 ; Dithyr. Brit. p. 6.—FLEM. Brit. Anim. p. 456.—BROWN, Ill. Conch. G. B. p. 114, pl. 48, f. 1 to 5. — M'G. Moll. Aberd. p. 306 ; Brit. Marine Conch. p. 29.—DILLW. Recent Shells, i. p. 40. WOOD, Gen. Conch. p. 81, pl. 15, f. 3, 4, 5.—HANL. Recent Shells, p. 7, pl. 2, Phol. f. 5 ; Index Testac. pl. 2, Phol. f. 5. SPENGL. Skrivt. Naturhist. Selsk. vol. ii. part 1, p. 96.— LAM. Anim. s. Vert. ed. 2, vol. vi. p. 46.—CHEMN. Conch. Cab. vol. viii. p. 369, pl. 102, f. 872, 873, 874.—GOULD, Invert. Massach. p. 27.—CUV. Règne Anim. ed. grande, pl. 113, f. 3 (animal).—DEKAY, New York Mollusc. p. 247, pl. 32, f. 506.

„ *bifrons*, DA COSTA, Brit. Shells, p. 242, pl. 16, f. 4.

„ *parva*, „ „ p. 247.—DONOV. Brit. Shells, ii. pl. 69. —Encycl. Méth. Vers. pl. 169, f. 5.—LIST. Hist. Conch. pl. 436, f. 279.

This coarse-looking shell is of a somewhat oval shape, rather strong (often becoming thick and heavy in aged individuals), greatly inflated, dull whitish, inequilateral, and

so excessively gaping at both ends that the valves only
touch each other at the hinge and in the middle of the opposite margin. The surface is rather obliquely divided
into two nearly equal portions by a broad groove-like channel which, proceeding from the umbones to the middle of
the extremely-arcuated ventral margin, is internally indicated by a corresponding costa or rib-like elevation. The
anterior portion, which is eminently tumid, is covered with
rather close-set concentric laminar striæ, whose free edge
is less closely dentated in radiating rows, which do not
quite extend to the dividing channel, posterior to which
the shell is flatter, and only marked with the concentric
wrinkles of increase. The anterior extremity forms a very
short obtuse beak, and the posterior termination broadly
rounded. The dorsal edges, which are but little sloping,
are incurved near the hinge. The hinge-margin is broadly
reflected, simple, and unprovided with denticles. The subumbonal tooth is long, flat, subspatulate, but little concave
at its extremity, and much curved. The single testaceous
accessory plate is small, but solid, and is situated at the
end of the skin which covers the front dorsal gape; it appears trigonal when imbedded, the sides being nearly
straight, and meeting in a rectangle, whose apex forms the
posterior termination of the plate, but when detached from
the shell more nearly approaches the form of an arrow-head,
the concealed underlapping portion constituting very
elongated barbs. The animal is dusky-white, its siphon
tinged with brown and rough with papillæ.

Our largest examples exceed three inches in length by
about one and three quarters in breadth. On the southern
shores of England it is reckoned among the less common
shells, but is occasionally found in smaller numbers imbedded along with the other *Pholades* at the Reculvers (S. H.),

Hastings (S. H.), &c. In the north it appears to be more abundant, and is taken at Liverpool (M'Andrew), Scarborough (Bean), in sand near Hartlepool in Durham (Jeffreys, cab.), in the shale rocks of Northumberland and Durham (Alder).

In Ireland it is dug from pure sand in an estuary near Dublin (from which vicinity have come some of the finest examples known to us), and is obtained, likewise, from Belfast and Dublin Bay (Thompson), the coast of Cork (R. Ball), &c.

Dead valves are frequently cast ashore on the Isle of Man (E. F.).

In Scotland, among other localities, may be mentioned the Murray Frith (M'Andrews), Frith of Forth, where it is found in abundance burrowing in the coal-shales exposed at low water, in company with *P. crispata* (E. F.), Clyde (Smith), Aberdeenshire (M'Gillivray).

Mr. Clark has obtained this species at Guernsey, " from the sandstone, from which the waterproof cement is made."

The *Pholas crispata* is distributed generally throughout the European seas, and is the only one of our *Pholades* which ranges to the shores of North America. It occurs on the coasts of Massachussets and New Jersey. This wide distribution is connected with its geological history. It is one of the species which ranged throughout the upper part of the northern hemisphere during the pleistocene or glacial epoch, in the ancient sea-beds of which time it is a common fossil. Before that period it had lived within our area during the successive epochs of the coralline and red crags. It is an interesting instance of a littoral, or sublittoral shell, capable of bearing many varieties of climate, having consequently a great range in time, and in the end a wide and peculiar geographical distribution.

PHOLAS CANDIDA, Linnæus.

Valves not beaked ; surface not divided by a radiating grove ; dorsal plate single.

Plate IV. figures 1, 2.

Pholas candida, LINN. Syst. Nat. ed. 12, p. 1111(not Spengler).—PENN. Brit.Zol. ed. 1, vol. iv. p. 76, pl. 39, f. 11. — DA COSTA, Brit. Conch. p.246. Pulteney,in Hutchin's Hist.Dorset,p .26.— DONOV. Brit. Shells, vol. iv. pl. 132. —MONT. Test. Brit. p. 2.--Dorset Catal. p. 27, pl. 1, f. 12.—Linn. Tr. vol. viii. p. 81.—TURT. Conch. Diction. p. 144, f. 79 ; Dithyr. Brit. p. 10.—FLEM. Brit. Anim. p. 457. — M'GIL. Moll. Aberd. p. 306. —Brit. Marine Conch. p. 31.—BROWN, Ill. Conch. G. B. p. 115, pl. 48, f. 6, 7, 8, 9, 10.—CHEMN. Conch. Cabinet, vol. viii. p. 358 (not variety), pl. 101, f. 861.—WOOD, General Conch. p. 79, pl. 14, f. 3, 4. — DILLW. Recent Shells, vol. i. p. 36. (not variety).—LAM. Anim. s. Vert. ed. 2, vol. vi. p. 44.— BURROWS, Elem. Conch. pl. 3, f. 4.—MAWE, Introd. Conch. pl. 3, f. 2.—WOOD, Ind. Testac. pl. 2, Phol. f. 3.—CROUCH, Introd. Conch. pl. 2, f. 11.—PHILIPPI, Moll. Sicil. vol. i. p. 3, and vol. ii. p. 4.—HANL. Recent Shells, p. 5, pl. 2, Phol. f. 3. —DESH. Exp. Sc. Algér. p. 109, pl. IX. D. I. f. 4, 5 (animal).

 „ *papyracea*, SPENGL. Skrivt. Naturhist. Selakab. vol. ii, part 1, pl. 1, f. 4 (not of his diagnosis).—LIST. Hist. Conch. pl. 435, f. 278.

The outline of this fragile shell varies from oblong to elongated oblong ; it is thin, semi-pellucid, dull white, and moderately inflated. Its posterior gape is the more considerable, the valves being nearly closed anteriorly. Their surface is simple, covered with fine moderately-distant radiating lines, and closer set concentric sublaminar striæ, which, at their intersection, give birth to very short and rather broad prickles or spines, which are chiefly evident at the front of the shell, where the radiating lines are broader and, in most specimens, more distant. The ventral edge is uniformly convex or subarcuated, and slopes upwards anteriorly: the dorsal edges are convex, but little sloping behind, more so in front. The sides are very unequal, and both are rounded at their termination ; the posterior end is the more attenuated. The hinge-margin is reflected, but neither chambered, nor extending over any considerable portion of the umbonal region. The solitary accessory plate, which rests upon the front dorsal edges, is rather large, fragile, testaceous, elongated, tapering off to a more or less rounded point anteriorly, and posteriorly subtruncated and bending inwards. Its sides are retuse in the middle; the surface concentrically striolated, and divided lengthways by a distinct, shallow, groove-like excavation. The subumbonal tooth-like apophysis is peculiarly slender, flat, arcuated, rather oblique, and but little expanding at its extremity. The hinge-margins are armed with an extremely oblique tooth-like process, attached by its entire length, and only projecting above it in one valve.

Animal elongated, white, body oblong; siphonal tube very long, pale brown, minutely dotted with tawny or red; covered with closely-studded papillæ (which, under the microscope, appear hollow), towards the extremity. Orifices dusky-rayed, or longitudinally banded with purplish-brown, internally; the branchial with twelve rays or long cirrhi, and intermediate smaller ones; the anal plain. Mantle in front dotted with opaque, white specks, foot oblong-lanceolate, truncate. This animal can close its shell much more completely than the other British *Pholades* but its siphon is scarcely so retractile. It is highly muscular. *Pholas candidus* is very active, rapid in its motions within its hole, withdrawing to its inmost recesses speedily on being disturbed.

The absence of a beak, combined with the possession of a single accessorial plate, easily distinguish the shell of this species from its English congeners. It never attains to any considerable size, rarely exceeding two inches in length, and five-sixths of an inch in breadth, and is much more usually only obtained of by far smaller dimensions. Although common, its range does not appear so extended as that of *dactylus*, in whose company, however, it is often taken. It is met with towards low-water mark, embedded in chalk, limestone, red sandstone, hard clay, decayed wood, &c., in many parts of England, and is peculiarly plentiful at Margate and other parts of the Kentish coast (S. H.), is found also at Weymouth (S. H.), Liverpool (M'Andrew), Torquay (S. H.), Exmouth, in pure sand (Clark), Salcombe, Hastings (S. H.), Lyme Regis, in lias (E. F.), Scarborough (Bean), in the shale-rocks of Northumberland and Durham (Alder). In Wales, at Oxwich Bay, in Glamorganshire (Jeffreys). In Ireland, Dublin Bay (Thompson), Youghal (R. Ball), Ballycotton (Jeff. cab.), Waterford, Belfast, and Birterbie Bay (Dr. Farran). In Scotland, it occurs plentifully boring in the coal-shales of the Frith of Forth (E. F.), Aberdeenshire (M'Gillivray), Loch Ryan (Smith).

This species made its first appearance in the British seas during the epoch of the red crag. It is now distributed throughout the seas of Europe.

Under the manuscript name of *P. Nana* of Solander, Dr. Pulteney, in 1799, first introduced this species to us as British, in his catalogue of the birds and shells of Dorsetshire, defining it, however, rather by his synonymy than by his very bald diagnosis. At that period a less strict regard was paid to the necessity of confining the term indigenous to such species as actually propagate upon our coast, and of not bestowing it alike upon all such as may be discovered, however manifestly of casual foreign importation, in a living state within our waters. Nevertheless, the doctor cautiously modifies his introduction with, "I doubt whether they breed upon the English coast. I have seen it in the sides of the ships, whilst careening, in great numbers, both at Poole and Weymouth." Montagu, after an accurate description of it, adds, "Whether this species can strictly be said to be British may be doubted." The careful and long-continued observations of our living naturalists confirm the justice of these doubts; it being universally now acknowledged to be solely taken, "occasionally alive" (Bean), from vessels which have entered our harbours from foreign ports, or "from wood washed ashore only" (Thompson), as was the case with the specimens recorded in the "Annals of Natural History," vol. xiii. p. 434, to have been discovered "in water-logged mahogany, near Killala, Sligo; also on the coast of Clare (W. Thompson). Montagu has remarked the fact, that whilst the general habit of the shipworms is to bore parallel with the grain, the *Pholas* perforates the wood across the grain.

Although known to Linnæus, and referred to in his "Systema Naturæ," it was first clearly characterised by Parsons who, in the "Acta Anglica," gives us an excellent representation of it, not, however, as an English shell, but as avowedly taken out of a Spanish vessel.

P. STRIATA, Linnæus.

Pholas striata, LINN. Syst. Nat. 1111.—MONT. Test. Brit. p. 26 and 559.— Dorset Catal. p. 27, pl. 1, f. 7.—Linn. Trans. vol. viii. p. 31. —TURT. Conch. Diction. p. 147 ; Dithyra Brit. p. 11.—Brit. Marine Conch. p. 31.—BROWN, Illus. Conch. G. B. p. 115, pl. 49, f. 5, 8.—WOOD, General Conch. p. 83, pl. 16, f. 1, 2, 3, 4, 8.—MAWE, Conch. pl. 3, f. 1.—Index Testac. pl. 2, Phol. f. 7. —REES, Cyclop. Shells, pl. 8.—SOWERBY, Genera Sh. Pholas, f. 1, 2.—REEVE, Conch. System, pl. 24, f. 2.

   ,,   *nana*, PULTENEY, Dorset. p. 27.

   ,,   *pusilla*, LINN. Syst. Nat. p. 1111.—DONOV. Brit. Shells, vol. iv. pl. 117. —CHEMN. Conch. Cab. vol. viii. p. 365, pl. 102, f. 867 to 871. —SPENGLER, Skrivt. Naturhist. Selskab. vol. ii. part 1, p. 95. —DILLW. Recent Shells, vol. i. p. 38.

   ,,   *lignorum*, SPENGLER, Beschaft. Berlin Ges.Naturf. vol. iv. pl. 5, f. 1 to 5.

   ,,   *conoides*, FLEM. Brit. Animals, p. 457.

   ,,   *clavata*, LAMARCK, Anim. s- Vert. ed. 2, p. 46 (excluding var. C.)— HANL. Recent Shells, p. 7.—Encyclop. Méthod. Mollusq. pl. 170, Phol. f. 1, 2, 3.

The shape is somewhat conoid, being broad, and rounded in front, and strongly tapering to a more or less obtuse point posteriorly. The valves are similarly compressed behind, but ventricose, or even tumid anteriorly; their texture is very thin and fragile, and under a more or less distinctly visible yellow epidermis, they are of a dull white. The surface is vertically divided a little before the middle by an extreme and abrupt difference of sculpture; the posterior area being distinguished by concentric elevated plicæ, which become more or less obsolete as they recede from the beaks and the line of separation, where they are strongly indicated; whilst the anterior portion is more or less closely covered with rather strong oblique laminar crenulated striæ, which form distinct angles towards their middle, at which point the foremost ones diverge, and the following ones converge. A thin, smooth, tumid, triangular space near the front ventral margin, covers in the adult the vast gape which is there present in the immature examples. The extremity of the posterior side, which is greatly the longer, is slightly hiant, and the ventral edges are prevented approaching each other by an elongated testaceous accessory plate, which lies between their hinder edges. There is a kind of double appressed reflection of the front dorsal edge over the umbones, which supports the large and somewhat heart-shaped shield which entirely conceals them. This latter, which is rather blunted in front, and profoundly incurved behind, is followed by a third accessory testaceous plate, which separates the posterior dorsal margins, and is elongated and narrow in shape. The subumbonal toothlike apophysis is flattened but slender; and there is a deep umbilicus-like impression in front of the beak, caused by the primary and more abrupt reflection of the dorsal margin.

At the first glance this species bears a strong resemblance to the *P. cuneiformis* (Journ. Ac. Sci. Philad. vol. ii. p. 322.—Dekay, New York Moll. p. 248) of Say, which, not being very clearly characterized by its author, seems but little known in England; it may, however, readily be distinguished by the acuminated hinder termination of its smaller and more solid umbonal shield, and in all stages of growth by the non-angulation of its elevated anterior striæ.

The specimens taken in England rarely exceed an inch in length, and even the more strictly exotic ones are not greatly larger. They peculiarly affect mahogany.

PHOLADIDEA, Leach.

Shell more or less globose or oblong, equivalve, inequilateral, surface of valves similar to those of *Pholas;* their beaks not covered by callosities ; accessory plates small. Muscular impressions as in *Pholas.* Anterior extremity open in the immature, but closed in the adult shell by a thin papyraceous permanent shelly coat, with a small opening centrally and anteriorly for the foot. Posterior extremity truncated and gaping, usually furnished with an expanded coriaceous cup.

Animal claviform ; the mantle closed in front, except a small opening for the passage of a truncated suckershaped foot. Siphonal tube long, terminating in a disk surrounded by cirrhi, encircling the openings of the branchial and anal siphons, each of which are also surrounded by radiating cirrhi.

The separation of the calyciferous *Pholades* from their allies of the last-described genus, was, we believe, first suggested on conchological grounds, by Dr. Goodall to Dr. Turton, who, in his " Conchological Dictionary," gives the name of *Pholadidea Loscombiana* to our British species. In the thirty-ninth volume of the " Diction. des Sciences Naturelles," the group is characterised under the name of *Pholadidea,* and made a sub-genus of *Pholas.* Swainson, in his " Elements of Conchology" (1835) called the genus *Pholidea,* and in his more recent " Treatise on Malacology" in Lardner's Cyclopedia, writes it *Pholidæa,* and refers to Leach as the founder.

The genus is a good one, seeing that both shell and animal afford excellent distinctive characters, which are pre-

sented equally by British and exotic species. The
remarkable cup-shaped appendage surrounding the base of
the united siphons may be regarded as a rudimentary tube
for their protection—especially for the protection of the
complicated cirrhigerous disk which surrounds the openings
of the branchial and anal siphons in *Pholadideæ*, and which
is so characteristic of them. M. Deshayes regards this
group as intermediate between *Pholas* and *Teredina*, whilst
the latter is intermediate between *Pholadidea* and *Teredo*.*
In some respects, however, the passage seems rather from
Pholas towards *Gastrochæna* and its allies, and in such a
position we have placed it here.

P. PAPYRACEA, Solander.

Plate V. Figs. 3, 4, 5, 6, and Plate II. Fig. 1, and (animal) Plate F. f. 4.

Pholas papyracea, TURT. Dithyr. Brit. p. 2, pl. 1, f. 1 to 4.—BROWN, Ill.
Conch. G. B. p. 114, pl. 49, f. 4, 6, 7, 9. — Brit. Marine
Conch. p. 29.—SOWERB. Gen. Shells. Pholas, f. 3.—
REEVE, Conch. System. pl. 24, f. 3. — MAWE, Conch.
pl. 3, f. 5.—Sow. Conch. Man. f. 56.— HANL. Recent
Sh. p. 9, sup. pl. 1. Phol. f. 1, 3.—Ind. Testac. sup. pl.
1. Phol. f. 1.

„ *Lamellata*, TURT. Dithyr. Brit. p. 4, pl. 1, f. 5, 6.—FLEM. Br. Anim. p.
456. — BROWN, Ill. Conch. G. B. p. 114, pl. 49, f. 10, 11.
—Ind. Testac. sup. pl. 1. Phol. f. 3.

Pholadidea Loscombiana, TURT. Conch. Dict. p. 147.

Pholas (Pholadidea) Goodallii, Dict. Sc. Nat. vol. xxxvii. p. 532.

„ *striata*, CUV. Anim. King. (edit. Griffith) pl. 8, f. 1.—Cuv. Anim. King.
(Henderson's edit.) pl. 41. f. 1.

Pholade striée, BLAINV. Manuel Malacol. pl. 80 *bis*, f. 7.

This delicate and remarkable shell, whose different
aspects in its mature and undeveloped state, have caused
so much controversy among English conchologists, is of
an elongated ovate shape, ventricose, very thin, not glossy,

* Traité Elementaire de Conchyliologie, p. 75.

whitish, and moderately inequilateral. It is closed and
tumid in front, somewhat linearly gaping, and provided
with a cup-like appendage behind, which, projecting about
three-eighths of an inch beyond the extremity of the shell,
and composed of two papyraceous vaulted laminæ of a very
pale brown colour, suggests the idea of the attachment of
a portion of another specimen to its valves. An oblique
line from the umbones, forming a rib internally, divides the
surface into two nearly equal parts, the hinder of which is
merely marked with broad and not very close concentric
wrinkles; the anterior, however, is again diagonally subdivided, the portion nearer the beaks being most closely
and obliquely sculptured with curling laminar striæ, whilst
the excessively thin and almost semi-transparent matter,
which in the adult fills up the expanded front ventral gape
of the immature shell, is perfectly smooth. The ventral
margin is nearly straight or but slightly convex; the hinder
dorsal, whose edges being turned outwards cause a lip-like
projection near the beaks, is similarly but slightly convex,
and is but little inclined. The posterior extremity is
obtusely biangulated, the anterior peculiarly rounded.
The front hinge-margin, which is elevated above the dorsal
line, and at first reflected towards the umbones, again
recurves, and forms a kind of crest which is abruptly truncated posteriorly at the beaks, where it is terminated by two
minute somewhat rhomboidal testaceous accessory valves.
The hinge is furnished with a rather large, erect, thin, subtriangular tooth-like lamina in one valve, and a smaller and
more caducous one in the other. The subumbonal blade is
short, flat, curved, and scarcely expanding at the tip.

The young of this beautiful shell (which stage constitutes the *Pholas lamellata* of Turton) assumes so different
an aspect, that few would recognize it from a description or

figure of the adult. As yet unprovided with the calyx, its posterior end, instead of being truncated, is rounded and somewhat attenuated, whilst the dome-like structure of its anterior extremity is replaced by a gaping expanse, above which the side is obtusely angulated.

This non-formation of parts and deferred enclosure of the gape with shelly matter, until the last stage of growth, is not confined to *P. papyracea*, but prevails likewise in many *Pholadidæ* of the American seas.

Dr. Turton's specimen of his *Pholas lamellata* is not merely the young of this species, but seemingly a kind of monstrosity, or at least a specimen of an unusual growth ; for instead of the animal attempting as usual to enclose the front ventral gape with testaceous matter, upon the completion of the immature stage of growth, it has contented itself with solidifying the entire shell, and reflecting the edge of its anterior ventral margin. This form is extremely rare, but differs in no other respects from the ordinary aspect of the young *papyracea*. There is a dwarf variety figured in our plates which, instead of being littoral, is taken by the dredge in detached lumps of rock five or six miles from the shore. This is supposed by many collectors, who regard *lamellata* as a distinct species, to be the true young of *papyracea*, and not an adult form depauperated by the unfavourable influence of an unnatural locality.

Mrs. Griffith has kindly furnished us with coloured drawings of the animals of the two forms taken from life, and Dr. Battersby with good specimens of *P. papyracea* in spirits. Mrs. Griffith regards both shells and animals of each as indicating distinct species ; but the apparent differences presented in the figures of the latter seem to depend upon different states of the creatures at the moment when pourtrayed, for the characters noticed as distinctive of the form *lamellata* are all present in that termed *papyracea*, as we have convinced ourselves by an examination of preserved specimens, and as Mr. Clark had previously observed and drawn from life in each variety. The account of them in the manuscripts of that excellent malacologist, communicated by Mr. Jeffreys, is so full and clear, and his opinion in consequence so important on this disputed point, that we cannot do better than give it in his own words, though at the risk of some repetition :—" This animal, in consequence of its shell having been taken under very different appearances of form, has, when from circumstances it has not formed the testaceous membrane that often covers its anterior ventral gape and the testaceous cup-like process at the posterior end, been considered a distinct species, and named by Dr. Turton and others the *Pholas lamellata ;* but when it had acquired those appendages, it was named *Pholas papyracea.* But having this summer (1835) studied the animal under both forms, we are fully enabled to confirm Mr. G. B. Sowerby's opinion, stated in his ' Genera,' that the two shells are one species under different forms. We do not, however, think that the form styled *P. lamellata* is the young of the shell styled *P. papyracea,* but that they each maintain their respective forms when of all sizes, from circumstances dependent on peculiarities of animal economy. In corroboration of this opinion, we can state that we have seen what is called the *P. lamellata* equal in size to the largest *papyracea,* and, on the other hand, we have seen what is called the *P. papyracea* completely formed, with the cup and testaceous ventral membrane not more than a quarter of an inch in length ; and we believe that when peculiar circumstances, most probably attendant on habitat and animal economy arise, the animal has then the power of forming the cup and membrane. The cup we consider as nothing more than an incipient shelly lining of its habitation for the protection of some part of its tubes, probably the ciliated orifices, which are more complex in this species than in any of the others, and is, in some measure, analogous to the shelly linings of the *Teredo* and *Gastrochœna*. An inspection of the tubes of the animals which are precisely similar, and which differ most conspicuously from all the other *Pholads*, will at once convince the most sceptical of their identity. The orifices of the two tubes are placed in a distinct finely-fringed circle, unlike in this to all our other *Pholades*. The branchial tube has around its orifice twelve rays, with a smaller one between each. The upper or anal tube is plain and closely united to the lower, and both are placed within a finely white-fringed circle. The tube is pale reddish brown to within about a quarter of an inch of its extremity, where it is of a pearly white. The rays and orifices within the white-fringed circle are pale reddish brown. The foot is small, oval, and somewhat pointed before and behind. The belly of the animal is white, mottled with intensely white flaky points or dots, as in *Pholas candida*."

Pholadidea papyracea must be considered not only a very local shell, but one difficult to procure even at most of the spots from whence only it can be obtained. It is met with at very low tides imbedded in reddish sandstone (*Trias*) at Exmouth, Teignmouth, Torquay, and other towns of the South Devon coast; but its extreme fragility renders its safe extraction, and the subsequent removal of the animal matter, a work of delicate manipulation. The dwarf variety we have figured was dredged some five or six miles from land in lumps of indurated red clay, by Mr. Clark, of Exmouth. Portrush, in the north of Ire-

land, is likewise given as a locality for the species in the
" Annals of Natural History," on the authority of two
specimens thus labelled in the Ordnance Museum ; and an
example, believed to have been dredged between Howth
and Lambay, was taken from a fishing-boat in Dublin Bay,
imbedded in a sandy conglomerate of shelly matter. (W.
Thompson, in Ann. N. H. vol. xiii. p. 434.) Few specimens attain to greater dimensions than an inch and a half
in length, and about half that breadth.

In Captain Brown's " Conchological Illustrations" is a
Pholas sulcata* (p. 115, pl. 48, f. 17, 18), which more
nearly agrees with the young of this than with any of our
known British *Pholades*. Its Scotch locality (Dunbar ;
in the collection of David Falconer, of Carlowrie,) is, however, against this supposition.

* Since writing the above paragraph, we have received a letter from Captain
Brown, in which he assures us that this species, of which only a single valve was
found, is neither a fossil nor a variety of *papyracea*. We append, therefore, his
description, much regretting that the specimen is inaccessible to us.

   " *P. sulcata*, BROWN, Ill. Conch. G. B. p. 115, pl. 48, f. 17, 18.

" Oblong-ovate ; hinge-line nearly parallel ; almost equally rounded at both
extremities ; a thickening and slight flexure of the superior margin, extending to
the anterior side ; from the umbonal region emanate two obliquely longitudinal
narrow furrows, and terminate on the basal margin, at which point the shell is
longest ; anterior to the sulci the surface is covered with close-set waved transverse striæ, and the posterior side with irregular broken concentric striæ ; external
surface of a yellowish or pale brown hue ; inside smooth, white ; a curved flattened, tooth-like process under the umbones, a small denticle at the central point
of the umbonal region, and an oblique longitudinal rib, corresponding to the external furrows."—*This shell was found at Dunbar, and is in the collection of David
Falconer, Esq. of Carlowrie.*

II. GASTROCHÆNIDÆ.

WE have seen that several of the mollusks of the preceding family secrete a testaceous tube, which lines their
habitations and protects their siphons. This character was
laid undue stress upon by Lamarck, who united with the
tube-forming species of *Pholadidæ* the genera *Fistulana*,
Clavagella and *Aspergillum*, and constituted thus his
family of *Tubicola*. This family was afterwards reformed
by Deshayes, and restricted to the three last-named Lamarckian genera, which were retained by him as *Aspergillum*, *Clavagella*, and *Gastrochæna*. The tube-making
character is, however, as unessential here as it is in the
Pholadidæ; and, as we shall see presently, the genus *Saxicava*, which is always free, must take rank next after and
along with *Gastrochæna*, whilst *Petricola*, and probably
Venerupis, have strong claims to a similar position.

The animals of this family are oblong or claviform, and
often provided with very long siphons, united almost to
their extremities, where their orifices are ornamented with
cirrhi. The mantle is closed in front, except a small opening for the passage of a very small digitiform foot, very
different from that of the *Pholas* tribe. The margin of the
mantle around this opening is plain. The shell is equivalve and often gaping, with valves often very inequilateral, united by a simple rudiment, or in some cases a
toothed hinge, often variable even in the species of a single
genus. They have no spoon-shaped apophysis under the
beaks, nor accessory plates behind them. A calcareous

tube sometimes protects the valves, and in certain genera
unites with them. These tubes are very regular and curious
in some of the exotic species, especially in those which live
buried in sand. This habit is not merely the living habitually and freely in sand, as the razor fish do, but rather
the treating of it in the manner of a substance bored into,
and the tubes are to be regarded as the linings of the
perforations so made. All the species of the family are
borers, most of them preferring calcareous rock.

GASTROCHÆNA, Spengler.

Shell cuneiform, equivalve, widely gaping, valves very
inequilateral ; hinge simple, linear, toothless, but furnished
with a small spathulate lamina ; ligament external, long ;
muscular impressions small, distant, connected by a slightly-
marked, sinuated, palleal impression.

Tube calcareous, claviform, free or fixed, often incom-
plete.

Animal cuneiform, or when the siphons, which are separate only at their extremities, are extended, elongated ;
orifices fringed ; mantle closed, and thickened when expanded ; with a very small opening for the small, pointed,
curved, finger-shaped foot, which sometimes spins a delicate
byssus. Mouth with two equal, simple lips, and a pair of
sickle-shaped labial tentacula.

This genus is chiefly interesting on account of the curious
tubes which are formed by the several species, often enveloping them in the manner of a flask. M. Deshayes believes* that the animal, at certain periods, can dissolve a
part of its tube, and so enlarge its capacity, observing with

* Mollusques d'Algerie, p. 24.

respect to the allied genus *Clavagella*, in which the valves
of the shell adhere to the tube, that we cannot otherwise
understand their growth, since it becomes necessary that
the wall of the tube should disappear; then it is replaced
by the shell. He describes a peculiar organ connected with
the mantle, which he believes to secrete an acid for the
purpose of destroying a part of the tube, and permitting of
the enlargement of the cavity inhabited by the animal.
This organ he supposes to have alternations of activity and
repose. Such an explanation, however, is too hypothetical
to be admitted without question, and the purpose of the
structure, which the distinguished French malacologist
terms an acid-secreting organ, is by no means clearly made
out. We should rather be inclined to believe that the enlargement of the tube was effected by some process of
absorption and replacement; but for light upon this as
upon many other obscure though highly interesting phenomena in the economy of these mollusks, we must wait for
further researches and careful observations on the habits of
living animals. In the British seas *Gastrochæna* are not so
generally distributed or so plentiful as to afford convenient
opportunities for such observations; but the naturalists
who live on the coasts of the Mediterranean would do well
to direct their attention to the subject.

The genus, though including comparatively few species,
is almost cosmopolitan, having representatives in most seas.
Geological researches shew that it was even less extensively
developed in the pre-adamic epochs than now.

G. MODIOLINA, Lamarck.

Plate II. figs. 5, 6, 7, 8 ; and (animal) Plate F. f. 5.

Mya dubia, PENN. Brit. Zool. ed. 1777, vol. iv. p. 82, pl. 44, f. 19.—DONOV. Br.
    Shells, vol. iii. pl. 108.—Dorset. Catal. p. 27, pl. 1, f. 11.—Linn.
    Trans. vol. viii. p. 33.—TURT. Conch. Diction. p. 104.—WOOD.
    General Conch. p. 102, pl. 25, f. 2, 3.
Chama parva, DA COSTA, Brit. Conch. p. 234.
Mya pholadia, MONT. Test. Brit. vol. i. pp. 28, 559, and Suppl. p. 20.
Pholas faba, PULTENEY, Hutchin's Hist. Dorset, p. 27.
Mytilus ambiguus, DILLW. Recent Shells, vol. i. p. 304.
Gastrochæna modiolina, LAM. Anim. s. Vert. ed. 2, vol. iv. p. 49. — SOW.
    Genera Shells, Gastrochæna, f. 1, 2; Conch. Manual,
    f. 52.—REEVE, Conch. System, pl. 20, f. 1, 2.—
    HANL. Recent Shells, p. 10.—Brit. Marine Conch.
    p. 33.
    „   *pholadia*, TURT. Dithyra Brit, p. 18, pl. 2, f. 8, 9.—Magazine of
        Nat. Hist. vol. vi. p. 404, f. 52. — BROWN, Ill.
        Conch. G. B. p. 116, pl. 48, f. 13, 14.
    „   *hians*, FLEM. Brit. Anim. p. 458.
    „   *dubia*, DESH. Traité Elem. Conch. pl. 2, f. 4, 5.—PHILIPPI, in
        Wiegman Archiv. Natur. 1845, pl. 7, f. 1.

The paucity of known species belonging to the genus
Gastrochæna, gives an interest, independent of peculiarities
of habitat and infrequency of occurrence, to the only one
inhabiting our British seas. This is obliquely oval-oblong,
in shape, cuneiform in convexity, being ventricose in front,
and compressed behind, rather thin and fragile, and of a
somewhat opaque white. The surface, which in living
examples is very slightly glossy, is merely marked with fine
concentric wrinkles, which are chiefly evident in front and
below. The large hiatus, which is fig-shaped, being
rounded in front, and produced and tapering behind to an
acuminated point, occupies nearly the entire ventral margin ; the shell is strictly closed at its posterior termination.
The sides are excessively unequal, but the umbones which
are decidedly prominent and curving forward, are not

quite terminal, as there exists a very short front dorsal edge, about equal to one-sixth of the hinder dorsal line as measured from the beaks to the extreme termination of the shell. The edges of this short dorsal line, which is scarcely convex and but very slightly declining, are reflected, and in consequence the small surrounding region appears somewhat excavated. The hinder dorsal margin, which for a considerable distance is straightish and not at all sloping but rather ascending, finally forming one line with the posterior, sweeps downward with a convex curve, attenuating the rounded extremity of the hinder side. The ventral margin, just by its anterior termination, is rounded, and very obliquely ascends in a scarcely convex line towards the front dorsal, by its juncture with which the anterior end is rather sharply angulated. The ligament is rufous, rather long, and slightly prominent: there is not the slightest indication of an umbonal ridge. The hinge consists of a not peculiarly small, somewhat spoon-shaped lamina, which projects inwards at some little distance from the anterior extremity.

The valves rarely exceed three quarters of an inch in length, and about half that measurement in breadth.

The valves are entirely concealed in a bottle-shaped sheath, of which the bulb is usually an excavation lined with shelly matter, and the neck which projects from the imbedded mass, a bipartite tube, resembling two cylinders laterally fastened together with their touching edges filed away. Authors do not appear to have universally noticed the existence of this envelope, which, however curious in its structure, is certainly a generic and not a specific characteristic, since we possess other *Gastrochæna* of exotic origin, which, although perfectly distinct in the form and character of their valves, have their protecting cells of precisely similar architecture. On the subject of these cases, there may be found an interesting paper in the sixth volume of the "Magazine of Natural History," written by Mr. Lukis, a gentleman from whose cabinet, Dr. Turton derived a considerable portion of his information upon the shells of the Channel Islands. From that paper we extract the following sentences, which are equally applicable to the case we have figured (from Ireland,) as to the Guernsey individuals, from which the somewhat rude wood-cuts referred to in the text were sketched: "In a country destitute of limestone or soft rock, these animals are indebted to other means for supplying them with a habitation. The *G. pholadia* accommodates itself to crevices, not the interior of rocks, where it forms its residence by covering its shell as here exhibited. It is found among madrepores and shelly fragments, thrown up with alluvial sand and rubbish on the sides of rocks. The cases here shewn are composed of broken shells and gravel, mixed with fragments of felspar, hornblende, and sand, (these latter substances are not present in our own examples,) strongly agglutinated together. The inside is smooth, and consists of thin layers of the calcareous secretion applied by the animal in the formation of this chamber, which somewhat resembles a flask; the lengthened neck through which the animal passes the double tube, is formed of concentric layers of the same substance, preserving to a certain depth, the same figure as at the summit of it."

The animal of *Gastrochæna modiolina* was first observed and figured by Delle Chiaje. It has recently attracted the attention of Philippi and of Deshayes, both of whom have published figures and accounts of its structure, external and internal. On the British shores it has been carefully examined by Mr. Clark. The body is claviform, broad

anteriorly, tapering posteriorly, the siphonal tube capable
of considerable extension. The mantle is entirely closed,
with the exception of a small aperture in front, for the
passage of the small finger-shaped pointed foot, which has
a byssal groove at its base. That part of the mantle which
is exposed is strong and thick. " Its inner surface," writes
Mr. Clark, " is fortified by a muscular substance of a pale
green colour, disposed in folds and rugosities." This is
probably the same body which M. Deshayes regards as an
acid-secreting organ. The siphonal tubes are capable of
being either almost withdrawn into the shell or protruded
to three times its length. They are united almost quite
to their extremities. Both the orifices are surrounded by
cirrhi. These, according to Philippi, are short and red,
and appear to spring from the margin of the opening in the
lower siphon, but are removed to some distance from it in
the upper.* Mr. Clark describes the branchiæ as of a pale
brown colour; they run longitudinally, and nearly parallel
to each other, and are of small depth, the upper one less
than the lower. On each side of the mouth is a pair of
short finely-pectinated tentacula, nearly equal in length.
The body of the animal is of a flaky white hue ; the siphons
reddish brown, more deeply coloured at their extremities.

With regard to its locality, we look upon Torbay as the
most prolific seat of it upon the English coast, and Birterbuy Bay, in Connemara, as the most populous of its Irish
habitats. From the former, at the depth of ten fathoms,
we have taken masses of limestone well honeycombed by
its excavations, and tenanted by several individuals, both
living and dead ; from the latter came numerous examples,
dredged by Dr. Farren and Mr. Barlee, of that interesting
variety with the more elaborate case, of which a repre-

* Philippi, in Wiegman's Archiv. 1845, pl. 187, p. 7, f. 14.

sentation appears among our engravings (pl. ii. fig. 8). It
is not, however, to be regarded as common, but few
localities yielding it in any abundance; and the frequent
accidental destruction of its tender valves, during the process of disinterring it, renders it of course a less frequent
sojourner in the cabinets of the collector. Among other
localities we may enumerate, Exmouth (Clark); off Weymouth, alive (M'Andrew); Guernsey, in thick valves of
dead oysters (Hanley); South Isles of Arran, off Galway
Bay, and Youghal, County Cork (R. Ball). (W. T. Ann.
N. H. vol. xiii. p. 434.)

It is a common inhabitant of the Lusitanian and Mediterranean, as well as of a great part of the Celtic regions of
the European seas, and occurs fossil in the newer pleistocene
beds of Italy. Philippi, however, considers the Mediterranean form a distinct species, and describes it under the
name of *Poliana*.* It was an inhabitant of the British
seas during the epochs of the coralline and red crags, but
retired for a time, when glacial conditions prevailed.

SAXICAVA, Fleuriau de Bellevue.

Shell oblong or rhomboidal, equivalve, more or less inequilateral and gaping: beaks prominent: hinge furnished
with cardinal teeth in some stages of its growth, never with
lateral: ligament external, more or less projecting: muscular impressions strong, distant, connected by a sinuated
pallial impression. No enveloping tube.

Animal oblong or claviform: mantle closed in front,
except a very small opening for the passage of a digitiform
foot, which is furnished with a byssal groove: siphons
united nearly to the extremities: branchial and anal orifices
large, margined with a fringe of (simple) cirrhi.

* Wiegmann's Archiv. 1845, p. 186.

When we compare the animal of *Saxicava* with that of *Gastrochæna*, we are at once struck with the near resemblance and evident affinity of the two genera, so near, indeed, that it is difficult to draw a well-marked line between them. We find the same structure of mantle, the same form of foot, and very similar siphons in each.   The shells are also very similar, and some of the varieties of *Saxicava rugosa* are so like in every respect to *Gastrochæna*, that, did we not know their history, it would be difficult, if not impossible, to pronounce on their generic position.   But when we attend to the changes which the former shell presents in the course of its growth, and compare the several congeneric species at different ages, we recognise a marked source of distinction, which, combined with the habit in *Saxicava* of never forming a tube, whilst *Gastrochæna* always, if possible, makes one, warrants the separation of the two genera. Those naturalists who have either not been acquainted with, or have not understood the animal of *Saxicava* have been extremely puzzled as to its true position, whilst the variable characters of the hinges of our European species have increased the difficulty and led to the institution of several spurious genera. The generic terms *Byssomya*, *Hiatella*, *Rhomboides*, *Biapholius*, and *Agina*, have not been proposed as mere synonyms of *Saxicava*, but as so many allied genera of equal rank, all constituted out of the typical species of the genus; whilst *Mya*, *Solen*, *Donax*, *Mytilus*, and *Anatina*, have at various times, and some simultaneously, numbered among their spurious adherents varieties of the same Protean shell.   Its true position has been equally misunderstood, its close affinity with *Gastrochæna* having rarely been recognised: more usually it has been placed between *Solen* and *Mya*, a false position assigned to it even by Cuvier. This is the more remarkable, seeing that

Otto Frederic Müller had long ago correctly delineated its animal.

The *Saxicavæ* are borers, although the habit of boring does not seem necessary to their existence, since we find them very commonly free. If there be a crevice, however, in rock, shell, coral, or seaweed, into which they can thrust themselves, they do so; and if near a limestone rock perforate it, and form crypts in which they live. Mr. Osler states that, when young they are very active animals, and soon commence to perforate. Both that gentleman and Mr. Garner have noticed that their excavations are not round, nor the sides smoothed off like those of the holes made by *Pholas*. As for us, we only know of their boring into calcareous rocks, but Mr. Clark has noticed an instance of their perforating triassic sandstone at Exmouth. Wherever we have a sea-coast of mountain limestone, the surface of the rocks is almost invariably found riddled by *Saxicava*. The whole front of the Plymouth breakwater has been attacked by it, and much alarm for its safety excited. Mr. Couch observes that the *Saxicava* never bores deeper than six inches, and that, consequently, unless a new surface be exposed by the destruction of the perforated part, there is not much danger. Owing, however, to the thinness of the partitions, which often are the only separations between the crypts of these mollusks, there is a great probability of the action of the sea rapidly forming new surfaces in such cases. How they bore has been as much discussed as the question how *Pholas* bores. The general opinion has been, that *Saxicava* bores by means of an acid secretion; an opinion held by many who will not admit the probability of such an agent being used by the *Pholadidæ*. Mr. Osler, though inclined to such a view, could detect no acid, nor, for reasons previously stated, is it likely. Mr. Hancock, as

we have seen when treating of *Pholas*, expressly asserts
that the *Saxicava* bore by rasping, effected by means of
siliceous particles contained in the anterior part of the
mantle. Mr. Couch entertains a similar view. We have
not been able to satisfy ourselves of the presence of such
particles, though inclined to regard such a view with favour,
as in this case the surface of the shell does not seem devised
for rasping as is that of the shells of the last tribe.

Great interest attaches to the British species of this
genus in a geological point of view; one, if not both of
them, owing a wide distribution, in the present epoch, to
events which occurred in pre-adamite ages. The researches
of geologists have made known to us, that, previous to the
present state of things, within the area of our islands, there
existed climatal conditions much more severe than those
which now prevail,—that, in fact, the climate of Greenland, and the fauna and flora of the regions in which that
climate is now met with, then extended over the greater
part of Europe and Northern Asia, having its southern
bounds somewhere in a line with the southernmost part of
the British Islands as they are now constituted. At that
time, however, the greater part of our country was under
water, and represented by ridges of land and small islands,
rising in the midst of an icy sea. During this chilly epoch
the *Saxicava* extended their range almost round the whole
of the northern hemisphere, and, when the bed of the
glacial ocean was upheaved,—as geological research proves
to have been the case, previous to the present arrangements
of our region, and preparatory to a more genial assemblage of conditions,—the shells of these mollusks were preserved in the raised sea-beds, and are found in them now,
even at elevations of several hundred feet about the level of
the present sea. Thus we find them in Sweden, where

their inland position attracted the attention of Linnæus,
whose all-inquiring mind was deeply impressed with this
curious, and, in his time, inexplicable phenomenon;* in
Norway, where the importance of the fact was fully recognised by the great German geologist, Baron Von Buch; in
Canada, whence we have seen specimens brought home by
Mr. Lyell; in distant and inland regions of Russia, where
the glacial beds were traced by Sir Roderic Murchison and
M. de Verneuil; and at home, where numerous observers
have noted the inland occurrence of the *Saxicava*—above
all, Mr. Smith of Jordanhill, who, bringing the knowledge
of the conchologist, and the discrimination of the field-
naturalist, to bear upon these critical investigations, was
the first to shew that these shells alone, from peculiarities
of variation and locality, indicated of themselves that the
conditions under which they lived were dissimilar from
those now regulating the distribution of animals in our
seas.   We could scarcely cite a more triumphant instance
of the necessity of a minute study of the character and
habits of our native shells to the geologist who seeks to in-
terpret the complicated phenomena of the changes which
preceded the present epoch; whilst, on the other hand, he
may fairly appeal to the naturalist equally to recognise the
services rendered, in return, by geological research; for
assuredly it is as vain to attempt to explain the distribution of existing beings on the surface of the globe, without
the aid of geological science, as it is to work out its physical geography without a careful study of the changes the
earth has undergone in time.

* Linnæus, West-Gotha Resa. p. 198.

1. S. ARCTICA, Linnæus.

Anterior extremity attenuated and cuneiform, with a lunule-like excavation in front of the prominent beaks; posterior extremity always the broader; ligamental edge almost always incurved; linear ridges spinous except in very aged individuals; hinge toothed.

Plate VI. figures 4, 5, 6.

Mya arctica, LINN. Syst. Nat. p. 1113.—O. FABR. Fauna Grœnl. p. 407.—TURT. Conch. Diction. p. 104.—WOOD, General Conch. p. 95.
Solen minutus, LINN. Syst. Nat. p. 1114.—MONT. Test. Brit. p. 53, pl. 1, f. 4.—SPENGL. Skrivt. Naturh. Selskab. vol. iii. part 2, p. 113.—Linn. Trans. vol. viii. p. 47.—TURT. Conch. Diction. p. 161.—CHEMN. Conch. Cab. vol. vi. p. 67, pl. 6, f. 51, 52.—WOOD, General Conch. p. 139, pl. 34, f. 5, 6.—DILLW. Recent Shells, vol. i. p. 69.—LAM. Anim. s. Vert. ed. 2, vol. vi. p. 57. — Index Testaceol. pl. 3, f. 33.
Donax rhomboides, POLI, Test. Sicil. pl. 15, f. 12, 15.
Mytilus præcinus, MONT. Test. Brit. p. 165.—Linn. Trans. vol. viii. p. 112.—DILLW. Recent Shells, p. 305.
Hiatella arctica, LAM. Anim. s. Vert. ed. 2, vol. vi. p. 443.—FLEM. Brit. Anim. p. 461.—Brit. Marine Conch. p. 59.—BOWDICH, Conchology, Biv. f. 40.—CROUCH, Introd. Conch. pl. 8, f. 6.—HANL. Recent Shells, p. 150.—CUVIER, R. Anim. (ed. Croch.) pl. 110, f. 1.
Anatina Arctica, TURT. Dithyra Brit. p. 49, pl. 4, f. 7, 8.—Brit. Mar. Conch. p. 42.
Agina purpurea, TURT. Dithyra Brit. p. 54, pl. 4, f. 9.—Brit. Marine Conch. p. 60.
Solen purpureus, FLEM. Brit. Anim. p. 459.
Saxicava rhomboides, DESH. in Lam. ed. 2, vol. vi. p. 153.
Saxicava arctica, DESH. Elem. Conch. pl. 12, f. 8, 9.—PHIL. Moll. Sicil. vol. i. p. 20, pl. 3, f. 5, and vol. ii. p. 19.—MACGILL. Moll. Aber. p. 285.—LOVEN, Ind. Moll. Sueciæ, p. 40.
Hiatella minuta, TURT. Dithyra Brit. p. 24, pl. 2, f. 12.—BROWN, Ill. Conch. G. B. p. 103, pl. 47. f. 1, 16.
Saxicava purpurea, BROWN, Ill. Conch. G. B. pl. 42, f. 30, 31.
Saxicava rubra, DESH. Exp. Algérie, Moll. pl. 66, f. 18, 19 (shell and animal).
Hiatella, CHEMU, Traité Element. p. 58, f. 206.

Nothing but the most searching scrutiny will distinguish this closely allied *Saxicava* from its congener *rugosa*, the young of which is often confused in cabinets with that of this species, owing to the erroneous but current belief that *arctica* is distinguished from *rugosa* by being armed with spinous scales. This character, however, is shared, although less strongly so, by the young of the latter, and is completely lost in the aged examples of either species. Neither will the presence of teeth upon the hinge margin of *arctica* suffice for its ready separation, even though conjoined with the previously mentioned character, since the young *rugosa* have likewise teeth, although most feebly developed. It is requisite, then, to discover some permanent distinctive characteristic, which may assist the eye in the determination of the two species, that organ frequently enabling the collecting naturalist to ascertain the aggregate value of specific differences, which neither his tongue nor his pen can analytically define. This method, however allowable to collectors, is most reprehensible in authors, too many of whom have indolently preferred trusting the establishment of their discoveries to the skilful pencil of the artist, rather than themselves laboriously pourtray with their pen those several features, from the combination of which specific identity is constituted; thus entailing upon every author of a cyclopædia of species the necessity of personally examining each individual one, a labour which, however possible and desirable in a local or partial Fauna, must, in a general descriptive catalogue, be practically unattainable.

The tangible mark of distinction between *arctica* and *rugosa* consists in the constant presence of an excavated lunule in front of the beaks, which are moreover acute, leaning forward, and, when viewed in front, sufficiently prominent. The anterior extremity is more or less cuneiform, and is always attenuated; whereas in *rugosa* that portion is usually rounded and frequently broad: in that shell, likewise, the downward inclination of the front dorsal margin is almost invariably arcuated or convex, whilst in the present species it is oblique, and for a considerable distance incurved, only becoming convex near its ventral termination, which consequently is its most projecting part, the chief prominence in *rugosa* being, on the contrary, usually situated nearer the dorsal side.

The form is rhomboidal, with the length double or triple the breadth of the shell, the former chiefly in the adult, the latter frequently in the younger or immature individuals. The dorsal and ventral margins are more or less subparallel, and both exhibit a decided tendency to incurvation, whenever permitted by the circumstances of growth to assume an unrestricted outline. The valves are tolerably strong (solid in aged specimens, which stage of growth seems by no means common in collections), but rather fragile in the young, opaquely white under a lighter or darker brownish yellow epidermis, coarsely wrinkled concentrically, and otherwise only marked with two widely diverging elevated lines which run from the beaks posteriorward, one diagonally to the ventral side of the hinder extremity, the other adjacent to (but not parallel with) the posterior dorsal margin. These lines are armed (except in aged examples, where even the upper line itself is almost obsolete, and the lower resembles an umbonal ridge,) with rather strong and moderately sized scaly prickles, the narrow triangular area between which series is usually slightly concave. The front side is very short, occupying less more frequently than beyond one quarter of the entire length; the hinder side is greatly produced, and abruptly (not obliquely) subtruncated and bluntly biangulated at its termination, which does not taper off as in the typical *rugosa*, but is the broader of the two extremities. The

Ligament is small, sunken, and of a yellowish brown; the beaks sharply defined, acute, rather prominent, and leaning forward; having in front of them a deeply impressed, more or less ovate lunule. The interior is of a pure glossy white (sometimes subnacreous beneath the umbones), the margin entire, and the hinge, when not entirely obliterated with age (in which case the margin itself displays a considerable callosity), consisting of a single strong acute primary tooth in the right valve, interlocking between a rather smaller and a perfectly rudimentary one in the left valve. This latter minute denticle is sometimes present, but more usually absent, in both valves. The convexity of the valves sometimes amounts to ventricosity, more ordinarily they are but moderately convex, but there is always an appearance of compression upon the umbonal region, owing to the constant concavity of that portion of the surface which precedes the diagonal elevation.

The size of our British specimens is greatly inferior to that of foreign examples, and almost always with us is less than in the succeeding species, the average of individuals not exceeding two-thirds of an inch in length, and two-fifths of an inch, at most, in breadth.

The animal of this species is oblong or cylindrical, its mantle closed in front except a small orifice for the passage of the foot, which is very small and conical, and furnished with a byssal groove. The siphonal tubes are short, nearly equal, and united very nearly to their extremities, which are each furnished with about ten or twelve cirrhi. The body and foot are usually white or yellowish, the tubes orange, rose-colour, or brownish, varying much in intensity of colour.

The *Hiatella arctica*, though distributed throughout the British seas, is far more abundant in the north than in the south; the reverse of which is the case with the next species. It is found sometimes imbedded in stones or old shells, as oysters; sometimes and very commonly attached by a slight byssus to corallines, especially *Sertulariæ* and *Antennulariæ*, also in the meshes of intertwining *Serpulæ*, especially in the complicated interlacements of the curious *Filopora filograna*, and in the interstices of marine plants, such as the coral-like *Nullipore* and the roots of *Laminaria digitata*. It ranges from low water mark to very great depths, and appears to prefer gravelly ground. Though found almost every where on our coasts, when conditions are favourable, and consequently enumerated in all our local Faunas, a few localities may be specified in illustration of its habits and range. In the south of England it occurs boring into hard limestone at Plymouth (Montagu), and red sandstone at Exmouth (Clark); free in twenty fathoms water off the Land's End (R. M'Andrew and E. F.); in seven fathoms, stony ground, Weymouth (M'Andrew); Swansea (Jeffreys); Anglesea (Eyton); in twenty-five fathoms, eight miles from land, north of Anglesea (M'Andrew); on shell bank, twenty fathoms, north of the Isle of Man, and twelve fathoms south (E. F.). Dead valves in from one hundred and ten to one hundred and forty fathoms, off the Mull of Galloway (Capt. Beechey, R.N.); all round Ireland (Thompson); everywhere in the Hebrides; in fifty fathoms, five miles from land, off Cape Wrath (M'Andrew); in crevices of stones, fifty fathoms on the high banks, and alive in eighty fathoms off the west coast of Zetland (M'Andrew and E. F.); dead valves in one hundred fathoms, twenty-five miles from land off the east coast of Zetland (M'Andrew). This species ranges throughout the boreal and arctic provinces of the North Atlantic. It is found rarely and of small size in the Mediterranean.

S. RUGOSA, Linnæus.

Anterior extremity usually broad and rounded, no decided lunule-like excavation in front of the beaks ; posterior extremity frequently the narrower, ligamental edge rarely much incurved, more often convex ; linear ridges only spinous in the young shell ; hinge margin of the mature shell edentulous.

Plate VI. figures 7, 8, and (Animal) Plate F. fig. 6.

Mytilus rugosus, PENN. Brit. Zool. ed. 1, vol. iv. p. 110, p. 62, f. 72.—PULTENEY, Hutchins Dorset, p. 37.—MONT. Test. Brit. p. 164.—DONOV. Brit. Shells, vol. iv. p. 141,—Linn. Trans. vol. viii. p. 105.— Dorset Catalogue, p. 39, pl. 13, f. 5.—TURT. Conch. Diction. p. 113.—DILLW. Recent Shells, vol. i. p. 304.—Index Testacoolog. pl. 12. Mytil. f. 9.

Mytilus pholadis, LINN. Mantissa? p. 548.—MULLER, Zool. Danica, pl. 87, f. 1, 2, 3.

Mya byssifera, O. FABRIC. Fauna Greenland. p. 408.

Saxicava rugosa, LAM. Anim. s. Vert. ed. 2, vol. vi. p. 152.—TURT. Dithyra Brit. p. 20, pl. 2, f.10.—MACGILLIV. Moll. Aberd. p. 285.— BROWN, Illust. Conch. G. B. p. 103, pl. 47, f. 14, 16.— CROUCH, Introd. Conch. pl. 5. f. 3. — SOWERBY, Genera Shells, Saxicava, f. 2, 3, 4.—REEVE, Conch. Icon. vol. i. pl. 50, f. 2, 3, 4.—HANL. Recent Shells, p. 50.

Saxicava Gallicana, LAM. Anim. s. Vert. ed. 2, vol. vi. p. 152.—DELES. Rec. Coq. pl. 4, f. 9.—DESH. Elem. Conch. pl. 12, f. 1, 2, 3.— HANL. Recent Shells, suppl. pl. 9, f. 5.

Saxicava pholadis, LAM. Anim. s. Vert. ed. 2, vol. 6, p. 152.—TURT. Dithyra Brit. p. 21, pl. 2, f. 11.—HANL. Recent Shells, p. 50.

Saxicava distorta, GOULD, Invert. Massach. p. 61, f. 40.

Byssomya pholadis, BOWDICH, Bivalves, f. 43.

Hiatella oblonga, (young) TURT. Dithyra Brit. p. 25, pl. 2, f. 13.

Hiatella rugosa, FLEM. Brit. Anim. p. 461.—Brit. Marine Conch. p. 58.

Saxicava ridée, CHENU, Traité Elem. p. 58, f. 197, 198.

There scarcely exists a molluscous animal, whose testaceous covering is more affected by circumstances of habitation, than this ancient and widely extended species. Subject to almost every distortion of shape, it has received several appellations. The valves, when uninterruptedly developed, are generally of an oval-oblong shape ; they are solid, ventricose, opaque, white, covered with a dull or

scarcely at all glossy, paler or darker, brownish yellow
epidermis, beneath which the surface is utterly devoid of
lustre, and very coarsely wrinkled in a concentric direction.
From the beaks to either side of the posterior extremity, runs
a more or less obsolete elevated line, which is prickled with
small and rather elongated vaulted scales, but only entirely
so in the very young, and partially so (in the vicinity of
the beaks) in the middle-aged specimens, the full grown aged
examples rarely presenting the slightest trace of their previous existence. Both the beaks, which are simply incurved,
and the umbones, are very far from prominent, and exhibit
no trace of a lunule in front of them, the lips of the anterior
dorsal edge more frequently on the contrary protruding
outwards.   The front side is invariably much shorter than
the hinder one, which is at the least twice and a half its
length, but its proportion to the entire area is generally
much greater than in *arctica*, owing to the anterior extremity being typically round and never sharply cuneiform,
the curve of the anterior outline sweeping outwards, not
bending inwards.   The ventral edge is generally inclined
to retusion a little before the middle, and runs nearly
parallel to the hinder dorsal, which latter, however retuse
it may be near the beaks, always becomes convex before
its termination.   The hinder extremity is more or less obtusely subbiangulated, but never so distinctly and sharply
as in *arctica*; moreover, it is always, when freely developed, disposed to taper a little just before its termination,
and in one narrow variety which has its posterior side
greatly produced, and its anterior one correspondingly
abbreviated, this attenuation is most distinctly visible.
The ligament is brown, (yellowish or ashy brown in the
young,) and in typical examples is prominent and forms
one piece with the epidermis, but these characters are rarely

observable, as the majority of specimens are rubbed and distorted.

The hinge margin is destitute of any teeth, and is greatly thickened in the more aged shells; the very immature ones have usually, however, two or three rudimental primary teeth, but these, in most of our English specimens are very minute and caducous. The palleal scar is situated very high up, not easily discernible and flexuous. Examples are rarely obtained which exceed an inch in length, and about half an inch in breadth; the proportions are, however, very variable, as the longer shells are often the least wide ones.

The animal is oblong, somewhat claviform, or, when the siphons are contracted, oval. The mantle is completely closed, except a small round orifice in the centre of the widest part (that occupying the gape of the shell) through which it can protrude a linear, linguiform, triangular pointed foot, having a byssal groove at its base. This foot is sometimes entirely withdrawn, sometimes only protruded as far as the point, and occasionally thrust out to a considerable distance.   Mr. Clark has observed a substance lining the mantle, similar to that noticed in *Gastrochæna*, but white. That part of the front of the mantle, where the edges of the valves approach, is brownish and ligamentous.   Immediately beyond it is the base of the united siphons, which are separated only at their extremities, which are nearly equally, but not quite, on a level. The margins of the branchial and anal orifices are minutely cirrhated; the cirrhi appear to be simple.   There are about thirty around each. The whole animal is more or less tinged with yellow, which colour is palest in the central part of the mantle. The anterior extremity, and the siphons, are of an orange hue, often very bright and intense.

On the southern coasts this species may be regarded as a very common and abundant shell ; in the north it is not so plentiful. It is found near low-water mark upon the shores of Kent and Sussex, buried in large masses of chalk (S. H.), and is dredged as well as found upon the beach in detached portions of limestone rocks at Torquay, Weymouth, and other parts of Devonshire and Dorset (S. H.) : in the west bay of Portland it is dredged alive in twenty fathoms water (R. M'Andrew and E. F.) ; common at Scarborough (Bean) ; Swansea (Jeffreys) ; around the Irish Coast (Thompson). In twenty fathoms water off the Isle of Man (E. F.) ; Zetland, Ullapool, Loch Carron, and other localities on the west of Scotland (Jeffreys and Barlee) ; Lerwick, in seven fathoms, among *Laminariæ* (M'Andrew) ; Frith of Forth, in seven fathoms (E. F.). In local lists, this and the last species are so often mentioned under the same name, that it is difficult to discriminate their several localities.

It ranges throughout the Boreal and Celtic regions of the North Atlantic. Mr. M'Andrew has dredged it on the north coast of Spain. It is more abundant as a pleistocene fossil than the last species.

Some curious little shells, of which a few pair were dredged by Mr. Hanley, not far from the pier at Ryde, in the Isle of Wight, and an odd valve or two were procured by Mr. Jeffreys in the Island of Skye, have been figured, (Plate VI. figs. 1, 2, 3,) but not designated by us, under the supposition that, however different in aspect, they may prove to be merely the young of the last species. Their shape is ovate-oblong, but more rounded above than below ; the texture is thin and fragile, but not transparent, and the

valves are moderately convex, but compressed subcentrally.
Externally the colour is dirty-whitish, internally of a very
slightly nacreous porcelain white. The outer surface is nearly
smooth, but minutely and irregularly wrinkled concentrically at the narrower extremity, and in some specimens appears delicately and distantly sublaminated, through a kind
of imbricated elevation of the former stages of growth. This
latter feature can, however, be only regarded as an accidental
and not a permanent characteristic. The ventral margin is
nearly straight, with sometimes a slight retusion towards
the front ; the anterior dorsal edge slopes but very moderately, and almost in a straight line; the hinder dorsal line is
elevated above the level of the beaks, ascending from them
with a very trifling slope, in nearly a rectilinear or scarcely
convex course, and uniting near its close with the posterior
margin in a bold and arcuated outward sweep to the lower
corner of the hinder extremity. The hinder side is thus
dilated, and contains nearly quadruple the area of that of
the anterior: this latter, which is not more than half as
long as the posterior, is narrow, attenuated, and obtusely
rounded at its commencement. The umbonal ridge is remarkably developed, running very obliquely and most
prominently, so as to cut off a large posterior convex space.
Although much elevated, it is not acute, and does not exhibit
the slightest trace of any aculeation. Before it, a somewhat
triangular surface, occupying about the same space as that
succeeding it, is depressed below the level of the remainder
of the shell. The beaks are distinct, but small, and apparently do not incline to either side ; the umbones appear
depressed when examined from the posterior side; but are
much raised above the level of the front dorsal margin.
There is no vestige of a lunule, and the ligament is almost
minute, of an ashy hue, and scarcely projecting. No teeth

can be perceived with a lens of the highest power ; there is, however, a distinct callus beneath the ligament.

PETRICOLA, LAMARCK.

Shell ovate or subtrigonal, ventricose, equivalve, inequilateral, gaping : hinge with two cardinal teeth in each valve, or two in one, and one in the other valve. Ligament external short. Pallial impression, with an ample and rounded sinus.

Animal oval. Mantle closed in front except a small opening for a lanceolate and pointed foot. Siphons united for nearly half their lengths; their orifices fringed with a double series of cirrhi, the longer ones pinnated on one side.

Notwithstanding that the *Petricolæ*, from the comparatively impregnable nature of the fortifications in which they entrench themselves, are justly esteemed among the less frequent sojourners in our cabinets, the genus has a very wide distribution, pervading the temperate and southern parts of Europe, the Red Sea, the islands of the S. Pacific, Australia, and the shores of South-Western and North America.

P. LITHOPHAGA, Retzius.

Plate VI. figs. 9, 10, and (animal) Plate G. f. 1.

Venus lithophaga ,RETZIUS, Trans. Turin. 1786.

(*Unnamed.*)   POLI, Test. Sicil. vol. i. pl. 7, f. 14, 15.

Mya decussata, MONT. Test. Brit. Suppl. p. 20, pl. 28. f. 1.—TURT. Conch.
              Diction. p. 102.—FLEM. Brit. Anim. p. 466.—Brit. Marine
              Conch. p. 41.—WOOD, General Conch. p. 99.—DILLW. Recent Shells, vol. i. p. 46.—Index Test. pl. 2, Mya, f. 17.

Petricola striata, LAM. Anim. a. Vert. ed. 2, vol. vi. p. 158.—DELES. Rec.
              Coquil. pl. 4, f. 11.—HANL. Recent Shells. p. 52, suppl. pl.
              11, f. 44.

Petricola costellata,   LAM. Anim. s. Vert. ed. 2, vol. vi. p. 158.—DELES. Rec.
Coquil. pl. 4, f. 12.—HANL. Recent Shells, p. 52, suppl.
pl. 11, f. 45.

"   *roccellaria*,   LAM. Anim. s. Vert. ed. 2, vol. vi. p. 158.—DESH. Elem.
Conch. pl. 12, f. 7.—DELES. Rec. Coquil. pl. 4, f. 13.—
HANL. Recent Shells, p. 52, suppl. pl. 11, f. 46.

"   *ruperella*,   LAM. Anim. s. Vert. ed. 2, vol. vi. p. 159.—DELES. Rec.
Coquil. pl. 4, f. 14.—HANL. Recent Shells, p. 52, suppl.
pl. 11, f. 47.

Vénérupe pétricola,   BLAINV. Man. Malac. pl. 76, f. 2.

Petricola lithophaga,   PHILIPPI, Moll. Sicil. vol. i. p. 21, pl. 3, f. 6, and vol. ii. p.
20.—PHIL. in Wiegmann Archiv. Naturg., 1845, p. 188,
p. 7, f. 11 to 14 (animal). — Exped. Scient. Algérie,
Moll. pl. 66, f. 5 to 9 (shell), and pl. 67 (anatomy).

Sphænia decussata,   TURT. Dithyra, Brit. p. 38.—BROWN, Illust. Conch. G. B.
p. 104, pl. 45, f. 3.

Pétricole costellée,   CHENU, Traité Elem. p. 200, f. 59.

The shape of this Petricola varies from obovate to
elongated ovate, and the solidity from rather thin to
moderately strong. It is typically very inequilateral, but
the inequality of its sides is often rendered less observable
by the impeded development of the hinder one: this
character, however, is almost always observable by noting
the direction of the earlier lines of increase. The valves
are ventricose, and sometimes even tumid in front, the
hinder portion being always less convex. They are of a
dull lustreless white, with, in one (the largest) specimen,
an internal purplish stain at the posterior extremity. The
surface is roughened by numerous radiating elevated lines,
which, in the only two British examples we have seen, become narrow ribs posteriorly; and gradually diminish in
breadth, but with an increasing proximity to each other,
towards the anterior extremity, before arriving at which,
they become obsolete or very nearly so. A kind of decussation is produced from these lines being traversed by
minute concentric wrinkles and striæ of increase, but in
ordinary (Mediterranean) specimens this is by no means

a striking characteristic. A narrow strip near the hinder
dorsal edge is often free from the radiation, and here the
concentric wrinkles are usually the most evident. The
ventral edge is much arcuated, ascending at both extremities, but more suddenly so anteriorly. · The front dorsal
edge is elongated, and not greatly declining, its outline
has some disposition to convexity after quitting the
ligament which appears to be dark, of moderate size, and
rather prominent, but an examination of more specimens is
required before this can be asserted with certainty. The
(strictly limited) front dorsal edge is extremely short, and
scarcely sloping, but it almost forms one sweep with the
arcuated anterior margin. The front side of the shell is
broad and very short; its extremity is rounded, but not
symmetrically so, owing to the upper portion not curving
equally with the lower. The produced posterior side becomes attenuated towards its extremity, which is more
or less bluntly rounded. In the specimen figured this
is more attenuated and elongated than is usual in the
species, and the elevated radiating lines are coarser than in
our Mediterranean examples. The umbones are tumid
and rather prominent, and the beaks are small, much
inflected, and scarcely leaning to either side. There is
neither lunule nor umbonal ridge. The hinge consists of
two primary teeth in each valve, which are small, narrow,
much elevated, projecting inward, and very caducous:
the larger of these two, which is the anterior in the
left, and the posterior in the right valve, is deeply cloven
at its apex, where it is broader than at its base, which
sulcus is continued below, even to the hinge margin; the
smaller tooth is less raised, simple, narrow, and more
oblique. The inner margin is not crenated; the palleal
sinus is ample and rounded.

We have never had an opportunity of observing the animal of this interesting shell in the living state. Philippi has been more fortunate, and we quote his account of it,[*] and copy the figure appended : " The animal has a mantle which is entirely closed, with the exception of a small aperture in front for the passage of the foot. Posteriorly it is extended into two siphons united for nearly half their length. When I observed the animal alive the free parts alone projected from the shell, and scarcely extended to a third of its length. They were brown towards the apertures, which were surrounded by extremely delicate cirrhi. Between them the margin of each orifice is striped or puckered, and nearer the interior are other comb-like cirrhi, ciliated on one side. The foot, which extends itself about two lines, is thin and sharply pointed. I think it has a byssus." Deshayes has given some figures illustrative of its anatomy in his great work on the Mollusca of Algeria.

The *Mya decussata* of Montagu, owing to the imperfect dentition of the original specimen, and its inadequate representation in the " Testacea Britannica," has long been regarded as a lost species, and even its generic appellation has been at most hypothetical. The redis- covery of two specimens, each by a different individual, have enabled us to ascertain its identity with a *petricola*, which, although abundant on the opposite coast of France, has rarely been met with upon our own shores. The larger of the examples alluded to was taken by Mr. J. S. Miller, at Bristol, in clay, the other, which is above the average size of the Mediterranean ones, two-thirds of an inch long, and not quite half an inch at the broadest part, rewarded the researches of Mr. Hum-

* Wiegmann's Archiv. 1845, p. 168.

phreys in Cork Harbour. Both shells are now in the almost perfect British collection of our friend, Mr. Jeffreys of Swansea. The only other recorded specimen was the original one obtained by Mr. Laskey from the Frith of Forth, near Dunbar, and described and figured by Col. Montagu. It is very doubtful, however, whether we can regard the Scottish specimen as indigenous, and not improbable, that it was taken out of ballast. The Atlantic coasts of France and Spain, and the Western Mediterranean are the regions where this mollusk is most at home.

VENERUPIS, Lamarck.

Shell oblong, somewhat compressed, equivalve, inequilateral. Hinge, with two cardinal teeth in one valve and three in the other, or with three cardinal teeth in both valves, the central one more or less bifid. Ligament oblong, external. Palleal impression with a well-marked oblong sinus.

Animal oblong, thick, mantle closed in front for the passage of a compressed and lanceolate foot. Siphons united for about half their lengths, their orifice fringed with a double series of cirrhi, the longer ones pectinated.

This genus and the last approach very closely, and both present features which indicate an affinity with the *Veneridæ*, though the characters of the mantle, and the manners of the species induce us rather to associate them with the family in which we have placed them here. Possibly, when their exotic allies have been more carefully studied, and the characters of their animal inhabitants better known, one or other genus may form the type of a family apart from the *Gastrochænidæ*.

V. irus, Linnæus.

Plate VII. figs. 1, 2, 3, and (animal) Plate G. f. 2.

Donax Irus, Linn. Syst. Nat. ed. 12, p. 1128.—Pultwney, Hutchins Dorset,
p. 32.—Donov. Brit. Shells, vol. i. pl. 29, f. 2.—Mont. Test.
Brit. pp. 108, 573.—Linn. Trans. vol. viii. p. 77.—Dorset Cat.
p. 34, pl. 12, f. 6 (badly).—Turt. Conch. Diction. p. 43.—
Chemn. Conch. Cab. vol. vi. p. 271, pl. 26, f. 268, 269, 270.—
Poli, Test. Sicil. pl. 10, f. 1, 2, 3, and pl. 19, f. 25, 26.—Dillw.
Recent Shells, vol. i. p. 156.—Index Testaceolog. pl. 6, Donax,
f. 21.

Tellina Cornubiensis, Penn. Brit. Zool. ed. 4 (from Borlase's Cornwall, pl. 28,
f. 23).

Osmeus foliatus, Da Costa, Brit. Conch. p. 204, pl. 15, f. 6, on the left.

Venerupis Irus, Lam. Anim. s. Vert. ed. 2, vol. vi. p. 163.—Flem. Brit. Anim.
p. 451.—Brit. Marine Conch. p. 60.—Desh. Elem. Conch. pl.
12, f. 16, 17, 18.—Philippi, Moll. Sicil. vol. i. p. 21 ; and vol.
ii. p. 20.—Hanl. Recent Shells, p. 54.—Exped. Scient. Algérie, Moll. pl. 66, f. 14 to 17 (animal).

Petricola Irus, Turt. Dithyra Brit. p. 26, pl. 2, f. 14.

Pullastra Irus, Brown, Illust. Conch. G. B. p. 89, pl. 37, f. 9.

No minute and prolonged investigation is demanded, for
the discrimination of this rock-borer from any of the
hitherto-found Testacea of our shores, the remarkable
lamellation of its surface, enabling us immediately to
separate it : the chief difficulty rests in discovering strictly
permanent characteristics which may distinguish it from
its foreign congeners, a few of which might easily be
reckoned by the inexperienced, as but aberrant varieties of
the same species.   The shape is of course modified by that
of its habitation, but is typically subrhomboidal, at times
its length scarcely exceeds its breadth by one-fourth, more
usually, however, it nearly doubles it, and certain specimens
are even still more longitudinally produced.   The more
beautiful live shells (as they are technically called) are
of a pure slightly translucent white; such, however, are
rare, and indeed but few specimens comparatively are
taken with the animal in them.   Most examples are of
an uniform opaque dirty-white, or pale drab, externally:

the interior is of a similar paleness to the exterior, but is
always stained with purple or brown on the hinder hinge
margin, and is usually tinged or dyed with similar colours
near its posterior extremity. It never attains any considerable size. Its surface is more or less convex, at times
even ventricose, and is totally devoid of lustre. Its solidity
is extremely variable, it being sometimes decidedly thick
and strong, but quite as often thin and fragile. The sides
are extremely unequal, the front occupying ordinarily about
one-fourth the length of the shell. The surface is adorned
with thin-edged concentric lamellæ, which vary in approximation from distant to rather close-set, (the commoner form
appears to be rather remote,) and in elevation from depressed to erect. These have a decided tendency to enlarge
posteriorly, and are fimbriated by the very crowded
radiating striæ, which become elevated in the interstices.
The front extremity is always a little narrowed at its
termination by the very decided slope of its upper or dorsal
margin, and the ascent of its lower one; which latter,
although adapting itself to the circumstances of its dwelling-
place, is typically rather convex and a little retuse near the
middle, as an examination of the direction of the upper
or undisturbed lamellæ will demonstrate. The hinder extremity is always more or less biangulated, and sometimes
a little attenuated: the hinder dorsal margin is straight,
convex, or even incurved, but never much declining. The
beaks are curved forward, and are not preceded by a
lunule; the ligament is small, sunken, and narrow. The
hinge consists of three primary diverging teeth in each
valve; the central strong, and bifid or even bipartite, the
front in one, and the hinder in the other valve, almost
equally as large, but not always so evidently bifid, whilst
the third in each is simple, narrow, and at times almost

entirely obsolete. The inner margin is not crenated.
Were it not for this last character, the *Pectunculus
truncatus* of Da Costa, who, not delineating the species himself, refers for its representation to Borlase, whose figure
clearly is meant for *Irus*, might not unreasonably be
deemed an old worn example of this *Venerupis*. But as
Montagu justly observes, his species is involved in great
obscurity; from which uncertainty, the language of its
author not strictly applicable to any British species, and
equally suited to more than one exotic bivalve, forbids all
hope of our being able to extricate it.   .

Poli has remarked that it is very singular, whilst shells
of the *Venerupis irus* are cast up in profusion on the coasts
of Sicily, the animal is rarely found in them; indeed, he
himself had never been able to meet with it. Common as
the shell is in the south, few observations have been made
upon its constructor. Deshayes has given an outline figure
of the animal in his "Mollusques d'Algérie." He represents the siphons as united for a considerable length, and
when separated of unequal lengths. One of them has the
fringe of cirrhi placed immediately around the margin; the
other has a tube-like continuation beyond the fringe.
The cirrhi themselves are of two orders, the shorter one,
reflexed and simple, the longer projecting and pinnate.

The valves rarely exceed half an inch in length and
three-quarters of an inch in breadth. They are found imbedded in limestone rocks at Plymouth and other parts of
Devonshire (Montagu); in large masses of rock opposite the
old castle at Weymouth (S. H.) Dead shells are frequent
in shell-sand all along the Southern coast. In S. Wales it
has been found at Langland bay, near Swansea (Jeffreys).
In Ireland at Youghal (R. Ball); Howth (Turton); in
sponges and sea-weed at Miltown Malbay (W. Harvey).

On the whole it may be considered as a southern species
so far as the coasts of Britain are concerned. Indeed it
does not appear to range further north, and is most
abundant in the southern part of the Celtic province
(Atlantic coast of France) and in the Lusitanian and
Mediterranean regions of the European seas. Geologically
it dates as far back as the epoch of the Red Crag, but
retired for a time from our seas during the unfavourable
conditions of the pleistocene period. It is an inhabitant of
the littoral and laminarian zones, and rarely occurs even
dead in the dredge, unless in very shallow water and close
to shore.

SPURIOUS.

Venus substriata, MONT. Test. Brit. suppl. p. 48, pl. 29, f. 6.—TURT. Conch.
  Diction. p. 245.— TURT. Dithyra Brit. p. 152.— FLEM.
  Brit. Anim. p. 448.—Brit. Marine Conch. p. 91.
Venerupis decussata, PHILIPPI, Moll. Sicil. vol. i. p. 22, pl. 3, f. 5, and vol. ii. p.
  20.—Exped. Scien. Algérie, Moll. p. 66. f. 10 to 13 (shell
  and animal).

Rounded, subquadrangular, solid, opaque, more or less ventricose, rather dull, of an uniform white both within and without,
most crowdedly set with radiating elevated striæ, which assume
a subgranular appearance, especially in front, by being decussated with irregular concentric wrinkles, which are more manifest anteriorly. Ventral margin but little convex, ascending in
front, not crenated within: hinder dorsal edge straightish, and
not declining ; front dorsal edge straightish, and considerably
sloping. Anterior side much attenuated, very small, tolerably
rounded at the extremity : posterior termination broadly subbiangulated, the angles being rounded off, and the extreme edge
somewhat convex. Ligament almost concealed ; umbones prominent ; beaks incurved and distinct ; no lunule. Two divergent compressed primary teeth in the right valve ; three, of
which the bifid central is the largest, in the other. Length $\frac{5}{8}$,
breadth $\frac{1}{2}$ of an inch. *A Mediterranean shell, introduced by
Montagu, as dredged by Mr. Laskey, off the Isle of May, in the
Frith of Forth. Probably brought in ballast.*

III. MYADÆ.

THE GAPER TRIBE.

To arrange Mollusks, or the genera of any other class of animals, in a sequence of their natural affinities, is not possible in a written treatise, and can be done only by means of diagrams. The tribe of bivalve shell-fish which has now to engage our attention is an instance in point, for in many respects the animal of a *Mya* is much more nearly allied to an *Ascidia* than are most of the genera of the two tribes we have just passed in review. Yet to introduce the *Myadæ* between the *Pholadidæ* and *Gastrochænidæ* would be to separate, by an unnatural break, most natural alliances. The family before us, if indicated in a diagram, would rather take rank alongside the *Pholas* tribe, and like it be seen conducting us by gradual transitions from the *Tunicata* towards the more typical *Lamelli branchiata*. The aspect of a *Mya*, when clothed with its coriaceous epidermis is that of an elongated *Cynthia*, against whose sides two plates of shell have been appressed, and no better mode could be devised of impressing on the tyro in malacology the close affinity of two great sections, so unlike in most of their proper members, than the placing before him, side by side, examples of the two genera just mentioned.

The popular appellations of "Gapers" may be applied to the whole tribe. The shells are oblong and somewhat rude in appearance, always more or less gaping, and often very widely, at the two extremities. Some of the species grow to a very large size. The valves are united by a hinge of variable character. The ligament is in some genera external, in others internal. The animal has its mantle closed in front, except for the passage of a foot, which is seldom developed in proportion to the mass of the body. The siphons are greatly prolonged, and united almost to their extremities; their orifices are fringed. Both body and shell are often invested in a coarse and wrinkled epidermis. All the Mollusks of this tribe bury themselves in sand, gravel, or mud. They are palatable articles of food, and are much sought after in many places.

The evidence of geology would go to shew that this family was much more developed in the earlier epochs of the world than now, since, during the Jurassic period especially, many more species of *Myadæ*, mostly belonging to peculiar generic groups, lived than are now known to exist.

Not a few of the extinct forms, even of those oldest in time, bear a striking resemblance to their living allies, and are with difficulty discriminated from one another; a difficulty which is increased by the state in which these fossils are found, being most usually only external casts, so that in a majority of instances the structure of the hinge cannot be perceived. The general similarity of the members of this family depends on the slight amount of variation of shape and sculpture of surface presented by their shells. Professor Agassiz has attempted to group them into many genera, chiefly founded on the modifications of the latter character, but these are too slight and uncertain to permit of the adoption of such sections with safety either by the naturalist or geologist.

Judging from their associates, the *Myadæ*, at the epoch

of their greatest development, were abundant inhabitants
of warm seas, and, within the British area at least, gradually diminished in numbers as more temperate conditions
prevailed.   Now, however, some of the most characteristic
forms are among the most arctic of mollusca.

MYA, Linnæus.

Shell more or less oblong or rhomboidal, equivalve,
gaping at the extremities.   External surface of the valves
more or less furrowed or striated transversely, and furnished with a wrinkled epidermis, which is continued over
the mantle and tubes of the animal; beak depressed;
hinge composed of a dilated, ascending spathulate tooth in
the left valve, connected by a short thick internal ligament with a corresponding socket in the right.   Muscular
impressions distant, well-marked, and connected by a deeply sinuated palleal impression.

Animal oblong, with long tubes, enclosed in a strong
case-like coriaceous epidermis.   Mantle closed in front, except anteriorly, where there is an opening for the passage
of a small conical foot.   Siphons united nearly to their extremities, which have fimbriated orifices.   Labial palpi striated.

The genus *Mya*, as originally constituted, included mollusks of very different families, whose shells presented
similarities in the construction of the hinge.   It is now a
limited and very natural group, represented by few, but
well-marked species, most of which are inhabitants of the
temperate and colder seas of the northern hemisphere.
They are all borers in mud and sand, where they live
buried beneath the surface in an erect position, their
hiding-places being indicated by holes corresponding to the
extremities of their tubes.   They are excellent articles of

food; and both the following species are eaten in some parts of Britain and in North America. They are relished also by animals; and, in Greenland, according to Otho Fabricius, are much sought after by the walrus, the arctic fox, and various northern birds.

Few mollusks are more widely distributed than our native species of *Mya*, ranging as they do throughout the arctic seas, owing to the same causes which we have noticed as having brought about the extensive distribution of the *Saxicavæ*. Their range southwards, however, is not so great, for Cape Cod and New York respectively limit it on the American shores, and neither of the species reach the Mediterranean on those of Europe, although, during the glacial period, the *Mya truncata* was once an inhabitant of that sea, and has been found by Philippi fossil in very recent tertiaries on the coast of Sicily. It is not improbable that the original centre of the last-named species was on the European side of the Atlantic, and that of *Mya arenaria* on the American. The power each possesses in a remarkable degree, of enduring changes in the amount of saltness of the water, is no doubt a chief cause of their wide distribution now.

M. TRUNCATA, Linnæus.

Valves, when adult, abruptly truncated behind.

Plate X. f. 1, 2, 3, and (animal) Plate H. f. 1.

LIST. Hist. Conch. pl. 428, f. 269.

Mya truncata, LINN. Syst. Nat. p. 1112.—PENN. Brit. Zool. ed. 4, vol. iv. p. 78, pl. 41, f. 14.—PULTENEY, Dorset, p. 27.—DONOV. Brit. Shells, vol. iii. p. 92.—Dorset Catal. p. 27, pl. 3, f. 1.—MONT. Test. Brit. p. 32.—Linn. Trans. vol. viii. p. 35.—TURT. Conch. Diction. p. 97.— TURT. Dithyra Brit. p. 81.—FLEM. Brit. Anim. p. 462.—MACGIL. Moll. Aberd. p. 298.—Brit. Marine Conch. p. 40.—BROWN, Illus. Conch. G. B. p. 111, pl. 45, f. 2.— FABR. Fauna Grœnl. p. 404.—CHEMN. Conch. Cab. vol.

vi. p. 8, pl. 1, f. 1, 2—SPENGL. Skrivt. Naturh. Selskab. vol.
iii. part 1, p. 28.—WOOD, General Conch. p. 90, pl. 17, f. 1,
2.—DILLW. Recent Shells, p. 42.—LAM. Anim. s. Vert. ed. 2,
vol. vi. p. 73.—BURROWS, Conch. pl. 4, f. 1, 2.—Ind. Testac.
pl. 2, Mya f. 2.—CROUCH, Introd. Conch. pl. 3, f. 6, 7.—SOW.
Conch. Manual, f. 71.—DESH. Elem. Conch. pl. 8, f. 2.—
HANL. Recent Shells, p. 19, pl. 2, Mya f. 2.—GOULD, Invert.
Massac. p. 42.—DEKAY, New York Mollusc. p. 240, pl. 29,
f. 289.

Chama truncata, DA COSTA, Brit. Conch. p. 233, pl. 16, f. 1.
Mya ovalis, (IMMATURE.) TURT. Dithy. Brit. p. 33, pl. 3, f. 1, 2.
Sphenia Swainsoni, (FRY.) TURT. Dithy. Brit. p. 37, pl. 19, f. 2.—FLEM. Brit.
        Anim. p. 466.—Brit. Marine Conch. p. 57.
Mye tronquée, CHENU, Traité Elem. p. 48, f. 152.
Ency. Méth. Vers. pl. 229, f. 2.

This ancient and well-known shell is of a sub-oval form,
which is at times produced, but more generally abbreviated, subequilateral, more or less solid, opaque, and ventricose. This latter characteristic is, however, chiefly
manifested towards the rounded end, there being a considerable degree of flattening of the central surface, which,
after a slight retusion, again swells out at the truncated
tips of the posterior extremity, of which latter the hiatus is
extremely large, more or less oval in shape, and not extending below beyond the ventral margin; the lips of this
gape are reflexed, and there is not any tendency to stricture. A loose, yellowish-grey epidermis (which is continued posteriorly beyond the shell to the animal,) covers
the entire valves, which beneath it are of a more or less
squalid dull uniform white, and concentrically traversed by
irregular but very distinct wrinkles, which are often almost
pliciform at the sides, where they are always most developed. The dorsal and ventral margins are almost parallel;
the latter is more or less straight, a little retuse at or behind the middle, more convex in front, and more ascending
posteriorly. The former, immediately adjacent to the umbones, is subretuse in front, and not at all declining; but,

after running a short distance, bends down in an arcuated curve to the ventral, which does not equally rise to meet it ; hence the more or less broad anterior extremity, is well but not symmetrically rounded. The general direction of the hinder dorsal edge is subretuse or straight, and its slope is almost imperceptible. The hinder side, which is barely the shorter, is truncated at its termination, the truncation being almost direct, and not oblique ; the posterior, however, is rather convex than otherwise, and the hinder extremity not absolutely biangulated, but with the angulation a little softened off by the terminal convexity of the upper and lower margins. The posterior side is without any manifest umbonal ridge ; but a marked, though broad and undefined, ridge-like elevation very frequently runs anteriorward from the umbones, in a very oblique direction. The umbones are for the most part unequally prominent, the beaks are small, acute, much incurved, and a little inclined forwards ; in front of them there is seen a false lunule, being a kind of amorphous depression, which is continued also beneath the beaks to the opposite side. The whole interior is white and glossy ; the muscular impressions are not large, the posterior one is by far the more profound ; the sinus of the palleal impression is very large, and somewhat squared. The hinge consists of a very large, broad, solid, erect, complicated tooth in the left valve, of which the lower surface is convex and simple, but the upper is flattened and subdivided, the central triangular portion forming a very shallow pit for the adhesion of the cartilage, bounded by an obliquely-radiating, narrow fold in front, with a similar, but much more obscure one, at its posterior termination ; a third well developed fold-like projection is visible at the strengthened posterior extreme. In the right valve there is only a small oblique, fold-like

tooth, which, scarcely elevated above the hinge-margin,
lies in front of the cartilage-pit, which latter shelves down
almost at right-angles to the dorsal line.

The proportion of length to breadth is not constant;
specimens which are two inches wide, measuring from three
and a quarter down to two and a half inches only between
their lateral extremities.

The animal is oval with very long siphons, the epidermic coat, which invests the mantle and tubes, is rugose and
brown; beneath it the surface is white, or tinged with
yellow, so also is the foot. The viscera are of a pale
brown hue. The mantle is entirely closed in front except
a small aperture anteriorly for the narrow linguiform foot,
which is straight, and furnished with a byssal groove. The
suture of the united margins of the mantle is conspicuously
seen when the investing coat is removed. That part of the
sheath which surrounds the siphons is marked dorsally and
ventrally by a ridge or suture. The siphonal tubes are
united to their extremities, or very nearly so. They are
both surrounded at the point of separation by a circle of
filaments, the bases of which are tinged with brown. The
branchial orifice is especially fimbriated. A tubular membrane is protruded from the interior of the anal orifice.
The branchiæ are partly continued into the tube. The
labial tentacles are large, triangular, acute, and striated
upon their inner sides.

In Zetland, this animal is boiled and eaten. It is there
called "Smurslin." The species is abundant on the coast
of Newfoundland, where it is said to be a favourite food of
the cod-fish.

Our association of *Sphænia Swainsoni* and *Mya ovalis*
with the present species, results from a careful examination
of Turton's original types, which are still preserved and in

the possession of Mr. Jeffreys. The characteristic truncation of the adult is not present in the earlier stages
of growth, which may be seen by examining the earlier
concentric stages of growth in the mature valves.

This is both a deep sea and littoral species. It is often
found lurking in the sand towards low-water mark, with its
shell embedded to the depth of three or four inches. Although actually abundant and very widely diffused, fine
and perfect examples are not common in the cabinets of
collectors, not alone from their proneness to distortion, but
rather from the unpleasant and often baffling necessity of
digging them out from the wet spots where they are more
usually found. We have likewise met them, along with
Pholades, in chalk at Margate (S. H.), in which vicinity,
and also at Sandwich, the single valves are very common.
The species is abundant "at the mouths of rivers and in
bays, along with *arenaria,* in a mixture of gravel and mud"
(Alder); Exmouth (Clark); Portsmouth Harbour (Jeffreys); Dartmouth in seven fathoms (E. F. & R. M'A);
Liverpool (M'Andrew); Scarborough (Bean); in twenty-
five fathoms water, five miles from land off the coast of
Ballaugh, Isle of Man (E. F.); Swansea (Jeffreys); Tenby
(Lyons); Anglesea in seven fathoms (M'Andrew); "suitable localities on every side of the Irish coast" (Thompson);
Frith of Forth at low water and to a depth of seven
fathoms (E. F.); Aberdeenshire (M'Gillivray); "Oban,
Ullapool, Lochs Shieldaig, and Carron, Shetland and the
Orkneys" (Jeffreys and Barlee); dead valves in thirty-four
fathoms, ten miles from shore off Elgin, (R. M'A.) may be
enumerated among other habitats. Single valves are occasionally met with at extreme depths. One is recorded
by Mr. Thompson (Ann. Nat. Hist. vol. x. p. 22), to have
been dredged by Captain Beechey from Beaufort's Dyke at

the Mull of Galloway, in about 145 fathoms of water.
Mr. M'Andrew has taken them in 100 fathoms water,
twenty-five miles to the east of Zetland.

This species is not rare in the fossil state; a variety
with the posterior end extremely short, is the most frequent fossil form, and still lives in Greenland and the seas
of Boreal America. This is the *Mya Uddevallensis* of some
authors, examples of which, (but whether recent or fossil
is uncertain,) surmised to have been brought from a shell-
bank lying about twenty-five miles to the east of Fern
Islands, were procured by Mr. King from some Northumbrian fishing-boats. (Ann. N. H. 18, p. 236.)   As a British
species, *Mya truncata* dates from the epoch of the coralline crag.

M. ARENARIA, Linnæus.

Ovate-oblong, subequilateral, not tumid, merely marked with
concentric wrinkles of growth, rounded anteriorly, tapering posteriorly to a blunted point.

Plate X. f. 4, 5, 6.

Mya arenaria, LINN. Syst. Nat. ed. 12, p. 1112.—PENN. Brit. Zool. ed. 4, vol.
iv. p. 79, pl. 42, f. 16.—DONOV. Brit. Shells, vol. iii. pl. 85.
—MONT. Test. Brit. p. 30.—Linn. Trans. vol. viii. p. 35.—
Dorset Catal. p. 28, pl. 4. f. 2.—TURT. Conch. Diction. p. 98.
—TURT. Dithyra Brit. p. 32.—FLEM. Brit. Anim. p. 463.
—MACGIL. Moll. Aberd. p. 298.—Brit. Marine Conch. p. 40.—
BROWN, Ill. Conch. G. B. p. 111, pl. 45, f. 1.—O. FABR. Fauna
Grœnl. p. 405.—CHEMN. Conch. Cab. vol. vi. p. 10, pl. 1, f.
3, 4.—SPENGL. Skrivt. Naturh. Selskab. vol. iii. part 1, p. 30.
WOOD, General Conch. p. 91, pl. 17, f. 3. — DILLW. Recent
Shells, vol. i. p. 42.—LAM. Anim. s. Vert. ed. 2, vol. vi. p. 74.
—Index Testac. pl. 2, Mya, f. 2.—MAWE, Conchology, pl.
4, f. 1. — SOWERBY, Genera Shells. — BLAINV. Man. Malac.
pl. 77, f. 1.—REEVE, Conch. System, pl. 33.—CONRAD, Amer.
Mar. Conch. p. 42, pl. 9, f. 1.— GOULD, Invert. Massach. p.
40.—HANL. Recent Shells, p. 19.—DEKAY, New York Moll. p.
240, pl. 30, f. 290.

Chama arenaria, DA COSTA, Brit. Conch. p. 232.
Mye des sables, CHEM, Traité Elem. p. 48, f. 149, 150 (hinge).
Mya mercenaria, and M. acuta, SAY. J. Ac. N. S. Philad. vol. ii. p. 313 (fide de Gould).

This coarse and homely-looking shell has an oblong-oval contour, and a strong and solid texture, so as not unfrequently to be of considerable weight. The valves, which when most perfect have an ochraceous tint or are of a darker or paler sand colour, are frequently stained black, owing to the nature of the soil in which they are embedded; they are not uncommonly distorted or irregular in their growth, and are more or less ventricose, particularly upon the anterior side. Their surface is entirely devoid of lustre, and is rudely traversed concentrically by irregular wrinkles and lines of increase. The ash-coloured epidermis is but thinly spread over the surface, and is often entirely obsolete, or only visible towards the ventral margin. This latter is more or less retuse a little behind the middle, slightly convex posteriorly, and ascending and arcuated anteriorly. The sides are almost equal, the posterior, if either, being rather the longer, and bluntly acuminated below at its termination; the front side, which is also the more ample one, is nearly equally rounded above and below at its extremity. The front dorsal edge, which is convex or even arcuated, declines but slightly, the hinder, which is produced and comparatively straight, though still somewhat convex, is decidedly sloping. The umbones are by no means peculiarly prominent, and are often flattened above; the beaks are sometimes almost directly inflected, but more generally incline forwards; there is no vestige of an impression on either side of them; neither is there any distinct umbonal ridge. The shell gapes at both extremities, but much more so upon the narrower side, where neither the upper nor lower edges

touch each other from the centre of the shell to its hinder termination: the posterior dorsal margins bend outwards.*
The hinge consists of a remarkably large, solid, and erect tooth in the left valve, and an appressed subtriangular and oblique excavation under the umbones of the opposite

* Our friend Dr. Carpenter, whose researches into the microscopic structure of shells rank among the most important of recent contributions to Malacology, has examined with great care the structure of this species, and gives the following account of it in his forthcoming report : " The indications of cellular structure are of a peculiarly interesting nature in *Mya arenaria*, the careful examination of whose shell has thrown much light on several doubtful points of my inquiry. We have here a distinct cellular structure in some parts giving way by such imperceptible gradations to an almost perfectly homogeneous arrangement in others, that no separation can be made between them, so that we must regard the latter as having had the same origin with the former, although its primary characteristic has been lost. Near the external surface of the shell is a layer of cells, having very distinct boundaries and large dark nuclear spots ; and yet in other parts of the same layer the boundaries of the cells are completely obliterated, and only the dark nuclear spots remain to shew their original divisions. In some instances the continuous cells seem to coalesce in sinuous rows, so that wavy lines are left (somewhat resembling the boundaries of the furrows of Mæandrina) dividing one series from another (fig. 24).* Near the external surface some very large cells are disposed without any regularity, amongst those of which the layer is chiefly made up (fig. 25) ; and the external surface itself is composed of small cells of rounded form, in by no means close approximation with each other. In the tooth, also, we find a considerable variety of structure, in addition to those forms presented by the shell. Thus, in fig. 26, is seen a group of large cells, the calcareous contents of which are disposed in a very regular radiating Aragonite or Wavellite. The borders of this group pass into another cluster of cells (fig. 27) that presents no trace of this curious structure (of which, however, there are some indications in shell) ; whilst the latter gradually passes, by the obliteration of its cell-boundaries, into a layer of very homogeneous aspect. Besides these, there are several curious forms of elongated cells, some of them with square terminations, as in fig. 28, and some pointed or fusiform, as in fig. 29. In these last may be seen transverse striæ, closely resembling those of the long prismatic cells of Pinna, and probably due to the same cause, namely, the spaces between the striæ which indicate their lines of junction. Upon this last circumstance I am disposed to lay much stress, as indicating the really compound nature of the long fusiform cells, of which we have already seen some examples, but which are peculiarly characteristic of the univalve group. Neither in the shells nor the tooth of *Mya arenaria* is there animal matter enough to give anything more than a delicate membranous residuum, in which no vestige of cell walls can be traced."

* The figures refer to Dr. Carpenter's plate.

valve. Between them lies the rich brown cartilage, for
the reception of which there is a shallow indentation on the
external surface of the greatly projecting tooth.   Neither
the cartilage receptacle in the right valve, nor the opposing
tooth of the left, can be termed simple; there being a
broad ledge-like anterior detached margin to the former,
whilst the posterior scarcely elevated linear tooth forms
a lateral denticle near the base of the latter, which, moreover, is decidedly convex internally, with its apex arcuated
and its front almost rectilinear or truncated, and bending
over so as to form a margin for the cartilage on that side.
The inner surface is white and often glossy, and the sinus
of the palleal scar, which is rather remote from the margin
and a little undulated in its impression, is elongated and
narrow.

The animal of this species in its general features
resembles the last.   When stripped of its epidermis it is
of a yellowish-white colour, the orifices tinged with red.

The average size of the shell is about four inches long
and two and a third broad, but examples are often found
of much larger dimensions.   Although locally abundant,
for it is a gregarious species, and tolerably diffused throughout our coast, it is less frequently met with, especially in
fine condition, than might be imagined.   It is dug out of
a gravelly, sandy, or clayey bottom near low water mark,
usually in or near estuaries, and is found, among other
spots, at Herne Bay in Kent (S. H.); "Portsmouth, the
Isle of Wight, Southampton" (Jeffreys' cab. and M'Andrew), where, according to Montagu, they are called "old
maids," and are sometimes collected for food; Tenby in
Pembrokeshire (S. H.); Red Wharf Bay, Mackruss, Borth
(Eyton); "in suitable localities on every side of the Irish
coast" (Thompson); Dublin Bay and Cork Harbour (Jeff-

reys' cab.); "at Rothesay Bay both this and *truncata* are used by the fishermen for bait" (Alder); Frith of Forth (E. F.); Aberdeenshire, abundant in the Outer Hebrides (Macgillivray). The specimens found in sand are, as Montagu observes, far more smooth and regularly grown than those extracted from gravel, and are covered with a distinct epidermis. They are discovered by a small hole on the surface, through which on pressure the animal ejects a considerable quantity of water. It burrows to the depth of more than a foot.

The *Mya arenaria* is occasionally found in brackish water, and is then subject to dwarfing and distortion. Such is the condition of the specimens in the Loch of Stennis in Orkney, famous for the part it plays in the scenery of Scott's admirable novel of the "Pirate." In that lake we find *Limnei*, *Neritinæ*, and other fresh-water Mollusks, along with the *Myæ*, which now, however, appear to be nearly, if not altogether, extinct. Before they became so, they had greatly diminished in size, and become variously distorted. In this instance the cause is to be sought for in a very recent elevation of the land, which has gradually converted what was originally an arm of the sea into a brackish pool, only occasionally flooded with salt water, and probably destined eventually to become a fresh-water lake. In Mr. Cuming's collection are some remarkably distorted *Myæ* of this species from the sluices at Ostend, where their deformities are most likely also due to the pernicious influence of fresh water. To the same cause we may attribute the numerous and singular varieties of this shell, such as the so-called species, *M. lata* and *pullus*, found in the mamaliferous crag of the east of England, a formation in which many of the mollusca are deformed. The melting of the icebergs which then chilled our region doubtless furnished the disturbing medium. These dangerous and disastrous consequences of too great an imbibition of the " pure element" present a timely warning to the votaries of teetotalism.

PANOPÆA, MENARD DE LA GROYE.

Shell transversely oblong, rather compressed, equivalve, more or less inequilateral, gaping at both extremities ; surface of the valves nearly smooth or transversely furrowed, never longitudinally ribbed ; pallial impression in each valve very strongly marked, with a deep triangular sinus posteriorly ; muscular impressions strong and oblong ; hinge formed of a conic cardinal tooth in each valve lodged in a cavity in the valve opposite ; ligament external, short, prominent, attached to strong nymphal callosities.

Animal oblong, and furnished with a very long and extensible siphonal tube ; body and tube invested with a wrinkled brown leathery epidermis, continuous with the shell ; mantle closed throughout its length, except a small opening with thickened lips in front anteally for the passage of a short stout muscular foot ; adductor muscles very strong ; mouth surrounded by thickened lips bearing four labial palpi ; siphonal tubes united to their extremities ; orifices inconspicuously fimbriated.

This genus was founded by Menard de la Groye in the ninth volume of the "Annales du Museum" (1807), for the reception of an Italian tertiary fossil, closely related to the "*Chama glycimeris*" of Aldrovandus, a shell which had latterly been known as *Mya glycimeris*. The founder of the genus recognised their affinity, and also their relationship to *Mya* and neighbouring genera. The *Panopææ* indeed closely resemble *Myæ*, both in the general aspect of the shell and in the principal features of the animal. Their external ligament, and the absence of the spoon-shaped process of hinge, distinguish the former : the peculiar structure of the mantle and foot are characteristic of the latter. The animal of this genus was not known to Menard, and remained undescribed until 1839, when a valuable monograph on *Panopæa* was published by Valenciennes in the first volume of the "Archives du Museum." In that memoir an account was given of the animal of *Panopæa australis*, a south African species. The officers of a French frigate visiting Port Natal observed the tubes of a Mollusk projecting from the sand in one of the bays. The sailors endeavoured to draw the creature out of its habitation by the tube, but in vain ; for the siphons, after offering considerable resistance, in every instance gave way, and often were withdrawn entire in spite of the grasp of its persecutor. Curious to know the nature of the being which thus escaped them, they dug for it with spades, and at length uncovered the *Panopæa* buried several feet below the surface of the sand, and gregarious.

This genus was anciently of more importance than now, for during the Jurassic epoch there existed many species in our seas. They gradually decreased in numbers till the present time. The few species known now are natives of the North Atlantic, Lusitanian, South African, Patagonian, and New Zealand seas, one only inhabiting each region.

P. Norvegica, Spengler.

Plate XI. (slightly enlarged).

Mya Norvegica, Spengler, Skrivt. Naturh. Selskab. vol. iii. part 1, p. 46, pl. 2, f. 18.
Glycimeris arctica, Lam. Anim. s. Vert. (Desh. ed. 2) vol. vi. p. 70.

Panopæa glycimeris, BEAN, Mag. Nat. Hist. vol. viii. p. 562, f. 50, 51.
Panopæa arctica, GOULD, Invert. Massach. p. 37, f. 27.—HANL. Recent Shells,
        p. 18, suppl. 10, f. 43.—Brit. Marine Conch. p. 36.—
        DEKAY, New York Moll. p. 246.
Panopæa Spengleri, VALENC. Archiv. de Mus. vol. i. p. 15, pl. 5, f. 3 (not exact).
        —CHENU, Ill. Conch. Panopæa, p. 4, pl. 4, f. 4.
   "   *Norvegica*, LOVEN, Ind. Moll. Sueciæ, p. 49.
   "   *Bivonæ*, SMITH, Wern. Mem. vol. viii. p. 107, pl. 2, fig. 4.

The shape of this interesting shell is oblong, with a
slight tendency to be rhomboidal behind. It is extremely
thick and heavy, and very decidedly inequilateral. The
valves are ventricose, and appear peculiarly so when
united, as their edges only touch at the callus near the
beaks, and at a point in the ventral margin, which is
nearly opposite; the shell gaping at every other portion of
its margin, and particularly at the hinder extremity, where
the bending outwards of the edges of the shell increase
the hiatus. The outer surface is rather rough, being
marked with coarse concentric wrinkles and somewhat
obsolete ridges of growth; but that which chiefly characterises it is the presence of a broad triangular excavated
area, which radiates from the beaks subcentrally, and
rapidly enlarges as it nears the lower margin. A shallower and narrower space runs likewise to the lower
posterior corner from the hinder part of the umbones,
and thus the intervening surface assumes the appearance
of a broad and very oblique obtuse rib, which parts off
about two-fifths of the entire surface. The remaining
area is nearly equally divided between the impressed
triangle and the convex front terminal surface, the sudden
posterior cessation of whose convexity makes it appear
similarly but not equally like a perpendicularly radiating
obsolete ridge, which indeed it is generally described as
being, but which, from the specimen before us, we do not

feel ourselves justified in terming it, since, although there is
a slight flattening of the surface between it and the front
extremity, there is no defined anterior limit to the so-called
ridge.   The exterior is of an ashy buff colour, and utterly
devoid of lustre ; the interior is paler or darker ochraceous,
and moderately glossy.

The ventral margin is much incurved in the middle,
swelling out at the extremities, and rapidly and obliquely
ascending in front.   The dorsal margin for the most part
runs nearly parallel with the ventral, scarcely declining at
all behind, (where it is incurved, and where the dorsal surface is flattened,) but in front forming an uniform convex
or arcuated sweep with the anterior outline, by which that
extremity is distinctly rounded, yet not symmetrically so,
owing to the trifling declination of the upper portion, compared with the longer and more abrupt curve of the lower
one.   The hinder side is nearly twice as long as the front,
and is very bluntly biangulated at its termination, which
is broad and not at all tapering : the hinder edge is nearly
straight, and inclines a little obliquely outward from its
dorsal commencement.   The umbones project but slightly
above the cardinal edge, being rather flattened above, and
the beaks are very small and lean almost directly inwards.   The ligament is broad and rather prominent, but
not very elongated, and in the few shells we have seen
is of a dark colour.   Notwithstanding the solidity of the
shell, the edges are acute and simple, and for the most
part incline outward.   The hinge margin is very broad,
and is merely provided in each valve with a remarkably
small apical tooth, and an adjacent receptacle for that of
the opposite one: these occupy but little of the hinge
plate, which is there shallowly excavated, with its lower
edge, to which they scarcely reach half way, minutely

indented beneath the tooth. In addition, there is a remarkably elevated nymphal callosity just under the ligament, to which indeed it serves as a support. One of the larger examples measures three inches and a half in length, and rather more than two and a quarter in breadth. The hinge margin is often obsoletely and minutely denticulated within.

The following graphic account of Mr. Bean's discovery of this extremely scarce species is extracted from the " Magazine of Natural History," wherein the shell was first actually published as a native of our seas, although under the erroneous impression that it was the *Panopæa* which had been previously figured by Donovan:—" We have obtained at Scarborough three specimens of this, in every sense of the word, gigantic prize. To some of the fishermen of our coast it appeared to be well known by the name of the *'bacca-box*, from a fancied resemblance to one of their most useful household gods. They were all caught by the hook, and rescued from destruction in a singular manner. The first, from which our figure was taken, was destined for a tobacco-box; the second had the honour of holding the grease belonging to the boat establishment; and the third, after amusing them (the members of a philosophical society) by squirting water to the ceiling, was at last seen by a learned friend, purchased for a trifle, and generously placed in our cabinet. The animal we have not seen, but its colour is black." Three additional individuals have since then been obtained by Mr. Bean from the same locality, and two single valves have been dredged by Mr. M'Andrew in ninety fathoms water, twenty-five miles east of Zetland. It is likewise captured, though very rarely, in deep water off the Northumberland and Durham coasts (King and Alder).

SPURIOUS.

P. Aldrovandi, Lamarck.

Lister. Hist. Conch. pl. 414.
Mya glycimeris, Born, Mus. Cæs. Vind. p. 20, pl. 1, f. 8.—Chemn. Conch. Cab. vol. vi. p. 33, pl. 3, f. 25.—Donov. Brit. Shells, vol. iv. pl. 143.—Mont. Test. Brit. Supp. p. 19.—Linn. Trans. vol. viii. p. 54.—Turt. Conch. Diction. p. 107. — Wood, General Conch. p. 14, pl. 25, f. 1.—Dillw. Recent Shells, vol. i. p. 42.
Panopæa Aldrovandi, Lam. Anim. s. Vert. (ed. Desh.) vol. vi. p. 67.—Flem. Brit. Anim. p. 462.—Crouch, Introd. Conch. pl. 3, f. 1.— Phil. Moll. Sicil. vol. i. p. 7, pl. 2, f. 2, and vol. ii. p. 6.—Hanl. Recent Shells, p. 18.—Valenc. Archiv. de Mus. vol. i. p. 9, pl. 4, f. 1.—Chenu, Ill. Conch. Panop. p. 1, pl. 1.
  „ *glycimeris*, Turt. Dithyra Brit. p. 42.—Desh. Elem. Conch. pl. 7, f. 1.
Panopés d'Aldrovande, Chenu, Traité Elem. p. 46, f. 144 (hinge).

A Mediterranean shell, introduced by Donovan, from the general and correct belief that a Panopæa (evidently Norvegica, which was not at that time distinguished by English writers) had been fished up in the deep waters between the Dogger Bank and the eastern coast of England.

CORBULIDÆ.

This tribe is composed of bivalves, all of comparatively
small dimensions, the majority very small. Most of them
have inequivalve shells, and all have their hinder extremities more or less produced, and easily distinguished by
the tendency to form a beak from the anterior or buccal
end. The last mentioned is the most constant character,
for the hinge, presence or absence of epidermis, thickness
and sculpture of shell, and even position of the ligament,
vary considerably in the several genera composing the
tribe. The animals of all, however, are very nearly allied,
and easily distinguished, for all have extremely short
united siphons, with fimbriated extremities, the anal one
always provided with a conspicuous membranous tube.
The mantle is closed, except a passage for a narrow foot,
not unlike that of the *Gastrochænidæ*, to which family the
Corbula tribe has very close affinity. Most of the British
members of this tribe are either rare or very recent discoveries, and several of them we have to figure for the first
time as natives of our seas.

CORBULA, Bruguiere.

Shell suborbicular or oval, tumid or depressed, very inequivalve, slightly inequilateral, rounded anteriorly, more
or less truncated posteriorly; beaks prominent; surface of
the valves more or less furrowed or transversely striated,
covered with an epidermis. Hinge composed of a recurved

primary tooth in one or both valves, with corresponding socket and ligamental pit beside it. Ligament small, interior. Muscular impressions slightly marked, united by a pallial one with a very slight sinus.

Animal short, with very short united siphonal tubes. Orifices fimbriated. Mantle closed, except in front, where there is an opening for a bony, narrow, thick foot of considerable dimensions. Anal siphon with a conspicuous tubular membrane. Labial tentacles slender.

This is one of those genera which have diminished with the course of time. *Corbulæ* were abundant in the European seas during the earlier part of the tertiary epoch, and even before. They are now reduced to a very few species. The genus has more representatives at present in tropical seas.

The microscopic structure of the shell has been examined by Dr. Carpenter. He finds the outer layer to consist of large fusiform cells; the inner to be nearly homogeneous. "At the lines of junction of the successive additions to the margin is a yellow layer, probably owing its colour to an intermixture of horny matter, such as might, if poured out upon the surface, have formed a periostracum. In this layer there is a very definite and beautiful cellular arrangement, the cells being in some parts polygonal, and having their edges in contact, whilst in others they are rounded and isolated."—(*Report*, p. 104.)

C. NUCLEUS, Lamarck.

Rather obliquely subtriangular, very solid, not polished, subinequilateral, whitish, with the larger valve sometimes rayed with pale crimson, and the smaller one always covered with a stiff umberbrown epidermis : ventral edge arcuated, ascending and straighter posteriorly ; dorsal edges moderately and subequally sloping, and nearly straight. Valves excessively unequal, ventri-

cose; the smaller one only marked with a few central and rather
remote elevated lines : the larger one simply and closely grooved
concentrically, its umbo greatly projecting beyond the other.
Anterior extremity rounded ; posterior termination rapidly attenuated, and obtusely subbiangulated. Umbonal ridge obsolete.

Plate IX., figs. 7 to 12, and (animal) Plate G, fig. 3.

Tellina gibba, OLIVI, Zoolog. Adriat. p. 101.
Mya inæquivalvis, MONT. Test. Brit. p. 38, suppl. pl. 26, f. 7.—Linn. Trans.
             vol. viii. p. 40, pl. 1, f. 6.—TURT. Conch. Diction. p. 107.
             —WOOD, General Conch. p. 113.—DILLW. Recent Shells,
             p. 55.—Index Testaceolog. pl. 3, f. 40.
Corbula nucleus, LAM. Anim. s. Vert. (ed. Desh.) vol. vi. p. 139.—TURT. Dithyra
             Brit. p. 39, pl. 3, f. 8, 9, 10.— Brit. Marine Conch. p. 56.—
             BROWN, Ill. Conch. G. B. p. 105, pl. 42, f. 7, 8, 9.—SOWER-
             BY, Genera Shells, Corbula, f. 1.—DESH. Elem. Conch. pl. 8,
             f. 7, 8, 9.—PHIL. Moll. Sicil. vol. i. p. 16, and vol. ii. p. 12.
             —SOWERBY, Conch. Manual, f. 89.—REEVE, Conch. Sys-
             temat. pl. 36, f. 1.—HANL. Recent Shells, p. 46.—REEVE,
             Conch. Iconica, Corbula, pl. 2, f. 10.
    "   *striata,* FLEM. Brit. Anim. p. 425.—DESH. Exp. Scien. Algérie, Moll.
             p. 231.
    "   *olympica,* COSTA, Test. Sicil. p. 27.
    "   *inæquivalvis,* MACGILLIV. Moll. Aberd. p. 303.
    "   *rotundata,* SOWERBY, Min. Conch. pl. 572.
             Encyclopédie Méthodique, Vers, pl. 230, f. 4.

Whilst the naturalist, whose efforts at collecting are confined to the rocks, sands, briny pools, and streamlets of our
coast, is apt to regard the species under consideration as of
unfrequent occurrence, its extreme prevalence is a subject
of almost petulant complaint from the habitual dredger.

The shape of this *Corbula* is more or less triangular, and
its texture very solid and opaque. The valves are remarkably unequal; the right, or larger one, not merely overlapping the other at the base, and exceeding it, ventricose
as it is, in profundity, but projecting beyond it at the umbones in a most remarkable manner, its broader beak curling over, and resting, as it were, upon the margin of the
lesser valve. They are both of them nearly devoid of

lustre, and the smaller one is clothed with an umber-brown, tolerably thick epidermis, beneath which the surface is whitish, or a very pale pink madder colour; its only sculpture consists of a few rather distant elevated lines, which radiate, with but little divergence, down the central area of it. The larger valve is of a squalid white, not unfrequently adorned, in fine examples, with more or less broad rays of darker or paler crimson, and closely grooved throughout with simple concentric sulci. The ventral margin is more or less arched, and is typically straighter, and more ascending posteriorly, but is very variable in outline, although usually more tumid in front, from whence proceeds that slight obliquity so generally apparent in its contour. The sides are rarely equal, but usually the anterior, though occasionally the posterior, is the more produced. The dorsal edges are nearly straight, and moderately, but decidedly sloping, the amount of declination not being widely different on either side. The front extremity is rounded, and the hinder one attenuated and obtusely biangulated, the posterior edge is slightly convex. The umbonal ridge is obsolete; the beak of the lesser valve is acute: and there is a strong though undefined depression on either side of the umbones. The interior is almost always devoid of colour; and the palleal scar, without forming a distinct sinus, makes at the posterior extremity a very slightly obtuse angle with the former line of its direction. In the right valve is a posterior, strong, simple, and somewhat recurved, pointed primary tooth, with an adjacent cavity in front, which is partly occupied by the cartilage: in the left valve, behind the receptacle for the opposite tooth, is a kind of excavated one, of which the middle portion is hollowed out for containing the cartilage; but the basal and especially the hinder rim is elevated above the dorsal surface.

Common as this mollusk is, it is so excessively shy when taken from its home in the sea-bed, and placed in a vessel of sea-water, that it rarely exhibits under such circumstances either its foot or its siphons. This is probably the cause of the very contradictory statements which have been offered respecting the animal of this genus, for, when examined in a preserved state, only a very slight lesion of the tissues is apt to lead us to erroneous conclusions with respect to its systematic position. Mr. Clark seems to have been especially happy in his opportunities of observing the creature, and his account of it is so much more complete than either published statements or our own notes furnish, that we cannot do better than give it in his own words. " Animal subtriangular, thick, of a yellowish-white colour, having the mantle closed, except anteriorly, where there is an orifice, whose circumference is finely notched, for the passage of a moderately long, narrow, but rather thick foot ; posteriorly it forms two very short, united orifices, with eight or ten rays each. The upper, or anal one, has a tubular retractile membrane, which the animal often protrudes and retracts. We presume the sudden protrusion of this organ is to give force to the propulsion of the fæces. On each side of the animal there is a pair of very unequal branchiæ, which hang very obliquely from the dorsal line, the upper one being rather narrow, the lower much larger and triangular. They are of a brown colour, and finely pectinated. There are also two rather long and slender labial tentacles on each side. The tubes are yellow, the branchial one having a circle of red around its orifices, and the upper only a red mark or two."

Ordinary specimens of this shell do not exceed half an inch in length, and about one-fourth less in breadth. It is most abundant, often occurring in immense numbers and gregarious, in the lower part of the laminarian zone, especially when the bottom is mud or muddy sand. It is frequent in the coralline zone, and ranges even into the region of the deep-sea corals. The greatest depths at which it has been taken alive in our seas are sixty fathoms, twelve miles from shore, off Cape Clear, by Mr. M'Andrew, and eighty fathoms, ten miles from the west coast of Zetland. It is distributed very generally around the British coasts. A few localities may be specified as examples of its range: Guernsey (S. H.); fifteen miles from shore off the coast of Devon, in sand (M'Andrew and E. F.); in ten fathoms off the mouth of the Ex (M'Andrew and E. F.); Torquay (S. H.); West Bay of Portland, in fifteen fathoms, and Weymouth in seven fathoms; off the Thames (Lieut. Thomas, R.N.); Norfolk Coast (Capt. Stanley, R.N.); Scarborough (Bean); Northumberland (Alder); South Wales, at Oxwich and Fishguard (Jeffreys); in twelve fathoms, Anglesey (M'Andrew and E. F.); in fifteen fathoms, Laxey Bay, Isle of Man (E. F.); on each side of the Irish Coast, but not generally distributed (W. Thompson); Dublin Bay, Bantry, Youghal (Humphreys and Jeff. cab.); Frith of Clyde and Gairloch (Smith and E. F.); in from fifteen to twenty fathoms, Oban, Mull, &c., abundant (M'Andrew and E. F.); Loch Kishon, Loch Alsh, Loch Torridon, Loch Shieldaig (Jeffreys and Barlee); Frith of Forth (E. F.); " On hard ground in rather deep water, Aberdeenshire" (M'Gillivray); Orkneys, in four to fifty fathoms (Lieut. Thomas, R.N.); in six fathoms, Balta Sound, Unst (M'Andrew.)*

Corbula gibba is distributed throughout the European seas. In the Mediterranean it has been taken ranging

---

* In citing localities for a common species such as this *Corbula*, we omit instances already published, unless interesting or important.

from seven to eighty fathoms (E. F.).   To its capacity for
enduring many conditions of depth is doubtless due its long
range in time, for it has inhabited our area ever since the
epoch of the coralline crag.

C. ROSEA, Brown.

Subtriangularly oval, subequilateral, but moderately ventricose, glossy, fulvous (when adult), with a short dark roseate
streak on each valve, which diverges widely on either side of the
umbones, but does not reach to the margin.   Valves not peculiarly
unequal, the umbo of the larger and slightly more convex one
not projecting greatly beyond the other ; smaller valve almost
smooth ; larger valve simply but closely grooved concentrically,
the sulci only apparent in the adult towards the margins.   Extremities attenuated, the front one rounded, the hinder one most
obtusely and subbiangulately pointed.   Dorsal slopes moderate,
the anterior one nearly straight, the posterior slightly retuse :
ventral margin convex or subarcuated.   Umbonal ridge obsolete.

Plate IX. figs. 13, 14.

Corbula rosea, BROWN, Ill. Conch. G. B. p. 105, pl. 42, f. 6.—HANL. Recent
     Shells, supp. pl. 12, f. 33.—LOVEN, Moll. Suecie, p. 49 (from
     specimen).

It is with considerable hesitation that we admit this
distinct species of *Corbula* into our Fauna : we wish it to
be regarded, then, as only provisionally included until
either clearer proofs of its positive indigenousness, or of the
greater probability of its being solely exotic, are afforded,
than our own inquiries have been able to eliminate.   The
original specimens upon which the name *rosea* was bestowed belonged to Dr. Leach, and are stated to have been
dredged at Falmouth : numerous others were in the cabinet of the late Mrs. Loscombe, mixed with *nucleus*.   Those

from which we derive our own description and delineation
are declared to have been (*once*) dredged at Weymouth, in
Dorsetshire. They are not, however, quite mature, so
that it is necessary to amend their characters from adult
examples, which appear in tolerable abundance, but without any locality appended, in some of the larger general
collections of shells.

The shape is oval, and a little triangular, and the valves
for their genus are not much inequilateral or swollen,
although both are tolerably ventricose, and their sides
clearly unequal. It is, perhaps, less solid than the average
of *Corbulæ*, but is tolerably strong, opaque, and when adult
of a roseate buff or dark fulvous, with two short rays, of
a brownish rose-colour, which so widely diverge from the
beaks on either side as almost to run parallel with the dorsal margins: these rays are of a purplish rose-colour in the
young, where the ground is whitish, and the smaller valve
at least covered with a glossy yellowish brown epidermis.
The inequality of the valves, although manifest, is not
greatly displayed at the umbones, that of the larger one
not projecting beyond the other in so marked a manner as
in *nucleus*. This distinction, however, although observable
in the young, is most evident in the adult, which is extremely glossy, a character not belonging to the preceding
species, and preserved, although faintly, in the younger
examples. The smaller valve is almost smooth, the larger
is grooved in the young, with fine and closely-disposed
simple sulci, which almost entirely disappear in the adult,
usually leaving its entire area devoid of sculpture, excepting at the broader end, and closely adjacent to the ventral
margin. This latter is moderately arcuated, but always
less so than in *nucleus*. The beaks, which are but slightly
inclined and a little acute, being situated only a little in
advance of the middle, the sides do not greatly differ in
length; both extremities are attenuated, and the front one
is rounded, but not symmetrically, whilst the hinder is
narrowed to a very bluntly subbiangulated point. The
dorsal edges are almost equally and very moderately

sloping; that of the anterior side is almost straight; that of the posterior is very slightly retuse. There is no particular depression on either side of the umbones, which latter are tolerably prominent, and not peculiarly unequal in size or projection. The umbonal ridge is obsolete in both valves; the interior surface, which, in the few specimens examined by us, partakes of the external colouring, is said to be typically pink. The small example, from which the enlarged figure has been engraved in our plates, is only a little more than a quarter of an inch in length, and about one-third less in breadth; the width, however, of the fully adult shell is five-sixteenths, and the entire length full seven-sixteenths of an inch.

The supposed Weymouth specimens, collected, as Mr. Jeffreys assures us, by Mrs. Rd. Smith, of Bishopstoke, near Bristol, were found enveloped in a kind of net-work of broken cases of *terebellæ*, and other loose textures of known British origin; a strong, though not conclusive argument, for their being esteemed indigenous. It is taken chiefly in Sweden and the north of Europe.

C. ovata, Forbes.

Plate IX. Fig. 15.

Corbula ovata, FORBES, Malacol. Monensis, p. 53, pl. 2, f. 8, 9.—BROWN, Illust. Conch. G. B. p. 105, pl. 42, f. 32, 33.—REEVE, Conch. Iconica, Corbula, pl. 3, f. 18.

Although the original describer (E. F.) of this shell took it himself from the root of a *Laminaria* cast ashore at Ballaugh, in the Isle of Man, he prefers leaving it among the doubtful species rather than stamp with the authority of mature deliberation the previous introduction into our Fauna of a species which by its presence there would vio-

late the probabilities of geographical distribution. About
ten years have now elapsed since the date of its publication (1838), during which period no second example has
been discovered : should no further specimens then be
procured upon our coast, the finding of the only recorded
one must be attributed to some such incident as the im-
bedding of the living mollusk in the tangled roots of some
fucus clinging to the oysters or cirrhipedes so wont to con-
gregate upon ship timber, in a foreign port, and the subsequent detachment of the sea-weed, either in the process
of careening, or perchance by the breaking up of the vessel
itself.

As but a single specimen of this shell has ever been
taken upon the coasts of Great Britain, the following description must rather be regarded as the portraiture of an
individual than as a specific definition ; since the latter
may not be depended upon, unless based, not merely upon
the characters present in one example, but from the aggregate of features existing in several, which remaining un-
changed amid the many modifications of form, colour, or
sculpture to which every shell is liable, may reasonably be
supposed to be the permanent characteristics.

The shape is oblong-elliptic, and very nearly, if not
quite, equilateral ; the valves, which are opaque and not
very solid, although rather ventricose at the umbonal
region, are but moderately convex upon the whole, and
differ but little from each other in either size or profundity ; the right one, however, very slightly overlaps
the other below, and very slightly projects beyond it
above.   There is an appearance of erosion at the umbones,
which prevents the accurate determination of this latter
point.   The surface is devoid of sculpture in both valves,
unless we reckon a few antiquated lines of growth as such ;
it is dull white, and is covered with a lustreless skin of
squalid white, becoming of an ashy ferruginous cast (possibly a mere extraneous coating), chiefly in the vicinity of
the lower margin of the lesser valve, where it becomes
more or less distinctly wrinkled in a concentric direction.

There is no other painting or division of surface, neither is there any carination of the umbonal ridge, which is by no means strongly marked. The ventral margin is but moderately convex, and neither peculiarly arcuated nor bulging out either laterally or medially. The dorsal slopes are but trifling, and almost equal to each other in declination; the front one is straight; the hinder is slightly convex, but chiefly so near its termination. Both extremities taper a little; the posterior is rounded, the anterior subangulated above, but well rounded below. This subangulation is more evident in the smaller valve. The umbones are not prominent, and there is not the least appearance of a lunule in front of them: the dorsal surface is, however, rather depressed on both sides, but not peculiarly flattened in either valve. The teeth are those of the section (or subgenus?) *Potamomya*, and appear identical with those of the *Corbula ustulata* of Reeve (Conch. Iconica), to the young of which species it altogether bears so remarkable a likeness, that we would not venture to assert its specific distinctiveness. The anterior subangulation is not, however, there present, and the posterior termination has a slight angularity at its lower extremity. The interior of *ovata* is white, and rather dull. The breadth of the solitary example (which does not appear full grown, and is in a good state of preservation) is one quarter of an inch, and its length is almost twice that measurement.

SPHÆNIA, Turton.

Shell oblong, inequivalve, inequilateral, more or less gaping anteriorly. Surface of the valve smooth or rugose, covered with an epidermis. Beaks incurved. Hinge composed of an erect dilated laminar tooth in one valve, with a corresponding pit in the other. Ligament internal. Pallial impression with a slight sinuation.

Animal ovate; mantle closed in front, except an opening for the passage of a small digitiform foot, furnished with a byssal groove. Siphons united to their extremities; their orifices cirrhated. Anal siphon with a tubular membranous valve projecting beyond the orifice.

This rare and curious genus is as yet but very imperfectly known, and, thanks to the observations of Mr. Clark, we are enabled now, for the first time, to give some account of its animal. In his manuscripts he offers the following remarks with respect to its systematic position :— " Though not far removed from *Mya* and *Saxicava*, the animal is perfectly distinct, and so similar to *Corbula*, that it is difficult to point out more than a specific difference. Dr. Turton is perfectly right (though, we presume, by chance) in placing this species of *Sphænia* next to *Corbula*."

The shell has evidently, at a glance, a striking resemblance to the *Saxicava*, and may be passed over as such; but the notes of Mr. Clark on the animal remove it to another family. In some respects it has considerable affinity with certain exotic forms of the genus *Lyonsia*, and thus aids in maintaining the passage evident in several of the *Corbulidæ* from the gapers and borers to *Thracia* and its allies.

S. Binghami, Turton.

Sphænia Binghami, Turt. Dithyra Brit. p. 36, pl. 3, f. 3, 4, 5.—Flem. Brit. Anim. p. 465.—Brit. Marine Conch. p. 57, f. 32, 33.— Brown, Illust. Conch. G. B. p. 104, pl. 42, f. 17, 18, 22. —Sowerby, Conch. Manual, f. 96.

Corbula   „   Hanl. Recent Shells, p. 47, suppl. pl. 12, f. 4.

Typically of a more or less rhomboidal contour, this interesting bivalve is wont notwithstanding to assume from its terebrating powers, and its ability to adapt its shape to the circumstances of habitation, very numerous modifications of its primary form. It is extremely inequilateral, opaque, but not solid, and decidedly inequivalve; the left valve being both smaller and flatter than the right, a character chiefly observable towards the lower margin and posteriorly, the convexity (which is very moderate) being almost equal at the umbones of either valve: these vary, however, in elevation, that of the smaller being the less projecting. Both valves are covered with a dull yellow closely-attached epidermis, beneath which the surface is nearly smooth or merely wrinkled with concentric, and ordinarily rather distant, wrinkles of growth. The ventral margin is usually more or less straightish, and generally ascends a little behind; the produced posterior dorsal edge, which is a little retuse, runs nearly parallel to it; the front dorsal edge, which varies from almost straight to moderately convex, declines so abruptly that the anterior side appears almost truncated.

The extremity of the remarkably short anterior side is occasionally of an abbreviated wedge-shape, but more frequently is rounded off below; that of the elongated hinder side is broad, and either biangulated or subrectangular above, and more or less rounded off at the lower angle, the front edge being straightish or slightly convex, and but little swerving from the perpendicular. The right umbo projects moderately above the dorsal line; the beaks are acute, and incurved; in front of them lies a sort of lunule-like depression, owing to the inflection of the valves at that point. There is an umbonal ridge in both valves, but it is more or less obtuse, and neither carinated nor suc-

ceeded by any marked concavity. By this, and the absence of a ligament, its external aspect is most readily
distinguishable from *Hiatella arctica*, to whose general
features it bears no slight resemblance.

The interior is of an uniform white. The hinge consists,
in the left valve, of an erect, subtrigonal, laminar primary
tooth, which forms an obtuse angle at its apex, being subtruncated in front, and produced behind. It lies almost
entirely on the posterior side, and is subdivided by the
slightly more concave anterior portion, forming a shallow
cartilage pit: this division is likewise indicated by the
flexure of the upper margin, which, more arcuated in front,
becomes nearly straight posteriorly. A corresponding
deeply-seated tooth-receptacle is present in the right valve,
with, according to Turton, a denticle in front of it, which
latter, however, we have not discerned.

The animal of this curious shell has been observed and
examined by Mr. Clark, from whose manuscripts we extract the following account of it, dated, "Exmouth, August 7, 1836 : animal elongated, compressed, pale yellowish-white; mantle closed, except a passage anteriorly for
a small, narrow, subcylindrical foot of a bluish milky transparent colour, having at its root a byssal groove, from
whence a few rather coarse filaments issue, by which the
animal is often attached; posteriorly, the mantle forms the
anal and branchial tubes, which are very short and not in
the least divided; both are at their margins furnished with
about eight or ten rather rough white cilia; from the anal
tube there is frequently protruded a blue, milk-white, transparent, tubular membrane or valve, which is more than twice
the length of the tube; it is then suddenly retracted and
again protruded. The branchiæ and labia, on account of
the minute size of the shell, could not be observed."

Individuals exceeding a quarter of an inch in breadth, and four-ninths of an inch in length, must be regarded as fine and uncommon examples. But the relative proportions of length and breadth vary considerably in different specimens; occasionally, the former is greatly increased by the under side being so produced (in which case the posterior termination is much attenuated) as to resemble a dwarf *Mya truncata* with its tube attached. Indeed, it has been supposed that the present shell is only the fry of the above-mentioned bivalve; but, having examined the several stages of *Mya truncata*, we positively state the contrary, the likeness being confined to the truncated outline of the adult: neither is there any possibility of confounding it with the young of *M. arenaria*.

Very solid and aged single valves of the common oyster seem its favourite burrowing place, from which habitat it has been taken in comparative abundance (for so rare a species) near St. Peter's Port, Guernsey (S. H.); at Torquay it is occasionally found in limestone, dredged in company with *Gastrochæna* from about ten fathoms depth (S. H.); it is obtained likewise at Scarborough (Bean); Isle of Man, on both north and east coasts, in from twelve to twenty fathoms (E. F.); in twenty-five fathoms, eight miles from the north coast of Anglesey (M'Andrew and E. F.); at Tenby, and in the vicinity of Swansea (Jeffreys).

"Two valves were found at Bray by Mr. W. H. Harvey" (Thompson); Frith of Forth (E. F.).

Mr. M'Andrew (who has taken it likewise in Spain) procured it also from the Frith of Clyde.

NEÆRA, Gray.

Shell transversely ovato-pyriform, inequivalve, inequilateral, more or less beaked and gaping posteriorly; surface smooth, or striated, or ribbed longitudinally, never punctated, with or without an epidermis; valves strengthened internally with a longitudinal rib; hinge composed of a cartilage-fulcrum, usually oblique and spathulate in each valve, sometimes with a minute tooth beside it, and a more or less developed lateral tooth on the rostral side of one or both valves; ligament external, small; muscular impressions large; pallial with a very shallow sinus.

Animal oblong, mantle closed in front, except a plain-edged orifice for the passage of a lanceolate foot; siphons short, united, unequal, the branchial largest, both bearing a few long filiform cirrhi at their sides, extending beyond the orifices; anal siphon with a very extensile membranous valve.

When the only species of this genus hitherto figured as British, was first made known, our conchologists were inclined to question its indigenousness, and to regard it as accidentally introduced. Yet now not only is the *Neæra cuspidata* extant in many British collections, but two other species have been added to keep it company within the last three years; of those two, one until very recently was known only in the fossil state, and both till within the last three years were supposed to be peculiar to the Mediterranean Sea. Such advances in our knowledge of a genus so little known to most collectors as *Neæra* have been due entirely to the more active employment of the dredge, and the greater energy and adventure of the naturalists who have, with such excellent results, kept that invaluable instrument of submarine research in continual motion.

The genus before us includes some of the most curious, delicate, and beautiful among the bivalves of our seas. It also includes not a few exotic species, mostly made known for the first time by the late Mr. Hinds, a gentleman whose active and intelligent exertions during the few but productive years that he directed his attention to natural history gave great promise of future researches, too soon to be blighted by death. The amiable spirit of fellowship and kindness in which he pursued his studies calls forth this passing tribute of regret and admiration in connection with the mention of a genus so ably elucidated by his labours.

Geologically, the genus *Neæra* can be traced as far back as the oolitic period, of which date a large and beautiful species has lately been brought to light by Captain Ibbetson. Since then it has gradually increased in number of species to the present time.

N. CUSPIDATA, Olivi.

Of moderate size, strong, fawn coloured ; beak more or less produced ; surface not sculptured ; no radiating linear carina.

Plate VII. figs. 4, 5, 6, and (animal) Plate G, figs. 4, 5, 6, 7.

Tellina cuspidata, OLIVI, Zoolog. Adriatica, p. 101, pl. 4, f. 8, a, b, c.
Erycina cuspidata, RISSO, Hist. Nat. de l'Europe Méridion. vol. iv. p. 366, pl. 12, f. 170.
Anatina brevirostris, BROWN, Edinb. Jl. of Nat. and Geograph. Science, vol. i. p. 11, pl. 1, f. 1, 2, 3, 4.
Thracia brevirostra, BROWN, Illust. Conch. G. B. p. 110, pl. 44, f. 11, 12, 13, 14.
Neæra brevirostris, LOVEN, Index Moll. Suecise, p. 48.

The shape of this graceful shell somewhat resembles a fig, being dilated in front and tapering behind to a very

narrow termination. Although semi-transparent, and very
far from strong or solid in texture, yet for its genus it is by
no means fragile, as far exceeding in firmness as in size the
remaining *Neæræ* of our shores. The broader portion is
extremely tumid, and this ventricosity, which prevails over
two-thirds of the surface, is rather suddenly exchanged for
compression at the commencement of the beak-like extremity of the hinder side. The external surface is not at
all glossy, but possesses a kind of silky lustre upon the
epidermis with which it is covered; the latter is of a fawn
colour, varying in intensity according to individuals, but
ordinarily paler towards the beaks, and always of a deeper
tint upon the right valve; beneath it, the shell is smooth,
or merely concentrically striolated, presenting no trace of
further sculpture. The umbones are excessively oblique
and decidedly prominent, and the beaks curve both forward and inward; in front of them the valves are somewhat flattened near the dorsal margin. The ventral
outline is strongly arcuated, but sinuated near its hinder
extremity, where it forms a moderately long, subcentral,
straight, and somewhat acuminated rostrum, at its junction with the incurved edge of the posterior dorsal margin,
which slopes moderately to its termination. The end of
this rostrum is somewhat cylindrical, and a convexly elevated, narrow, sub-triangular area runs from it alongside
of the upper margin of the shell; the anterior end is somewhat attenuately rounded, with its upper edge a little
convex and greatly declining. The interior is of a somewhat pearly white; the ligament, which although external
is so depressed that one hardly perceives its existence until
the valves are opened, is situated in a narrow triangular
cavity of the hinge margin in one valve, and immediately
beneath the beaks; the minute cartilage lies in a very

small sunken receptacle which inclines hindward, and seems generally to project more below the surface of the hinge-margin in the left valve than in the right. There is but a single tooth, namely, a very large and elongated approximate lateral one, which is laminar and trigonal: it is situated on the posterior side, and leans inwardly with the apex curving again outwards and upwards.

There are two very distinct varieties; the one which is the more frequently obtained has the rostrum remarkably short, and the ventral edge peculiarly bulging out; the other, which we have only received from Loch Fyne, has a much more produced rostrum, and a far more slender shape altogether. It is from the latter then, which is connected with the former variety by imperceptible gradations, that we consider the identity of our species with that of the Mediterranean to be established. Olivi's original figure is somewhat rude, indeed; but, making allowance for the inaccuracies of engraving at that period, sufficiently coincides with our specimens: Risso's rough drawing is not an uncharacteristic representation of the ordinary and larger form.

Animal white, mantle united except for a space anteriorly, where a white lanceolate foot is protruded. Siphons short, united, the branchial largest and longest, tawny with reddish dots. From the anal is protruded a slender pellucid lancet-shaped tube, or veil, with two bright-red dots at its base. These marks are between and among three white filamentary cirrhi with lobed extremities. Four similar organs are placed at either side of the branchial siphon, and all appear to spring as it were from a split sheath.

As a native of Great Britain, the merit of the discovery of this curious and interesting shell is due to Mr.

James Gerard, who obtained it from the Frith of Forth
(Brown), and of its publication as such, to Captain Brown,
who admirably described and figured it (October 1829), in
the "Edinburgh Journal of Natural and Geographical
Science." The same gentleman states in his "Illustrations
of the Conchology of Great Britain and Ireland," that he
obtained a specimen also near Port Seaton. It is only
within a very few years past that any tolerable supply of
specimens has been taken. On the English shores it has
occurred only on the coast of Northumberland (Alder).
Lieutenant Thomas has taken it thirty miles from land
alive in mud, forty-five fathoms water in latitude of Tynemouth. The only Irish locality as yet discovered is off
Cape Clear, where it was dredged in sixty fathoms water,
twelve miles from land, by Mr. M'Andrew. On the east
coast of Scotland, besides the locality mentioned, it has
occurred off Fedra, Frith of Forth in seventeen fathoms,
mud (Thomas). On the western side it is more frequent.
In the Clyde district, where it was first noticed by
Mr. Smith, it has been taken frequently (Jeffreys, M'Andrew, Barlee); also around Mull and Skye. At Oban it
has occurred in fifteen fathoms water. Off the Zetland Isles
it has been taken in various depths from twelve to eighty
fathoms, and as far as thirty miles from land, living in sand
which forms a thick crust around it when it is taken up
(M'Andrew & E. F.).

As a foreign species, this shell occurs throughout the
Mediterranean Sea, having a wide range in depth (from
12 to 185 fathoms, E. F.). Loven records it as an
inhabitant of the coasts of Norway and Sweden. It is
known as a European fossil in beds of the older pliocene
epoch.

N. COSTELLATA, Deshayes.

Small, white, beak produced, surface more or less sculptured with radiating costellæ.

Plate VII. figs. 8, 9 (the smaller figures represent the natural size), and (animal) Plate G, figs. 8, 9.

Corbula costellata, DESH. Exped. Scient. Morée, Mollusques, p. 86, pl. 24, f. 1, 2, 3.
Neæra costellata, HINDS, Proc. Zoolog. Soc. 1843, p. 77.—JEFFREYS, Ann. Nat. Hist. July, 1847, p. 19.
   „   *sulcata*, LOVÉN, Index Mollus. Sueciæ, p. 48.

The outline of this extremely rare and recent addition to our Fauna, is rather obliquely pear-shaped, the resemblance to the contour of that fruit not being disturbed as in *cuspidata*, by any projection of the umbones. The valves are much less inflated than in the other two species, being but moderately ventricose. The epidermis which, however, is rarely preserved, appears when present to be of a pale-ash colour, becoming olivaceous towards the lower margin ; the shell itself is white, thin, fragile, and very nearly equilateral ; and is adorned with a very variable number of radiating linear ribs, which, commencing anteriorly to the concavity which precedes the rostrum, diminish in elevation, and become more approximate to each other as they recede from that part, either disappearing or changing into mere radiating lines near the anterior extremity, and upon the front umbonal region. The actual costellæ (not the radiating lines), seem to be fewer on the right or larger valve, than on the other one. The ventral margin is moderately subarcuated, the chief swell being near the anterior extremity ; it rises posteriorly and, forming a rather profound sinus on arriving at the very oblique linear rib, which is the hindmost of the series of costellæ,

again rises with a slightly convex inclination, forming, with
the incurved and moderately-sloping opposite dorsal edge a
slender and tubular rostrum, of which the somewhat acuminated extremity curves slightly upwards. The anterior
dorsal edge runs for a short distance in a nearly straight
and slightly ascending direction, forming a trifling angulation with the front margin, which sweeps obliquely and
without much arcuation to the projecting and well-rounded
lower corner of the anterior extremity. The beaks are
small, and the umbones, especially that of the smaller
valves, are scarcely raised above the dorsal line. The cardinal process is small and depressed, with a short and
strong lateral tooth contiguous to it; the ossicle is strong,
solid, elongated, and glossy.

The larger of the specimens from which this account
was drawn up measured nearly three-eighths of an inch in
length, and rather more than half as broad.

The animal has a white mantle, with its margins united
in front, except anteriorly, where there is a passage for
a lanceolate white foot. Siphons united the branchial
longest, largest, and firmest; the anal short and narrow,
but provided with a very fine white extensile membrane to
its orifice, which is protruded at pretty regular intervals
even beyond the branchial, and, unless closely observed,
appears of a lancet-shape, as if it were a membranous
blade. The main part of both siphons is cylindrical,
opaque, and of a yellow colour, with reddish or orange
markings; the branchial tube is surrounded by several
simple white filamentary processes or cirrhi, which extend
beyond its extremity.

As yet very few examples of this beautiful shell have
been found in the British seas. It was first taken in 1845
by Mr. M'Andrew and Professor E. Forbes in forty

fathoms water Loch Fyne. Three specimens were found, one alive and in fine condition. Mr. Barlee has since dredged a single example in the same locality. A comparison of British specimens with those of *Neæra sulcata*, sent from Sweden by Professor Loven, and now in the cabinets of Mr. Hanley and Mr. Cuming, has proved the identity of the species, and examples from the Ægean, where it was first discovered in a living state by one of the authors, who found it not uncommon, living in various depths of water, through the great range of from 20 to 185 fathoms, agree equally well. The shell varies not a little in shape, and the Mediterranean specimens are usually intermediate in character between those of Norway and of our own seas. The species was originally described and figured by Deshayes from fossil examples brought to France from the tertiaries of Greece. His figures agree well with the recent shell, but that figured by Philippi (Enum. Moll. Sicil. v. ii. p. 13, pl. 13, f. 9), is too doubtful to permit of our quoting it as a synonym. Some species of *Neæra* in the Cumingian cabinet, chiefly from the Indian seas, come remarkably near *Neæra costellata*, especially *N. concinna*, *Gouldiana*, and *Singaporensis*.

N. ABBREVIATA, Forbes.

Very small ; fragile ; pale ; beak very short, a radiating linear carina bounding it anteriorly : no ribs nor costellæ.

Plate VII. fig. 7.

Neæra abbreviata, FORBES, Proc. Zoolog. Soc. 1843, p. 75.
„ *vitrea*, LOVEN, Ind. Moll. Suecie, p. 48.

In general shape and appearance this, our smallest *Neæra*, bears no inconsiderable resemblance to the young of *cuspidata*, but is easily recognised by the linear elevation

which anteriorly bounds the rostrum by which the hinder
side is terminated.   The fragility of its valves is excessive;
they are transparent white, and so peculiarly delicate in
structure as almost to be membranaceous.   The epidermis
is slightly cinereous, or at most faintly ochraceous, presenting, however, scarcely any tinge of colouring; and the surface, which is rather glossy, and elsewhere nearly smooth,
exhibits anteriorly, in the fully developed specimens, some
obsolete narrow concentric plicæ.   The beaks are acute
and incurved, and the umbones sufficiently prominent to
disturb, by their projection, the otherwise ovate or obovate
contour.   Behind them, a more or less raised, not particularly oblique line, succeeded by a marked concavity,
divides the shell into two portions, which widely differ
both in convexity and size ; the front being ventricose,
and occupying more than three-fourths of the entire area,
whilst the hinder one, which is small, triangular, and
comparatively compressed, forms a short and very obtuse
beak, the lower edge of which is retuse or incurved, the
upper convex, and the extremity very distinctly hiant.
The ventral margin is arcuated, and much ascending at
each extremity ; the dorsal slopes are consequently very
trifling, and deviate but little from the rectilinear, except
at their extremities, which are more or less convex.   The
front side, which is very decidedly the larger, is irregularly
rounded at its margin.   The lateral tooth is obsolete.

   Our British specimens rarely, if ever, exceed one-third of
an inch in length, and somewhat less in breadth : indeed,
they are generally of far smaller dimensions.   As a native
of our Isles, its existence was first published by Mr. Jeffreys, who stated in the " Annals of Natural History," for
May 1847, p. 314, that Mr. Barlee had taken from seventy
to eighty individuals in Loch Fyne, from which locality

Mr. M'Andrew had previously procured some examples, dredging them at the depth of forty fathoms. In the Ægean, where it was first met with, dead valves are frequent in mud, taken between the great depths of 80 to 200 fathoms. It is now known also as an inhabitant of the Norwegian seas. The *Neœra tenuis* of Hinds is nearly allied to this species.

POROMYA, Forbes.

Shell ovate or suborbicular, equivalve, inequilateral, slightly produced posteriorly; surface invested with a scabrous epidermis, beneath which it is pearly and minutely punctated; hinge of a minute cardinal ossicle or erect tooth in one valve lodged in a pit or rather impression in the other; no lateral teeth; ligament external; pallial impression very slightly sinuated.

Animal unknown; but probably closely resembling that of *Neœra*.

This genus was founded for the reception of a Mediterranean shell which proved eventually to be identical with the tertiary fossil described by Nyst, under the name of *Corbula granulata*. Subsequently, the beautiful shell described by Mr. Hinds under the name of *Neœra hyalina*, and now in the Cumingian cabinet, proved to be congeneric, and afforded better opportunities than the fragmentary and rare shell before mentioned, for an investigation of the character of the hinge. Two remarkable cretaceous fossils from Pondicherry, and a European species of the same age, all presenting similar peculiarities of structure, were afterwards associated with it,[*] and very recently a new living

---

[*] Forbes on Fossils of Southern India. Geol. Trans. 2nd Ser. vol. vii. p. 140.

species has been brought to light by Sir Edward Belcher. The genus *Embla* of Loven is possibly nearly allied.

We see in *Poromya* characters which conduct us very naturally from *Corbula* towards *Thracia* and its allies.

P. GRANULATA, Nyst and Westendorp.

Plate IX. figs. 4, 5, 6.

Corbula ? granulata, NYST and WESTENDORP (1839), Nouv. Recherch. Coq.
    foss. d'Anvers, p. 6, no. 10, pl. 3, f. 3.—NYST, Descr.
    Coq. foss. des Terr. tert. de la Belgique, 1843, p. 71, pl.
    1, f. 6.—JEFFREYS, Ann. Nat. Hist. vol. xix. p. 314,
    and vol. xx. p. 19.
Poromya anatinoides, FORBES, Brit. Associat. Report, 1843, p. 191.

It is to the zeal and science of Mr. Jeffreys, through whose distant and laborious dredgings, natural history has been enriched with many rare and interesting discoveries, whilst his careful guardianship of the collection of Turton has thrown full light upon the many doubtful and spurious species of that author, that the conchologist is indebted for the discovery and publication of this most important generic addition to our Fauna.

The contour of the unique specimen from whence we have derived our drawing and description, and which at the first glance, might possibly be deemed a variety of *Kellia suborbicularis*, to which it bears some very slight resemblance in general aspect, is somewhat rhombic, and the length exceeds the breadth by about one-third. The texture is extremely thin and delicately fragile, yet is not so transparent as from its slight fabric might be expected, owing to the nature of its peculiar surface. This, which is of a pale clay colour, and utterly devoid of lustre, appears, when highly magnified, to be most minutely and crowdedly

scabrous, the asperities not being arranged in any deter-
minate figure. Where these have been abraded, the surface
appears of a pearly white, pricked over with but slightly-
indented wavy punctures. The valves are rather ventricose; and very inequilateral, and are internally of a nacreous
white. The ventral edge is merely convex, but rises a little
behind, where for a short space it is slightly incurved as it
approaches the extremity of the linear but almost obsolete
umbonal ridge, which runs very obliquely from the umbones
to the lower corner of the posterior side, behind which the
surface is slightly depressed. The hinder side is nearly
twice as long as the other, and appears very indistinctly
biangulated, its posterior edge being scarcely convex, and
its dorsal one but very little sloping, and though slightly
curved, not far removed from rectilinear. The anterior extremity is obtusely rounded, the downward curve of the
upper margin being subarcuated, and rather sudden. The
beaks are acute, prominent, and leaning forward, without
any lunule in front of them.

A single living example of this curious shell was dredged
by Mr. Jeffreys off the Island of Skye, in fifty fathoms
water. It was first captured in a recent state by Professor
E. Forbes in the Ægean, where it occurs at various depths
between forty and one hundred and fifty fathoms; chiefly
below ninety fathoms. As a fossil it occurs in the upper
tertiary beds of Belgium, and in the coralline crag of England, where it was found by Mr. Searles Wood.

PANDORIDÆ.

THE PANDORA TRIBE.

THE genus *Pandora*, and its foreign ally, *Myodora*, present peculiarities which prevent our including them, as many have done, in the tribe of which *Corbula* is the type. Their extremely unequal and irregular shells, and peculiar modifications of hinge and, above all, the minute structure of the shell, which resembles that of the margaritaceous bivalves, afford sufficient and easily-recognizable characters, derived from the hard parts; whilst the singular conformation of the branchiæ, partially reduced by suppression, the small foot, and the united tubes with diverging orifices, present a combination of features in the animal strikingly distinguishing it from that of the neighbouring tribes with closed mantles. The small extent of the family, as at present known, is no objection to its claim to rank as such: value of character, and not number of species, must ever be the only sound ground for the limitation of either tribe or genus.

PANDORA, LAMARCK.

Shell inequivalve, inequilateral, nacreous; one valve flat, the other more or less convex. Hinge composed of a primary tooth in each valve, with corresponding pits. Ligament internal. Muscular impressions weak, rounded; palleal with a very slight sinus.

Animal oval, compressed; the mantle closed, except for the passage of a narrow, tongue-shaped foot. Siphons very short, united nearly to their orifices, which are divergent and fringed. Branchiæ of each side united into one. Labial tentacles triangular.

This curious and beautiful genus includes some fifteen species, mostly exotic, though two of them range to our shores. The margaritaceous aspect of the shell is a striking character, and depends on a structure which has been investigated by Dr. Carpenter, according to whom " the exterior presents a regular prismatic arrangement of cellular tissue, the axes of the prisms being perpendicular to the surface. Between these are distinct membranous partitions, forming a tenacious membrane, that is left after decalcification. The interior is truly nacreous." * In the animal of this genus, according to Mr. Garner,† the only appearance of the internal laminæ of the branchiæ consists of two very narrow strips at the base of the others.

P. ROSTRATA, Lamarck.

Form rather elongated, anterior end the broader, posterior end attenuated and somewhat beaked; ventral margin most swollen in front and subcentrally; hinder dorsal edge retuse, or incurved, and somewhat declining.

Plate VIII. figs. 1 to 4.

Tellina inæquivalvis, LINN. Syst. Nat. ed. 12, p. 1118.—DONOV. Brit. Shells, vol. ii. pl. 41, f. 1.—MONT. Test. Brit. p. 75.—Linn. Trans. vol. viii. p. 50.—TURT. Conch. Diction. p. 172. (not remarks).—CHEMN. Conch. Cab. vol. vi. p. 115, pl. 11, f. 106. — SPENG. Beschaft Berlinisch. Ges. Natur. vol. iii. pl. 7, f. 25 to 28.—WOOD, General Conch. p. 201, pl. 47, f. 2, 3, 4.—DILLW. Recent Shells, vol. i. p. 86.—Index Testaceol. pl. 5, f. 97.

---

* Report Brit. Assoc. for 1846, p. 105.   † Zool. Trans. vol. ii. p. 92.

Pandora rostrata, LAM. Anim. s. Vert. (ed. Desh.) vol. vi. p. 145.—Brit. Marine
    Conch. p. 58.—BROWN, Illust. Conch. G. B. p. 104, pl. 47,
    f. 5, 12, 13.—SOWERBY, Gen. Shells, Pandora, f. 1, 2, 3.—
    CROUCH, Introd. Conch. pl. 5, f. 2.—SOWERBY, Spec.
    Conchylior. Pandora, p. 2, f. 7, 8, 9.—SOWERBY, Conch.
    Manual, f. 90.—DESH. Elem. Conch. pl. 8, f. 10, 11.—
    REEVE, Conch. Systemat. pl. 37, f. 1, 2, 3.—HANL. Re-
    cent Shells, p. 48.—DESH. Exp. Scient. Algérie, Moll. pl.
    24 (animal).
    „   *margaritacea,* TURT. Dithyra Brit. p. 40, pl. 3, f. 11 to 14.
    „   *inaquivalvis,* FLEM. Brit. Anim. p. 466 (chiefly).
Pandore rostrée, CHENU, Traité Element. p. 58, f. 194, 195.

This peculiarly graceful bivalve, which we may reckon among the rarer shells of the British Fauna, is of an elongated oblong shape, extremely inequivalve, and for its genus sufficiently strong. It is semitransparent, and coated with a thin layer of yellowish white; beneath which it is pearly; and, indeed, the nacreous lustre is more or less visible, especially in the young, upon the outer surface also. The valves are remarkably unequal; the left one being greatly convex, and smooth, with the exception of some irregular concentric striulæ towards the side; the right being almost flat throughout (a little concave in the young, and towards the beaks), with similar most closely-disposed irregular minute striulæ at the sides, and especially in front, besides obsoletely indented folds toward the upper portion of the area. The ventral margin is not (for a *Pandora*) greatly arcuated, being even in certain examples a little flattened in the middle of the arch; its chief swell is in front, becoming less convex, but gradually and most distinctly ascending, posteriorly. A perpendicular let fall from the beaks (which, although by no means prominent, are, nevertheless, through the inflection of the hinder dorsal margin, more manifest than in the succeeding species,) would about equal a similar one dropped from any other portion of the upper edge, and would sever an anterior

side of only about one quarter the length of the produced
posterior one. The front dorsal edge, at least in the less
shallow valve, is convex, and moderately declining; the
hinder dorsal edge is more or less (but not profoundly so)
concave, and slightly, yet decidedly sloping. The front
is the broader extremity, and is subangularly rounded;
the hinder is much attenuated, but not very acutely beaked, as there is no distinct ventral inflection beneath it, and
the tip is obtuse, more or less squared above, and not very
projecting or ascending. The front hinge margin of the left
valve is externally sharp, and elevated above that of the
other; the hinder of the right valve, as is usual in the
genus, is flattened down, and overlaps that of the other;
but is not concave, nor at all excavated. The umbonal
ridge is best indicated in the more convex valve, where two
rather broad and approximate elevated lines run from the
beaks to its extremity, becoming more obtuse as they advance; corresponding, but very feeble grooves, are visible
in the opposite valve.

The most elongated specimen we possess is an inch and a
third in length, and five-eighths of an inch in breadth; the
widest is a trifle more broad, and the sixth of an inch less
in length.

The animal is figured by Poli, and represented as having
yellowish-brown tubes.

Although by common report ascribed to Weymouth and
South Devon, we have no certain testimony of its being
found in any of these spots; it is, however, abundant on
the sandy shores of Gorey and St. Helier, in Jersey (S. H.);
Guernsey (Clark). It occurs fossil in both red and coralline
crags (S. V. Wood), and ranges at present to the Mediterranean.

P. obtusa, Leach.

Form somewhat abbreviated ; posterior end the broader, anterior end very narrow : ventral margin most swollen behind : hinder dorsal edge rectilinear, and not at all sloping.

Plate VIII. fig. 5, and (Animal) Plate G. fig. 10.

Solen Pinna, Mont. Test. Brit. p. 567.—Linn. Trans. vol. viii. p. 48.—Wood, General Conch. p. 141.—Index Testaceol. pl. 3, f. 35.

Pandora obtusa, Leach in Lam. (ed. Desh.), vol. vi. p. 145.—Brit. Marine Conch. p. 57, f. 15.—Sowerby, Species Conch. Pandora, p. 2, f. 1, 2, 3.—Delba. Rec. Coquil. pl. 4, f. 8.—Hanl. Recent Shells, p. 48, pl. 3, f. 35.—Philippi, Moll. Sicil. vol. ii. p. 14, pl. 13, f. 13.

Notwithstanding that several writers upon British conchology have supposed this to be merely the young of the preceding shell, no species of *Pandora* can be more radically different, a mere glance at the extremities at once determining to which of the two a specimen belongs. To prevent all chance of the recurrence of such an hypothesis, we have figured the true young of the latter shell.

The shape of *P. obtusa* is subrhombically subovate, and never elongated, and the valves are very dissimilar and unequal, the left one being strongly convex, whilst the right one is actually concave ; in colour, lustre, nacre, and general sculpture it is similar to *rostrata*, but is decidedly thinner, the flat valve being of considerable tenuity and great fragility ; the elevated lines which run along the umbonal ridge of that species are likewise altogether wanting, or at most but feebly evident towards the beaks, the umbonal ridge itself being almost if not quite obsolete. There seem generally, in adult examples, a few raised delicate radiating lines towards the lower margin of the concave valve ; we hesitate, however, in regarding these as permanently characteristic. The ventral margin is greatly arcuated, and swells out chiefly behind, the front portion of it ascending in a much less convex line; the broadest part of the shell is by no means between the beaks and the opposite margin, but not far from the hinder termination, from whence the width gradually diminishes to the very narrow extremity of the anterior side. This latter is sometimes equal to a third, sometimes to a fourth only, of the length of the posterior side, its superficial inequality is infinitely greater; the front dorsal edge is decidedly and retusely sloping; the hinder dorsal margin is straight, and either horizontal or slightly ascending; the posterior end is by far the broader, being expanded, almost rectangular above, and rounded beneath. The umbonal ridge is obsolete, and the beaks depressed; the nacre is within of a silvery pearl, and greatly iridescent; the tooth of the left valve elongated, shelving, subtrigonal, laminar, confined to the anterior side, and truncated behind; that of the right valve is small, narrow, perpendicular, and central; the cartilage is oblique, and not immediately adjacent to the teeth, but forms an acute angle with them at its apex.

The size of rather a large example is seven-eighths of an inch in length, and half an inch across at the broadest part.

Mr. Clark has observed the animal, and describes it as of an elongated suboval form, having the left side much more tumid than the right. The mantle is entirely closed, except a small fissure at the anterior end for the passage of the foot: posteriorly it forms a sheath, from which two very short tubes issue, rounded and very slightly separated at their points; their extremities have fine white rays, and the tubes themselves are aspersed with exceedingly minute intensely white spots, like grains of sand. [In Mediter-

ranean examples we have observed vivid orange specks
around the orifices of the tubes.] The foot is of a white
colour, flat, and tongue-shaped. " There is only one
branchial lamina at each side, having a furrow at its
uppermost margin, and a very fine rather indented line
above it, which may be the termination of each transverse thread of the branchial leaf, or possibly the rudiment
of an upper branchial plate, which certainly is wanting in
this species; at the anterior end on each side there are
two small triangular rather rigid labial appendages, each
united with the other by a small membrane around the
mouth. They are of precisely equal size, lying one on
the other, both (on each side) plain on their outer surfaces,
and strongly pectinated on the inner; the labia are so precisely of a size, and cover each other so exactly, that they
may be mistaken for a single labium on each side."

It is frequently obtained alive by dredging on many
parts of our coast in the west and south, usually on muddy
ground.   Off Portland (S. H.); in twenty-seven fathoms
water, eight miles off Dartmouth (M'Andrew and E. F.);
at Exmouth (Clark); Torbay (S. H.); Cornwall, in seven
fathoms, Weymouth (M'Andrew and E. F.); Isle of Man
(E. F.); Anglesea, in twelve fathoms (M'Andrew);
Guernsey (S. H.)

In Ireland it is very rare, specimens have, however,
been " dredged off Carrickfergus, Sept. 1835 (Mr. Hyndman); subsequently by Mr. H. and myself in Strangford
Lough" (W. T. Ann. Nat. H., vol. v. p. 14); in sixty
fathoms off Cape Clear (M'Andrew); in twenty to twenty-
five fathoms, Skye, and in ninety fathoms off the south
coast of Mull (M'Andrew and E. F.); "Oban, Loch
Shieldaig, Hebrides" (Jeffreys); Loch Fyne (Barlee).

It ranges to the Mediterranean.

LYONSIA, Turton.

Shell inequivalve, more or less inequilateral, both valves convex. Surface often striated and invested with an epidermis. Hinge without teeth, but provided with a movable testaceous ossicle, connected with each valve by cartilage; ligament internal. Muscular and palleal impressions weakly marked, the latter sinuated.

Animal oblong; mantle closed, except a fimbriated opening anteriorly for the passage of a tongue-shaped grooved foot; siphons very short, united nearly to their orifices, which are fringed. Labial tentacles triangular, small.

Although there are few better marked genera among the European bivalves than this, the nomenclature and synonomy of our native species are singularly varied and confused, owing, chiefly, to the comparative rarity of the shell, and the imperfect state in which it not unfrequently found its way into cabinets. The genus, however, is an excellent one, and important in a systematic point of view, since it constitutes an excellent transition from *Pandora* to *Anatina* and its allies. The peculiar nacreous structure of the shell, first examined microscopically by Dr. Carpenter, links it rather with the former tribe, an union which is borne out by features in the anatomy of the animal, especially the peculiarities of its respiratory system.

The species of *Lyonsia* are few, but distributed through arctic, temperate, and tropical seas. Some forms from the Indian seas indicate a generic affinity with *Sphenia*. The history of its fossil members has not yet been clearly made out. Some tolerably well marked species occur in strata of the Cretaceous epoch.

L. NORVEGICA, Chemnitz.

Plate VIII. fig. 6 to 9, and (animal) Plate H. fig. 3.

Mya Norvegica, CHEMN. Conch. Cab. vol. x. (1788), p. 345, pl. 170, f. 1647, 1648.—TURT. Conch. Diction. p. 100, f. 100.—FLEM. Brit. Anim. p. 466.—WOOD, General Conch. p. 98, pl. 18, f. 4, 5. —DILLW. Recent Shells, vol. i. p. 48.—Index Testaceol. pl. 2, Mya, f. 13.

Mya nitida, FABRIC. Skrivt. Natur. Selskab. (1798), vol. iv. part 2, pl. 10, f. 10.

Amphidesma Corbuloides, LAM. Anim. s. Vert. ed. 2, vol. vi. p. 129.

Mya striata, MONT. Linn. Trans. vol. xi. p. 188, pl. 1, f. 13.—TURT. Conch. Diction. p. 105.

Mya pellucida, BROWN, Mem. Wern. Soc. vol. ii. p. 505, pl. 24, f. 1.

Lyonsia striata, TURT. Dithyra Brit. p. 35, pl. 3, f. 6, 7.

Anatina Norvegica, SOWERB. Genera Shells, Anatina, f. 2.—REEVE, Conch. System. pl. 34, f. 2.

Osteodesma Corbuloides, DESH. in Lam. Anim. s. Vert. vol. vi, p. 85.—DESH. Elem. Conch. pl. 8, f. 12, 13, 14.—HANL. Recent Shells, p. 24.

Lyonsia Norvegica, SOWERB. Conch. Manual, ed. 2, f. 491, 492.—MACGILL. Moll. Aberd. p. 300.

Myatella Montagui, BROWN, Illust. Conch. G. B. p. 111, pl. 40, f. 26, 27.

Magdala striata, BROWN, Illust. Conch. G. B. p. 111, pl. 44, f. 1, 2, 10.

Ostéodesme Corbuloïde, CHENU, Traité Elem. p. 51, f. 164, 165, 166.

VAR.—*Tellina coruscans*, SCACCH. Osserv. Zool. p. 14.

Pandorina „ SCACCH. Catalog. p. 6.—Ann. N. H. vol. iv. p. 294, pl. 14, f. 1 to 4.

Osteodesma coruscans, PHILIPPI, Moll. Sicil. vol. ii. p. 15, pl. 14, f. 1.

Anatina truncata, LAM. Anim. s. Vert. (DESH. ed.) vol. vi. p. 77 (in part).—DESH. (not Deles. nor Hanl.) Encycl. Méth. vol. ii. p. 40.

Lyonsia elongata, GRAY, in British Museum.—HANL. Recent Shells, p. 25, suppl. pl. 13, f. 27.

„ *coruscans*, DESH. Exped. Scient. Algérie, Moll. pl. 25. A.

From the ossicle of Montagu's shell having been represented as fixed, Captain Brown has instituted a genus based upon the figured type for its sole reception. Having examined Mr. Lyons's own specimen, and conferred with him upon the subject, we are enabled positively to assert its identity with the present species. The general contour is oblong, the texture very thin, brittle, and somewhat translucent, externally dull whitish, and internally of a

silvery pearl-like nacre. Both valves are decidedly convex, or rather subventricose, but that which is very slightly
the less so, is reflexed at the lower edge (which is peculiarly sinuated in its outline when viewed from below),
and overlapped by the margin of the larger valve. The
surface is covered with an extremely thin ash-coloured
epidermis, which is much wrinkled concentrically beyond
the almost obsolete umbonal ridge, where the valves are
compressed, and marked with a shallow excavation. This
membrane is frequently covered with grains of sand, and
beneath it the shell is closely radiated with delicate raised
rugose striæ, the interstices of which are microscopically
granulated. The dorsal and ventral edges are somewhat
parallel; the front superior margin is very retuse, and instead of declining, curves upward at its termination, the
hinder dorsal margin is slightly convex, and very moderately sloping. The inferior or ventral margin (looked
upon from the larger valve) is arcuated, and rises considerably behind to meet the slightly retuse and reflected posterior edge, which latter almost forms a rectangle with the
dorsal margin. The anterior side is regularly rounded at
its extremity; the posterior, which is nearly half as long
again, gapes at its narrowed and subtruncated termination.
The beaks are obliquely inflected, and are preceded by a
rather large lanceolate, and but slightly excavated lunule,
which is most easily distinguished by the absence of radiating striæ. The dorsal edge of the lesser valve somewhat
overlaps the other, of which the umbo is decidedly the more
prominent. There is no external ligament. The hinge
is destitute of fixed teeth, but is provided with a movable,
somewhat heart-shaped, testaceous ossicle, which is united
to both the valves by a cartilaginous deposit.

The animal of this interesting bivalve has received considerable attention, and has been more or less completely noticed by Philippi, Deshayes, and Gray. We have ourselves examined it in its living state in the British seas, and as long ago as 1835, it was carefully observed by Mr. Clark. It is oblong, and of a yellowish white hue. The mantle is closed throughout, except where there is an opening towards the anterior extremity for the passage of a white linguiform foot, flat and straight, long, rather pointed, and marked by a byssal groove. Deshayes has observed a byssus. Posteriorly the mantle forms two short tubes, which are united nearly to their orifices. These tubes are white, speckled with minute black dots. Both have about twelve cirrhi around their openings. The labial palpi are narrow, and plicated on their internal surfaces. According to Mr. Clark, there is only one elongated branchial leaf on each side, attached to the dorsal range, and running straight to the tubes. Each leaf is divided into two equal parts by a depressed groove or furrow, and is coarsely pectinated and doubled upon itself on the inner surface, rather more than half-way up its height, the extent of the duplication being marked by the external furrow. In consequence of this arrangement, each branchial lamina, though really single, appears as if it were one-and-a-half on each side.

The finest specimens we know of are those dredged off Weymouth, (near Portland,) which measure fully an inch and three-quarters in length, and seven-eighths of an inch in breadth. The species is likewise taken at Cullercoats, near Newcastle (Alder); at Scarborough (Bean); in twenty-seven fathoms, the Coquet (Thomas); in fifteen fathoms West Bay of Portland, and twenty-five fathoms Penzance Bay (M'Andrew and E. F.); in fifteen to twenty fathoms Isle of Man (E. F.).

It is by no means plentiful at Tenby (its original locality), and although "inhabiting each side of the Irish coast,
is very scarce" (Thompson). Among other places in Ireland where it may be found, may be specified Birterbuy
Bay in Connemara (Barlee) ; and the bays of Dublin
(Jeff.) ; and Bantry (Brown).

In Scotland it is dredged from Oban, Inverary, Lochs
Shieldag and Torridon (Jeffreys) ; the Orkneys, Hebrides, and Shetland Islands (M'Andrew), where it
has occurred in five, thirty, seventy, and eighty fathoms
water, and as far as twenty-five miles from land ; also in
thirty-four fathoms on the Elginshire coast, Aberdeenshire
(Macgillivray).

SPURIOUS.

To this genus belongs the *Mytilus plicatus* of Laskey and
Montagu, a species which we, in common with other
students of British Conchology, had regarded as lost to
science, until, searching in our national museum for the
remnants of Colonel Montagu's collection, we lighted upon
a specimen so exactly agreeing with the only extant figure
in the Wernerian Memoirs, and named on the tablet " Lyonsia plicata," that the supposition is not unreasonable that
it was the identical individual described and figured by our
authors. From this and a few other examples, we have
described the species, giving a more detailed account of it
than is our wont with the spuriously British shells, from
our conviction that it is by no means generally known to
the authors of works upon general Conchology. It is a
native of the West Indies (Guilding).

L. PLICATA, Montagu.

Mytilus plicatus, Mont. (not Chemn.) Test. Brit. Suppl. p. 70. — Laskey, Wern. Mem. vol. i. pl. 8, f. 2.—Turt. Conch. Diction. p. 114.

Saxicava plicata, Turt. Dithyra Brit. p. 22.

The shape is more or less rhomboidal, but evidently variable, from a liability to distortion ; it is excessively inequilateral, being truncated in front, and dilated and produced behind. The valves seem very nearly, if not quite equal, and are thin, but not transparent, of a subnacreous white, veiled, when perfect, with a pale yellowish drab-coloured epidermis, beneath which the surface is almost smooth, or, at most, rather distantly antiquated by the concentric layers of growth. The convexity is unequally distributed, the chief elevation, amounting at times to tumidity, being subcentrally from the umbones to the posterior side of the ventral margin ; the upper area of the posterior side, as well as the front extremity, is considerably more depressed. The ventral margin, which varies from slightly retuse to actually inflected in front, is more or less arcuated behind. The anterior edge abruptly slopes from the beaks in a more or less straightish line, (at times subretuse, at times a little convex,) causing the extremity of the almost truncated anterior side to appear abbreviately subcuneiform, or rectangular below. The termination of the elongated posterior side is more or less angulated above, and obliquely rounded below, the chief projection being more adjacent to the dorsal than to the ventral margin ; the former is produced, more or less ascending, and in the more naturally developed examples straightish, but occasionally convex, or even arcuated. The umbones project a little above the dorsal outline ; the beaks are small, and much incurved, (in one specimen they lean a little forward,) in front of them is situated a large and distinct lunule-like impression. The interior is of a silvery pearl, the hinder dorsal edges are not inflected, and the hinge plate resembles that of *cuneata.*

The ossicle of the specimens from whence we have drawn up the above description, is unfortunately wanting. The larger individuals were about five-sevenths of an inch in length, and at most half an inch in breadth. They appear most nearly allied to *cuneata,* which differs from them in the absence of a lunule, and in the attenuation of its hinder side.

ANATINIDÆ.

This tribe consists of a very natural assemblage of acephalous mollusks, closely allied to those of the last two families. The shells it includes are of a more or less oblong form, often tumid, sometimes compressed, mostly fragile in comparison with their dimensions; all inequivalve and gaping at the hinder extremity. The surface is dull-coloured or white, rarely conspicuously ornamented, though often minutely scabrous. The hinge varies, being in some furnished with spoon-shaped fulcra, in others deprived of such substitutes for teeth, and furnished with a free shelly ossicle fixed to each valve by a cartilage. The ligament is internal, or both internal and external. The animals have mantles, closed, except where the foot, which is more or less linguiform, protrudes. Their siphons are separated, moderately long, and furnished with fringed orifices. They are closely allied to the members of the last family in the characters of the respiratory system, a single branchial leaflet only being developed fully on each side. They live buried in mud or sand, sometimes in cavities of rock, and have a wide range, extending from low water mark to very great depths. Members of this family are distinctly recognized as fossil during the early stages of the oolitic period.

THRACIA, Leach.

Shell transversely ovate, tumid, or compressed, generally thin, inequivalve, often nearly equilateral, more or less gaping posteriorly; surface nearly smooth, or minutely scabrous, sometimes covered by an epidermis. Muscular scars unequal, united by a strongly sinuated palleal impression. Hinge composed of a thickened shelly, more or less prominent fulcrum in each valve; ligament partly internal; cartilage furnished with a free crescentic ossicle. Beaks entire.

Animal ovate. Mantle closed, except for the passage of a compressed linguiform foot. Siphons rather long, separated to their origins, and furnished with fimbriated orifices, which are "often inflated into a globular form" (Clark). A single branchial lamina developed on each side. Labial appendages triangular, pectinated.

The shells of this genus are not remarkable for beauty, being all white or dusky in colour, and not distinguished by any conspicuous ornaments. The scabrous, or shagreen-like structure, which the surfaces of many of them present, has been investigated by Dr. Carpenter, who finds it to depend upon "the presence of numerous large isolated cells, filled with calcareous matter, which form a superficial coating superposed upon the ordinary external layer, the periostracum being continued over them, and sinking down into their interspaces, just as the human epidermis covers the papillary surface of the true skin. The proper external layer is composed of polygonal cells, with sharply defined boundaries having large nuclear spots."

T. PHASEOLINA, Lamarck.

Small, white, oblong, rather oblique, more or less glossy, smooth, except posteriorly ; anterior side the longer ; posterior termination subtruncated : ossicle broader in the middle.

Plate XVII. fig. 5, 6, and (animal) Plate H, fig. 4.

Tellina fragilis? PENN. Brit. Zool. ed. 4, pl. 47, f. 25.
Mya declivis, TURT. Conch. Diction. p. 98.—Index Testac. pl. 2, Mya, f. 4.
   ,,   ,, *young*, WOOD, General Conch. pl. 18, f. 3.
   ,, *pubescens, young*, TURT. Dithyra Brit. pl. 4, f. 3.
Anatina declivis, TURT. Dithyra Brit. p. 47.—Brit. Marine Conch. p. 42.
Amphidesma declivis, FLEM. Brit. Anim. p. 432.
   ,,   *phaseolina*, LAM. Anim. s. Vert. (ed. Desh.) vol. vi. p. 129 (badly).
Thracia phaseolina, KIENER, Coq. Viv. Thracia, pl. 2, f. 4.—STORER, Translat.
        Kiener, p. 7.—DESH. Elem. Conch. pl. 9, f. 4, 5.—
        COUTHOUY, Bost. J. of Nat. Hist. vol. ii. p. 147.—HANL.
        Recent Shells, p. 22, supp. pl. 10, f. 35,—PHILIPPI, Moll.
        Sicil. vol. ii. p. 16.—LOVEN, Ind. Moll. Scandin. p. 46
        (probably).
Odoncineta papyracea, COSTA, Test. Sicil. p. 23, pl. 2, f. 1, 2, 3, 4.
Thracia pubescens, MACGILLIVRAY, Moll. Aberd. p. 296.—BROWN, Ill. Conch.
        G. B. p. 110, pl. 44, f. 6.
  ,, *declivis*, Brit. Marine Conch. f. 70.

Dr. Turton, who was the first British writer to detect the specific distinctness of the present species, has curiously enough figured a variety of it as the young of *pubescens*. Its nearest congener is, however, the *T. villosiuscula*, to which species we refer our readers, for the exposition of their points of difference. The *T. phaseolina* is of an oval oblong shape, very thin and fragile, snowy white under its yellowish epidermis, not at all pellucid, rather glossy, and very inequivalve ; the margin of the more convex valve (and both are moderately so) embracing the other through-out its entire circumference. The surface, which is marked with obsolete concentric wrinkles, only appears shagreened when viewed with a powerful lens or microscope. The ventral margin, which in front varies from arcuated to moderately convex, and ascends behind in a rectilinear or

but slightly convex line, is sometimes, but not invariably,
a little retuse, adjacent to the obtusely-biangulated posterior extremity of the shell. The anterior side is rounded;
the posterior narrowed, and always decidedly the shorter,
although the range of variation as to the extent of inequality is tolerably extensive. The front dorsal edge is
typically arcuated, but in some specimens is decidedly
sloping, and in others is but slightly convex. The hinder
dorsal line slopes but little, and after being excavated for
the insertion of the ligament, curves out gently to the subtruncated and linearly gaping posterior extremity. The
beaks are inflected and oblique, the umbone of the larger
valve prominent, and the ligament short, somewhat sunken,
and of a yellowish olive colour. The umbonal ridge is very
distinctly defined; a shallow excavation divides it from the
dorsal edge. The hinge consists of a simple, small, not very
thick triangular plate, which is slightly hollowed out upon
the top, excepting at its broader end, which causes that
portion to appear possessed of a denticle, or incipient tooth.
This plate is not divided by any medial tooth, and, being
entirely posterior, leaves the umbonal cavity exposed. The
ossicle, or moveable shelly plate, (which lies immediately
beneath the beaks in front of the hinge-plate, clasping the
edge of either valve so as to present to the eye, when attached, only its arcuated edge,) is moderate in size, and of
a broad crescent-shape. When detached (and, unfortunately, this almost always occurs before its capture, or else
in the excision of the animal,) it appears to be very convex
on one side, but flat, with a large and deep excavation near
the concave edge, on the other. It never attains to any
considerable size, and rarely exceeds the dimensions of the
specimen we have delineated.

"Animal oval, elongated, moderately thick, having the

mantle closed throughout, except quite anteriorly, where there is a fissure for the passage of a compressed, not very large linguiform foot; and posteriorly for the issue of two large rather long tubes, which are separate nearly their whole length, and divergent at their extremities, which have each a few rays. The branchiæ consist of only one lobe on each side, which has a longitudinal furrow in the middle, and is reflected for half its height, on the inner surface, precisely in a similar manner with that described as occurring in *Lyonsia Norvegica*. There are on each side the branchial lobes two small triangular labia. The animal is of a white colour throughout."—Clark MSS.

This is by far the most abundant of our *Thracias*, being a tolerably plentiful bivalve, and one that is widely diffused. It is taken in Northumberland (Alder); Scarborough (Bean); Weymouth (S. H.); various spots in S. Devon (Jeffreys); and on the sandy shores of both eastern and western coasts, from Cornwall to the Shetland Islands (M'Andrew). A variety is met with at Plymouth, in which the length is twice and a half the breadth (Jeffreys cab.). At Tenby it is peculiarly abundant (S. H.), and is likewise procured at Swansea, and the neighbouring coves (Jeffreys). Among its Irish localities we may specify Belfast, Strangford, Dublin, and Bantry Bays (Thompson), and Cork Harbour (Humphreys). It has a wide range in depth, having been taken alive in five fathoms at Unst, and dead in thirty, seventy, and a hundred fathoms, around the Shetland Isles, sometimes more than twenty miles from land. Lieut. Thomas has dredged it in twenty-seven fathoms off the coast of Northumberland.

This species ranges from the coasts of Norway to the Levant. It is the most ancient of our *Thracias*, being found fossil in the coralline crag.

T. villosiuscula, Macgillivray.

Like *T. phaseolina*, but rather shorter, dull, scabrous, and not at all oblique ; ossicle not broader in the middle.

Plate XVII. fig. 4, 7.

Anatina villosiuscula, Macgilliv. Edinburgh Philos. Journal (Jameson's), 1827, p. 370, pl. 11, f. 6.
Thracia ovata, Brown, Illust. Conch. G. B. p. 110, pl. 44, f. 4.

Although most closely allied to the *T. phaseolina*, this little known species possesses distinctive features, which, although apparently trifling, are nevertheless important from their constancy. These characters had long been noticed by that most accurate observer Mr. Clark, who had separated it in his cabinet, under the name *intermedia*. The general outline is nearly oblong, with a tendency to angularity at the beaks ; and the valves rather thin, fragile, somewhat inclined to be ventricose, but moderately unequal in area and convexity, and of a dull opaque white. The surface, even when examined with a lens of low power, is distinctly shagreened, and is usually coarse-looking, from the great irregularity of its unsymmetrically concentric wrinkles of growth, and the indentations by which it is not unfrequently deformed. The ventral margin is more or less inclined to be rectilinear ; it is sometimes however decidedly convex, but scarcely ever ascends much at its hinder termination. The dorsal edges are both moderately and nearly equally sloping, the anterior declination is ordinarily the greater ; they are both nearly straight, the front being scarcely convex, and the hinder hardly retuse, but with its extremity a little rounded and bending downwards. The sides are unequal, the anterior always being the longer (and typically much so,) but the amount of inequality is very

variable; the front extremity is rounded, but rarely symmetrically so, and is almost always attenuated and narrower
than the hinder termination; this latter is bluntly biangulated, with the upper edge in typical examples projecting
beyond the lower, so that a perpendicular line drawn from
the dorsal end would fall beyond the ventral margin. The
umbonal ridge is distinctly indicated, is not very oblique,
and has a rather large area behind it. The beaks project
moderately, and do not lean to either side; the ligament
is rather large and prominent, elongated, and of a buff
yellow. The cardinal plate which supports the ligament is
very narrow, peculiarly trigonal, and inclining outwards.
The ossicle is solid, longer than in *phaseolina*, and almost
linear, resembling a portion of a broken ring.

The preceding species, although very nearly allied to the
present, has a more elongated and oblique contour, a more
delicate texture, and a smoother surface. Its dorsal edges
are less sloping; the front one, which is convex or even
arcuated, scarcely declines at all, so that the anterior side
is much the broader; the ventral edge too both rises more
behind and swells out more in front. The beaks are more
inclined; the ligament smaller and darker; and the ossicle
is filled up, as it were, in the middle by shelly matter. In
the more typical examples of *phaseolina*, the hinder termination is usually coated with a rust-like substance, and
projects below as much at least as it does above; its
dorsal edge inclines upward. The cardinal plate is rather
stronger, and produced more under the umbo, making
the sinus more oblique; the muscular impression beneath
the beaks is rather broader, and the sinus of the palleal
impression more profound and running more to a point
below.

The superficial dimensions are almost the same as in the

preceding, but the shell is rather broader in proportion, from its more abbreviated shape.

The animal, according to Mr. Clark, is in every respect similar to that of *T. phaseolina*. It is occasionally taken in deep water upon the Northumbrian coast (Alder); at Exmouth (Clark); and in Cornwall (Alder): Swansea, Bantry bay, Ross-shire, and Lerwick (Jeffreys). It is not uncommon on the west coast of Scotland (Alder), where it was first discovered and named by Professor Macgillivray.

T. PUBESCENS, Pulteney.

Oval-oblong, biangulated behind, of a pale sand colour, never pure white, devoid of all lustre, scabrous : sides equal or very nearly so ; hinder dorsal edge moderately sloping : hinge-plate, notched in front.

Plate XVI. figs. 2, 3.

? *Mya declivis*, PENNANT, Brit. Zool. ed. 4, vol. iv. p. 79.

Mya pubescens, PULTENEY in Hutchins's Dorset, p. 27.—MONT. Test. Brit. p. 40, and Suppl. p. 166 (chiefly).—TURT. Conch. Diction. p. 99, f. 35.

„ *declivis*, DONOV. Brit. Shells, vol. iii. pl. 82.—Linn. Trans. vol. viii. p. 36. —Dorset Catal. p. 28, pl. 4, f. 6.—WOOD, General Conch. p. 93, pl. 18, f. 1, 2.—DILLW. Recent Shells, vol. i. p. 43 (not variety).

Anatina Myalis, LAM. Anim. s. Vert. (ed. Desh.) vol. vi. p. 80.—CROUCH, Introd. Conch. pl. 4, f. 1.—DELESS. Recueil Coquilles, pl. 3, f. 3.

Anatina pubescens, TURT. Dithyra Brit. p. 45.—Brit. Marine Conch. p. 41.

Thracia pubescens, KIENER, Coq. Viv. Thracia, p. 5, pl. 2, f. 2.—STORER, trans-lat. Kien. Thracia, p. 5.—COUTHOUY, Boston J. Nat. Hist. vol. ii. p. 135.—DESH. Encyclop. Méthod. Vers, vol. iii. p. 1039.—Exp. Morée Zool. p. 87, 3rd ser. pl. 18, f. 1, 2.—HANL. Recent Shells, p. 21.

Amphidesma pubescens, FLEM. Brit. Anim. p. 431.

Thracia declivis, BROWN, Ill. Conch. G. B. p. 109, pl. 44, f. 5.

It is by no means improbable that Pennant's *Mya declivis* was identical with this species ; at least, Montagu declares that the Portland specimen, the traditional type of

that shell, was similar to, though smaller than, his own
pubescens. As, however, the last-named author has confused our next species with the present one, and regarded
convexa as identical with *distorta*, we cannot look upon
him as a high authority upon the *Thracias*; and the description of Pennant being so brief and inadequate, we
have, in accordance with the opinion of our best conchologists, preferred expunging altogether the name *declivis*
to sanctioning the dangerous practice of hypothetically
determining an undefined object.

This large *Thracia* has an oval-oblong figure, is rather
thin, inequivalve, subventricose, devoid of lustre, and of
a pale sand-colour; the surface is distinctly shagreened,
and marked with coarse, irregular, concentric wrinkles;
the ventral edge is almost straight, or even very slightly
retuse on the posterior side, and slightly convex on the
anterior. These distinctions are most apparent upon the
more ventricose valve, which overlaps the lesser one both
above and below. The sides of the adult are nearly equal,
the front one rounded, the hinder tapering and bluntly
biangulated at its termination; the dorsal edge, which
anteriorly is very convex and moderately sloping, after
permitting by a slight concavity the insertion of the ash-
coloured and rather small sunken ligament, runs with but
little convexity and very moderate slope to the almost
straight posterior edge, the dorsal extremity of which is
rather the more projecting; there is a broad depressed
umbonal ridge, between which and the margin exists a
shallow excavation; both these, however, are most readily
observable in the more convex valve, the umbo of which
is very prominent, and often worn away by the obliquity
of the incurved beak of the lesser valve; the surface of
the hinder part of the shell is flattened near the dorsal

edge; the inside is white, and the hinge-plate consists of
a large and very strong prominent tooth-like callus, whose
upper surface (which in the lesser valve is above, and in
the larger beneath the level of the margins,) is hollowed
out slightly near the middle, and profoundly so in front, for
the insertion of the ossicle, the intermediate space thus presenting the appearance of a very blunt tooth; this callus,
being entirely seated upon the angulated side, exposes the
cavity of the umbones in front, and is continued posteriorly
in a narrow rib-like line, which runs parallel to the margin,
and causes the intervening space to appear grooved.

From the very rare occurrence of the young of this
species, whose extreme fragility materially diminished the
chances of its being captured in a good state of preservation, Montagu erroneously supposed that *T. phaseolina* was
its immature state. Turton, too, although separating the
species, has delineated a large specimen of that shell as the
young of *pubescens*. This error we have avoided from an
examination of the long suite of examples belonging to
Mr. Jeffreys (taken at Exmouth by Mr. Clark), from
whence we are enabled to specify the points in which they
differ from *phaseolinæ* of equal length. They are much
thinner and excessively brittle, much more scabrous, and
furnished with coarse concentric wrinkles, which become
folds upon the umbones. Moreover, their shape is very
dissimilar, the proportional distance from the beaks to the
ventral margin being considerably greater, and the hinder
dorsal edges (which are both of them flattened above)
being much incurved; the ligament, likewise, is more
cinereous, and the cartilage plate more solid.

The size of full-grown individuals is occasionally three
inches and a half in length, and two inches and a third in
breadth.

Devon and Cornwall appear to be the only counties of England which furnish us with this interesting bivalve: in the former it is occasionally taken at Dawlish (Clark), Plymouth (Montagu), and other parts of the southern coast, in the latter at Falmouth (Couch).

In Ireland it is taken on the Dublin coast and in Belfast Bay (Thompson); Birterbuy Bay (Barlee).

T. CONVEXA, Wood.

Subtriangular, inflated, cuneiform in convexity, ferruginous, subequilateral; dorsal edges peculiarly sloping: umbones excessively prominent : hinge plate extremely narrow.

Plate XVI. figs. 1, 4.

Ligula distorta, MONT. Test. Brit. Suppl. (not his original species), p. 166.
Mya convexa, WOOD, General Conch. p. 92, pl. 18, f. 1.—TURT. Conch. Diction. p. 100.—Index Testaceol. pl. 2, Mya, f. 3.
Anatina convexa, TURT. Conch. Dithyra Brit. p. 45, pl. 4, f. 1, 2.—Brit. Marine Conch. p. 41.
Amphidesma convexum, FLEM. Brit. Anim. p. 431.
Thracia convexa, COUTHOUY, Bost. Journ. N. H. vol. ii. p. 140.—BROWN, Ill. Conch. G. B. p. 110, pl. 44, f. 3.—HANL. Recent Shells, p. 22.
„ *declivis*, MACGILL. Moll. Aberd. p. 296.

Perhaps the most important feature of this rare shell, which, to the best of our knowledge, has never yet been found elsewhere than in the British islands, where it is reckoned one of our rarest species, is its peculiar inflation ; the lesser valve (for it is inequivalve, although less strikingly so than our other *Thracias*) almost vying in that particular with the larger. The shape is oval triangular, the umbones being remarkably prominent. The texture is thin but not remarkably so, and under a slight ochraceous epidermis, the colour varies from pale ferruginous to orange buff colour. The surface is not shagreened, but merely traversed by the concentric wrinkles of increase, which, however, are

very numerous upon the larger valve, especially beyond the
umbonal ridge.   The ventral or lower edge is incurved near
the middle, but decidedly convex in front.   Both the upper
or dorsal edges are convex in outline, and slope greatly,
especially the front one which thus attenuates the rounded
extremity of the anterior side.   The termination of the
hinder side, which is barely the longer and most obtusely
wedge-shaped, is rather peculiar in its contour, the upper
end of the convex posterior edge projecting further outward
than the lower one.   The beaks, which are incurved and reflected, press most closely upon each other, and the umbones,
which are tumid, are elevated far above the dorsal line.
In front of them, upon the opposite side to the extremely
short ligament, the shell, which elsewhere upon the anterior
side is distinctly the more ventricose, is retuse.   The umbonal ridge, that is to say, the obsolete fold which stretches
posterior-ward from the beaks to the end of the ventral
margin, is rounded but very distinct.   The hinge-plate is
extremely narrow, and the ossicle very small.

Large examples attain to an inch and a half in breadth,
and nearly two inches and a half in length.

The S. Devonshire coast has produced the greater part
of the specimens existing in cabinets.   In Torbay (S. H.)
it is occasionally, though very rarely, brought in by the
trawlers, who know it by the name of the *Golden hen*, possibly in allusion to the comparatively high price they have
obtained for it, or perhaps solely in consequence of its rich
yellow colouring.   Mr. Clark, whose dredging of shells upon
the Devonshire coast extended over a long series of years,
remarks that it is obtained at Teignmouth by trawling, and
at Exmouth is taken in the dredge; but the specimens are
always (in the latter case) small, and rarely if ever alive.
Mr. M'Andrew and Professor Forbes procured it in Corn-

wall ; and Mr. Alder has taken some odd valves upon the coast of Northumberland.

In Ireland it has been taken alive by Mr. Warren on the Dublin coast (Thompson), and has likewise been met with in Cork harbour (Humphrey), in Strangford Lough, and near Belfast (Thompson), and in Bantry bay (M'Andrew).

Some single valves have also been found at Arran (Alder). It occurs fossil in pleistocene clays at Belfast. An account of the animal of this remarkable shell is much to be desired.

T. DISTORTA, Montagu.

Small, variously-shaped, almost always indented at the margin, shorter in front ; umbones not prominent ; cardinal plate rounded and projecting.

Plate XVII. fig. 1, 2, 3, 8, and (animal) Plate H. fig. 5.

Mya distorta, MONT. Test. Brit. p. 42, pl. 1, f. 1.—Linn. Trans. vol. viii. p. 37.
    —TURT. Conch. Diction. p. 101.—WOOD, General Conch. p. 98.—DILLW. Recent Shells, vol. i. p. 45.—Index Testac. pl. 2, Mya, f. 15.
Anatina ———, TURT. Dithyra Brit. p. 48, pl. 4, f. 5.—Brit. Marine Conch. p. 43.—HANL. Recent Shells, p. 23.
Amphidesma distortum, FLEM. Brit. Anim. p. 432.
Thracia distorta, BROWN, Ill. Conch. G. B. p. 110, pl. 44, f. 7.—LOVEN, Index Moll. Scand. p. 47.
Anatina rupicola, LAM. Anim. s. Vert. (ed. Desh.) vol. vi. p. 80.—DELESSERT, Rec. Coquil. pl. 3, f. 4.
    „   *truncata*, (VARIETY,) TURT. Dithyr. Brit. p. 46, pl. 4, f. 6.—Brit. Marine Conch. p. 41.—HANL. Recent Shells, vol. i. p. 48.
Amphidesma truncatum, FLEM. Brit. Anim. p. 431.
Thracia truncata, BROWN Ill. Conch. G. B. p. 110, pl. 42, f. 28.

From the nature of its habitat, and the various distortions assumed for the purpose of accommodating itself to the cavity in which it may be lying, this shell, like other rock-dwelling species, is extremely variable in contour. Hence it has happened, that examples in which the growth

has more regularly proceeded than was the case with that
figured by Montagu, have been separated by Turton, and
established as distinct under the name *truncata*. Its
shape varies then from suborbicular, in which state the
lower margin is always more or less distorted or sinuated,
to subrhombiform, with the ventral edge perfectly free from
any irregularity. The valves are slightly unequal, and
somewhat ventricose, of a dull whitish hue externally, and
internally of a more or less pearly-white, which is sometimes even iridescent (varying in solidity from fragile to
' moderately strong). The outer surface is minutely shagreened, appearing under a powerful glass crowdedly set with
microscopic grains of sand, and is more or less strongly
marked with concentric wrinkles of growth, which sometimes, though rarely, are elevated at irregular intervals into
fine laminæ. The general inclination of the ventral edge
(which is variously indented) is to convexity, with a disposition to form a slight retusion towards the front. The
anterior dorsal margin is always peculiarly sloping, and
in the more perfectly and quietly developed specimens is
arcuated or at least convex; the hinder dorsal edge is inferior both in convexity and declination, being typically
scarcely sloping, and only slightly curved outward. Near
its extremity the sides are plainly unequal, the anterior one,
whose extremity is irregularly rounded or very obtusely
wedge-shaped, being invariably the shorter; and in the
rhomboidal shapes this inequality is so considerable, that
the hinder is often more than twice as long as the front
portion. The posterior termination is almost always more
or less obtusely angulated above, and frequently so beneath,
but is there as often rounded. The umbonal ridge is very
blunt and often obscure; and the beaks are small, acute,
and incurved. The ligament is depressed, buff-coloured,

and remarkably small; the umbones are not very prominent; and the hinge consists of a strong and rather narrow
oblique triangular plate, situated close under the beaks on
the posterior side, which is more or less deeply hollowed at
the top for the reception of the cartilage, and whose free
extremity curves upward in both valves, but is only elevated
above the surface in the right one. By careful examination
there is to be perceived in the upper part of its front edge
an emargination adapted to the size of its most minute
moveable ossicle.

This bivalve never attains to any considerable size; the
largest specimen we know of not exceeding three quarters
of an inch in length, and not quite half an inch in breadth ;
ordinary examples are one-third less, but the breadth often
equals the length.

The animal of this species, according to the notes of Mr.
Clark and Mr. Alder, appears to differ from its congeners
but slightly. It is more or less suborbicular in shape,
entirely white, and has the mantle closed, except a small
aperture for the passage of a small, oval, linguiform, flat
foot ; the tubes are rather short, and slightly more united
at their origins than in the other British *Thraciæ;* the
branchial siphon is often extended more than half an inch,
whilst the anal remains quiescent ; previously to its being
retracted, it is always globularly inflated at its extremity,
which inflation increases in size until its near approach to
the margin of the shell, and then suddenly disappears ;
when inflated, all signs of the cirrhi are lost, and they only
become visible when the tube is at rest. This operation
seems to be performed for the purpose of ejecting water
and rejectamenta with greater force (Clark). The branchiæ
are large and brown, one lobed on each side ; the labial
tentacles are nearly equal and pectinated.

The *Thracia distorta* is sometimes mistaken for a borer, on account of its habit of inserting itself into crevices of rock, where it assumes not unfrequently those eccentric variations of form which have given rise to its specific appellation.

Though on the whole to be regarded as a scarce shell, it is very generally distributed. We have dredged it in about ten fathoms water at Torquay, alive and embedded in masses of limestone (S. H.) It has been taken at Exmouth (Clark) and Falmouth, where the variety *truncata* occurs (Jeffreys). We have taken dead valves from the rocks upon the shore at Weymouth, nearly opposite the old castle (S. H.), and have dredged it at Guernsey (S. H.), lodged in a very thick oyster-shell. Lieut. Thomas has dredged it alive on a stony bottom in twenty-seven fathoms water off the coast of Northumberland. On the Welsh coast Mr. Jeffreys has taken it at Swansea and the adjacent bays, and Mr. Lyons at Tenby. We have dredged it off the Isle of Man (E. F.) In Ireland it was found on the north coast by Mr. W. Thompson, and at Youghal by Mr. Ball. In Scotland Mr. Jeffreys takes it at Tarbert Island, and Mr. M'Andrew in the Hebrides. The Rev. G. Laing communicates it from the Orkneys, and we have found it in the Frith of Forth (E. F.) Laskey long ago recorded it from Dunbar.

It is not known fossil; as a foreign shell, it is recorded from the north-west coasts of Norway by Löven, and the *Thracia brevis* of Deshayes (Moll. Algér., pl. 81) from the coast of Algiers does not seem materially to differ from it.

COCHLODESMA, Couthouy.

Shell transversely ovate, rather compressed, thin, inequi-valve, nearly equilateral. Surface nearly smooth, or mi-nutely scabrous, with a fine epidermis. Muscular impres-sions slight, connected by deeply sinuated palleal impres-sions; hinge formed of a spoon-shaped horizontal process in each valve, connected by a cartilage. Ligament external and slight; internal surface of valves strengthened by ob-lique divergent ribs. Beaks fissured.

Animal, according to Couthouy, " compressed, mantle closed, except anteriorly for the broad compressed foot; siphons long, slender, divided in their whole extent." Ac-cording to Mr. Clark, the characters of the animal closely resemble those of *Thracia*.

This genus was founded by the distinguished American conchologist, whom we have just quoted, for a small but very distinct group of bivalves, previously confounded with *Thracia* and *Anatina*, but conspicuously distinguished by the peculiar structure of the hinge.

C. PRÆTENUE, Pulteney.

Plate XV. fig. 4.

Mya prætenuis, PULTENEY, in Hutchin's Dorset, p. 28.—Dorset Catal. p. 28, pl. 4, f. 7.—MONT. Test. Brit. p. 41, pl. 1, f. 2.—Linn. Trans. vol. viii. p. 37.—DONOV. Brit. Shells, vol. v. pl. 176. —TURT. Conch. Diction. p. 101.—WOOD, General Conch. p. 94, pl. 24, f. 7, 8, 9.—DILLW. Recent Shells, vol. i. p. 48. —Index Testac. pl. 2, Mya, f. 5.

Anatina prætenuis, TURT. Dithyra Brit. p. 48, pl. 4, f. 4.—MACG. Moll. Aberd. p. 294.—Brit. Marine Conch. p. 43.—HANL. Recent Shells, p. 23.

Amphidesma prætenue, FLEM. Brit. Anim. p. 432.

Ligula pratenuis, Mont. Test. Brit. Suppl.—Brown, Ill. Conch. G. B. p. 106, pl. 42, f. 1.—Recluz, Revue Zool. Soc. Cuvier. 1845. p. 416.
Cochlodesma pratenue, Couthouy, Boston Journal Nat. Hist. 1839.
Thracia pratenuis, Loven, Index Moll. Scandin, p. 47.

This scarce and interesting bivalve, which appears to be little known to the naturalists of the continent, is of a somewhat oval or of an elongated ovate form, and rather tortuous ; it is thin and brittle, rather pellucid, compressed, and of an uniform scarcely glossy subnacreous white. The surface, which when recent is covered by an extremely delicate pale yellowish epidermis, is almost smooth, or only faintly striolate, (being merely marked with the lines of increase,) except behind the obsolete umbonal ridge, where it is rendered minutely scabrous by almost microscopic papillæ. The lower edge is convex, or even subarcuated, in front, but rises behind where it is very faintly retuse. The sides are nearly equal ; the anterior, which is rather the longer, tapers but little, and is regularly rounded at its extremity ; the posterior termination, which in the lesser valve is rounded and attenuated, is subtruncated in the larger one. The front dorsal margin is very much arched, and slopes but very moderately ; the hinder dorsal edge, which declines rather more, especially in the left valve, is straightish, or occasionally even subretuse, at its commencement, but a little convex at its extremity. The umbones which are moderately prominent, are much inclined; the beaks are small and inflected. There is an obtuse umbonal ridge, at whose origin near the beaks is a short linear fissure, and internally a very narrow rib-like fold, the triangular space near which is brilliantly pearly, a character more peculiarly marked in the dead specimens, from the general dulness of the surrounding surface. Both extremities are a little gaping. The hinge consists of an hori-

zontal spoon-shaped lamina, which projects with a forward
inclination from the posterior hinge-margin, upon which it
is entirely seated, and is strengthened there by a callosity
running between the beaks and the hinder muscular impression. The umbonal cavities, from the front edge of
the lamina being unattached, and the dorsal edge being
simple and not margined, are exposed even to the tip of the
beaks. The ossicle, which forms a small segment of a
circle, is moderately convex on one side, and excavated in
the middle of the other.

We had always regarded this as one of the rarest of our
British bivalves, since, although not confined to one or two
localities, it was no where obtained in any abundance, a
specimen or two being the average fruit of a season's
dredging. We learn, however, from a recent publication
of Professor Macgillivray's, that it is not unfrequently
brought up by the fishing-lines from deep water off Aberdeen, and of dimensions (nearly an inch and a half long
and an inch broad) far above the average of English examples. " It is not uncommonly dredged from Falmouth
Harbour, but mostly single valves; is also found on the
south coast of Devon, where we have taken perfect shells "
(Mont.). Dr. Pulteney procured it on the coast between
Weymouth and Portland, and on the north shore near
Brownsea Isle, Dorsetshire. Exmouth (Clark); Torbay,
Falmouth (Jeffreys); Penzance, in twenty-five fathoms
(M'Andrew and E. F.). It is obtained, though rarely, at
Scarborough (Bean); at Newbiggin in Northumberland
(Alder); the Isle of Man (M'Andrew and E. F.). " It is
rather a scarce species on the Irish Coast; found at Magil-
ligan, Dublin, and Cork Coasts " (Thompson); at Kenmare
River, in Kerry (Jeff. cab.); Coast of Down (Patterson);
Bantry Bay (Miss M. Ball). In Scotland Mr. Jeffreys has

taken it at Oban; on the Ross Coast; and at Lerwick. Mr. M'Andrew has taken it in sixty fathoms water, twenty miles westwards from the Zetland Coast. It is taken from sandy bays in the Orkneys (Thomas and Laing); the Murray Firth (M'Andrew); and the Frith of Forth, where it was noticed by Laskey. It ranges to the Norwegian seas. It is not known in a fossil state.

The only information we possess of the animal of this interesting shell is derived from a note of Mr. Clark, who describes it as closely resembling that of the several British species of *Thracia*. Its foot is situated very anteriorly, and similar in shape to that of its allies. The tubes appear also to be similar, and the mantle closed to the same extent. "The branchiæ are completely similar, being composed of one oblique lamina fastened dorsally and facing ventrally, pectinated in a marked manner. There are two small labia on each side the mouth. The branchial plate is divided by an oblique furrow into two parts, the upper being less in depth than the lower portion."—*Clark MSS.*

NOTE.—It is with regret that we allude to a paper on the *Anatinidæ* by M. Reclus, in the "Revue Zoologique" for 1845 (p. 407), but his positive assertions respecting the species of British *Thracia* must not pass uncontradicted. His erroneous impressions respecting them have arisen from his constant habit of trusting to the language and figures of writers, without correcting his views by the personal examination of typical specimens. His declaring (p. 414) that the name *declivis* originated from Donovan; his boldly naming (p. 414) the *Anatina distorta* of Turton, *Th. Turtoniana*, under the idea that *that* author had not divined the Montaguian species, which he states is identical with *Th. corbuloides* of Kiener (he has likewise proposed the name *Beauiana* for what he calls the *Thr. declivis* of Sowerby and of Thorpe; we know not where the former was published, the latter was figured from Mr. Hanley's cabinet, and is our *phaseolina*) —his denial of an apical fissure to *C. pratensis*, &c. &c. have rendered us, perhaps erroneously, adverse—from want of confidence in his statements—to that separation of *pratensis* from *Cochlodesma*, as *Ligula* proper (the name retained to it alone of the *Thracia Syndosmya* and *Scrobicularia*, confused together in that ill constituted genus), which is urged by an author who displays a minute research and a knowledge of our conchological literature which demands our high respect.

SOLENIDÆ.

THE RAZOR-FISHES.

A SMALL but important tribe of bivalves, remarkable for the extreme transverse elongation of their shells, and the large development of foot in their animals. The razor-fishes, so called on account of their peculiar shape and the sharp edges of their valves, constitute a very natural group, confined almost entirely to a single genus. Their short, united, fimbriated siphons, and thick, elongated, truncated foot, which emerges from one extremity of the elsewhere united lobes of the mantle, furnish excellent distinctive characters. Lamarck constituted the family *Solenacées* for their reception, associating with the true razor-fishes, however, the very dissimilar genera *Glycimeris* and *Panopæa*. Deshayes, in 1839, restricted the family to the genera *Solemya*, *Solen*, and *Solecurtus;* but the animal of the last-named genus is too distinct to be placed in the same group with the true *Solen*. Agassiz, in the same year, included in this family the genera named *Psammobia* and *Sanguinolaria*, a still more unnatural assemblage. D'Orbigny has lately placed *Solen* among the *Myacidæ*, alongside of *Panopæa*, *Pholadomya*, *Mya*, and *Lutraria*, but removes *Solecurtus* to another family. Such differences of opinion respecting the true position and associates of a very natural and defined genus, are sufficient of themselves to warrant our regarding it as probably the type of a distinct family.

SOLEN, Linnæus.

Shell transversely greatly elongated, subcylindrical, more
or less compressed, equivalve, inequilateral, gaping at both
extremities; surface diagonally comparted, invested with
an epidermis. Muscular impressions distinctly marked,
dissimilar, the posteal oblong, the anteal greatly elongated;
palleal impression with a wide, short sinus at its posterior
extremity. Hinge variable in structure and position, sometimes terminal, sometimes subcentral; usually composed of
well-defined cardinal teeth and a lateral ligamental fulcrum
in each valve. Ligament external, elongated. Valves
beneath the hinge internally strengthened by a more or
less distinct and oblique rib.

Animal very narrow, more or less cylindrical or compressed; mantle united at the borders, except anteriorly,
where it opens for the passage of a large, long, thick,
oblique, truncated foot. Siphons short, united, their orifices fimbriated. Branchiæ prolonged into the inferior
siphon. Labial palpi long, narrow, and triangular.

Aristotle, in his "History of Animals," mentions more
than once a shell-fish under the name of σωλην, in such
expressive terms that we can scarcely doubt its identity
with the razor-fish, in all probability the first of the
species to be hereafter described. He states that it buries
itself in sand, perpendicularly, even to a depth of two
feet, and can rise and sink in, but does not leave its hole;
that it does not spin a byssus wherewith to fix itself, like
other testacea; that it is alarmed by noise, and buries
itself rapidly when frightened; that the valves of the shell
are connected together at both sides, and that their surface
is smooth. Such an enumeration of character indicates

how carefully the great philosopher studied razor-fishes, and with what interest he watched their doings and chronicled their fears.

In more modern times, about the commencement of the last century, they had equal attraction for Reaumur, who, as we shall have occasion to shew presently, observed their habits with like interest and care. The razor-fishes, however, would scarcely have attracted such attention had it not been for their excellent qualities as articles of food. They are among the most delicious of shell-fish when properly cooked—broiling is the best method—and are eaten in many parts of Britain, as well as abroad. They bury in sand, mostly near low-water mark; but many species are only to be obtained by dredging, and some of the smaller kinds live at very great depths. The valves of the shell, being connected by epidermis, serve at once as a protection and as a lining to their holes. Their powerful foot, with its broad, finger-like extremity, enables them to sink in sand or mud with great rapidity. It is curious that Pliny, and after him Rondeletius, distinguished between male and female *Solens*,—in their cases a distinction probably fanciful, but worthy of note as a blind anticipation of the later discovery of the bisexuality of Acephalous Mollusca.

The *Solens* are remarkable for presenting the greatest length and least breadth of all the bivalves.

We find traces of this genus in shells presenting a close similarity of external form among palæozoic fossils. Not until we reach the tertiary epoch do we find remains of species very distinctly allied to such as now live. In beds of the pleistocene epoch they become comparatively abundant, but the genus must be considered rather as belonging to the present than to any former period. The

existing species are distributed all over the world, without
regard to climate, those from tropical seas often closely
simulating those from arctic regions, though specifically
distinct.

S. MARGINATUS, Pulteney.

Straight, margined by a stricture in front ; hinge terminal ;
a single tooth in each valve.

Plate XIV. fig. 1, and (animal, siphon only) Plate I. f. 3.

Solen vagina, PENN. (not LINN.) Brit. Zool. ed. 4, vol. iv. p. 83, pl. 46, f. 3.—
MONT. Test. Brit. p. 48, and Suppl. p. 25. — Dorset Catal. p.
28, pl. 4, f. 8.—TURT. Conch. Diction. p. 159 ; Dithyra Brit.
p. 79, pl. 6, f. 4.—FLEM. Brit. Anim. p. 458.—Brit. Marine
Conch. p. 34.—BROWN, Ill. Conch. G. B. p. 112, pl. 47, f. 2.—
POLI, Testac. Sicil. vol. i. pl. 10, f. 5, 6.—WOOD, General
Conch. p. 119, pl. 27, f. 1.—DILLW. Recent Shells, p. 57.—
LAM. Anim. s. Vert. (ed. Desh.) vol. vi. p. 53 (not vars.).—Index
Testaceol. pl. 3, Solen, f. 3.—MAWE, Conchology, pl. 5, f. 3.—
DESH. Elem. Conch. pl. 6, f. 4, 5, 6.—PHIL. Moll. Sicil. vol. i.
p. 4 and vol. ii. p. 4.—HANL. Recent Shells, p. 11.—CHENU,
Ill. Conch. Solen, pl. 1, f. 1.—PHIL. Neu Conch. Solen, pl. 1,
f. 4.—CUVIER, R. Anim. (ed. Croch.) 111. f. 3.—Exped.
Scien. Algér. Moll. p. 179, pl. 10, f. 1, to 5 (shell and
animal).

Solen marginatus, PULTENEY, in Hutchins' Dorset, p. 28.—DONOV. Brit. Shells,
vol. iv. pl. 110.

THE valves of this species, which is longitudinally elongated, the length averaging about six times the breadth,
are quite straight, rather solid, and of a somewhat compressed subcylindrical form. They are less shallow than
in the two succeeding *Solens*, and when in fine condition,
are partially covered with a rather glossy ashy-olivaceous
very thin and caducous epidermis, beneath which the surface, which is almost smooth, or, at most concentrically
substriated, is of an uniform tint, being whitish, or tinged
with alternately deeper and paler shades of orange buff-
colour. The dorsal and ventral margins run parallel to each

other; there is, however, a slight contraction of them near the ligament, which is the narrowest portion of the shell. A broad groove-like excavation runs from the terminal beaks to the opposite margin, stricturing as it were the anterior extremity; this latter is subtruncated, but the edge is convex, and but little oblique; the posterior termination, which is, if anything, the broadest part of the valves, is decidedly and almost rectangularly truncated. The interior either partakes of the external colouring, or is of an uniform whitish hue. The hinge is destitute of lateral laminæ, and consists of a single primary greatly compressed prominent semicircular tooth in each valve, applied to the corresponding surface of the other.

The animal of *Solen vagina* is well known, having frequently attracted the attention of malacologists for more than a century. It differs considerably from that of either of the preceding species; the differences, however, are only of specific value. It is elongated and subcylindrical, the mantle brownish-white, closed in front, and open anteriorly for the passage of an oblong, compressed, yellowish-white foot, which, when at rest, is subcylindrical, with an oblique clavate extremity. The siphons are united to their extremities, the tube so formed long as compared with that of allied species, yellowish, and marked with concentric bands of linear or moniliform brownish spots of unequal dimensions. These circles seem to indicate so many stages of growth, since they are evidently the remains of the brown markings which surrounded the very short tentacles or cirrhi fringing the siphonal orifices. The branchial orifice has an obsoletely fimbriated margin, and a circle of very short cirrhi beyond it; the margin of the anal aperture is plain, but bordered beyond by a similar tentacular circle. The branchiæ are long, linear, and of an orange brown colour, and the labial tentacles large, very long, triangular, and acute.

The habits of this species were made the subject of investigation by the celebrated Reaumur, who published an account of them, illustrated by figures, in the "Memoires de l'Academie des Sciences," for 1712. It burrows in sand near low water-mark, spring tides, to the depth of from a foot and a half to two feet. The *Solens* lie in their holes nearly vertical, and their places are marked by perforations shaped like keyholes, corresponding to the form of the extremities of their united siphons. They are nearly vertical, and do not remain quiet, but rise up and down now and then, shifting themselves partly above the sand, as if to learn what is going on in the world above. When the tide goes out they sink deeper. The fishermen then endeavour to tempt them out as little boys would catch birds if they could—by putting salt on their tails. The salt penetrating the perforation reaches and irritates the extremities of the siphons, and the *Solen*, annoyed and pained, rises suddenly to clear itself of the nuisance. His vigilant human enemy watches the moment and seizes the opportunity,—and the *Solen*, if he can catch it; but unless very quick in his motions, those of the *Solen* may be quicker, and once aware of the danger impending, the sensible shell-fish will not rise again, but submits patiently to the indignity of being salted alive, rather than run the risk of being caught and roasted, or else cut up for bait. But if it be not touched, a second dose of salt will cause it again to rise, which shows that knowledge and recollection of the danger is the impediment to its reappearance in the former case. Fishermen in England have a queer but absurd fancy that when the razor-fish feels the salt, it thinks the tide is coming in, and therefore rises in its hole.

If the *Solen* be taken out of its hole, and placed upon the sand, it immediately prepares to re-bury itself. It stretches out its foot to full length, and then bends it so as to use the extremity as a kind of auger. When the end has sunk into the sand, it draws up its shell, which, first oblique, and afterwards perpendicular, soon becomes immersed, and rapidly disappears. M. Deshayes, during his Algerian researches, observed a remarkable instinct of *Solen marginatus* to swim, when desirous of changing its locality. When it finds itself on ground too hard to be penetrated by its foot, it fills the cavity of its mantle with water, and then contracting, and closing exactly at the same time its siphonal orifices, elongates its foot; then recontracting that organ, it ejects the water with force from the tubes, and thus propels itself, after the manner of a cuttle-fish, for a foot or two forwards. Then, if it finds the surface favourable, it bores and buries itself; but if not, makes another leap, to try its chance anew.

The ordinary size of our British specimens is about four and a half inches in length, and three quarters of an inch in breadth; those from the Mediterranean appear to be of far smaller dimensions. The species is by no means so common as *Siliqua* or *Ensis*, but is sufficiently abundant in certain localities. Amongst others, we may mention the sands between Tenby and Langharne, in Caermarthenshire (S. H.); Exmouth, on the cockle-sands near Lympstone (Clark); Anglesea (M'Andrew); and the isles of Guernsey and Jersey (S. H.), as peculiarly productive. It is obtained also in the neighbourhood of Swansea (Jeffreys). It is enumerated by Mr. Smith among the shells of the Clyde; but, if a Scottish shell, is certainly a very rare and local species.

"On the Irish coast it is local, inhabiting very extensive

sandy beaches, as those of Magilligan, and of the counties
Dublin and Cork" (Thompson). In eight fathoms, Bangor,
County Down, dead (Patterson).

Abroad it has a wide range. Löven enumerates it
among the mollusca of Norway. Southwards it extends
into the Mediterranean, and Philippi records it as occur-
ing among the shells collected by Ehrenberg and Von
Hemprich in the Red Sea.

S. siliqua, Linnæus.

Straight, not margined by a stricture in front ; hinge terminal,
two teeth in one valve.

Plate XIV. fig. 3, and (animal) Plate I. f. 1.

LISTER, Hist. Conch. pl. 409, f. 255.

Solen siliqua, LINN. Syst. Nat. p.1113.—PENN. Brit. Zool. ed. 4, vol. iv. p. 83, pl.
45, f. 20.—DA COSTA, Brit. Conch. p. 236, pl. 17, f. 5.—
PULTENEY, Hutchins Hist. Dorset, p. 28. — DONOV. Brit.
Shells, vol. ii. pl. 46.—MONT. Test. Brit. p. 46.—Linn. Trans.
vol. viii. p. 43.— Dorset Catal. p. 28, pl. 2, f. 5.— TURT.
Conch. Diction. p. 158 ; Dithyra Brit. p. 80, pl. 6, f. 5.—
FLEM. Brit. Anim. p. 459.—MACGILL. Moll. Aberd. p. 282.—
Brit. Marine Conch. p. 35.—BROWN, Ill. Conch. G. B. p. 112,
pl. 47, f. 33.*—POLI, Testac. Sicil. vol. i. pl. 10, f. 7, 11.—
WOOD, General Conch. p. 118, pl. 26, f. 1, 2.—DILLW. Recent
Shells, vol. i. p. 59.—LAM. Anim. s. Vert. (ed. Desh.) vol. vi. p.
55.—Index Testac. pl. 3, Solen, f. 1.—DESH. Elem. Conch. pl.
6, f. 1, 2, 3.—PHILIPPI, Moll. Sicil. vol. i. p. 4, and vol. ii.
p. 5.—HANL. Recent Shells, vol. i. p. 11.—DESH. Exp. Scien.
Algér. Moll. p. 181.

Solen novacula, MONT. Test. Brit. p. 47.—Linn. Trans. vol. viii. p. 44.—TURT.
Conch. Diction. p. 159 ; Dithyra Brit. p. 80.—FLEM. Brit.
Anim. p. 459.—Brit. Marine Conch. p. 35.—WOOD, General
Conch. p. 119.—DILLW. Recent Shells, vol. i. p. 58.

,, Ligula, TURT. Dithyra Brit. p. 82, pl. 6, f. 6.—BROWN, Ill. Conch. G.
B. p. 112, pl. 47, upper f. 2.

THE valves of this well-known species are of an elongated
greatly compressed cylindrical shape, their length averaging six or seven times their breadth ; they are fragile, al-

though usually of moderate thickness, and are scarcely, if
at all, curved. The exterior is almost smooth, or at most
concentrically striolate, and is covered with a membranaceous, strong, highly polished, yellowish-green, or olivaceous yellow epidermis, beneath which the shell is whitish,
with irregular interrupted concentric bands of a purplish
liver colour. The colouring is most profusely displayed
upon the hinder area, which is diagonally divided from the
other by an imaginary line drawn from the beaks to the
posterior corner, behind which the surface is slightly more
elevated, again becoming suddenly flattened towards the
dorsal margin, where the edges have a tendency to bend
outward, instead of curving inwards. The dorsal and
ventral margins are almost parallel, both sloping a little
upwards at the rather narrower anterior extremity. This
latter, as well as the posterior termination, is truncated,
the edges descending abruptly, yet not without some degree of convexity, especially in front, to the ventral margin.
There is no stricture nor internal callus in front, neither is
there any attenuation of the valves at the hinder extremity, which, on the contrary, is broad, and almost rectangularly biangulated. The inside is white, exhibiting in the
thinner and younger specimens the external colouring.
The hinge, which is terminal, and whose entire length is
not equal to one half of the ligamental callus, is furnished
in the left valve with two rather solid and closely approximating fang-shaped primary teeth, which admit between
them the peculiarly thin and laterally compressed tooth of
the other. This latter, when in fine preservation, (which
is rarely the case, being almost invariably broken in ex-
tracting the animal) is bifid at its apex, and strengthened
at its base in the more delicate individuals by a more or
less distinct and semicircular horizontal plate. There are,

moreover, three lateral laminæ, two in the left valve, and
one in the right valve, whose length is but trifling, and
whose extremities curve upwards and outwards.

Although rarely attaining to such dimensions, the length
is occasionally as much as eight inches, and the breadth fully
one inch. It is decidedly the largest of the British *Solens*.
We have included in our synonymy the *S. ligula* of Turton,
and the *S. novacula* of Montagu, having taken the former
from the Tor Abbey sands, (the indicated locality,) and
ascertained with certainty that its dentition, (the sole
reason for its specific separation) is that of the perfect
siliqua before age has obscured the sharpness of its outlines.
The latter we have been enabled to determine, by an examination of the individual forwarded to Mr. Dillwyn by Col.
Montagu, in compliance with that gentleman's request for
information as to his species. The absence of lateral
laminæ (the distinctive feature of the diagnosis) was in
all probability the result of accidental fracture, as they
are distinctly present in that typical specimen.

The animal is elongated, thick, and of a yellowish-white
colour; its foot is very long and large, thick and white,
slightly angular and truncated at the extremity. The
base of the foot occupies about the middle of the shell, between which point and the siphons the mantle is closed.
At the point where it opens to let the foot pass, its margins
are minutely fringed. The posterior extremity is truncated, the truncation being occupied by the very short
siphons, each with an orifice surrounded by a double fringe
of cirrhi. The margin of the mantles near the siphons is
slightly tinged with brown, as are also the siphons themselves. The labial palpi are larger and narrower than in
the next species.

" This shell is common on most of our sandy shores,

found buried to the depth of a foot or more, near low-water mark ; it frequently elevates one end a little above the surface, and protrudes its body in search of food ; upon being disturbed it suddenly recedes. This place is known by a small depression on the surface. In many places it is sought after for food by the common people" (Montagu). The mode in which a dishful of these esculents is rapidly collected by children, might successfully be imitated by conchologists, for other than culinary purposes. A long narrow wire, bent and sharpened at one end is suddenly thrust into the hollows of the sands indicative of the pre-sence of these animals, and passing between the valves, the barbed portion fixes itself on retraction in the animal, and forces it to the surface.

The species is both abundant and diffused. It is plen-tiful at Scarborough (Bean), and the North (Alder), and is taken from the South of England up to Shetland (M'An-drew). " It inhabits Dublin Bay, and the sandy coast of Ireland generally" (Thompson) ; and is found on both the east and west sides of Scotland. Dead valves are occa-sionally dredged in various depths of water, and as far as five miles from shore on some of our coasts (E. F.) ; but it probably does not extend its true range beyond the lami-narian zone. It is distributed throughout the European seas, and is found fossil in tertiary beds of more than one epoch. It appeared in the British seas during the period of the Red Crag and is a common fossil, though usually in a fragmentary condition, in the glacial beds of the Clyde, Ireland, and Bramerton ; a good indication of the littoral origin of part of these deposits.

S. ENSIS, Linnæus.

Resembling *S. siliqua*, but arcuated, and generally more slender.

Plate XIV, fig. 2.

Solen ensis, LINN. Syst. Nat. p. 1114.—PENN. Brit. Zool. ed. 4, vol. iv. p. 84, pl. 45, f. 22.—DA COSTA, Brit. Conch. p. 237.—PULTENEY, Dorset, p. 28.—DONOV. Brit. Shells, vol. ii. pl. 50.—MONT. Testac. Brit. p. 48.—Linn. Trans. vol. viii. p. 44.—TURT. Conch. Diction. p. 160, f. 61 ; Dithyra Brit. p. 82.—FLEM. Brit. Anim. p. 459.—MACGILL. Moll. Aberd. p. 282.—Brit. Marine Conch. p. 35.—BROWN, Ill. Conch. G. B. p. 113, pl. 47, f. 10.—CHEMN. Conch. Cab. vol. vi. p. 47, pl. 4, f. 30 and C.—POLI, Test. Sicil, pl. 11, f. 14.—WOOD, General Conch. p. 122, pl. 28, f. 1, 2.—DILLW. Recent Shells, vol. i. p. 59.—LAMARCK, Anim. s. Vert. (ed. Desh.) vol. vi. p. 55.—Index Test. pl. 3, Solen, f. 6.—BURROWS. Conch. pl. 4, f. 3, 4.—PHILIPPI, Moll. Sicil. vol. i. p. 4, and vol. ii. p. 5. —SOWERBY, Conch. Manual. f. 60.—HANL. Recent Shells, p. 11.—DESH. Exp. Scien. Algér. Moll. p. 184, pl. XI. f. 1, 4. (animal).
Solen Sabre, CHENU, Traité Elem. p. 41, f. 126, and pl. 1, f. 1. Encycl. Méthod. Vers, pl. 223, f. 2.

THE description of *siliqua* is so nearly applicable to the present species, that it is only necessary to particularize those few points of difference by which they may be distinguished from each other.

Of these, the most readily perceptible is the decided arcuation of the valves in *ensis*, which typically, likewise, is far more slender in proportion, the length of ordinary individuals being eight times their breadth. The anterior extremity, moreover, is not truncated but rounded, whereas in characteristic examples of the preceding species, the convexity of the front margin is so trifling as scarcely to be noticeable. The posterior side is likewise a little tapering near its termination. The colouring matter is perhaps of a browner tint, and the epidermis, which, as in *siliqua*, is transparent and colourless upon the diagonally-parted-off posterior area, usually, assumes a chesnut or rusty cast towards the ventral margin and the anterior side.

The valves seem slightly more convex, and the extreme difference of size between adult individuals of the usual dimensions belonging to the two species is so marked as almost to merit being regarded as characteristic. There is, however, a variety, a scarce one though, whose amplitude is on a par with that of *siliqua*; but in general the valves do not attain four inches in length, nor exceed half an inch in width.

Turton is in error when he declares the solitary tooth of the right valve to be simple; it is distinctly, but most delicately, grooved at its rounded apex.

The animal of *Solen ensis* has been examined and figured by M. Deshayes. It is very closely allied, as might be expected, to that of *siliqua*. The siphons are very short, the branchial one having a fringe of tentacula, irregular, but simple, around its orifice, and a second circle of similar organs just below. The anal has the second series only developed, but its margins are slightly scalloped. Both tubes are white below the second circle of cirrhi, but above it they are minutely speckled with brown. The foot is of a dull flesh-colour at the sides, its end paler, and obliquely truncated.

It is an inhabitant of rather deeper water than the last species, ranging from five to fifteen fathoms, the ground sand or shelly sand.

Equally with *siliqua*, this species is at once both numerous in individuals, and most widely diffused. It is abundant at Scarborough and the North (Bean and Alder); occurs at intervals along the eastern coast, from thence to Devonshire (S. H.); and is common on sandy shores from the south of England to Shetland (M'Andrew). "It inhabits the sandy coast generally of Ireland" (Thompson) ; and is taken at Lochs Carron, Kishon, Torridon (Jeffreys), and other parts of Scotland.   It ranges throughout the European Seas, and occurs fossil in Pleistocene beds.

The *S. ensis* of transatlantic writers, judging from the description of Gould (Invert. Massachus. p. 28), and the figure of Conrad (Americ. Marine Conch. pl. 5, f. 1,) does not exactly coincide with our shell ; it is represented by the latter as of a much more abbreviated form, and as obliquely truncated at the shorter end.

S. PELLUCIDUS, Pennant.

Small, subarcuated, very thin ; the hinge not terminal.

Plate XIII. fig. 3. and (animal) Plate I. f. 2.

Solen pellucidus, PENN. Brit. Zool. ed. 4, vol. iv. p. 84, pl. 46, f. 23 (not Spengler, 1794).—MONT. Test. Brit. pp. 49, 565.—DONOV. Brit. Shells, vol. v. pl. 153.—Linn. Trans. vol. viii. p. 44.— TURT. Conch. Diction. p. 160 ; Dithyra Brit. p. 83.—FLEM. Brit. Anim. p. 459.—MACGILL. Moll. Aberd. p. 283.—Brit. Marine Conch. p. 35, f. 106.—BROWN, Ill. Conch. G. B. p. 113, pl. 47, f. 4.—WOOD, General Conch. p. 123, pl. 28, f. 3.—DILLW. Recent Shells, vol. i. p. 60.

Solen pygmæus, LAM. Anim. s. Vert. (ed. Desh.) vol. vi. p. 56.

Solen tenuis (?) PHILIPPI, Moll. Sic. vol. i. p. 6, pl. 1, f. 2.

This delicate and fragile shell is of a linear and slightly-arcuated form, very thin, more or less compressed, and everywhere covered by a polished epidermis of a greenish yellow, beneath which the surface is uniformly whitish, both externally and internally.   The length of the valves is about four times their breadth ; they are extremely inequilateral, semi-pellucid, gaping at both extremities (particularly in front, where their margins are reflected), and devoid of all sculpture or markings.   The ventral and dorsal edges run nearly parallel, so that the latter is retuse,

and the former subarcuated; but, as both extremities are a
little attenuated, the ventral effects this by rising at each
end, and thus its general curve appears to exceed that of
the upper margin. The umbones are rather depressed than
otherwise, the beaks almost undefined, but not terminal;
so that there is an anterior side, although a very small
one, it not being quite equal in length to the ligament,
which latter is not peculiarly depressed, and occupies about
a sixth of the entire dorsal outline. The front extremity is
remarkably well rounded, particularly below; the posterior
termination is bluntly subtruncated. The front dorsal edge
is convex and moderately sloping. The hinge occupies a
very small space, and closely resembles that of *legumen*.
It consists in the right valve of a single small compressed
primary tooth, and an adjacent posterior sublateral lamina,
which is rather short, and obliquely projects beyond the
hinge-margin. In the left valve is a curved posterior sublateral denticle, a somewhat conical front primary tooth
with a posterior inclination, and a large central compound
tooth (that of the immature shell, when viewed from above,
reminds one of a high-heeled boot), forming with the two
preceding ones receptacles for the opposing teeth, and consisting of a small acutely pointed conical primary tooth,
and a short sublateral lamina on the same base.

The length of one of our larger specimens, which is at
least of the average size, is an inch and a half; its extreme breadth is three-eighths of an inch.

The animal of *Solen pellucidus*, is of a lanceolate form,
and not so thick in proportion to the shell as the other
species of this genus. Its siphons are very short, of a
tawny or dull orange yellow colour, united to their extremities, and fringed at their orifices. The foot is long, compressed, and obliquely truncated at the extremity; it is of

a rose colour, paler at the end and base. The epidermic membrane, which closes the front of the shell, is colourless and almost transparent. Through it shine the yellow-tinged mantle and branchiæ.

This elegant little *Solen* has an immense range in depth, from six to one hundred fathoms, and appears to be as much at home in shallow as in deep water. Pure sand and sandy mud are the bottoms in which it thrives. It is distributed all round our shores. A few selected localities, illustrative of its range and distribution, may be mentioned: in the south, Guernsey (S. H.); in seven fathoms at Weymouth and Dartmouth, and in from ten to twenty-seven fathoms at various distances from shore, off the coasts of Dorset and Devon (M'Andrew and E. F.). On the east coast, off Kent (Capt. Stanley); Scarborough (Bean); Northumberland (Alder); in sixty fathoms off Durham (Howse). On the west coast, Ilfracombe, Tenby, and Fishguard (Jeffreys); off Ormeshead in twelve fathoms, and Isle of Man twelve to thirty fathoms (M'Andrew and E. F.); in Scotland, Hebrides, and coast of Ross-shire (Jeffreys); Clyde (Smith); Loch Fyne (Barlee); in Zetland alive in seven, sixty, seventy, eighty, and a hundred fathoms, and as far as twenty-five and thirty miles from land (M'Andrew and E. F.); Orkney (Thomas); Murray Firth in from fifteen to thirty-four fathoms (M'Andrew). Aberdeenshire (Macgillivray); Frith of Forth (Thomas and Knapp). In Ireland, "though not a common species, it is found on every side of the coast" (W. Thompson); Cape Clear in sixty fathoms, and Bantry Bay in fifteen fathoms (M'Andrew); Coast of Down eight fathoms (Patterson).

It ranges throughout the European seas.

SOLECURTIDÆ.

WE follow M. Alcide d'Orbigny in considering *Solecurtus* as the type of a family separate from the true razorfishes. Not only have the shells a habit which at once distinguishes them from their neighbours, but the animals are also essentially different, especially in the arrangement of their siphons, which, instead of being united as in the last tribe, are separated for more than half their length. On this account we have removed the *Solen legumen* of authors from among the *Solens*, and constituted for that singular shell a special genus. It forms the connecting link between the *Solenidæ* and *Solecurtidæ*.

CERATISOLEN. FORBES.

(*κεφατιον*, a pod, and *σωλην*.)

Shell greatly elongated transversely, compressed, equivalve more or less inequilateral, thin, gaping at the extremities. Surface diagonally comparted, centrally radiatostriate, invested with an epidermis. Muscular impressions distinctly marked, dissimilar, resembling those of *Solen*; pallial impression with a wide short sinus. Hinge subcentral, complicated, composed as described in *C. legumen*. Ligament external. Valves beneath the hinge strengthened by a strong oblique rib.

Animal compressed, narrow; mantle closed in front, open anteriorly. Foot ovate, elongated, truncate. Siphons separate, diverging with fringed orifices.

According to Mr. Gray, the generic name *Pharus* is applied to the *Solen legumen* in the manuscripts of Dr. Leach. No characters being appended, and the name itself too closely resembling *Phorus*, a genus of Gasteropoda, we do not adopt it here.

C. LEGUMEN, Linnæus.

Plate XIII. fig. 2, (under the name of *Solen legumen*), and (animal) Plate I. f. 4.

LISTER, Hist. Conch. pl. 420, f. 264.

Solen legumen, LINN. Syst. p. 1114.—PENN. Brit. Zool. ed. 4, vol. iv, p. 84. pl. 46, f. 24.—DA COSTA, Brit. Conch. p. 238.—DONOV. Brit. Shells, vol. ii. pl. 53.—Dorset Catal. p. 29, pl. 4, f. 4.—MONT. Test. Brit. p. 50.—Linn. Trans. vol. viii. p. 45.—TURT. Conch. Diction. p. 162.—FLEM. Brit. Anim. p. 459.—Brit. Marine Conch. p. 36.— BORN, Mus. Cæs. pl. 2, f. 1, 2.—CHEMN. Conch. Cab. vol. vi. p. 49, pl. 5, f. 32, 33, 34.—WOOD, General Conch. p. 124, pl. 28, f. 4.—POLI, Test. Sicil. vol. i. pl. 11, f. 15.—DILLW. Recent Shells, vol. i. p. 60.—LAM. Anim. s. Vert. (ed. Desh.) vol. vi. p. 57.—WOODARCH, Conch. ed. 2. pl. 1, f. 9.—Index Testac. pl. 3, Solen, f. 8.—PHILIPPI, Moll. Sicil. vol. i. p. 4, and vol. ii. p. 5.—DESH. Elem. Conch. pl. 6, f. 8, 9, 10.—HANL. Recent Shells, p. 13, pl. 3, Solen, f. 8.— CHENU, Ill. Conch. Solen, pl. 2, f. 1.— DESH. Exp. Scien. Algér. Moll. p. 185.

Psammobia ——, TURT. Dithyra Brit. p. 90.
Solenocurtus ——, BROWN, Ill. Conch. G. B. p. 113, pl. 47, f. 8, 9, 9.*
Solen gousse, CHENU, Traité Elem. p. 42, f. 132 (hinge).
Encyc. Méth. vers. pl. 226, f. 3.

This graceful bivalve is of an elongated shape, the length averaging about four-and-a-half times the width of the shell. The valves are very fragile, thin, more or less transparent, greatly compressed, whitish, and covered with a polished light greenish-yellow epidermis, beneath which the surface is almost smooth, or at most concentrically striolated. The ventral margin is almost straight for the greater part of its extent, if anything slightly retuse near the middle, and rounding off at each extremity; to this the dorsal edges run nearly parallel, but both converge a little anteriorly, so that the anteal extremity is the more tapering; both the front and hinder dorsal edges are almost straight, but the former is slightly the more sloping, and the latter exhibits a very trifling degree of convexity. Neither the beaks nor the umbones are at all conspicuous; the blackish ligament, which is large and somewhat triangular, expanding greatly behind, does not project above the dorsal line, an incision being made in the valves for its reception; its hinder termination is about the centre of the hinge-margin. The posterior side is nearly double the length of the anterior one, and is rather broad and very obtusely rounded at its termination; the upper side of the attenuated front- extremity projects in a trifling degree beyond the lower one, so that the anterior outline is obliquely rounded below, and obsoletely subangulated above. There is no appearance of any umbonal ridge, nor the slightest inflection of the margin on either side of the beaks.

The inside is usually whitish, but is sometimes stained with orange upon the subumbonal region. The hinge is very complicated; the hinge-margin is strengthened near the beaks, in both valves, by a very short obliquely radiating rib-like callosity; in the left valve there is a single upright greatly compressed primary tooth, and an extremely approximate bifid sublateral one juts out beyond the hinge-margin, which ceases near the commencement of the ligament. In the right valve are three teeth, the posterior sublateral a mere denticle, and the central broadly based and bifurcated; which two constitute, with the curved posteriorly inclined primary anterior one, a double pair of nipper-like receptacles for the teeth of the opposite valve.

The animal is of a linear oblong shape; its mantle, of a yellowish-white colour, is closed in front, and open anteriorly for the passage of the foot. Its edges at the opening are fimbriated above and below, but not at the extremity. The foot is of a reddish-purple hue, and when contracted is thick, ovate, and truncate; when extended it presents the form of a pedunculated disk. The siphons are separate and diverging, and of a reddish colour. Their orifices are fringed with short tentacula.

The largest of the individuals, from which collectively we have drawn up our description, measures three and a half inches in length, and three-quarters of an inch in breadth; occasionally valves are found of four inches in length, and of proportionate width. (Montagu.)

As an English species, it must be accounted rare, although locally abundant at Biddeford Bay in North Devon (Mont.); it is obtained likewise at Exmouth (Clark); and near Liverpool. (M'Andrew.)

In Wales it is frequently met with, as at Swansea and its vicinity (Jeffreys); Tenby and other parts of Caermarthenshire (S. H.); Aberystwith (S. H.); Anglesea. (M'Andrew.)

In Ireland " it inhabits the extensive sandy coasts of the counties of Louth and Dublin, and likewise Bantry Bay; Captain Brown's remark, that it is plentiful on the eastern coast between Cork and Belfast, gives too extensive an idea of its distribution." (Thompson.)

It is essentially a species of southern origin, Britain being its most northern limit. It occurs on the coasts of Spain and Portugal, throughout the Mediterranean, and is recorded as an inhabitant of the shores of Senegal and of the Red Sea.

SOLECURTUS, BLAINVILLE.

Shell transversely oblong, compressed, equivalve, sub-equilateral, rounded and gaping at both extremities. Surface more or less invested with an epidermis, sometimes nearly smooth, sometimes ornamented with oblique grooves. Hinge composed of two fine divergent primary teeth in each valve. Ligament external. Inside of valves with two strong muscular impressions, the anterior largest and lobed; the pallial impression deeply sinuated.

Animal very large and thick in proportion to the shell, oblong; mantle closed in front, widely open anteally for the passage of a large linguiform foot, and posteriorly for the siphons, which are deeply separated at their extremities, united and forming a thick mass at their bases. Labial palpi triangular, narrow, lamellated on their inner sides. A large portion of the branchiæ are lodged in the branchial siphon.

This very natural genus, which from habit many authors have persisted in retaining as a portion of *Solen*, presents affinities, both of shell and animal, with *Lutraria* on the one hand, and *Psammobia* on the other. *Solemya* is perhaps its nearest ally. It dates from the cretaceous, perhaps from the oolitic period, and shells allied to it occur in still older strata. Very near allies of existing forms are found in the oldest of the tertiaries.

S. COARCTATUS, Gmelin.

Surface striated only by concentric lines of growth.

Plate XV. fig. 3, and (animal) Plate I. fig. 5.

Solen cultellus, PENNANT (not Linn.) Brit. Zool. ed. 4, vol. iv. p. 85, pl. 46, f. 25.
Chama Solen, DA COSTA, Brit. Conch. p. 238.

Solen angustior, constrictus, &c.   CHEMN. Conch. Cab. vol. vi. p. 62, pl. 6, f. 45.

Solen coarctatus, GMEL. (1788) p. 3224.—Brit. Marine Conch. p. 36.—DILLW.
        Recent Shells, vol. i. p. 64.—PHILIPPI, Moll. Sicil. vol. i. p.
        6, and vol. ii. p. 5.—HANL. Recent Shells, p. 14.

Solen emarginatus, SPENGLER, Skrivt. Naturh. Selskab. vol. iii. pt. ii. p. 103.

Solen antiquatus, PULTENEY (1799), Hutchins Dorset. p. 28.—DONOV. Brit.
        Shells, vol. iv. pl. 114.—MONT. Test. Brit. p. 52.—Linn.
        Trans. vol. viii. p. 46.—Dorset Catalog. p. 29. — TURT.
        Conch. Diction. p. 162. — FLEM. Brit. Anim. p. 460.—
        WOOD, General Conch, p. 125, pl. 29, f. 3.—LAM. Anim.
        s. Vert. (ed. Desh.) vol. vi. p. 59.—Index Testaceol. pl. 3,
        Solen, f. 10.—CHENU, Illust. Conchyliolog. Solen, pl. 6, f. 8.

Psammobia antiquata, TURT. Dithyra Brit. p. 91.

Solecurtus antiquatus, DESH. Elem. Conch. pl. 5, f. 8 ; Exp. Scient. Algérie,
        Mollus. p. 210.

Azor antiquatus, BROWN, Illus. Conch. G. B. p. 113, pl. 47, f. 6, 7.

It is with some hesitation that we have substituted the
more expressive epithet bestowed upon this species by
Gmelin, for that by which it has been more generally
known among British writers ; since, notwithstanding that
the law of priority imperiously demands the establishment
of the first name correctly given to a species, so inadequately defined is the *S. coarctatus* of Gmelin, and so entirely dependent for identification upon two somewhat dissimilar figures, that a kind of injustice seems inflicted upon
authors who have clearly and comprehensively characterized the shell, in denying them the honour of its
nomination. Pennant, who first noticed this shell, mistook
it for the Linnean *S. cultellus* ; Da Costa used an objec-
tionable generic compound ; Chemnitz omitted the designation of it by a single appellation ; consequently, Gmelin,
whose sole merit is the attachment of a name to a drawing,
obtains the credit of creating the species.

The shape of this bivalve is more or less obliquely oblong, and occasionally somewhat elongated ; the texture is
opaque, and tolerably strong. The valves, without being
particularly shallow, are decidedly compressed near the

middle, and even retuse towards the incurved ventral margin. The surface which is devoid of regular sculpture, merely showing a few antiquated lines of growth, which are occasionally almost obsolete, is whitish both externally and internally, and exhibits but little if any lustre. Its dull yellowish-olive, or olivaceous straw-coloured epidermis, (in exotic specimens this is sometimes of a drab or fawn-colour,) is strongly wrinkled at each extremity. The sides are very nearly equal ; the anterior, however, is rather the shorter, and its dorsal margin very slightly sloping, and barely convex ; that of the posterior side declines still less, and is almost rectilinear, but is incurved near the short and prominent ligament. Both extremities are bluntly rounded ; the upper part of the anterior one is the more projecting, the lower portion being obliquely rounded from the greater ascent of the ventral margin on that side of the shell. The lower corner of the hinder termination is well rounded ; there is a trifling angularity at the upper corner, which projects almost as far as the other, owing to the absence of declination in the dorsal edge ; the posterior outline is convex.

The umbones are dorsally depressed, and the beaks incurved, and not peculiarly distinct. The umbonal ridge is broad, but not greatly elevated ; a corresponding ridge appears from the intervening concavity, to run from the beaks to the front ventral corner, but this is not preceded by any depression of the surface on the other side. The lateral hiation is remarkably ample, the valves only touching at the beaks and at the opposite incurved portion of the ventral edge. The hinge is furnished with two primary teeth in each valve, of which the hinder of the left valve is very oblique, laminar, and very caducous ; the rest are much elevated, recurved, and extending beyond the margin ; the hinder of the right valve is slightly cloven. The palleal sinus is very large. The full average length of examples may be estimated at an inch and three-quarters; their breadth at about seven-eighths of an inch.

The animal is oblong, rather compressed, entirely white. The mantle is closed centrally in front, widely open anteriorly, for the thick, oblong, rather compressed linguiform foot. The lips of the opening are fringed with short cirrhi. The tubes are united for a considerable distance at their bases, thick and fleshy, separated at their extremities, the anal one with a plain orifice, the branchial slightly fimbriated or rather scalloped. Mr. Clark observes, that " the surface of the tubes is clothed with fine white hairs ;" this appearance we have not noticed. He further remarks, that " the animal is continually dilating both tubes to sometimes thrice their ordinary diameter, and then suddenly contracting them." We have seen it break up its tubes voluntarily into fragments in the manner of the Mediterranean *Solecurtus strigilatus*. The branchiæ are long, linear, narrow ; the upper much shorter than the lower. The labial tentacles are rather long.

Though rather widely distributed, this is a scarce shell, and never occurs in any abundance, even locally. It inhabits moderately deep water, usually in the coralline region. In England it has been dredged alive at Exmouth (Clark) ; in fifteen fathoms, west bay of Portland, and twenty-five fathoms off Plymouth (M'Andrew and E. F.). Mr. Jeffreys has it from Dawlish, Torbay, and Falmouth. It occurs in the Irish sea off Anglesey, and the Isle of Man. In Scotland it inhabits the Frith of Clyde (Smith) ; and the Hebrides (Jeffreys) ; off Armadale, Sound of Skye, alive in twenty-five fathoms (M'Andrew and E. F.).

In Ireland " it inhabits some of the bays of the Down and Antrim coasts" (Thompson) ; and is also met with at Dublin (Turton).

It ranges from Sweden (Loven) to the Ægean (E. F.).

S. CANDIDUS, Renieri.

With oblique striæ.

Plate XV. fig. 1, 2.

Soleni strigilati varietas, CHEMN. Conch. Cab. vol. vi. p. 60, pl. 6, f. 43.

Solen candidus, RENIERI, Tavola Alph. Adriat. (from Philippi).—Brit. Marine Conch. p. 38,—HANL. Recent Shells, p. 14, suppl. pl. 11, f. 31.

Solen strigilatus, TURT. (not Linn.) Conch. Diction. p. 161, (not his figure, which is from an exotic example.) — PHIL. Moll. Sicil. vol. i. p. 5, var. β.

Psammobia strigilata, TURT. Dithyra Brit. p. 97, pl. 6, f. 13.—FLEM. Brit. Anim. p. 439.

Solecurtus candidus, DESH. Elem. Conch. p. 122, pl. 6, f. 11, 12 (broader than usual).—PHIL. Moll. Sicil. vol. ii. p. 5.—DESH. in Exp. Algér. Moll. p. 208. pl. 10, f. 1 to 5 (shell and animal.)

Psammobia scopula (YOUNG), TURT. Dithyra Brit. pp. 98, 259, pl. 6, f. 11, 12. —FLEM. Brit. Anim. p. 439.—Brit. Marine Conch. p. 38.

Solen scopula, CHENU, Ill. Conch. SOLEN, pl. 6, f. 7.

The shape of this curiously sculptured shell, which may be reckoned among our rarer species, notwithstanding that single specimens are usually described in the cabinets of the more active collectors, is elongated oblong, and frequently somewhat reniform. The valves, although sufficiently convex, are compressed in the middle, and strongly gaping at either extremity, the apices of the beaks and that portion of the ventral margin which is immediately opposite them being the sole touching points. The surface varies in lustre, but when in perfection is moderately glossy, and provided (at least towards the margins) with an olivaceous yellow epidermis; it is ornamented for about three quarters

of its area, with profound oblique more or less curved radiating striæ, which are so graven that each appears to imbri-
cate the succeeding.   Those striæ which are beyond the
almost obsolete umbonal ridge, are more closely disposed
than the more distant ones situated in advance of it, from
which latter they diverge at acute angles, irregularly uniting
with them, and not leaving any intermediate unoccupied
space. A larger or smaller triangular surface, extending
from the acute sub-central but by no means prominent
beaks, is free from all sculpture, except a few antiquated
wrinkles which concentrically traverse the entire shell.
The sides, although nearly equal, vary a little in this
respect, at some the anterior, at others the posterior, being
the more produced; both the extremities are rounded, but
assume nevertheless a very different aspect, the hinder
being very slightly attenuated and more symmetrically
arcuated, whilst the front, owing to the absence of declination, and the rectilinear outline of the anterior dorsal edge,
is bluntly angulated above, although strongly and obliquely
arcuated below.   The hinder dorsal margin is slightly
retuse near the large and very broad olivaceous prominent
ligament, and slopes in but a very trifling degree, although
exceeding the anterior in that respect; the ventral margin
is more or less incurved in the middle, and slightly convex
at either side, but rather more so anteriorly, where it curves
rapidly up in forming the front extremity. The structure
of the adult is firm or even solid, opaque, and of an uniform
dirty white externally: within it is of a purer white and
often polished.   The hinge, which however is very rarely
found perfect, consists of two primary teeth in each valve,
variable in obliquity or erectness; those of the right valve
are strongly curved and much elevated, the hinder tooth
being greatly the longer, but from its compression at the

base by far the more caducous; the front one is shorter and unguiform. In the opposite valve, interlocking with these, is a strong central greatly curved erect tooth, and behind it a depressed narrow very oblique laminar one. The nymphæ are strong and moderately projecting.

The animal has recently been described and figured by Deshayes, who has shown that its characters are very distinct from those of *S. strigilatus.* It is much too large for the shell, of a brilliant orange colour; the mantle is rather paler towards the margin, closed in front, open widely anteriorly for the passage of a very large orange foot, with a whitish base. A glistening crucial ligament shines through the mantle. The branchial tubes are united at their bases (where the siphonal mass is large and thick), and separated at their extremities; the orifices are fimbriated. Its habits are probably similar to those of *S. strigilatus,* which lives very deeply buried in pure sand, its place marked by perforations on the surface. Deshayes compares the colour of this animal to that of the pulp of an apricot.

Fine specimens occasionally attain to the length of two inches and a quarter, and the breadth of an inch.

In England, it has not to our knowledge been detected on the eastern coast, and is sufficiently rare elsewere to be much prized. It is dredged (but without the mollusk) at Exmouth (Clark); Torbay (Jeffreys, &c.); Falmouth (S. H.); Penzance (M'Andrew and E. F.); and the Isle of Man (E. F.). In the two last instances it occurred in twenty-five fathoms water, which appears to be its most usual depth. The finest valves we have ever seen came from Bantry bay (Humphreys); it is likewise taken at Howth (Turton); and Dr. Lloyd (Thompson) procured it from Malahide on the Dublin coast.

Mr. M'Andrew dredged it in the Hebrides, Zetland, and off Caithness (but never alive); it has also been met with in Skye by Mr. Barlee (Jeffreys, Ann. Nat. H. vol. xix. p. 314).

It ranges to the Mediterranean.

SPURIOUS.

S. BIDENS, Chemnitz.

Solen divisus, SPENG. Skrivt. Nat. Selskab. vol. iii. pt. ii. (1794), p. 96, (from O. FABR. Skriv. Nat. Selsk. vol. iv. pt. ii. pl. 10, f. 11, 12.

Solen bidens, CHEMN. Conch. Cab. vol. xi. p. 203, pl. 198, f. 1939.—HANL. Recent Shells, p. 16.

Solen fragilis, PULTENEY, Hutchins Hist. Dorset (1799), p. 28.—MONT. Test. Brit. pp. 51, 565, and Suppl. p. 26 ; Dorset Catal. p. 29, pl. 4, f. 5.—TURT. Conch. Diction. p. 163.—FLEM. Brit. Anim. p. 460.—WOOD, General Conch. p. 126, pl. 29, f. 4, 5; Brit. Marine Conch. p. 37.—DILLW. Recent Shells, vol. i. p. 65.—Index Testac. pl. 3, Solen, f. 11.—GOULD, Invert. Massachus. p. 31.—CONRAD, Americ. Mar. Conch. pl. 4.

Solen centralis, SAY, Jour. Ac. Philadelp. vol. ii. p. 316 (*fide* GOULD).

Psammobia læviata, TURT. Dithyra Brit. p. 85.

Elongated-suboval, (not unlike a bean-pod,) not strong, nor opaque, subequilateral, covered with a yellowish drab-coloured or olivaceous yellow epidermis, which is more or less firm and glossy, and is wrinkled posteriorly. Valves smooth, rather compressed, contracted in the middle, white both within and without, with a short and almost perpendicular broad, purplish ray under the beaks, and a tinge of the same colour, occasionally ray-shaped, under the ligament, besides two narrow, approximate, white oblique rays behind the central one, which are visible beneath the epidermis, but become obsolete in aged specimens. Ventral margin incurved, not rising but well arcuated at both extremities. Dorsal edges scarcely at all sloping, their declination almost equal, both very slightly convex. Both extremities simply rounded, that of the hinder side (which is very slightly the longer) rather the more so. Hinder tooth of the right valve erect, peculiarly expanded at its apex, and sublaterally bifid. 1¾—⅜. *W. Indies, &c.: introduced as from Dorsetshire by Dr. Pulteney. The name of Spengler, whether it be* bidentatus, *as asserted by Chemnitz, or divisus, as the examination of the engraving of Fabricius would lead us to imagine, not being accompanied by a figure, and not being defined by a Latin diagnosis, loses the right of priority.*

SPURIOUS.

S. GIBBUS, Spengler.

LISTER, Hist. Conch. pl. 421, f. 265.

Solen gibbus, SPENGLER, Skrivt. Nat. Selskab. vol. iii. pt. ii. (1794), p. 104.

Solen Guineensis, CHEMN. Conch. Cab. vol. xi. (1795), p. 202, pl. 198, f. 1937.—WOOD, General Conch. p. 129.

Solen Caribæus, LAM. (1818), Anim. s. Vert. ed. 2, vol. vi. p. 58.—HANL. Recent Shells, p. 14.

Solen declivis, TURT. Conch. Diction. (1819), p. 164, f. 80.—FLEM. Brit. Anim. p. 460; Brit. Marine Conch. p. 37.

Psammobia declivis, TURT. Dithyra Brit. p. 91.

Solecurtus Caribæus, GOULD, Invert. Massach. p. 36. — DEKAY, N. York Mollus. p. 243, pl. 52, f. 302.

Solen Bouchardii, POTIEZ, Gal. Mollusq. de Douai, vol. ii. p. 261, pl. 68, f. 4, 5.

Encyclop. Méth. Vers, pl. 226, f. 1.

Elongated oblong, moderately strong, opaque, decidedly convex, but depressed near the umbones, not lustrous, almost smooth, scarcely inequilateral. Surface covered, when fresh, with a dull asparagus-green coloured epidermis, which rarely extends to the umbones, and is more or less coarsely wrinkled at the sides; beneath this, the valves are stained with lighter and darker shades of liquorice brown, and not unfrequently marked near the middle with perpendicular, scattered, scratch like lines. Ventral margin subparallel to the dorsal, but retuse or incurved; dorsal edges nearly straight, scarcely declining, the front one the more elevated, and if anything slightly convex, the hinder just retuse. Anterior side the longer, occupying nearly three-fifths of the entire length; its extremity bluntly subangulated, projecting above, very obliquely rounded below; posterior termination most bluntly subbiangulated, and rather the more projecting (as usual) below. Inside white; two erect curved simple primary teeth (of which the hinder is the broader) in the right valve; two smaller oblique incurved ones in the left. Length 3 inches, breadth 1 inch and an ½. *N. America, W. Indies, &c. Introduced by Dr. Turton, as from the Scilly Isles.*

SPURIOUS.

S. STRIGILATUS, Linnæus.

Solen strigilatus, LINN. Syst. Nat. ed. 12, p. 1115 (chiefly). — TURT. Conch.
　　　　Diction. fig. 53.—CHEMN. Conch. Cab. vol. vi. pl. 6, f. 41, 42.
　　　　—POLI, Test. Sicil. pl. 12.—WOOD, General Conch. p. 127,
　　　　pl. 30, f. 1. — LAM. Anim. s. Vert. (ed. Desh.) vol. vi. p. 60.
　　　　—Index Testaceolog. pl. 3, Solen, f. 12.—REEVE, Cyclopædia.—
　　　　PHILIPPI, Moll. Sicil. vol. i. p. 5.—REEVE, Conch. Systemat.
　　　　vol. i. pl. 26, f. 3, 4.—CUVIER, Règne Anim. (ed. Croch.) pl.
　　　　111, f. 2. — CHENU, Illus. Conchyliol. Solen, pl. 4, f. 1, and
　　　　pl. 6, f. 1.
Solecurtus strigilatus, PHILIPPI, Moll. Sicil. vol. ii. p 5. — DESH. Exped. Scient.
　　　　Algérie, Moll. p. 207.
Solecurte rose, CHENU, Traité Element. p. 42, f. 135, and pl. 1, f. 8.
Encyclopédie Méthodique, Vers, pl. 224, f. 3.

*A Mediterranean shell; introduced by Turton among the figures
of his Conchological Dictionary, from supposing the S. candidus to
be a colourless variety of it. The animal as well as the shell are,
however, very distinct.*

TELLINIDÆ.

THE TELLEN TRIBE.

A LARGE family of bivalves, often remarkable for elegance of form, delicacy of sculpture, and beauty of colour. Some of our most vividly painted British shells are members of this tribe. The majority of species are thin, fragile, and compressed. Whilst they present a general resemblance of external form, although with many modifications of outline, the internal structure, so far as the hinge is concerned, is very different in different genera. The small value of the hinge-characters for indicating mutual affinities is, indeed, strikingly shewn in this group; as examples we may cite *Psammobia* and *Tellina*, and contrast them with *Syndosmya* and *Scrobicularia*.

The animals, however, of all the genera of Tellinidæ are strikingly similar. They have all very slender, separate, diverging siphons, often very long, the orifices of which are either quite plain or slightly fimbriated. The margins of their mantles are widely open, and usually furnished with fine short filaments. The foot is broad, geniculated, and linguiform. Although their shells are often painted with glowing hues, the animals are almost always white or colourless. The *Tellens* are mostly inhabitants of the littoral and laminarian zones, but many species have great ranges in depth, and some are among the inhabitants of the deepest sea-beds yet explored.

Through *Psammobia*, they are evidently related to the

Solecurtidæ; through *Syndosmya* and *Scrobicularia* with
the *Mactradæ.*

PSAMMOBIA, LAMARCK.

SHELL transversely oblong, equivalve, subinequilateral,
slightly gaping at the extremities; surface smooth, or
transversely, and more or less radiatingly striated, invested
with a thin epidermis. Muscular impression round; pallial sinus strongly marked. Hinge composed of cardinal
teeth, two or a single bifid tooth in one valve, and one in
the other; supplementary laminæ small, and often obsolete. Ligament prominent, external.

The animal is oblong and compressed; its mantle is
open throughout its length, and bordered by a fringe of
fine simple filaments; the siphons are very long, slender,
and delicate, marked with longitudinal ciliated lines, which
terminate in more or less conspicuous cirrhi, few (six or
eight) in number, surrounding their orifices. The foot is
rather large, and linguiform. The labial tentacles are triangular, and internally pectinated. One of the branchial
leaflets on each side is shorter than the other.

The *Psammobiæ* are inhabitants of most seas, though
sparingly distributed, and may be traced, though doubtfully, far back in time. They live buried in sand or
gravelly mud, some in the littoral, some in the laminarian
and coralline zones, and several species have a considerable
range in depth. Our native examples are all shells
remarkable for elegance and beauty. The animals are not
of dull and torpid habits, but active in their motions,
though moving about below the surface of the sea-bed.

P. VESPERTINA, Chemnitz.

Rather strong, somewhat compressed, rayed with livid pink and white, merely marked with obsolete concentric striæ; hinder end very bluntly biangulated; hinder dorsal edge almost straight, and scarcely sloping; ligament large, and prominent.

Plate xix. fig. 1, 2.

Lœa vespertina, CHEMN. Conch. Cab. vol. vi. p. 72, pl. 7, f. 59, 60.
Tellina depressa, PENN. (not Linn.) Brit. Zool. ed. 4, vol. iv. p. 87, pl. 47, f. 27.
—— *variabilis*, PULT. in Hutchins' Dorset, p. 29.—DON. vol. ii. pl. 41, f. 2.
Solen pictus (partly), SPENGLER, Skrivt. af Naturhist. Selskab. vol. iii. part 2, p. 107.
Tellina Gari, POLI (not Linn.), Test. Sicil. pl. 15, f. 19, 21, 23.
Solen vespertinus, MONT. Test. Brit. p. 54.—Linn. Trans. vol. viii. p. 47.—Dorset Catal. p. 29, pl. 5, f. 1.—TURT. Conch. Diction. p. 163.
—WOOD, General Conch. p. 135, pl. 33, f. 2, 3.
Tellina albida, DILLW. (of Linn. ?) Recent Shells, vol. i. p. 78.
Psammobia vespertina, LAM. Anim. s. Vert. (ed. Desh.) vol. vi. p. 173.—TURT. Dithyra Brit. p. 92, pl. 6, f. 10 (young).—BROWN, Illus. Conch. G. B. p. 102, pl. 40, f. 3.—PHILIPPI, Moll. Sicil. vol. i. p. 22, and vol. ii. p. 21.—HANL. Recent Shells, p. 57.—CUV. Règne Anim. (ed. Croch.) pl. 111, bis, f. 2 (animal).
Psammobia florida, LAMARCK, Anim. s. Vert. (ed. Desh.) vol. vi. p. 174 (fide Payand. and Philippi).
Sanguinolaria vespertina, FLEM. Brit. Anim. p. 460. — Brit. Marine Conch. p. 65.

The *Setting Sun*, as the present species, from its peculiar style of colouring, has poetically, and not inappropriately, been termed, is of an oval-oblong shape, nearly equilateral, tolerably strong, opaque, and rather compressed (particularly in front). The surface, beneath the ashy olive-coloured epidermis, which partly conceals it, and which, except in the very young, is destitute of lustre, is shining, and only obsoletely striated in a concentric direction. The colouring consists of numerous alternate rays of carnation or livid pink and white, the preponderance of each hue varying in different examples. The coloured rays are almost invariably mottled, and indeed this speckled appearance not unfrequently pervades the white rays also. The ventral margin is, for the most part, nearly straight, but is moderately convex and sharply ascending in front. The dorsal edges possess but little convexity; the front indeed is inclined to retusion, and is scarcely at all sloping; the hinder declination likewise, although greater, is but very moderate. The anterior side, which is decidedly the narrower, is well rounded at its extremity. The posterior termination is very bluntly biangulated, the hinder edge being distinctly convex, and the angles (particularly the lower one) rounded off. The ligament is very large, dusky brown, and prominent; the beaks are small, and not at all projecting; and the umbonal ridge is quite obsolete. In most specimens the inner surface is highly polished, and of a porcelain white; it is sometimes, however, (as in foreign examples,) richly tinted with yellow or purple. The hinge consists in the right valve of a very strong simple broadly based anterior tooth, and a less solid, narrow-based posterior one; in the left valve, of an exactly central rather narrow bifid tooth, with a very oblique simple laminar posterior one, which latter is so extremely thin and fragile as generally to be wanting in our cabinet specimens; from which circumstance this species is usually described as having only a solitary tooth in one of the valves.

The average size of the valves is about two inches in length, and rather more than one inch in breadth. Young specimens are usually of an uniform pale yellowish hue, with their ligaments of a yellow brown. Those mentioned by Montagu as adorned with a more vivid colouring than the adult, were, in all probability, the species subsequently called *florida* by Dr. Turton.

For an account of the animal of this shell, we are indebted to Mr. Clark, who examined and noted living specimens at Exmouth, as long ago as 1835. It is suboval, elongated, compressed, and of a yellowish-white colour throughout. The edges of the mantle are finely fimbriated. The tubes are long, and appear to be rather wider than in the following species. The lower one is usually, though not always, curved shorter than the upper, truncate at its extremity, and perforated with six rays. The upper siphon is curved, and terminates in an irregular margin. The foot is very large, broad, rather thick and linguiform. The branchiæ hang obliquely from the dorsal range, and consist of a pair on each side, the upper being shorter and smaller than the lower, of a brown colour, rather coarsely pectinated, each pair united with the opposite pair posteriorly, and each branchial lamina free at its lower edge. There are also a pair on each side of lighter coloured, elongated, pointed, triangular labia, smooth on their outer surface, well pectinated on the inner, nearly lying on each other, and of equal length; each pair is connected with the other by a membrane surrounding the mouth.

It is a locally abundant shell, and is usually collected upon the sands after a succession of rough gales; it dwells near the shore, and may be taken at low tides in muddy sand, burrowing but a little depth from the surface. Among its localities we may enumerate Scarborough (Bean); Northumberland (Alder); at both which places it is rare; Weymouth (S. H.); Poole (Pulteney); Exmouth (Clark); Torbay (S. H.); Falmouth (Jeff. cab.); West bay of Portland in fifteen fathoms, dead (M'Andrew and E. F.); Tenby (Lyons); Pwlheli (M'Andrew); near Milford Haven (Lyons); "Bantry, Cork, Youghal"

(Humphreys and Jeff. cab.). In Scotland it occurs abundantly and of large size in Loch Ryan (Nicol); Dunbar (Laskey), &c.; Islet of Herm near Guernsey (S. H.).

A livid variety is sometimes met with, and valves with a purple interior occur at Ullapool (Jeffreys).

It ranges along the south-western and southern shores of Europe.

P. Ferroensis, Chemnitz.

With raised concentric striæ, which are decussated behind by a few elevated radiating lines.

Plate XIX. fig. 8.

Tellina incarnata, Penn. (not Linn.) Brit. Zool. ed. 4, vol. iv. p. 88, pl. 47, f. 31.
———— *radiata*, Da Costa (not Linn.), Brit. Conch. p. 209, pl. 14, f. 1.
———— *trifasciata*, Donov. (not Linn.) Brit. Shells, vol. ii. pl. 60.
———— *Ferroensis*, Chemn. Conch. Cab. vol. vi. p.99, pl. 10, f. 91 (badly).—
Pulteney, Hutchins Hist. Dorset, p.29.—Linn. Trans. vol. viii. p. 49.— Dorset Catal. p. 29, pl. 6, f. 1.— Turt. Conch. Diction. p. 171.—Wood, General Conch. p. 164, pl. 45, f. 1.—Dillw. Recent Shells, vol. i. p. 77.—Index Testaceol. pl. 4, f. 36.—Mawe, Conch. pl. 6, f. 1.
———— *truncata*, Spengler (not Linn.), Skriv. Nat. Selsk. vol. iv. part 2, p. 10.
———— *ferroensis*, Gmel. Syst. Nat. p. 3235.—Mont. Test. Brit. p. 55.
Psammobia Ferroensis, Lam. Anim. s. Vert. (ed. Desh.) vol. vi. p. 172.—Turt. Dithyra Brit. p. 94, pl. 8, f. 1.—Flem. Brit. Anim. p. 438.—Macgill. Moll. Aberd. p. 284.—Brit. Marine Conch. p. 64.—Brown, Illust. Conch. G. B. p. 101, pl. 40, f. 1, 2.—Sowerby, Conch. Manual, f. 100.—Desh. Elem. Conch. pl. 15, f. 9, 10.—Philippi, Moll. Sicil. vol. i. p. 23, pl. 3, f. 7; and vol. ii. p. 20. —Hanl. Recent Shells, vol. i. p. 57.
Encyclopédie Méthodique, Vers, pl. 227, f. 5.

From the peculiar character of its sculpture, the *P. Ferroensis* incurs but little risk of being confounded with any other of its genus, either native or foreign. It is of an elongated oblong figure, much compressed, tolerably strong, opaque, nearly equilateral, and with the valves more or less twisted, and not perfectly equal in depth. When fresh taken it is usually covered with a dull ashy olive-coloured epidermis, beneath which the surface, which possesses but little if any lustre, is either rayed with madder-lake and white, (the preponderance of colour varying with the individual) or marbled in a linear fashion, with the former, on a whitish or pale-coloured ground. It is closely striated for its entire length with raised concentric lines, which not unfrequently at their posterior termination dentate the hinder dorsal edge. These striæ are decussated beyond the umbonal ridge, which is indicated by a sharp elevated line, by a few fine radiating ones, which in the adult, however, do not quite proceed to the extremity of the shell. The ventral margin is nearly straight in the middle, but ascends (and convexly so anteriorly) at either extremity. The dorsal edges are flattened above; the front one is slightly convex, and but little sloping, the hinder one is subretuse, and scarcely at all declining. The front extremity of the shell is rounded and a little tapering, the hinder termination is perfectly biangulated, the lower angle projecting further than the upper. There is a slight ventral flexure before the umbonal ridge; the ligament is long, prominent, moderately large, rich brown in the adult, and brownish-yellow in the young; the beaks are acute but small, and not much projecting. The interior, which is highly polished, is white or lilac; the teeth, which are rather small, consist in the left valve of a deeply cloven narrow central, and a very small rudimentary laminar one, the latter lying obliquely behind the former, and being very caducous is usually wanting; in the right valve, of a simple anterior, and a bifid posterior one, the former of which is the more solid.

Individuals which have attained to two inches in length,

and about seven-eighths of an inch in breadth, may be considered as of the full ordinary size, the majority of examples being of rather less dimensions. A very beautiful rayless variety of a rich maroon colour is preserved, without a locality, in the collection of Mr. Hanley; we are not aware, however, that any such have hitherto been taken in this country.

The animal of *Psammobia Ferroensis* is white, like its congeners, and differs but little in form from that of the last species. The tubes are long and rather more slender; their extremities are finely fimbriated, especially that of the branchial tube. The foot is very large, strong, and fleshy, linguiform and apiculated. The branchiæ are of a reddish hue.

This species is well known all round our shores, and is not unfrequently cast on shore after storms. On the south coast it occurs at Torquay and elsewhere in Devonshire (S. H.); at Poole, in Dorsetshire, where it was first noticed by Pulteney (E. F.). On the west, at Tenby (Lyons); Oxwich Bay and St. David's (Jeffreys); Anglesea (M'Andrews); Isle of Man (E. F.). On the east, it is plentiful at Scarborough (Bean); and on the coast of Northumberland (Alder). In Ireland it is generally distributed along both east and west coasts. In Scotland it is frequent in the Clyde (Smith); Hebrides (Jeffreys); Orkney and Zetland (M'Andrew); Moray Frith (M'Andrew); Aberdeenshire (Macgillivray); Firth of Forth (E. F.) It ranges on our shores from three fathoms to as deep as ninety. The coralline zone appears to be its favourite locality.

It ranges throughout the European seas, but becomes scarcer as we proceed southwards. As a fossil it is found in tertiaries of Meiocene, Pliocene, and Pleistocene ages.

P. TELLINELLA, Lamarck.

Small, convex, smooth, not distinctly rayed, tinged with orange or livid flesh-colour or purple, almost always with a red or dark-hued short linear ray on the anterior side of the beaks. Ventral margin convex or subarcuated; both dorsal edges slightly convex: hinder end not biangulated. Ligament small, and not prominent; cardinal teeth very small.

Plate XIX. fig. 4, and (animal) Plate K. fig. 1.

Psammobia Tellinella, LAM. Anim. s. Vert. (ed. Desh.) vol. vi. p. 177.—Brit. Marine Conch. p. 62.—BROWN, Illust. Conch. G.B. p. 102, and 133, pl. 39, f. 30.—HANL. Recent Shells, p. 58, suppl. pl. 11, f. 11.

——— *florida,* TURT. Dithyra Brit. p. 86, pl. 6, f. 9.—FLEM. Brit. Anim. p. 437.

This pretty little *Psammobia,* which was first specifically distinguished in England by Dr. Turton, having previously, in all probability, been regarded as the young of *vespertina,* is, like it, of an oval-oblong contour, and almost equilateral. It is rather convex upon the umbonal region, not strong but opaque, and at most possesses an extremely thin yellowish epidermis, and a very trifling degree of glossiness; its surface is smooth, and offers a great variety of colouring in different examples. The more usual one consists of irregularly radiating specks of orange or livid flesh colour, on a paler ground of the same tint, and a very short orange-red linear ray in front of the whitish or very pale beaks, with a similar, though less distinct and still smaller one (which is sometimes obsolete), lying behind them; more rarely the valves are of an almost uniform purple, with the anterior streak, however, still perceptible, and often of a deeper purple. The ventral margin is convex, or even subarcuated; the front dorsal edge but slightly convex or sloping, and the hinder one

still less so, the degree of convexity and inclination in both
being in inverse proportion to that of the ventral margin.
The anterior side is the narrower, and tapers to a well
rounded extremity; the posterior termination is also
rounded, but irregularly so, manifesting in but a very
trifling degree that tendency to biangulation which is almost typical of the genus. The umbonal ridge is perfectly obsolete; the beaks are depressed, and the ligament
is small, of a yellowish-brown, and by no means prominent. The interior is frequently stained with brilliant
orange or purple, with a white area or ray beneath the
beaks; it is sometimes livid or lilac, and more rarely
whitish, with the external red ray equally visible on the
inner disk. The teeth are remarkably small, but resemble in other respects those of *vespertina*; the laminar
denticle is, however, rarely if ever present.

The dorsal edges are often stained with red at irregular
intervals, and the ligament is very frequently barred with
roseate brown. For size, an inch in length, and a little more
than half that space in breadth, may be regarded as a fair
average.

The animal is entirely white; its mantle is conspicuously fimbriated. The siphons are slender, the upper
one with eight, the lower with six ciliated ridges; the
cirrhi of their extremities are small. The foot is thick
and linguiform. The labial tentacles are lanceolate. When
placed in a vessel of sea water, with a supply of sand, it is
very active, moving about in all directions, and evidently
has considerable power of changing place.

Though formerly esteemed rare, it appears to be a widely
diffused and plentiful shell. Whilst it has not been found
at such great depths as *P. Ferroensis*, it appears to be habitually a resident in deeper water than that species, and is not

so often cast on shore. It occurs at Guernsey and Exmouth (Clark, Metcalfe, S. H.) ; Falmouth (Jeffreys) ; Portland in fifteen, Plymouth in twenty-five, and Penzance in twenty fathoms, where a white variety was taken (M'Andrew and E. F.) ; Tenby (S. H.) ; Cardigan Bay (M'Andrew) ; Bantry in fifteen fathoms (M'Andrew) ; Cork, Youghal (Humphreys and Jeffreys) ; Oban, and lochs of the west of Scotland (Jeffreys) ; Outer Hebrides (M'Andrew) ; Zetland in depths from five to fifty fathoms, often in shelly gravel (M'Andrew and E. F.). On the whole, it appears to be a western shell. It occurs fossil in the coralline crag.

P. COSTULATA, Turton.

Smooth, except at the posterior end, where it is rayed with costellæ or elevated striæ.

Plate XIX. fig. 5.

Psammobia costulata, TURT. Dithyra Brit. p. 87, pl. 6, f. 8.—FLEM. Brit. Anim. p. 437.—Brit. Marine Conch. p. 62.— BROWN, Illus. Conch. G. B. pp. 102, 133, pl. 39, f. 34.—HANL. Recent Shells, p. 59.—PHILIPPI, Moll. Sicil. vol. ii. p. 21. —PHILIPPI, Neu. Conch. Psammobia, pl. 1, f. 3, 4.

————— discors, PHILIPPI, Moll. Sicil. vol. i. p. 23, pl. 3, f. 8.

This small species, which is most closely allied in shape and general character to *Tellinella*, is principally distinguished from it by the sculpture upon its posterior side. It is rather thin, but not transparent, nearly equilateral, and moderately convex ; the chief profundity is at the umbonal region. The outline is nearly oblong ; the front extremity is rounded and distinctly attenuated, and the hinder (from the convexity of the posterior edge) is only bluntly subbiangulated. The external surface is almost devoid of lustre, and in the adult is closely set with concentric, irregularly-disposed wrinkles, which become obsolete upon the

umbones, and vary in their intensity with different individuals.   These rugæ usually become more or less indistinct
beyond the ordinary position of the umbonal ridge, (which
is almost entirely obsolete,) where the area is adorned by
about fourteen obliquely-radiating costellæ, which constitute
the peculiar feature of the shell.   The colouring is beautiful
but very variable ; ranging from pale yellow, mottled or
specked with small livid-red markings, to purple, merely variegated with minute whitish speckles.   The ventral margin
is decidedly convex or even subarcuated, and rises, but not
equally, at both extremities, ascending rather more in front.
The dorsal edges scarcely slope downwards ; the front one
is the more (though very slightly) convex, the hinder one
being almost straight.   The anterior side is rather the
longer, and is a little tapering and well-rounded at its
extremity ; the posterior extremity is likewise rounded,
the terminal hinder outline, though arcuated, notwithstanding exhibits some slight traces of the ordinary generic biangulation.   The ligament is yellowish brown, and
neither large nor prominent.   The umbones are depressed ;
the beaks small, acute, and scarcely leaning to either side.
The interior is polished and usually tinted with a deeper
shade of the external colouring, (sometimes with the hue of
the peach-blossom,) and is invariably adorned, beneath the
umbones, with two short, ray-like blotches of livid-red or
purple, (the intervening space being usually pale or white,)
one on either side of the beaks, of which the hinder is
decidedly the larger, and is evident (more or less distinctly) upon the external surface likewise.   The teeth
are very small, and consist of a single primary one in the
left valve, interlocking between two (of which the front is
the more divergent) in the opposite valve.   The nymphæ
project but little.

We know of no examples which exceed an inch in length, and about half that measurement in breadth.

This is decidedly the scarcest of our *Psammobiæ*, and, moreover, one of our rarest bivalves to obtain in a living state. Not that the species is confined to one or two spots, being there gregarious and tolerably plentiful, for, on the contrary, our list of its habitats is tolerably full, but that in no one locality is it taken in abundance, two or three specimens, at the most, rewarding indefatigable research, so that even single valves are not held despicable by any of our collectors.

Dr. Turton, who first recognized the specific value of its distinctive characters, obtained it at Torbay and in the Channel; to this locality we may add Exmouth, in deep water, though rarely alive (Clark); Port Carnow Cove in Cornwall (Miss Lavers); Penzance, in twenty fathoms (M'Andrew and E. F.); St. Peter's Port at Guernsey in nine fathoms (Metcalfe and Hanley); Cork (Humphreys); Isle of Skye (Jeffreys and Barlee); one living specimen from St. Magnus bay in Zetland (M'Andrew).

The only recorded foreign locality is Sicily, where it is stated by Dr. Philippi to be one of the scarcer shells. It occurs also on the coast of Greece (Graves and Spratt).

SPURIOUS.

P. Laskeyi, Montagu.

Tellina Laskeyi, Mont. Test. Brit. Suppl. p. 28, pl. 28, f. 3.—Turt. Conch.
Diction. p. 175.—Wood, General Conch. p. 179.
Psammobia ———, Turt. Dithyra Brit. p. 89.—Flem. Brit. Anim. p. 438.—
Brit. Marine Conch. p. 63.—Brown, Illust. Conch. G. B.
p. 103, pl. 39, f. 32.

As very little is known of this pretty bivalve, and its presence is rare even in the larger exotic collections, we have been in-

duced to draw up a more diffuse description of it than is our
wont with species of such undeniably foreign extraction.

Its general shape is more or less oblong, and the texture opaque
and tolerably strong. The valves are somewhat ventricose or decidedly convex; the profundity is, however, chiefly apparent
upon the subumbonal region; they are but little inequilateral,
and covered with a shining olivaceous yellow or buff-coloured,
somewhat corneous epidermis, beneath which the shell is whitish,
and more or less clouded with violet stains, which latter are, in
the immature examples only, arranged in concentrically-disposed
flexuous lines; at this stage, too, there are a pair of paler very
narrow rays at no great distance from the posterior extremity.
The surface is almost smooth; there are often, however, a few
antiquated concentric lines in front near the lower margin, and
almost always some rather closely-set inferior subimbricated
concentric lines upon and beyond the rather obscure umbonal
ridge. The ventral margin, which is moderately convex (but
not arcuated) in front, rises obliquely and rather considerably
upon that side, becoming nearly straight or very slightly inflected
near its posterior termination. Both dorsal edges are subrectilinear; the front one, which in the young is slightly convex, but
becomes flattened down with age, slopes in a very trifling degree;
the hinder one, which in aged specimens is somewhat retuse and
moderately sloping, declines but little in the younger examples.
The anterior side is rather the longer, and tapers but little at its
extremity, where it is obliquely rounded off below, but is subangulated above; the front margin is curved, and its chief swell
is above the middle. The posterior termination, which becomes
almost wedge-shaped in the adult, where the tip, however, is
always rounded off, is in the younger shell (whose extremity is
not more attenuated than in front) very obtusely and indistinctly
subbiangulated; in this stage, its chief swell is below the middle
of the side, and the narrow tip is subrectilinear. The umbones
do not appear prominent (they are generally a little eroded) nor
the beaks acute; the ligament is wanting in all the specimens
we have examined, but judging from the rather projecting nymphal callosities, must be of both moderate length and projection.
There is no appearance of a lunule; the hinder dorsal surface
seems linearly sunken (as in most of the *Donaces*). The interior
is glossy, and more or less mottled with violet; the edge is quite

entire; the hinge-margin moderately wide; and the palleal sinus
very large. The teeth, which are obscure and very small, are
stated by Montagu, who had probably the opportunity of examining them in a more perfect state than we had, to consist of
two approximate sub-bifid ones, interlocking with the solitary
one of the opposite valve. The hinge-margin of the right valve
is a little channelled in front, where it becomes slightly broader;
there are no lateral teeth. The length of a large single valve
was eight-ninths of an inch, and its breadth all but half an inch;
these are, however, beyond the average dimensions. *Introduced
by Montagu, as dredged by Laskey in the Frith of Forth : according to the late Mr. Humphreys, it is an inhabitant of the shores of
the West Indies.*

DIODONTA, Deshayes.

Shell subequivalve, inequilateral, both valves convex.
Surface more or less striated or ridged transversely, not
invested with an epidermis. Hinge composed of two primary teeth in one valve and one bifid tooth in the other;
no lateral teeth. Ligament external. Muscular and palleal impressions strongly marked. The former oblong and
nearly equal; the latter with a very deep and wide sinus.

Animal ovate; mantle open, its margins fimbriated; siphons separated to their bases, unequal, their orifices
fimbriated. Foot linguiform. Branchiæ equal. Labial
tentacles triangular, rather large.

The animal of *D. fragilis* has been examined by Philippi
and by Deshayes, both of whom have given figures of it.
The mantle is freely open in front, and, like the rest of the
body, of a yellowish white colour. Its margin is fimbriated. The siphons are separated throughout their length
and very unequal, the branchial one much the longest, and
having a corrugated brownish base. The branchial orifice

is six-rayed or fimbriated, the anal eight-rayed.   The foot
is rather large, and has no byssal groove.   The labial palpi
are of considerable size.

D. FRAGILIS, Linnæus.

Plate XXI. fig. 3, and Plate K. f. 2 (animal).

Tellina fragilis, LINN. Syst. Nat. ed. 12, p. 1117.—TURT. Conch. Diction. p. 166.
—CHEMN. Conch. Cab. vol. vi. p. 95, pl. 9, f. 84.—POLI, Test.
Sicil. vol. i. pl. 15, f. 22, 24.—DILLW. Recent Shells, vol. i. p.
78.—Index Testaceolog. pl. 3, Tellina, f. 7.—PHILIPPI, Moll.
Sicil. vol. i. p. 27, and vol. ii. p. 22.—PHILIPPI, in Wiegm.
Archiv. f. Natur. 1845, p. 190, pl. 7, f. 19, 20 (animal).—
HANL. in Sow. Thesaur. Conch. vol. i. p. 319, pl. 56, f. 14, and
pl. 60, f. 149.
Petricola ochroleuca, LAM. Anim. s. Vert. (ed. Desh.) vol. vi. p. 157.—SOWERBY,
Genera Shells, Petricola, f. 4.—PAYRAUD. Cat. Moll. Corse,
pl. 1, f. 9, 10.—DESHAYES, Elem. Conch. pl. 12, f. 13,
14, 15.—REEVE, Conch. Systemat. pl. 51, f. 4.—HANL.
Recent Shells, p. 52, suppl. pl. 1, Tellina, f. 6.
Psammotæa Tarentina, LAM. Anim. s. Vert. (ed. Desh.) vol. vi. p. 183.—DE-
LESSERT, Rec. Coquilles, pl. 5, f. 11.—HANL. Recent
Shells, p. 60.
Tellina jugosa, BROWN, Werner. Memoirs, vol. ii. p. 506, pl. 24, f. 2.
Psammobia fragilis, TURT. Dithyra Brit. p. 88, pl. 7, f. 11, 12.—FLEM. Brit.
Anim. p. 438.—Brit. Marine Conch. p. 62.
Tellina ochroleuca, WOOD, Index Test. suppl. pl. 1, Tellina, f. 6.
Psammobia jugosa, BROWN, Illust. Conch. G. B. p. 102, pl. 40, f. 4, 5, 6.
. *Diodonta fragilis*, DESH. Exped. Sci. Algérie, Moll. pl. 68 (animal, &c.).

The range of variation permitted to the *Diodonta fragilis*
is very remarkable, extending, as it does, not merely to
shape and colour, but likewise to sculpture.   In the Mediterranean. examples, the shell is comparatively smooth and
fragile ; those from Africa are occasionally beautifully lamellated ; whilst in the British and northern specimens the
valves, which are coarser and stronger, have the lamellæ
very irregularly developed.

Our native variety is of a produced ovate or slightly trigonal form, more or less strong, almost opaque, and sub-ventricose or even slightly inflated. It is decidedly in-equilateral, almost devoid of lustre, and when fresh, usually tinted externally with brownish saffron. The surface, which is apt to be indented in various places, is wrought with concentric, elevated, somewhat undulated laminar striæ, (which are occasionally almost obsolete,) varying in their approximation to each other, and in the distinctness or obscurity of the very minute radiating lines which de-cussate their interstices. The ventral margin, whose out-line is often wavy, is moderately convex; the dorsal edges are very slightly retuse on either side of the beaks, then convex and rather sloping in front, and almost straight and decidedly sloping behind. The anterior side, which is conspicuously the shorter, is broadly rounded at its ex-tremity; the posterior termination is bluntly acuminated, and very slightly subrostrated. The umbonal fold is broad and rather obtuse, the ventral flexure is tolerably evident. The beaks are small, acute, and almost directly inflected, scarcely leaning to either side; the umbones are sufficiently prominent; the ligament is rather large, and moderately projecting. The dorsal lips bend considerably inward in front of the beaks. The interior is either of a dirty white or stained with the external colouring. The hinge is not provided with any distinct lateral teeth; there are two moderately sized divergent primary teeth in the right valve, which become much more elevated towards the internal edge, and a single broad and very large bipartite subre-flected central tooth in the left valve. There appears to be a very thin oblique laminar denticle behind this tooth, but it is so extremely caducous, that it is rarely present. The palleal sinus is extremely large. The length of rather a large specimen is an inch and a half, and its breadth slightly exceeds one inch.

This is a rare shell, for which we know no English locality; in Ireland, it is taken in Dublin, Bantry, and Valentia bays (Turton); and in Wales, it has been picked up on a sandy beach about two miles from Tenby (Lyons).

It ranges to the Mediterranean and along the north-west coast of Africa.[*]

TELLINA, Linnæus.

Shell ovate, oblong or rounded, compressed, subequivalve, subinequilateral, marked with an umbonal fold, sometimes nearly obsolete; surface smooth, or marked with transverse, oblique, or radiating striæ; inner margin of valves smooth. Hinge with one or two primary teeth in each valve; lateral teeth present in some species, obsolete in others. Ligament external. Muscular impressions

---

[*] It seems highly probable that the *T. polygona* of Montagu, stated to have been dredged by Mr. Laskey off Cramond Island in the Frith of Forth, was a young variety of this shell, with which it agrees far better than with the exotic *Guinaica* of Chemnitz (Conch. Cab. vol. x. p. 348, pl. 170, f. 1651, 1652, 1653,) to which (from the want of more characteristic figures) it is referred by its describer.

Tellina polygona, Mont. Test. Brit. suppl. p. 27, pl. 28, f. 4.—Turt. Conch.
    Diction. p. 180.—Brit. Marine Conch. p. 63.—Brown, Illust.
    Conch. G. B. p. 102, pl. 39, f. 53.— Index Testaceolog. pl. 4,
    f. 80.

Tellina Guinaica, Dillwyn, Recent Shells, vol. i. p. 96.

Psammobia polygona, Turt. Dithyra Brit. p. 96.—Flem. Brit. Anim. p. 439.

"Subovate, suborbicular, of a dirty-white colour, wrought with very fine concentric striæ, which are crossed with excessively fine lines not visible to the naked eye; the umbo is small, not central, nor turning to either side; the shorter end is subtruncated and subangulated : the larger end is rounded. Inside not very smooth, the margin uneven: teeth in one valve two, large, and distant (? distinct); in the other one very large, triangular, bifid tooth, with an approximate small one, that might easily be passed unnoticed. Length, half an inch, breadth rather more. The umbo in the only specimen we have examined is ferruginous, but this might have been stained." All the descriptions and delineations cited by us have been drawn from Laskey's solitary specimen.

oblong, the posterior one widest ; pallial impression with a deep and wide sinus.

Animal ovate, compressed, mantle entirely open in front, its margin fimbriated ; siphons long, separate throughout, usually nearly equal, their orifices plain, or very indistinctly toothed. Foot large, triangular, compressed, apiculate. Labial palpi large, lanceolate. Branchial leaflets united in pairs on each side.

The mollusks of this genus live in sand or sandy mud, buried beneath the surface ; the majority at low watermark, or in considerable depths. A few species have a range as deep as the coralline zone. The number of known kinds of *Tellinæ* exceeds two hundred. They occur in all seas, but more than a third of them are inhabitants of the Indian Ocean. Many species are found also in the West Indian region, and on the west coast of South America. They increase in numbers from the poles to the equator. The arctic forms are squalid and unattractive ; those inhabiting the tropics, on the contrary, gaily-coloured and ornamental, so as to be sought after for decorative purposes. Their range in time is not so certainly known, though several Palæozoic and secondary shells have been assigned to this generic group. In the upper part of the cretaceous system, and in beds of the tertiary (especially Eocene) epoch they are distinctly present.

The structure of the branchial and the labial palpi, with the simple character of the extremities of the tubes, distinguish the animals of this genus from those of *Psammobia*, whilst the shells may usually be distinguished with facility by their umbonal folds and dentition. Nevertheless the two genera are exceedingly closely allied.

T. CRASSA, Pennant.

Rounded oval; strong, concentrically grooved; with lateral teeth.

Plate XX. figs. 1, 2.

LISTER, Hist. Conch. pl. 299, f. 136.

Tellina crassa, PENN. Brit. Zool. ed. 4, vol. iv. p. 87, pl. 48, f. 28.—MONT. Test. Brit. p. 65.—Linn. Trans. vol. viii. p. 55.—Dorset Catalog. p. 30, pl. 7, f. 4.—TURT. Conch. Diction. p. 173.—TURT. Dithyra Brit. p. 109, pl. 7, f. 2.—FLEM. Brit. Anim. p. 436.—MACGILL. Moll. Aberd. p. 280.—Brit. Marine Conch. p. 80.—WOOD, General Conch. p. 186, pl. 40, f. 1.—DILLW. Recent Shells, vol. i. p. 96.—LAM. Anim. s. Vert. (ed. Desh.) vol. vi. p. 201.— WOOD, Index Testaceolog. pl. 4, fig. 75.—MAWE. Conchology, pl. 6, f. 7.—HANL. Recent Shells, p. 68, pl. 4, f. 75.—HANL. in Sow. Thesaur. Conch. p. 265, pl. 61, f. 169, 173.

? Pectunculus depressus, DA COSTA, Brit. Conch. p. 194, pl. 13, f. 4 (right hand fig.)

Tellina maculata, ADAMS, Linn. Trans. vol. iii. p. 252.—Linn. Trans. vol. viii. p. 48.—TURT. Conch. Diction. p. 173, f. 13.—TURT. Dithyra Brit. p. 108, pl. 6, f. 7.—FLEM. Brit. Anim. p. 436.—Brit. Marine Conch, p. 70.—WOOD, General Conch. p. 153.

Tellina rigida, PULTENEY, in Hutchins' Hist. Dorset, p. 30.—DONOV. Brit. Shells, vol. iii. pl. 103.

Arcopagia crassa, BROWN, Illust. Conch. G. B. p. 99, pl. 40, f. 8.

„   *ovata*, BROWN, Illust. Conch. G. B. p. 99, pl. 40, f. 9, 10.

Tellina obtusa, SOWERBY, Min. Conch. pl. 179, f. 4.

Of a rounded oval form, very inequilateral, and of a solid opaque texture, the valves of this pretty shell are rather ventricose when united, but not quite equal in profundity, the left being rather the more depressed. The exterior, which is rather dull, and of a more or less squalid white, is usually adorned with narrow rays of crimson red, but is occasionally devoid of any painting: it is likewise most closely, coarsely, and rather irregularly grooved concentrically; there is no interstitial decussation. The ventral margin is well arcuated, and rises far more on the posterior side, the chief swell being in front of the shell. The anterior side is the more produced, and a little attenuated at its well-rounded extremity; its dorsal edge is moderately sloping, and more or less convex. The hinder side is short, its termination is bluntly subangulated below, and its dorsal edge is arcuated, and much declining. The umbones are rather prominent, and incline forward; the beaks are small, and the ligament is depressed, but elongated and rather large. There is a very small and narrow excavated lunule; the umbonal ridge is indistinct, the ventral flexure small, but tolerably evident. The interior is usually more or less richly stained with reddish-orange, but is sometimes merely white. The hinge margin is not only furnished with the ordinary primary teeth, but in the right valve with two lateral ones, of which the posterior is distant, and the anterior rather approximate.

The measured breadth of rather a fine specimen, was an inch and three quarters, and its length rather more than two inches. The *T. maculata* of Turton's cabinet, is merely a dead discoloured specimen of this shell.

This species has a considerable range in depth, extending from low water-mark to below fifty fathoms. Its favourite habitat appears to be in the upper part of the coralline zone, where it lives buried in gravelly sand. In the Islet of Herm, near Guernsey, it is dug out of sand at low water, and is plentiful (S. H.); in the Isle of Man it occurs, though not abundantly, under similar circumstances (E. F.). Though generally distributed, it is local. On the south coast it occurs off Hastings, Poole, and Weymouth (S. H.); Portland bay, west, in fifteen fathoms, gravel (M'Andrew and E. F.); Exmouth (Clark); Torbay (Alder and S. H.); Plymouth (Jeffreys); Salcomb, Falmouth, and Helford (Montagu); Penzance, in twenty fathoms (M'Andrew and E. F.). On the Welsh coast it has been taken at Langharne (Jeffreys); Tenby (Lyons);

Cardigan and Caernarvon bays, and Anglesea, in ten
fathoms water (M'Andrew). On the east coast it is not
uncommon on the shores of Northumberland (Alder). In
Ireland it is generally distributed, but is especially abundant
in Bantry bay, becoming comparatively rare northwards
(W. Thompson). It is found on both sides of Scotland;
Hebrides; Skye, in forty fathoms, dead; in various localities and at considerable depths on the Shetland coast
(M'Andrew); alive in twenty-five fathoms, Eda Sound,
Orkney (Thomas); on the Aberdeenshire coast (Macgillivray); Firth of Forth (Knapp and E. F.).

Abroad this mollusk is confined to the Celtic and Boreal
coasts of Europe, ranging as far north as Bergen (Loven).
It appears to be extinct now in the Mediterranean, but
inhabited that region during the Glacial Epoch, as we know
from the occurrence of its fossil remains in the Sicilian tertiaries. It ranges throughout the Meiocene, Pleiocene,
and Pleistocene beds of Britain.

T. BALAUSTINA, Linnæus.

Suborbicular, not grooved; with two lateral teeth in one valve.

Plate XXI. fig. 2.

Tellina balaustina, LINNÆUS, Syst. Nat. ed. 12, p. 1119.—THOMPSON, Annals
Nat. Hist. vol. xviii. p. 385.—JEFFREYS, ditto, vol. xix. p.
313.—POLI, Test. Sicil. vol. i. pl. 14, f. 17.—DESH. in
Lam. Anim. s. Vert. vol. vi. p. 209.—PHILIPPI, Moll. Sicil.
vol. i. p. 25, and vol. ii. p. 21.—HANL. Recent Shells, p.
72, suppl. pl. 9, f. 17.—HANL. in Sow. Thesaur. Conch.
vol. i. p. 253, pl. 56, f. 10.
Lucina   „   PAYRAUDEAU, Cat. Moll. Cors. pl. 1, f. 21, 22.

This recent and very beautiful addition to our Fauna,
varies in shape from suborbicular to obovate, is moderately
firm in texture, opaque, and decidedly convex or even sub-

ventricose. The surface of specimens in fine condition possesses but little lustre, and is closely set with very delicate
membranaceous concentric striulæ, but these are usually
worn away, and the valves appear smooth and rather glossy.
The colouring is elegant, consisting of very numerous narrow rays of a scarlet red upon a ground of pale yellow or
white. The ventral margin is strongly arcuated; and
rather the more ascending behind; both dorsal edges are
but moderately sloping, the convexity of the hinder, which
is the more elevated, is but trifling, that of the anterior,
after passing the lunule-like depression in front of the beaks,
is more decided. The sides are very nearly equal; the front
extremity is symmetrically rounded; the hinder termination is most bluntly subangulated. The umbones are prominent, and often of a rich yellow; the beaks are acute,
and directly inflected, not leaning to either side. The
ligament is narrow, and by no means projecting; the umbonal ridge and the ventral flexure not very marked; and
the interior is generally more or less profusely tinted with
yellow. The primary teeth are small, but the two nearly
equidistant (the front one is rather the more approximate,)
lateral teeth are rather large.

The magnificent shell (belonging to Mr. Jeffreys,) from
which our engraving has been taken, is of more ample
dimensions than any Mediterranean specimens we have ever
seen, measuring seven-eighths of an inch from side to side,
and about three-quarters of an inch from the beaks to the
opposite margin. It is more fragile and ventricose, likewise, than foreign examples, and does not vie with them in
that golden hue, which so often adorns their umbonal region
and interior surface. The species was first discovered, as
a native of the British seas, by that enterprizing and indefatigable dredger, Mr. Barlee, who obtained it at Birterbuy

Bay, in Connemara (Thomp. Ann. Nat. H. vol. xviii, p. 385), and subsequently procured it from the Island of Skye and at Stornoway (Jeff. Ann. Nat. H. vol. xix. p. 313). A fresh and beautifully perfect but pale tinted individual, measuring almost an inch in length, nearly three-quarters in breadth, and containing the animal, was purchased in 1848 by Mrs. Gulson of Exmouth, from a fisherman at Falmouth, who dredged it along with other undoubted British species. It is a Lusitanian shell, and ranges into the Mediterranean, where it is not rare in six or seven fathoms water.

T. DONACINA, Linnæus.

Elongated, concentrically striated; posterior end short and wedge-shaped; with two lateral teeth in the right valve.

Plate XX. figs. 3, 4, and (animal) Plate K. fig. 4.

Tellina Donacina, LINN. Syst. Nat. ed. 12, p. 1118.—PULTENEY, in Hutchins' Hist. Dorset, p. 29.—MONT. Test. Brit. p. 58.—Linn. Trans. vol. viii. p. 50. pl. 1, f. 7.—Dorset Catalog. p. 29, pl. 12, f. 3, b.—TURT. Conch. Diction. p. 170.—TURT. Dithyra Brit. p. 102, pl. 8, f. 4.—FLEM. Brit. Anim. p. 485.—Brit. Marine Conch. p. 67.—BROWN, Illust. Conch. G. B. p. 101, pl. 40, f. 16.—WOOD, General Conch. p. 161, pl. 45, f. 5.—DILLW. Recent Shells, vol. i. p. 89.—LAM. Anim. s. Vert. (ed. Desh.) vol. vi. p. 198.—DESHAYES, Elem. Conch. pl. 14, f. 1, 2, 3.—PHILIPPI, Moll. Sicil. vol. i. p. 24, and vol. ii. p. 21.—HANL. Recent Shells, p. 64.—HANL. in Sow. Thesaur. Conch. vol. i. p. 232, pl. 56, f. 12, and pl. 66, f. 259.—DESH. Exped. Scient. Algér. Moll. pl. 69, f. 1 to 3 (with animal).

Tellina trifasciata, PENN. Brit. Zool. ed. 4, (fide last edit.) p. 88.
  „   *variegata*, POLI, Test. Sicil. vol. i. plate 15, f. 10.
  „   *Llantivyi*, PAYRAUDEAU, Catal. Moll. Corse, p. 40. pl. 1, fig. 13, 14.

Uniting the peculiar contour of the *Donaces* to the gorgeous colouring of the typical *Tellinæ*, this pretty bivalve is of an oblong shape, tolerably firm in texture, nearly opaque, moderately convex, and very inequilateral. Its exterior, which is not lustrous, is yet occasionally glossy, and densely striated in both valves with concentric and subimbricated lines, one half of which disappear on reaching the umbonal fold. The ordinary colouring consists of very numerous interrupted rays of a carnation red upon a whitish or yellowish ground, with the environs of the ligament, the inflected hinder dorsal area (which is narrow or even linear), and a short direct ray which emanates from behind the beaks, all stained with the same brilliant dye. Not unfrequently, also, the surface is zoned with lighter and darker shades of pink or yellow. We have figured likewise a beautiful and uncommon variety (from Portland) in which the ground colour is crimson, and the rays, zones, and apices are white. The ventral margin which exhibits the generic flexuosity (the curvature of the posterior side to the right being very distinct) is comparatively straight behind, but arches out moderately in front where it very obliquely ascends in an uninterrupted sweep to the dorsal edge, which being scarcely convex, barely declining, and much produced, the anterior extremity (although the tip is arched) is not rounded symmetrically, and the chief swell is above and not beneath the middle. The posterior side, which is scarcely half the length of the anterior one, is abbreviatedly wedge-shaped, as the hinder dorsal margin rather abruptly declines in a straightish line, which however becomes convex near its termination, thus rounding off the posterior tip. The ligament is large and prominent. The interior is either stained with rich yellow, displaying the rosy apical ray and the dorsal stains, or faintly exhibits the external colouring. The hinge of the right valve is furnished, in addition to its primary teeth, with two lateral laminæ, of which the front one is decidedly the larger and the more approximate.

An example is recorded by Turton, which measured an inch and a quarter in length, and three-quarters of an inch in breadth, dimensions far exceeding those that are ordinarily met with.

The animal is entirely white and of the same shape as the shell; compressed and oblong. The mantle is freely open, and its margin conspicuously fringed. The siphonal tubes are very long and slender, distinct from each other throughout their lengths, plain at their extremities, marked at their sides by whitish lines, what appears to be ciliciferous. The foot is ovate, acute, and compressed. The labial palpi are narrow.

This is a widely distributed shell and one of our prettiest Tellens. It occurs at Guernsey (S. H.); and all along the coasts of Dorset, Devon, and Cornwall. At W. Portland bay it occurred alive in fifteen fathoms water, and at Penzance in twenty (M'Andrew and E. F.). It has been taken at Tenby (Lyons); and on the north coast of Wales in from twelve to more fathoms (M'Andrew and E. F.). On the east coast it occurs at Scarborough (Bean); off Norfolk (Stanley); and on the coast of Northumberland (Alder). In Ireland it is abundant in Bantry Bay, rare and occasional in the north, as at Strangford and Portmarnock (W. Thompson). It is frequent in the Clyde district (Smith); the Hebrides (Jeffreys); and the Orkney, Zetland, and Moray Firth coasts (M'Andrew); but is apt to be confounded with the following species. In those localities, it and its ally have been taken alive at various depths from five to fifty fathoms. It occurs also in the Forth district.

Abroad it is a common inhabitant of the southern coasts of Europe, but does not extend its range northwards of Britain, being replaced in the Norwegian seas by *T. pygmæa.*

It inhabited the British seas as early as the epoch of the Coralline crag.

T. PYGMÆA, Philippi.

Like *Donacina*, but very small ; the hinder end blunter, the sides still more unequal, and the lateral teeth equally approximate.

Plate XIX. figs. 6, 7.

Tellina pygmæa, PHILIPPI, in Loven, Index Moll. Sueciæ, p. 42.—ALDER, Cat. Northumb. and Durham Moll. p. 88.

This pretty little shell, which for its size is by no means thin or fragile, being tolerable solid in the adult, but always a little transparent, has a narrow, oblong contour ; its external surface is more or less glossy, its internal area is shining ; the colouring is infinitely diversified, specimens from the same locality being rose, orange, sulphur tinted, or white, and at times of almost an uniform colour, but more usually variegated by greatly interrupted more or less narrow rays of a darker hue, which are most distinctly apparent at the concentric zones of growth. The most common variety is pale yellow with crimson rays, but examples with rosaceous orange rays on an orange yellow ground seem nearly equally abundant. There is often, but not invariably, a short, broad, perpendicular ray of orange or crimson, extending scarcely half way from the beaks to the lower margin, and sometimes a similar oblique and rather longer one running anteriorward, and dilating as it becomes fainter. The line of the interior is either as that of the exterior, or yellow with the abbreviated ray or rays more visible than externally ; the valves are convex or even subventricose, and are regularly though delicately

striolate concentrically, the striulæ being remarkably close
set; the ventral margin is convex, but not quite symmetrical, the anterior portion being the more arcuated; the
front dorsal outline is nearly straight, produced, and scarcely at all sloping, the hinder is extremely short and moderately declining; both extremities are rounded, but neither
symmetrically, that is to say, with an equal arcuation
above and below, the extremely blunt subangulation of the
posterior termination forbidding it behind, and the slight-
ness of the front dorsal slope preventing it in front; this
character, however, is not so peculiarly evident as in *Donacina*; the sides are excessively unequal, the front being
twice or even thrice the length of the hinder; the ligament is prominent, but very short, the ventral flexure
distinct, but the umbonal fold almost obsolete; there is
a linear, lunule-like excavation along the front dorsal edge,
which is only at times stained with reddish crimson internally; besides the narrow, simple, and small bifid tooth
of each valve, the right possesses a large anterior and a
small posterior lateral tooth, which are moderately and
equally distant from the former. Although most closely
bordering upon *T. donacina*, this beautiful and diminutive
species appears to us specifically distinct, and not merely,
as has been conjectured by some, a dwarf variety of that
long-known shell. It does not seem, indeed, to have been
found at all by the older conchologists, with the exception
of Mr. Humphreys of Cork, in whose cabinet it is still
preserved; so that whether the sum of its difference from
its nearest congener be varied or specific has not yet been
mooted among us. In his interesting Prodromus of the
shells of Sweden, Löven has lately constituted it a species,
and to his opinion we assent, in common with those other
British conchologists who have devoted their attention to

the comparison of the two shells; for, independently of the largest known specimens (from L. Carron and L. Alsh) never attaining to quite half an inch in length and a quarter of an inch in breadth, and these are not young fragile shells, but manifesting their adolescence by their solidity; the posterior end is not wedge-shaped but blunt, and the sides are far more unequal than even in *Donacina*. In proportion to its size it is more convex too, and this convexity is more evenly diffused, there being no posterior compression as in that species; it has striulæ, not striæ, and certain characteristics, as the short red perpendicular ray, and the crimson stain upon the front dorsal edge, which appear permanent in the latter, are by no means so in *pygmæa*. The lesser development of its umbonal ridge, and, above all, the different approximation of the lateral teeth to the cardinal, must not be passed over, the front lateral of *Donacina* being invariably the closer to the primary teeth.

In England it has been taken at Holy Island in Northumberland (Alder); at Whitesand Bay in Devon, and Port Carnow Cove in Cornwall (Jeff. cab.) In Ireland in Cork Harbour (Humphreys), and Galway (Barlee). In Scotland it has been dredged by Mr. M'Andrew from a sandy bottom of from eight to fifty fathoms at Cape Wrath, the Hebrides, Orkneys, and Shetland Islands; and by Messrs. Jeffreys and Barlee at Lochs Alsh, Kishon, Carron, &c. Abroad it is recorded as an inhabitant of the coasts of Sweden and Norway.

T. INCARNATA, Linnæus.

Oblong, subequilateral, compressed, acuminated behind ; right valve with regular concentric striulæ : one or more lateral teeth.

Plate XX. fig. 5.

Tellina incarnata, LINN. Syst. Nat. ed. 12, p. 1118. — POLI, Test. Sicil. pl. 15.
    f. 1.—HANL. in Thesaur. Conch. vol. i. p. 283, pl. 60, f.
    142, and pl. 66, f. 265.
  „ *squalida*, PULTENEY, Hutchins, Hist. Dorset. p. 29.—MONT. Test. Brit.
    p. 56.—FLEM. Brit. Anim. p. 436.—Rees' Cyclopædia, pl. 5.
  „ *depressa*, DONOV. Brit. Shells, vol. v. pl. 163.—Linn. Trans. vol. viii. p. 51.
    —TURT. Conch. Diction. p. 171.—TURT. Dithyra Brit. p. 105,
    pl. 8, f. 6.—Brit. Marine Conch. p. 68.—Dorset Catalog. p.
    30, pl. 5, f. 2.—BROWN, Illust. Conch. G. B. p. 100, pl. 40,
    f. 12.—WOOD, General Conch. p. 171. pl. 45, f. 3.—DILLW.
    Recent Shells, vol. i. p. 91.—LAM. Anim. s. Vert. (ed. Desh.)
    vol. vi. p. 195.—PHILIPPI, Moll. Sicil. vol. i. p. 27, and vol.
    ii. p. 22.—HANL. Recent Shells, p. 63.

We have changed the name by which this species is ordinarily designated, in consequence of a careful examination of the original type of Linnæus, which is still preserved in his cabinet at Soho Square. The shape is oblong oval, the texture rather thin, or but moderately strong, and not quite opaque. The valves are almost equilateral, compressed, and of a more or less glossy pale orange, or reddish flesh-colour, (the latter hue is extremely rare in British examples, but is the ordinary tint of the Mediterranean specimens, which are much more delicate and lustrous than our own,) with two whitish or paler approximate linear rays, adjacent to the umbonal fold, which latter, as well as the ventral flexure, is well marked. These rays are most evident in the younger shells, and become occasionally indistinct in the more aged examples. The right valve is closely striolated in a concentric direction; the left valve is comparatively smooth, though concentric subimbricated

lines are not unfrequently wont to appear in front and towards the lower margin. The ventral edge is generally
more convex in front than behind; both dorsal margins are
comparatively straight, the anterior being more inclined to
retusion, the posterior to convexity; the declination of the
hinder one is moderate, the front slope is but trifling. The
anterior side is rather the longer, its extremity is a little
attenuated, and well rounded both above and below. The
posterior end forms an acute angle, or imperfect rostrum,
which is situated below the middle of the side. The umbones project but little, and are slightly recurved; the
beaks are small and acute. The ligament is sunken. Internally the colouring is usually of a deeper tone than it is
externally; the hinge margin is rather narrow, and only
provided, in addition to the ordinary primary teeth, with
a single, rather approximate lateral lamina in the right
valve.

Poli describes the animal as having very long rose-
coloured, speckled plain siphons, a strongly fimbriated
mantle, and a large flesh-coloured foot.

The length of rather a large example was an inch and
three-quarters; its breadth exactly one inch. It is a scarce
British shell, and is taken sparingly in Guernsey, South
Devon, and Cornwall (Mont. &c.); Weymouth in seven
fathoms (M'Andrew and E. F.); Guernsey (S. H.); Irish
Sea (E. F.); Oxwich Bay in Glamorganshire (Jeffreys);
Tenby (Lyons and S. H.); Bantry Bay (Jeff. cab.); and
other parts of the Irish coast (W. Thompson). Lamlash
Bay, in Arran (Smith, Alder); and various parts of the
west of Scotland (Barlee).

It is on the whole a southern shell, and a member of the
Lusitanian Fauna.

T. TENUIS, Da Costa.

Suboval, compressed, glossy, devoid of epidermis, smooth, not
acuminated behind ; a single lateral tooth.

Plate XIX. fig. 8. and (animal) Plate K. fig. 3.

Tellina incarnata, LISTER, Hist. Conch. pl. 405, f. 251.
    „   „   CHEMN. (not Linn.) vol. vi. p. 119, pl. 12, f. 110.
    „ *planata*, PENN. (not Linn.) Brit. Zool. ed. 4, vol. iv. p. 87, pl. 48, f. 29.
               —BURROWS, Introd. Conch. pl. 5, f. 3.
    „ *polita*, PULTENEY, Hutchins, Dorset, p. 29.
    „ *tenuis*, DA COSTA, Brit. Conch. p. 210.—DONOV. Brit. Shells, vol. i. pl.
             19, f. 2.—MONT. Test. Brit. p. 59.—Linn. Trans. vol. viii.
             p. 52.—Dorset Catal. p. 30, pl. 5, f. 3.—TURT. Conch. Diction.
             p. 169.—TURT. Dithyra Brit. p. 107.—FLEM. Brit. Anim. p.
             436.—MACGILL. Moll. Aberd. p. 280.—Brit. Marine Conch.
             p. 69.—BROWN, Illust. Conch. G. B. p. 100, pl. 40, f. 19.—
             WOOD, General Conch. p. 155, pl. 44, f. 3, 4.—LAM. Anim. s.
             Vert. (ed. Desh.) vol. vi. p. 197. — Index Testaceol. pl. 3,
             Tell. f. 22.—PHILIPPI, Moll. Sicil. vol. i. p. 26, and vol. ii.
             p. 22.—HANL. Recent Shells, p. 64.—HANL. in Thesaur.
             Conch. vol. i. p. 287, pl. 58, f. 81, 82.
    „ *exigua* (VAR.), POLI, Test. Sicil. vol. i. pl. 15, f. 15, 17.
    „ *balaustina*, DILLW. (not Linn.) Recent Shells, vol. i. p. 93.—CHEMN.
             Conch. Cab. vol. vi. p. 124, pl. 12, f. 117 ?

This pretty and well-known species is of a suboval shape,
very thin, translucent, extremely glossy, and, especially the
left valve, much compressed. It is not greatly inequilateral ; the surface is almost smooth, and extremely variable ' in colouring, ranging from pale crimson, through
orange and yellow, to almost white, and often shaded with
paler and darker zones of the same tint, but never rayed,
spotted, or marbled. The ventral margin is convex in
front, and straighter, less ascending, and subinflected behind. The anterior side is rather the longer, and tapers a
little at the extremity, where it is well rounded, the front
dorsal edge declines but very moderately, and is more or
less convex or even subarcuated. The posterior termina-

tion is subangulated below, but rounded off at the tip ; the
hinder dorsal edge is straight, and unites itself in an almost
uninterrupted line with the convex and very obliquely
sloping posterior margin. The umbones project but little ;
the beaks are very small, and almost directly inflected ; the
umbonal ridge is almost, but not quite, obsolete ; and the
ligament is large, elongated, and prominent. The interior
is coloured similarly to the exterior ; the teeth are very
small, and the hinge of the right valve exhibits an approximate lateral in addition to, and immediately preceding, the
primary teeth.

The average size of the full grown shell is nearly one
inch in length, and five-eighths of an inch in breadth.

The animal, respecting which we have ample notes by
Mr. Clark and sketches by Mr. Alder, is subtriangular
and very much compressed. Its mantle is open throughout
in front, and finely fringed at its edges. The siphonal
tubes are long and slender, separate through their whole
length, both somewhat curving upwards, often extended to
equal lengths, or having one or other alternately the longer,
most frequently the branchial being the shorter. The foot
is large, broad at the base, rather long, linguiform, and not
very acutely pointed. The branchiæ consist of a single
large triangular leaf, on each side divided by a line into
two parts and finely pectinated. On each side of the
mouth there is a pair of long, rather narrow, pointed,
labial palps, smooth on their outsides and pectinated very
strongly within. The colour of the animal is yellowish
white. The tubes are nearly hyaline, and the branchiæ
light brown.

This is one of our commonest and prettiest bivalves. It
occurs in abundance on most of our sandy shores all round
Britain and Ireland ; so generally, indeed, that to cite lo-

calities would be superfluous. It lives at or near low water-
mark, and ranges a fathom or two below it, buried in sand.
Specimens of remarkable size and brilliancy are found
both on the northernmost and southernmost of our sandy
bays.

Abroad it ranges from the coasts of Finmark to the
Mediterranean, everywhere littoral. As a fossil it occurs
in beds of the glacial epoch, but does not appear to extend
farther back in time.

T. FABULA, Gronovius.

Ovate-oblong, with oblique striæ on one of the valves.

Plate XIX. fig. 9.

Tellina fabula, GRONOV. Zoophyl. p. 263, no. 1111, pl. 18, f. 9.—DONOV. Brit.
          Shells, vol. iii. pl. 97.—MONT. Test. Brit. p. 61.—Linn. Trans.
          vol. viii. pl. 52.—Dorset Catalog. p. 30, pl. 12, f. 3 and 3 A.—
          TURT. Conch. Diction. p. 170.—TURT. Dithyra Brit. p. 101.
          —FLEM. Brit. Anim. p. 435.—MACGIL. Moll. Aberd. p. 260.
          —Brit. Marine Conch. p. 66.—BROWN, Illust. Conch. G. B.
          p. 101, pl. 40, f. 18.—WOOD, General Conch. p. 156, pl. 45,
          f. 4.—DILLW. Recent Shells, vol. i. p. 91.—LAM. Anim. s.
          Vert. (ed. Desh.) vol. vi. p. 197.—Index Testaceol. pl. 3, f. 23.
          —RERS, Cyclop. Shells, pl. 5.—PHILIPPI, Moll. Sicil. vol. i. p.
          26, pl. 3, f. 10, and vol. ii. p. 22.—DELESS. Rec. Coquil. pl. 6,
          f. 5.—HANL. Recent Shells, p. 64.—HANL. in Thes. Conch.
          Hist. vol. i. p. 287, pl. 57, f. 62.

„   *discors*, PULTENEY, Hutchins, Dorset, p. 54.

This Tellen, which, from its peculiar sculpture, is easily
distinguished from any of our British shells, is of an ovate-
oblong shape, compressed, thin, semi-transparent, lustrous,
subequilateral, occasionally somewhat iridescent, and both
externally and internally of a somewhat pearly white, frequently stained on the umbones with orange or blush, but
never rayed nor uniformly tinted with those or any other
colours. The valves are rather flexuous, their front portion

bending to the left, their hinder to the right ; their surfaces are very different, the left being almost smooth or merely marked with concentric lines of increase, whilst the right is diagonally striated with most delicate and crowded oblique lines, which run from the upper part of the anterior side towards the lower end of the hinder extremity. These lines usually become converted into concentric striæ adjacent to the front extremity, and do not cross the umbonal fold (which is but little elevated) posteriorly. The ventral margin is usually but little rounded, and is but slightly inflected behind, where it is ordinarily straightish and but little ascending. The sides are all but equal, the front is well-rounded and but slightly tapering at its extremity, whilst the hinder termination is attenuated below to an obtuse point. The front dorsal edge, which slopes but little, although straightish near the acute and rather projecting beaks, becomes more or less arcuated near the extremity ; the hinder dorsal slope is very decided, and its outline, which beneath the large and prominent ligament is retuse, becomes convex near its termination. The posterior tip is rounded. The front dorsal area is very slightly inflected. The hinge of the right valve is furnished with an approximate front lateral lamina in addition to its primary teeth.

The ordinary size of this shell is about four-fifths of an inch, and its breadth not quite half an inch at the widest part. We have figured in plate XXVI. (f. 3), an interesting variety of this shell, observed by Mr. Jeffreys, in which the oblique striæ, gradually becoming indistinct anteriorly, wholly vanish near the front extremity. The shape is likewise more abbreviated than in the typical form, and the hinder termination is less attenuated than usual.

The animal closely resembles that of *Tellina tenuis*, though differing of course materially in its outlines. Its siphonal tubes appear to be rather longer than in that species. It is entirely white.

Wherever the coast exhibits a long expanse of sand, this species is almost invariably present; and almost always in considerable abundance. Localities need not be cited, as it occurs in all favourable places around England, Scotland, and Ireland, from north to south. Like the last species, it is usually a littoral shell, but ranges deeper, occurring occasionally at a depth of ten or twelve fathoms. It ranges throughout the Celtic and Lusitanian regions of the European seas, but is not enumerated by Löven among the mollusks of Scandinavia. It is found fossil in the mammaliferous crag of Southwold.

T. SOLIDULA, Pulteney.

Roundish-ovate; convex or subventricose, smooth; teeth very small, no lateral ones.

Plate XX. fig. 6.

LISTER, Hist. Conch. pl. 405, f. 250.

Tellina carnaria, PENN. (not Linn.) Brit. Zool. ed. 4, vol. iv. p. 88, pl. 49, f. 32.
„   *rubra*, DA COSTA, Brit. Conch. p. 211, pl. 12, f. 4.
„   *solidula*, PULTENEY, in Hutchins' Hist. Dorset, p. 29.—MONT. Test. Brit. p. 63.—Linn. Trans. vol. viii. p. 58.—Dorset Catalog. p. 31, pl. 8, f. 4.—TURT. Conch. Diction. p. 177.—MACGILLIV. Moll. Aberdeen, p. 279.—Brit. Marine Conch. p. 70.—BROWN, Illust. Conch. G. B. p. 101, pl. 40, f. 14.—WOOD, General Conch. p. 193, pl. 46, f. 2.—LAM. Anim. s. Vert. (ed. Deah.) vol. vi. p. 206.—Index Testaceolog. pl. 4, f. 84.—HANL. Recent Shells, p. 70.—HANL. in Sowerb. Thesaur. Conch. p. 318, pl. 59, f. 109, 110.—LÖVEN, Moll. Suecim, pl. 41.

Tellina zonata, DILLW. Recent Shells, vol. i. p. 100.
Psammobia solidula, TURT. Dithyra Brit. p. 95, pl. 8, f. 2.—FLEM. Brit. Anim. p. 438.
Tellina Balthica, PHILIPPI, Moll. Sicil. vol. i. p. 28, and vol. ii. p. 22.—FORBES, Mem. Geol. Surv. vol. i. p. 411.

Although the name *solidula* is well established, the specific appellation *rubra* was previously bestowed upon this shell by Da Costa, an epithet which we wish not to resuscitate, since not only is it peculiarly unsuited to a shell with so variable a colouring, but emanates likewise from an author who, having wilfully passed over the just claims of his predecessors in nomenclature, has forfeited the right of challenging for himself the law of priority. It is by no means certain after all, that this bivalve is specifically distinct from the *Balthica* of Linnæus; the differences at least, although sufficiently definite, not being greater than what are avowedly induced in other species by the peculiar nature of the waters of the Baltic sea, under whose influence the majority of the marine shells become depauperated.

The form is rounded, ovate, and longer than broad (more rarely suborbicular); the valves are equilateral, opaque, strong, and more or less ventricose, the convexity being most marked near the umbonal region, diminishing below it, and more especially lessening towards the pointed extremity. The surface, except in aged examples, is more or less glossy, and both externally and internally of the same hue, although the interior is frequently of a deeper tone. The colouring matter is often disposed in darker and paler zones, and never in rays or spots; it is infinite in diversity, various shades of yellow, flesh, orange, and pink, occupying the entire surface; the valves more rarely are almost white. There are neither striæ nor sulci, but only a few antiquated lines of growth. The ventral margin is well arcuated in front, but becomes straighter and somewhat ascending behind, where it forms an acute angle below with the much declining and scarcely convex dorsal edge.

The declination of the front dorsal margin adjacent to the beaks, (where it is almost straight) is very inconsiderable ; the outline subsequently becomes arcuated and moderately sloping.　The anterior side is a trifle the longer ; its extremity is broadly but not symmetrically rounded, there being an occasional obscure subangulation at the cessation of straightness in the dorsal edge, and the rise of the lower margin exceeding the descent of the upper one. The umbones are rather prominent ; the beaks acute, and hardly leaning forward in the least, in front of them exists (in the adult only) a linear pseudo-lunule, which is more evident in the right than in the left valve.　The ligament is long, very prominent, and usually dark coloured.

The ventral flexure is almost obsolete, the umbonal fold, which runs adjacent to, and almost parallel with, the dorsal margin, is chiefly distinguishable by the depression of the surface behind it, which, in the right valve, obscurely subangulates it.

The hinge margin is rather broad ; there are two very caducous almost rudimentary cardinal teeth in each valve but no lateral laminæ.

The length of a good sized specimen is rather more than one inch, and its breadth about three-quarters of an inch. A curious variety is found where fresh water mingles with the sea.　There is a suborbicular form taken at Southampton, with a peculiarly dull surface, and much arched ventral margin ; and the declination of the hinder dorsal edge, so abrupt as materially to diminish the ordinary angulation of the posterior extremity.

The animal is suborbicular, thick, and convex ; its mantle is open, and ornamented at the margin with fine white filaments.　The two siphons are nearly hyaline, of moderate length, and quite plain at their orifices ; the anal one is usually curved upwards. Mr. Clark describes the arrangements of the branchial and labial palps to be similar to those of *T. tenuis*, except that the latter are broader. The foot is white, flat, linguiform, rather pointed, bent at the base, and of moderate dimensions. The colour of the animal is yellowish, tinged slightly, especially the branchiæ with reddish-brown.

" This species," observes Montagu, "is found common on most of the British coasts, particularly the sandy bays and inlets, buried four or five inches beneath the surface." It is indeed universally distributed, and often occurs in vast abundance in suitable localities. It is distributed throughout the European seas, and ranges as far as the Euxine. It is as common fossil in beds of the pleistocene epoch, wherein it makes its first appearance, as on existing shores, and unerringly marks the shallow waters under which such formations were accumulated.

T. PROXIMA, Brown.

Obovate ; compressed, smooth, never glossy, usually provided with an epidermis ; no lateral teeth.

Plate XXI. fig. 1.

Macroma tenera, LEACH, Appendix to Ross's Voyage.
Tellina proxima, BROWN, Zoolog. Beechey Voyage, p. 154, pl. 44, f. 4.—SMITH, Wern. Mem. 8, p. 105, pl. 1, f. 21.—Brit. Marine Conch. p. 246.—MACGILLIV. Moll. Aberd. p. 340.—JEFFREYS, Ann. Nat. Hist. vol. xx. p. 19.—PHILIPPI, Neu Conch. vol. ii. Tellina, pl. 5, f. 4.—HANL. in Sow. Thesaur. Conch. vol. i. p. 313, pl. 66, f. 264, and pl. 59, f. 115.
Tellina sordida, COUTHOUY, Boston Journ. Nat. Hist. vol. ii. p. 59, pl. 3, f. 11.
Sanguinolaria sordida, GOULD, Invert. Massach. p. 67.
Tellina lata, GMELIN, only from figure of List. pl. 407, f. 253.—LOVEN, Ind. Moll. Sueciæ, p. 41.
   „   *calcarea*, LYELL, Phil. Trans. 1836.—FORBES, Mem. Geol. Surv. vol. i p. 411.
   „   *ovalis*, WOODWARD, Geol. Norfk. pl. 2, f. 11.
   „   *ovata*, Sow. Min. Conch. pl. 161, f. 2.
   „   *obliqua*, Sow. Min. Conch. pl. 161, f. 1.

The shape of *T. proxima*, which is intermediate between that of *solidula* and *tenuis*, is very variable, but when fully developed in specimens of a larger growth, is rather obliquely obovate; but becomes more or less abbreviated slightly sub-trigonal and more oblique in others which have lived under less favourable circumstances. The valves, which are rather thin, and usually much bent, do not appear perfectly equal, one being frequently flatter than the other; both are, how-ever, more or less shallow, of an opaque and rather dull white colour within and without, and almost smooth, being merely marked with minute concentric wrinkles, chiefly apparent at the sides. They are clothed with an olivaceous or ash-coloured epidermis, which is frequently only present towards the lower margin. The ventral edge, which is greatly arcuated in front, is scarcely convex, but much ascending behind; the front dorsal outline, excepting near the beaks, is more or less arcuated or at least convex, whilst the hinder dorsal edge is almost rectilinear or even subre-tuse, curving out very slightly, however, near its termina-tion. The degree of declination in the dorsal margin is not constant, but typically is rather trifling anteriorly, and only moderate posteriorly, but in many specimens these slopes, although still preserving their relative proportions, are much more decided. The beaks (when not eroded) are acute and a little projecting; they are situated much nearer to the hinder termination, which is bluntly angulated below, than to the rounded extremity of the anterior side, which is consequently much produced. The umbonal ridge, although present, is much depressed and almost obsolete; the ligament is large and prominent. The hinge margin is rather broad; there are no lateral teeth, and the primary are very caduc-ous; when the hinge, however, is perfect, one of the teeth is bifurcated in each valve. The pallial sinus is rather large.

The few specimens which have been dredged in Britain are much smaller than the exotic ones, none which we have seen exceeding three-quarters of an inch in length, and about half an inch in breadth.

It is a very rare shell, and wholly confined to North Britain, where as yet no living example has been taken. Indeed, in despite of the beautiful state of preservation in which the valves are found, we would not vouch for their not being fossils; the species is, however, most certainly found in a living state a little more northward, being an inhabitant of the shores of Sweden and the colder parts of Europe as well as of the United States of America. The small but perfect and fresh-looking valve delineated in our engraving was dredged by Mr. Jeffreys in fifty-three fathoms water off Croulin's Island, Skye; Mr. M'Andrew has likewise obtained two valves from Loch Fyne, and Mr. Macgillivray relates that a decayed one was brought up by the lines off Aberdeen. As a fossil it is well known, commencing its existence in the coralline crag. During the pleistocene epoch it was widely spread and plentiful, occurring in Sweden, Russia, and Canada, besides our own seas. The retrocession of glacial conditions probably caused its retirement northwards.

T. BIMACULATA, Linnæus.

Tellina bimaculata, LINN. Syst. Nat. p. 1120.—DA COSTA, Brit. Conch. p. 213. — PULTENEY, Hutchins, Hist. Dorset. p. 70.— DONOV. Brit. Shells, vol. i. pl. 19, f. 1. — MONT. Test. Brit. p. 69. — Linn. Trans. vol. viii. p. 57.— Dorset Catalog. p. 31, pl. 8, f. 7.—TURT. Conch. Diction. p. 178.—TURT. Dithyr. Brit. p. 104, pl. 8, f. 5. — FLEM. Brit. Anim. p. 435. — Brit. Marine Conch. p. 68. —CHEMN. Conch. Cab. vol. vi. p. 132, pl. 13, f. 127, 132. — DILLW. Recent Shells, vol. i. p. 101.—LAM. Anim. s. Vert. (ed. Desh.) vol. vi. p. 207.—

Index Testaceolog. pl. 4, f. 83.— HANL. in Sow. Thesaur.
Conch. vol. i. p. 250, pl. 56, f. 16, 19, 20, 21, 22.
Tellina sea radiata, LAM. Anim. s. Vert. (ed. Desh.) vol. vi. p. 207.— Index
Testaceolog. Suppl. pl. 11, f. 37.

Our description of the *T. bimaculata* is drawn up from
foreign examples, the great range of variation not being
adequately represented by the scattered individuals reported to have been taken upon our shores. The shape
varies from ovate to rounded ovate ; the valves are equal,
thick, opaque, simply convex, almost smooth, and rather
glossy. The diversity of colouring is infinite ; the principal variations are as follows :—violet, white, orange-red,
rich yellow, or pinkish red (either uniform or rayed with
purple, the white specimens with usually two lateral internal spots of deep crimson) ; whitish or yellowish, with
narrow interrupted violet rays, which often assume the
appearance of arrow-heads ; violet, rayed with white ; and
whitish, with broad fawn-coloured and narrower purplish
rays. The ventral margin, which is often a little inflected
at the posterior end, ranges in the middle from merely convex to arcuated. The sides are decidedly unequal ; the
front one is the longer, and tapers considerably to a rounded
extremity, the dorsal edge sloping greatly, but with little
convexity ; the hinder termination is bluntly biangulated,
and its dorsal edge straight, short, and but little declining.
The umbonal ridge is not much marked ; the ligament is
short, projecting, and rather large ; the beaks are acute,
and lean slightly backward ; the nymphæ great and prominent. The primary teeth are large, the lateral, which
are occasionally obsolete, are short, thick, and nearly equidistant. The sinus of the palleal impression is much expanded, straight above, and bluntly rounded in front. Our
largest example measures two-thirds of an inch in length,
and full three-quarters of an inch in breadth.

"As this species is considered by some naturalists to
have been erroneously introduced into our catalogues, it
may be stated that Mr. R. Ball has specimens of it collected on the coasts of Clare and Cork, and that Mr. Warren
of Dublin, obtained one in a living state at Ardmore,

county Waterford." (Thompson on the Fauna of Ireland,
in the Report of the British Association for 1843.) Three
more individuals are likewise stated, on credible authority,
to have been taken on the coasts of Cork and Waterford.
(Thompson.) Da Costa observes, that he has received the
species from Hampshire and Lancashire; Pulteney mentions it among his Dorset shells; and Turton ascribes it to
the " Western coasts." Modern researches have not confirmed the correctness of the English localities cited by
authors notoriously lax upon the question of indigenousness. Its occasional appearance on our shores is, probably,
to be ascribed to the frequent wreck of vessels from the
West Indies, where it is most abundant.

SPURIOUS.

We owe to the kindness of Dr. Fleming the opportunity of describing an interesting shell, which was mentioned (p. 434) in
his " History of British Animals," under the supposition that it
was the *T. fragilis* of Pennant, to whose figure indeed (pl. 47, f.
26) it bears some resemblance, but is broader, more inequilateral,
and more swollen at the front ventral margin. As the teeth of
the two specimens, which are otherwise in excellent preservation,
are either accidentally broken or naturally obsolete, the generic
allocation can only be regarded as hypothetical, the general aspect
being equally like a *Thracia*.

T. FRAGILIS, Fleming (not Linnæus).

Suboval, solid, opaque, of a shining squalid white externally,
dull white internally. Valves unequal; the right the larger and
the more convex, the left the shallower, but not flattened. Exterior somewhat obsoletely sulcated or even subplicated in a
concentric direction, and behind the umbonal ridge or indistinct
fold, where the surface becomes duller, more or less distinctly
marked with fine elevated wrinkles. Ventral margin arcuated
in front, ascending and subretuse behind. Anterior side decid-

edly, and occasionally much, the longer; its dorsal edge not
greatly declining, and becoming convex or subarcuated as it
recedes from the rather prominent beaks: its extremity well-
rounded both above and below. Posterior side truncated at its
narrowed termination, the upper angle rather the more projecting; its dorsal slope moderate or considerable, retuse or incurved.
Ligament very large, prominent, of an ashy yellowish brown.
Umbones eroded (in these examples). Inside with radiating
wrinkles; front muscular impression slightly lunate, moderately
large; hinder scar small, rounded, reniform; palleal sinus short,
rounded at the apex; margins acute. Length an inch and a
sixth : breadth five-sixths of an inch.

In reference to these shells, Dr. Fleming writes, "I believe I
got them as specimens of *Tellina fragilis* of Pennant, and from
Plymouth. This was my conviction at the time, but the founda-
tion of it I cannot now illustrate. Since the publication of the
'British Animals,' I have repeatedly thought they had an out-
landish character."

T. PISIFORMIS, Linnæus.

Tellina pisiformis, LINN. Syst. Nat. ed. 12, p. 1120.—Linn. Trans. vol. viii. p. 67.
            TURT. Conch. Diction. p. 178.—SPENGLER, Skrivt. Nat.
            Selskab. Kioben. vol. iv. pt. 2, p. 117.—WOOD, General
            Conch. p. 194.—DILLW. Recent Shells, vol. i. p. 102.—
            HANLEY, in Sow. Thesaur. Conch. vol. i. p. 261, pl. 56, f. 30.
            —PHILIPPI, Neu. Conch. Tellina, pl. 4, f. 7.
Cardium discors, MONTAGU, Test. Brit. p. 84.
Strigilla pisiformis, TURTON, Dithyra Brit. p. 119.
Lucina   „   FLEM. Brit. Anim. p. 442.—Brit. Marine Conch. p. 76.

*A West Indian shell, introduced as British with hesitation by
Montagu, who picked a single dead specimen from the sand of Falmouth harbour. As this example is no longer to be found, and
the Card. discors is not so minutely defined as to determine whether
it belongs to the pale variety of pisiformis, or is the flexuosa of Say
(J. Acad. N. S. Philadelph. vol. ii. p. 303), wherein the oblique
striæ change their directions several times at the posterior termination, it is assigned, with some little doubt, to the former.*

T. CARNARIA, Linnæus.

Tellina carnaria, LINN. Syst. Nat. ed. 12, p. 1119,—DONOV. Brit. Shells, vol. ii.
pl. 47.—MONT. Test. Brit. p. 73.—Linn. Trans. vol. viii. p.
57.—Dorset Catalog. p. 31, pl. 5, f. 6.—TURT. Conch. Diction.
p. 177.—CHEMN. Conch. Cab. vol. vi. p. 130, pl. 13, f. 126.
— WOOD, General Conch. pl. 40, f. 4. — DILLW. Recent
Shells, vol. i. p. 100.—Index Testac. pl. 4, f. 79.—DESH. in
Anim. s. Vert. vol. vi. p. 209.—HANL. Recent Shells, vol. i.
p. 72, pl. 4, f. 79 ; in Sowerb. Thesaur. Conch. vol. i. p. 260,
pl. 56, f. 37, 38.
Cardium corneceum, DA COSTA, Brit. Conch. p. 181.
Lucina carnaria, LAM. Anim. s. Vert. (ed. Desh.) vol. vi. p. 227.—FLEM. Brit.
Anim. p. 442.—Brit. Marine Conch. p. 75.
Strigilla carnaria, TURT. Dithyra Brit. p. 118, pl. 7, f. 15.

*A West Indian shell ; introduced by Da Costa, as received from
Scarborough, Devonshire, and Cornwall.*

T. FAUSTA, Pulteney.

LISTER, Hist. Conch. pl. 266, f. 102.
Tellina remies, BORN (not Linn.), Mus. Cæs. p. 36, pl. 2, f. 11.—CHEMN. Conch.
Cab. vol. vi. pl. 12, f. 112.—LAM. Anim. s. Vert. (ed. Desh.)
vol. vi. p. 199.
,, *fausta*, PULTENEY, in Hutchins' Dorset, p. 29.—DONOV. Brit. Shells, vol.
iii. pl. 98.—MONT. Test. Brit. p. 64.—Linn Trans. vol. viii. p.
55, pl. 1, f. 3.—Dorset Catal. p. 30, pl. 5, f. 5.—TURT. Conch.
Diction. p. 175.—DILLW. Recent Shells, vol. i. p. 94.—HANL.
in Thes. Conch. p. 256, pl. 64, f. 260, 264.
,, *lævis*, WOOD, General Conch. p. 181, pl. 37, f. 1.

*A West Indian shell, introduced by Dr. Pulteney as dredged
at Weymouth.*

T. STRIATA, Chemnitz.

Tellina striata, CHEMNITZ, Conch. Cab. vol. 10, p. 349, pl. 170, f. 1654, 1655.—
HANL. in Thesaur. Conch. vol. i. p. 240, pl. 61, f. 161.
,, *angulosa*, GMELIN, Syst. Nat. p. 3244.
,, *lata*, PULTENEY, Hutchins' Hist. Dorset, p. 29 (from his own shells).—
MONT. Test. Brit. p, 57.
Donax Martinicensis, LAM. Anim. s. Vert, (fide Deles. Rec. Coq. pl. 6, f. 15.)
Tellina punicea, TURT. Conch. Diction. p. 171 and Dithyra Brit. p. 100 (certo
from specimens).—FLEM. Brit. Anim. p. 435 (partly).

*A West Indian shell, introduced by Dr. Pulteney as obtained in
Dorsetshire.*

T. PUNICEA, Born.

Tellina punicea, BORN, Testacea Mus. Cæs. Vind. p. 33, pl. 2, f. 2.—Dorset
    Catal. p. 30, pl. 7, f. 5.—Linn. Trans. vol. viii. p. 50.—Brit.
    Marine Conch. p. 66 (badly).—BROWN, Ill. Conch. G. B.
    p. 100.—GMEL. Syst. Nat. p. 3239.—LAM. Anim. s. Vert.
    (ed. Desh.) vol. vi. p. 196.—HANL. in Sow. Thesaur. Conch.
    vol. i. p. 239, pl. 58, f. 89, and pl. 60, f. 154.
Encycl. Méthod. Vers, pl. 291, f. 2.

*A West Indian shell, introduced into our Fauna through having
been figured in the Dorset Catalogue as identical with the preceding.*

T. INÆQUISTRIATA, Donovan.

Tellina inæquistriata, DONOV. Brit. Shells, vol. iv. pl. 123.—HANL. in Thesaur.
    Conch. vol. i. p. 238, pl. 57, pl. 58, and pl. 58, f. 80.
    ,, *sanguinea,* WOOD, General Conch. p. 159, pl. 44, f. 2.—HANL. Recent
    Shells, p. 67, pl. 4, f. 27.

*Inhabits the bay of Guayaquil ; was introduced by Donovan,
who only surmised that it had been taken by Dr. Pulteney on the
Dorset coast.*

T. SIMILIS, Sowerby.

Tellina similis, SOWERBY, Brit. Miscellany, pl. 75.—MONT. Test. Brit. Suppl.
    p. 167.—TURT. Conch. Diction. p. 170.—TURT. Dithyra Brit.
    p. 102.—FLEM. Brit. Anim. p. 435.—Brit. Marine Conch. p.
    67.—BROWN, Illust, Conch. G. B. p. 101, pl. 39, f. 35.—PHI-
    LIPPI, Neu. Conch. Tellina, pl. 3, f. 7.—HANL. in Thesaur.
    Conch. vol. i. p. 285, pl. 57, f. 65.

*A West Indian shell, introduced by Mr. Sowerby as taken at
Brighton.*

T. LINEATA, Turton.

Tellina Brasiliana, LAM. (not Spengler), Anim. s. Vert. (ed. Desh.) vol. vi. p.
    205.—HANL. Recent Shells, p. 70, Suppl. pl. 9, f. 3.
    ,, *striata,* MONT. (not Chemn.) Test. Brit. p. 60, pl. 27, f, 2.—Linn. Trans.
    vol. viii. p. 54.—TURT. Conch. Diction. p. 169 ; Dithyra
    Brit. p. 106.—FLEM. Brit. Anim. p. 436.—Brit. Marine
    Conch. p. 69.—DILLW. Recent Shells vol. i. p. 92.

Tellina lineata, TURT. Conch. Diction. p. 168, f. 16 ; Dithyra Brit. p. 99, pl. 7,
f. 1.—FLEM. Brit. Anim. p. 435.—Brit. Marine Conch. p.
65.—BROWN, Illust. Conch. G. B. p. 100, pl. 40, f. 15.—
PHILIPPI, Neu. Conch. Tellina, pl. 4, f. 6.—HANL. in
Thesaur. Conch. vol. i. p. 233, pl. 56, f. 35, 36, and pl. 57,
f. 46, 47.

*A Brazilian species, introduced by Montagu as picked up by
Mr. Bryer on the shore between Weymouth and Portland. In
this and the preceding cases of exotic species being enumerated as
British, there is no reason to suspect wilful deception : they were
probably taken from heaps of foreign ballast.*

SYNDOSMYA, RECLUZ.

Shell thin, transversely more or less oblong or elongated,
equilateral or inequilateral, slightly gaping at the extremities, surface smooth, invested with a thin and deciduous
epidermis ; muscular impressions rounded or oblong ; pallial sinus deep and wide ; hinge composed of an oblique
spathulate fulcrum in each valve, in the pit of which a
cartilage is lodged, and two distinct lateral teeth in one
or both valves ; primary teeth small or wanting ; ligament
rather short, partially external.

Animal oblong, compressed, its mantle open throughout,
and finely fringed at the margin ; the siphons separated
throughout, long, slender, the upper one invested with a
fine wrinkled epidermis ; their orifices plain ; foot linguiform, large, apiculated ; labial tentacles triangular, sometimes obscure.

The shells of this genus have been designated by so
many generic names, that some of our British conchologists will hardly recognise them under the appellation we
have here adopted. *Mactra, Amphidesma, Ligula, Erycina,* and *Abra* have at various times numbered them in
their ranks ; and, had the last-named designation ever

been accompanied by a distinct diagnosis, it might have
been as well to adopt it. As it is, the last name, that
given by Recluz, claims the place of honour. The species
are not remarkable for beauty or singularity. They are
small bivalves, mostly northern, living in all depths of
water, from the laminarian zone to the deepest explored
regions. They bury in sand and mud, and appear to be
active creatures of their kind, capable of enduring many
vicissitudes of conditions.

S. ALBA, Wood.

More or less oval, not at all elongated ; sides very unequal.

Plate XVII., fig. 12, 13, 14.

Mactra alba, WOOD, Linn. Trans. vol. vi. pl. 18, f. 9 to 12.
Mactra Boysii, MONT. Test. Brit. p. 98, pl. 3, f. 7.—Linn. Trans. vol. viii. p. 72,
pl. 1, f. 12.—Dorset Catalog. p. 33, pl. 12, f. 7.—TURT. Conch.
Diction. p. 84.—DILLW. Recent Shells, p. 143.—Index Testa-
ceol. pl. 6, Mactra, f. 27.
Amphidesma Boysii, LAMARCK, Anim. s. Vert. (ed. Desh.) vol. vi. p. 128.—TURT.
Dithyra Brit. p. 53. pl. 5, f. 4, 5.—Brit. Marine Conch.
p. 55.—BROWN, Ill. Conch. G. B. p. 105, pl. 42, f. 3.—
HANL. Recent Shells, p. 42, pl. 6, Mactra, f. 27.
Amphidesma album, FLEM. Brit. Anim. p. 432.—MACGILLIV. Moll. Aberd. p. 293.
Syndosmya alba, RECLUZ, Revue Cuv. Zool. 1843, p. 362.—RECLUZ, in Chenu's
Illustrat. Conch. Syndosmya, p. 3. — LÖVEN, Index Moll.
Scandinav. p. 44.

Notwithstanding that the epithet *alba* is peculiarly devoid of significance in the genus *Syndosmya*, we are not
at liberty to reject it for the subsequent one of *Boysii*,
although the latter commemorates in some measure the
services rendered to Conchology by one of the authors
of the "Testacea Minuta Rariora," a work too frequently
attributed solely to Walker, who was merely the engraver
of the plates.

This well-known bivalve is of an oval shape, very thin
and fragile, but not pellucid, of an uniform white under

a glossy, very thin, yellowish, and evenly spread epidermis, which is at times slightly opalescent; the valves are rather compressed, though not particularly so for this genus, and their surface is nearly smooth. The sides are distinctly unequal, the front exceeding the hinder by nearly one half its length; the ventral edge is simply arcuated, and both the dorsal margins are more or less convex, the front one but little sloping, the hinder one greatly declining. The anterior extremity is rounded, but not broadly so, the posterior end is obtusely angulated below; the umbonal ridge is entirely obsolete; the beaks are small and inflected, not leaning to either side; the ligament is very little, and often of a chestnut colour. The inside is more or less nacreous and iridescent; the cartilage-pit is rather large, curved, and subtriangular upon the hinder side just under the beaks, leans obliquely backward, and contains a rufous orange-coloured cartilage; the two lateral laminæ are large, raised, approximate, and nearly equal, their edges are slightly concave, and form an obtuse or right angle near their termination; the space between their apices occupies one third of the entire hinge-margin.

The measured length of a large Scotch specimen (the northern far exceed the southern in dimensions) was very nearly one inch, and its breadth was one third less: this is at least one fourth larger than the size of any of our English examples.

The animal has very lately been submitted to a most careful scrutiny by Mr. Clarke; and, as his notes are much fuller than our own, we draw from them the greater part of the following description. It is compressed, subovate, and of a very pale bluish-white hue; the mantle is open, and very finely fringed with short filaments; the branchial and anal tubes are completely separated from

their bases, and are eminently elastic both longitudinally
and laterally; when fully extended they are cylindrical,
and very little short of the length of the shell: the animal
has the power of inflating them to three times their ordinary diameter; they are of a light brownish colour, the
effect of an epidermis, which, when the tubes are half
exserted, exhibits in the branchial and rather longer one
about thirty-five annular corrugations, and in the anal
twenty-five; the colour of the true tubes under this epidermis, which is sometimes obsolete, is very pale whitish-
yellow; their epidermic cases are prolongations of the
investment of the shell; the branchial tube is truncate
and plain at the orifice, the anal furnished with a tubular
hyaline valve. The foot is compressed and muscular, large
in proportion to the animal: it presents no trace of a
byssal groove. The ventral portion of the body is marked
with intensely flake-white polymorphous spots; its dorsal
range is chiefly occupied by the liver, which appears of
a green colour through its investing membrane; the
branchiæ are white, two on each side of the body.

The *Syndosmya alba* is a very plentiful shell in most
sandy and muddy localities around all our coasts, and is
so generally distributed that all our maritime provinces
may rank it among their inhabitants. It often occurs
gregarious in considerable numbers, and is frequently cast
on shore. It ranges from one to forty fathoms, and is
most abundant in between ten and fifteen. The localities
which have furnished the finest specimens are Deal Voe
in the Zetlands (Jeffreys) and Loch Long (M'Andrew).
It ranges throughout the European seas from Norway
to the Mediterranean, and as a fossil commences its appearance in the coralline crag. It lived within our area
also during the pleistocene epoch.

S. INTERMEDIA, Thompson.

Elongated, ovate, almost equilateral.

Plate XVII. fig. 9, 10, and (Animal) Plate K, fig. 5.

? *Mya nitida*, MULLER, Prodr. No. 2963, (Not of O. Fabric.)
Amphidesma intermedia, THOMPSON, Ann. Nat. Hist. vol. xv. p. 318, pl. 19. f. 6.
Abra profundissima, (YOUNG) JEFF. Ann. Nat. Hist. vol. xx. p, 19 (not of
FORBES).
Syndosmya nitida, LÖVEN, Index Moll. Skandinav. p. 44.

It is by no means improbable that Müller intended to
indicate this graceful shell, under the name of *Mya nitida*,
but as his description, which is unaccompanied by any
figure, so inadequately defines it, as to leave much room
for conjecture, we have preferred to retain the appellation
given by the distinguished naturalist who first introduced
it into our Fauna.

The shell has an oblong, or rather elongated ovate-form,
and is of a brilliant porcelain white beneath the extremely
thin and almost imperceptible iridescent epidermidal surface. It is subdiaphanous, exceedingly thin and fragile,
compressed, (particularly behind,) and almost entirely
smooth, or at most marked with indistinct striulæ. The
anterior side, which is slightly but decidedly the more
produced, is rounded at its extremity, but not equally above
and below, since the front dorsal edge, which is barely convex, slopes but little downwards, the rotundity being effected
by the ventral margin, which, although straight and sometimes almost subretuse in the middle, rapidly ascends at
either extremity and particularly and arcuatedly so in front.
The posterior side is attenuated to a more or less acute or
obtuse subcentral point ; the hinder dorsal edge, after passing the extremely short, small, and olivaceous ash-coloured
ligament (which scarcely projects,) slopes very moderately,
yet more so than the front one, to its termination, exhibit-

ing ordinarily in the adult but little convexity of outline.
The beaks are depressed and minute, and scarcely incline
to either side.   The saffron-coloured cartilage is situated in
rather a large subtrigonal spoon-shaped projecting receptacle; on either side of this (in the right valve only) is an
approximate sublateral lamina, the front one of which is the
longer. The valves gape in a remarkable degree at each
extremity.

The animal is white, ovate and compressed. The edges
of the mantle are free and finely fringed. The anal siphon
is dusky, and, as if invested with a brownish corrugated or
ringed epidermis. The branchial one is transparent, and
presents a reticulated appearance. The foot is linguiform
and very changeable.

It lives buried in slimy mud in various depths, from six
to one hundred fathoms, and appears to be a species of
boreal origin, occurring chiefly in the neighbourhood of the
pleistocene deposits of Scotland, and in peculiar localities in
the Zetland isles, and on the west and south of Ireland.   It
was first found by Mr. Ball, Mr. Thompson, and Mr.
Forbes, in the bay of Killery, in Connemara, and afterwards by Mr. Thompson, in six fathoms, in Strangford
Loch. As it is a rare British shell we mention all the other
localities; Loch Fyne in fifty fathoms; Dunstaffnage;
Armadale in Skye, in from fifteen to forty fathoms. St.
Magnus bay twenty-one miles east of Brassay in seventy
fathoms; and twenty-five miles east of Noss in one hundred
fathoms, all in Zetland (MacAndrew); Deal Voe, Zetland
(Jeffreys); Birterbuy bay, in Connemara (Barlee and
Farren); and Cape Clear in sixty fathoms (MacAndrew).

It is essentially a northern species, and is recorded as an
inhabitant of the Norwegian seas (Löven) and the Straits
of Oresund (Öersted).

S. PRISMATICA, Montagu.

Much elongated, very inequilateral.

Plate XVII. fig. 15.

Ligula prismatica, MONT. Test. Brit. Sup. p. 23, pl. 26, f. 3.
Mya prismatica, TURT. Conch. Diction. p. 103.—WOOD, General Conch. p. 101.
        DILLW. Recent Shells, vol. i. p. 47.—Index Testaceol. pl. 2,
        Mya, f. 21.
Amphidesma prismatica, LAM. Anim. s. Vert. (ed. Desh.) vol. vi. p. 128.—TURT.
        Dithyra Brit. p. 52, pl. 5, f. 3.—MACGIL. Moll.
        Aberd. p. 294.—Brit. Marine Conch. p. 54.—BROWN,
        Ill. Conch. G. B. p. 105, pl. 42, f. 5.—HANL. Recent
        Shells, vol. i. p. 42, pl. 2, Mya, f. 21.
Syndosmya prismatica, RECLUZ, Rev. Cuv. Zool. 1843, p. 367; in Chenu, Illus.
        Conch. Syndos. p. 4.—LÖVEN, Index Moll. Skandi-
        navia. p. 45.

The *iridescent Syndosmya* (not that the iridescence is confined to this species) is of an elongated oblong shape, the length more than doubling the breadth; is extremely inequilateral, much compressed, and gaping slightly at both ends. The texture is very thin and fragile, of a translucent white, which in some specimens is more or less iridescent; and the surface is polished and almost smooth. The anterior side, which is nearly twice as long as the posterior, has its extremity rounded, but not symmetrically so, as the front dorsal edge which is slightly convex is scarcely or but little sloping, whilst the ventral edge which is arcuated in front, curves more or less obliquely upward to meet it. The hinder portion of the lower margin is more rectilinear, and even indistinctly retuse near its termination, but ascends equally as much as in front, forming a subcentral rounded off acute angle, with the arcuated and moderately sloping dorsal margin. The posterior termination is somewhat bent. The umbonal ridge is almost entirely obsolete: the beaks are small, very slightly inclined forward and but little

projecting.   The ligament is of a yellowish olive colour, and
but little prominent.   The hinge consists of a curved subtriangular cartilage pit situated just behind the beaks, and
inclining posteriorward, having in one valve a very small
apical triangular tooth above it in front, and an approximate
little elevated lateral lamina on either side of it, but unaccompanied by any teeth in the other valve.

   The length of a specimen of moderate size is seven-
eighths of an inch, which is just double the measure of
its breadth.

   " Animal sub-oval, compressed, with the mantle open
throughout its margins, finely fringed.   Siphonal tubes long,
slender, separated throughout, the upper one usually longest
and plain at its orifice.   The lower with about six short
points or scallops.   The foot is compressed, moderately
long, linguiform broad at its base with a slight shoulder,
tapering to a not very rounded termination.   Labia two,
very large, triangular, smooth externally, pectinated within.
Colour pearly-white, the tubes hyaline, the branchiæ tinged
with light brown."—CLARK, MSS. 1835.

   Though by no means so common a shell as *S. alba*, it is
not unfrequent on many parts of our coast.   It lives in sandy
mud, and has a great range in depth, extending from shal-
lows, whence it is occasionally cast on shore by the waves,
to beneath one hundred fathoms.   Between twenty and
fifty fathoms is its favourite region.   A few out of many
localities may be mentioned ; Weymouth (S. H.) ; Exmouth (Clark) ; Swansea and Fishguard (Jeffreys) ; Isle
of Man in twenty fathoms (E. F.) ; German Ocean,
southern parts, (Stanley) ; Scarborough (Bean) ; Northumberland (Alder) ; off Tynemouth, in fine sand and mud,
from four or five to fifty fathoms (Thomas) ; Frith of Forth
(E. F.) ; Aberdeenshire (Macgillivray) ; Orkney (Tho-

mas); Zetland, in from five fathoms, as at Balta Sound,
to one hundred, as it occurred at twenty-five miles east from
Noss (MacAndrew); Skye in twenty fathoms, Loch Fyne
in fifty fathoms (MacAndrew and E. F.); Mull of Galloway (Beechey); " Found on all sides of Ireland : thrown
ashore at Magilligan, Belfast bay and Dublin coast;
dredged by Mr. Hyndman in twenty fathoms, in Belfast
bay, and from fifty fathoms off the South Rock, Down.
Found in spring in the stomachs of haddocks and flat fish
along the eastern coasts " (Thompson). In sixty fathoms
off Cape Clear (MacAndrew).

Abroad this species ranges from the seas of Norway to
the Ægean. As a fossil it occurs in the coralline crag.

S. TENUIS, Montagu.

Subtriangular, almost equilateral ; breadth and length nearly
equal.

Plate XVII. fig. 11.

Mactra tenuis, MONT. Test. Brit. p. 572, pl. 17, f. 7.—Linn. Trans. vol. viii. p.
72.—Dorset Catalog. p. 53.—TURT. Conch. Diction. p. 84.—
FLEM. Brit. Anim. p. 433.—DILLW. Recent Shells, vol. i. p.
142.—Index Testaceolog. pl. 6, Mactra, f. 26.

Amphidesma tenue, LAM. Anim. s. Vert. (ed. Desh.) vol. vi. p. 126.—TURT.
Dithyra. Brit. p. 53.—FLEM. Brit. Anim. p. 432.—MAC-
GILLIV. Moll. Aberd. p. 293.—Brit. Marine Conch. p. 55,
f. 24.—BROWN, Ill. Conch. G. B. p. 105, pl. 45, f. 2.—
DELESSERT, Recueil Coquilles, pl. 4, f. 6. —HANL. Recent
Shells, p. 42.

Syndosmya tenuis, RECLUZ, Revue Cuv. Zool. 1843, p. 366.—RECLUZ, in Chenu's
Ill. Conch. Syndosmya, p. 3.

This small *Syndosmya* is nearly equilateral, subtriangular, very thin and fragile, somewhat translucent, and
under a very delicate sallow and slightly concentrically
wrinkled epidermis, of a dirty white hue, occasionally
somewhat iridescent, and but rarely glossy. The surface is

moderately convex, and almost smooth, and the shell is a
little open at either extremity. The lower margin is simply
arcuated, with the arch a little flattened near the middle ;
both the upper edges are almost straight, and profoundly
and almost equally sloping.   The sides are very nearly
alike in size, the front one is rounded below, and obtuse
above, the hinder is bluntly angulated. The beaks are
small, but acute and prominent, and are directly inflected,
not turning towards either side. The ligament is very minute,
and lies at the bottom of the narrow escutcheon formed by
the compression of the hinder dorsal margin.   There is also
a similar though less evident compression in front, whence
originates a false or incipient lunule. No umbonal ridge
is present. The hinge is only furnished in the left valve
with a single denticle ; the right valve has two denticles,
and two lateral laminæ, of which the hinder is large and
more remote, and the front more approximate and decidedly
smaller. The cartilage pit is large, much curved, and not
at all angular.   The length is not quite three-eighths of an
inch, and the breadth is about one-sixth less.

Notwithstanding that it is locally abundant, this cannot
be considered a very common species, being found in but
very few localities. Perhaps a few miles beyond Portland
bridge in Dorsetshire (S. H.), where the high water-mark
is indicated upon the muddy surface by the copiously scattered shells of this and other Mollusks, may be regarded
as its most prolific site. It has occasionally been taken
in Northumberland (Alder) ; at Ramsgate (Sowerby,
M‘Andrew); at Portsea and Southampton (Jeffreys); Torbay (Alder) ; and met with, though rarely, at Scarborough
(Bean) ; and Littlehampton in Sussex (Strickland).

Mr. Thompson has received some individuals from Larne
Lough in Antrim (Ann. N. H. vol. xiii. p. 433), the only

Irish locality from which he has seen unquestionable specimens.

The *Syndosmya truncata* of Recluz (Revue Zoologique, 1843, p. 368 ; in Chenu, Illust. Conch. Syndos. p. 4,) is entirely constructed from the *Amphidesma truncatum* of Brown's Illustrations of the Conchology of Great Britain, p. 106, pl. 42, f. 4, a species which is rendered peculiarly obscure, through the drawing and description being at variance, an error which, unfortunately, the author's memory is unable to account for. Neither of them, however, suggests to us the idea of its belonging to this genus, the figure, especially as regards the hinge, not being unlike the young of our solitary species of *Scrobicularia*. The reference to the species so named in Fleming's work on the British Animals, would have led us to the supposition that it was a *Thracia*, that shell being avowedly the *Anatina truncata* of Turton, which we know from the types to be a variety of *Thracia distorta*, but the indicated teeth of the following description are entirely adverse to such a conclusion.

" Subovate, rather convex, oblique, anterior side produced ; posterior side rather straight and subtruncated below ; with a flexure emanating from the umbo, and terminating on the margin ; umbones small, nearly central and slightly inflected, beneath them a lanceolate cavity or lunule, covered with transverse nearly obsolete striæ and wrinkles ; surface white, smooth, and glossy ; hinge with a double primary tooth in each valve, and a small tooth-like knob in the left valve, locking into a cavity for its reception in the opposite one ; inside smooth, glossy, and white ; each valve provided with two large muscular impressions ; margins rather thick for the size of the shell. Length three-eighths of an inch ; breadth half an inch. Found at Greenock by Stewart Ker, Esq. and is in the cabinet of Lady Jardine.

SCROBICULARIA, Schumacher.

SHELL compressed, subequivalve, dull, nearly smooth or marked by lines of growth. Muscular impressions round, pallial sinus ample. Hinge with small and narrow primary teeth, one or two in each valve ; no lateral teeth ; spathulate triangular fulcra in each valve with connecting cartilage. Ligament small, narrow, partially external.

Animal compressed, oblong or suborbicular ; mantle open, its margins distinctly denticulated. Siphonal tubes long, separated throughout, their orifices plain. Foot large, linguiform, compressed. Labial palps large and triangular.

This genus is closely allied to the last, though there are
sufficient distinctions between both shell and animal—distinctions of more consequence than those which separate
Psammobia from *Tellina*.   The only British shell included
in it has had the felicity of enjoying at various times not
fewer than a dozen generic titles.   The few known species
live in the mud of estuaries, and are gregarious.

S. PIPERATA, Gmelin.

Plate XV. fig. 5, and (Animal) Plate K. fig. 6.

LIST. Hist. Conch. pl. 253, f. 88.
Mya Hispanica, CHEMN. Conch. vol. vi. p. 31, pl. 3, f. 21.
Venus Borealis, PENN. (not Linn.) ed. 4, vol. iv. p. 96, pl. 48, f. 28 (badly).
Trigonella plana, DA COSTA, Brit. Conch. p. 200, pl. 13, f. 1.—Exp. Scient.
            Algerie, Moll. pl. 44 to 64 (shell, animal, and anatomy).
Mya Gaditana, GMELIN, Syst. Nat. p. 3221 (made from figure only).
Mactra Listeri, GMELIN, Syst. Nat. p. 3261.—Linn. Trans. vol. viii. p. 71.—
            Dorset Catal. p. 33, pl. 7, f. 1.—TURT. Conch. Diction. p. 83.
            —Index Testac. pl. 6, Mactra, f. 25.
Mactra piperata, GMELIN, Syst. Nat. p. 3261.—DILLW. Recent Shells, vol. i.
            p. 142.
Mactra compressa, PULTENEY, in Hutchins' Dorset, p. 31.—MONT. Test.
            Brit. p. 96 and 570.
Tellina plana, DONOV. British Shells, vol. ii. pl. 64, f. 1.
Lutraria compressa, LAM. Anim. s. Vert. (ed. Desh.) vol. vi. p. 91. — CROUCH,
            Introd. Conch. pl. 4, f. 3.—HANL. Recent Shells, p. 27.—
            CHENU, Ill. Conch. Lutraria, pl. 1, f. 7. — BROWN, Ill.
            Conch. G. B. p. 109, pl. 43, f. 4.
Lutraria piperata, LAM. Anim. s. Vert. (ed. Desh.) vol. vi. p. 92.—PHILIPPI,
            Moll. Sicil. vol. i. p. 9.
Listera compressa, TURT. Dithyra Brit. p. 51, pl. 5, f. 1, 2.—Brit. Marine Conch.
            p. 45.
Lutricola compressa, BLAINV. Malac. pl. 77, f. 2.
Scrobicularia piperata, PHILIPPI, Moll. Sicil. vol. ii. p. 8.
Lutraria Listeri, MACGILLIV. Moll. Aberd. p. 291.
Lavigno calcinella, RECLUZ, Ill. Conch. Lavigno, p. 8.
Amphidesma transversum, SAY, Americ. Conch. pl. 28, mid. figures (fide Recluz).

So peculiarly wide a variation of outline seems permitted
to this species, that until very lately, the elliptic specimens
of the Mediterranean have been specifically separated from

their more trigonal brethren of the Atlantic Ocean. Our
British examples, which all display a certain degree of tri-
angularity, vary in shape from elliptic to suborbicular, the
length being, however, always greater than the breadth.
The valves are subequilateral, compressed, dull, or but
very slightly glossy, and of an uniform squalid white, but
very frequently stained black by the colour of the mud in
which they are imbedded : they are opaque, fragile, though
not particularly thin, and either smooth, or marked with
very delicate concentric wrinkles, and more distant stages
of growth. The ventral margin is not much arcuated, and
whatever degree of ascent exists at its extremity, is almost
always straightish, or even at times slightly retuse, near the
middle. The dorsal edges vary greatly in the amount of
declination, but are always more or less straight, and the
ligamental one is generally the more sloping. The anterior
side is very slightly the shorter, its extremity is rounded,
but more regularly so below than above. The posterior
side is but little attenuated at its extremity, which is
bluntly subangulated, and situated rather below than above
the middle of the side, its exact elevation being dependent
upon the greater or lesser rise of the ventral margin posteriorward. The umbones are rather prominent ; the beaks
acute and incurved, not leaning to either side, nor preceded
by any lunule-like depression. The ligament is small and
narrow, but rather projecting : there is a certain degree of
depression at the hinder dorsal surface of the shell. There is
little or no elevation of the umbonal ridge, but there is usually
a more or less obsolete shallow groove adjacent to its site.
The inner surface is of a glossy white, occasionally, but
rarely, stained slightly with yellow : the cartilage pit is
triangular, and rather large ; in front of it lie the small and
extremely narrow primary teeth, a simple and solitary one

in the left valve, interlocking between what may either be
regarded as twin narrow teeth, or as a most broadly and
profoundly cloven single one. The pallial sinus is of the
most ample magnitude. Fine specimens occasionally reach
the size of two inches in length, and one-and-a-half in
breadth: the exact proportions are, however, very fluc-
tuating.

   The animal of this species has been frequently submitted
to examination, and some good figures of it have been published: it is subtriangular, compressed, and yellowish, or
pale orange; the mantle is freely open, and the margins
are only slightly and distantly fringed, or rather denticulated, so that they sometimes appear as if quite plain;
the siphonal tubes are long, yellowish, and separate, their
extremities plain: they are very contractile; the foot is
large, white, flat, tongue-shaped, and geniculated; the
labia are very large, triangular, and pointed. Elaborate
figures of the anatomy of this animal have lately been published by Deshayes in his gorgeous work on the Mollusca
of Algeria.

   As Montagu remarks, it is "chiefly found at the mouths
of rivers or inlets not remote from fresh water; and though
never beyond the flux of the tide, yet it delights in situa-
tions where fresh water is occasionally flowing over. It
principally inhabits sludge or muddy places, buried to the
depth of five or six inches." It is from the comparative
inaccessibility of such spots, that the species, although most
abundant, is not frequently taken alive, and that cabinets
are usually only furnished with dead valves washed on
shore after rough weather. It is common at Scarborough
(Bean); Liverpool (E. F.); Shellness, near Ramsgate (S.
H.); Littlehampton in Sussex, and Southend in Essex
(Strickland); in four fathoms near the Nore light, and

northwards to the Dudgeon, but not farther (Thomas);
Swansea and Langland Bay (Jeffreys); near Langharne
(S. H.); Cork (Humphreys); "in suitable places on each
side of the Irish coast" (Thompson); Clyde (Smith);
Skye and Frith of Forth (E. F.).

SPURIOUS.

AMPHIDESMA RETICULATUM, Linnæus.

Tellina reticulata, LINNÆUS, Syst. Nat. ed. 12, p. 1119.—Linn. Trans. vol. viii.
    p. 54, pl. 1, f. 9.—Dorset Catalog. p. 30, pl. 5, f. 4.—TURT.
    Conch. Diction. p. 174.—CHEMN. Conch. Cab. vol. vi. p. 124.
    pl. 12, f. 118.—WOOD, General Conch. p. 182, pl. 42, f. 2, 3.
    DILLW. Recent Shells, vol. i. p. 470.—Index Testaceol. pl.
    4, f. 70.

Tellina proficua, PULTENEY, Hutchins, Dorset, p. 29, pl. 5, f. 4.—MONT. Test.
    Brit. p. 66.

Amphidesma reticulatum, SOWERBY, Genera Shells, Amphid. f. 2.—CROUCH, In-
    trod. Conch. pl. 4, f. 9.—SOWERBY, Conch. Man. f. 85.—
    DESH. Encycl. Méthod. Vers, vol. ii. p. 25.

Suborbicular, a little oblique, moderately strong, somewhat
translucent near the beaks, moderately convex, umbones and interior rich yellow, elsewhere white; surface with moderately close
set concentric little elevated laminæ (usually obsolete above), the
interstices of which are delicately radiated with very small
raised wrinkles. Lower edge strongly arched, ascending posteriorly: beaks curved forward, subcentral. Dorsal edges very
moderately sloping, the front one straightish, the hinder one
decidedly convex or subarcuated. Both extremities rounded,
the posterior one rather obtusely. Two small primary and two
short strong approximate lateral teeth in one valve; cartilage
pit narrow, triangular; hinder dorsal area with a slight and
narrow depression. Diameter an inch and a quarter.

*A native of Brazil (?), introduced by Dr. Pulteney as taken at
Poole and Weymouth.*

SPURIOUS.

SANGUINOLARIA DEFLORATA, Linnæus.

Venus deflorata, LINN. Syst. Nat. p. 1133.—PENN. Brit. Zool. ed. 4, vol. iv. p.
   96, pl. 57, f. 54.—MONT. Test. Brit. p. 123, pl. 3. f. 4.—
   Linn. Trans. vol. viii. p. 123.—TURT. Conch. Diction. p. 240.
Tellina anomala, CHEMN. Conch. Cab. vol. vi. p. 93, pl. 9, f. 79 to 82.
Sanguinolaria rugosa, LAM. Anim. s. Vert. (ed. Desh.) vol. vi. p. 170 (in part).—
   Brit. Marine Conch. p. 64.
Psammobia deflorata, TURT. Dithyra Brit. p. 93.
Sanguinolaria deflorata, FLEM. Brit. Anim. p. 461.
Psammobia rugosa, SOWERBY, Genera Shells, Psammobia, f. 1.—REEVE, Conch.
   Systemat. pl. 53, f. 1.
Capsa deflorata, CONRAD, Americ. Marine Conch. pl. 17, f. 2.
Sanguinolaire ridée, CHENU, Traité Element. p. 60, f. 208.
Encyclop. Méthod. Vers, pl. 531, f. 3, 4.

*An exotic species, introduced by Pennant, of which a single
individual was obtained by Montagu in Falmouth Harbour.
Touching this last locality, so frequently quoted by our earlier
writers for doubtfully indigenous species, we fully agree with Mr.
Alder, who, referring to the large quantity of foreign ballast continually thrown into it, observes, "that no dependence can be
placed on the indigenousness of any shell, which has solely been
found in that harbour." As there are at least two varieties (?) of
the Lamarckian Sanguinolaria rugosa, besides the S. dichotoma
(Chemnitz, Conch. Cab. vol. vi. pl. 9, f. 83,) which has justly been
held specifically distinct by Anton (Vers. Conch. p. 4,) we may
remark that our pseudo-British one is the West Indian and South
American shell, which differs from the Oriental individuals, among
other respects, in being less inequilateral, less coarsely and more
crowdedly ribbed, and in having the lower or ventral margin much
less arcuated.*

831

DONACIDÆ.

This small tribe is nearly allied to the last. The shells are usually of much stronger and more compact texture, and their hinges, though variable, more highly developed, and provided with conspicuous primary teeth. The animal is often more or less brightly coloured, and is strikingly distinguished by the great development of the cirrhi around the orifices of the rather strong siphons, those of the branchial tubes being more or less pinnated and ciliated. The margin of the mantle, which was almost always fringed in the last tribe, in this is indifferently plain or cirrhigerous, even in the same generic group. The foot is very large, thick, sharp-edged, and not furnished with a byssal groove. The species of this tribe live buried in sand, most of them near the water's edge, and are, on the whole, members of southern and even tropical regions. They rarely occur in the fossil state, their littoral habits being unfavourable to their preservation.

DONAX, Linnæus.

Shell rather strong, more or less triangularly wedge-shaped, equivalve, very inequilateral; posterior side shortest; surface smooth, or radiato-striate, or decussate, covered by a distinct epidermis. Inner margin plain or denticulated; muscular impressions rounded or oblong; pallial sinus wide and deep, its outer edge rather distant

from the margin. Hinge composed of two primary teeth
in one valve, and one in the other, with accessory lateral
teeth. Ligament short, external.

Animal oblong, its mantle freely open in front, with
fringed, or partially fringed (or plain!) margins. Siphons
separated to their bases, the branchial with pinnated cirrhi
around its orifices, the anal with simple denticulations.
Foot very large, apiculated, sharp-edged. Branchial
laminæ on each side distinctly separated. Labial palps
long and triangular.

D. ANATINUS, Lamarck.

Inner margin crenulated ; hinge with lateral teeth.

Plate XXI. figs. 4, 5, and 6, and (animal) Plate K. fig. 7.

LISTER, Hist. Conch. pl. 376, f. 217.

Donax trunculus, LINN. Syst. Nat. ed. 12, p. 1127, partly (not of Mus. Ulric.).
—PENN. Brit. Zool. ed. 4, vol. iv. p. 93, pl. 55, f. 45.—
POULTENEY, Hutchins, Dorset, p. 32.—DONOV. British Shells,
vol. i. pl. 29, f. 1.—MONT. Testacea Brit. pt. i. p. 103.—
Dorset Catalog. p. 33, pl. 6, f. 3.—TURT. Conch. Diction.
p. 41.—TURT. Dithyra Brit. p. 123.—Flem. Brit. Anim. p.
433.—MACGILLIV. Moll. Aberd. p. 275.—Brit. Marine
Conch. p. 77.—BROWN, Ill. Conch. G. B. p. 97, pl. 39, f. 11.
—DILLW. Recent Shells, vol. i. p. 150.—Index Testaceolog.
pl. 6, Donax, f. 5.—MAWE, Conchology, pl. 9, f. 5.—
CROUCH, Introd. Conch. pl. 6, f. 5.

Cuneus vittatus, DA COSTA, Brit. Conch. p. 207, pl. 14, f. 3.

Donax anatinum, LAM. Anim. s. Vert. (ed. Desh.) vol. vi. p. 249.—HANL. Recent Shells, vol. i. p. 83.

Donax ruber (YOUNG), TURT. Dithyra Brit. p. 127, pl. 10, f. 14.—FLEM.
Brit. Anim. p. 434.—Brit. Marine Conch. p. 79.—
BROWN, Ill. Conch. G. B. p. 97, pl. 13, f. 13.

This extremely common shell is not the *D. trunculus* of
Continental writers, although perhaps equally entitled
(since both conjointly received this epithet from Linnæus)
to be termed so ; nevertheless, as the appellation cannot
be retained for more than one of them, it is held advisable

to yield the name to the Mediterranean species, not only
from its being almost universally so designated throughout
Europe, but likewise from there existing a slight balance
in its favour, on weighing the rival claims by the evidence
of the original synonymy and descriptions.

The shape of our British species is oblong-cuneiform,
and the texture is always more or less firm; although
most decidedly inequilateral, for its genus it is less so than
usual. Typically it is compressed, but certain solid and
gigantic specimens from Stornaway are convex or even
subventricose. The exterior is more or less glossy, and is
sculptured with fine rather closely set radiating simple
striæ, which diverge rather widely towards the margin,
and do not extend to the front portion or the hinder area;
these in many specimens (but not invariably) are decussated by still finer irregular scratch-like concentric lines on
the hinder side. Beneath the shining epidermis, which
passes from a lighter or darker oil-coloured yellow, almost
into olivaceous, the surface is generally tinged with livid
lilac of different shades (more rarely being pure white both
within and without), sometimes uniform, but frequently
with two paler or even white central diverging rays proceeding from the beaks, with the lines of increase indicated
by deeper belts of a livid hue: internally the colour ranges
from white to the darkest violet. The ventral margin is
more or less sinuous, presenting a slight and often almost
imperceptible trace of retusion posteriorly, but bulging out
anteriorward ere it abruptly ascends at the obtusely rounded front extremity. The dorsal edges are nearly straight
(yet always sinuous in some trifling degree), and in ordinary
sized specimens the front one scarcely declines, and the hinder one but moderately; the extent of declination increases,
however, in the young, and in the large variety we have

previously mentioned. The extremity of the posterior side, which is about half as long as the other, is very bluntly wedge-shaped; its dorsal area is more or less slightly flattened (with the lips, however, projecting), and excepting near the acute and slightly inclined beaks, traversed by more or less close concentric striæ, and occasionally even by some minute crowded radiating striæ near the ligament. The umbonal ridge is well developed, but obtuse. The inner edge is finely crenated posteriorly, and very strongly so at the ventral portion of it; anteriorly it is simple. The central triangular primary tooth of the right valve is profoundly bifid, or even bicuspidate, the broadly diverging narrow ones of the opposite valve are simple; there are two small approximate lateral teeth in the left valve, of which the anterior is nearly rudimentary, and almost adjacent to the primary.

The average size of specimens is about an inch and a fifth in length, and about eleven-sixteenths of an inch in breadth; the Stornaway variety exceeds an inch and a half in length, and is of proportionate width likewise.

The fry of this species is certainly the *D. ruber* of Turton's Dithyra, as we have ascertained from his cabinet; possibly also that of Montagu (Test. Brit. Suppl. p. 38.— Turt. Conch. Dict. p. 43), but the fact is not equally well assured. Young shells are almost destitute of any striation; they retain, however, their characteristic form, and are peculiarly and tolerably evenly compressed.

The animal is oblong, and rather thick. Its mantle is freely open in front, and has the margins fimbriated. According to Mr. Clark, the edges are double, the outer one plain or slightly crenulated, the inner furnished with a close set fine white fringe every where bordering it, except at the ligament, and composed of alternately longer and shorter cirrhi, all being longer in the neighbourhood of the tubes than elsewhere. The tubes are separated throughout, and rather long. The orifice of the branchial siphon has eight principal cirrhi ramifying, or pinnated and ciliated at their extremities; the anal is surrounded by six short single points. Both are of a pale orange colour, and often marked above and below by deeper bands of the same tint. The foot is yellowish, very large, pointed, and sharp-edged, plaited at the base when retracted, and not furnished with a byssal groove. The labial palps are brownish, very long, triangular, and pointed. The animal is sluggish when removed from its native locality, but is capable of active motion.

Few if any bivalves seem more universally diffused around our coasts. Wherever there exists a wide range of unmixed sand, there they are ordinarily met with in the greatest abundance, buried an inch or two from the surface, towards low water-mark.

The *D. fabagella* of Lamarck (judging at least from a specimen which we received in Paris from M. Recluz, as having been compared with the original type) is precisely identical in contour; it is, however, distinctly sulcated, and not merely striolate throughout the posterior half, and the radiating striæ appear entirely obsolete on the anterior side. The *D. venusta* of Poli is equally allied, but has, in all stages of its growth, strong and rather remote sulci upon its hinder dorsal area. The entire absence of these latter in the real *D. trunculus*, forms one of the most immediately perceptible marks of its distinctness from the present species.

D. POLITUS, Poli.

Inner margin entire.

Plate XXI. fig. 7.

LISTER, Hist. Conch. pl. 384. f. 227.

Tellina polita, POLI, Test. Siciliæ, pl. 21, f. 14, 15.

Donax complanatus, MONT. Test. Brit. p. 106, pl. 5, f. 4.—Linn. Trans. vol. viii.
p. 75.—TURT. Conch. Diction. p. 42.—TURT. Dithyra
Brit. p. 125, pl. 7, f. 13, 14.—FLEM. Brit. Anim. p. 433.
Brit. Marine Conch. p. 78.—DILLW. Recent Shells, vol. i.
p. 150.—LAM. Anim. s. Vert. (ed. Desh.) vol. vi. p. 249.
—Index Testaceolog. pl. 6, Donax, f. 6.

Psammobia polita, COSTA, Catal. Test. Siciliæ, p. 20.

Capsa complanata, SOWERBY, Genera Shells, Capsa, f. 2.—BROWN, Ill. Conch.
G. B. p. 96, pl. 39, f. 10.—PAYRAUDEAU, Cat. Moll.
Corse, p. 46.—REEVE, Conchol. Systemat. pl. 61, f. 2.—
HANL. Recent Shells, p. 86, pl. 6, Donax, f. 6.

Donax longa, PHILIPPI, Moll. Sicil. p. 57, pl. 3, f. 13.

Among our more beautiful shells, must certainly be
reckoned the *D. complanatus* of Montagu, its vivid tinting
presenting one of the few exceptions to that tameness of colouring which characterises the testacea of the less sunny
climates of Europe. We have allowed to Poli the meed
of priority in nomenclature, although he has erroneously
placed it in the genus Tellina; but his error is excusable,
from its being so aberrant a *Donax* as to justify that position in a Linnean arrangement.

The shape is of an elongated subcuneiform oblong, and the
texture, although tolerably firm, is by no means typically
solid. Its convexity is not great, the inclination being
rather to compression than otherwise. The exterior,
which is entirely devoid of any sculpture whatsoever, is
covered with a delicate yellow highly polished epidermis,
beneath which it is angularly mottled with liver-colour or
rich brown, varying much in intensity of hue. A single,

rather broad, conspicuous white ray runs from the beaks,
with but very trifling obliquity, to the commencement of
the posterior third of the ventral margin. This latter is
comparatively straight, the anterior portion bending but
little from its regular curve, and ascending with a moderate
upward inclination to the well-rounded anterior extremity.
The dorsal edges are tolerably straight, the front is but
little, and the hinder but very moderately sloping. Hence
the posterior wedge-shaped termination is very blunt, the
tip being rather broad and well-rounded. As the umbonal
ridge is rather obscure, the hinder area is not distinctly
defined; it is not, however, flattened, and the lips pout,
or project outwards. The sides for a *Donax* are not peculiarly unequal, the anterior one not being quite double
the length of the other. The ligament is short, prominent, and of a rich fulvous brown; the lunule is very indistinctly impressed. The beaks, which are by no means
prominent, are yet sufficiently acute at their apices, which
are scarcely inclined, and are sometimes purple, sometimes
orange yellow, and sometimes white. One of the more
beautiful varieties has the umbonal region of a deep violet,
with the beaks of a snowy whiteness. The interior of the
shell, which has its margins simple and not crenated, is
usually of a rich purple or violet; sometimes, however, it
is white, somewhat radiatingly stained with purple, and
the vicinity of the beaks adorned with a deep and brilliant
orange. The hinge of the right valve presents the ordinary solid bifid hinder primary tooth, and the very oblique
and almost linear front one, with a rudimentary linear intermediate one (to be met with in many, if not most of
this genus); in the right valve, in addition to the divergent narrow almost simple primary teeth, are two small
approximate sublateral ones, of which the anterior is so

immediately adjacent that the term lateral is almost inappropriate.

The animal, according to Poli, has long divided siphons, of a bright yellow colour, with orange stripes and pink cirrhi. The foot is large and white.

The largest specimens we have seen came from the Channel Islands, and were almost an inch and a half in length, and about half that space in breadth. These dimensions far exceed, however, the average size of specimens; those from Ireland are generally much smaller, but of more vivid painting. Although found in many localities, it is never common, and is generally prized by collectors. It is occasionally met with at Exmouth, Dawlish, Falmouth, Milton in South Devon, Looe in Cornwall. (Mont.)

In Ireland it is chiefly procured from Bantry Bay. (Humphreys.)

Mr. Hanley has received from Dr. Philippi an almost colourless and rayless variety from the Mediterranean, with the information that it is rarely met with. We are not aware that this has hitherto been discovered on our own coast.

D. TRUNCULUS, Linnæus.

Donax trunculus, LINN. Syst. Nat. ed. 12, p. 1127.—BORN, Mus. Cæs. pl. 4, f. 3, 4.—CHEMN. Conch. Cab. vol. vi. pl. 26, f. 253, 254.—POLI, Test. Sicil. pl. 19, f. 12, 13.—LAM. Anim. s. Vert. (ed. Desh.) vol. vi. p. 248.—PHILIPPI, Moll. Sicil. vol. i. p. 36, and vol. ii. p. 28.—DESH. Exped. Scient. Algérie, Moll. pl. 74, f. 1 to 5, and pl. 75 (anatomy).
Capsa „ HANL. Recent Shells, p. 87, pl. 11, f. 38.
Encyclop. Méthod. Vers. pl. 262, f. 1.

Although placed in this second section of very uncertain if not solely exotic species, it is by no means impossible, when the differences between this and the *trunculus* of the British conchologists are clearly understood, the discrimination of other individuals may establish a claim for this shell to be regarded as indigenous. At present the sole specimen we have seen, now in the collection of Mr. Metcalfe, was taken (not living) by Dr. Battersby, at Torquay. As that gentleman has no foreign collection, and is of the most unimpeachable veracity, no doubts could rest upon its British origin, were it not that Torquay has for years been so closely investigated, as to render it extremely improbable, supposing the species to be truly native, that other examples should not exist in some of the numerous collections continually being formed at that attractive watering place.

Hence, from what may not unlikely be esteemed an over-cautiousness, we prefer at present regarding it among our doubtful species; indeed, its mention at all, contrary to our usual rule of confining our attention among the supposed spuriously indigenous, to those mentioned in print (for otherwise the number of the excluded would far exceed those of undoubted British origin), is solely owing to the highly respectable authority of the naturalist we have mentioned.

The valves are oblong wedge-shaped, very inequilateral, strong, and not very convex. They are covered with a very thin epidermis, of darker or lighter shades of fulvous or buff-coloured yellow, beneath which the surface is usually of a glossy liver-colour, with often linear paler rays, but sometimes even of a pure uniform white. The ventral margin slightly bulges out anteriorly, and greatly ascends at that extremity which is obtusely rounded, and not much attenuated. The hinder side is scarcely equal to one fourth of the front; its blunted wedge-shaped termination is very abrupt, as the hinder dorsal edge slopes most suddenly and deeply from the ligament; the front dorsal edge is tolerably straight and but slightly declining. The beaks are somewhat inclined, and not acute; the lunule is linear and deeply excavated, and the posterior

340

area, which is defined by a very obtuse umbonal ridge, is
generally convex (invariably, however, with the lips pouting), and perfectly destitute of any sculpture. The interior of the shell is of a violet or purple cast, the lower edge
is strongly crenated, but the posterior crenulations do not
extend to the ligament. The hinge is destitute of lateral
teeth. The size is about seventeen lines in length, by
about eight and a half in breadth, and five and two thirds
in depth. It is one of the commonest species of the Mediterranean, replacing, as it were, the *anatinus* of the colder
shores of Europe.

SPURIOUS.

D. DENTICULATUS, Linnæus.

Donax denticulata, LIN. Syst. Nat. ed. 12, p. 1127.—PULTENEY, in Hutchins,
   Hist. Dorset, p. 32.—MONT. Test. Brit. p. 104.—Linn.
   Trans. vol. viii. p. 76.—Dorset Catal. p. 34, pl. 5, f. 12.—
   TURT. Conch. Diction. p. 41.—TURT. Dithyra Brit. p.
   124.—FLEM. Brit. Anim. p. 433.—MACGIL. Moll. Aberd.
   p. 275.—Brit. Marine Conch. p. 78.—DILLW. Recent Sh.
   vol. i. p. 151.—LAM. Anim. s. Vert. (ed. Desh.) vol. vi.
   p. 246.—HANL. Recent Sh. p. 82, pl. 6, Donax, f. 8.
   „ *punctata*, CHEMN. Conch. Cab. vol. vi. p. 262, pl. 26, f. 256.
   „ *crenulata*, DONOV. Brit. Shells, vol. i. pl. 24.

*A West Indian shell first introduced as British by Da Costa,
under the name of* Cuneus truncatus. *As regards the* denticulatus
*of Pennant, (ed. 1, vol. iv., p. 93, pl. 55, f. 46,) neither the draw-
ing nor the language of that author sufficiently coincide with the
characters of this well-known Donax, to render the identity at all
probable. Indeed the elongated form of his engraved figure,
(which bears more resemblance to the true* rugosus *of Linnæus,)
supported by his assertion of its exceeding the length of* anatinus,
*must be fatal to such an hypothesis. Several of our British authors
have admitted it in their works, but, we believe, no proof of its indigenousness has yet been furnished. Mr. Bean informs us that
very many years ago he took a valve from a fishing-boat at Scarborough; but as, during his many years' subsequent residence on*

the same spot, he has never procured a second example we think it most probable that the shell came from some foreign vessel.

ERVILIA, Turton.

Shell more or less solid, equivalve, inequilateral, oblong, depressed, closed. Surface transversely striate or nearly smooth. Two diverging teeth in each valve, one of them in the right valve high and projecting: a cartilage pit in each for the reception of the connecting internal cartilage. No lateral teeth. Muscular impressions strong; pallial sinus large and broad.

Animal unknown.

This genus, which was constituted by Turton for the *Mya nitens* of Montagu, has lately been revised and redefined by Recluz.[*] It has considerable relations with *Mesodesma*, but until the animal shall have been observed, its true position can only be assigned by analogy, as indicated by the shell alone. The species here described are all which have as yet been enumerated as members of the group.

E. castanea, Montagu.

Plate XXXI. figs. 5, 6.

Donax castanea, Mont. Test. Brit. p. 573.—Linn. Trans. vol. viii. p. 77.—Turt. Conch. Diction. p. 42.—Dillw. Recent Shells, vol. i. p. 152.—Index Testac. pl. 6, Donax, f. 10.

Capsa castanea, Turt. Dithyra Brit. p. 128, pl. 10, f. 13.—Flem. Brit. Anim. p. 434.—Brown, Ill. Conch. G. B. p. 96, pl. 39, f. 12.

Mesodesma castanea, Brit. Marine Conch. p. 54.

Ervilia castanea, Recluz, Mag. de Zool. 1845, pl. 95.—Recluz, in Chenu Ill. Conch. Ervilia, p. 3.

The shape of this interesting and rare shell, erroneously placed by Dr. Turton in the genus *Capsa* (which has a

[*] Revue Zoologique par la Soc. Cuvierienne, March, 1844.

prominent external ligament), is oblong elliptic, its length
being nearly double its breadth. It is solid, opaque, and
tolerably convex, the swell diminishing moderately and
evenly from the umbones on either side. The colouring
is slightly variable, but always of darker or lighter tints
of warm chestnut, the ground-colour being usually pale
or almost whitish (but sometimes decided chestnut), with
an almost vertical ray of dark chestnut-brown, which is
usually narrow, and does not reach to the beaks, lying
almost directly beneath them, and very slightly curving to
the longer side : the extreme posterior portion is likewise
stained with a similar brown tinge, forming a kind of
obsolete broad ray externally, but usually displayed more
distinctly upon the interior ; there is often too a third but
almost obsolete ray-like stain adjacent to the anterior
extremity. The surface is slightly glossed, and, from the
more or less abraded state of our English specimens, is
quite smooth ; in the living examples, however, it is concentrically substriolate, the striulæ being more closely and
regularly disposed on the anterior side. The ventral margin is convex or subarcuated, and rises the more anteriorly,
where it often forms a slight subangulation above with the
dorsal edge, which margin is more or less rectilinear towards
the beaks, but subsequently has a tendency to display
convexity. The produced posterior side is attenuated and
bluntly rounded at its termination ; the anterior varies
in these respects, but is more usually narrowed and only
rounded below, yet occasionally is rather the broader end,
and rounded both above and below ; the hinder dorsal
margin is retuse near the beaks, then straightish, and
finally just convex ; its declination is very trifling, that
of the shorter extremity is rather more considerable. The
beaks, which are acute and rather prominent, are situated

at two-fifths the distance from the shorter end, and lean
slightly backward : there is no lunular depression upon
the dorsal area. The inner margin is quite entire ; the
hinge-margin is wide and shelving inward near the beaks.
The hinge, which is destitute of lateral teeth, consists of a
broad and profound central triangular cartilage pit, preceded in the right valve by a strong but narrow triangular
highly projecting primary tooth, and succeeded by a still
narrower very oblique laminar one, which defines it posteriorly and occasionally leans over it ; in the left valve
the tooth-receptacle is scarcely divided from the cartilage-
pit by a narrow and hardly raised wall, and is bounded
in front by a very oblique and but little elevated lamina ;
a similar but more indistinct one succeeds the cartilage-
pit, but the majority of specimens (being worn) display
scarcely any traces of dentition in this valve ; none of the
teeth are cloven. The muscular impressions are seated high
up, and are profoundly impressed ; the pallial sinus is
rather large, and not much attenuated at its extremity.

The ordinary length of the larger shells is nearly half
an inch ; their breadth is rather more than half this measurement.

The animal is unknown.

Notwithstanding that numerous examples have been
procured from Cornwall and the Scilly Isles (the only
habitats on the British shores), none but single, and more
or less worn, valves have hitherto been detected. As
the species is taken alive (and in that state it is very
beautiful, the interior being rich violet, the external rays
of a deep chocolate, and the intermediate spaces whitish
or tinged with violet) in the Red Sea, we might have
supposed them the produce of some wrecked vessel, but
they have been taken continually in these localities from

the days of Montagu to the most recent period, and not merely cast upon the shores, but by dredging (S. H. 1848) in deep water in fifty-four fathoms between Scilly and Cornwall (M'Andrew); and in twenty fathoms near Penzance (M'Andrew and E. F.). In a recent state these valves are partially covered by a slight yellowish epidermis, of a somewhat horny texture.

SPURIOUS.

E. NITENS, Montagu.

Mya nitens, MONT. Test. Brit. Suppl. p. 165.—TURT. Conch. Diction. p. 103.—
       LASKEY, in Werner. Memoirs, vol. i. pl. 8, f. 4.—WOOD, General Conch. p. 101.—DILLW. Recent Shells, vol. i. p. 47.
Amphidesma purpurascens, LAM. Anim. s. Vert. (ed. Desh.) vol. vi. p. 129.—
       HANL. Recent Shells, vol. i. p. 43.
Ervilia nitens, TURT. Dithyra Brit. p. 56, pl. 19, f. 4.—FLEM. Brit. Anim. p. 431.
       —Brit. Marine Conch. p. 5.—SOWERB. Conch. Manual, f. 497.
       —HANL. Recent Shells, p. 43.—RECLUZ, Mag. de Zool. 1845,
       . Moll. pl. 96.—RECLUZ, in Chenu, Ill. Conch. Ervilia, p. 3.—
       PHILIPPI, Wiegman's Archiv. f. Naturg. 1847, pl. 3, f. 9.
Syndosmya purpurascens, RECLUZ, Rev. Cuvier. Zool. 1843, p. 365.

The contour is oval and very slightly oblique, and the valves glossy, tolerably strong, compressed, and regularly and closely sculptured with concentric striæ, which usually cover the entire surface; we possess, however, a young variety differing in no other respect, in which they are entirely obsolete on the longer side. The colouring (which is both externally and internally the same), varies from uniform rose colour to almost pure white, but is usually of a darker or lighter tint of the former, becoming pale or colourless towards the ventral margin and at the shorter side. The valves are devoid of any umbonal ridge, and rounded at both extremities, the front tapering in some degree, and the hinder termination being considerably attenuated. The ventral edge (which is entire within), is considerably, yet not regularly, arcuated, ascending chiefly in front; the dorsal margin slopes decidedly on either side, but more so in front, where it is nearly rectilinear, than behind, where, as it recedes from the middle of the shell, it becomes convex or even subarcuated. The posterior side is about half as long again as the anterior. The beaks are very acute, moderately prominent, not leaning to either side, and preceded and succeeded by a small depression, but no distinct lunule nor escutcheon.

The hinge consists in the right valve of a very strong highly-projecting primary tooth situated just in front of the apex, which is subtriangular in shape, and directed forward, in front of which the hinge margin, which is very thick and strong, is somewhat excavated; behind it, and exactly beneath the apex, is the large triangular cartilage cavity, the front edge of which is perpendicular, and the hinder very oblique; there is also a fine linear excavation running along the posterior hinge margin. In the other valve, the margin on either side of the beaks is elevated so as to simulate two laminar diverging teeth, the broadly-triangular interstice being divided into a narrow and trigonal hollow for the reception of the opposite tooth, and a broader cartilage plate which projects in front beyond the basal line and whose anterior edge is elevated so as to resemble a linear tooth. The cartilage is inserted between a cut in the apices. The ordinary length is about three-eighths of an inch, and the breadth about one-fifth.

A West Indian shell, introduced by Montagu as taken near Dunbar by Mr. Laskey. It is not unimportant to remark, as accounting in some measure for the very considerable number of exotic shells introduced from the neighbourhood of Dunbar by Mr. Laskey, that several vessels from foreign ports had, just before that gentleman's investigation, visited his subsequent dredging-ground, and their ballast was in all probability the fertile source of most of his additions to British Conchology, as it has in like manner added not a few spurious species to the Flora of the neighbouring district.

* An *Ervilia pellucida* has been added to this genus by Professor Macgillivray, which we vainly hoped to have examined before the publication of this sheet, as that gentleman had promised to forward us any of his species we might desire to investigate. Judging only from the description, we feel little doubt that it is merely the fry of a described species, and certainly not the *Tellina pellucida* of Brown, to which it was referred in the Molluscous Animals of Aberdeenshire, &c. (p. 341, copied in the British Marine Conchology, p. 245,) which is a full quarter of an inch in length, and smooth in surface, &c.; while *this* is described as being but three-fourths of a line only, and concentrically sulcated. We owe to the kindness of Sir Walter Trevelyan (who found it at Seaton, in Durham,) an

SPURIOUS.

Under the name of *Mactra deaurata*, Dr. Turton has introduced into our Fauna a species of the genus *Mesodesma*, stating that it was dredged up in the offing of Exmouth. One of our most assiduous and scientific collectors, Mr. Clark of Bath, whose researches in that neighbourhood extended over a period of twenty years, during that long space of time never once procured a single specimen, a strong, although negative, proof of the individual shell described by the doctor being of foreign importation, and not of native origin. The species is an inhabitant of the Gulf of St. Lawrence, Newfoundland, and does not range to the European seas. Inquiries instituted on the Devonshire coast have enabled us to solve the mystery of the discovery of this and other transatlantic shells in spots so utterly at variance with their known habitats. We find that during many years several vessels from those parts were engaged in prosecuting the Newfoundland fisheries; so that the accidental appearance of a few specimens of northern shells may readily be accounted for, as they frequently are mingled with the ballast of ships. A comparison of the original type with its delineation in the Conchylia Dithyra, compels the remark, that it is represented as more narrow and elongated than nature has shaped it, and enables us to declare its perfect identity with examples of the *Mesodesma Jauresii*, received by us from North America.

M. DEAURATA, Turton.

Mactra deaurata, TURT. Dithyra, Brit. p. 71, pl. 5, f. 6.—FLEM. Brit. Anim. p. 427.
„ *denticulata*, Index Test. Suppl. pl. 1, Mactra, f. 9.
Mesodesma denticulata, GRAY, Cuv. Anim. King. (ed. Grif.) pl. 22, f. 2.

---

inspection of the typical example of *Tellina pellucida*, which, crushed as it unfortunately then was through transmission by post, still remained sufficiently united to enable us to state with certainty that it is not an adult shell, (it was not unlike the fry of *Scrobicularia piperata*,) and that the engraving of it (Ill. Conch. G. B. pl. 40, f. 22) scarcely presents any resemblance to the species, the dorsal edge not being incurved, and the hinder termination not being rounded (as delineated) but subangular.

Mesodesma Jauresii, DE JOANNIS, Mag. de Zool. 1834, Moll. pl. 54.—GOULD,
      Invert. Massach. p. 58, f. 38.—DEKAY, New York Moll.
      p. 231.
  „   *decuratum*, HANL. Recent Shells, p. 39, suppl. pl. 1, Mactra, f. 9.—
      Brit. Marine Conch. p. 53.

Somewhat triangularly subovate, thick, heavy, opaque, very
inequilateral, moderately convex behind, compressed in front ;
valves, when young, perfectly smooth and covered with a shining
yellow epidermis ; when aged, antiquated, and the epidermis
olivaceous or dusky brown, beneath which the surface is whitish,
or pale reddish brown. The anterior side is nearly double the
length of the posterior, and tapers to a rounded extremity, the
ventral margin, which is straightish near the middle, strongly
ascends anteriorly in an arcuated sweep ; the hinder extremity
is most bluntly subcuneiform, the tip being broad and slightly
rounded. The inclination of the front dorsal edge is very trifling,
that of the hinder is much greater, but still moderate ; the convexity of both of them is so slight as scarcely to be apparent.
The beaks are not greatly elevated, but are rather acute when
not eroded, and do not lean to either side ; there is a slight flattening of the dorsal edge in front of them, but no lunule. The
interior is more or less white, and the margins entire ; the cartilage pit is broad, deep, and subtriangular, shelving downward
so that its base is below the level of the inferior edge of the hinge
margin, and appressed upon the subumbonal region ; its lower
edge is convex. The lateral teeth are remarkably strong and
solid, and are more or less coarsely sculptured with raised perpendicular striæ ; both of them are approximate, and the anterior is
distinctly the more produced. A small semicircular posterior
sinus alone prevents the pallial impression from being simple.

The full dimensions assigned to it by Dr. Gould are an inch
and three-quarters in length, by a little more than an inch in
breadth. Our own and Dr. Turton's examples, are far less. The
American author, whose opportunities of examining numerous
specimens were of course superior to ours, remarks, that, on the
anterior edge of the deep spoon-shaped cartilage-pit "is the vestige of a short, widely diverging, V-shaped tooth, which will
seldom be found, as it is scarcely possible to open the valves without destroying it."

MESODESMA CORNEA, Poli (not Lamarck).

Mactra cornea, POLI, Test. Sicil. vol. ii. pl. 19, f. 8 to 11.
Donax plebeia, PULTENEY, Hutchins Hist. Dorset, p. 32.—MONT. Test. Britan.
  p. 107, pl. 5, f. 2.—Dorset Catalog. p. 34, pl. 5, f. 13.—TURT.
  Conch. Diction. p. 42.—TURT. Dithyra Brit. p. 126.—FLEM.
  Brit. Anim. p. 434.—DILLW. Recent Shells, vol. i. p. 152.—
  Index Testaceolog. pl. 6, Donax, f. 9.
Amphidesma Donacilla, LAM. Anim. s. Vert. (ed. Desh.) vol. vi. p. 126.
Erycina plebeia, SOWERBY, Genera Shells, Erycina, f. 3.—SOWERBY, Conch.
  Manual, f. 86.
Mesoderma Donacillum, DESH. in Lam. Anim. s. Vert. (ed. Desh.) vol. vi. p.
  183.—Brit. Marine Conch. p. 53.—REEVE, Conch.
  System. pl. 45, f. 5.—HANL. Recent Shells, p. 39,
  suppl. pl. 11, f. 41.—PHILIPPI, Moll. Sicil. vol. ii.
  p. 29.—DESH. Exp. Scient. Algérie, Moll. pl. 39, 40,
  41, 42. (shell and animal).
Donacilla Lamarckii, PHILIPPI, Moll. Sicil. vol. i. p. 37.

An inhabitant of the Mediterranean ; introduced by Dr. Pulteney as taken at Weymouth. The original specimens of plebeia *are still preserved in the doctor's collection at the Linnean Museum, and are clearly identical (which some have doubted) with the* Donacilla *of Lamarck.*

MACTRIDÆ.

More than once we have had occasion to remark on the impossibility of arranging genera and tribes in order of affinity, and at the same time of maintaining a continuous sequence in a single line. The family before us is an instance; for, whilst there can be no question that it has close affinities with the *Veneridæ*, it presents so many features which remind us of the *Myadæ* that we seem to have separated it from the last-named tribe by a forced and unnatural barrier when we marshalled the Tellens and their allies in the interspace. Yet they too afford indications of near affinity — relations which the microscope has confirmed ; for we find Dr. Carpenter describing the texture of the shell of *Mactra* as resembling that of the *Tellinidæ*, but presenting more distinct indications of organic structure, exhibiting an unquestionable cellular layer though not definitely developed, on the external surface, and an inner layer of elongated cells with distinct boundaries.*

The *Mactridæ* have variously shaped, often tumid, shells, sometimes thick, sometimes thin and invested externally with a strong epidermis ; most of them are smooth, or merely striated across externally. The valves are connected together by a hinge consisting of a forked diverging tooth in one raised on a ligamental fulcrum, lodged in a cavity, which is marginated, in the other, a con-

* Carpenter, *loc. cit.* p. 103:

necting cartilage and small external ligament completing
the union ; the inner surface of the valves invariably presents a considerable pallial sinus. The animals have their
mantles variously open, often with the margins united for
a considerable distance in front ; the siphons are united
and fringed with simple cirrhi at their orifices.

MACTRA, Linnæus.

Shell more or less triangular, solid or thin, equivalve,
more or less inequilateral, sometimes nearly equilateral,
slightly gaping at the extremities ; surface smooth or transversely striated, invested with a striated epidermis ; muscular impressions rounded or oblong ; pallial sinus shallow,
but wide ; hinge composed of a V-shaped cardinal tooth
in one valve, locking into a marginated pit in the other,
and a long lateral tooth on each side of the same valve
which like the primary one is lodged in a deep groove with
tooth-like margins in the other ; cartilage pit triangular,
a small external ligament immediately behind it.

Animal triangular or oblong ; its mantle freely open in
front as far as the siphons, the margins more or less distinctly fringed ; the siphons are united to their extremities,
which are surrounded with fringes of simple cirrhi ; the
foot is strong, changeable in shape, linguiform, and geniculated ; the labial tentacles are long and pointed, pectinated on their inner sides ; the outermost branchial leaflet
in each pair is shorter than the other.

The *Mactræ* are found on sandy coasts at various depths,
though the majority of species, and especially the larger
kinds, are littoral. Shells of this genus are often cast on
shore by the waves. The animals live buried in sand at a
small depth beneath the surface, and are active and power-

ful for their size; some exotic species attain considerable
dimensions. More than fifty species of this genus are
clearly ascertained; they are found in all seas, but the
most beautiful are tropical forms. Few fossil examples
occur, except in tertiary strata.

M. SOLIDA, Linnæus.

Oval or subtriangular, equilateral, or almost so, solid, more or
less rounded at both extremities, smooth; dorsal areas grooved
concentrically, not much depressed: umbones not greatly prominent; ventral edge not strongly arcuated: lateral teeth
grooved.

Plate XXII. figs. 1, 5, and (siphons) Plate L. f. 2.

Mactra solida, LINN. Syst. Nat. ed. 12, p. 1126.—PENN. Brit. Zool. ed. 4, vol.
iv. p. 92, pl. 51, f. 43 A, and pl. 52, f. 43.—PULTENEY,
Dorset. p. 31.—DONOV. Brit. Shells, vol. ii. pl. 61, f. 1, 3, 4,
5.—MONT. Test. Brit. p. 92.—Linn. Trans. vol. viii. p. 70.—
Dorset Catal. p. 32, pl. 12, f. 1.—TURT. Conch. Diction. p. 81.
—TURT. Dithyra Brit. p. 67.—FLEM. Brit. Anim. p. 426.—
MACGIL. Moll. Aberd. p. 288.—Brit. Marine Conch. p. 46.—
BROWN, Ill. Conch. G. B. p. 108, pl. 41, f. 3, 4.—CHEMN.
Conch. Cab. vol. vi. p. 230, pl. 23, f. 229.—SPENGL. Skriv.
Naturh. Selskab. vol. v. part 2, p. 113.—DILLW. Recent Shells,
vol. i. p. 140.—LAM. Anim. s. Vert. (ed. Desh.) vol. vi. p. 104.
—Index Testac. pl. 6, Mactra, f. 21.—PHIL. Moll. Sicil. vol.
i. p. 11, and vol. ii. p. 10.—HANL. Recent Shells, p. 31.
Trigonella zonaria, DA COSTA, Brit. Zool. p. 197, pl. 15, f. 1.
„   *gallina,* DA COSTA, Brit. Zool. p. 199, pl. 14, f. 6.
Mactra truncata, TURT. (not Mont.) Dithyra Brit. p. 68 (from type).
Mactra dubia and *M. ovalis,* Sow. Min. Conch. pl. 160.

The shape of the species which we are about to describe
is very variable, ranging from simply oval to subtriangular.
It is solid, opaque, subequilateral, glossy, and of an uniform
white under the ordinarily dull yellowish ash-coloured epidermis, which veils its outer surface. This latter is almost
smooth throughout, except occasionally a few scattered
antiquated or obsolete concentric furrows; the dorsal areas

are, however, closely grooved in a concentric direction with
abruptly terminating furrows.   The valves are but moderately ventricose, and the convexity is evenly enough
diffused, not being confined to the umbones as in certain
other *Mactræ*.   The ventral margin is simply convex, and
rises equally at either extremity.   The dorsal edges are
more or less convex, and the declination nearly equal on
both sides; the curve of the anterior is, however, greater
than that of the higher posterior one; and the degree of
slope varies from slightly to decidedly declining, according
to the greater or lesser disposition toward angularity in the
example.   The dorsal areas are but little flattened, the
hinder is the more so; the adjacent umbonal ridge is evident, but is not a prominent character.   The sides are
very nearly, if not quite equal; if either, the anterior one
is very slightly the longer, and is attenuatedly rounded
at its extremity, the most elevated portion of the arch not
being subcentral, but below the middle of the shell; the
posterior termination is almost rounded, being only very
bluntly subangulated towards the lower margin.   The lips
of the dorsal slopes are elevated or pouting, and not inwardly inclined; the umbones are not prominent, and the
beaks, which are small and in no way remarkable, lean a
little forward.

The internal surface is of a polished but not a snowy
white; the scars, which are profound, are moderate in size,
the pallial sinus is small.   The teeth are strong, the lateral
ones of moderate length and transversely grooved, both of
them approximate, but the hinder one the more closely so,
and subtruncated near the V-shaped primary denticle;
their upper edges are but little convex, and often nearly
straight, so as to appear subtruncated above: the cartilage
is not very large.

The length of an ordinary-sized example is about an inch and three-quarters, and its breadth about an inch and two-fifths. " Worn shells frequently become deeply furrowed or zoned with grey or slate-colour and sometimes yellow." (Mont.)

" Animal yellowish white or pale orange, subtriangular, thick, the mantles freely open in front and fringed at the margins. Siphons short, united to their extremities, the branchial orifice rather larger than the anal one, the former surrounded by about sixteen cirrhi, the latter with about twenty, shorter and more regular than those of the branchial tube. Both tubes of a pale yellow, pale brown, pale reddish, or flake-white colour, varying in examples from different localities. Foot large, fleshy, pointed when extended and not furrowed by a byssal groove. By means of its powerful agency the animal can leap for some distance. Branchiæ and labial palps of a reddish brown colour ; the latter long, narrow, pointed, and triangular." (Clark, MSS.) We find the animals of young and true specimens of this species to differ from that of *Mactra subtruncata*, in having the sides of the united siphons smooth, and only faint traces of a scabrous keel on the back of the anal one. The orifice of the latter is furnished with a tubular valve, which can be projected beyond the cirrhi.

The *Mactra solida* is a common frequenter of most of our sandy coasts all round Britain and Ireland. It is usually a littoral species, burying in sand or gravelly sand near low water-mark. Thence it ranges, if the ground be continuous and favourable, to a depth of fifteen fathoms, (as in the west bay of Portland,) being most abundant in about five or seven fathoms (as in the Frith of Forth). In one instance it was dredged from water as deep as thirty-five fathoms, at a distance of fifteen miles from

Duncansby Head (M'Andrew). It delights in estuaries, though some of the largest varieties occur in localities away from the neighbourhood of fresh-water, as on the coasts of Lewis. It ranges throughout the European seas, and has inhabited them ever since the epoch of the coralline crag.

M. TRUNCATA, Montagu.

Solid, rounded, triangular, subequilateral; umbones oblique and very prominent; dorsal areas and lateral teeth grooved.

Plate XXIII. fig. 1.

LISTER, Hist. Conch. pl. 253, f. 87.
Mactra truncata, MONT. (not of Turt. Dithyra Brit.) Test. Brit. Supplement p. 34.
    —TURT. Conch. Diction. p. 81.—FLEM. Brit. Anim. p. 427.
    —Brit. Marine Conch. p. 46.—DILLW. Recent Shells, vol. i.
    p. 140.—HANL. Recent Shells, p. 32, sup. pl. 9, f. 1.
  „ *subtruncata*, DONOV. Brit. Shells, vol. iv. pl. 126.
  „ *crassa*, TURT. Dithyra Brit. pp. 69, 258, pl. 5, f. 7.

The *Mactra truncata* of Montagu is most closely allied to that ancient species the *M. solida*; but although requiring the strictest scrutiny to discriminate it from certain forms of that shell, nevertheless appears, throughout the long series of specimens in all stages of growth and collected in various localities which we have examined, to preserve its peculiar distinctive characters. The contour is rounded-triangular; the texture thick, solid, opaque, and of an uniform dirty white; the surface dull or but very moderately glossy, and more or less evidently marked, in a concentric direction, with regular rather broad striæ, which, however, very readily become wholly or partially obsolete. The ventral margin is irregularly arcuated in the middle, and both dorsal edges meet it in a single uninterrupted rapid slope, whence arises the trigonal outline of the shell. The valves are ventricose and subequilateral,

the anterior side being, if either, the more produced. Both
extremities are somewhat attenuated, but whilst the front
is rounded, the hinder is angulated below, the anterior
dorsal slope being strongly arcuated, and the posterior one
far more rectilinear. The umbones, which are elevated,
very prominent, and oblique, curve forward at their acute
apices; on either side of them there is a considerable flattening of the sides of the shell, which are invariably
grooved with crowded narrow sulci. This depression is
more marked behind, where it is defined by an indistinct
umbonal ridge, than in front, where it is confined to the
beaks, and is not co-extensive with the sulci. The ligament, cartilage, teeth, and inner margin are similar to those
of *solida*.

The length of the largest specimen we have seen was
two inches, and its breadth an inch and three-quarters. It
is distinguished from *M. solida* by the great projection of
its umbones, its triangular contour, the arcuation of its
ventral margin, the profundity of its valves, and, in the
more typical examples, the production of its anterior side
and its concentric striæ.

The animal closely resembles that of the last species.

This shell is stated by Montagu to be extremely common
on the shores of the Frith of Forth,—where we have dredged
it in seven fathoms (E. F.),—and was dredged by Turton
in the Irish Channel. It is occasionally taken at Tenby
(S. H.), and is met with also in Cork harbour and
Dublin bay (Humphreys and Jeff. cab.); Bangor bay,
Down (Patterson). It is stated by Mr. Couch to inhabit
the shores of Cornwall, and is a littoral species at Stronsa
in Orkney (Thomas).

It occurs fossil in the glacial beds of the Clyde (Smith).

M. ELLIPTICA, Brown.

Elliptic, thin, quite smooth, subequilateral ; epidermis glossy ;
dorsal areas not grooved ; lateral teeth striated.

Plate XXII. fig. 3, and (animal) Plate L. fig. 1.

Mactra elliptica, BROWN, Illust. Conch. G. B. p. 108, pl. 41, f. 6.—FORBES,
     Malacol. Monensis, p. 48.—MACGILLIV. Moll. Aberdeen, p.
     288.—Brit. Marine Conch. p. 244, f. 28.—LÖVÉN, Ind.
     Moll. Skandinaviæ, p. 45.
  „ *solida* (partly), DONOV. Brit. Shells, vol. ii. pl. 61, f. 2.

Mactra elliptica, although bearing a very close resemblance to *M. solida*, may, nevertheless, without any great
difficulty, be distinguished from it by its lesser solidity,
more produced shape, its comparatively glossy epidermis,
and above all by the absence of those regular sulci which
invariably roughen the dorsal slopes of the latter species.
The shape is elliptical, with a slight tendency in the adult
to become trigonal, owing to the greater declination of the
dorsal edges in the final stage of growth ; the texture is
but moderately solid, and the valves are subventricose in
the adult, but simply convex in the young ; the surface
is nearly smooth, being free, even upon the dorsal slopes,
from all regular striæ, sulci, or other sculpture, and merely
marked with a few antiquated lines at the stages of increase, and sometimes irregular concentric wrinkles and
striulæ towards the extremities.   Beneath the smooth
and sometimes glossy epidermis, which in the young is
entirely buff-coloured, becoming ashy, except at the
margin, in specimens of more advanced age the shell is
white.   The ventral edge is straightish towards the middle,
and convex at each end.   The front dorsal edge, whose
slope instead of being depressed has its lips peculiarly
prominent, is arcuated and moderately declining ; the
hinder, which in the young is almost symmetrical with

the anterior, becomes somewhat rectilinear in the adult,
and its declination is similarly moderate. The beaks are
very nearly central, very depressed, acute at their apices, and
almost directly inflected, projecting, however, very slightly
forward. The anterior side is, if either, a little the shorter, and is somewhat rounded, but not symmetrically, at its
extremity; the posterior termination is subangulated below in the adult, but more rounded when immature.
The hinge occupies four-ninths of the entire length of the
valves; the cartilage-pit is triangular, oblique, and rectangular in front at the base; the primary teeth occupy nearly
the entire breadth of the margin, and have the lobes nearly
equal in the left valve. The lateral laminæ are nearly equally
approximate, elongated, and very solid, rather flat-topped,
and most delicately grooved perpendicularly; these in *solida*
are thicker, and less closely but more strongly sulcated.

The largest example we have ever seen was an inch
and a half long, and four-fifths of an inch broad, which
we regard as a comparatively gigantic shell, being nearly
double the ordinary dimensions.

The animal varies in colour from pale orange-yellow
to tawny, siphons, foot, and mantle being all of the same
hue; the margins of the mantle are firmly and conspicuously fringed; the siphons are united to their extremities, where both are surrounded by prominent cirrhi,
and the anal one is provided with a tubular valve, which
it projects beyond the fringe; the sides and back of the
siphonal tubes are smooth; the foot is digitiform, and not
so large as usual in this genus: it is very extensile, and
when the animal is placed on the surface of the sand,
it can extend its foot for a great distance, and feel with
it in all directions as if with a finger. When in the act of
leaping, both foot and siphons are projected very far.

This very distinct species, which was long confounded with the *Mactra solida*, and was first distinguished by the sagacity of Captain Brown, is by no means an uncommon shell, occurring on all parts of our coast from Jersey (S. H.) to Zetland (E. F.), usually in deeper water than its congeners. It was first observed, however, at low water in the Frith of Forth. We mention a few localities to shew its range in depth: Penzance, twenty fathoms (M'Andrew and E. F.); Fishguard in eighteen fathoms (Jeffreys); Anglesey in nine to twelve fathoms (M'Andrew); Isle of Man in fifteen to twenty-five fathoms (E. F.); North Sea off Norfolk in twenty-five fathoms (Stanley); Cape Wrath in fifty fathoms gravel, and in the same depth on the Lingbanks off Zetland, forty miles from shore (M'Andrew). Its range on the Irish coast is equally extensive.

Löven enumerates it among Scandinavian shells, ranging as far north as Finmark.

M. SUBTRUNCATA, Da Costa.

Decidedly inequilateral, triangular or trigonally ovate; surface partially covered with regular concentric grooves; posterior end more or less acutely angulated below: umbones prominent: dorsal areas and lateral teeth sulcated.

Plates XXI. fig. 8, XXII. f. 2. and (siphons) Plate L, fig. 3.

Mactra subtruncata, DA COSTA, Brit. Conch. p. 198.—MONT. Test. Brit. p. 93, and Suppl. p. 37, pl. 27, f. 1.—Linn. Trans. vol. viii. p. 71, pl. 1, f. 11, (badly).—Dorset Catal. p. 32, pl. 5, f. 10.—TURT. Conch. Diction. p. 82.—TURT. Dithyra Brit. p. 70.—FLEM. Brit. Anim. p. 427.—MACGIL. Moll. Aberd. p. 289.—Brit. Marine Conch. p. 47.—BROWN, Ill. Conch. G. B. p. 108, pl. 41, f. 7.—Index Testac. pl. 6, f. 23.—MAWE, Conchol. pl. 8, f. 4.—PHILIPPI, Neuer Conchyl. Mactra, pl. 1, f. 4.

Mactra stultorum, PENN. Brit. Zool. ed. 4, vol. iv. p. 92, pl. 52, f. 42.
 „   *lactea*, POLI, Testac. Sicil. pl. 18, f. 13, 14.
 „   *triangula*, PHILIPPI, Moll. Sicil. vol. i. p. 11, and vol. ii. p. 10
        (from specimen).—HANL. Recent Shells, sup. pl. 10, f. 40
        (copied from Poli).
 „   *crassatella*, LAM. Anim. s. Vert. (ed. Desh.) vol. vi. p. 107 (variety).—
        DELESS. Rec. Coquill. Lam. pl. 3, f. 6.
 „   *cuneata*, SOW. Min. Conch. pl. 160. f. 7.—WOODWARD, Geol. Norf. 62.
        f. 10.

The *M. subtruncata* is of a triangular or trigonally ovate
shape, very inequilateral, more or less solid, opaque, and
glossy; it varies in convexity from scarcely ventricose to
almost tumid, in the majority of examples, however, it
is merely subventricose; the valves are of an uniform
whitish hue, covered with a very thin cinereous epidermis, which has often a yellowish tinge; their surface has
its dorsal areas closely and more or less strongly grooved
concentrically, the anterior sulci being continued so as
to traverse a greater or smaller portion of the shell.
There are two well-marked varieties: the one which has
these sulci occupying almost its entire superficies is more
ventricose and abbreviated in form; the other, in which
they are confined to the front extremity and the vicinity
of the lower margin, so that the general surface is smooth,
is more produced, being trigonally ovate and comparatively compressed. The ventral margin is nearly straight
in the middle, and rises anteriorly; the declination of
both dorsal margins is very considerable, particularly of the
front one, which, as it recedes from the beaks, is more
or less arcuated; there is a great tendency to straightness
in the hinder dorsal or rather posterior outline. The hinder
dorsal area is greatly flattened, the front one is defined
by an angulated line running to the ventral corner from
the apex of the shell, which results from a slight depression
of that area, whose lips, however, distinctly project. The

umbones are remarkably prominent; the beaks are acute
and directly inflected. The anterior extremity is rounded,
but with a slight angulation a little below the middle;
the posterior side, which is much the longer of the two,
is attenuated at its termination and acutely angulated
below; the umbonal ridge, which bounds the hinder dorsal area, is tolerably evident, being distinguished by the
roughness of the epidermis upon it. The interior is of a
pure glossy white. The lateral teeth are moderately elongated, strong, and vertically sulcated, the front one flattened
at its apex where the hinder one is rounded.

The majority of specimens are not an inch long, nor
quite three quarters of an inch broad: the Irish example,
delineated in plate XXI, is of unusual magnitude.

The animal is triangular, and thick; the edges of its
mantle are not so distinctly fringed as in the other. British species, but rather crenated or serrated. The siphons,
which are united to their extremities, vary in colour from
reddish to yellowish, or white. Their orifices are thickly
fringed at the margins by a double row of cirrhi, and the
anal one often projects its tubular valve. The sides of the
siphons are scabrous at intervals, and the back of the anal
tube is rough with a serrated keel. The foot is large, tapering, and of a yellowish white colour.

This shell is universally distributed, and extremely common in all sandy localities around our coast, being equally
a littoral and moderately deep-water species, inhabiting
sand, sandy gravel, and even occasionally sandy mud. A
few localities will serve to mark its range in depth. Low
water in sand, Swansea and adjacent bays (Jeffreys);
Frith of Forth (E. F.); Clyde (Smith); and Orkney
(Thomas); in seven fathoms, Weymouth; twelve fathoms,
Anglesey; and four to seven fathoms, Zetland (M'An-

drew and E. F.); in three to four fathoms, Clew-bay, and elsewhere in the west of Ireland (W. Thompson, R. Ball, and E. F.); in fifteen fathoms, Moray Firth (M'Andrew), and twenty-seven fathoms, eight miles from land, off Dartmouth (M'Andrew and E. F.); in twenty-four fathoms, off Norfolk (Stanley); and very common generally in deep water, North Sea (Thomas). "A large, and much produced variety is very common in the Ardrossan sands in Ayrshire; a similar, but smaller one, is also common in Lamlash-bay, Isle of Arran, where it is gathered alive at low water, to feed pigs" (Alder).

It ranges from the Mediterranean to the south of Norway, and appeared in the Celtic seas during the epoch of the red crag, living there through the glacial period.

* We transcribe from the "Illustrations of the Recent Conchology of G. Britain and Ireland " (p. 108) the following description, which we have reason to believe is merely that of an aberrant variety of *M. subtruncata* ; the original shell, now in the collection of Sir W. Jardine, was not accessible up to the time of the printing of this sheet.

" *M. striata*, (pl. 41, f. 10,) BROWN.

" Shell transversely elongated, rather strong ; umbones small, subcentral ; anterior side subdepressed, and rounded ; posterior side elongated, and subovate : its superior line gently arcuated, as well as the basal margin ; surface brownish yellow, covered with strong tranverse equidistant striæ ; inside smooth, white.

This species bears a strong similitude to *M. subtruncata*, but differs in the posterior side being less acute, the umbones being much smaller in proportion to the size of the shell, in the striæ assuming nearly the character of ribs, and in the shell being considerably larger. I procured this species in Lough Strangford, county of Down, Ireland."

M. STULTORUM, Linnæus.

Rather thin, inclined to be trigonal, equilateral; beaks white: dorsal areas never chestnut at the junction of the valves: lateral teeth smooth.

Plate XXII. figs. 4, 6, and Plate XXVI. fig. 2.

Cardium stultorum, LINNÆUS, Syst. Nat. ed. 10, p. 681.
Mactra stultorum, PULTENEY, Hutchins Hist. Dorset, p. 31.—DONOV. Brit.
　　　Shells, vol. iii. pl. 106.—MONT. Test. Brit. p. 94.—Linn.
　　　Trans. vol. viii. p. 69.—Dorset Catalogue, p. 32, pl. 3, f.
　　　3.—TURT. Conch. Diction. p. 31.—TURT. Dithyra Brit.
　　　p. 72.—FLEM. Brit. Anim. p. 427.—MACGILL. Moll.
　　　Aberd. p. 287.—Brit. Marine Conch. p. 47.—BROWN,
　　　Illust. Conch. G. B. p. 107.—DILLW. Recent Shells, vol.
　　　i. p. 138.—LAM. Anim. s. Vert. (ed. Desh.) vol. vi. p. 99.
　　　(in part)—MAWE, Conchology, pl. 8, f. 5.—CROUCH, Introd.
　　　Conch. pl. 4, f. 4.—SOWERBY, Conch. Manual, f. 79.—
　　　HANL. Recent Shells, p. 29.—CHENU, Illust. Conchyliol.
　　　Mactra, pl. 3, f. 3.
Tellina radiata, PENN. Brit. Zool. ed. 4, vol. iv. p. 87. pl. 49, f. 30.
Trigonella radiata, DA COSTA, Brit. Conch. p. 196, pl. 12, f. 3.
Mactra cinerea, MONT. Test. Brit. Suppl. p. 35.—TURT. Dithyra Brit. p. 73.—
　　　FLEM. Brit. Anim. p. 428.—Brit. Marine Conch. p. 47.
　　　　　magna, WOODWARD, Geol. Norf. pl. 2, f. 10.

Although not exactly identical with the Linnæan type, which comes nearer to the *inflata* of Philippi (En. Moll. Sic. vol. i. p. 11, pl. 3, f. 1), we have not ventured to regard the differences as of more than varial importance; for a more diffuse dissertation upon the typical *stultorum*, we must refer our readers to the " Ipsa Linnæi Conchylia " of Mr. Hanley, the publication of which has been deferred, owing to the present work occupying his entire time.

Both in shape and colouring this is a very variable shell. The former ranges from simply elliptical to broadly subtriangular; the latter from fawn-coloured, covered with more or less narrow white rays, and generally adorned with paler zones, to an uniform ash-colour, passing through pale livid, only diversified by an obscure and partial radiation. The pale subtriangular variety, which is much less common than the more oval one, constitutes the *M. cinerea* of Montagu. The rays, although never broad, vary in relative width upon the same specimen; there is frequently a tinge of purplish liver-colour upon the umbones (not the beaks, which are usually paler), and there is often a stain of fawn-colour beyond the umbonal ridge, even when the rest of the surface is almost devoid of colouring. Less frequently the rays are fawn-coloured upon a paler ground. The valves are rather thin, not quite opaque, and more usually semipellucid; they are glossy, and almost smooth, being neither striated nor grooved; when magnified, however, a kind of crowded concentric subimbricated wrinkle-like lineolation displays itself, especially upon the umbonal fold, and towards the lower margin. Recent examples are covered with an epidermis of a cinereous brown, straw-coloured drab, or yellowish ash-colour, which is most closely and delicately wrinkled in a concentric direction. The valves are rather swollen, the chief profundity being at the subumbonal region, from whence it diminishes with tolerable evenness on either side; there is a slight, but evident flattening of surface upon both dorsal areas, which are equally free from sculpture with the rest of the shell; the hinder area is the more depressed. The amount of this dorsal compression mainly determines the contour of the shell, which, when it is but very trifling, and the lips of the suture pout, the slopes being more or less arcuated, is oval; but when more violent, so that the lips do not pout, and the slopes are comparatively rectilinear, becomes subtrigonal. The front dorsal edge is, however, almost invariably arched below, and its declination, though decided, is not quite equal to the produced, and rather ab-

rupt one, of the posterior side. The ventral margin is
more or less regularly subarcuated ; the sides are equal,
and not very unsymmetrical ; they taper a little at their
extremities, which are not regularly rounded, both (especially the hinder one) displaying a more or less slight angulation near the lower margin. The umbones are rather
prominent ; the beaks are more or less acute, lean forward, and do not approach closely to each other. The
umbonal fold is sufficiently evident, but neither carinated
nor peculiarly angulated. The interior varies from pale lilac
to white ; the teeth are very large, but thin, the cartilage
pit is rather narrow, and the lateral laminæ, which are of
about the same size and distance, are perfectly free from
crenation.

The dimensions of rather a large example were, an inch
and five eighths in breadth, and rather more than two
inches in length. The dorsal lips of the young specimens
project greatly, and their arcuation is very considerable.

The following full account of the animal was drawn up
by Mr. Clark this summer, and kindly communicated to
us by that gentleman, on the value of all whose observations we lay the greatest stress. "Animal suboval, tumid,
of the palest bluish-white, with its mantle entirely open,
the margins thereof clothed with an intensely white delicate fringe, formed of linear short filaments ; the ventral
portion of the body is white, and the dorsal, containing
the mass of the liver and other viscera, of a duller and
more opaque white ; the siphonal tubes are short, of the
same length, and united to their extremities, and are
never, in their utmost extension, exserted more than three-
fifths or half an inch ; the orifices of the tubes are truncate
and furnished with pale, dirty-red cirrhi, the branchial
rather the longest in diameter, with from twelve to six-

teen of moderate though irregular lengths, the anal with
about sixteen or twenty finer, shorter, and more even ;
the colour of the tubes is pale brown, with a reddish
tinge. The foot is white, large, and thick, long and tapering to a fine edge, and extensible into every form, from
a blunt mass to a very sharp lanceolate termination : it has
no byssal groove ; there are on each side two branchiæ
of a brown colour, the outer the smaller and overlapping the
under one very obliquely ; the latter is hung more transversely from the dorsal portion of the body ; a pair of
labial palps are united on each side of the buccal orifice,
and hang from it in long, subtriangular, pointed leaflets
of a paler brown and marked with stronger striæ, especially on their inner sides, than the branchiæ."

This is a most abundant shell everywhere on our sandy
beaches, littoral in its habits, and rarely taken by the
dredge except near shore and on a continuous tract of
sand, when, as off Ormeshead, it may be taken as deep
as twelve fathoms. As it ranges from one end to the
other of the British Isles with no restriction save unsuita-
bility of ground, to enumerate localities would be superfluous.

It is distributed ·generally through the European seas
as far north as the south of Norway, where the long
range of rocky coasts and deep water of the west inter-
rupt its progress. Philippi mentions it as a species collected by Ehrenberg and Van Hemprich in the Red Sea.
As a fossil it occurs in the red and mammaliferous crags.

M. HELVACEA, Chemnitz.

Shape inclined to oval, inequilateral ; dorsal area chestnut to the very lips ; beaks coloured : lateral teeth smooth.

Plate XXIII. fig. 2.

Mactra helvacea, CHEMN. Conch. Cab. vol. vi. p. 234, pl. 23, f. 232, 233.—LAM. Anim. s. Vert. (ed. Desh.) vol. vi. p. 99.—PHILIPPI, Moll. Sicil. vol. i. p. 10, and vol. ii. p. 9.—CHENU, Ill. Conch. Mactra, pl. 2, f. 4.

„   *glauca,* GMELIN, Syst. Nat. p. 3260.—DONOV. Brit. Shells, vol. iv. pl. 125.—MONT. Test. Brit. p. 571.—Linn. Trans. vol. viii. p. 68.—Dorset Catal. p. 68.—TURT. Conch. Diction. p. 80.—TURT. Dithyra Brit. pp. 73, 258.—FLEM. Brit. Anim. p. 428.—Brit. Marine Conch. p. 48.—BROWN, Ill. Conch. G. B. p. 107, pl. 41, f. 1.—SPENGLER, Skrivt. Natur. Selskab. vol. v. pt. 2, pl. 3.—DILLW. Recent Shells, vol. i. p. 144.—Index Testac. pl. 6, Mactra, f. 30.—HANL. Recent Shells, p. 29, pl. 6, Mactra, f. 30.

„   *Neapolitana,* POLI, Test. Sicil. vol. i. pl. 18, f. 1, 2, 3. Encyclop. Méthodique, Vers, pl. 256, f. 1.

This fine *Mactra* very closely resembles the preceding in its general aspect and features. Its contour ranges from simply oval to ovato-trigonal ; it is by no means solid, is inequilateral, semipellucid, and though decidedly convex, is, for its size, comparatively compressed. The convexity gradually, and nearly equably, diminishes on either side, from the subumbonal region ; the hinder dorsal area is flattened in the adult, but there is no peculiar angulation at the umbonal ridge, which is occasionally wrinkled concentrically in the full-grown examples. The entire surface is free from grooves or striæ, being smooth, more or less glossy, and of a pale fulvous or light rufous, adorned all over with numerous, and not very broad rays of a rufous or livid rufous hue, with which colouring the dorsal areas

are stained for the most part likewise. In the more recent specimens a tawny or yellowish brown closely-adhe-
rent epidermis somewhat obscures the vividness of the
radiation. The ventral margin, which is not particularly
arcuated, rises the more behind, where it forms a subangulation with the produced and but moderately sloping posterior dorsal, which edge is but very moderately convex in
the adult; the hinder extremity is a little attenuated.
The anterior side is manifestly, though not very greatly,
the shorter, and tapers at the extremity (which is well,
but not symmetrically rounded) from the great declination
of the dorsal margin, the lips of which are pouting, but the
outline not in general arcuated. The umbones do not
greatly project, but incline a little forward; the beaks are
blunt, not quite close to each other, and not preceded by
any concavity. The interior is whitish, or faintly exhibits
the external colouring; the teeth are large and thin, and
the lateral laminæ perfectly free from sulcation.

The shell we have figured (which, being bleached by the
sun, is not so distinctly rayed as in the engraving, where
the colouring is restored from an exotic specimen) is about
the average size of those picked up on the English coast;
foreign examples attain to the dimensions of four inches in
length and nearly three inches in breadth.

The animal is figured by Poli, and appears closely to
resemble that of *M. stultorum*. Almost all the British
examples consist of the worn valves which were obtained
by Miss Pocock (1801) from the sands of Hale in Cornwall, and appear to have passed from her hands into the
cabinets of several collectors. It was from one of her specimens that Donovan, the original introducer of the species
into our Fauna, derived his figure and description. We
only know of two examples with the valves united; these

Mr. Lukis, of St. Peter's Port, Guernsey, assures us (S. H.) were dug out from a little sandy nook of the adjacent islet of Herm. It is chiefly taken on the coasts of France, Sicily, and the warmer parts of Europe.

SPURIOUS.

M. FRAGILIS, Chemnitz.

Mactra fragilis, CHEMN. Conch. Cab. vol. vi. p. 236, pl. 24, f. 235.—TURT. Dithyra Brit. pl. 4, f. 10.—FLEM. Brit. Anim. p. 428.—Brit. Marine Conch. p. 48.—DILLW. Recent Shells, vol. i. p. 144. —CONRAD, Amer. Marine Conch. pl. 14, f. 3.

„   *dealbata,* PULTENEY, Hutchins, Hist. Dorset, p. 31.—MONT. Test. Brit. p. 95, pl. 5, f. 1.—Linn. Trans. vol. viii. p. 68, pl. 1, f. 10.— Dorset Catalog. p. 32, pl. 7, f. 7.—TURT. Conch. Diction. p. 80.—FLEM. Brit. Anim. p. 428.—BROWN, Illust. Conch. G. B. p. 107, pl. 41, f. 8, 9.

„   *Braziliana,* LAM. Anim. s. Vert. (ed. Desh.) vol. vi. p. 106.—HANL. Recent Shells, p. 31, Suppl. pl. 10, f. 60.

An American shell introduced by Dr. Pulteney as a native of Dorset. Having seen the examples delineated by our English authors, we are enabled to state that they really belong to the same species, a conclusion which the engravings referred to would scarcely have borne out.

LUTRARIA, Lamarck.

Shell oblong, equivalve, inequilateral, gaping at both extremities; external surface transversely striated or furrowed, invested with an epidermis; edges sharp and smooth; hinge formed of a more or less prominent spoon-shaped fulcrum in each valve, accompanied in the right one by an erect primary tooth, which locks into a pit with laminar tooth-like edges in the left: the greater part of the fulcrum in each valve is occupied by a wide ligamental pit. Ligament partly internal, partly external. Muscular impressions strong; pallial impression with a deep linguiform sinus.

Animal thick, oblong, with much-produced siphonal tubes, which are united almost to their extremities. Mantle closed, except a rather large anterior opening for a foot of considerable dimensions; both it and the siphons partially invested with an epidermic sheath. Orifices of the tube fimbriated. Labial tentacles narrow, triangular, pointed.

The animals of this genus form large and conspicuous shells, not remarkable for their beauty. They live habitually buried in mud, for the most part near low water, or at very moderate depths. The systematic position of *Lutraria* has been much disputed. Cuvier, Blainville, and very recently D'Orbigny, have placed it beside *Mya*, and in the same family, whilst Linnæus, Lamarck, and Deshayes have maintained its near affinity to *Mactra*. The shell presents considerable resemblances to that of the latter genus, yet the animal is in many respects nearly related to that of *Mya*. We place it for the present in the former group, regarding it as an aberrant form of the

Mactridæ, though with considerable hesitation, and only as an arrangement for convenience.

The shell of *Lutraria* is found by Dr. Carpenter to be composed of elongated fusiform cells, their extremities cropping out, one set above another. The species of this genus chiefly affect temperate seas. Many *Lutrariæ* are recorded in lists of fossils, but their affinities with existing forms is doubtful. One of our native species, the *Lutraria elliptica*, which now ranges throughout the European seas, anciently inhabited our area even so far back as the epoch of the coralline crag, and has maintained its place near the British shores throughout all the ups and downs of geological change which have disturbed them, even to the present time.

L. ELLIPTICA, Lamarck.

Somewhat elliptic, not at all arcuated.

Plate XII ; and (animal) Plate H. fig. 2.

Mactra lutraria, LINN. Syst. Nat. ed. 12, p. 1126.—PENN. Brit. Zool. ed. 4, vol. iv. p. 92, pl. 55, f. 44.—PULTENEY, Hutchins, Dorset Hist. p. 32.—Dorset Catalog. p. 33, pl. 5, f. 11.—MONT. Test. Brit. p. 99.—DONOV. Brit. Shells, vol. ii. pl. 58.—Linn. Trans. vol. viii. p. 73.—TURT. Conch. Diction. p. 84.—CHEMN. Conch. Cab. vol. vi. p. 239, pl. 24, f. 240, 241.—DILLW. Recent Shells, p. 146.

Lutraria elliptica, LAM. Anim. s. Vert. (ed. Desh.), vol. vi. p. 90.—TURT. Dithyr. Brit. p. 65.—Brit. Marine Conch. p. 45.—BROWN, Ill. Conch. G. B. p. 109, pl. 43, f. 2, 3.—MACGIL. Moll. Aberd. p. 291.—PHILIPPI, Moll. Sicil. vol. i. p. 9, and vol. ii. p. 7.—HANL. Recent Shells, p. 26.—CHENU, Ill. Conch. Lutr. pl. 1, f. 10.—DESH. Exp. Scient. Algér. Moll. pl. 33, 35, 36 (animal).

„ *vulgaris*, FLEM. Brit. Anim. p. 464.

Lutraire elliptique, CHENU, Traité Elém. p. 170, f. 52 (hinge).

LIST. Hist. Conch. pl. 415, f. 259.—Encycl. Méth. Vers, pl. 258, f. 3.

Of a produced elliptic form, the valves of this shell, which may be reckoned one of our largest bivalves, are, although by no means solid for their size, yet sufficiently strong, almost opaque, and decidedly shallow. This compression is very manifest upon the umbonal region, from whence to the ventral margin there is often indeed a slight retusion of the external surface: the hiation is very considerable, the valves merely touching each other at the beaks and along the middle portion of their lower margins, and gaping more particularly at the hinder extremity. The outer surface is nearly smooth, or at most concentrically wrinkled by coarse irregular lines of growth; it is of a squalid white, or stained with a reddish rust colour, covered, when recent, with a thin but rather tenacious epidermis, of an ashy olive colour (almost passing into drab in a foreign variety), which is smoothly laid on, and varies in lustre from dull to moderately glossy. The ventral margin is almost straight or somewhat retuse in the middle; from thence becoming convex on either side, it ascends very obliquely and considerably in front, rising far more moderately behind. The anterior side is much the smaller, occupying, in some examples, not more than one-half the entire length of the shell: it is liable to great variation in shape from the absence or existence of depression at its upper or dorsal margin. This edge, in very large individuals, where the lips are apt to expand, or become in a degree subreflected, is convex and moderately sloping; but in the majority of specimens (those of average size), is more or less retuse, and not much declining; in the former case, the lower corner of the front extremity being invariably rounded off, there is only a slight subcentral angulation at the anterior end; but in the latter event, a distinct upper angle. The posterior termination is rounded both above and below, yet not equally so, the chief swell of the hinder outline being rather above the middle, as the

hinder dorsal edge, which is the more elevated one, is
almost straight, and declines in but a very trifling degree.
The umbones are not very projecting; the beaks, which
are incurved and acute, lean scarcely, if at all, to either
side. There is no umbonal ridge, nor the slightest appearance of a distinct lunule. The internal surface is of a
glossy bluish white; in the left valve, in advance of the
large curved triangular cartilage-pit, is a solid truncated
reversed V-shaped primary tooth (which does not reach
the basal line of the hinge-margin), preceded by a very
thin lamellar sub-pyramidal one : in the right valve is only
the very thin and fragile anterior wall of the cartilage-pit,
which resembles a tooth, and a rather curved slanting anterior laminar one, which is considerably elevated at its
lower extremity, and acutely pointed.

The largest of our specimens (from the Welsh coast)
measures five inches and a half from side to side, and three
inches from the umbones to the opposite margin. These
proportions are not universal, as the breadth of another
example of four inches in length is only two inches.

The animal is sub-cylindrical, with a siphonal tube fully
as long as the body, or longer. The mantle is closed posteriorly and frontally; anteriorly there is rather a large
opening for the passage of the thick, long, white foot,
which does not appear to be furnished with a byssal
groove. The siphons are united almost to their extremities, which are but very slightly separated from each other.
The tube is white, thick, and corrugated at the base,
thinner and yellow, speckled with brown towards the extremity. " The branchial tube," according to Mr. Clark,
" is clotted with about ten yellow rays, dotted with minute points, and each ray more or less ciliated on one or
both sides; the anal tube turns upwards, and has around

its orifice about thirty slender yellow rays, each ray being alternately dotted with a minute red and yellow point." These dots are analogous to the coloured points or ocelli which we have noticed in describing the *Ascidiæ*, where they are conspicuously seen around the branchial and anal orifices. The tube and mantle are more or less invested with a thin, wrinkled, brownish epidermis. The branchiæ are of a brownish hue. On each side of the mouth is a pair of narrow, triangular, pointed labial tentacles.

Notwithstanding that fine shells, of this species, are not easily procurable, (their habitat, a moist oozy sand or mud repulsing the less sturdy and zealous collectors,) it is abundantly prolific and sufficiently diffused. We may enumerate among other localities Scarborough, where it is common (Bean) ; Exmouth (Clark); Torbay (Jeff. cab.) ; the Islet of Herm near Guernsey (S. H.) ; Oxwich Bay, in Glamorganshire and Laugharne (Jeffreys) ; Tenby, where the shores are strewed with dead valves (S. H.) ; in twelve fathoms, Anglesea (E. F.) ; Isle of Man (E. F.) ; "Bantry, Dublin Bay, and Cork Harbour" (Humphreys and Jeffreys) ; and in other "suitable localities on each side of the Irish coast" (Thompson) ; Frith of Forth (E. F.) ; Aberdeenshire (Macgillivray) ; St. Andrews, abundant (E. F.) ; the west coast of Scotland (Barlee and Jeffreys); Murray Frith, and the Hebrides (M'Andrew) ; Lerwick (Jeffreys); Balta Sound, Unst in six fathoms (M'Andrew).

L. OBLONGA, Chemnitz.

Extremely inequilateral, arcuated, of a compressed cylindraceous form.

Plate XIII. fig. 1.

Chama magna, DA COSTA, Brit. Conch. p. 230, pl. 17, f. 4.
Mya oblonga, CHEMNITZ, Conch. Cab. vol. vi. p. 27, pl. 2, f. 12 (badly).—
    GMELIN, Syst. Nat. p. 3221.
Mactra hians, PULTENEY, Hutchins, Hist. Dorset, p. 32.—MONT. Test. Brit. p.
    101.—DONOV. British Shells, vol. iv. pl. 140.—Linn. Trans.
    vol. viii. p. 74.—Dorset Catalog. p. 33, pl. 2, f. 4.—TURT.
    Conch. Diction. p. 85, f. 41.—DILLW. Recent Shells, vol. i. p.
    146.—Index Testaceol. pl. 6, f. 37.
Lutraria oblonga, TURT. Dithyra Brit. p. 64, pl. 5, f. 6.—Brit. Marine Conch.
    p. 44.
    „   *Solenoides,* LAM. Anim. s. Vert. (ed. Desh.) vol. vi. p. 90.—BROWN,
            Ill. Conch. G. B. p. 109, pl. 43, f. 1.—SOWERBY, Conch.
            Manual, f. 78.—HANL. Recent Shells, vol. i. p. 26.—
            CHENU, Illust. Conch. Lutraria, pl. 1, f. 9.—DESH. Exp.
            Sc. Algérie, Moll. pl. 31, 32 (anatomy).
    „   *hians,* FLEM. Brit. Anim. p. 465.
Lutricola Solenoides, BLAINV. Malacol. pl. 77, f. 3.

Were it allowable, we should have preferred the signifi-
cant appellation of *Solenoides,* bestowed upon this species
by Lamarck, to its prior name of *oblonga,* which denotes a
character appertaining to most of the restricted genus
Lutraria, and not confined to this species individually.
We may remark, as an excuse for the ordinary neglect of
the Chemnitzian name, that both the description and the
drawing of the *Mya oblonga,* are most infelicitously executed.

Of an elongated oblong and subarcuated form, this
species may readily be distinguished from the preceding, by
the incurvation of its hinder dorsal edge, and the great inequality of its sides. It is solid, opaque, coarse-looking,
and subventricose; the convexity, however, is diffused,

not being peculiarly apparent upon the umbonal region.
The valves, which gape most widely at the extremities,
and especially at the posterior end, where they are more or
less reflected, are of a squalid white (often stained with
darker tints from the soil they inhabit), covered with a
brownish or dark ash-coloured epidermis which is generally
more permanent, wrinkled, and deeper coloured near the
posterior extremity. The surface is roughened by coarse
wrinkles of growth, which are sometimes almost pliciform
along the course of the somewhat obsolete umbonal ridge.
The ventral margin, whose middle course is straightish, or
even subretuse, rises very considerably at each extremity,
and more particularly in front. The anterior side, which
occupies but little more than one-fourth of the entire
length, and from the sub-attenuation of its well-rounded
extremity even a still less portion of the area of the valves,
has its upper or dorsal edge, which is at first almost straight
and scarcely sloping, and then convex and very moderately
declining, united to the anterior outline without any
marked angularity. The posterior extremity, which although the broader one is still slightly attenuated, is more
bluntly rounded than the other, but is equally devoid of
angularity. The hinder dorsal edge is much incurved, and
upon the whole, declines but slightly, its termination not
being greatly below the level of the but moderately prominent umbones. The beaks are obtuse and incurved ; there
is no depression in front of them, but the dorsal outline behind them is a little flattened. The interior is of a pure
white. In the left hinge a single rather large primary
tooth, whose lower surface is broadly grooved, interlocks
between the great thin laminar oblique posterior and the
smaller bifurcated anterior one of the opposite valve.

The dimensions assigned to this species by Montagu are

five inches in length and two inches and a quarter in
breadth: specimens of such magnitude, however, are but
rarely met with.

However abundant, or rather diffused, in other parts of
Europe, this bivalve is justly esteemed by our shell
collectors as one of our less frequent native species.
Nevertheless, it is recorded by Montagu as not uncommon
in the river between Truro and Falmouth (in the recent
Cornish Fauna by Mr. Couch, it is termed "rare or
local"), and as frequently brought up with sea-sand, for
manure, to the former place. It is occasionally obtained
at Exmouth (Clark); Torbay (Jeff. cab.); and in Salcombe Bay (Alder); the Dorset coast (Pulteney); dead
valves in twenty-five fathoms, Penzance Bay (M'Andrew
and E. F.). A few specimens were dug out of sandy mud
near low-water mark at the little islet of Herm, near
Guernsey (S. H.); they are sometimes taken at Fishguard, and Caldy Island in Pembrokeshire (Lyons); and
appear not unfrequent in Ireland, being found " in suitable
places on each side of the coast" (Thompson).

VENERIDÆ.

THE VENUS TRIBE.

Most of the tribes, of which we have hitherto described British representatives, are such as severally included forms of shell very different, with animals strikingly similar. In that now before us, the aspect of the shells, though variable, always indicates their natural affinity with each other, whilst many characters in their animals, hitherto of great sectional value, become variable, and, at most, generic. The shells of the *Veneridæ* present numerous modifications of colour and sculpture, and are often of considerable thickness; their hinge is always considerably developed, and the teeth strongly marked and distinct; their margin is in some plain, in others crenulated, indicating differences, usually of generic value, in the structure of the mantle; the ligament is external; the muscular impressions are always strongly marked, and the pallial has a conspicuous sinus; the animal has its mantle rather freely open in front for the passage of a large and thick foot; the siphons are united or separate, according to the genus, and have their margins either fringed or almost plain. The species of the several divisions have very different habits of life.

Dr. Carpenter's researches shew that the shells of this tribe present little organic structure, and are among the hardest of bivalves, approaching the porcellanous univalves

in density, and in the almost entire absence of any trace
of animal matter.

TAPES, MEGERLE.

This genus consists of a very natural assemblage of
Veneridæ, distinguished by marked characters of both shell
and animal, and by a general habit recognisable at a
glance.

Shell solid, transversely oblong, or, more rarely, obliquely
subtriangular, equivalve, inequilateral, closed, the posteal
extremity always longest; surface smooth, or transversely
striated; inner margins smooth; muscular scars strongly
impressed, semicircular, the posteal always largest; beaks
not prominent; pallial sinus deep, oblong, rounded at the
extremity; hinge composed of three scarcely diverging
primary teeth, two of which are usually bifid on each
valve, and a ridge bounding the groove for the ligament,
which is external.

Animal shaped as the shell, rather thick, having the
mantle freely open in front, its margins either plain or
partially plain, or, if fringed, bordered by fine filaments
and not by strong scallops; siphons moderately long, more
or less separated, sometimes for half their length, sometimes throughout; both branchial and anal orifices bordered by cirrhi, those of the former ciliated; labial palps
rather long, lanceolate; foot lanceolate, thick, with a
byssal groove, a structure which conspicuously distinguishes
this animal from *Venus*, and allies it, as well as the shape
of the shell, with *Petricola*. The species of *Tapes* inhabit
all climates, those of the tropics being most brightly coloured. Except the tertiary forms, most of the older
fossil species are doubtfully referred to this genus. They
inhabit the littoral, and, more rarely, the laminarian and
coralline zones.

T. DECUSSATA, Linnæus.

Suboval, subrhombic, coarsely decussated by concentric sulci and radiating striæ, verrucose in radiating rows at the posterior extremity: front dorsal edge moderately long; umbones rather prominent: pallial sinus not peculiarly large.

Plate XXV. fig. 1.

LISTER, Hist. Conch. pl. 423, f. 271.

Venus decussata, LINN. Syst. Nat. p. 1135.—PULTENEY. Hutchins, Dorset. p. 34 (chiefly).—DONOV. British Shells, vol. ii. pl. 67.—MONT. Test. Brit. p. 124.—Linn. Trans. vol. viii. p. 88, pl. 2, f. 6. —Dorset Catalogue, p. 36, pl. 6, f. 4, (not well).—TURT. Conch. Diction. p. 244.—TURT. Dithyra Brit. p. 158, pl. 8, f. 10.—Brit. Marine Conch. p. 93.—CHEMNITZ, Conch. Cab. vol. vii. p. 58, pl. 43, f. 455, 456.—DILLW. Recent Shells, vol. i. p. 206.—LAM. Anim. a. Vert. (ed. Desh.) vol. vi. p. 357 (not var. 4.)—Index Testaceolog. pl. viii. f. 107.—PHILIPPI, Moll. Sicil. vol. i. p. 45, pl. 4, f. 11, and vol. ii. p. 35. —HANL. Recent Shells, p. 122, vol. i. pl. 8. f. 107.

Venus litterata (not of Linn.) PENN. Brit. Zool. ed. 4, vol. iv. p. 96, pl. 57, f. 53.

Cuneus reticulatus, DA COSTA, Brit. Conch. p. 203 (in part), pl. 14, f. 4 (badly).

Venus florida, POLI, Test. Sicil. pl. 21, f. 16, 17.

Venerupis decussata, FLEM. Brit. Anim. p. 451.—MACGILLIV. Moll. Aberd. p. 339.

Pullastra decussata, BROWN, Ill. Conch. G. B. p. 88, pl. 37, f. 5, 6.

The shape of *V. decussata,* whose valves are destitute of lustre, opaque, solid, ventricose, and extremely variable in painting, is suboval and subrhomboidal; its convexity is most apparent around the umbonal region, the sides being comparatively flattened. As respects colouring, our British specimens do not quite display so brilliant a diversity of painting as the continental ones, but exhibit various shades of buff, drab, or rufous, rayed, freckled, or zig-zagged with markings of a deeper tint, with generally more or less of a livid tinge; occasionally, they are of an uniform reddish cast, but we have rarely met with any of that chalky whiteness which is so common in *pullastra.* The

beautiful variety figured by Turton (so common in the
Adriatic), in which the pattern is composed of radiating
rows of smoke-coloured, irregularly-shaped spots (not a
little resembling the Chinese style of writing) upon a
ground of bluish-grey, is not of frequent occurrence upon
our coasts. The sculpture (which is coarser in our examples than in the majority of those we receive from the
Mediterranean) consists of most closely arranged and rather
wavy concentric sulci, decussated throughout by radiating
striæ; the latter are more crowded in the middle area
(where the concentric sulci often disappear or become fainter), are stronger and more remote in front, and behind the
umbonal slope lose all claim to be held as striæ, forming
shallow interstitial grooves to the apparently radiating
rows of compressed bead-like prominences, which the in-
tersected sulci there present. The ventral margin is
moderately convex in the middle, and rises greatly at the
sides, particularly in front; the declination, as well as
the convexity, of the hinder dorsal edge is very trifling;
the front dorsal edge slopes almost rectilinearly, and rather
profoundly, to about the middle of the narrow anterior
side, whose extremity is well rounded and rather attenuated; the hinder side is about twice as long as the other,
and has the appearance of being subtruncated at its extremity, from the posterior edge being but little convex,
and not greatly oblique; the posterior termination is broad,
and almost biangulated, the lower angle being, however,
rounded off in the young (at which stage the angulation
in shells is always most apparent); the ligament is rather
large, yellowish brown, and not much elevated. The
lunule is not usually much depressed, and is frequently
only defined by its freedom from decussation; its lips, too,
except in aged examples, are elevated, not sunken; the

shape is cordate lanceolate. The umbones are rather prominent, and somewhat inclined; the beaks small, very
acute, and much inflected; the internal surface is whitish,
with generally a stain of purple behind the teeth; the
hinge as in *aurea*. The form is occasionally abbreviated,
and the beaks, though rarely, if ever, in our native examples, are stained with a beautiful violet. The length of
our largest example is about two inches and a quarter, and
its breadth an inch and five-eighths.

The animal of *Tapes decussata* has frequently been observed; indeed, considering what a favourite article of
food it is in many parts of the continent, it would have
been very strange had everybody swallowed it without examination. As long ago as 1710 it was figured and described by Reaumur. It is oval, white and thick, and
has the margins of the mantle, which are freely open, ornamented with a conspicuous scalloped white fringe. The
siphons are separate to their bases and equal, yellowish and
white, dotted towards the base and centre, marked with
tawny or reddish or dark-brown specklings and cloudings
near their orifices. These are fringed, the branchial with a
double border of twelve long cirrhi and as many alternating
small ones, the anal with nearly twenty or so simple cirrhi,
in both cases of a brown colour. The branchial, according
to Mr. Clark, are suboval, the upper the smaller, and all of
a pale brown colour. The labial palps are proportionally
small and triangular. The foot is large, white, lanceolate,
and furnished with a byssal groove.

Except locally, this is rather a scarce shell. It is usually
dug out near the shore, being rarely, if ever, taken by the
dredge. It is sometimes, but seldom, procured on the
Northumbrian coast (Alder); and at Scarborough (Bean);
on the south-west it is more frequent, occurring at Little-

hampton (Strickland); Hastings (S. H.); Weymouth
(S. H.); and is captured at Exmouth (Clark); Torquay
(S. H.); and other parts of South Devon, as "the in-
let between Kingsbridge and Salcombe at the mouth of
the Aun" (Mont.); Falmouth (Cocks); Swansea and its
vicinity (Jeffreys); Caldy Island, near Tenby (Lyons);
Pwllheli (M'Andrew). It occurs of large size buried in
gravel at low-water mark on the shores of Skye and Zetland (E. F.); Bantry and Dublin bays (Jeff. cab.).

It does not appear to range northward of the British
seas, but is very abundant in the Lusitanian and Mediterranean provinces. It ranges southwards to the shores of
Senegal, and is said to inhabit the Red Sea. As a fossil it
occurs very generally in the newer pliocene beds of Europe,
and appears to have originated in the Lusitanian region.
Everywhere it is a littoral shell.

T. PULLASTRA, Wood.

Suboval, subrhomboidal, finely decussated by concentric striæ
and radiating striulæ; front dorsal edge very short; posterior
extremity often concentrically sublamellar: umbones obtuse:
pallial sinus very large; teeth very narrow, recurved, nearly equal
and much elevated.

Plate XXV. figs. 2, 3, and, animal, Plate L. fig. 5 and 5 a.

9 *Tellina rugosa*, PENN. Brit. Zool. ed. 4, p. 88, pl. 57, f. 34.
Venus pullastra, MONT. Test. Brit. p. 125.—Linn. Trans. vol. viii. p. 88, pl. 2,
    f. 7.—Dorset Catal. p. 36, pl. 1, f. 8 (not well).—TURT.
    Conch. Diction. p. 244.—TURT. Dithyra Brit. p. 159.—
    FORBES, Malacol. Monens. p. 53.—Brit. Marine Conch. p.
    94.—Index Testaceolog. pl. 8, f. 109.—LAM. Anim. s. Vert.
    (ed. Desh.) vol. vi. p. 358. HANL. Recent Shells, p. 122.
Venus perforans, MONT. Test. Brit. p. 127, pl. 3, f. 6.—Linn. Trans. vol. viii. p.
    89.—TURT. Conch. Diction. p 245.—DILLW. Recent Shells,
    vol. i. p. 206.—Index Testaceolog. pl. 8, f. 108.
Venus Senegalensis, DILLW. Recent Shells, vol. i. p. 206.

Venerupis perforans, LAM. Anim. s. Vert. (ed. Desh.) vol. vi. p. 162.—TURT. Dithyra Brit. p. 29, pl. 2, f. 15 to 18.—FLEM. Brit. Anim. p. 451.—Brit. Marine Conch. p. 61.—CROUCH, Introd. Conch. pl. 5, f. 5.—HANL. Recent Shells, p. 54. —PHILIPPI, Wiegm. Archiv. f. Natur 1845, p.190, pl. 7, f. 15 to 18.

Venerupis nuclous, LAM. Anim. s. Vert. (ed. Desh.) vol. vi. p. 162.—MACGILLIV. Edin. New Phil. Journ.(Jameson's) 1827, p. 370.—DELES. Rec. Coquilles, pl. 5, f. 1.—HANL. Recent Shells, p. 54.

Venus palustris, MAWE, Lin. Conchology, pl. 16, f. 3.

Venerupis pullastra, FLEM. Brit. Anim. p. 451.—MACGILLIV. Moll. Aberd. p. 269.

Venerupis vulgaris, SOWERBY, Concholog. Manual, f. 97.

Venus vulgaris, BRODERIP, Penny Cyclop. vol. xxvi. p. 211.

Pullastra vulgaris, BROWN, Illust. Conch. G. B. p. 89, pl. 37, f. 7.

Pullastra perforans, BROWN, Illust. Conch. G. B. p. 89, pl. 37, f. 10.

Venus plagia, (VAR.) JEFFREYS, Ann. Nat. His. vol. xix. p. 313.

The *V. pullastra* was long regarded as at most a variety of the preceding, to which alone of our British shells it bears much resemblance. Its distinctness from *decussata* was first pointed out by Mr. Wood, (the author of a valuable work entitled, "General Conchology," containing figures and descriptions of many rare species, which are hardly to be met with elsewhere,) who founded his separating characters chiefly from the structure of the hinge. The more easily distinguishable differential features, are stated by Colonel Montagu to consist of its smaller size, the greater delicacy of its decussation, (which, moreover, is never verrucose anteriorly, and which posteriorly has a concentric and not a radiating arrangement,) the greater regularity and approximation of its teeth, and the more ample sinus of the pallial impression. To these we may add, the greater shortness and usually lesser declination of the front dorsal margin. The animal is also sufficiently distinct. An examination of a long series of specimens, which clearly connect the rock-dwelling *perforans,* with its type *pullastra,* and display the want of permanency in the supposed specific characters of the former, compels us to unite the two under one appellation.

The general outline is subrhomboidal, and suboval (typically it is more elongated than the preceding); the valves are moderately strong, opaque, very inequilateral, and more or less ventricose, the convexity being more evenly diffused than in *decussata*. The outer surface is almost entirely devoid of lustre, and is usually of a chalky or dirty-white, which shades into a browner tint in the adult; this is very rarely destitute of markings, being almost always diversified by radiating angulated spots, and zigzag confluent splotches of a livid brown; occasionally the entire surface is finely reticulated, (though usually but faintly so,) with angular lines of that hue, but the colouring matter is generally more lavishly displayed on the posterior extremity, to which portion occasionally the pencilling is confined. Crowded and wavy striæ, which are coarser at the extremities, and of which the interstices have a tendency to become imbricated and lamellar at the posterior end, traverse the entire shell in a concentric direction, and are most finely decussated by radiating striulæ, which are very closely disposed, and become obsolete towards the beaks. The ventral margin is convex, but usually inclines to straightness near the middle, though rising greatly and arcuatedly in front, and moderately so behind. The anterior side is very short, occupying but little more than one-fourth of the entire length; its extremity is very narrow and obliquely rounded below, but is very slightly angulated above, owing to the straightness of its extremely short dorsal margin.

The termination of the produced posterior side is subbiangulated and broad, the convex, or subarcuated hinder margin, which is but slightly oblique, forming an obtuse angle with the almost rectilinear and scarcely in the least declining dorsal edge; the lower angle is rounded off. The ligament is tolerably large, but not at all elevated; the

lunule ovato-lanceolate, often coloured, and not sunken or
well defined; the umbones depressed, and the beaks small,
inflected and leaning a little forward. The interior is of a
chalky-white, with often a violet or purple stain at the posterior extremity. The pallial sinus is very large.

The teeth, as regards being cloven or simple, are, as usual
in this genus; viz., the two last of the right hinge and the
two first of the left more or less bifid; they are, however,
peculiarly elevated and narrow, the central one of the left
valve not exceeding (as in *decussata*,) the other two in
breadth. They lean outwards, their inner sides being remarkably curved, and the supporting portion of the hinge-
margin arching out below, and bulging out in front much
beyond the level of the remainder.

The length of our largest specimen is about two inches,
and its breadth one inch and a quarter; these dimensions,
however, are but rarely attained to, the majority of examples being about an inch and a half only in length, and
of proportionate width.

Animal oblong, thick, yellowish-white or tinged with
pink, the extremities of the siphons variously tinged with
brown, black, red, or orange. Mantle freely open in front,
plain at the edge except for a short space around the anterior end. Tubes united for half their length, and then
diverging; the upper or anal one smallest. Their orifices
are fringed; the branchial with from nine to fifteen ciliated
rays, and the anal with from fifteen to twenty-five. The
foot is linguiform, fleshy, flat-heeled, and furnished with a
byssal groove. The palps are of moderate length, narrow
and triangular.

We have often compared the animal of the ordinary or
pullastra form of this species with that of the " *Venus perforans*," but could find no distinctions. As long ago as

1835, Mr. Clark had carefully investigated this point, and
his observations, which on account of their value, we quote
at full, appear to us decisive. " Having dissected," writes
that most careful observer, " examined, and compared
many of the animals of these hitherto-considered distinct
species, I have found that in every respect they agree with
each other, and that there is not even the slightest variation
in the conformation of any of their organs either external or
internal. The branchiæ of the two, in colour and form, are
exactly the same. The foot has precisely the same slit in
its centre for the byssal filaments, and we have seen the one
imbedded in its cavity attached by them, and the other
naked, from the shingle attached in like manner to particular stones. The margins of the mantle are the same in
both. The tubes extend, bifurcate, and vary in their rays
and ciliations in the same degree in both. In short, we
cannot point out any particular organ but what is exactly
similar. We are therefore compelled by the force of facts
to come to the conclusion that the two are identical ; and
though the shells of each seem to present greater differences than their animals, still the principal form and outline of both, with their striæ of growth and decussations,
are essentially of the same character ; the variations are
mere modifications of similar elements dependent on habitat, deprivation of light, or exposure to it, for when the
shells are embedded in the cavities of rocks they are subject to variations of form, and being deprived of light, they
are usually colourless and without markings ; and not
being rubbed by the action of the waves amongst the
shingly beaches, their striæ are sharper and more foliaceous.
Amongst shingle, where they are free, or if the current be
strong, attached by their filaments to stones, and exposed
to light and the action of the sea, they are of regular form,

often beautifully coloured with smoother striæ and decussations. In the former case they are the *Venus perforans*; in the latter the *Venus pullastra* of authors."

This shell is littoral, and does not appear ever to range beyond the laminarian zone. It lives buried in gravelly sand, muddy gravel, or in crevices of rocks, and roots of Laminariæ. It is very generally distributed around our coast, but rather local; usually, however, plentiful wherever it does occur. Among localities may be cited:— Gorey in Jersey, in crevices of submarine granite rocks (S. H.); "Plymouth in hard limestone" (Montagu); Falmouth (Cocks); Exmouth in the shingles near the new rope-walk (Clark); Dartmouth in seven fathoms water, dead (M‘Andrew and E. F.); Poole (E. F.); at Hastings and at Margate, in blocks of chalk near the jetty (S. H.); Littlehampton (Strickland); Scarborough abundantly (Bean); not uncommon in the shale rocks of Durham and Northumberland (Alder); Swansea and other places in South Wales (Jeffreys); Anglesea (M‘Andrew); Isle of Man, but scarce (E. F.); Clyde (Smith); Hebrides (Jeffreys); Zetland, littoral and as deep as seven fathoms (Jeffreys, M‘Andrew, E. F.); Aberdeen and Banff, both varieties (Macgillivray); Frith of Forth, plentiful at low water, especially near Newhaven and Cramond (E. F.); Ireland.

The *Tapes pullastra* is confined to the Celtic and Scandinavian seas, and dates its origin from the Pleistocene epoch.

T. VIRGINEA, Linnæus.

Subcordate, suboval, glossy, very inequilateral ; surface smooth towards the beaks, elsewhere merely concentrically striated ; ventral edge subarcuated : umbones obtuse, and much inclined forwards : inner surface white or pink.

Plate XXV. fig. 4, 6.

LISTER, Hist. Conch. pl. 403, f. 247.

Venus virginea, LINN. Syst. Nat. ed. 12, p. 1136.—PULTENEY, Hutchins, Dorset, p. 34.—MONT. Test. Brit. pp. 128, 576.—Linn. Trans. vol. viii. p. 89, pl. 2, f. 8.—Dorset Catalog. p. 36, pl. 12, f. 1.—TURT. Conch. Diction. p. 246.—TURT. Dithyra Brit. p. 156, pl. 8, f. 8. —FORBES, Malacol. Monensis, p. 53.—Brit. Marine Conch. p. 92.—DILLWYN, Recent Shells, vol. 1, p. 207.—LAM. Anim. s. Vert. (ed. Desh.) vol. vi. p. 360.—Index Testaceolog. pl. 8, f. 110.—HANL. Recent Shells, p. 123, pl. 8, f. 110.

Venus rhomboides, PEN. Brit. Zool. ed. 4, vol. iv. p. 97, pl. 55, f. (omitted).

Cuneus fasciatus, DA COSTA, Brit. Conch. p. 204.

Venus Sarniensis (VARIETY), TURT. Dithyra Brit. p. 153, pl. 10, f. 6.—Brit. Marine Conch. p. 91.

Venerupis „ (VARIETY), FLEM. Brit. Anim. p. 452.

Venerupis virginea, FLEM. Brit. Anim. p. 452.—MACGILLIV. Moll. Aberd. p. 269.

Pullastra virginea, BROWN, Ill. Conch. G. B., p. 89, pl. 37, f. 8, 9, and pl. 36, f. 6.

Venus virago, LOVEN, Index Moll. Skandinaviæ, p. 40.

Tellina elliptica (FRY)? BROWN, Ill. Conch. G. B., p. 101, pl. 40, f. 20, 21.

By far the most beautiful in painting of our *Veneridæ*, is that which we are about to describe. In form it is of a somewhat heart-shaped oval, and is strong, opaque, and very inequilateral ; its valves are moderately ventricose, but the convexity is tolerably evenly diffused, and not chiefly confined to the umbonal region. The surface, which is glossy, is merely striated in a concentric direction with coarse moderately distant lines, which are not regularly parallel, but approximate in front, becoming more remote at the hinder part of the central disk. These striæ are entirely obsolete towards the beaks, and anteriorly have a

tendency to imbrication. The variety of colouring is almost
infinite in patterns, but is generally compounded of pencil-
lings of pink, or various shades of dark or ruddy flesh-
colour and white. Very rarely it is of a pure milk-white,
and devoid of all painting; more usually the darker are
the prevailing tints from the crowded masses of zigzag lines
which cover the surface so closely that the white is only
visible at the triangular interstices of this net-work, or
in the shape of two more or less broad ray-like streaks.
One of these latter, is ordinarily placed at about one-third
the distance from the anterior end (and this is almost perpendicular); the other, which is very oblique, along the
ordinary site of an umbonal ridge. Occasionally, where
the entire surface is thus reticulated, or assumes an uniform
or slightly mottled tint from the extreme minuteness of the
linear zigzags, there are from two to four rays which are
chiefly manifested by there being a lesser preponderance of
dark markings upon those areas, and sometimes too by the
occurrence of angulated spots of a deeper shade than the
prevailing colour; these last are occasionally confluent, and
run alongside of the white or paler rays. Occasionally the
rays are wholly composed of more or less interrupted obscure markings of a deeper tint than the almost uniform
ruddy hue of the ground.

The ventral margin is convex or subarcuated, rising at
each end, but particularly in front: the declination of the
front dorsal is short, moderate, and straight, or but slightly
retuse, that of the hinder one is very trifling, and almost
rectilinear in the young, becoming stronger and more convex
with increasing age. The anterior side, whose extremity is
attenuately rounded, varies from occupying one-third, to
only making one-fifth, of the entire length: the posterior
end, which, in the young, is somewhat biangulated, (the

lower angle is, however, always rounded off) becomes only
obsoletely so in the more aged examples; from a similar
rounding off of the upper angle, the hinder margin is convex and oblique. The ligament is large, yellowish-brown,
and not elevated above the dorsal line. The lunule is lanceolate, moderately large, but neither profoundly impressed
nor sharply defined; it is often of an uniform liver-colour.
The umbones are not at all prominent, but are much inclined forwards, the beaks are obtuse, and curve both inwards and anteriorward. The inner surface is white or
stained with pink; the pallial sinus semi-elliptic. The
teeth are divergent, the extremes forming at least a right
angle; the central of the left valve, and the posterior and
the central of the right valve are bifid.

The ordinary run of specimens do not generally exceed
an inch and a half in length, and half an inch less in
breadth; we have, however, an individual now before us
which has the large dimensions of nearly two inches and
a-half in length, and almost an inch and three-quarters in
breadth. Young examples are perfectly smooth. The
variety termed *Sarniensis*, by Dr. Turton, is usually of a
coarser texture, lighter colour, and rather more ventricose;
its concentric striæ are generally closer, and their tendency
to become more remote posteriorward is consequently less
distinctly manifested. These characters are, however,
rarely all evident in the same specimen, the union between the type and the variety being perfect in gradation.
There is a great bluntness or absence of angularity in the
outline of *virginea*, as compared with that of its British
congeners.

The animal of *T. virginea* resembles, in most of its characters, that of the other forms of the genus. It is entirely
of a cream-white hue, except the extremity of the branch-

ial siphon, which is tinged with red. The siphons are united for more than half their length, and then diverge. The foot is not very large in proportion to the body.

This species is chiefly found in the coralline region of depth; very rarely littoral. The most brilliantly-coloured examples are dredged in about seven or eight fathoms water, at Guernsey, where it is excessively abundant (S. H.); it is, indeed, one of our most plentiful species, yet in many localities scarcely a specimen is to be obtained. It is rare in Dorsetshire and Devonshire (Mont.); it has been taken at Falmouth by Mr. Jeffreys and by Mr. Cocks; in twenty fathoms near Penzance, and in fifteen fathoms West Bay of Portland (M'Andrew and E. F.); off Poole (E. F.); Scarborough (Bean); Tenby (Lyons); Pwllheli and Anglesea, in twelve fathoms (M'Andrew); Isle of Man, on north and east coasts, in from fifteen to twenty-five fathoms, plentiful and very varied in its colours (E. F.); on the east coast of Scotland and north-east of England it is either very rare or absent, not occurring in the copious lists of either Macgillivray or Alder. On the west and north, however, it is frequent; Ullapool, Loch Carron, Deal Voe, and Lerwick (Barlee and Jeffreys); Clyde, Hebrides, and Shetland Isles, ranging from five to thirty-five fathoms (M'Andrew); Orkneys (Thomas), where it is both littoral and in deep water.

This is one of the species which were dredged by Captain Beechey in a submarine ravine off the Mull of Galloway, at a depth ranging from a hundred and ten to a hundred and forty-five fathoms (W. T. Ann. N. H. vol. x. p. 21). The variety *Sarniensis* is not confined to the Channel Islands, but has been dredged likewise upon the Dublin coast by Dr. Loyd, of Malahide (W. T. Ann. N. H. vol. v. p. 13); Bantry Bay, Youghal (Jeffreys and Ball);

Donaghadee, in eight fathoms (Patterson); north of Ireland, in various localities (Thompson and Hyndman).

It ranges from Norway to the Mediterranean, but its capital is in the Celtic province. As a fossil it dates its appearance from the epoch of the red crag.

T. AUREA, Gmelin.

Subcordate, subovate, concentrically closely sulcated, sulci not becoming more distant posteriorly; sides not particularly unequal; ventral margin more or less arcuated: umbones ventricose, and rather prominent: inner surface of a deeper or paler yellow.

Plate XXV: fig. 5.

Venus aurea, GMELIN, Syst. Nat. p. 3288.—MONT. Test. Brit. pp. 129, and 576.
—Linn. Trans. vol. viii. p. 90, pl. 2, f. 9.—Dorset Catalog. p. 36, pl. 13, f. 3.—TURT. Conch. Diction. p. 247.—FLEM. Brit. Anim. p. 449.—Brit. Marine Conch. p. 92.—DILLW. Recent Shells, p. 207.—LAMARCK, Anim. s. Vert. (ed. Desh.) vol. vi. p. 360.—Index Testaceol. pl. 8, f. 111.—PHILIPPI, Moll. Sicil. vol. i. [p. 47, and vol. ii. p. 35.—HANL. Recent Shells, vol. i. p. 123, pl. 8, f. 111.—TURT. Conch. Diction. p. 248.
Venus nebulosa, PULTENEY, Hutchins, Hist. Dorset, p. 34.
Venus cnea, TURT. Conch. Dithyra Brit. p. 152, pl. 10, f. 7.—FLEM. Brit. Anim. p. 449.—Brit. Marine Conch, p. 91.
Venus nitens, TURT. Conch. Diction. p. 247.—Turt. Dithyra Brit. p. 157, pl. 10, f. 8.—FLEM. Brit. Anim. p. 449.—Brit. Marine Conch. p. 93.
Venus sinuata, TURT. (not Penn.) Conch. Diction. p. 242.—TURT. Dithyra Brit. p. 155, pl. 9, f. 7, 8.—FLEM. Brit. Anim. p. 449.—Brit. Marine Conch. p. 92.
Pullastra aurea, BROWN, Ill. Conch. G. B. p. 89, pl. 36, f. 5, 7, 8.

The subject of our description is prone to much variation both in form and markings, our ordinary British specimens being in proportion so much broader than those of the Mediterranean, that the identity of the two might almost be doubted, did not intermediate gradations definitely establish it. Its general outline is subovate and subcordiform; it is tolerably strong, opaque, moderately inequilateral,

and rather glossy. The valves are more or less ventricose,
the umbones being disposed to tumidity ; and their surface
is concentrically traversed by close-set not strictly parallel
narrow sulci, the interstices of which are often bifurcated,
and not unfrequently become obtuse costellæ, especially in
front and towards the lower margin. This sculpture,
which has a tendency to become obsolete upon the most
swollen portion of the shell, the hinder part of the umbonal region, is indistinctly decussated by impressed radiating lineoles. The ground-colour, which is usually of a
pale golden yellow, or creamy hue, often whitish, is most
frequently marbled with linear or cloudy zigzags of many
shades of liver and smoke-colour, differing in various examples in respect to the size and propinquity of markings. More rarely, the shell is perfectly devoid of any
variegation, and is of an uniform pale yellow, or white.
The ventral margin is always more or less subarcuated,
and is usually a little contracted posteriorly in the adult.
The declination of the front dorsal edge is retuse, and
always more or less strong ; that of the hinder one is considerably less, and convex, though frequently but slightly
so. The anterior side, which occupies from one-third to
two-fifths of the entire length, is well rounded at its
extremity, which from its greater or lesser attenuation
often appears strikingly projecting. The posterior termination is very variable in its contour ; in the younger shell,
it is generally more or less bluntly and obliquely subbiangulated ; in the adult it is more nearly rounded, and often-
times is produced attenuated and thoroughly rounded.
The lunule is very large, ovately lanceolate, not profound,
but defined by a shallow line. There is no posterior
escutcheon. The umbones are more or less prominent, and
the beaks are very acute, small, and inclined forwards.

The ligament is rather large, yellowish brown, and not elevated beyond the dorsal line.

The internal colouring is typically of a rich golden yellow, but is often pale, and has usually more or less extensive stains of brilliant purple upon the hinge margin. Of the three primary teeth, the two hinder are bifid in the right valve ; in the left hinge the central alone is invariably cloven, the anterior not being always distinctly bifid : the right anterior and the left posterior are thin, laminar, and oblique.

Some of the larger of our specimens, are fully an inch and a half in length, and at least an inch in breadth ; these, however, may be regarded as rather exceeding the average size of examples.

We consider this a locally abundant, but by no means common shell. Mr. Alder remarks, that it is very frequent in Falmouth harbour, and at Helford river in Cornwall, where the shells are more produced in shape, and more elegantly marbled than the ordinary run of specimens. It is likewise obtained at Little Hampton, Sussex (Strickland) ; Weymouth (S. H.) ; Portsmouth and Plymouth (Jeffreys) ; the Scilly Isles, where it grows to a very large size (M'Andrew) ; Tenby (Lyons) ; Pwllheli (M'And.) ; Clew Bay, in from three to ten fathoms (R. Ball, W. Thompson, and E. F.) ; Birterbuy Bay in Connemara (Farren and Barlee) ; Bantry Bay (Jeffreys cab.) ; Youghal (Ball). In Scotland it has been certainly found only in the extreme south-west : Mr. Smith recording it from Ayr, and Mr. Nicol from Loch Ryan. Laskey's locality of it in the Frith of Forth is probably a mistake. Abroad it ranges from Scandinavia to the Mediterranean.

It is only known as a British fossil in certain beds, probably of Pleistocene age, near Dublin, where the stained specimens were mistaken for a distinct living species by Dr. Turton, and named *Venus ænea*. It is also found in the Newer Pliocene strata of Sicily.

CYTHEREA. LAMARCK.

SHELL solid, equivalve, inequilateral, closed, usually more or less transversely oblong, with slightly prominent and recurved beaks. Surface sometimes sulcated or striated transversely, usually nearly smooth. Muscular impressions ovate ; pallial sinus wide, ovate, obtusely pointed. Margins always smooth. Hinge composed usually of four diverging teeth in one valve, and three in the other, with corresponding pits. Ligament external, rather long.

Animal oblong, with its mantle freely open, and plain at the margins. Foot large, linguiform, not furnished with a byssal groove ; siphons united nearly to their extremities, orifices of both with (simple) cirrhi.

This genus is rejected by Deshayes, Rang, and D'Orbigny, and many modern malacologists, on the plea of its being entirely artificial. It is maintained by others as a convenient section of a group containing an immense and inconvenient number of species, which the genus VENUS in the sense used by the authors mentioned is. In a scientific treatise, such as we wish this to be, no such plea could be admitted. We adopt this Lamarckian group on higher grounds, and maintain it because it includes a very natural assemblage of forms, presenting certain important characters in common, both of shell and animal, sufficiently separating them from the true *Veneres*. In our seas we have only a single representative of this beautiful section— that one among our most beautiful indigenous mollusks. In tropical seas they abound, and are remarkable for ele-

gance of form and brilliancy of colour. The majority of
the more ancient fossil *Veneridæ* appear to belong to *Cytherea*.

C. CHIONE, Linnæus.

Plate XXVII., and animal, Plate L. fig. 8.

Venus Chione, LINN. Syst. Nat. p. 1131.—PULTENEY, Hutchins, Dorset, p. 33.
—DONOV. Brit. Shells, vol. i. pl. 17.—MONT. Test. Brit. p. 115.
—Linn. Trans. vol. viii. p. 84.—Dorset Catalog. p. 35, pl. 6, f. 7.
—TURT. Conch. Diction. p. 239.—CHEMN. Conch. Cab. vol. vi.
p. 344, pl. 32, f. 343.—POLI, Test. Sicil. pl. 20, f. 1, 2.—
DILLW. Recent Shells, vol. i. p. 176.—Index Testaceolog. pl.
7, f. 44.—BLAINV. Man. Malacol. pl. 74, f. 5.
Pectunculus glaber, DA COSTA, Brit. Conchology, p. 184, pl. 14, f. 7.
Cytherea Chione, LAM. Anim. s. Vert. (ed. Desh.) vol. vi. p. 305.—TURT. Conch.
Dithyra, p. 160, pl. 8, f. 11.—FLEM. Brit. Anim. p. 444.—
Brit. Marine Conch. p. 83.—BROWN, Ill. Conch. G. B. p. 91,
pl. 37, f. 2.—DESH. Elem. Conch. pl. 19, f. 4, 5.—PHILIPPI,
Moll. Sicil. vol. i. p. 40, and vol. ii. p. 31.—HANL. Recent
Shells, p. 98, pl. 7, f. 44.
Cythérée fauve, CHENU, Traité Elem. pl. 3, f. 10.
Cytherea nitidula, (YOUNG) LAM. Anim. s. Vert. (ed. Desh.) vol. vi. p. 305 (fide
Reclus, and Philippi).
REGENFUSS, Choix Coquil. pl. 8, f. 17.—Encyclop. Méthod. Vers. pl. 266, f. 1.

This magnificent bivalve has a somewhat heart-shaped
ovate contour, is strong, solid, opaque, glossy, and decidedly inequilateral, but yet for its genus not particularly
so. Although, for a *Cytherea*, it may be termed compressed, it is often somewhat ventricose, though never inflated; the profundity is manifestly greater behind than in
front. The exterior, which is smooth, or merely marked
in a concentric direction with obsolete shallow indented
folds (and these are confined to the vicinity of the sides
and lower margin), is of a pale but warm chestnut tint
(which varies in intensity) copiously adorned with broader
and narrower rays of a more livid cast. These rays, from
the colouring matter being deposited in paler and darker

zones, have oftentimes (especially in young individuals, and upon the umbonal region of the adult) an interrupted appearance; the beaks, too, have almost invariably three short indistinct ray-like colourless markings proceeding from them, of which the central is the shortest, and the others margin the commencement of the lunule and the ligament. The ventral outline is moderately and tolerably evenly curved; the declination of the hinder dorsal edge is very moderate, and slightly convex; that of the front dorsal is stronger, incurved or retuse at first, and arched at its termination. The anterior side, which occupies about one-third of the shell, is attenuated at its extremity where it is rounded both above and below; the posterior side likewise tapers more or less, and is bluntly and unsymmetrically rounded at its termination. The umbones project very considerably forward, but are not swollen; the beaks, which are acute and inflected, are preceded by a very large oval-lanceolate lunule, which is well defined, yet not greatly depressed, and rises or pouts at the rather tortuous seam. The ligament is long, moderately prominent below, but overhung above by the projection of the valves at the umbonal region, the hinder dorsal areas inclining inwards but not forming any excavation or lozenge-like area. The inside is of an uniform white, its margin is blunt and entire. The hinge consists in the right valve of two central entire primary teeth, (of which the front one is the thinner and shorter, and the posterior shelves greatly behind) and an extremely oblique somewhat bifid produced hinder one. Before all these stands the receptacle for the front sublateral lamina of the left valve, which latter has in addition a central cloven but very erect and narrow primary tooth, behind which is a much more solid entire one, and a third excessively oblique almost linear one adjacent to the ligament.   The pallial sinus is pointed, or scalpel-shaped.

The largest of our specimens measured nearly three inches and three-quarters in length, and not quite two inches and three-quarters in breadth.   The three whitish markings at the umbones are an useful character for distinguishing the species from its nearest exotic congeners (*squalida*, &c.).

We have never had an opportunity of examining the animal alive, but a good drawing of it, which we have copied, is given in Poli's magnificent work on the " Mollusca of Naples."   He figures and describes it as having the mantle freely open, with thick and slightly undulated, but not fringed, margins of an orange flesh colour.   The siphons are long and united nearly to their extremities, which are each surrounded by a circle of simple cirrhi.   The tubes themselves are of a deep orange colour with fleshy stripes ; their extremities dusky-striped ; the tips of their fringes black.   The foot is very large, thick, and of a dark pinkish flesh-colour.

Upon the whole, this, although so frequent abroad, must rank with our rarer bivalves, being taken in but few localities, and those only in the south-west.   Of these Plymouth (S. H.), is, perhaps, the most prolific, but other parts of South Devon, as Teignmouth, &c. (S. H.); with Falmouth, Mount's Bay (Jeffreys), and other parts of Cornwall, off which coast it has been dredged in twenty fathoms (M'Andrew and E. F.), likewise yield specimens in tolerable plenty.   Mr. M'Andrew has also dredged it in twelve fathoms water Caernarvon Bay, which appears to be its most northern station.   Living shells are ordinarily brought in by the trawling vessels, whence we may conclude that they do not very closely approach the shore.

Abroad it has its chief centre in the Lusitanian Province, and is abundant in the Mediterranean. It was an inhabitant of our seas as long ago as the epoch of the coralline crag but retired southwards during the prevalence of glacial conditions, and afterwards returned.

SPURIOUS.

C. CIRCINATA, Born.

Venus circinata, BORN, Mus. Cæs. Vindob. p. 61, pl. 4, f. 8. — CHEMN. Conch. Cab. vol. vi. p. 312, pl. 30, f. 311.—DILLW. Recent Shells, vol. i. p. 169.

Venus Guineensis, GMELIN, Syst. Nat. p. 3270.—MONT. Test. Brit. Suppl. pp. 48, 168.—Dorset Catalog. p. 35.—TURT. Conch. Diction. p. 237.

Cytherea Guineensis, LAM. Anim. s. Vert. (ed. Desh.) vol. vi. p. 311.—TURT. Dithyra. Brit. p. 161.—FLEM. Brit. Anim. p. 445.— Brit. Marine Conch. p. 84.—HANL. Recent Shells. p. 100. Encyclop. Méthod. Vers. pl. 265, f. 1.

Inhabits the S. Atlantic Ocean; was introduced by Montagu, as taken in the Frith of Forth by Mr. Laskey.

VENUS, LINNÆUS.

SHELL often thick, equivalve, closed, more or less suborbicular or transversely ovate, generally ornamented by concentric ribs or striæ, in some species decussated by longitudinal furrows, often brightly coloured. Margin crenated. Beaks prominent. Hinge composed in each valve of three diverging cardinal teeth. Ligament strong, external, lodged in a well-defined area. Lunule well-marked. Muscular impressions rounded, strongly marked. Pallial sinus lanceolate, wide.

Animal ovate or suborbicular, thick; its mantle open throughout, and fringed or furbelowed at the margins. Siphons separate, and diverging, or partially, or even en-

tirely united to their extremities, where the orifices are
surrounded by fringes of cirrhi. Foot linguiform, apiculate, not furnished with a byssal groove ; labial tentacles
lanceolate.

This beautiful and extensive group of bivalves includes
more than a hundred distinct forms, of which the majority
are remarkable either for elegance of shape or brilliancy of
colour.   But few of these range to the British Seas ;
those·which do, however, are among our most attractive
shells. Since northwards of our region these are not replaced by new forms, we may regard ourselves on the out-
skirts of the generic province, especially as the majority of
Veneres, and the larger and more beautiful kinds are either
tropical or subtropical.   The vertical range of the several
species is very variable, extending from low-water mark to
great oceanic depths.   Some kinds are confined to the
water's edge, others inhabit exclusively the abysses of
ocean, whilst not a few have very extensive ranges, as in
the instances of *Venus striatula* and *Venus ovata*, both of
which live indifferently at the margin of the sea, and beneath a depth of more than one hundred fathoms.   Such
capacity for enduring great differences of pressure warn us
not to lay too great stress on that influence as a regulator
of distribution, the more so as examples of these mollusks
drawn suddenly up from very great depths appear to experience no inconvenience from the rapid change of conditions,
and display their siphons and other organs as readily in a
basin of sea-water as they could ever have done in the profound recesses of their birth.

Whilst some conchologists object to the separation of
Venus from *Cytherea* and *Tapes*, others would divide this
group into numerous lesser genera. Thus, *Venus casina* represents the genus *Clausina* of Brown ; *Venus striatula* his

Ortygia ; Venus ovata is the type of *Timoclea* in Leach's arrangement ; and the genera *Dosina* of Gray, *Chione* of Megerle, and *Antigone* of Schumacher, are in the same category. Such subdivisions, founded in all cases on mere conchological characters, do not seem to us describable.

V. verrucosa, Linnæus.

With concentric ribs, which are broken into wart-like tubercles at the sides.

Plate XXIV. fig. 3.

Lister, Hist. Conch. pl. 284, f. 122.

Venus verrucosa, Linn. Syst. Nat. ed. 12, p. 1130.—Pulteney, Hutchins, Dorset. p. 32.—Donov. Brit. Shells, vol. ii. pl. 44.—Mont. Test. Brit. p. 112.—Linn. Trans. vol. viii. p. 78.—Dorset Catalog. p. 34, pl. 8, f. 1.—Turt. Conch. Diction. p. 231.—Turt. Dithyra Brit. p. 140.—Flem. Brit. Anim. p. 446.—Brit. Marine Conch. p. 85.—Brown, Ill. Conch. G. B. p. 90. pl. 36, f. 16.*—Born, Mus. Cæs. Vind. pl. 4, f. 7.—Chemn. Conch. Cab. vol. vi. p. 303, pl. 29, f. 299, 300.—Poli, Test. Sicil. pl. 21, f. 18, 19.—Lam. Anim. s. Vert. (ed. Desh.) vol. vi. p. 339 (not varieties).—Dillw. Recent Shells, vol. i. p. 163.—Index Testac. pl. 7, f. 12.—Crouch, Introd. Conch. pl. 7, f. 6.—Sowerb. Conch. Man. f. 119, a.—Desh. Elem. Conch. pl. 21, f. 1, 2.—Philip. Moll. Sicil. vol. i. p. 43 ; and vol. ii. p. 34.—Hanl. Recent Shells, p. 110.

Venus Erycina, Penn. Brit. Zool. ed. 4, vol. iv. p. 94, pl. 54, f. 48.

Pectunculus strigosus, Da Costa, Brit. Conch. p. 185, pl. 12, f. 1.

Venus cancellata (Young), Donovan, Brit. Shells, vol. iv. pl. 115? (fide Mont.)—Mont. Test. Brit. p. 574.—Turt. Dithyra Brit. p. 144, pl. 10, f. 3.—Flem. Brit. Anim. p. 447.—Brit. Marine Conch. p. 87.

Venus Lemanii (Young), Payraudeau, Moll. Corse, p. 53, pl. 1, f. 29, 30, 31 (fide Desh. and Recluz, from types).

The peculiar wart-like tubercles give so remarkable an aspect to this solid and coarse-looking bivalve, as to render its separation from its congeners a comparatively easy task. It is of a somewhat heart-shaped obovate form, very strong, generally heavy, decidedly inequilateral, and of a

paler or darker rusty-brown, occasionally adorned, but
chiefly in the younger examples, with rather indistinct
linear zigzag markings, or with about three obscure rays of
livid brown.   When adult it is more or less ventricose, or
even inflated ; the convexity is broadly and tolerably evenly
diffused, although the valves are slightly more compressed
anteriorly.   The surface is covered with numerous concentric much-elevated solid laminar ridges, which are closely
arranged, somewhat reflected or bending towards the beaks
(thus appearing hollowed out beneath, when examined
from above), and more or less distinctly indented at their
edges.   These ridges at both ends, but far more evidently behind, are broken up into rather large and horizontally
compressed wart-like tubercles, which form radiatingly
divergent rows.   The interstices of the ridges are usually
traversed by one or two raised concentric lines, and towards the umbones with depressed and rather distant
radiating ribs, which in some examples quickly become obsolete, but are continued in others almost to the base of the
shell.   The ventral margin is more or less arcuated, and
rises far more in front than behind, thus attenuating below
the short and tolerably-rounded anterior side.   The posterior termination is rather broad, and very obscurely sub-
biangulated, the lower angle being almost entirely rounded
off in the adult, though sufficiently manifest in the immature individuals ; the posterior margin is more or less convex.   The front dorsal edge is short, and rather rapidly declining, its slope is not incurved as the lunule pouts very
manifest at the lips; the declination of the hinder dorsal margin is by no means considerable ; it is comparatively
rectilinear in the young, and becomes more curved in the
aged examples.   The umbones are prominent, and, as well
as the beaks, incline much forward ; the latter are acute,

and are preceded by a rather large heart-shaped lunule, which is well defined by being laterally sunken, though elevated in the middle, and is concentrically substriated, and usually tortuous at the suture. The ligament, which is rather large when not concealed by the overlapping of the hinder dorsal lips, is seated in a tolerably ample and somewhat shallow lanceolate excavation, which is smooth, and in the left valve, where it is more manifest, is adorned with a few more or less flexuous cross-bars of a livid smoke-colour. The interior is of an uniform white; the edge is obtuse, and distinctly but not coarsely crenated, except posteriorly, where it is usually more or less entire. The hinge-margin is broad, and is furnished in each valve with three divergent teeth, of which the anterior in the right valve is very short (not reaching to the margin), and the central only subbifid; the two front teeth of the opposite valve are generally more or less cloven when young.

The fry, being far more angular in shape, and having the ridges thinner, the radiating costellæ more apparent, and the tubercles not yet developed, has erroneously been condered a distinct species, and separated under the name of *cancellata*. The shell so named in Donovan, and which is referred by Montagu to the present species, seems to bear an at least equal resemblance to *striatula*.

We possess foreign examples which are two inches and a half in length, and two inches and a third in breadth; but know of no British specimens approaching these dimensions.

The animal is suborbicular, very thick, and of a pale yellowish-white colour. The mantle is freely open from the tubes to the anterior adductor muscles; its edges are serrated or fringed, presenting more or less of a furbelowed aspect. The siphons are short, but well separated, and of a yellowish-white colour, with tawny specks or dark grey spots, lines, and small blotches. The orifice of the branchial tube is surrounded by a double series of cirrhi, the longer ones, about twenty in number, being simple. There are only about ten simple and shorter filaments around the anal orifice: it is furnished with a prominent tubular valve. The foot is white, moderately long, linguiform, pointed, and, when at rest, of a securiform shape. It presents no traces of a byssal groove. The branchiæ are subcircular, free, of a brown colour, coarsely pectinated, the upper part as usual smaller than the under one. The labial palps are rather small and narrow. (Clark MSS., Deshayes.)

The *Venus verrucosa* is a southern species on our coasts, and does not range northwards beyond the British shores. Mr. Bean states that it occurs, though rarely, at Scarborough, and it is recorded from the coast of Northumberland, though we are inclined, with Mr. Alder, to suspect that the specimens have been imported with ballast. In the English Channel it is tolerably abundant, as on the Devonshire coast (Clark); Cornwall and the Scilly islands (M'Andrew); Weymouth, dredged in seven fathoms (M'Andrew and E. F.); and Littlehampton (Strickland). In the islet of Herm, near Guernsey, it is collected for eating from the small pools between the rocks at low-water (S. H.). In Wales it is taken at Milfordhaven (M'Andrew and E. F.), and as far north as Pwllheli (M'Andrew). In Ireland it occurs at Youghal and Bantry bays (Jeffreys); and on the west coast as far north as the county of Sligo (W. Thompson).

It is a characteristic Lusitanian mollusk, and ranges throughout the Mediterranean. It extends as far south as Senegal (Adanson), and the Canaries (Webb), and is recorded as a Red Sea species by Ehrenberg. It is not known as a fossil in British strata of older date than beds

of the glacial epoch, and in them have only been found in
their southernmost portions, in Ireland, where it was discovered by Captain James, R.E., during the researches of
the Geological Survey.

V. CASINA, Linnæus.

Suborbicular, or subquadrate, either whitish, or with a few
roseate rays; rough with numerous lamellæ : hinder dorsal area
never lineated.

Plate XXIV. figs. 1, 5, 6.

Venus casina, LINN. Syst. Nat. p. 1130.—Linn. Trans. vol. viii. p. 79, pl. 2, f.
	1.—MONT. Test. Brit. Suppl. p. 47.—TURT. Conch. Diction. p.
	252 ; Dithyra Brit. p. 141, pl. 9, f. 1.—FLEMING, Brit. Anim.
	p. 446.— MACGILLIV. Moll. Aberd. p. 264.— Brit. Marine
	Conch. p. 86.—BROWN, Ill. Conch. G. B. p. 90, pl. 36, f. 15.*—
	CHEMN. Conch. Cab. vol. vi. p. 306, pl. 29, f. 301, 302.—DILLW.
	Recent Shells, vol. i. p. 165.—LAM. Anim. s. Vert. (ed. Desh.)
	vol. vi. p. 340.—Index Testaceolog. pl. 7, f. 14.—HANL. Re-
	cent Shells, p. 111.—LÖVEN, Ind. Moll. Suecize, p. 39.
Pectunculus membranaceus, DA COSTA, Brit. Conch. p. 193, pl. 13, f. 4 (on the left).
Venus reflexa, (VAR.) MONT. Test. Brit. Suppl. pp. 41, 168.—Mem. Wer-
	ner. Soc. vol. i. pl. 8, f. 1 (badly).—TURT. Conch. Diction. p.
	253 ; Dithyra Brit. p. 142, pl. 10, f. 1, 2.—FLEM. Brit.
	Anim. p. 446.—MACGILLIV. Moll. Aberd. p. 264.—DILLW.
	Recent Shells, vol. i. p. 168.—HANL. Recent Shells, p. 110,
	suppl. pl. 16, f. 10.
Venus lactea, DONOV. Brit. Shells, vol. v. pl. 149.—Linn. Trans. vol. viii. p. 79.
	—MONT. Test. Brit. Suppl. p. 46.
Venus discina, LAM. Anim. s. Vert. (ed. Desh.) vol. vi. p. 338.—Brit. Marine
	Conch. p. 86.
Venus Rusterucii (YOUNG) PAYRAUDEAU, Moll. Cors. p. 52, pl. 1, f. 26, 27, 28.
Cytherea reflexa, COUCH, Cornish Fauna, pt. 2, p. 26.

This handsome bivalve being liable to certain modifications of form and colouring, has been subdivided into two
species, *casina* and *reflexa;* but as their distinctive features
so merge into each other that it is often impossible to de-
cide to which of them a specimen would belong, we have
regarded the latter as merely a variety of the earlier known
and more commonly diffused *casina.*

The general form is subquadrate and suborbicular, and
the profundity, which varies from actually ventricose to
but moderately convex, is always more marked behind
than in front.   The valves are extremely inequilateral,
strong (not unfrequently thick and heavy), opaque, but
moderately glossy, whitish, pale ferruginous brown, or
cream coloured, and occasionally painted with from one
to three rosy-red more or less interrupted rays, which are
not particularly broad, and are often partially indistinct,
the one which runs from behind the beaks to the lower
posterior corner being least liable to become obsolete.   The
exterior is covered with very numerous concentric laminar
simple (not fimbriated) much elevated plates, which are
more solid depressed and closely set in front, bend towards the beaks in the middle, and become erect, or even
deflected, behind.   Their interstices are not decussated by
any radiating striæ or costellæ, but are often subdivided by
irregular concentric striæ or incipient lamellæ.   In the
young, and upon the umbonal region of the adult, these
plates are rather thin, but usually become more or less
solid towards the ventral margin.   This latter is decidedly
arcuated, and rises the more in front.   The anterior side is
not merely very short,—for it occupies ordinarily but one-
fourth, and frequently a still less proportion of the entire
length,—but is likewise much narrower than the hinder extremity, its extent being diminished as well by the ascent
of the lower margin, as by the more or less rapid declination of the upper one.   The general inclination of the front
dorsal edge is, from the pouting of the lips of the lunule
(which latter is large, heart-shaped, and strongly defined
by being sunk below the general level at its margin), nearly
rectilinear; the front extremity is narrowed, and unsymmetrically rounded.   The hinder termination is broad and

sub-biangulated (the upper angle is the more distinct, and
generally is the more projecting), the posterior edge being
more or less perpendicular; the hinder dorsal edge, which in
the young is straightish, becomes convex, or even arcuated,
in the adult, but never slopes to any considerable extent, and
not unfrequently declines in but a very trifling degree. The
umbones lean remarkably forward, but are not by any
means prominent; the beaks are acute and distinct. The
ligament, which is sunken and moderately large, occupies
about one-half the length of the not very profound dorsal
excavation or lozenge, whose shelving and subequal sides
are either colourless, or only irregularly painted. The
lunule is rather short, and often rufous. The interior is of
an uniform whitish hue; the muscular scars are large, and
the pallial sinus rather small and abbreviately linguiform;
the basal margin, which is very broad, is strongly but
finely and very closely crenated. Besides the three very
divergent teeth (of which the central, by far the largest, is
subbifid in the left valve), there is a minute anterior denticle at the lower part of the hinge margin in the left valve,
and a corresponding indistinct socket in the right one.

Fine examples occasionally attain to the length of two
inches; their breadth is somewhat less. The animal is
thick and white; but the details of its structure have yet
to be observed.

This is one of our least common Veneres, and is rarely
obtained in any abundance. It is occasionally taken in
Northumberland and Durham (Alder); at Scarborough
(Bean); West Bay of Portland in fifteen fathoms (M'A.
and E. F.); South Devon (Mont.); Guernsey (S. H.);
Milford Haven (M'Andrew and E. F.), and elsewhere on
the Welsh coast. In from twelve to twenty-five fathoms
on the Manx Coast (E. F.). Both sides of Ireland (Thomp-

son); Youghal and Bantry Bay (Humphreys); Oban,
Loch Carron, Skye (Jeffreys); Orkney in twelve fathoms,
and Foula eighty fathoms, Copenhaw Head forty fathoms,
Cape Wrath fifty to seventy fathoms (M'Andrew); the
Mull of Galloway from fifty to one hundred and forty-five
fathoms (Beechey); thirty-five fathoms off the Staples and
east coast of Scotland (Thomas). It occurs in the Scandinavian seas and more rarely in the Lusitanian, where
it was more common during the newer pliocene epoch.

The *V. casinula* of Deshayes (Exp. Morée, p. 101, pl.
18, f. 18, 19; *V. casina*, Philippi, Moll. Sicil. vol. ii. p.
33) scarcely differs from our variety *reflexa*; its shape,
however, is more elongated, its front dorsal slope is longer in proportion, and its lamellæ in general are more
closely disposed.

V. STRIATULA, Donovan.

Triangular-heart-shaped; if coloured, painted with delicate
zigzag lines: sulcated or costellated (if lamellar, the shape elongated): hinder dorsal area flexuously lineated.

Plate XXIII. fig. 4, Plate XXIV. fig. 4, and Plate XXVI. figs. 9, 10, 11.

LIST. Hist. Conch. pl. 282, f. 120.
Pectunculus striatulus, DA COSTA, Brit. Conch. p. 191, pl. 12, f. 2.
Venus casina, (not of Linn.) PULTENEY, Hutchins, Hist. Dorset, p. 33.
„ *striatula*, DONOVAN, British Shells, vol. ii. pl. 68.—MONT. Test. Brit. p.
113.—LÖVEN, Ind. Moll. Skandin. p. 39.
Venus gallina, MATON AND RACKETT, Linn. Trans. vol. viii. p. 82. — Dorset
Catalog. p. 35, pl. 8, f. 2.—TURT. Conch. Diction. p. 234, f.
65 (execrably); Dithyra Brit. p. 149, pl. 9, f. 2. — FLEM.
Brit. Anim. p. 448.—MACGILLIV. Moll. Aberd. p. 265.—
Brit. Marine Conch. p. 89.—BROWN, Ill. Conch. G. B. p. 89,
pl. 36, f. 11.—ALDER, Northumb. and Durham Mollus. p. 85.
—DILLW. Recent Shells, p. 168.—LAM. Anim. s. Vert. (ed.
Desh.) vol. vi. p. 347 (in part).—Index Testaceolog. pl. 7, f.
23.—HANL. Recent Shells, p. 115.

Venus Pennantii, FORBES, Malac. Monens. p. 52.

„ *laminosa*,* TURT. Conch. Diction. p. 233 (except the description of the hinge, which is copied from Montagu) ; Dithyra Brit. p. 148, pl. 10, f. 4.—Brit. Marine Conch. p. 89.—HANL. Recent Shells, suppl. pl. 16, f. 11.

„ *rugosa*, PENN. Brit. Zool. vol. iv. p 95, pl. 56, f. 50.—FLEM. Brit. Anim. p. 448.—BROWN, Illust. Conch. G. B. p. 90, pl. 36, f. 14.

„ *Prideauxiana*, COUCH, Cornish Fauna, pt. 2, p. 26.—MACGILLIV. Moll. Aberdeenshire, p. 266.

„ *sulcata*, Brown, Ill. Conch. G. B. p. 90, pl. 36, f. 12.

„ *costata*, BROWN, Ill. Conch. G. B. p. 90, pl. 36, f. 13.

A reference to the tenth edition of the " Systema Naturæ" will convince our readers that the *Venus gallina* of Linnæus [CHEMN. Conch. Cab. vol. vi. p. 311, pl. 30, f. 308, 309, 310.—POLI, Test. Sicil. pl. 21, f. 5, 6, 7.—PHILIPPI, Moll. Sicil. vol. i. p. 44, and vol. ii. p. 34.—HANL. Recent Shells, suppl. pl. 16, f. 42,] is the shell so named by those who have illustrated the conchology of the Mediterranean. It is perhaps a matter of

* *Venus laminosa*, MONT. Test. Brit. Suppl. p. 58.—LASKEY, Memoirs Wernerian Soc. vol. i. p. 384, pl. 8, f. 16.—BROWN, Illust. Conch. G. B. p. 90, pl. 87, f. 14, 15 (copied from last).

We have not ventured to assert the identity of the *V. laminosa* of Montagu and Laskey with that of Turton, owing principally to the dentition assigned to the former in the Testacea Britannica. Nevertheless, it is highly probable that the general belief of collectors (the tradition, if we may so term it) is not unfounded, and that the species was established upon an aged example of that variety of *striatula* termed *rugosa* by Pennant and Brown, in which some peculiar distortion of the cardinal edge misled the author and induced him to attribute to it the hinge of a *Cytherea*. That no known species of the latter genus (*tortuosa* is, perhaps, the nearest) will accord with the figure in the Wernerian Memoirs, which is exactly like a swollen example of the produced (but generally compressed) variety of *striatula* is an additional argument in favour of the traditionary hypothesis. We subjoin the original description.

" Shell ovate, with numerous concentric laminar ridges, very little reflected ; these ridges are not quite regular nor equidistant, but so thin as to be almost membranaceous ; between the ridges about the umbonal region where a natural decortication has taken place, it is finely striated in the longitudinal direction, which shews that younger specimens are more generally furnished with such

controversy, whether that species is specifically distinct
from the one so designated by the British writers; we
subjoin, therefore, a brief digest of the more striking
points of difference. The valves of *gallina* are always
more or less inflated, or at least ventricose, and their surface covered with distant subimbricated grooves, which are
so peculiarly irregular as scarcely to be concentric (characters even more fully evident in the young than in the
old), their ventral margin is very strongly arcuated, and
their front dorsal edge short and much incurved; internally
the hinder extremity, or the muscular scar, is almost invariably stained with purple; the crenations are coarse,
and not particularly numerous, and the sinus of the pallial
impression is remarkably short. In *striatula*, on the contrary, the valves, whose shape is much more trigonal, are
frequently compressed, and very rarely are even ventricose; the surface, especially upon the umbones and in the
younger shells, is girt with distinct costellæ, which are by
no means peculiarly irregular, and, if distant, change into
lamellæ; the arcuation of the lower edge is not remarkable; the front dorsal margin is long, and not strongly in-

striæ; but in the only large specimen we have had an opportunity of examining,
scarcely any such markings were observed but where the old shell had been super-
ficially separated: the umbo is pointed and much reclined to one side, beneath
which is a broad cordiform depression; but neither this nor the cartilage slope
differs in colour from the rest of the shell, which is wholly of a dirty-white. Inside white: hinge furnished with four teeth in each valve, but the outer one
above the cordiform depression in one valve is obsolete, or formed only by a
cavity for the reception of the corresponding tooth in the opposite valve: the margin is finely crenulated. Length (breadth) more than an inch; breadth (length)
above an inch and a quarter.

The above description is taken from a shell in the cabinet of Mr. Laskey,
who assured us he took it by dredging off the Isle of May, in the Frith of Forth,
in the year 1804. In our cabinet is a single valve of about half the size of that
before described, which was found in Devonshire; in this the longitudinal
striæ are evident by the assistance of a lens, in the sulci between the tranverse
ridges."

curved, and the interior is of an uniform white, with the marginal crenations extremely small and very numerous; the pallial sinus, too, is sublanceolate, and is half as long again as the adjacent muscular impression.

The species even thus restricted exhibits a remarkable latitude of variation in form, sculpture, and colouring; but these varieties are inseparably connected by intermediate gradations. The general contour is heart-shaped, but differs greatly from being at times produced and therefore subovate, at times abbreviated, and consequently subtriangular. The convexity, likewise, is subject to great variation, some examples being decidedly ventricose, whilst others, being merely convex, are for *Veneres* comparatively compressed. In the ordinary intermediate specimens, the chief swell is rather behind the subumbonal region, and the chief compression at the anterior extremity. The valves are opaque, more or less solid, and almost entirely devoid of lustre; the ordinary and more typical examples are variegated, upon a whitish or cream-coloured ground, with extremely numerous and very fine linear zigzag markings of a livid chestnut, or reddish liver colour, which not unfrequently give an appearance of crenation to the concentric sculpture. The majority of individuals are adorned with three more or less distinct broader or narrower rays, which are never of an uniform colour, but appear mottled, being composed of the more thickly clustered interlacements of the lineation previously mentioned, which usually becomes of a darker colour, and rather broader character on these parts. Occasionally, and especially in the younger shells, there are two white and widely separated rays, sometimes only a single subposterior one, with the commencement of the second visible at the umbones; sometimes, too, both the white and dark rays are present in the same individual, occasionally the colouring matter is almost or entirely absent from the general surface, but whenever present is, when closely examined, composed of linear painting, and always exists upon the hinder dorsal area. The diversity of its sculpture is not less striking. This is solely composed of concentric costellæ, or laminar striæ, which vary considerably in thickness, elevation, distance, and, consequently, number. In the ordinary or typical form, they are extremely numerous, slightly irregular, tolerably strong, rounded above, and very closely disposed. These costellæ, in the more elongated and compressed varieties, become converted into sharp laminæ, whose interstices when highly magnified appear radiated with very delicate and scarcely distinct striulæ, which are never broad or greatly elevated, and range in approximation to each other from closely disposed to moderately distant; in the former case they are so acute as almost to resemble raised striæ, and occasionally retain their richer colouring and radiated markings (we have figured one also which is completely destitute of all lineation, except upon the hinder dorsal slope); in the latter case the painting is almost wholly absent.

The ventral margin is arcuated, particularly in front, where it rises to the dorsal edge in an undisturbed sweep. The front dorsal margin is but moderately incurved and extremely sloping, the hinder one is typically subarcuated, produced, and much declining: these characters in the most aberrant variety are somewhat modified.

The anterior side is only about half the length of the posterior, and tapers very considerably at its extremity, where it is centrally subangulated. The hinder termination is either subangulated below, or if much attenuated, then bluntly subbiangulated.

The umbones are prominent, but not swollen; they in-

cline much forward. The beaks, which are very distinct
and acute, are preceded by a large impressed and well-defined lunule, which is more or less heart-shaped and devoid
of any sculpture, unless we regard as such the concentric
lines of growth. The ligament, which is of a moderate
size, not at all concealed, and usually of a fulvous or yellowish hue, is seated in a peculiarly large moderately excavated area, which is almost smooth, and not limited by
any carination, though its boundaries are more or less angulated. In this excavation the breadth, as well as the
bevelling of edges, is equal in both valves; but the left
valve is decidedly the smoother.

The interior is of an uniform white; the hinder teeth are
so thin as occasionally to become almost obsolete in one or
both valves: the inner margin is very finely crenulated;
the pallial sinus is moderately large.

The length of a fine example is nearly an inch and a
half, and the breadth about an inch and a fifth.

Having had ample opportunities of observing the animal,
we can confidently assert the distinctness of its characters,
as well as the shell, from those of the true *gallina*, of which
a good representation has lately been given by Deshayes in
the "Mollusques d'Algerie." The two species differ most
materially in the structure of their siphons. In our British
one the siphonal tubes are united to their extremities; in
the Mediterranean form they are not only much shorter,
but diverge considerably: their orifices in the former are
fringed with few and very inconspicuous cirrhi; in the
latter the cirrhi are numerous and conspicuous. The animal
of *striatula* may, indeed, be regarded as an aberrant form
in its genus, whereas that of *gallina* presents the ordinary
characters of its congeners.

The body of the animal of *Venus striatula* partakes of

the shape of the shell, but is prolonged anteriorly into two smooth slender completely-united tubes, forming a single siphonal process. The anal tube is much smaller than the branchial, and its orifice is separated only in the slightest and almost imperceptible degree. Mr. Clark has observed ten cirrhi, and intermediate shorter ones around the branchial orifice, and ten around the anal. In several specimens which we have examined we found the cirrhi of the branchial orifice rather more numerous, but very short and inconspicuous, and could only distinguish them as denticles on the anal margin. Both tubes are of a pale sulphur-yellow, in some examples slightly tinged with rose around their extremities. They may be extended to a length very nearly equalling the breadth of the shell. The mantle is freely open, and is of a yellowish-white colour ; it is fringed by cirrhi or fimbriations, which are fasciculated so that it appears to be sinuous, and bordered by a series of little tufts. The foot is large, fleshy, white, linguiform, and geniculated. Mr. Clark has observed that the branchiæ on one side are very unequal, the upper being much shorter than the lower. The animal in confinement is rather sluggish.

This is one of our commonest shells, occurring everywhere upon our sandy coasts, and ranging to the greatest depths as yet explored in the British seas. Some of its numerous varieties, especially that termed *sulcata* by Captain Brown, are however rare. It is so generally distributed that to specify localities would be to enumerate almost every point explored where the bottom was sand or sandy mud. The form generally thrown up on the shore lives in sandy tracts near low-water mark, but the lamellated kinds inhabit deeper water. Specimens dredged by Mr. M'Andrew in depths between eighty and one hundred fathoms, at considerable distances from the shores of the Zetland Isles, are remarkable for their deficiency of colour.

The species appears to have commenced its existence during the Newer Pliocene epoch, and occurs abundantly in many of the Glacial-drift deposits.

V. FASCIATA, Donovan.

Triangular; the adult with broad and flattened ribs; the young lamellar, the lamellæ few and distant.

Plate XXIII. fig. 3, Plate XXVI. f. 7, and (Animal) Plate L. f. 7.

Pectunculus fasciatus, DA COSTA, Brit. Conch. p. 188, pl. 13, f. 3.
Venus Paphia, PULTENEY, (not Linn.) Hutchins, Hist. Dorset, p. 33.—MONT. Test. Brit. p. 110.
Venus fasciata, DONOV. Brit. Shells, vol. v. pl. 170.—Linn. Trans. vol. viii. p. 80.—Dorset Catalog. p. 34, pl. 7, f. 3.—TURT. Conch. Diction. p. 234; Dithyra Brit. p. 146, pl. 8, f. 9.—FLEM. Brit. Anim. p. 447.—FORBES, Malac. Monens. p 52.—MACGILLIV. Moll. Aberd. p. 267.—Brit. Marine Conch. p. 88.—BROWN, Ill. Conch. G. B. p. 91, pl. 36, f. 10.—BURROWS, Elem. Conchology, pl. 7, f. 2.—DILLW. Recent Shells, vol. i. p. 159.—DESH. in Lam. Anim. s. Vert. (ed. Desh.) vol. vi. p. 371; Elem. Conch. pl. 20, f. 4, 5.—HANL. Recent Shells, vol. i. p. 412.—PHIL. Moll. Sicil. vol. ii. p. 34.
Venus Brogniarti, PAYRAUDEAU, Moll. Corse, p. 51, pl. 1, f. 23, 24, 25.—PHILIPPI, Moll. Sicil. vol. i. p. 43.

The *V. fasciata* is subtriangular, suborbicular, and a little heart-shaped, very strong, solid, and heavy; opaque, but slightly glossy, and not greatly inequilateral: in convexity it varies from compressed (which is the more typical state) to subventricose, the young being the former, the aged not unfrequently the latter. The diversity of its painting, not so much as regards the colours, which are almost invariably orange or roseate-brown on a paler or whitish ground, as their disposition, is almost infinite, but never devoid of gracefulness. Ordinarily there are three

or four simple or interrupted, lighter or darker, broader or
narrower-coloured rays, on a very pale or whitish ground;
sometimes but two remarkably broad orange-brown rays,
which are occasionally more or less distinctly edged with
very small linear markings of a darker hue.   More
rarely the entire surface is of an uniform white, but where
colour is present at all, the rays seem always more or
less developed, though frequently only composed of confluent linear markings. A kind of obscure reticulation,
formed by short and crowded minute coloured lines, or
small dots, is very prevalent, especially in specimens from
Guernsey and the warmer portions of our coast: where
this pattern is peculiarly distinct, the rays are usually of a
dark roseate-brown, and the general effect of colouring
remarkably rich.

The great alteration of the sculpture with age has been
the cause of the immature state being regarded as a distinct
species. In its most typical stage the surface is covered
with not very numerous broad and but little elevated obtuse
belts, separated by shallow and much narrower smooth interstices.   The fry have only crowded and rather depressed fine concentric costellæ; in the earlier stages concentric
recurved laminæ often arise, which, gradually becoming
solid with age, form laminar belts which are solid and
shelving below, but hollow and recurved above: at these
periods the interstices are at least as broad as the elevations, usually diminishing in width as age advances.

In certain examples the hinder dorsal slope is coarsely
dentated, as it were, by the projection and abrupt termination of the laminar belts; this does not take place, however, in the full-grown shells, where the belts at once
diminish in elevation at the posterior extremity.   The
ventral margin is always more or less arcuated, rises greatly

at the sides, and is finely and closely crenulated within. The anterior side, which is rather the shorter, and is well rounded below, appears to project with an upward inclination owing to the rapid declination of the more or less long and incurved dorsal slope.

The hinder side is sub-angulated below, the angulation becoming less manifest in the older shells; its dorsal edge is produced, sloping and curved, the elongation declivity and arcuation becoming more marked as age advances. The lunule is sub-angularly heart-shaped, not profound, rather large, pouting in the young, and usually more or less stained with colouring matter; the lozenge is large, rather profoundly excavated, and generally lineated. The ligament is sunken, and so extremely narrow as scarcely to be visible. The umbones are more or less compressed, and very prominent; the beaks are remarkably distinct, small, and acute, leaning most decidedly both forward and inwards. The interior is generally white, but occasionally of a brilliant reddish-purple; the margins, except the posterior dorsal, are minutely but closely and distinctly crenulated. The hinge margin is rather broad, and is furnished in the right valve with a subtriangular central tooth, which is the largest of the three, and shelves inward and posteriorward, being more elevated in front, and diminishing in height as it widens from its somewhat truncated and slightly bifid apex; preceding this is a small and very oblique laminar tooth, and behind it lies an elongated more or less bifid solid one. In the opposite valve, the central tooth is similarly shelving and the broadest, but the front one, which is curved and subtrigonal, is the most elevated, whilst the hinder one is depressed, linear, and indistinct. The muscular impressions are strongly marked, the pallial sinus is extremely small, and more or less angulated.

The length does not greatly exceed an inch, and the breadth, except in the young, is not much inferior.

The animal has been observed by Mr. Clark, Mr. Alder, and ourselves. It is triangularly suborbicular, and rather thick. The mantle is freely open in front, of a yellowish-white colour, and furnished with a fine white fringe, bordered by a reddish line. The tubes are short and united, except near their extremities, where they become separate and diverge. Their orifices are furnished with cirrhi; those of the branchial are largest and most conspicuous, and are about sixteen or twenty in number. The tubes and cirrhi are of a sulphur-yellow colour, tinged with pale red flakes towards their orifices. The foot is sub-compressed, and moderately long. " The branchiæ are composed of a pair of unequal plates on each side, the upper being much smaller than the lower. The labial palps are small." (Clark.) This animal is very sluggish, and, when kept in confinement, is very shy of exhibiting either its foot or siphons.

Venus fasciata inhabits for the most part gravelly sand, or gravel within the coralline zone. It has a wide range, even from four to sixty fathoms, in our seas. It is very generally diffused, and sometimes occurs in considerable numbers. On the south and west coasts it is especially common, and is very abundant in the Irish sea. ` A few localities illustrative of its vertical range may be mentioned :—Herm near Guernsey, very vividly coloured, alive on the long beach (S. H.) ; off Portland in fifteen fathoms, Penzance in twenty fathoms, and Milford in ten fathoms (M'Andrew and E. F.) ; off Cape Clear in forty fathoms, and Kinsale in sixty fathoms (M'Andrew) ; Cape Wrath in fifty-five fathoms, St. Magnus' Bay, Zetland, in forty-five fathoms, and Stornaway in four fathoms (M'Andrew) ; Eda Sound, in

Orkney, in sixteen fathoms (Thomas); Isle of Man in twenty-five fathoms (E. F.); rare on the Northumberland coast (Alder); at Scarborough (Bean). Mr Jeffreys has taken it in many localities in the Hebrides, and Mr. Thompson records it from all round the Irish coast.

As a foreign shell it ranges from the Mediterranean, where it lies as deep as forty fathoms (E. F.), to the shores of Norway. Mr. M'Andrew has taken it on the Atlantic coast of Spain. It commenced its existence within our area, as far back as the epoch of the coralline crag.

V. ovata, Pennant.

With crowded radiating costellæ, which are concentrically decussated by very closely set elevated striulæ.

Plate XXIV. fig. 2, Plate XXVI. f. 1, and (animal) Plate L. f. 6.

Venus ovata, Penn. Brit. Zool. ed. 4, vol. iv. p. 97, pl. 56, f. 56.—Mont. Test. Brit. p. 120.—Linn. Trans. vol. viii. p. 85, pl. 2, f. 4.—Dorset Catalog. p. 35, pl. 1, f. 15.—Turt. Conch. Diction. p. 239 ; Dithyra Brit. p. 150, pl. 9, f. 3.—Forbes, Mal. Monensis, p. 52.—Macgilliv. Moll. Aberd. p. 267.—Brit. Marine Conch. p. 90.—Brown, Ill. Conch. G. B. p. 91, pl. 37, f. 11.—Dillw. Recent Shells, p. 171.—Lam. Anim. s. Vert. (ed. Desh.) vol. vi. p. 370.—Index Testaceol. pl. 7, f. 30.—Mawe, Conchology, pl. 10, f. 5.—Hanl. Recent Shells, p. 116.

Venus pectinula, Lam. Anim. s. Vert. (ed. Desh.) vol. vi. p. 348.

Cytherea ovata, Flem. Brit. Anim. p. 445.

Venus radiata, Philippi, Moll. Sicil. vol. i. p. 44, and vol. ii. p. 34.—Deshayes, Elem. Conch. pl. 20, f. 17, 18.

The ordinary outline of the *Venus ovata* is, as its name implies, egg-shaped, but both the fry and some of the more aged examples, are of a less elongated form. The valves, which are decidedly, but not particularly, inequilateral, are tolerably strong, opaque, lustreless, at most subventricose, and much more frequently are still less swollen ;

the convexity is broadly diffused, and diminishes in nearly
an even ratio at either extremity. The exterior, which is
ordinarily of a rulous flesh-colour, generally variegated in
the younger examples with amorphous stains of a deeper
tint, but which occasionally, though very rarely, is in the
northern shells of an uniform chalky white, is rayed with
extremely numerous narrow ribs, which near their termination become divided by a groove, but not bifurcated,
and are much more closely set in front than beyond the
umbonal ridge, behind which they are replaced by most
crowded and elevated radiating striæ ; these, as well as the
preceding costellæ, are concentrically decussated by raised
lines. This decussation exhibits itself upon the striæ in
continuous concentric series of sublunate scales (the last
five or six are not affected by it), and forms somewhat
tubercular rows of crenæ upon the ribs, but is not usually
distinct in their interstices, which occasionally are subdivided by a still narrower costella. The crenæ are generally less marked upon the hinder ribs, and in a very rare
variety are altogether converted into scales. The northern
examples have their ribs in general rather further apart,
and somewhat more elevated and square-topped than the
southern ones, but never deviate so far from the typical
character as to have them remote or much raised.

The ventral margin is moderately curved, and rises
rather the more in front, where it is more or less arcuated.
The anterior side is the shorter, and tapers a little at its
extremity, which is better rounded below than above. The
posterior termination is attenuated, but rounded at the tip.
The dorsal edges are moderate in both convexity and slope,
the front never being incurved, as in most of the *Veneres*,
and the hinder being almost straight, and scarcely declining as far as the ligament extends. This latter is ex-

tremely narrow, small, and not at all projecting. The
lunule is rather large, very ill defined, not sunken, but, on
the contrary, pouting at the lips; it is not free from the
ribs which traverse the rest of the exterior. The umbones
are moderately prominent, and incline a little forward; the
beaks are not acute. The interior is whitish or flesh-
coloured, with the disk occasionally of a fine reddish-purple
or lilac hue; the inner margin is everywhere very delicately but quite distinctly crenated. The hinge-margin is
moderately broad, and is furnished in the right valve with
an anterior simple and almost laminar tooth, which is so
oblique as almost to lie adjacent to the upper margin: both
the other teeth are triangular, somewhat bifid, and tolerably strong. The central of the left valve is bifid and rather
broad; both the others are simple, narrow, and very
oblique.

Our engraving represents the ordinary size of fine examples of the adult shell.

The animal is yellowish-white, ovate, and has very short
tubes. The margins of the mantle are finely scalloped,
and fringed and marked with reddish lineations. The tubes
are united nearly to their orifices, where they diverge;
around the openings of each are about twenty slender and
conspicuous cirrhi. The colour of the tubes is sulphur-
yellow; between each pair of cirrhi is a red dot. The anal
valve is very conspicuous. The foot is compressed and
linguiform, geniculated at the base. The branchiæ are
pale-brown.

The *Venus ovata* is universally diffused throughout the
British seas, inhabiting all depths of water between three
and nearly one hundred fathoms, often excessively abundant. It seems to have a preference for a gravelly-sand
bottom. Southern specimens are often more brightly-

coloured than those from the north; and examples from
very deep water off Zetland, taken by Mr. M'Andrew, are
of a chalky whiteness. Abroad it ranges throughout the
European seas, and in the Mediterranean has been taken
as deep as one hundred and thirty fathoms (E. F.). As
a fossil it is known from the Coralline Crag; during
the formation of which stratum it inhabited our area, and
has never since departed. This long and continuous
range in time is coincident with its wide distribution at
present.

V. PALLIDA, Turton.

Venus pallida, TURTON, Dithyra Brit. p. 150, pl. 10, f. 5.—FLEMING, Brit.
Anim. p. 448.—Brit. Marine Conch. p. 90.

We found two specimens thus named in Dr. Turton's
collection, of which one was manifestly a very worn
example of *V. striatula*, and still exhibited traces of its peculiar colouring. The other, which we regard as the sole
type, being the individual delineated and described by the
author, presents to the eye certain features which distinguish it as well from *striatula*, its nearest congener apparently, as from any of the very numerous members of this
extensive genus with which we are acquainted. We hesitate,
however, to consider it a distinct British species on the authority of the single worn example said to have been found
at Dawlish.

The shell is triangular heart-shaped, decidedly inequilateral, and of an uniform yellowish white; the valves are
thin but opaque, and rather compressed except at the umbones, which are moderately ventricose; their outer surface
is but slightly glossy; the interior is entirely white, and its
margin is most finely and closely crenated. The raised
concentriæ striæ (their elevation is scarcely sufficient for

the term lamellæ), which gird the entire exterior, become
very closely disposed near the lower margin, but are much
more distant towards the beaks. These striæ are radiatingly decussated by elevated and crowded lines, which
appear more or less distinctly to traverse them, and not to
be confined to their interstices.

The ventral margin is arcuated, and rises considerably at
both extremities. The declination of both dorsal edges is
likewise considerable; the front one is incurved, somewhat
abrupt, and rather longer than is usual in the genus; the
hinder, which is of moderate length, slopes with but little
convexity, except near the prominent beaks (which are very
acute and curve peculiarly forward), to the ventral margin,
with which it forms a rather narrow subangulation. The
front extremity is narrow, well rounded below, but less
distinctly so above. The lunule is large, elongated-cordate,
and profoundly impressed; the hinder dorsal area is rather
broad, flattened, and a little retuse: the ligament, though
not prominent, is very distinct. The dentition is that of
striatula.

The length of the individual we have been describing is
full eleven lines; its breadth is four-fifths of an inch.

SPURIOUS.

Venus subcordata, Mont. Test. Brit. p. 121, pl. 3, f. 1.—Linn. Trans. vol. viii.
p. 82.—Turt. Conch. Diction. p. 237 ; Dithyra Brit. p. 143.
—Flem. Brit. Anim. p. 447.—Brit. Marine Conch. p. 87.—
Index Testaceol. pl. 7, f. 16.—Dillw. Recent Shells, vol. i.
p. 166.

Although we regard the *V. subcordata* of Montagu, whose
type is still preserved in our National Museum, as only the immature state of the *V. radiata* of Chemnitz (Conch. Cab. vol.
vi. p. 371, pl. 36. f. 386.—Dillw. Recent Shells, vol. i. p. 189),
we have preferred drawing up our description from that stage, as,

in the event of others not coinciding with our views of its affilia-
tion, we shall, at least, have enabled them more readily to com-
prehend what was intended by Montagu, by redescribing the
species from the original type (which is sadly broken), and its
exact but perfect facsimiles from the coast of the West Indian
Islands.   The epithet *radiata* was bestowed on the species,
through the presence of a character in the described individual,
which is rather exceptional than constant.

Somewhat ovately cordate, solid, opaque, not particularly inequilateral (the front being at least half the length of the hinder
side), rather dull, more or less ventricose, profundity rather less
in front : exterior whitish, adorned with thin, short, concentric
lamellæ, which are rendered wavy by the very closely disposed
simple radiating interstitial costellæ, and become extremely
crowded near the lower edge, but are less so in the very young,
and upon the umbonal region of the adult.   Ventral margin more
or less subarcuated, a little flattened in the middle.   Anterior
side tapering to a rounded extremity ; the declination of the
upper edge (which is straightish near the beaks) moderate, but
not equal to the rise of the lower margin.   Hinder dorsal edge
moderately sloping, and not very convex ; hinder termination
attenuated, subangulated in the middle.   Ligament small.   Umbones rather prominent ; beaks acute, leaning forward, and preceded by a large cordate lunule, which is well defined by a
groove, but not much sunken nor yet smooth, possessing, though
obscurely, the general sculpture.   Hinder dorsal area large, deeply
and equally excavated in either valve, but remotely cross-barred
with chocolate colour in the left valve only.   Inside white, or
tinged on the disk with flesh-colour ; hinge-margin broadish,
stained with purplish chocolate behind.   Front and lower edges
crenated within.

*Introduced as British with doubt by Montagu, who had taken
a single valve from the sand of Falmouth harbour.   It is a native
of the West Indies and of the shores of Central America.*

V. CANCELLATA, Gronovius.

Venus cancellata, GRONOV. Zoophylac. fasc. 3, pl. 1, f. 8, No. 1149, p. 270.—
LAM. (ed. Desh.) vol. vi. p. 341.—HANL. Recent Shells,
p. 112, pl. 7, f. 6.
Venus Dysera, MONT. Test. Brit. Suppl. p. 43.—TURT. Conch. Diction. p. 237 ;
Dithyra Brit. p. 147, pl. 9, f. 4.—FLEM. Brit. Anim. p. 447.—
CHEMN. Conch. Cab. vol. vi. p. 294 (partly), pl. 28, f. 289.—
REEVE, Conchol. Systemat. pl. 68, f. 2.
Venus cingenda, DILLW. Recent Shells, vol. i. p. 161.—Index Testaceolog. pl. 7,
f. 6.
Venus elevata, SAY, Journ. Ac. Philad. vol. ii. p. 272.
Encyclop. Méthod. Vers, pl. 268, f. 1.

*A West Indian shell ; introduced by Montagu, from Mr. Las-
key having found some worn valves in the Frith of Forth. We
have found valves of it ourselves on the shore near Birkenhead in
the Mersey, evidently derived from ballast.*

V. GRANULATA, Gmelin.

Venus Marica, BORN (not Linn.), Mus. Cæs. Vind. p. 59, pl. 4, f. 5, 6.
Venus Marica-spuria, CHEMN. Conch. Cab. vol. vi. p. 314, pl. 30, f. 313.
Venus granulata, GMELIN, Syst. Nat. p. 3277.—DONOV. British Shells, vol. iii.
pl. 83.—MONT. Test. Brit. p. 122.—Linn. Trans. vol. viii.
p. 85.—TURT. Conch. Diction. p. 240 ; Dithyra Brit. p. 145.
—FLEM. Brit. Anim. p. 447.—Brit. Marine Conch. p. 88.—
DILLW. Recent Shells, p. 171.—Index Testacool. pl. 7, f. 29.
—LAM. Anim. s. Vert. (ed. Desh.) vol. vi. p. 344.—HANL.
Recent Shells, vol. i. p. 114, pl. 7, f. 29.

*A West Indian shell ; introduced by Donovan as British from
a small one having been said to have been found on the Cornish
coast.*

V. PAPHIA, Linnæus.

LISTER, Hist. Conch. pl. 279,—KNORR, Verg. vol. ii. pl. 28. f. 2.—
REGENFUSS, Choix Coquill. pl. 7, f. 11.
Venus Paphia, LINN. Syst. Nat. p. 1129.—CHEMN. Conch. Cab. vol. vi. p. 267,
pl. 27, f. 274, 275, 276.—DILLW. Recent Shells, vol. i. p. 159.
—Index Testaceolog. pl. 7, f. 2.—DESH. in Lam. Anim. s. Vert.
(ed. Desh.) vol. vi. p. 371.—HANL. Recent Shells, vol. i. p. 112.
Venus vetula, DA COSTA, British Conchology, p. 190, pl. 13, f. 5.

A West Indian shell; introduced, without any specified locality, by Da Costa (who became aware of his error after publication), from merely having seen it, in a collector's cabinet, as a British production.

We have appended as a note to the *Veneres* the original description (from whence all the others have been abridged) of the *Venus subrhomboidea* of Montagu, not because we consider it a true Venus (for that, at least, the bidentate hinge will certify), but solely from the extreme uncertainty of its actual generic position, which, if determined without examination of the original specimen, must, of course, be conjectural. Had the *Venerupis Irus* been found so far north, our suspicions would certainly have inclined to the supposition that it was only a distorted individual of that species, with the hinge imperfectly developed; and our inference from the language of Montagu (we may remark, by the bye, that he uses the word "behind," in the above description, in a different sense from his usual one, as the figure—which evidently represents a distorted and probably lithodomous shell—shews the replication to be on that side usually called the anterior or front one, by the writers of the Linnean school,) would rather have led to our placing it with *Petricola*, than, as Turton has done, with *Astarte*, the large pallial sinus forbidding its admission into the latter genus :—

Venus subrhomboidea, MONT. Test. Brit. Suppl. p. 49, pl. 28, f. 2.—TURT. Conch.
　　　　　　　　Diction. p. 246.—FLEM. Brit. Anim. p. 448.
Crassina ―――, TURT. Dithyra Brit. p. 128.

"Shell subrhomboidal, rounded at one end, truncated at the other, and irregularly wrinkled concentrically, especially towards the margin, where the ridges are prominent but obtuse; these are decussated by extremely fine approximate longitudinal striæ; umbo small and nearly central, but the beak reclines to one side; the colour is white, with a tinge of rufous at the truncated end. The inside is white, with a dash of purple at that part which is rufous on the outside; the margin is plain; cicatrix broad, spreading half across the shell: the hinge is singularly formed; in each valve are two strong, plain teeth, one of which stands very oblique; behind these the margin projects inward, and then doubling back, forms a smooth replication and a cavity between it and the exterior edge of the shell behind the umbo for the connecting cartilage. Length half an inch; breadth three-quarters."

"A single specimen (in a living state) is recorded to have been dredged by Mr. Laskey off St. Abb's Head, in the Frith of Forth. It bore the most marked resemblance to *Venerupis Irus*, but differed in the closeness of its striæ, the absence of thin membranaceous ridges, the replication of the hinge margin, and by its dentition exhibiting only two simple teeth in each valve."

ARTEMIS, Poll.

Shell suborbicular, more or less strong, equivalve, closed; surface concentrically striated; inner margins entire. Muscular impressions oblong, nearly equal; pallial sinus lanceolate, acute, deep, oblique. Hinge strong, composed of three diverging teeth in one valve, and four in the other. Ligament external, sunken, rather long; lunule strongly defined.

Animal suborbicular, its mantle freely open, the margins entire, or only partially serrated. Siphonal tubes long, united to their extremities, margins of their orifices fimbriated. Foot semilunar.

This well-marked group was constituted by Poli; the habit and characters of both shell and animal evince its very natural constitution. Common as the two species which inhabit our seas are, our knowledge of their construction, however, is almost entirely derived from the observations of the distinguished Neapolitan naturalist who founded the genus. It too often happens that whilst the animals of the rarer shells are carefully observed, noted, and drawn, we are apt to neglect those most abundant, fancying they are always at hand. Guilty of this crime, and confessing our guilt as a warning to others, we are obliged to content ourselves for the present with a very imperfect notice of these mollusks, but, before the completion of our work, hope to present our readers with a full and original account of them.

A. EXOLETA, Linnæus.

Striæ not very closely arranged; surface generally rayed, or variegated; hinder dorsal edge straightish, and scarcely sloping; lunule generally coloured; hinder dorsal area not flattened.

Plate XXIII. fig. 3, 4.

Venus exoleta, LINN. Syst. Nat. ed. 12, p. 1134.—PENN. Brit. Zool. ed. 4, vol. iv. p. 95. pl. 54, f. 49, A. (as variety.)—PULTENEY, Hutchins, Hist. Dorset, p. 34.—DONOV. Brit. Shells, vol. ii. pl. 42, f. 1.—MONT. Test. Brit. p. 116 (chiefly).—Linn. Trans. vol. viii. p. 87, pl. 3, f. 1.—Dorset Catalog. p. 35, pl. 8, f. 5.—TURT. Conch. Diction. p. 241.—BORN, Mus. Cæs. Vind. pl. 5, f. 9.—CHEMN. Conch. Cab. vol. vii. p. 18 (partly), pl. 38, f. 404.—POLI, Test. Sicil. pl. 21, f. 9, 10, 11.—DILLW. Recent Shells, vol. i. p. 195 (partly).—Index Testaceol. pl. 8, f. 33.—BLAINV. Manuel Malacol. pl. 74, f. 2.

Pectunculus capillaceus, DA COSTA, Brit. Conch. p. 187, pl. 12, f. 5.

Cytherea exoleta, LAM. Anim. s. Vert. (ed Desh.) vol. vi. p. 314.—TURT. Dithyra Brit. p. 162, pl. 8, f. 7, and (as *sinuata*) pl. 10, f. 10, 11.—FLEM. Brit. Anim. p. 445.—MACGILLIV. Moll. Aberd. p. 262.—Brit. Marine Conch. p. 84.—PHILIPPI, Moll. Sicil. vol. i. p. 41, and vol. ii. p. 32.—HANL. Recent Shells, p. 102.

Arthemis exoleta, DESH. Elem. Conch. pl. 20, f. 9, 10, 11.—PHILIPPI, Neu. Conch. vol. i. p. 171.

Artemis exoleta, FORBES, Malac. Monensis, p. 51.—BROWN, Ill. Conch. G. B. p. 92, pl. 36, f. 1, 3.

The shape is suborbicular, but with a slight tendency to squareness; the length is more usually (but not invariably) slightly superior to the breadth. The valves, which are opaque, solid, occasionally ponderous, and, when adult, almost entirely devoid of lustre, are probably, although not vieing in this respect with the succeeding species, rather above than below the average convexity of this genus, being subventricose; they are decidedly inequilateral, the hinder side being nearly twice as long as the front one. The external surface, which is never of a pure white, is of a pale cream colour, almost invariably adorned with livid red

markings, either disposed in linear zigzags (more rarely
clouded ones), or in numerous narrow rays (which are generally rather interrupted), or in two or three broad (and
usually continuous) ones. The irregularity of the concentric striæ, by which it is roughened, and the strongly
marked lines of increase give it a very coarse and subimbricated appearance ; the closely set interstitial spaces look,
when magnified, like large and elevated striæ. There is
no radiating sculpture whatsoever, nor are the striæ-like
lines raised into lamellæ at their extremities or elsewhere.
The ventral margin is moderately arcuated, and has a tendency to rise rather the more anteriorward. The declination of the dorsal edges is remarkably trifling ; the front
one is extremely short, and, from the peculiarity of the
lunule, appears deeply incurved, although when examined
internally its outline is actually a little convex ; the hinder
one, which is very manifestly the higher margin, is at first
subrectilinear and scarcely sloping, increasing afterwards in
convexity and declivity, its termination, except in aged individuals, is usually above or on a par with the level of that
of the anterior dorsal. Both upper corners are slightly
angulated, both lower ones are thoroughly rounded. The
posterior side is decidedly the broader ; its edge, as well as
that of the anterior extremity, is at its upper part rather
perpendicular and not greatly curved. The umbones are
not very prominent ; and the beaks, which are acute, distinct, and not coloured, turn very considerably forward ; in
front of them is a very deeply impressed heart-shaped
lunule, which is not abbreviated in shape, is almost invariably coloured, and whose lips are almost always more
or less pouting. The sunken ligament is almost entirely
concealed ; there is neither a flattening nor the slightest
excavation of the posterior dorsal surface. The interior is

pure white, but rarely, if ever, glossy, except towards the margin, which is more or less flexuous, and is destitute of all crenation. The hinge margin is moderately but not peculiarly broad.

The length of a fair-sized individual when measured was an inch and seven-eighths, its breadth was an inch and three-quarters.

This common, though rather handsome shell, inhabits sandy ground in various depths, from low-water mark to seventy or eighty fathoms all round our coasts. Among its numerous localities, we may mention Guernsey (S. H.); Littlehampton, Sussex (Strickland); Exmouth (Clark); Penzance, in twenty fathoms, and Scilly Isles (M'Andrew); Bristol Channel (Jeffreys); Caernarvon Bay, in twelve fathoms (M'Andrew); Mochruss (Eyton); Isle of Man, in twelve to twenty-five fathoms (E.F.); Scarborough (Bean); Northumberland (Alder); Clyde (Smith); Hebrides (E. F.); in fifty, seventy, and eighty fathoms around Zetland, also, in from four to seven fathoms on the same coasts (M'Andrew and E. F.); Orkneys (Thomas); East coast of Scotland; plentiful in seven fathoms, Frith of Forth (E. F.); "all round the Irish coast in suitable localities" (W. Thompson). There is a marked difference in the aspect of most specimens of this species found on the western coasts as compared with the majority of those from the eastern.

Artemis exoleta ranges throughout the European seas, and is fossil in pleistocene formations.

A. LINCTA, Pulteney.

Striæ extremely delicate and most closely disposed ; surface not rayed or variegated ; hinder dorsal edge curved and moderately sloping ; posterior dorsal area flattened.

Plate XXVIII. Fig. 5, 6.

LISTER, Hist. Conch. pl. 290, f. 126.

Venus lincta, PULTENEY, Hutchins, Dorset, p. 34.

Venus exoleta, PENN. Brit. Zool. ed. 4, vol. iv. p. 94, pl. 56, f. 49.

"   "   *Var.* Linn. Trans. vol. viii. p. 87, pl. 3, f. 2.—Dorset Catalog. p. 35, pl. 1, f. 13.

Venus sinuata, TURT. Conch. Diction. p. 242.

Cytherea lincta, LAM. Anim. a. Vert. (ed. Desh.) vol. vi. p. 315.—FLEM. Brit. Anim. p. 445.—MACGILLIV. Moll. Aberd. p. 262.—Brit. Marine Conch. p. 84.—HANL. Recent Shells, vol. i. p. 102.

Cytherea sinuata, TURTON, Dithyra Brit. p. 165 (not var. nor figure).

Arthemis lincta, DESHAYES, Elem. Conch. pl. 20, f. 12, 13.—BROWN, Ill. Conch. G. B. p. 92, pl. 56, f. 2, 4.—PHILIPPI, Neu. Conch. (not Cytherea lincta of Moll. Sicil.) vol i. p. 171.

The contour of this shell is suborbicular as, indeed, is more or less the case in every *Artemis,* and the breadth of the adult habitually, but not invariably, exceeds the length. The valves are opaque, more or less strong, and ventricose or subventricose when mature, their profundity rapidly decreasing from the centre. The surface is more or less glossy, of an uniform soiled ivory white (occasionally tinged with livid brown, or with the umbones richly stained with orange), and is never rayed or variegated with coloured markings. The concentric striæ which form its sole sculpture, there being neither lateral lamellæ, nor radiating lines, are most closely and delicately engraved, and, by slightly widening at each extremity, convert their interstices into fine elevated and crowdedly-arranged striæ. The ventral margin is much arcuated, ascending in an uninterrupted sweep on either side to the dorsal edges, so that

the lower corners of the shell are perfectly free from angulation.   The dorsal edge, whose declination exceeds that of
exoleta, is in front short, rather strongly sloping, and with
its general inclination, though not its actual outline, incurved ; behind it is far more elevated, curved, and ranges
from very moderately to decidedly sloping.   There is a
manifest, although slight, flattening (but no excavation) of
the hinder dorsal surface.

Both sides are somewhat angulated above, and are
rounded below ; the front and hinder edges are more or less
convex.   The ligament, though plainly visible, is sunken ;
the umbones are very prominent, and bend considerably
forward ; in front of them is a large heart-shaped deeply
impressed lunule, with pouting lips, which is rarely if ever
stained with any colouring matter.   The beaks are very
acute, and rarely adorned with painting different from that
of the umbones ; but in a scarce northern variety are
purple.   The interior is of an uniform white, and is for
the most part devoid of lustre ; its margin, which is very
slightly flexuous, is perfectly free from crenation.

This species never attains to the dimensions of the preceding, its diameter rarely measuring an inch and a third.
From the greater declination of the dorsal lines the
adult shell appears to taper in some degree towards the
umbones.   The exquisite delicacy and crowded disposition
of its concentric lines, the absence of coloured markings,
and the flattening of the hinder dorsal surface, enable us
with facility to distinguish it from *exoleta*.

The *Artemis lincta* is nearly equally common with its
British congener, though not always occurring in the same
localities.   It has as great a range in depth, extending
from near low-water mark in some places to as deep
as sixty fathoms in others.   As instances of its distribu-

tion, may be mentioned Exmouth (Clark); Penzance, in
twenty fathoms, and Plymouth in twenty-five (M‘An-
drew and E. F.); Torbay and Falmouth (S. H. and
Alder); Scarborough (Bean); Northumberland (Alder);
Irish Sea (E. F.); Hebrides, as at Skye, in from seven-
teen to forty fathoms (M‘Andrew and E. F.); Clyde
(Smith); St. Magnus Bay, Zetland, in sixty fathoms;
Balta Sound, in from five to ten fathoms; also in the
Moray Frith, fifteen fathoms (M‘Andrew); in sand at low-
water, and also in thirty-five and forty fathoms, Orkneys
(Thomas); Aberdeenshire (Macgillivray); St. Andrews
(Knapp); Frith of Forth (E. F.); "general, around
Ireland in suitable localities" (W. Thompson); Bantry
Bay in fifteen fathoms, and off Cape Clear in sixty fathoms
(M‘Andrew); Birterbuy Bay, Connemara (Barlee).

This species ranges throughout the Celtic and southern
regions of the European seas.   Mr. Alder remarks, from a
comparison of specimens, that the *Artemis compta* of Löven
is identical with one of our British varieties of it. As a
fossil it occurs in both red and coralline crags.

LUCINOPSIS, Forbes and Hanley.

Shell more or less orbicular, rather thin, equivalve
slightly inequilateral, closed; surface smoothish or concentrically striated; inner margins entire; muscular impressions oblong or suborbicular, nearly equal; pallial sinus
wide, deep, central, obtuse. Hinge composed of two diverging primary teeth, one of which is bifid, in the right
valve, and three, the central one bifid, in the left. Ligament external, prominent, rather long; no defined lunule.

Animal suborbicular, its mantle freely open, the margins
entire. Siphonal tubes short, diverging, separate, the

branchial with its orifice fringed, the anal simple.   Foot
lanceolate.   Labial palps small, triangular.

We have constituted this genus for the reception of the
Venus undata of authors, a shell which has been now placed
in one group, now in another, as the inclinations of the
systematist may have directed, but always with a doubt
respecting its true position.   Presenting the external appearance of a *Lucina*, whilst its internal structure linked it
more closely with *Venus* and its allies, it had become a
sort of conchological puzzle, and yet, though many a shell
with fewer claims to distinction had been elevated to the
rank of a generic type, distrust respecting its true nature
seems to have prevented this one enjoying such an honour.
The deep pallial sinus should have shewn those who associated it with the *Lucinidæ* that it had no place in that
family.   Its evident affinities were with the *Venus* tribe,
but from *Venus* proper and equally from *Cytherea* and *Pullastra* marked features of dentition or margin, independent
of peculiarity of habit, separated it.   With *Artemis* it had
more connection, chiefly, however, in external aspect, for its
hinge and pallial sinus are very different.   The discovery of
the animal has shewn that its peculiarities indicate essential
differences in the organization also, and that the characters
of its foot, mantle, and siphon, are such as to place its
claim to generic rank beyond a question.   It seems to have
considerable affinity with the fossil genus *Thetis*, in which,
however, the pallial sinus is lanceolate and prolonged almost to the beaks, whilst the external surface is curiously
punctated.

L. UNDATA, Pennant.

Plate XXVIII. fig. 1, 2, and (Animal) plate M. fig. 2.

Venus undata, PENN. Brit. Zool. ed. 4, vol. iv. p. 95, pl. 55, f. 51.—MONT.
Test. Brit. p. 117.—DONOV. Brit. Shells, vol. iv, pl. 121.—Linn.
Trans. vol. viii. p. 86.—TURT. Conch. Diction. p. 241, f. 54.—
FLEM. Brit. Anim. p. 448.—DILWYN, Recent Shells, vol. i. p.
197.—Index Testaceol. pl. 8, f. 87.—PHILIPPI, Moll. Sicil. vol.
ii. p. 34.

Venus sinuosa, (monstrosity,) PENN. Brit. Zool. ed. 4, vol. iv. p. 95, pl. 55, f.
51 A.—MONT. Test. Brit. p. 120.—Linn. Trans. vol. viii. p. 90.

Lucina undata, TURT. Dithyra Brit. p. 115.—Brit. Marine Conch. p. 73.—
BROWN, Ill. Conch. G. B. p. 98, pl. 39, f. 1, 2.—LAM. Anim.
s. Vert. (ed. Desh.) vol. vi. p. 229.—HANL. Recent Shells, p. 76.

Venus incompta. PHILIPPI, Moll. Sicil. vol. i. p. 44, pl. 4. f. 9.

Cytherea undata, MACGILLIV. Moll. Aberd. p. 263.

Artemis undata, ALDER, Cat. Northumberl. and Durham Moll. p. 84.

The shape of this inelegant but peculiar shell, is suborbicular, with a slight tendency to squareness. The valves which are subventricose rather above the middle, become depressed towards the lower margin, and lessen in convexity almost equally on either side; their surface, however, is not evenly curved, appearing somewhat angulated owing to the slight flattening from the umbonal region downwards, and a similar one at the posterior side. They are opaque, brittle, more or less glossy, not very solid, and of a paler or deeper fawn colour, irregularly wrinkled in a concentric direction with very numerous and extremely fine lines, and occasionally marked here and there with concentric very shallow somewhat pliciform indentations. There is no other sculpture or division of surface whatsoever. The ventral margin is not very convex, and usually rises rather the more in front; the anterior dorsal edge is more or less retuse, and rather strongly sloping; the hinder dorsal edge is almost straight, and scarcely declining. The anterior side is very much the smaller, being hardly more than half the size of the posterior, its extremity is rather narrowed, and is rounded both above and below. The hinder termination is broad and sub-biangulated ; the posterior margin being somewhat straightened in the middle, and its inclination almost perpendicular, though slightly bending forward inferiorly. The umbones are rather swollen and prominent ; the beaks acute and incurved ; in front of them is a dorsal depression, but no defined lunule. The ligament is large and broad, but not at all projecting ; there is no excavation or depression of the hinder dorsal surface. The interior is white, the margin acute, entire, and decidedly flexuous. The hinge, considering the fragility of the valves, is rather strong, and consists in the right valve of two divergent primary teeth, of which the hinder is bifid, and the front one simple ; and in the left valve of three divergent cardinal ones, of which the central is much the largest, and very profoundly bifid, or rather reversed V-shaped, and the others simple and extremely narrow. The pallial sinus is very large, and runs slightly obliquely into the middle of the disk.

The average breadth does not much exceed an inch and a quarter, and the length is slightly superior. Although there is no difficulty in procuring dead examples of this interesting shell, we seldom meet with it in the living state, probably owing to the nature of the localities in which it buries itself. During the winter season it is occasionally thrown alive on the shore by storms, but is rarely so taken in the dredge. Only very recently have we been able, after many endeavours, both of our own and of numerous indefatigable friends, to obtain sufficient information respecting its animal constructor—one of the many obligations we owe to our invaluable correspondent Mr. Clark.

By that gentleman we have been furnished with the accompanying description and sketch.—Animal lentiform, subcompressed, mantle open, margin plain, produced posteriorly into two short siphonal tubes, separate from their bases and divergent. The branchial one is conical, pale yellow, with sulphur-coloured, flaky, irregular, subrotund blotches, marked with short dark lines around the orifice, giving it the appearance of a minute fringe; from this circle spring about fourteen rather long white cirrhi. The anal tube is also conical, shorter than the branchial, bluish hyaline, and quite plain at the orifice; these tubes are never protruded more than one-sixth of an inch, at least in the specimens examined, and are very delicate to external view, but on opening the animal they appear long, strong, cylindrical, corrugated, of the same length, lying parallel to each other at nearly the middle of the shell in the large vertical sinus in the mantle. The body is very small, pale brown, with a moderately long hyaline lanceolate foot attached to it. On each side the body is a pair of suboval almost hyaline branchiæ, the upper the smallest, most delicately pectinated; also small triangular palps more strongly striated, but of the same hyaline character.

Lucinopsis undata inhabits sandy ground, from a very few fathoms to as deep as eighty fathoms, rarely plentiful any where, though very generally distributed around the coast. Among localities may be mentioned Exmouth (Clark); Southampton (Jeffreys); Weymouth in seven fathoms, and Dartmouth in twenty-seven fathoms (M'Andrew and E. F.); British Channel (Jeffreys); Isle of Man in twelve to twenty fathoms (E. F.); Scarborough (Bean); Northumbrian coast, in deepish water (Alder); on the edge of the Dogger bank, sixty miles east off Sunderland in fifty fathoms water (King); Sana Island in forty fathoms

(Hyndman); Hebrides (Jeffreys); west of Zetland in
from four to seven fathoms (M'Andrew and E. F.);
Orkneys in fifteen fathoms, and almost littoral (Thomas);
Aberdeenshire in deep water, and cast on the beach (Macgillivray); St. Andrews and Frith of Forth (E. F.); all
round the Irish coast in suitable localities (W. Thompson);
in from three to ten fathoms, Killiries (E. F., R. Ball,
and W. T.); off Cape Clear alive in thirty fathoms
(M'Andrew).

Abroad it ranges from the shores of Norway to the
Ægean. It is a pleistocene fossil.

CYPRINIDÆ.

In the arrangements of the older conchologists many shells were associated with *Venus* which, though they bore a near resemblance to the true members of that group, so far as external aspect and characters of dentition went, presented an unsinuated pallial impression, thereby indicating a very differently formed animal. Among these were the shells out of which the genera *Cyprina* and *Astarte* were constituted. We associate with them in one family the *Venus minima* of Montagu, and the *Isocardia cor*.

The members of this family have substantial shells, often thick and heavy, almost always strong in proportion to their size, and frequently invested with a strongly-developed epidermis; some of them are very brilliantly coloured, others dull and dusky. Their surface is either smooth, or nearly so, or, if sculptured, marked with concentric striæ or furrows. The greater or less prominence and direction of the beaks, and the presence or absence of a lunule, are variable characters, and serve to distinguish the genera. The hinge has strongly developed cardinal teeth, and the ligament is well formed and external. The pallial impression is either quite entire, or presents only the slightest indication of a sinus. This depends on the peculiar feature in the organization of the animal, which has, instead of distinct and produced siphonal tubes, only rudimentary ones in the shape of two scarcely separated orifices. The foot is thick and linguiform, resembling that of the *Veneridæ*.

Whilst the last family appears to have increased in numbers upwards in time, until its maximum was attained in existing seas, this seems to have been chiefly developed during past epochs, and to be now in progress of diminution. The two groups may be regarded as to a certain extent successive in time.

M. Alcide d'Orbigny styles this family *Astartidæ*, and gives as prominent characters the absence of a distinct buccal siphon, and the shortness of the foot, both of which do not apply to any of the animals of the group examined by us. In the last arrangement by Mr. J. E. Gray, *Circe* is placed in one division of the *Veneridæ*, *Cyprina* in another, whilst *Astarte* and *Isocardia* form part of distinct families in a separate order from that to which the *Veneridæ* themselves are assigned. It would be interesting to know upon what principle so curious a disposition of these genera has been proposed.

CYPRINA, Lamarck.

Shell more or less suborbicular, solid, equivalve, closed, smooth, or concentrically striated, invested with an epidermis; beaks prominent, incurved; no lunule; margins smooth. Hinge composed of a lateral tooth, and three or four primaries in one valve, and of three primaries only in the other. Ligament well developed, conspicuous; pallial impression simple, muscular impressions oval.

Animal suborbicular; its mantle freely open, with plain or serrated edges. Siphonal orifices sessile, or nearly so, their margins fringed, the branchial largest. Foot large, linguiform; labial palps moderately long, triangular.

The *Cyprinæ* live in gravelly sand or mud, and are not remarkable for beauty, though often of considerable size. They are chiefly found in moderately deep water. Anciently they were much more abundant than now, and within our own area several well marked species lived at the commencement of the cretaceous epoch, apparently having similar habits with their existing congeners. The absence of the pallial sinus in the casts serves readily to distinguish between fossil species of *Cyprina* and *Venus* otherwise very nearly alike.

C. ISLANDICA, Linnæus.

Plate XXIX, and (animal) Plate M. Fig. 4.

Venus Islandica, LINN. Syst. Nat. ed. 12, p. 1131 (not of O. Fabr. Fauna Groenlandica, p. 411).—PULTENEY, Hutchins, Dorset p. 33.—DONOV. Brit. Shells, vol. iii. pl. 77.—MONT. Test. Brit. p. 114.—LINN. Trans. vol. viii. p. 83.—Dorset Catalog. p. 35, pl. 6, f. 5.—TURT. Conch. Diction. p. 238.—CHEMN. Conch. Cab. vol. vi. p. 340, pl. 32, f. 341, 342.— MULLER, Zool. Dan. pl. 28.—DILLW. Recent Shells, vol. i. p. 176.—Index Testaceolog. pl. 7, f. 41.

Venus mercenaria, (not of Linn.) PENN. Brit. Zool. ed. 4, vol. iv. p. 94, pl. 53, f. 47.

Pectunculus crassus, DA COSTA, Brit. Conch. p. 183, pl. 14, f. 5.

Cyprina Islandica, LAM. Anim. s. Vert. (ed. Desh.) vol. vi. p. 290.—TURT. Dithyra Brit. p. 135.—FLEM. Brit. Anim. p. 443. — MACGILLIV. Moll. Aberd. p. 257.—Brit. Marine Conch. p. 81.—CROUCH, Introd. Conch. pl. 7, f. 2.—BLAINV. Man. Malacol. pl. 70, bis, f. 5.—DESHAYES, Elem. Conch. pl. 18, f. 8, 9, 10.—GOULD, Invert. Massach. p. 82.—HANL. Recent Shells, vol. i. p. 95.

Cyprina vulgaris, SOWERBY, Genera Shells.—BROWN, Ill. Conch. G. B. p. 93, pl. 37, f. 1, and pl. 38, f. 11.—Sow. Conch. Manual, f. 116.—REEVE, Conchol. Systemat. pl. 65.

Cyprina d'Islande, CHENU, Traité Elem. p. 68, f. 243 (hinge).

The general form is suborbicular and somewhat heart-shaped; the valves are solid, often ponderous, moderately inequilateral, and ventricose; the convexity being chiefly

manifest upon the umbonal region, and diminishing more
rapidly and decidedly in front than behind. The surface,
which is of a reddish white, although neither striated nor
grooved, is not smooth, being more or less wrinkled irregularly in a concentric direction. Very fine and crowded
concentric wrinkles are also visible upon the thick epidermis which covers the entire exterior, and is of an uniform
more or less glossy fawn colour, becoming of a pitchy hue
in aged individuals. The ventral margin, which is internally simple and acute, is well arcuated throughout, and
ascends rather the more upon the anterior side. The front
dorsal edge, which at first subretuse, becomes eventually
convex or even arcuated, declines but moderately, not quite
rivalling the upward slope of the opposite lower margin.
The declination of the hinder dorsal edge is rather trifling
in the adult, but is proportionately more considerable in the
young ; this edge is much the more elevated, and excepting towards its termination is almost straight. The anterior extremity is narrow, and rounded both above and
below ; the posterior extremity is broad, and obtusely
rounded, or sometimes obsoletely sub-biangulated, the
lower angle being rounded off, and the upper being very
obscure, and often almost obsolete ; the middle of the posterior edge is, however, not unfrequently (especially in the
young) straight and perpendicular, which is the chief cause
of the slight angularity of that side of the shell. The umbones are situated at about two-fifths the distance from the
commencement of the shell ; they are swollen, rather prominent, and incline forward ; the beaks are acute, much
inflected, and not preceded by any lunule, the area in front
of them is, however, much depressed. The ligament though
ample is not particularly projecting. The interior is of an
uniform chalky white, and is almost totally devoid of lustre.

The hinge-margin is moderately broad, and is furnished in the right valve in addition to its remote, and not much projecting posterior lateral lamina, with four primary teeth, of which the hinder is very oblique, acutely edged, and much shelving anteriorward, the two middle are simple (not bifid), and do not extend to the extreme margin, whilst the fourth, which is a mere denticle, is adjacent to the interior edge, and looks rather like a somewhat divergent interrupted continuation of the preceding one, than a distinct and separate tooth.

In the left valve there is no lateral tooth, and of the three primary ones, the front is short and rather divergent, the middle one, which is nearer to the former than to the succeeding, is long and bifid, and the posterior is produced oblique and very narrow.

The Iceland specimens which have been held distinct by one of our most eminent Conchologists, who has consequently reserved the specific name *Islandica* for them alone, appear to us not to differ from the British examples in essentials, but only in such points as are invariably subject to modification through difference of climate. Their form is rounder, their hinder dorsal edge more sloping, and somewhat convex at its extremity, which almost or entirely destroys the slight angularity observable at the hinder termination of our own specimens; their epidermis looser, and of a reddish cast. We know not whether these features be permanent or not in this variety, as it is of rare occurrence in the museums of England. The examples still preserved in the cabinet of Linnæus are exactly identical with our British ones.

This is one of our largest shells, measuring occasionally four inches and a half in breadth, and an inch more in length (Brown); the ordinary size is not, however, beyond three inches and a half long, and about two and a half broad.

The animal, which was long ago figured and described by O. F. Müller, is orbicular and thick; its mantle freely open and finely serrated at the edges. The siphons project a little, their orifices are sessile and quite united, fringed at the margins, and partially so at the sides. They are red, with brownish markings near the openings. The foot is large, thick, and linguiform; both it and the mantle are of a yellowish-white hue. "The branchiæ," according to Mr. Clark, "are pale brown, unequal, coarsely pectinated, the outer leaflets more triangular, and much less than the inner, extending posteriorly to the siphons, and anteriorly to the mouth and labia, of which there are a pair on each side, pectinated, not very long, and of a triangular form, and rather pointed."

The *Cyprina Islandica* is essentially a northern species, although it ranges all round the British shores, and is sufficiently frequent as not to be considered rare in any district. Most commonly it is brought in by the trawlers, but inhabits all depths of water over a sea-bed of sandy mud. It is equally common in the Irish Sea and German Ocean, living in from five to twenty-five fathoms water. On the south it is very frequent off Weymouth (S. H.); and Poole (E. F.); but becomes rare about Devon and Cornwall, though frequent again on the Welsh coast and in the British Channel (Jeffreys). It occurs throughout the Hebrides and off the Zetland Isles, where Mr. M'Andrew has taken it alive in water as deep as seventy and eighty fathoms, forty miles from land, and has procured dead valves in one hundred fathoms water; whilst at Balta Sound in Unst, among the same islands, he found it living in from five to ten fathoms. Lieutenant Thomas states that he takes it among the Orkneys in all depths, and quite as large in seven as in forty fathoms. We have gathered it exposed alive at very low tides in the Frith of Forth. On the Irish coast it inhabits the northern, eastern, and southern shores, occurring on the first in from five to twenty-five fathoms (Thompson); and on the last as deep as sixty (M'Andrew).

The peculiarities of its distribution are very interesting, as this is one of the Mollusca common to European and North American seas, and a member of the faunas of all the crags. The remarkably wide bathymetrical range of so large a shell indicates a capacity for enduring many changes of conditions which illustrates strikingly the cause of its great geographical and geological extension. A species so constituted must be expected to present considerable variations, and we cannot admit the separation of its fossil representatives into distinct specific types, as has been done by Professor Agassiz, on account of slight variations in the degrees of their tumidity. Every British sea-going collector knows how variable living specimens are in this respect. Even Agassiz himself, however, though he endeavoured with earnest good-will to draw a line between the fossil specimens from the Clyde glacial beds and living examples, could not do it. The hair was too fine to split. During the glacial epoch this and a few other boreal Mollusks had extended their range to the Mediterranean, whence they have long disappeared, though their remains are preserved in the upheaved newer pliocene strata of Sicily.

CIRCE, Schumacher.

Shell more or less subtrigonal, solid, equivalve, closed; surface concentrically striated or grooved; beaks not very prominent; a distinct lunule; margins smooth. Hinge composed in each valve of three primary teeth, and a lateral lamina; ligament external, linear, and much sunken. Pallial impression with scarcely any traces of a sinuation; muscular impressions roundish or oblong.

Animal suborbicular; its mantle freely open, and slightly denticulated at the margin, closing posteriorly to form two siphonal orifices very slightly separated from each other, and scarcely projecting; the branchial one the largest; both fringed with short close-set cirrhi. Foot rather large, geniculated, linguiform. Labial palps long and linear-lanceolate.

We follow Mr. King in referring the *Venus minima* of British authors to the genus *Circe* of Schumacher, though not without doubts of the propriety of the reference. The characters we have given have special reference to our native species, and the features of the animal are now made known for the first time. They connect in a very satisfactory manner this genus with *Cyprina*, and it with *Astarte*. The habits of the species are those of the laminated *Veneres*.

C. minima, Montagu.

Plate XXVI. figs. 4, 5, 6, 8, and (Animal) Plate M. fig. 3.

Venus minima, Mont. Test. Brit. p. 121, pl. 3, f. 3.—Linn. Trans. vol. viii. p. 81.—Turt. Conch. Diction. p. 236.—Dillw. Recent Shells, vol. i. p. 166.—Index Testaceolog. pl. 7, f. 17.

Venus triangularis, Mont. Test. Brit. p. 577.—Linn. Trans. vol. viii. p. 83.—Turt. Conch. Diction. p. 238.—Index Testaceolog. pl. 7, f. 35.

Cyprina minima, Turt. Dithyra Brit. p. 137.—Flem. Brit. Anim. p. 444.—
          Brit. Marine Conch. p. 82, f. 102.—Hanl. Recent Shells,
          vol. i. p. 95.

Cyprina triangularis, Turt. Dithyra Brit. p. 136, pl. 11, f. 19, 20.—Flem.
          Brit. Anim. p. 444.—Brit. Marine Conch. p. 82.—Hanl.
          Recent Shells, vol. i. p. 95.

Cytherea triangularis, Macgilliv. Moll. Aberd. p. 268.

Cytherea apicalis, Philippi, Moll. Sicil. vol. i. p. 40, pl. 4, f. 5.

Circe triangularis, King, Ann. Nat. Hist. vol. xv. p. 112.

Cytherea Cyrilli, Philippi, Moll. Sicil. vol. ii. p. 32.—Hanl. Recent Shells,
          suppl. pl. 15, f. 26.

Cytherea minima, Brown, Ill. Conch. G. B. p. 92, pl. 37, f. 3.

Cytherea minuta, Brown, Ill. Conch. G. B. p. 92, pl. 37, f. 4.

Montagu having first established his *Venus minima* from
the young of the more rounded variety, subsequently
founded his *V. triangularis* upon the aberrant colourless
triangular form which is chiefly obtained in our more
northern waters. The subsequent discovery of intermediate examples has compelled us to unite these two shells.

The shape is rounded subtrigonal, and the valves are
solid, opaque, glossy, typically somewhat compressed, but
occasionally even subventricose; the convexity is about
equal on either side. The exterior of the shell, which is
not greatly inequilateral, is covered with broad and rather
unsymmetrical concentric grooves, which are disposed at
moderate distances from each other; their interstices in
certain examples assume the appearance of depressed concentric costellæ. The colouring is infinite in diversity;
sometimes the external surface is pure and unmixed white,
more frequently, however, the exterior is variegated with
larger or smaller pyramidal spots of a livid red, arranged
in one or two subcentral rays (which rarely commence at
the umbones); sometimes, too, these spots are squarish or
amorphous and very distant. One variety is of an uniform
pale livid lilac, another is entirely of a rich roseate flesh-
colour, another subradiatingly mottled with livid or brown-

ish flesh-colour. The variety of painting is indeed great; one of the prettiest consists of a delicate network of brown lines upon a white ground. The ventral margin which rises much more behind, where it slopes uninterruptedly without angulation to the dorsal edge (with which it forms a more or less distinct angle), is not particularly arcuated in the middle. Both dorsal margins are elongated, the front one, which is always the more sloping, is straight, the hinder one barely convex; in extent of declination they vary much, but always observe their relative proportion, the front slope being sometimes abrupt, and the hinder very decided, in which case the contour is almost triangular; when, on the contrary, the front slope is only moderate, and the hinder one rather slight, the contour then approaches a rounded oval. The anterior side, which although the shorter is often not greatly so, is subangulated below, the angle being rounded off; the most projecting part of the hinder termination is above the middle. The umbones are prominent, and lean a little forward; the beaks, which are very acute and obliquely inflected, are preceded by a large lunule of an elongated heartshape, which is not sunken, but defined by a groove. The hinder dorsal area is neither peculiarly flattened nor excavated; the ligament is either totally concealed or linear and sunken. The interior is white, or tinged with flesh colour on the disk, but never stained with any dark colour upon the hinder side or upon the hinge margin. The hinge is furnished in the left valve with a rather large approximate front lateral lamina, and three divergent primary teeth, of which the anterior one is bifid; in the right valve with three primary ones, the central of which is very indistinctly cloven, and a tooth-like receptacle for the opposite lamina. The inner margin is quite entire.

Fine examples attain to five-eighths of an inch in length, and usually a trifle less in breadth; in the more triangular specimens these proportions are reversed, the breadth a little exceeding the length.

The animal is orbicular and compressed, its texture not very solid. The mantle is freely open, and indistinctly fimbriated or denticulated, white with obscure dots. Posteriorly it projects a little, and is closed to form two siphonal orifices, the branchial much larger than the anal, the margins of each with a close-set fringe of short cirrhi, which are dusky or dotted with brown or red, varying in different examples. The foot is white, linguiform, and geniculated, resembling that of *Venus*. It can be projected to a considerable distance, and when protruded is acute. The branchiæ are yellowish-white, the liver dark brown. The labial palps are long, linear, and pointed. Its habits are rather sluggish.

Until lately the *Circe minima* was regarded as one of our rarest testacea, and specimens were not often to be seen in our collections. Those which Montagu examined were very small and in poor condition. The activity of scientific dredgers, during the last few years, has made it comparatively common; large and beautifully coloured British examples now decorate all our best cabinets. It is, however, still to be respected as one of our scarcer species, for, though plentiful in certain localities, it does not fall within every collector's reach. The largest and most brilliant individuals we know are dredged in about eight fathoms water off St. Peter's Port, in the island of Guernsey (S. H.). On the coast of Cornwall, it was noticed by Montagu, and we have taken it in twenty fathoms off Penzance; on the Welsh coast it is both remarkably abundant and beautiful in ten fathoms in Milford Haven (M'Andrew and E. F.). In

Scotland it is frequent in the Clyde (Smith); and Hebrides (Jeffreys, &c.). At Oban it occurred in fifteen
fathoms; off Mull in twenty; off Skye in twenty-five; and
in forty and fifty fathoms in the Minch (M'Andrew). On
the Zetland shores it lives chiefly in from fifteen to twenty
fathoms, and occurs on the Lingbank, forty miles west
of Zetland, in fifty fathoms (M'Andrew and E. F.).
Lieutenant Thomas takes it among nullipore and broken
shells in fifteen fathoms, Eda Sound, Orkney. Mr.
Thompson communicates the following note on its Irish
range. "I have seen it from the following localities on the
Irish coast, two specimens were dredged from eight to ten
fathoms in Belfast Bay in 1834 by Mr. Hyndman and
myself; Erris in Mayo; Birterbuy Bay (Farran, Barlee) ;
Miltown Malbay (W. H. Harvey); Bantry Bay (Humphreys); Youghal (Miss M. Ball)."

Its distribution on our shores indicates that it is a member of a southern fauna, spreading along our oceanic coasts.
Accordingly, whilst we find it plentiful in the Lusitanian
and Mediterranean regions, it does not range north of
Britain.

ASTARTE, Sowerby.

Shell oblong, suborbicular, or triangular, solid, equivalve
more or less inequilateral, sometimes nearly equilateral,
closed ; surface smooth, or transversely furrowed, and
covered by a conspicuous epidermis. Muscular impressions
ovate, strongly marked ; pallial impression simple, rather
distant from the margin. Hinge composed of two strong
diverging primary teeth in one valve, and a primary tooth
with a lesser supplementary one, which is sometimes
obsolete, in the other. Ligament external, elongated,

usually lodged in a lozenge. Lunule almost always distinct.

Animal of the shape of the shell, and never exceeding it; its mantle freely open, with plain (always!) margins, slightly united posteriorly at two points so as to form two siphonal orifices, both with simple edges. Foot linguiform, strong but not large. Labial tentacles large, lanceolate; leaflets of each pair of branchiæ equal or nearly so.

This genus is of very ancient origin, species of it appearing very far back in time, and abounding during the middle secondary period. The number of living species is inconsiderable as compared with the assemblage of them which existed even within our own limited area during some ancient geological epochs. It is curious to note that whilst at present the predominance of *Astartes* in a collection made at any particular though unknown locality, would lead the conchologist to infer that they had been gathered in an arctic or boreal region, such an inference would, most probably, be incorrect if drawn from a similar assemblage of fossils, for during the oolitic and cretaceous epochs the abundance of *Astartes* was associated with the presence of numerous tropical or subtropical forms of mollusks and zoophytes. In the upper tertiaries, however, an increase in the number of species and individuals of this genus is usually coincident with the advent of boreal or glacial conditions.

The members of this genus have a wide range in depth, but are never, at least in our seas, found littoral. They constitute a favourite food of many fishes of the cod tribe. Many of the species are remarkable for presenting variations in the characters of the inner margin and sculpture which, in neighbouring genera, would be of specific, or

even generic value, though in this, of only individual
importance. Mr. Searles Wood has suggested that the
difference in the margin may indicate sexual distinctions ;
an observation deserving of minute inquiry.

A. Sulcata,* Da Costa.

More or less convex, never elliptical ; ribs occupying the entire surface, not peculiarly close set : lower margin crenated in
the adult.

Plate XXX. fig. 6, (*A. Danmoniensis*) and (Animal) Plate M. fig. 5.

Pectunculus sulcatus, Da Costa, (1778) Brit. Conch. p. 192.
Venus borealis, (in part) Chemn. Conch. Cab. vol. vii. p. 26, pl. 39, f. 413.
  „   *Scotica,* Maton, Linn. Trans. vol. viii. (1807) p. 81, pl. 2, f. 3.—Mont. Test.
              Brit. Suppl. p. 44.—Turt. Conch. Diction. p. 236.—Lam.
              Anim. a. Vert. (ed. Desh.) vol. vi. p. 360.—Dillw. Recent
              Shells, vol. i. p. 167.—Index Testaceologic. pl. 7, f. 20.
  „   *Danmonia,* Mont. Test. Brit. Suppl. (1808) p. 45, pl. 29, f. 4.—Dillw.
              Recent Shells, vol. i. p. 167.—Index Testaceol. pl. 7, f. 21.
Crassina Danmoniensis, Lam. Anim. a. Vert. (ed. Desh.) vol. vi. p. 257.—Brit.
              Marine Conch. p. 80.—Brown, Ill. Conch. G. B. p.
              95, pl. 38, f. 1.—Crouch, Introd. Conch. pl. 6, f. 7.
              —Delessert, Rec. Coquil. pl. 7, f. 1.
Venus sulcata, Turt. Conch. Diction. p. 235.
Crassina Scotica, Turt. Conch. Dithyra Brit. p. 130, pl. 11, f. 3, 4.—Brit. Marine
              Conch. p. 79.—Brown, Ill. Conch. G. B. p. 95, pl. 38, f. 9.
              —Hanl. Recent Shells, vol. i. p. 87.
  „   *sulcata,* Turt. Conch. Dithyra Brit. p. 131, pl. 11, f. 1, 2.—Hanl.
              Recent Shells, vol. i. p. 87.
Astarte Scotica, Flem. Brit. Anim. p. 440.—Macgill. Moll. Aberd. p. 258.—
              Philippi, Neuer Conch. vol. ii. p. 56, Astarte, pl. 1, f. 3.—
              Loven, Index Moll. Skandinav. p. 36.
  „   *Danmoniensis,* Sowerby, Genera Shells, Astarte, f. 1, 2, 3.—Flem. Brit.
              Anim. p. 440.—Macg. Moll. Aberd. p. 258.—Reeve,
              Conch. Systemat. pl. 66, f. 1, 2, 3.—Sowerb. Conch.
              Man. f. 110.
  „   *sulcata,* Macgilliv. Moll. Aberd. p. 250.—Brit. Marine Conch. p. 247.—
              Phil. Neuer Conch. Astarte, vol. ii. p. 56, pl. 1, f. 4.
Crassine crassatellée, Chenu, Traité Elem. f. 232, 233.

---

* Da Costa's name has been preferred, not so much for its priority, as that,
through its adoption, we are enabled to include under one epithet both *Scotica*
and the subsequent *Danmoniensis*.

The union of *A. Scotica* with *A. Danmoniensis* may excite some little surprise and hesitation among naturalists, and, indeed, was only acceded to by ourselves after a protracted scrutiny, and the examination of some hundreds of specimens assembled from the widest range of localities. In no respect did individuals of the former differ from those of the latter variety, excepting in the crenulation of the margin, and as specific differs from varietal diversity mainly by the greater number of permanent distinctive characteristics, we cannot separate into two species shells only unlike in the presence or absence of a single feature. With regard to the greater or lesser approximation of the ribs, and their consequent proportion to the interstices, no stress can be laid upon this point, as the more rapid is the growth of the animal, the more remote do these become; thus, in the southern *Astartes*, which are more speedily developed, the ribs are more distant, whilst in the more northern examples, whose progress to maturity is more sluggish, and whose growth is not unfrequently stunted, they are sharper defined, and more closely arranged.

Like most of the *Astartes*, its contour is very variable; it is, however, longer than broad, and more or less sub-triangularly heart-shaped; some northern individuals, however, are so abbreviated in shape that their breadth nearly (but not quite) equals their length, and their form consequently becomes suborbicularly trigonal. The valves are always solid and opaque, more or less convex, at times even ventricose, and are covered with an unpolished cuticle or thick adherent epidermis, which varies in colouring from bright yellow to rufous chestnut; beneath this the surface is whitish, or pale rufous, and concentrically lyrated with from about twenty to thirty more or less elevated ribs, which are almost always, if not invariably,

narrower than their interstices, and are rarely if ever much
depressed or at all broad. They typically cover the entire
surface down to the ventral margin, excepting that they
usually vanish (but not in the young), beyond the ordinary
site of the obsolete umbonal ridge towards its extreme
termination, but are generally visible for about half-way
down that posterior area. Besides these ribs which,
moreover, continue *quite* down to the ventral margin,
which is always more or less convex, and at times (when
the declination of the dorsal edges is more than ordinarily
strong), is even arcuated, there is no sculpture. The
sides are unequal, but for the genus not particularly so, the
beaks, which are acute, prominent, and a little inclined,
being situated about one-fifth, at most, before the middle of
the dorsal edge. This latter is concave and greatly sloping
in front from the deep excavation of the very large lanceolate or ovato-lanceolate lunule, which, as well as the
linear lozenge running nearly the entire length of the
hinder dorsal margin, is perfectly smooth; the hinder edge
is by no means so sloping as the front one, but varies from
slightly to moderately declining. The ligament is small
and yellowish, and is seated in the lozenge of whose length
it only occupies about two-fifths. The anterior extremity
is well rounded; the hinder termination is more or less
bluntly biangulated, and in the young very broadly so. The
interior is usually white, a small northern variety is, however, of a reddish liver colour. The edges are adorned typically in the adult with closely-set bead-like elevations, excepting upon the hinge-margin, which is moderately broad,
and provided in the right valve, with a solid central simple
triangular tooth, which shelves inwards, the highest point
not being, as in most shells, at its lower end, but midway from the base of the margin; in the other valve a

similarly shelving, but narrower, simple tooth, diverges on
either side of the receptional cavity for the opposite tooth.
The elevation of the outer sides of the dental pits, in
the right valve, at times induces the surmise of there being
three teeth in one valve.

The size of the largest of the very numerous examples
which have furnished the materials for our description, is
an inch and three-eighths in length, by an inch and
one-eighth in breadth. With regard to crenation of edge, a
character which is typically proper to this species, it is
absent from immature shells, and such as have the edges
acute from a new costa being scarcely or not yet commenced; almost all which terminate ventrally in a fully-
formed rib have the margin thick and beaded.

The animal is more or less tinged with flesh-colour. The
mantle is freely open in front, plain at the margins, and
bordered by a narrow belt of orange. The siphonal openings are quite sessile, and but slightly separated from each
other; their edges are plain, and, like the mantle, bordered with orange. The foot is linguiform, not large in
proportion to the shell, and of a pale flesh or fawn colour.
The visceral mass is variegated with bright rose colour and
dusky green, the former hue appertaining to the reproductive organs, the latter to the liver. The branchiæ are of a
pale yellowish hue. The labial palps are rather large, of a
lanceolato-triangular shape, strongly striated externally,
and of a pale tawny colour. Its habits are sluggish.

Astarte Danmoniensis received its name from the coast of
Devon where, however, though not unfrequently procured
by trawlers, it is not nearly so common as in numerous
other localities. It is very generally distributed round our
coast, living in muddy sand, at various depths, from eight
to eighty fathoms. On the south coast of England, Devon

and Cornwall are its chief habitats (S. H.). On the east
coast, it is taken off Scarborough (Bean); and Northumberland (Alder). On the west, it occurs in the Bristol
Channel (Jeffreys); Milford Haven, in eight to twelve
fathoms, and off Anglesea in twelve fathoms (M'Andrew
and E. F.); the Isle of Man in twelve to twenty-five
fathoms (E. F.). It is abundant throughout the Hebrides,
most plentiful in from fifteen to twenty fathoms water. On
the Zetland coast it is common, and occurs at great depths,
as in seventy fathoms, thirty miles from Noss, and in eighty
fathoms on the west coast (M'Andrew). Along the east
coast of Scotland it is also not unfrequent, and has been
taken in thirty-four fathoms in the Moray Firth. "It is
dredged sparingly in Ireland all along the Antrim coast,
and in Belfast and Strangford Lough from eight to twenty-
five fathoms in sand and mud (Hyndman and W. T.);
Bray (Turton and Brown); rarely obtained at Youghal
and Cork" (W. Thompson). Bantry Bay (Mrs. Puxley).

As a foreign shell it ranges all along the European
coasts, but diminishes in numbers as we proceed southwards from Britain. It is known as a pleistocene fossil,
though very scarce as compared with *elliptica*.

A. CREBRICOSTATA, Forbes.

Concentrically lyrated with very numerous sharply defined
narrow ribs, which become obsolete posteriorly; ventral margin
internally crenated.

Plate XXX. fig. 9.

Astarte crebricostata, FORBES, Annals Nat. Hist. vol. xix. p. 98, pl. 9, f. 4.

The perfect condition in which pleistocene fossils are
found in many of the glacial beds on the coast of Scot-

land, is such that it becomes very difficult to draw a line
between recent and fossil examples of many of our boreal
species. This difficulty is greatly increased when the specimens are procured from a considerable depth of water.
The shell we have now to describe has only been taken in
a state much more ancient to appearance than most of our
pleistocene *Astartes*, yet we prefer describing it as an existing form, on account of the locality in which it was first
procured presenting no traces of the vicinity of pleistocene
strata, and because no fossil examples of it have ever occurred in beds of that age, which having been upheaved,
have undergone close scrutiny. Only odd valves of this
curious species have been taken; these valves are subtriangular, longer than broad, solid, opaque, and rather compressed; they are destitute of any epidermis, are of a dirty
or pale reddish-white colour; look slightly porous, and
feel harsh to the touch. There is not the least appearance
of lustre; and their only sculpture consists of very numerous (at the least thirty) and crowded concentric ribs, which
are sharply defined, extremely narrow, and extend the
entire distance from the beaks to the ventral margin, but
become obsolete upon and beyond the ordinary site of an
umbonal ridge. The interstices are simple, that is to say,
are not traversed by either longitudinal or transverse striæ,
and are for the most part rectangularly grooved out, the
edges of the ribs being usually but little, if at all, shelving.
The sides are unequal, but not particularly so; the hinder,
which is the longer, has its termination somewhat attenuated, and obtusely sub-biangulated, and its tip subrectilinear, or scarcely convex; the front extremity is
rounded, but not symmetrically, as the arch of its lower
portion is far more bowed out than its upper outline. The
declination of the dorsal edge (a character of little value in

Astarte), seems rather considerable, and neither accompanied by much convexity posteriorly, or very marked concavity anteriorly, The curve of the ventral margin is not unfrequently a little depressed towards the middle, but arcuated at each extremity. The umbones are not elevated or prominent, and the beaks when not eroded seem tolerably acute. The lunule is large, not very profoundly excavated, but acutely defined at the edges; the margins of the linear much elongated lozenge appear similarly well defined. None of our specimens exhibit a ligament. The second or posterior primary tooth of the right valve is clearly distinct (it is often rudimentary or obsolete in this genus); the muscular impressions are by no means peculiarly large, but rather the contrary; and the lower internal margins are strongly crenated.

The only British *Astarte* at all akin to *crebricostata*, is *sulcata*, to which it is also allied in being of similar dimensions, no other ribbed species possessing likewise a crenated rim; from this, however, the posterior cessation of its narrower and more crowdedly set costæ, affords a ready mark for discrimination.

The average length of the finer specimens was an inch and one-fifth, their breadth being but little inferior to that measurement.

Some single valves were dredged by Mr. M'Andrew on the west coast of Zetland; and one has since been obtained (Ann. Nat. Hist. 1847, vol. xix. p. 314) by Mr. Jeffreys, in forty fathoms off Croulin Island, the Isle of Skye, where it has also been taken by Mr. M'Andrew.

A. ELLIPTICA, Brown.

Elliptically or ovately suboordate, typically compressed, much produced and obtusely (but not broadly) biangulated behind, covered with a rufous chestnut or olivaceous brown cuticle, concentrically ribbed and striolate ; costæ rounded, more or less depressed, not crowded, as broad as their interstices, either not extending to the ventral margin, or growing obsolete at the lower posterior corner and along the hinder shelving area : inner margins quite entire ; scars large.

Plate XXX. fig. 8.

Crassina ovata, BROWN (not Smith) Edinb. Journal of Natur. and Geogr. Science, vol. i. p. 12, pl. 1, f. 8, 9.—BROWN, Illust. Conch. G. B. p. 96, pl. 38, f. 12, 13.

" *sulcata*, NILSON, (not Maton, Turt. nor Lam.) Nov. Act. Holm. 1822, p. 187, pl. 2, f. 1, 2.

" *elliptica*, HANL. Recent Shells, suppl. pl. 14, f. 36.—Brit. Marine Conch. p. 246, f. 107 (not well).—BROWN, Illust. Conch. G. B. p. 96, pl. 38, f. 3.

Astarte elliptica, MACGILLIV. Moll. Aberd. p. 259.

" *semisulcata*, (not of Leach) MÜLLER, Ind. Moll. Gröen (from type).—PHILIPPI, Neuer Conch. vol. ii. p. 57, Astarte, pl. 1, f. 10. —LOVEN, Ind. Moll. Skandin. p. 37 (from type).

Although to determine by the pen the exact limits between this and the preceding species demands a certain prolixity of diagnosis, the eye most readily discriminates them when mingled together. For no difficulty can occur in separating the fully developed shells, as the inner margins are so widely at variance; and if we compare the immature *sulcata* with the present shell in any stage of growth, we shall find the ribs of the former most sharply defined, and not at all obsolete towards the posterior corner or at the ventral margin, whilst those of the latter (and particularly in the young) are depressed and obsolete at one or both of those areas.

The typical form is elliptically heart-shaped, but the abbreviated variety is ovate-cordiform, and most closely

resembles that of *sulcata*. The valves are usually compressed (more rarely convex), not heavy, and only moderately solid, opaque, and covered with a rufous or, less
commonly, olivaceous brown cuticle, becoming fulvous upon
the umbones, beneath which the surface, as well as the interior, is of a more or less squalid white. The more or
less depressed and rounded ribs, which traverse the shell
concentrically, and are usually at least as broad as their
interstices, yet not very closely arranged, generally grow
faint or utterly vanish towards the ventral margin, and
always cease, excepting those in immediate proximity to
the beaks, beyond the site of the obsolete umbonal ridge.
The concentric striulæ, which are only occasionally met
with in *sulcata*, are here permanently characteristic, and
pervade the ribs as well as the interstices. The ventral margin is convex or subarcuated ; the front dorsal edge
concave, and decidedly sloping, but varying in intensity of
curve and declination ; the slope of the hinder dorsal edge,
whose convexity is by no means strong, is trifling or very
moderate. The beaks which are inclined, tolerably acute,
and not very prominent, are situated at about one-third the
distance from the rounded anterior extremity to the obtusely and not broadly, biangulated termination of the posterior side. The lunule, lozenge, hinge, and ligament, are
similar to those of the preceding species ; the two first are
perhaps more deeply excavated, and the last darker and
possibly larger. The inner surface of the margins is entirely free from crenulation, even in the most aged examples. The muscular impressions are nearly double the
size of those of *sulcata*. The dimensions of rather a
large specimen are an inch and a quarter in length, by
eight-ninths of an inch in breadth.

This shell appears to be almost wholly confined on our

shores to the coast of Scotland, where we have often taken
it, mixed with *sulcata*, but in far less abundance. It
is, however, not uncommon in mud at from five to ten
fathoms in depth, and has been dredged at Oban, Loch
Carron, Ullapool, Lerwick, Loch Gair, Stornoway, and
Skye, (M'Andrew, Jeffreys, and Barlee.) It was first
" discovered near Helensburgh, mouth of the Clyde, by H.
Witham, Esq., where it appears to be not uncommon."
(Brown.) The earlier specimens which found their way
into collections, were chiefly collected by Mr. W. Nicol, and
distributed under the MS. name of *Gairensis*. It ranges
from ten to forty fathoms, usually on a muddy bottom. It
occurs also on the north-east coast of Scotland (Macgillivray), where it has been dredged by Lieut. Thomas in
thirty-five fathoms water. Mr. Alder states that the
Rev. G. C. Abbes has met with valves evidently recent on
the coast of Northumberland. It ranges to the shores of
Finmark and Greenland, and is one of the most abundant
of pleistocene fossils.

A. ARCTICA, Gray.

Decidedly inequilateral, subcordate, very solid, almost smooth,
or only obsoletely sulcated, and never costellated (except slightly
at the beaks) ; epidermis chestnut coloured, fibrous at the base ;
ligament half the length of the lozenge : lower margin arcuated
and entire.

Plate XXX. fig. 7.

Venus borealis (not of Linn.), CHEMN. Conch. Cab. vol. vii. pl. 39, f. 412, (fide
  Lovén).
  „ *compressa*, Mont. Test. Brit. Suppl. (not desc.) pl. 26, lower f. l, l.
Crassina arctica, GRAY, Appendix to Parry's Voyage (from types).—HANL.
  Recent Shells, vol. i. p. 88.
  „ *borealis*, NILSON, Nov. Act. Holm. 1822, p. 188, pl. 2, f. 3, 4.
Astarte Cyprinoides, DUVAL, Revue Zoolog. Cuv. Soc. 1841, p. 278.—HANL.
  Recent Shells, suppl. pl. 14, f. 40.

Astarte compressa, MACGILLIV. Moll. Aberd. p. 261.—Brit. Marine Conch. p. 247.
Crassina compressa, BROWN, Illust. Conch. G. B. p. 96, pl. 38, f. 4, 5.
„   *corrugata*, BROWN, Illust. Conch. G. B. p. 96, pl. 40, f. 24.
Astarte borealis, PHILIPPI, Neuer Conch. vol. ii. p. 58, Astarte, pl. 1, f. 11. —
             FORBES, Memoirs Geol. Survey G. B. vol. i. p. 412 ; Ann.
             Nat. Hist. vol. xix. p. 98.
„   *corrugata*, LOVÈN, Index Moll. Skandinav. p. 37 (from types).
„   *plana*, SOWERBY, Min. Conch. pl. 179, f. 2.
„   *Withami*, BROWN, Wern. Mem. vol. viii. pl. 1, f. 24, 25.

This scarce and interesting bivalve assumes such various forms, that shape can scarcely be held characteristic in the species ; indeed, it seems somewhat debatable whether the outline of any *Astarte* is of specific importance. The contour, which is almost always somewhat triangularly subcordate, is subovate in most adult individuals, as the length in that stage generally exceeds, and very decidedly, the breadth ; but, the immature valves, and certain full-grown ones likewise, have their length and breadth nearly equal ; in which case the hinder termination becomes broad, and more or less triangular, instead of, as in the produced forms, rounded and somewhat tapering. The valves are rarely at all ventricose, and are usually shallow, becoming more rapidly so in front than behind. The sides, although unequal, are not greatly so for the genus, the posterior seldom occupying two-thirds of the entire length. The shell, which is often heavy, and always solid, opaque, and of a lighter or darker rufous tint, is covered by a fibrous chestnut-coloured epidermis, which has a silky lustre, is thinner towards the beaks, and becomes thicker, and with the fibres arranged so as to resemble crowded concentric striulæ towards the lower margin. This latter, which is quite entire within, is arcuated, and rises anteriorly with greater convexity and rapidity, generally forming a slight angle with the upper edge. Both dorsal slopes are more or less con-

siderable, and in general peculiarly straight, the front incurvation being usually very trifling, but rather elongated.
The external surface is not plicated, but is sculptured with
strong impressed concentric wrinkles at the umbonal region,
and is elsewhere smooth, or only obsoletely substriated in a
concentric direction. The umbones, which are never eroded,
are prominent; the beaks are acute, inflected, and lean
slightly forward. The lunule is remarkably profound, and
ranges from lanceolate to ovato-lanceolate. The ligament,
which is very large and broad, is seated in a lanceolate depression of twice its length. The whitish hue of the interior
has a bluish cast and more shining surface below the very
high-seated pallial impression, above which it becomes
squalid, or slightly embrowned. The hinge-margin is
extremely broad, and is furnished, in addition to the
primary teeth, with an indistinct rudimentary front lateral
one in the right valve. The muscular impressions are
large.

The example we have figured, which has evidently not
arrived at its full growth, measures an inch and a half in
length, and an inch and three-eighths in breadth. The
length of a more produced form (exotic) of the same
breadth, was an inch and two-thirds.

This is one of the rarest of our bivalves, of which the
first-recorded example was that figured by Montagu in his
Supplement to the "Testacea Britannica" as a large
growth of the *Astarte compressa*, and may be inferred, from
his language, to have been taken at Dunbar by Mr. Laskey.
The large dead valves, mentioned by Dr. Fleming in his
description of *A. compressa* as having been taken in St.
Andrew's Bay, likewise belong to this species, as one of
them, still preserved in our National Museum, distinctly
evidences. It has been captured in Aberdeenshire (Mac-

gillivray); and a fresh single valve has likewise been dredged in eighty fathoms water, forty miles to the west of the Mainland of Zetland (E. F. and M'Andrew). The beautiful and perfect specimen delineated in our engraving was procured from Loch Riden by Capt. Brown, to whose courtesy we are indebted for the loan of it.

It is a strictly boreal shell, and is chiefly obtained from Spitzbergen and Sweden, but is by no means common in the museums and private collections of England. The *A. semisulcata* of Leach (Appendix to Ross's Voyage), of which the young was figured in the Supplement to the "Index Testaceologicus," under the name of *Mactra Veneriformis* (we speak from an examination of the original types), is most closely allied to this species, but is generally more elliptical in shape, has broader and more manifest umbonal plicæ, eroded umbones (in the adult), and a somewhat different-looking epidermis. It occurs fossil in pleistocene strata of Britain, Northern Europe, and Boreal America.

A. COMPRESSA, Montagu.

Small, subtriangular, subequilateral, usually as broad as long, never elliptical; either traversed concentrically and entirely with most crowded and very narrow costellæ, or smooth, excepting at the beaks, which are always thus costellated. Epidermis yellowish or olivaceous, never chestnut nor fibrous, glossy. Beaks very prominent and acute. Ventral margin quite entire.

Plate XXX. fig. 1, 2, 3.

Venus compressa, MONT. Test. Brit. Suppl. p. 43, pl. 26, f. 1.
Venus Montagui, DILLW. Recent Shells, vol. i. p. 167.—TURT. Conch. Diction. p. 243.—Index Testaceol. pl. 7, f. 19.
Cyprina compressa, TURT. Dithyra Brit. p. 137, pl. 11, f. 22, 23.
Astarte compressa, FLEM. (not Macgil.) Brit. Anim. p. 440.
Crassina Montagui, GRAY, Ann. Phil. 1825, p. 136.—HANL. Recent Shells, vol. i. p. 88.
Astarte striata, BROWN, Ill. Conch. G. B. p. 96, pl. 38, f. 6, 7, 8.—LOVÉN, Index Moll. Skandinaviæ, p. 37.

Crassina compressa, Brit. Marine Conch. p. 80.
Astarte multicostata, MACGILL. (not Smith) Moll. Aberd. p. 260.—PHIL. Neuer
      Conchyl. vol. ii. p. 59, Astarte, pl. 1, f. 8.
  „ *Banksii*, LOVEN (not Leach nor Hanley) Index Mollusc. Skandinaviæ, p.
      38 (from specimens).

There are certain genera which appear to admit of a
much wider range of variation in their species, than others,
and pre-eminence in this respect may perhaps be claimed
for *Astarte*, so comparatively independent of form and
sculpture, do the true and permanent specific characters
in this genus appear to be. In diversity of variation, the
present species stands almost without a rival in its genus,
each locality, comparatively speaking, yielding its own
peculiar variety, yet so intimately connected by minute
gradations with the most apparently opposite examples,
that it seems utterly impossible that they can collectively
constitute more than a single species.

We conceive the typical form to be subtrigonal, and
equally broad as long, either almost smooth,—excepting
always more or less obsolete costellæ at the beaks,—or
much more usually entirely covered with most closely set
or crowded costellæ, which are thirty in number at the few-
est, but more frequently forty, or even more, and are never
much elevated, the valves seeming as it were sulcated rather
than ribbed. The interstices are simple and narrow. The
valves are almost equilateral, and vary from compressed to
ventricose, the ordinary rule being, that the more triangular
is the shell, the more ventricose will it be; they are always
small, strong, opaque, and covered with a smooth more or
less glossy strongly attached yellowish epidermis. The
swell of the ventral margin ranges from simple convexity to
full arcuation, and the declination in the dorsal edges increases in like proportion with the arcuation of the former,
yet typically is moderate and barely convex behind, but

always profound and incurved in front. The anterior
extremity is narrowed and rounded; the posterior termination is obtuse, but displays a more or less manifest tendency to biangulation. The beaks are acute and inclined,
and the umbones remarkably prominent. The dorsal impressions, but especially the hinder one, are large, and not
very profound; the lunule is lanceolate or ovato-lanceolate.
The ligament, which is, as usual, imbedded, is rather broad,
enlarged at its termination, and not much depressed; it
occupies two-fifths of the lozenge, and is yellow, or fulvous
brown. The internal surface is white, and its margin perfectly entire. The hinge consists in the left valve of two
rather narrow slightly divergent simple teeth, with a
cavity between them for the reception of the large solid
central simple tooth of the right valve, which has, besides,
an almost rudimentary one running nearly parallel with,
and adjacent to, the hinder dorsal margin. The front
extremity of the hinge margin of the latter valve frequently
also assumes the appearance of a distant lateral tooth.

A remarkable variety has been taken in North Britain,
which demands especial notice, approximating as it does
to the shape of *sulcata*, from which, however, the in-
tegrity of its solid margin, the smallness of its size compared with its solidity, and the closeness, depression, and
narrowness of its ribs, suffice to distinguish it. It is longer
in proportion to its breadth, than in the type, and has
fewer and broader ribs; its front extremity not unfrequently projects so that the anterior side is equal in length
to the posterior. This variety, however, appears to unite
with the type by almost imperceptible gradations. We
may remark, that the smooth variety is always the more
compressed one.

The animal has a plain edged mantle, with sessile siphonal orifices, and a white linguiform foot. The length or breadth of the shell rarely exceeds half an inch, and the average size of specimens is much less. It is obtained (the smooth variety) at Scarborough (Bean); and is not uncommonly dredged on the Northumbrian coast (Alder); in the mid-channel opposite Hampshire (Damon); Bantry Bay (Dillwyn). On the coast of Scotland it is much more abundant, occurring not uncommonly in the Hebrides and the lochs of the west coast. Mr. M'Andrew has dredged it in forty fathoms, muddy bottom off Skye, and as deep as seventy fathoms in the Zetland seas, where both smooth and ribbed forms are found, as also in the Moray Firth, in from eight to forty fathoms. In the Frith of Forth it is not rare on the oyster banks in seven to fourteen fathoms (E. F.). It is a Norwegian as well as British species, and is a common pleistocene fossil.

Crassina striata of Nilsson in the "Nova Acta Holmiæ" 1822, p. 189, pl. 2, f. 6, is probably this species; but the rudeness of the figure, and the brevity of the diagnosis, forbid our positively asserting so. The *Nicania striata* of Leach (Hanl. Recent Shells, suppl. pl. 14, f. 38), so imperfectly described in the Appendix to Ross's voyage, may possibly prove also identical, but is much less angular in outline, &c.

A. TRIANGULARIS, Montagu.

Very small, obliquely triangular, broader than long, quite smooth, typically crenated at the ventral margin; beaks extremely prominent; no dorsal impressions.

Plate XXX. fig. 4, 5.

Mactra triangularis, MONT. Test. Brit. p. 99, pl. 3, f. 5.—MATON and RACKETT, Linn. Trans. vol. viii. p. 72.—TURT. Conch. Diction. p. 82.—DILLW. Recent Shells, vol. i. p. 143.—Index Testaceol. pl. 6, Mactra, f. 28.

Mactra minutissima, MONT. Test. Brit. Suppl. p. 37.—TURT. Conch. Diction.
p. 83.—DILLW. Recent Shells, vol. i. p. 143.
Goodallia triangularis, TURT. Dithyra Brit. p. 77, pl. 6, f. 14.—FLEM. Brit.
Anim. p. 429.—MACGILLIV. Moll. Aberd. p. 289.—
Brit. Marine Conch. p. 49.
" *minutissima*, TURT. Dithyra Brit. p. 77, pl. 6, f. 15.—FLEM. Brit.
Anim. p. 429.—MACGILLIV. Moll. Aberd. p. 290.—
Brit. Marine Conch. p. 50.
Mactrina triangularis, BROWN, Ill. Conch. G. B. p. 108, pl. 40, f. 25.
" *minutissima*, BROWN, Ill. Conch. G. B. p. 108, pl. 42, f. 25, 26.

From the imperfect condition of the original specimens
of this minute *Astarte*, arose the error, which, by denying
the shell an external ligament, and thus severing it from its
kindred species, led to the construction of the ill-based
genus GOODALLIA. As the only permanent difference between
the *G. triangularis* and *minima* consists of the non-cre-
nation of the margin in the latter (which we are not at all
sure is ever the case with the adult), we are induced to
unite them as one species.

The contour of this shell is obliquely triangular, and
broader than long; for its size it is remarkably solid,
opaque, and perfectly smooth. Both externally and internally it is of a rich yellowish chestnut, either indistinctly
rayed with the same hue, but of a darker tint, or uniformly
coloured, although when the animal is not removed, there
is frequently a slightly mottled or even zoned appearance.
Excepting upon the umbones, the valves are rather compressed; the ventral margin is more or less arcuated, and
rises in front, whence originates the peculiar appearance of
obliquity in the valves. The anterior side which is decidedly the shorter, is rounded at its extremity, the front
dorsal edge descending with great abruptness, and but
trifling convexity to the ventral, without the interposition
of any anterior margin.

The posterior side is produced below; its dorsal edge is

much elongated, greatly sloping, and almost straight, being
very slightly retuse near the beaks, and not much convex
subsequently ; the hinder termination is well rounded and
projecting. There is neither lunule nor lozenge, but there
is a slight undefined depression or flattening of the sides,
both to the right and left of the umbones ; which latter
are remarkably prominent, but the beaks are neither acute
nor at all inclined. The ligament is very short, but not
depressed. Internally the lower margins are coarsely crenated, with raised bead-like projections, which, however,
do not always exist in the immature specimens. There
are two diverging central simple teeth in the right hinge,
and a large simple inwardly-sloping central tooth in the
other : the muscular scars are by no means large.

Examples which are equal to the eighth of an inch in
breadth, and the ninth or tenth of an inch in length, may
be regarded as fine ones, the ordinary run of specimens
being somewhat less.

It seems far more abundant in Scotland than in England,
where it is always held a very rare shell, and is dredged
(but usually in not very shallow water) at Scarborough
(Bean); the Fern Islands (Alder) ; Exmouth (Clark);
Plymouth and Whitesand Bay (Jeffreys) ; Falmouth
(Mont. and Jeffreys) ; the Scilly Islands (M'Andrew) ;
Guernsey (S. H.) ; Isle of Man, in fifteen fathoms (E. F.) ;
Langland Bay, in Glamorganshire, in twenty-five fathoms
sand (Jeffreys) ; Tenby (Lyons) ; Fishguard (Jeffreys).
Among Scottish localities may be mentioned, — Icolmkill,
very abundant in five fathoms, and equally plentiful in
fifty-five fathoms, off Cape Wrath (M'Andrew) ; in from
five to fifty fathoms on the Zetland Coast, and thirty-five
off Duncansby Head ; also in the Moray Firth (M'Andrew).   It is a rare pleistocene fossil.

SPURIOUS.

A representation occurs in the eighth volume of the Linnean Transactions, accompanying Maton and Rackett's Descriptive Catalogue of the British Testacea, of a shell previously described by Montagu, but not so characteristically indicated as usual; hence doubts have arisen as to the species of the two works being actually identical. The following passage in the " Testacea Britannica," has not only satisfied us of this, but enabled us, through the examination of the referred to type, positively to declare its identity with one of the varieties of Say's *Astarte castanea,* " It is marked in Dr. Pulteney's cabinet *Venus sulcata,* but he did not know it had ever been found in this country, nor did he believe it had ever been described, and therefore named it himself."

Its claims to be held British, were never of much weight, being merely the assertion of one individual, who had received it from the Duchess of Portland as such, that similar ones (in all probability the valves of *compressa* or *arctica*) had since been found in the North of Scotland ; and that Montagu had himself received it (without specified locality) from Mr. Sowerby as English. It is a common and well-known North American species.

A. CASTANEA, Say.

Venus sulcata, MONT. (not *Pectunc. sulcatus* of Da Costa) Test. Brit. p. 131.—MATON and RACK. Linn. Trans. vol. viii. p. 81, pl. 2, f. 2.—DILLW. Recent Shells, vol. i. p. 166.

„ *castanea,* SAY, Jour. Acad. Philad. vol. iv. p. 273.

Astarte castanea, SAY, Americ. Conch. pl. 1.—CONR. Amer. Mar. Conch. pl. 17, f. 3.—GOULD, Invert. Massach. p. 76, f. 45.—HANL. Recent Shells, suppl. pl. 9, f. 27.—PHIL. Neuer Conch. vol. ii. p. 57, Astarte, pl. 1, f. 2.—DEKAY, New York Moll. p. 220, pl. 28, f. 280.

„ *sulcata,* FLEM. Brit. Anim. p. 439.

Crassina castanea, DESH. in Lam. Anim. s. Vert. (ed. Desh.) vol. vi. p. 258.—HANL. Recent Shells, vol i. p. 88.

„ *sulcata,* BROWN, Illus. Conch. G. B. p. 96, pl. 38, f. 10.

Subtriangularly suborbicular, equally broad as long, thick, ponderous, opaque, moderately convex, covered with a tar-coloured or yellowish chestnut glossy epidermis, which is ordinarily adorned with darker and lighter concentric zones, beneath which it is externally and internally whitish. The entire outer surface is either smooth, or more rarely marked with obsoletely elevated broad belts. Ventral margin much arcuated; dorsal slopes strong, the front moderately incurved, the hinder more or less straight. Sides not greatly unequal; the anterior the shorter, and well rounded at its extremity; the posterior obtusely rounded, its extreme tip convex. Beaks nearly central, greatly elevated, a little inclined forwards; lunule ovato-lanceolate, rather deeply excavated, of a darker hue than the general colouring; lozenge not much impressed, the ligament occupying two-fifths of it at least. No umbonal ridge. Hinge margin very broad; muscular impressions profound, of moderate size; lower margins internally crenated. Diameter, an inch.

THE following description appears to apply to one of the fossil forms of *Astarte*, so common in our pleistocene strata :—

Crassina depressa, BROWN, Ill. Conch. O. B. p. 96, pl. 38, f. 2.

" Shell compressed, transversely and obliquely subovate, umbones rather prominent and slightly reflexed, with a lanceolate deep lunule under them ; colour of a dark reddish brown, with many flattened transverse ridges, and narrow shallow intervening furrows ; inside white, smooth ; margin plain, and slightly thickened in the edge. Length, nine-eighths of an inch ; breadth, nearly eleven-eighths. *This differs from* C. Scotica *in being more transversely elongated, oblique, more compressed, with the basal line more parallel, the transverse ridges more numerous, very flattened, and almost obsolete. Found in the Frith of Forth, but I have hitherto only met with dead and detached valves.*"

ISOCARDIA, LAMARCK.

Shell inflated, heart-shaped, equivalve, rather strong, smooth, or furrowed, with or without an investing epidermis; beaks very prominent and contorted; margins entire; muscular impressions small, no pallial sinus. Hinge composed of two erect primary teeth (one of them indented) parallel with the margin in one valve, and three in the other; a lateral tooth and tooth-like socket. Ligament external, furcated anteriorly. No defined lunule.

Animal shaped like the shell, open in front for the broad triangular, compressed, pointed foot. Siphonal orifices sessile, their margins fringed. Mantle double edged.

This remarkable genus may be regarded as constituting a connecting link between the *Cyprinidæ* and *Cardiadæ*, whilst its affinities with *Chama* and its associates are also not small. Our only British species is rather an exceptional form, and isolated from its tropical congeners by the possession of a highly developed epidermis. In British strata even as old as the oolitic formations, we have fossil examples of *Isocardiæ*, but all of them bear more resemblance to those now existing in the seas of warm regions, than to that about to be described.

I. COR, Linnæus.

Plate XXXIV. f. 2, and (Animal) Plate N. f. 6.

LISTER, Hist. Conch. pl. 275.—GUALTIERI, Index Test. pl. 71, f. E.—GINANNI, Opere Postume, vol. ii. pl. 19, f. 129.— KNORR. Delices des Yeux, pt. vi. pl. 8, f. 1.
Cardium humanum, LINN. Syst. Naturæ, ed, 10, p. 682 (badly).
Chama cor, LINN. Syst. Nat. ed. 12, p. 1137; Mus. Ulrica, p. 516.—MONT. Test. Brit. pp. 134, 578, and Sup. p. 50.—DONOVAN, Brit. Shells, vol. iv. pl. 134.—LASKEY, Mem. Werner. Soc. vol. i. pl. 8, f. 7.—TURT. Conch. Diction. p. 32, pl. 17.—BROWN, Mem.

Werner. Soc. vol. ii. pp. 511, 535.—BORN, Testacea Mus. Cæs.
Vind. p. 80.—CHEMN. Conch. Cab. vol. vii. pl. 48, f. 483.—POLI,
Test. 'Siciliæ, vol. ii. p. 213, pl. 23, f. 1, 2, 3.—DILLW. Recent
Shells, vol. i. p. 212.—Index Testaceolog. pl. 3, Chama, f. 1.

Cardita cor, BRUGUIÈRE, Encyclop. Méthod. Vers, vol. i. p. 403.

Isocardia cor, LAM. Anim. s. Vert. (ed. Desh.) vol. vi. p. 445.—TURT. Dithyra
Brit. p. 193, pl. 14.— FLEM. Brit. Anim. p. 419.— Brit.
Marine Conch, p. 100.—BROWN, Ill. Conch. G. B. p. 86, p. 30,
f. 9, and pl. 30,* f. 5.— SOWERBY, Genera Shells, Isocardia
f. 1, 2.—BULWER, Zool. Journal, vol. ii. p. 258, suppl. pl. 18.
— BLAINV. Manuel Malacologie, pl. 69, f. 2. — CROUCH, Introd. Conch. pl. 8, f. 7.—DESHAYES, Encycl. Méthod. Vers,
vol. ii. p. 321 ; Elem. Conch. pl. 23, f. 10, 11. — PHILIPPI,
Moll. Sicil. vol. i. p. 56, and vol. ii. p. 41.—REEVE, Conch.
System. pl. 78, f. 1, 2. — HANL. Recent Shells, vol. i. p. 150,
pl. 9, Chama, f. 1.

„   *Hibernica*, REEVE, Conchol. Icon. Isocardia, pl. 1, f. 4.

Encyclop. Méthodique, Vers, pl. 232.

We are not disposed to consider the slight differences
which exist between the Irish and Mediterranean examples
of this remarkable shell, as of essential or specific importance, but esteem them rather as contingent upon climate,
depth, food, or some of those multifarious causes which
induce variation.

The lateral contour is exactly heart-shaped, whence its
popular name of the *Heart Shell;* the general outline of
each valve is cordate-truncated, the lower angle of the
heart being as it were lopped off by the obtuse truncation
of the posterior extremity. The valves are solid, opaque,
much inflated, and under a rather thin and yellowish-
brown concentrically wrinkled epidermis, of a dirty white,
closely reticulated by delicate angular radiatingly-arranged
lineations, of a livid red, or fawn-colour, which are chiefly
apparent (partly from the abrasion of the epidermis at that
point) upon the swollen umbones, behind which they become so thickly clustered as to present an almost uniform
tint. The surface is devoid of either lustre or sculpture,
exhibiting only the more or less coarse concentric stages of

increase, which as usual become more marked as age advances. The ventral margin is arcuated, and rises sharply in front; the hinder dorsal edge is convex, and slopes so little (indeed it slightly ascends at first) as almost to be sub-parallel with the opposite margin. The front dorsal slope is short, incurved, and rather abrupt. The anterior extremity is angulated, the angle being, in the adult, above the middle of the side, and its tip rounded off; the posterior termination is rather broad, and very bluntly biangulated. The umbones are contorted, and project considerably forward, so as to appear subterminal; the beaks are so much inflected as almost to appear spiral, and so diverge from each other as to be widely sundered at their apices, which are very acute, and lean upward. The ligament, which, though sufficiently ample, is not particularly prominent, is divided anteriorly, and runs in a narrow slip along the base of each umbo. There is no defined lunule, but a very expansive hollow in front of the umbones; the dorsal lips, however, are elevated. Within, the surface is of a whitish hue, with occasionally a slight tinge of buff or flesh-colour upon its disk; the inner edge is sharp and simple. The teeth of the hinge are erect, and lie parallel with the margin; in the left valve the front one is very large, truncato-trigonal, indented at its apex so as at times almost to appear double, and impressed below by the opposing tooth; the hinder one is thin, laminar, and dorsal. Of the two strong front primary teeth of the right valve, which lie parallel with each other, the upper is semicircular and situated less forward, the lower one is the shorter, and more trigonal; the hinder tooth is laminar, and not peculiarly solid. The lateral tooth (and its tooth-like receptacle) are strong, posterior, and remote from the beaks, lying beyond the termination of the ligament.

The fry, which is very rarely to be met with in cabinets, is very thin, transparent, and of a subcordiform obovate shape. It is of an uniform whitish hue, and remarkable for its somewhat opaline diaphanous yellowish epidermis, which is studded with minute hairs in radiating series. This peculiarity is observable likewise under the lens in well preserved middle-aged specimens. The epidermis in the Mediterranean examples (which do not appear to reach the dimensions of the northern shell) is smoother, rather more shining, and of a ruddier cast.

The following interesting account of the animal and its habits was communicated by the Rev. James Bulwer to the 2nd volume of the Zoological Journal.

" Mantle completely lining the shell, double at the outer edge; exterior fold divided in front, open at each end; at the posterior end forming two short siphons or tubes, ciliated at the upper orifices; colour yellowish white; margin orange. Foot very muscular, broad, triangular, compressed, pointed, orange. Branchiæ external, concealed between the mantle and the body. Body soft, completely included within the valves. On being placed in a vessel of sea-water the valves of the shell gradually opened, to the extent represented in the drawing; the feelers or ciliated fringe of the upper orifice of the mantle moved slowly, as if in search of animalculæ. Having remained in this situation about ten minutes, water was ejected with considerable force from the lower orifice, which till now had remained motionless. The expulsion of the water appeared to be effected by a sudden contraction of the muscles, because this was never done without the valves nearly closing at the same instant. After a few seconds the valves gradually returned to their open position, and remained quiescent as before, till the water was again ejected with a

jerk; this alternating process was repeated at unequal intervals during the whole time my specimens were under
examination, but at shorter intervals on receiving fresh
supplies of sea-water, when I suppose food (its quality I
could not ascertain) was more abundant.

"The animal appears to be insensible both to sound and
light, as the presence or absence of either did not at all in-
terrupt its movements; but its sense of feeling appeared to
be very delicate, minute substances being dropped into the
orifice of the mantle instantly excited the animal, and a
column of water strongly directed expelled them from the
shell. With so much strength was the water in some
instances ejected, that it rose above the surface of 3 inches
of superincumbent fluid. Animal small in proportion to its
shell, occupying when dead barely a third of the space enclosed in the valves. Its mantle is slightly attached to the
shell, and to the epidermis at the margin, and appears to
be kept distended and in contact with the interior of the
valves, by the included water. The valves fit so closely
that the animal can remain two days or more without permitting a single drop of fluid to escape. Locomotion very
confined; it is capable, with the assistance of its foot,
which it uses in the same manner (but in a much more
limited degree) as the Cardiacea, of fixing itself firmly in
the sand, generally choosing to have the umbones covered
by it, and the orifices of the tubes of the mantle nearly
perpendicular. Resting in this position on the margin of a
sand bank, of which the surrounding soil is mud, at too
great a depth to be disturbed by storms, the Isocardia of
our Irish sea patiently collects its food from the surrounding element, assisted in its choice by the current it is capable of creating by the alternate opening and closing of its
valves."

The chief locality of this fine shell in the British seas is off the Dublin coast, where specimens are sometimes obtained in considerable abundance. It is also procured in deep water off the Cornish coast; and is brought in by fishermen at Falmouth (Cocks, Alder). Bantry Bay (Turton); and the Cove of Cork (Brown), are among its Irish southern habitats. It occurs in the Hebrides, living, as near Oban, in mud at a depth of fifteen fathoms, and dead in forty fathoms off Skye (M'Andrew and E. F.). Laskey recorded it from Icolmkill, and also from near St. Abb's Head. Abroad it ranges to the Mediterranean.

EXPLANATION OF THE PLATES OF ANIMALS.

SERIES I.

GENERA OF TUNICATA, ACEPHALA AND PTEROPODA.

PLATES A AND B.—1. *Aplidium fallax.* 2. *Sidnyum turbinatum*—both from specimens taken on the shores of the Isle of Man (E. F.). 3. *Polyclinum aurantium* (miscalled *gelatinosum* in Plate B). 4. *Amouroucium argus.* 5. *Leptoclinum gelatinosum.* 6. *Distoma rubrum.* 7. *Botryllus polycyclus.* 8. *Botrylloides albicans.* The figures of Plate A, from 3 to 6, and fig. 8, are after Milne Edwards. Those of Plate B are mostly after Savigny, and repre- ·sent (greatly magnified) the individual mollusks extracted from the common masses.

PLATE C.—1. *Ascidia mentula.* 2. *A. virginea.* 3. *A. scabra.* 4. *A. echinata.* 5. *Molgula tubulosa* (*arenosa* of Alder); all from life (E.F.).

PLATE D.—1. *Cynthia quadrangularis.* 2. *C. morus.* 3. *C. tessellata.* 4. *C. limacina.* 5. *C. aggregata,* 5. a. the tadpole of the last highly magnified. 6. *Molgula oculata,* adhering to a *Pecten,* and encrusted with shells and sand ; all from life (E. F.).

PLATE E.—1. *Clavellina lepadiformis, a.* natural size of a group of examples; *b.* a single individual magnified. 2. *Perophora Listeri, a.* of the natural size, upon a fucus; *b.* the same highly magnified. 3. *a.* and *b. Pelonaia glabra,* in different states of contraction. 4. *Pelonaia corrugata ;* all from life (E. F.). 5. The solitary, and 6. The aggregate individuals of *Salpa runcinata,* from specimens taken in the Scottish seas by Lieut. Thomas, R.N.

PLATE F.—1. Animal of a *Teredo;* the upper figure representing the siphonal extremity, magnified. 2. *Xylophaga dorsalis,* after a sketch and specimens communicated by the Rev. D. Landsborough ; the siphons, however, are not collateral at the extremity of the tube, as here represented. See note in vol. ii. p. 375. We have not been able to procure a fresh figure, as there promised. 3. *Pholas parva*, from life. 4. *Pholadidea papyracea*, the siphons only, after preserved specimens and a sketch by Mr. Clark. 5. *Gastrochæna modiolina*, and 6. *Saxicava rugosa*.

PLATE G.—1. *Petricola lithophaga* (after Philippi). 2. *Venerupis irus* (after Deshayes). 3. *Corbula nucleus*. 4 and 5. *Neæra cuspidata*. 6. Its siphons and their appendages, greatly magnified. 7. The orifices of the siphons. 8. *Neæra costellata*, and 9. its foot, all from life; as also 10. *Pandora obtusa*.

PLATE H.—1. *Mya truncata*. 2. *Lutraria elliptica*, and 2. a. its siphonal apertures. 3. *Lyonsia norvegica*. 4. *Thracia phaseolina*. 5. *Thracia distorta*.

PLATE I.—1. *Solen siliqua*. 2. *Solen pellucidus* : these and 5. *Solecurtus coarctatus* (the shell reversed by mistake), with 6. its siphons, are from life (E. F.). 3. The siphons of *Solen marginatus* (after Deshayes). 4. *Ceratisolen legumen* (shell reversed by error).

PLATE K.—1. *Psammobia tellinella*, and 1. a. its siphons. 2. *Diodonta fragilis* (after Deshayes). 3. *Tellina tenuis*, and 3. a. its siphons with part of mantle. 4. and 4. a. Similar figures of *Tellina donacina*. 5. and 5. a. Ditto of *Syndosmya intermedia*. 6. *Scrobicularia piperita* (lettered *compressa*). 7. *Donax anatinus*. 8. Siphons of *Mesodesma*, introduced for comparison (E. F.).

PLATE L.—1. *Mactra elliptica*. 2. Siphons of *M. solida*. 3. Those of *M. subtruncata*. 4. Those of *M. stultorum*. 5. *Tapes pullastra*, and 5. a. its siphons. 6. Siphons of *Venus ovata*. 7. *Venus fasciata*. 8. *Cytherea chione*.

PLATE M.—1. *Artemis lincta* (after Poli). 2. *Lucinopsis undata* (from sketch by Mr. Clark). 3. *Circe minima* (from a specimen dredged in Milford Haven). 4. *Cyprina islandica* (the beaks are turned the wrong way in the engraving). 5. *Astarte sulcata*, var. *Danmoniensis*. 6. *Lucina borealis* (from sketch by Mr. Alder). 7. *Diplodonta rotundata* (from sketch by Mr. Clark).

PLATE N.—1. *Cardium norvegicum*. 1. a. portion of the branchial siphon. 2. *Cardium pygmæum*. 3. *C. fasciatum*. 4. *C. echinatum*, junior. 5. Siphons of *C. edule*. 6. *Isocardia cor* (after Bulwer).

PLATE O.—1. *Turtonia minuta*, called *purpurea* on the plate ; the shell in this figure is reversed by mistake (see vol. ii. p. 375). 2. *Montacuta substriata*. 3. *Kellia rubra*. 4. and 4. a. *Kellia suborbicularis*. 5. *Galeomma Turtoni* (partly after Mittre). 6. *Lepton squamosum*. 7. *Cyclas calyculata*. 8. *Pisidium amnicum*. 9. *Pisidium pusillum*. The figures of *Kellia* and of *Lepton* are from drawings by Mr. Alder.

PLATE P.—1. *Arca tetragona*, with 1. a. its byssus. 2. *Leda caudata*, and 2. a. the expanded disk of its foot. 3. *Leda pygmæa.* 4. *Nucula nucleus.* 5. *Nucula tenuis.* 6. *Pectunculus glycimeris*, called *pilosus* on the plate. The drawing of 1. is by Mr. Alder; the others are from our own sketches after life.

PLATE Q.—1. *Cyclas rivicola.* 2. *Unio pictorum.* 3. *Anodonta cygnea*, with 3. a. its mantle-fringe. 4. *Dreissena polymorpha*, 4. a. and b. details of its siphons, after sketches by Mr. J. de C. Sowerby. 5. *Mytilus edulis*, and 5. a. part of its mantle-fringe. 6. *Modiola tulipa.* 7. *Crenella nigra* (after a drawing by Mr. Alder).

PLATE R.—*Lima hians* (under Turton's name of *L. tenera*). 1. and 2. different views of the animal fully expanded. 3. its foot. 4. one of the cirrhi highly magnified. The beautiful drawings from which these figures were engraved, are among the many favours we owe to the pencil and observation of our accomplished friend, Mr. Alder.

PLATE S.—1. *Pecten similis.* 2. *P. striatus*, and 2. a. a portion of its mantle highly magnified. 3. *P. niveus*, with 3. a. portion of its mantle. 4. *Avicula tarentina*, drawn from a living Mediterranean specimen (E. F.).

PLATE T.—1. *Ostrea edulis* (this beautiful figure was most kindly drawn and engraved from the living animal by Mr. J. de Carle Sowerby). 2. *Anomia ephippium.* 3. *Sphænia Binghami*, from a drawing by Mr. Spence Bate.

PLATE U.—1. *Terebratula caput-serpentis*, 1. b. the under valve, and 1. c. the upper valve, laid open, from living specimens taken in Loch Fyne. 2 *Crania norvegica.* 3. *Hyalæa trispinosa*, and 4. *Spirialis* (after Souleyet), named *Peracle* on plate.

PLATE W.—1. *Panopœa norvegica*, after a drawing from the living British specimen by Mr. Richard Howse. 2. *Poromya granulata*, after a sketch by Mr. M'Andrew. 3. *Appendicularia*, a slight sketch from a British example.

[PLATES X, Y, Z, no such plates].

SERIES II.

GENERA OF GASTEROPODA AND CEPHALOPODA.

PLATE AA.—1. *Patella (Patina) pellucida.* 2. *Acmœa testudinalis*, —2. a. and b. one of the articulations of the tongue. 3. *Pilidium fulvum*, with 3. a. its head, showing the eyeless tentacles, and 3. b. articulations of its tongue. 4. *Propilidium ancyloide*, with 4. a. under side of its head, and 4. b. upper side of its head and position of the two branchial plumes. 5. *Chiton asellus*, and 5. a. its head, seen in profile. 6. *Chiton ruber*. All from original drawings.

PLATE BB.—1. *Emarginula rosea*. 2. An enlarged view of its head and neighbouring parts seen from above; and 3. the same seen laterally. 4. *Puncturella noachina*, seen sideways. 5. The same from below, and 6. its head. 7. *Fissurella reticulata*. 8. *Calyptræa sinensis*, seen from below; 9. Its head; 10. Shell of the fry; 11. Head and neck of the fry; 12. and 13. Tongue. All from original drawings.

PLATE CC.—1. *Patella vulgata*. 2. *Emarginula crassa*. 3. *Haliotis tuberculata*. 4. and 4*. *Trochus helicinus*. 5. and 5*. *Pileopsis hungaricus*, from a half-grown example. Figures 2, 4, and 5, are from drawings by Mr. Alder.

PLATE DD.—1. *Trochus cinerarius*, and 1. a. its head and lobes (the right lateral lobe should be simple-edged, not crenated). 2. *T. tumidus*. 3. *T. magus*. 4. *T. granulatus*. 5. *Phasianella pullus*, and 5. a. its head: the second lateral filament should be shorter than the others. Fig. 2 is by Mr. Alder.

PLATE EE.—1. a. *Trochus ziziphinus*, from below; 1. b. the same, front view; 1. c. its head and tentacles; 1. d. a lateral filament; 1. e. its operculigerous lobe and tail; 1. f. the branchial plume; 1. g. branchial lamellæ very highly magnified. 2. a. *Trochus alabastrum* (misprinted *alabastrites*); 2. b. its head, tentacles, lateral and capital lobes, and the anterior portion of its foot.

PLATE FF.—1. *Scalaria Trevelyana*, showing the head and siphonal fold of mantle. 2. The same crawling. 3. Head and anterior portion of the foot seen from above. 4. *Chemnitzia fulvocincta*, under the name of *rufa*. 5. Head, &c. of *C. scalaris*. 6. *C. rufescens*. 7. *Eulimella Scillæ* (named *Chemnitzia MacAndrei*, on plate). 8. *Odostomia spiralis*. 9. and 10. *Truncatella truncatula*.

PLATE GG.—1. *Skenea planorbis*, and 1. a. the same seen crawling, so as to show its operculigerous lobe. 2. *Littorina rudis*, var. *patula*; 2. a. its foot seen from below. 3. Head of *Littorina littorea*. 4. and 4. a. *Lacuna vincta*. 5. Some stages of development of *Lacuna pallidula*; and 5. a. ova of that species clustered on a fucus, both from the drawings of Mr. Spence Bate.

PLATE HH.—1. *Neritina fluviatilis*. 2. *Paludina vivipara*; 2. a. its head and neck-lobes. 3. *Bithinia tentaculata*; and 3. a. its head and neck-lobes. 4. *B. Leachii*. 5. *Valvata cristata*; and 5. a. its head and front of foot. 6. *Assiminea Grayana*. All from original drawings.

PLATE II.—1. *Trichotropis borealis*. 2. and 2. a. *Cerithium reticulatum*. 3. *Aporrhais pes-pelecani*; and 3. a. its foot. 4. and 4. a. *Turritella communis*. All from drawings by Mr. Alder.

PLATE JJ.—1. and 1. a. *Jeffreysia diaphana;* 1. b. part of its head ; 1. c. d. e. its operculum. 2. Operculum of *Jeffreysia opalina,* all from drawings by Mr. Alder. 3. *Rissoa abyssicola.* 4. *R. cingillus;* and 4. a. its operculum. 5. *R. parva.* 6. Head of *R. labiosa.* 7. Head of *R. rufilabris.* 8. *R. ulvæ.*

PLATE KK.—1. *Cæcum trachea,* a. from the side ; b. from below; c. its head. 2. *Eulima polita,* var. *nitida* (wrongly labelled *E. nitida* on plate). 3. a. and b. *E. polita,* typical form (wrongly *E. nitida,* var. *polita,* on plate). 4. a. and b. *E. distorta.* 5. Anterior portion of *E. bilineata.*

PLATE LL.—1. and 1. a. *Nassa incrassata.* 2. and 2. a. *N. pygmæa* (called *N. varicosa* on plate). 3. *N. reticulata.* 4. *Purpura lapillus;* and 4. a. its head, seen from above. 5. *Buccinum undatum.*

PLATE MM.—1. *Spirialis Flemingii,* from living specimens off the coast of Skye. 2 a. and b. *Jeffreysia opalina,* after a drawing by Mr. Alder. 3. a. and b. *Assiminea littorea* (see Appendix): this is the *Rissoa littorea* of Plate lxxxi. figs. 6 and 7, after living specimens taken on the coast of the Isle of Wight. 4. *Rissoa vitrea,* from a specimen taken off Oban. 5. *Aclis supranitida,* after a sketch by Mr. Hanley.

PLATE NN.—1. 2. 4. *Ovula patula* (under the name *Volva patula*) ; and 3. its head. 5. 6. 7. *Cypræa europæa;* and 7. its head, seen from below. 8. *Marginella lævis;* and 9. its head.

PLATE OO.—1. a. b. and c. *Cerithiopsis tubercularis;* and 2. its operculum. 3. Operculum of *Cerithium reticulatum.* 4. *Otina otis.* 5. *Stilifer Turtonis.* (All from drawings by Mr. Alder.) 6. a. and b. *Velutina flexilis* (under the name of *V. plicatilis*). 7. *Velutina lævigata.*

PLATE PP.—1. a. b. c. *Lamellaria perspicua.* 2. *L. tentaculata* (after a drawing by Mr. Spence Bate). 3. *Natica sordida.* 4. *N. Montagui* (after a drawing by Mr. Alder). 5. *N. Alderi* (*N. nitida* of text). 6. *N. monilifera* (lettered *N. canrena* by a mistake); and 7. a. and b. its nidus (after drawings by Mr. Spence Bate).

[PLATE QQ, no such plate].

PLATE RR.—1. a. *Mangelia Leufroyi;* 1. b. its anterior portion ; 1. c. its tail. 2. a. *M. brachystoma;* 2. b. its anterior portion ; and 2. c. its tail. 3. a. *M. teres;* and 3. b. its head. 4. a. *M. costata* (after a sketch by Mr. Alder); 4. b. its head, from another drawing. 4*. its lingual denticles. 5. Head and anterior parts of *M. attenuata.* 6. *M. linearis.* 7. Head and tail of *M. nebula.* 8. *M. gracilis* (after a drawing by Mr. Alder).

PLATE SS.—1. *Fusus propinquus,* (drawn from life by Mr. Alder). 2. a. *Fusus islandicus ;* 2. b. its head ; and 2. c. its lingual dentition. 3. a. *Trophon clathratus* (as *Bamfium*) ; and 3. b. its lingual dentition. 4. a. *T. Barvicensis;* and 4. b. its head. 5. *T. muricatus* (under the name of *T. echinatum*); and 5. b. its head.

PLATE TT.—1. a. and b. *Murex erinaceus;* and 1. c. its lingual dentition. 2. a. and 2. b. *Mangelia (Bela) turricula;* and 2. d. its lingual dentition. 3. *M. (Bela septangularis).* 4. a. *M. (Bela) rufa;* and 4 b. its head. (Figs. 2. a. and 3. are from drawings by Mr. Alder.)

PLATE UU.—1. a. and b. *Bullæa* (or *Philine*) *aperta;* 1. c. its lingual dentition. 2. a. and b. *Amphisphyra hyalina;* 2. c. its lingual dentition. 3. *Bulla hydatis.* 4. *Philine (Bullæa) catena,* and *Philine (Bullæa) punctata.* All the figures on this plate are from drawings by Mr. Alder.

PLATE VV.—1. *Philine (Bullæa) scabra.* 2. *Bulla Cranchii.* 3. *Cylichna cylindracea.* 4. *C. truncata* (after a sketch by Mr. A. Alder); and 4. a. its lingual dentition. 5. *Scaphander lignaria.* 6. *Akera bullata.* 7. a. and b. *Tornatella fasciata* (*T. tornatilis* on plate).

PLATE XX.—1. *Pleurobranchus plumula.* 2. *P. membranaceus.* After drawings by Mr. Alder. A few impressions of this plate were issued, marked 88.

PLATE YY.—1. *Aplysia hybrida.* 2. *Doris coccinea.* 3. *Goniodoris nodosa* (these two figures are after drawings by Mr. Alder). 4. *Idalia inæqualis.* 5. *Polycera quadrilineata.*

PLATE ZZ.—1. *Hermæa dendritica.* 2. *Proctonotus mucroniferus.* 3. *Lomonotus marmoratus.* 4. *Ancula cristata.* 5. *Dendronotus arborescens* (all after the figures by Alder and Hancock).

PLATE AAA.—1. *Triopa claviger.* 2. *Ægirus punctilucens* (these figures are after Alder and Hancock). 3. *Tritonia Hombergi* (copied from the figure by Mrs. Johnston). 4. *Doto coronata.* 4.* *D. fragilis.* 5. *Scyllæa pelagica.*

PLATE BBB.—1. *Eolis papillosa,* var. *Zetlandica.* 2. *E. coronata,* from our drawing of the original specimen. 3. *E. viridis,* from a Cornish example. 4. *E. exigua,* after Mr. Alder's drawing. 5. *Embletonia minuta.* 6. *Antiopa cristata* (under the name of *A. splendida,* see note in Appendix) ; after Mr. Spence Bate's drawing.

PLATE CCC.—1. *Alderia modesta.* 2. *Runcina Hancocki.* 3. *Elysia viridis.* 4. *Limapontia nigra.* 5. *Acteonia corrugata.* 6. *Cenia Cocksii.* All from Mr. Alder's drawings, except the first, which is from a figure by Mr. Spence Bate.

PLATE DDD.—1. a. *Arion empiricorum;* 1. b. the same, at rest and contracted ; 1. c. part of the surface of its shield and body magnified. (This figure is referred to wrongly in vol. iv. p. 7, as fig. 4.

THE PLATES OF ANIMALS.

of his plate.)   2. a. *Limax cinereus;* 2. b. part of its surface
magnified ; 2. c. its shell (referred to as fig. 1. in text). 3. a.
Limax agrestis; 3. b. the same, at rest ; 3. c. part of surface magnified ; 3. d. its shell (referred to as fig. 2. in text). 4. a. *Limax
gagates;* 4. b. the same, at rest ; 4. c. part of surface magnified ;
4. d. its shell (referred to as fig. 3. in text).

PLATE EEE.—1. a. *Limax flavus;* 1. b. part of surface magnified ;
1. c. its shell. 2. a. *Limax arborum* (written *arboreus* on plate) ;
2. b. the same, at rest ; 2. c. part of surface magnified ; 2. d. its
shell. 3. a. *Limax Sowerbii;* 3. b. the same at rest ; 3. c. part of
the surface magnified ; 3. d. its shell.

[PLATE FFF. A few impressions were issued of a plate so marked;
these should be altered to GGG. There is no plate FFF.]

PLATE FFF.*—1. a. *Arion hortensis;* 1. b. portion of surface magnified.
2. a. *Arion flavus;* 2. b. the same, at rest (from a drawing by Mr.
Alder). 3. *Limax tenellus* (from a drawing by Mr. Alder). 4.
Limax brunneus (from a drawing by Mr. Alder). 5. *Geomalacus
maculosus* (after Dr. Allman's drawing). 6. *Onchidium celticum,*
from a specimen taken by Mr. Couch.

PLATE GGG.—1. *Helix hispida.* 2. *H. rotundata.* 3. *Zonites cellaria*
(written *Helix*). 4. *Helix fusca.* 5. *Zua lubrica.* 6. *Bulimus
acutus.*

PLATE HHH.—1. *Vitrina pellucida.* 2. *Clausilia plicatula.* 3.
C. laminata. 4. *Balea fragilis,* under the name of *perversa.* 5.
Pupa muscorum, called *marginata* on plate. 6. *Pupa umbilicata.*

PLATE III.—1. a. *Testacella haliotoidea* (referred to in text, by error,
as GGG. fig. 1.) ; and 1. b. its eggs. (This figure was engraved
from life, with the assistance of a drawing by Mr. S. P. Woodward.)
1. c. and 1. d. its shell. 2. a. *Limnæus pereger;* and 2. b. its head.
3. *Physa hypnorum* (after a drawing by Mr. Spence Bate). 4.
Planorbis vortex. 5. *Succinea putris.* 6. *S. oblonga* (these two
figures after drawings by Mr. Spence Bate). 7. *Conovulus denticulatus* (after a drawing by Mr. Alder).

PLATE JJJ.—1. *Physa fontinalis.* 2. *Achatina acicula.* 3. *Carychium minimum.* 4. *Limax agrestis,* a remarkable monstrosity,
taken by Mr. Gibbs at Sandown. 5. *Cyclostoma elegans.* 6.
Ancylus.

PLATE KKK.—1. 2. 3. *Diphyllidea lineata.* 4. *Eledone ventricosa*—
both from drawings by Mr. Alder.

PLATE LLL.—*Loligo vulgaris,* after drawing by Mr. Alder.

PLATE MMM.—1. a. *Eledone cirrhosus,* attitude when at rest ; and
1. b. portion of arm with suckers. 2. a. *Sepiola Atlantica,* from a
specimen taken off Skye ; 2. b. one of its lower arms, showing the
peculiar arrangement of the terminal suckers ; 2. c. portion of an

arm with suckers, much magnified; 2. d. its pen. (Both the preceding species were drawn from the living animal.) 3. a. outline
of *Sepiola Rondeletii*, from a British specimen, taken by Mr. Alder,
and preserved in spirits; 3. b. one of the arms; 3. c. termination
of one of the lower arms, showing the peculiar arrangement of the
suckers; 3. d. its pen.

PLATE NNN.—1. *Rossia macrosoma*, from an Irish specimen, in spirits,
in the Museum to Trinity College, Dublin; presented by Dr. R.
Ball. (The reference in the text is misprinted MMM. fig. 1.)
2. *Octopus vulgaris*, after the figure of a British specimen, by
Sowerby.

PLATE OOO.—*Sepia officinalis;* drawn from life by Mr. Bailey; the
specimen was taken by Mr. Mackie, off Folkestone.

PLATE PPP.—1. a. Under surface of the "bone" or shell of *Sepia
officinalis;* 1. b. side view; 1. c. lower part of back of the same.
2. a. under side of shell of *Sepia biserialis;* 2. b. upper side;
2. c. side view; from drawings by Mr. Alder of a British specimen.

PLATE QQQ.—1. a. *Loligo media*, dorsal surface; 1. b. another speci-
men, ventral surface; and 1. c. the pen. Drawn from the life by
Mr. Alder. 2. a. *Loligo marmoræ;* and 2. b. its pen. From an
Irish specimen taken by Dr. Robert Ball, and preserved in the
Museum of Trinity College, Dublin.

PLATE RRR.—1. *Ommastrephes sagittatus;* drawn by E. F. from a living
specimen obtained by the Marchioness of Hastings, off Brighton.
2. *Ommastrephes todarus;* from a drawing by Mr. Alder, of a
British example.

PLATE SSS.—1. *Rossia Owenii.* 2. *Ommastrephes Eblanæ;* both from
Irish specimens, taken by Dr. Robert Ball, and preserved in the
Museum of Trinity College, Dublin.

LONDON:
Printed by SAMUEL BENTLEY and Co.
Bangor House, Shoe Lane.

PLATE A.

1. Aplidium fallax.   2. Sidnyum turbinatum.

3. Polyclinum aurantium.   4. Amouroucium argus.

5. Leptoclinum gelatinosum.   6. Distoma rubrum.

7. Botryllus polycyclus.   8. Botrylloides albicans.

1 Aplidium fallax.   2 Sidnyum turbinatum.

3 Polyclinum gelatinosum   4.Amouroucium argus

5. Leptoclinum gelatinosum.   6 Distoma

7 Botryllus   8. Botrylloides.

PLATE C.

E Forbes, delt.

1. Ascidia mentula. 2. A virginea 3 A scabra.

4. A. echinata 5 Molgula tubulosa.

London Published by J. Van Voorst 1848

PLATE D.

1. Cynthia quadrangularis.   2. C. morus.

3. C. tessellata.   4. C. limacina.   5. C. aggregata & its tadpole.

6. Molgula oculata.

London, Published by John Van Voorst, 1848.

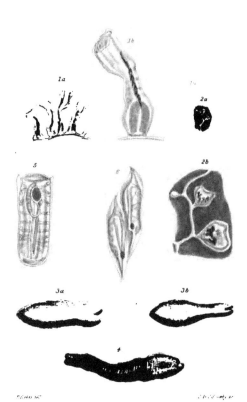

1. Clavelina lepadiformis.   2. Perophora Listeri.

3. Pelonaia glabra.   4. Pelonaia corrugata.

5 & 6. Salpa runcinata.

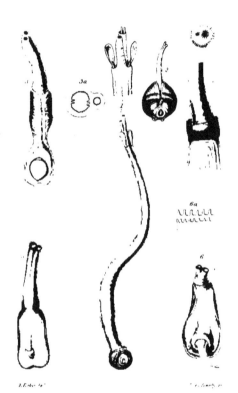

1. Teredo.   2. Xylophaga dorsalis.

3 Pholas parva.   4. Pholadidea papyracea (the siphons and cup)

5. Gastrochæna modiolina   6 Saxicava rugosa

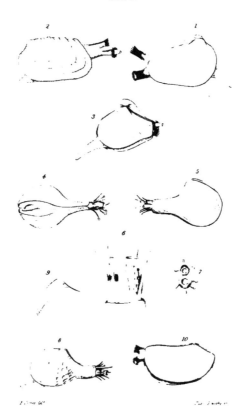

1. Petricola lithophaga.   2. Venerupis Irus.

3. Corbula nucleus.   4.5.6.7. Neæra cuspidata.

8.9. Neæra costellata.   10. Pandora obtusa.

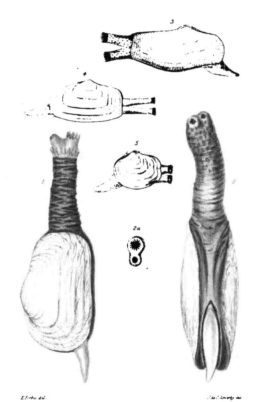

E.Forbes del.   I de C.Sowerby sc.

1. Mya truncata.   2. Lutraria elliptica.

3. Lyonsia norvegica   4. Thracia phaseolina.

5. Thracia distorta.

London Published by John Van Voorst. 1848.

PLATE I.

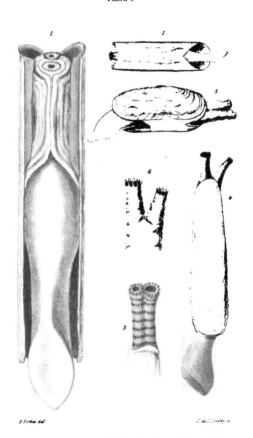

1. Solen siliqua.   2. Solen pellucidus.   3. siphons of Solen marginatus.

4. Ceratisolen legumen.   5. Solecurtus coarctatus.   6. its siphons.

London Published by John Van Voorst. 1848.

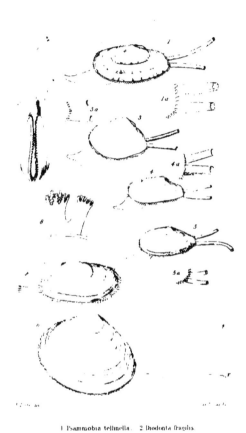

1 Psammobia tellinella. 2 Diodonta fragilis.

3 Tellina tenuis   4 Tellina donacina   5 Syndosmya intermedia

6 Scrobicularia compressa   7 Donax anatinum   8 Siphons of Mesodesma

PLATE I.

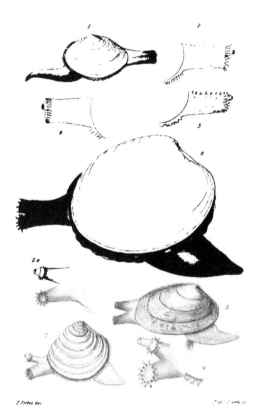

F.Forbes del.

1. Mactra elliptica. 2. Siphons of M. solida.

3. S. of M. subtruncata. 4 S. of M. stultorum. 5. Tapes pullastra.

6. S. of Venus ovata. 7. Venus fasciata. 8. Cytherea chione.

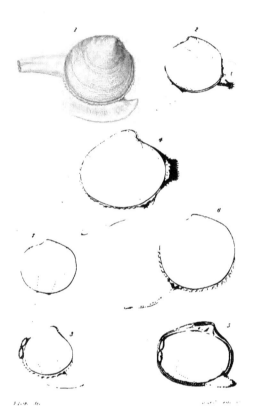

1.Artemis lincta. 2.Lucinopsis undata.

3.Circe minima. 4.Cyprina islandica. 5.Astarte danmoniensis.

6.Lucina borealis. 7.Diplodonta rotundata.

London Published by Jnn Van Voorst 1 48

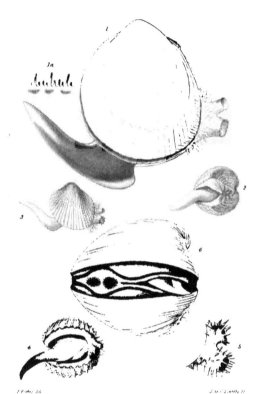

1. Cardium norvegicum.   2 C. pygmæum.   3. C. fasciatum.

4. C. echinatum .jun.   5. Siphons of C. edule   6 Isocardia cor.

London, Published by John Van Voorst, 1847.

P. Forbes del.

1. Turtonia purpurea. 2 Montacuta substriata . 3. Kellia rubra
4. Kellia suborbicularis. 5. Galeomma Turtoni. 6 Lepton squamosum .
7. Cyclas calyculata . 8. Pisidium amnicum . 9 Pisidium pusillum .

PLATE P

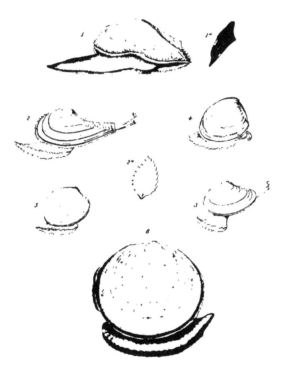

1. Arca tetragona   1ᵃ its byssal appendage
2. Leda caudata.   2ᵃ its disk.
3. Leda pygmæa.   4. Nucula nucleus.
5. Nucula tenuis.   6. Pectunculus pilosus.

PLATE Q

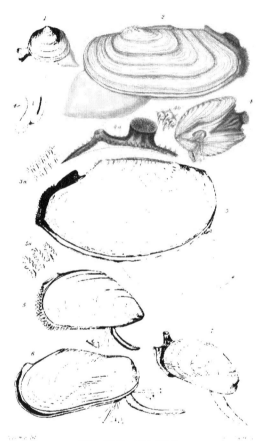

1. Cyclas rivicola.   2. Unio pictorum.

3. Anodonta cygnea.   4. Dreissena polymorpha.   5. Mytilus edulis.

6. Modiola tulipa.   7. Crenella nigra.

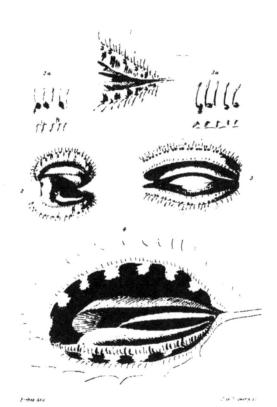

1 Pecten similis   2 P. striatus.   3 P. niveus.

4 Avicula tarentina

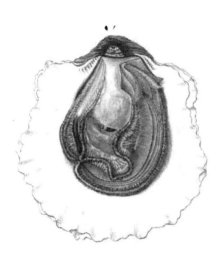

1. Ostrea edulis.   2. Anomia ephippium

3. Sphænia Binghami

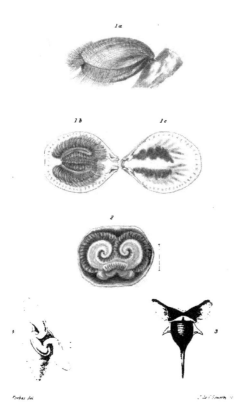

1 a

1 b　　　　　*1 c*

2

3

Forbes del.　　　　　　　　　　　　　J. de C. Sowerby sc.

1. Terebratula caput serpentis.

2. Crania norvegica. 3. Hyalæa trispinosa.

4. animal of a Peracle. (after Souleyet.)

PLATE W.

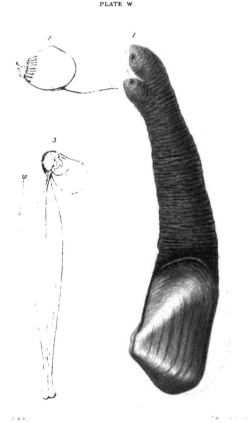

1. Panopæa norvegica.   2. Poromya granulata.

3. Appendicularia.

PLATE AA.

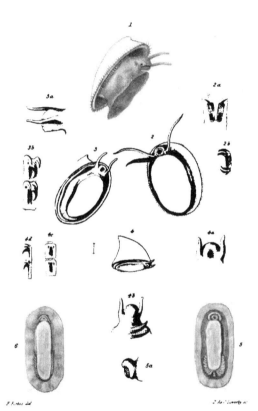

F. Forbes del.

J. de C. Sowerby sc.

1. Patella pellucida. 2. Acmæa testudinalis.

3 Tilidium fulvum. 4. Propilidium ancyloide.

5. Chiton asellus. 6. Chiton ruber.

London. Published by John Van Voorst, 1848.

E. Forbes del.   J. de C. Sowerby sc.

1,2 3 Emarginula rosea.   4,5,6. Puncturella Noachina.

7. Fissurella reticulata.   8 to 13. Calyptræa Sinensis.

PLATE C C

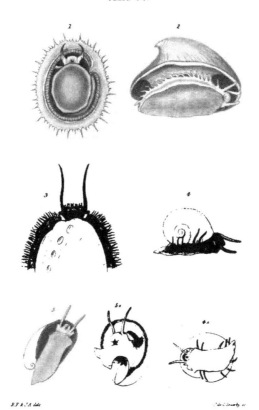

1. Patella vulgata.   2. Emarginula crassa.

3. Haliotis tuberculata   4. Trochus helicinus.

5. Pileopsis hungaricus.

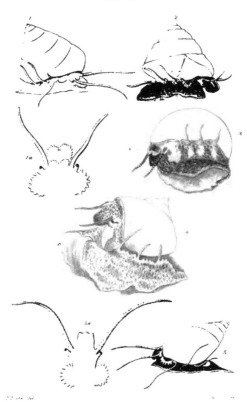

1. Trochus cinerarius.   2. T. tumidus.   3. T. Magus.

4. T. granulatus.   5. Phasianella pullus.

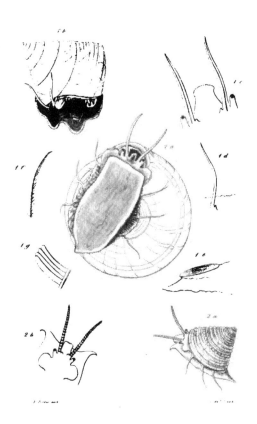

PLATE FF

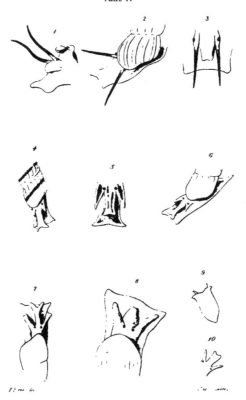

1 2 3 Scalaria Trevelyana. 4. Chemnitzia rufa.

5. C scalaris. 6 C rufescens. 7. C Mac Andrei.

8, 9, Odostomia spiralis. 10. Truncatella truncatula.

PLATE 66

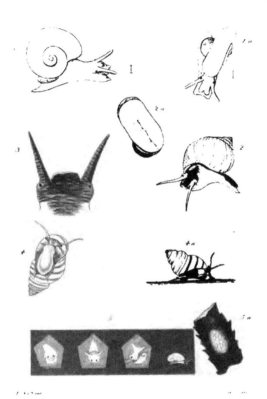

1 Skenea planorbis.　2. Littorina patula.

3. Littorina littorea　4. Lacuna vincta.

5. development of Lacuna pallidula.

•

PLATE II.II.

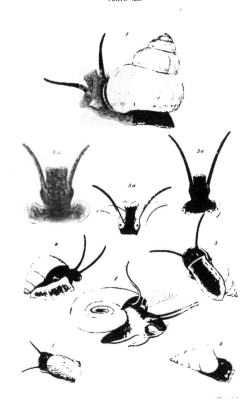

1. Neritina fluviatilis. 2. Paludina vivipara.

3. Bithinia tentaculata. 4. B. Leachii.

5. Valvata cristata. 6. Assiminea Grayana.

PLATE LI.

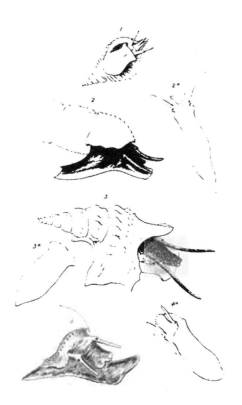

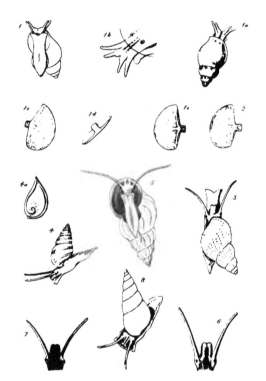

1. Jeffreysia diaphana & operculum.   2. Oper^m of Jeffreysia opalina.
3. Rissoa abyssicola.   4. R. cingillus & oper^m.   5. R. parva.
6. R. labiosa.   7. R. rufilabris   8. R. ulvæ.

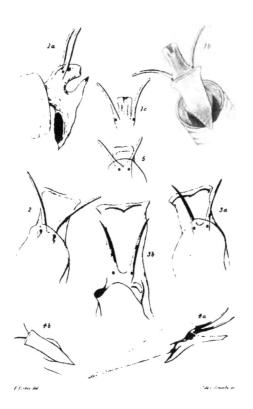

1. Cæcum trachea.   2. Eulima nitida.

3. E. nitida. var. polita.   4. E. distorta.   5. E. bilineata.

PLATE . K K .

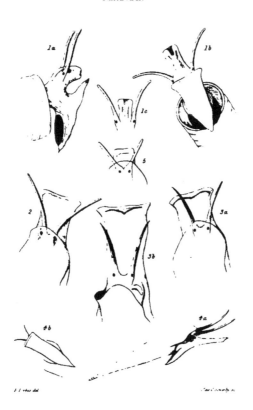

1. Cæcum trachea .   2. Eulima nitida .
3. E. nitida . var polita .   4. E. distorta .   5. E. bilineata .

PLATE L.L.

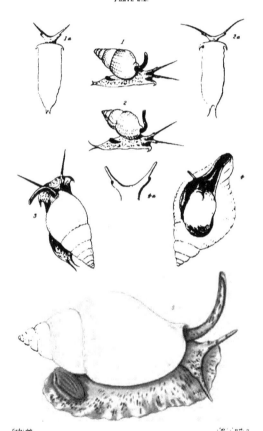

Forbes del.   Gale & March se.

1 Spirialis Flemingii.   2 Jeffreysia opalina.

3 Assiminea littorea.   4 Rissoa vitrea.

5 Achis supranitida

PLATE NN.

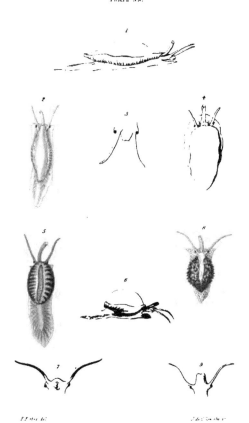

F.F .... del   J de ... ...

1 _ 4. Volva patula.   5 _ 7. Cypræa europæa.

8. 9. Marginella lœvis

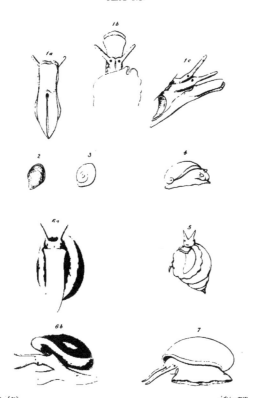

1 Cerithiopsis Tubercularis & 2 its operculum.

3. Operc. of Cerithium reticulatum. 4 Otina otis. 5. Stilifer Turtonis.

6 Velutina plicatilis 7. Velutina lævigata

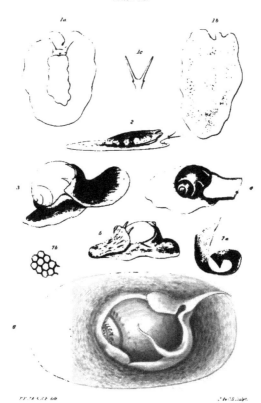

F.E. JEASE del.

J. de S. sculpt.

1 Lamellaria perspicua. 2.L..tentaculata.

3.Natica sordida. 4.N.Montagui. 5.N.Alderi.

6.N.canrena and 7 its spawn.

London Published by John Van Voorst. 1850.

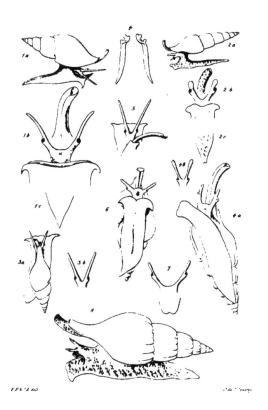

1 Mangelia Lefroyi.   2. M. brachystoma.   3 M. teres
4. M. costata.   5 M. attenuata.   6. M. linearis
7. M. nebula   8. M. gracilis

London Published by John Van Voorst 1857

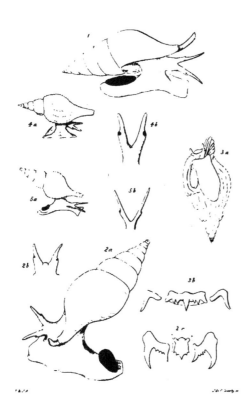

1 Fusus propinquus   2. Fusus islandicus.

3. Trophon Bamfium   5. T echinatum.

4. T. Barvicense.

London Published by ... ... 1821.

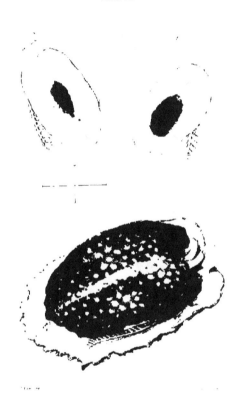

PLATE 88

1 Phumobranchus plumula   2 P membranaceus.

PLATE 88

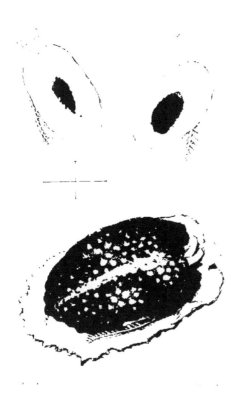

1 Pleurobranchus plumula   2 P. membranaceus

1 Murex erinaceus.   2. Mangelia (Bela) turricula.

3. M (Bela) septangularis   4. M.(Bela) rufa

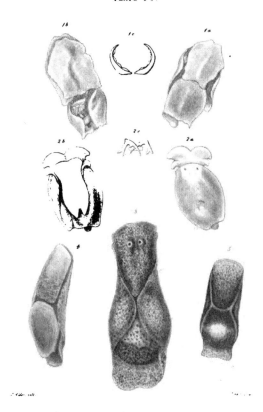

1. Bullæa aperta.   2. Amphisphyra hyalina.

3. Bulla hydatis.   4. Bullæa catena.

6. Bullæa punctata.

London Published by John Van ...... 1841.

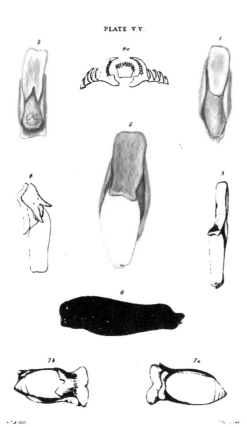

PLATE V.V.

1. Bullæa scabra.   2. Bulla Cranchii.
3. Cylichna cylindracea   4. C. truncata.
5. Scaphander lignaria.   6. Akera bullata.
7. Tornatella tornaulis.

PLATE Y Y.

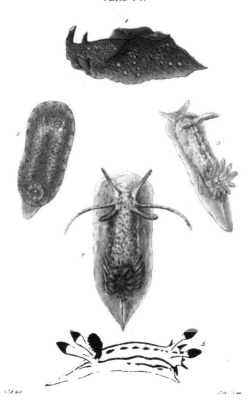

1. Aplysia hybrida.   2. Doris coccinea.

3. Goniodoris nodosa.   4. Idalia inæqualis.

5. Polycera quadri lineata.

1. Hermœa dendritica. 2. Proctonotus mucroniferus.

3. Lomonotus marmoratus. 4. Anctla cristata.

5. Dendronotus arborescens.

1. Triopa claviger.   2. Ægirus punctilucens.   3. Tritonia Hombergi.

4. Doto coronata.   4*. Doto fragilis

5. Scyllæa pelagica.

PLATE B.B.B.

1.Eolis papillosa. 2.E.coronata. 3.E.viridis. 4.E.exigua.

5.Embletonia minuta. 6.Antiopa splendida.

London Published by John Van Voorst 1851

PLATE C.C.C.

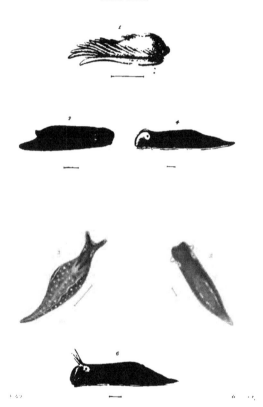

1 Alderia modesta.   2 Runcina Hancocki.

3. Elysia viridis.   4. Limapontia nigra.   5. Acteonia corrugata.

6. Cenia Cocksii.

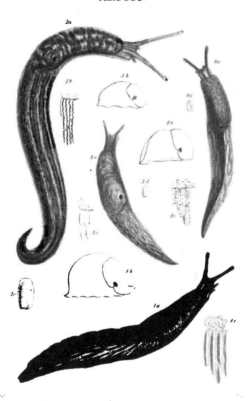

1 Arion empiricorum.   2. Limax cinereus.

3 Limax agrestis   4 Limax gagates

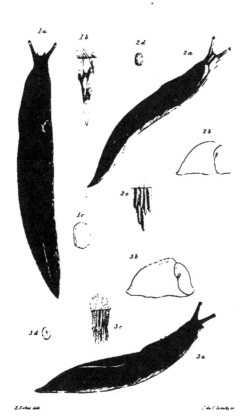

E. Forbes delt.   J. de C. Sowerby sc.

1 Limax flavus.   2 L. arboreus.   3 L. Sowerbii.

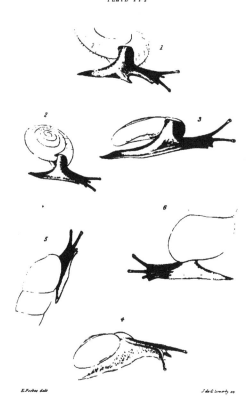

E.Forbes delt

J.de C.Sowerby sc

1.Helix hispida   2 H.rotundata   3 H.cellaria   4 H.fusca.

5.Zua lubrica   6 Bulimus acutus.

PLATE F.F.F.[#]

1. Arion hortensis.   2. A flavus   3. Limax tenellus.

4 Limax brunneus.   5 Geomalacus maculosus

6 Onchidium celticum.

1 Vitrina pellucida.　2 Clausilia plicatula　3 C. laminata

4 Balea perversa

5 Pupa marginata　6. Pupa umbilicata

PLATE LII.

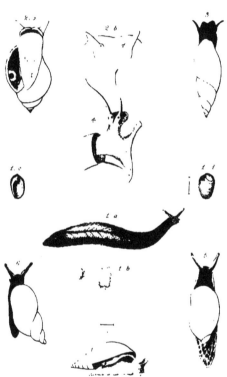

1. Testacella haliotoidea.   2. Limnæus pereger.

3. Physa hypnorum.   4. Planorbis vortex.

5. Succinea putris   6. S. oblonga.   7. Conovulus denticulatus.

London Published by I. Van Voorst 1845

1 Physa fontinalis.   2. Achatina acicula

3 Carychium minimum   4 Limax agrestis, monster

5 Cyclostoma elegans   6 Conovulus bidentatus

PLATE K.K.K

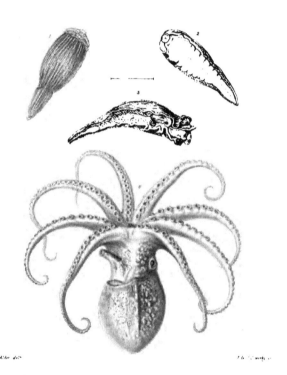

1.2.3 Diphyllidia lineata.   4. Eledone cirrhosus.

London, Published by John Van Voorst 1853

PLATE LLL

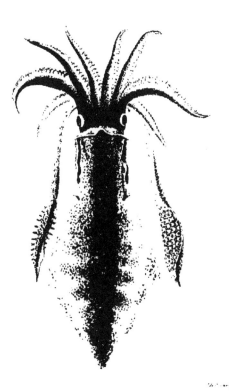

Loligo vulgaris.

PLATE LL L

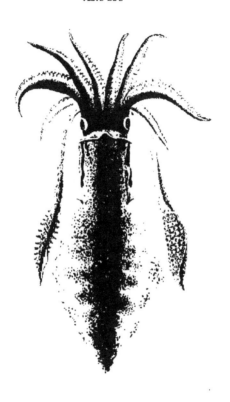

Lohgo vulgaris.

1. Eledone cirrhosus.   2. Sepiola atlantica.

3. Sepiola Rondeletii.

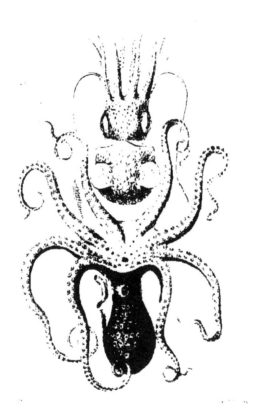

1 Rossia macrosoma   2 Octopus vulgaris

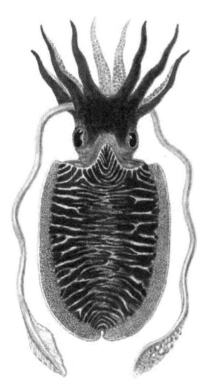

PLATE O.O.O.

W^m sculp. delt.   ...dw C.Sowerby sc.

Sepia Officinalis.

1 c

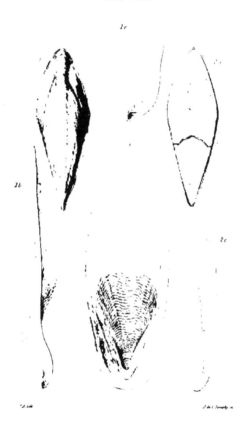

1 b

2 c

1. Sepia officinalis.   2. S. bisserialis.

PLATE Q Q Q.

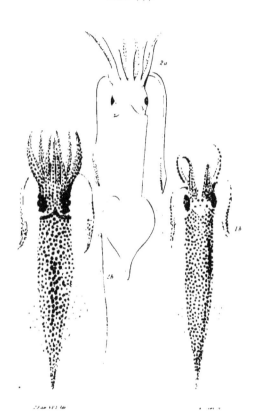

1. Loligo Media.   2. Loligo Marmorae

1 Ommastrephes sagittatus   2 O todarus

PLATE S.S S

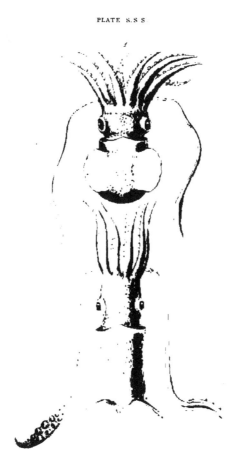

www.ingramcontent.com/pod-product-compliance
Lightning Source LLC
LaVergne TN
LVHW011941060326
832903LV00045B/216